TALKING VISIONS

new museum
NEW MUSEUM OF CONTEMPORARY ART

New Museum of Contemporary Art, New York
Documentary Sources in Contemporary Art
Series Editor: Marcia Tucker

New Museum of Contemporary Art,
583 Broadway, New York, New York 10012

The MIT Press, Massachusetts Institute of Technology
Five Cambridge Center, Cambridge, Massachusetts 02142

Cover Image: *Interior Cartography #1*, 1995
Gelatin Silver Print, 16×20"
Tatiana Parcero
courtesy of the artist

TALKING VISIONS

Multicultural Feminism in a Transnational Age

Ella Shohat, editor

Images selected by Coco Fusco/Ella Shohat

Foreword by Marcia Tucker

NEW MUSEUM OF CONTEMPORARY ART

New York, New York

The MIT Press

Cambridge, Massachusetts

London, England

This book was set in Bembo by Graphic Composition, Inc., and was printed and bound in Spain.

Library of Congress Cataloging-in-Publication Data

Talking visions : multicultural feminism in transnational age / edited by Ella Shohat ; foreword by Marcia Tucker.
    p.   cm.
    Includes bibliographical references and index.
    ISBN 0-262-69205-8 (pbk. : alk. paper)
    1. Feminism and the arts.   2. Arts and society—History—20th century.   3. Multiculturalism in art.   4. Gender identity in art.   I. Shohat, Ella.
NX180.F4T36   1998
700′.82—dc21   98-17423
                                                                  CIP

Contents

Contents   vii

Plate 1: *La Tetona Mendoza* (Big Tits Mendoza)
Earth Day, Mexico City, 1990
Yolanda Andrade
Courtesy of the artist

Foreword

There was a time, not so very long ago, when the terms "feminism" and "race," no matter how or by whom they were defined, belonged to separate worlds; only rarely could one hear a call echoing across the infinite chasms of difference that separated them. Race was "us" or "them," depending on who or where you were (or thought you were) in relation to everyone else; the first wave of feminism in America, in the late 1960s, seemed blind to all categories other than "male" or "female." Gay and lesbian studies; the notion of age as a social construction; theories of class and the effects of a rapidly growing global economy; the mutable and fluctuating borders that constantly redefine communities, languages, practices, and national, ethnic, and gender identities at the end of the millennium—none of these figured in the earliest attempts to postulate a politics of either "feminism" or "race."

As consciousness-raising techniques made women—and men—increasingly aware of how personal experience is molded by larger political structures and policies, feminists began to see how politics result from the ways that power is wielded within a given society, by whom, and to what ends.

An understanding that everyone is subject to the hierarchies of power has ultimately led to the breakdown of "race" and "feminism" as separate and distinct arenas of investigation and activity. An elaborate web of discursive structures now enmeshes them both, along with many other related concepts and categories, in an inextricable field of multiple meanings, representations, and narratives that have put an end to an identity politics consisting of competitive individual, immutable, and categorically succinct entities.

Nonetheless, in the Western European art worlds, women of color and their work have been largely invisible except as colonized objects of study, ghettoized into "special" exhibitions for the most part organized by people from outside the culture being studied. But traditional concepts of art history, museology, artistic practice, and cultural expression are also breaking down under critical analysis from both inside and outside the field, and are hastened by the constant challenge of a newly recognized global world. There is an increasing awareness that everyone is a racialized and gendered subject, created within and defined by the hierarchies of power. As the feminist critic and philosopher Gayatri Spivak constantly reminds us, we must always acknowledge not only who we are, but *where* we are, that is, where we are positioned in relation to those hierarchies, and to questions of authority and privilege.

Of course, there is no one way to address these complex issues, nor to respond to them. But if the essays in this volume lead to the next step for identity politics, the question must no longer simply be "Who are we?" but rather "What can we do for each other?"[1]

The genesis of this book, the fifth in the New Museum's *Documentary Sources in American Art* series, was a sequence of panels and discussions entitled *CrossTalk: A Multicultural Feminist Symposium* (July 5 and 6, 1993) held at The Drawing Center in New York and organized for the Museum by Ella Shohat and Susan Cahan, then the Museum's Curator of Education. It is an understatement to say that the symposium generated yet more talk, across and through races, classes, nationalities, language groups, ages, professions, and experiences among the audience. There was a lot of heated argument, and a great deal more listening than might be expected from the first large-scale public forum attempting to address both multiculturalism and feminism as inextricable and contingent discourses.

Most of the essays in this volume were adapted by their authors from the papers given during the two day long series of panels, lectures, and discussions. Others were added by Ella Shohat to complement and augment them. The volume is part of the New Museum's long-standing commitment to exhibitions, programs, and publications that address both feminist and multicultural issues and practices: *Minorities Dialogues* (1980), organized with Linda Goode Bryant, John Neeley, and Howardina Pindell; *Difference:*

---

1. June Jordan, cited in Elspeth Probyn, "Technologizing the Self," in Lawrence Grossberg, Cary Nelson, and Paula Treichler, eds., *Cultural Studies* (New York: Routledge, 1992), 508.

Marcia Tucker

On Representation and Sexuality (1984–5), by guest curator Kate Linker; *The Decade Show,* with the Studio Museum in Harlem and the Museum of Contemporary Hispanic Art (1990); *Africa Exlores* (1991); *Bad Girls* (1994); and solo exhibitions of the work of Ana Mendieta (1987–88), Nancy Spero (1989), Mary Kelly (1990), Carrie Mae Weems (1991), Carolee Schneemann (1996), Mona Hatoum (1997–98), and Faith Ringgold (1998), among many others.

Without the insight, leadership, and hard work of Ella Shohat, the editor of *Talking Visions,* who has been instrumental in every phase of this project, it could not have come to fruition; we are very grateful not only for her skills, but for her continued concern to explore a complex and controversial terrain in new and meaningful ways.

At the New Museum, Susan Cahan, now Director of Programs at the Eileen and Peter Norton Foundation, was the force behind the project during her tenure as Deputy Director, and it was thanks to her efforts that the Museum was able to undertake the co-publication of the book. I am also grateful to Brian Goldfarb, her successor, who took over its supervision as Curator of Education and smoothed its way to completion. Many thanks as well to Dennis Szakacs, Deputy Director of Planning and Development, and to Charlayne Haynes, former Managing Director, for their hard work and counsel on the project.

It has been our great pleasure to work once again with Roger Conover of The MIT Press, who is an inspired editor, extraordinary thinker, and patient collaborator in all phases of this and many other publications that we have undertaken together.

We are grateful above all to the writers and artists whose work is represented here for having led the way, with enormous courage and often at great personal cost, to a vision of the world in which respect for difference is a critical agent in the dismantling of the crippling social and political inequities that have kept us apart.

Marcia Tucker
Founding Director of the New Museum of Contemporary Art

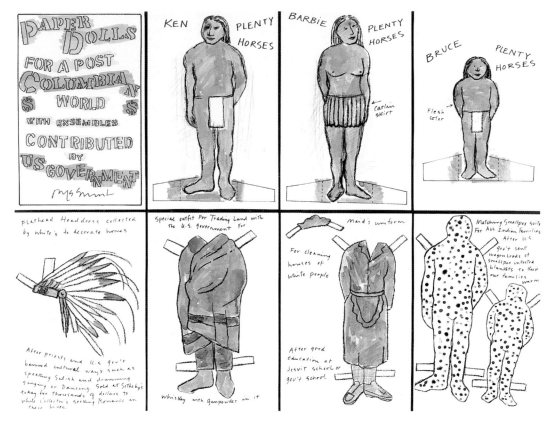

Plate 2: *Paper Dolls for a Post-Columbian World with Ensembles Contributed by U.S. Government*, 1991
Watercolor and pencil on photocopy, 8 of 13 panels, each 17 × 11″
© Jaune Quick-to-See Smith
Courtesy of Steinbaum Krauss Gallery, New York

Ella Shohat

Editor's Preface

The long voyage to produce *Talking Visions: Multicultural Feminism in a Transnational Age,* from its inception as a symposium to this book, has finally come to an end. The volume was conceived out of a desire to celebrate the accomplishments of activists, artists, curators, and scholars working on what I call here "multicultural feminism." Many of us had long lamented the lack of space for interacting, conversing, and dialoguing within the public sphere, and for me the symposium and the book formed welcome opportunities for forging such a space. Especially exciting for me was the idea of shaping synergies between diverse locations: academic fora, cultural institutions, political organizations, and community centers.

Despite my long years of scholarship, teaching, lecturing, and curatorial work, *Talking Visions* has been conceptually challenging because the theme of multicultural feminism is so broad, embracing so many communities and practices. Given my personal-familial trajectories across several countries (Iraq, Israel/Palestine, United States, Brazil), languages and cultures, and given the diverse U.S. communities represented in the book, I felt accountable, as an editor, to an extremely wide spectrum of constituencies. It was not always easy to orchestrate these diverse, at times conflictual, voices into a coherent volume.

The original public event, "Cross Talk: A Multicultural Feminist Symposium," which took place on June 5 and 6 in 1993, received an extremely enthusiastic response, followed by many inquiries about a future publication. My original purpose in organizing this event had little to do with publishing a book, but rather with a desire to talk, exchange, debate. But inquiries from conference and audience participants, as well as from those who missed the conference, convinced me to take on the project of putting the material together into a publication available for a wider audience.

Although based on the "Cross Talk" symposium, *Talking Visions* is also substantially different: it draws on moments from the conference while also bringing in new materials, all reshaped for a new totality. To begin with, I introduced a visual project that involved research into the work of several hundred artists, as well as collaboration with some of the artists who created or reworked images specifically for this book. I wish to thank all the artists who shared their excellent work with me, and to offer my apologies for not including much of it, since contractual limitations on space prevented me from including more images. I also thank Coco Fusco for responding to my invitation to collaborate on the selection of the images, and for sharing her wide knowledge of the contemporary art scene. I am indebted to Tatiana Parcero for her beautiful work on the book cover, and for patiently and creatively accommodating my requests concerning its visual aspects.

Talking Visions also does not fully coincide with the public event in terms of the format. In some cases, I felt a dialogue format would be more effective, and therefore asked Catherine Benamou to dialogue with the journalist Maria Hinojosa, while inviting two of my students at the CUNY-Graduate Center, Ginetta Candelario and Rocio Aranda-Alvarado, to conduct dialogue with the activists Marina Alvarez and Petra Allende, respectively. I furthermore sought the participation of contributors who were not part of the original public event, and assigned topics which were not addressed at the symposium. I would like to call attention, however, to those speakers who made strong contribution to the conference, but who for various reasons were unable to participate in the book: Rabab Abdul-Hadi, cofounder of the Union of Palestinian Women's Associations in North America; Anannya Bhattacharjee, Executive coordinator of SAKHI for South Asian women; Lisa Cartwright, Associate Professor of Media and Cultural Studies, The University of Rochester; Josanne Lopez, journalist and the founder of Dust Tracks Production; Jolene Rikard, artist, writer and scholar of the turtle clan of the Tuscarora people; Vanessa Jackson, a member of the Board of Directors of the National Black Women's Health Project; Ninotchka Rosca, writer and national chair of GABRIELA network and a member of the Executive Committee of PEN International Women Writers Committee.

My relationship with the New Museum of Contemporary Art came about through one of my students at the CUNY-Graduate Center, Susan Cahan, then curator of Education at the New Museum. In 1991 Susan invited me to work on an educational installation on colonial discourse and popular culture for the museum based on the themes of my seminar "Gen-

Ella Shohat

der and the Culture of Empire," in which she enrolled in the spring of 1990. We worked for about a year preparing this installation, which was ultimately canceled for lack of funds. Instead, I was invited to shape a conference or panel on the same theme. At that point I felt that I had already written and lectured extensively about these issues, and that there was a danger that seductive "exotic" issues were becoming chic in academia and the museums in ways that end up re-focussing attention on the "West," even while deconstructing its imagery. In the context of SOHO and the New Museum, I thought it would be more meaningful to stage a symposium on current work on questions of race, gender, sexuality, and nation. I also felt that in the context of a SOHO museum it would be just as important to engage with the work of flesh and blood activists and artists as to engage in the critique of imperial exoticism.

I worked as the program organizer along with the program coordinators for the New Museum, Susan Cahan and Jerry Philogene, who at the time was the museum's Education Associate. I wish to thank both Susan and Jerry for their skillful organizational efforts in putting together the "Cross Talk" symposium. Many people with whom we have been in touch gave useful suggestions; just to name a few of the long list: Gloria Anzaldua, Anne Belsamo, Hazel Carby, Gina Dent, Mallika Dutt, Angelika Festa, Elaine Kim, Gerry Kosasa, Karen Kosasa, Agustin Lao, Wahneema Lubiano, Margo Machida, Beckie Masaki, Maria Luisa "Papusa" Molina, Jennifer Terry, and Inderpal Grewal, who suggested the title "Cross Talk" for the conference (partially echoing a similar phrase from an article by Ruth Frankenberg and Lata Mani). I also wish to thank Ann Phiblin of the Drawing Center who hosted the event due to lack of space at the New Museum. The symposium was made possible with support from the New York State Council on the Arts, the New York City Department of Cultural Affairs, and individual and corporate members of the New Museum.

Following the success of the conference, I was approached by several publishers. I especially thank Cecelia Cancellaro of Routledge for her initial work in trying to get "Cross Talk" published as well as the supportive readers: Sumita Chakravarty, Alex Juhasz, and Kamala Visweswaran. Susan Cahan was instrumental in my decision to publish the project with MIT and the New Museum, and Brian Goldfarb was helpful as liaison after her departure. Jerry Philogene, with her enthusiastic identification with the project, greatly facilitated the transition back to the museum. I also appreciate all the good will shown by the people at MIT Press. I especially wish to thank my editors, Roger Conover and Katherine Arnoldi, as well as Julie Grimaldi. The book has also benefitted from the dedicated labor of the interns/assistants who at different points worked with me on the book. I value their commitment and excitement about the issues addressed here: Dorothy Désir-Davis, Rebecca Kaminsky, Rocio Aranda-Alvarado, Sofia Theodoropoulou, Anita Anantharam, Naama Oppenheim Kovner, Aline Duriaud, Barbara Winfree, Sreemala Nair, and Evelyn Alsultany. I especially thank Evelyn, who accompanied the project over the past two years, for her generosity, dedication, and for simply being her wonderful self.

I have been fortunate to have been invited to present my ideas on multicultural feminism in very diverse fora. I would like to acknowledge the institutions and individuals who invited me as well as the participants who contributed through questions at the following sites: U.C. Regents Lectureship at Davis; the MacArthur Interdisciplinary Program on Peace & International Cooperation at the Institute of International Relations, The University of Minnesota; The Center for Modern and Contemporary Studies, U.C.L.A.; The Irish Film Centre, Dublin, Ireland; The Consortium of Humanities Centers and Institutes, The University of Illinois at Chicago; Women's Studies, Hamilton College; English and Film Studies, Swarthmore College; The Center for the Humanities, The University of Oregon, Eugene; Gender Institute, Columbia University; Near Eastern Studies, Oxford University, England; Universidade Fernando Pessoa, Porto, Portugal; The 21st Century Fund and the Center for Women's and Development's seminar on Gender and Globalization, Neemrana, India; The Ford Foundation and The Curriculum Transformation Project, at The University of Maryland at College Park; The Committee on Culture and Cultures and the Comparative Studies in Race, Stanford University. I am also grateful to the students in my seminars on multicultural feminism at the City University of New York-Graduate Center and at U.C.L.A. for lively discussions, and for making teaching so pleasurable and meaningful.

In this long process many people have been helpful with advice, information, and support. I am extremely fortunate to have worked on both conference and book in constant and vital conversation on issues of postcolonialism, transnationalism, and feminism with my colleagues and friends Caren Kaplan and Inderpal Grewal. I thank them both not only for their many important suggestions for the book, but also for their touching solidarity, sharing the anxious and the exciting moments along the way. My introduction has benefited immensely from Caren's careful readings and insightful comments, as well as from her encouragement to always rethink and reformulate arguments whose implications I might have taken for

Ella Shohat

granted. In an academic environment keen on competition, Caren's sensitivity, generosity, and dialogical spirit are at once moving and inspiring. Inderpal too has generously commented on my introduction and on the book, making perceptive suggestions and useful recommendations whose impact is felt throughout. Her provocative questions have turned our exchange, especially on issues of immigration, into a stimulating intellectual journey.

I am also indebted to several other people who have read the introduction in parts or in whole: Meena Alexander, Catherine Benamou, Ginetta Candelario, May Joseph, David Frankel, Ivone Margulies, Chandra Talpade Mohanty, Satya Mohanty, John Mowitt. I wish to thank the following people for their assistance or supportive gestures at various moments during the course of producing this book: Brad Verebay, Wahneema Lubiano, Sherry Millner, Ayse Franko, Connie Katon, Dafne Depollo, Patricia Hoffbauer, George Sanchez, Irit Rogoff, Lynne Jackson, Ruth Tsoffar, Viola Shafik, Andrew Ross, Faye Ginsburg, Joseph Massad, Joao Luiz Vieira, Luiz Antonio Coelho, Kate Ramsey, Manthia Diawara, Mervat Hatem, Ranjani Mazumdar, Neery Melkonian, Parine Jaddo, Shoreh and Niloufar Esfandiar, Na'eema Itzahaik, Zaineb Istrabadi, Sholeh Vatanabadi, Eric Smoodin, Minoo Moallem, Norma Alarcon, David Roediger, Meir Gal, Sonia S'hiri, Anne McClintock, Ayisha Abraham, Azadeh Farahmand, and Arlindo Castro, whose untimely death saddened so many of us here and in Brazil. I also wish to express special gratitude to my colleagues George Custen, Mirella Affron, Electa Arenal and Jill Dolan for their support over the years, especially toward the institutional and curriculum battles to deghettoize alternative critical perspectives.

Finally, I thank Robert Stam, first for being the editor's editor. When, after working very closely on many of the essays here, I needed someone to look over my own writing, or discuss the many decisions that went into the making of *Talking Visions*, Robert was there. In moments when I felt that the work on the project was endless, when I was feeling drained from nurturing other writers and artists, I had his generosity to rely on. Robert has accompanied this book from its inception, reading and rereading my introduction, making insightful suggestions about style and organization. But most important, he eased the difficult moments along the bumpy road of producing this book with his great philosophical sense of humor. To him and to my loving family, especially Sasson, Aziza, Yvette, and Jacob, my gratitude is boundless.

Ella Shohat

Introduction

Talking Visions: Multicultural Feminism in a Transnational Age aims at a feminist reimagining of community affiliations and cultural practices, articulated not in isolation but rather in relation. It does not exalt one political concern (feminism) over another (multiculturalism); rather, it highlights and reinforces the mutual embeddedness between the two. By tying the two terms together, the volume refuses the hierarchy of class, racial, national, sexual, and gender-based struggles, highlighting instead the "political intersectionality" (Kimberle Crenshaw) of all these axes of stratification. This volume assumes, in other words, that genders, sexualities, races, classes, nations, and even continents exist not as hermetically sealed entities but rather as parts of a permeable interwoven relationality. Instead of segregating historical periods and geographical regions into neatly fenced off areas of expertise, it highlights the multiplicity of community histories and perspectives, as well as the hybrid culture of *all* communities, especially in a world increasingly characterized by the "traveling" of images, sounds, goods, and people. As a situated practice, multicultural feminism takes as its starting point the cultural consequences of the worldwide movements and dislocations of people associated with the development of "global" or "transnational" capitalism. Like national borders, disciplinary borders too are out of synch with such transnational movements. The relational feminist approach demands moving beyond nation-bound and discipline-bound teaching, curating, and organizing. *Talking Visions* attempts, in this sense, to place diverse gendered/sexed histories and geographies in dialogical relation in terms of the tensions and overlappings that take place "within" and "between" cultures, ethnicities, nations.

"Multiculturalism" here does not simply evoke the mere existence of multiple culture. Rather it designates a project which calls for envisioning world history and contemporary social life from the perspective of the radical equality of peoples. Unlike a liberal-pluralist discourse, a polycentric multiculturalism entails a profound reconceptualization and restructuring of intercommunal relations within and beyond the nation state.[1] It hopes to decolonize representation not only in terms of cultural artifacts (museum exhibitions, literary canons, film series) but also in terms of the communities "behind" the artifacts. This volume stands at the point of convergence of two practices—multiculturalism and feminism—that share the goal of transforming social stratifications and hegemonic epistemologies. And while there is no single comprehensive definition of feminism—one might better speak of "feminisms" in the plural—most feminisms share the critique of masculinist ideologies and the desire to undo patriarchal power regimes. Gay/lesbian/queer critique, meanwhile, has further complexified issues of gender and sexuality. Multicultural feminism takes on board all these critiques and ramifications, yoking multiculturalism and feminism not as distinct realms of politics imposed on each other, but rather as coming into political existence in and through relation to each other. Rather than simply a "touchy-feely" sensitivity toward a diffuse aggregate of victims, multicultural feminism animates a multifaceted "plurilogue" among diverse resistant practices: "First World" white feminism, socialism, anarchism, "Third World" nationalism, "Fourth World" Indigenism, anti-racist diasporic activism and gay/lesbian/bi/transsexual movements.[2] As a set of situated practices, multicultural feminism emphasizes not simply the *range* of culturally distinct gendered and sexualized subjects, but also the *contradictions* within this range, always in hopes of forging alternative epistemologies and imaginative alliances.

This project is above all multi-voiced. It orchestrates an ensemble of perspectives: of activist scholars, artists, curators, and political organizers, many of whom have worked at the forefront of the multicultural feminist project. Moving across the intersections of race and nation, gender and sexuality, *Talking Visions* links different yet co-implicated constituencies and arenas of struggle. Although a wide variety of feminists are represented here, this volume does not cover "all" races and ethnicities in an imperial sweep, nor does it pretend to probe all that matters for gender and sexuality. The volume forges a polyphonic[3] space where many critical voices engage in a dialogue in which no one voice hopefully muffles the others. *Talking Visions* does not force an artificial consensus; rather it aims at a dissonant polyphony. Multicultural feminism is not an easy Muzak-like harmony but rather a polyrhythmic staging of a full-throated counterpoint

Ella Shohat

where tensions are left unresolved. It does not offer a unified feminist subject, or a single ideological position, or a canonical repertoire of subversive acts. Rather than display women's diversity for the delectation of an imaginary "mainstream," the volume delineates a "world wide web" where feminist communities derive their identity and difference vis-à-vis multiple "others."

The volume is also *generically* polyphonic, in that its texts partake of many genres: reflective essay, testimonial dialogue, digital collage, prose poem, photo montage, performance piece. As part of a visual culture project, the images are more than illustrative. By mixing word and image, the volume eschews two forms of elitism: academic iconophobia rooted in reverence for the "sacred word," *and* art-world logophobia rooted in the fetishism of the image. Neither text nor image has so to speak the "last word." The two mutually amplify and contextualize one another, militating against any single authoritative history. The visible, the written, and even the aural here hybridize and play off each other. Whether through the texts/images themselves, or through their juxtaposition, this project challenges a whole series of discursive, communitarian, institutional, and disciplinary boundaries, undermining any univocal mode of feminist narrative, while revealing a glimpse of the vital possibilities of multicultural feminism in a transnational age.

Talking Visions comes at a particular moment in the development of anti-racist feminist and queer struggles, in a time when global flows of information, products, and people challenge a simplistic First World/Third World dichotomy. Although the participants in this volume are largely U.S.-based, the book's critical terrains are not nationalist in scope. In this text the U.S. is not a border-restrictive, arbitrary, or essence-producing parameter, but rather a circumstantial point-of-departure from which to examine issues of urban space, immigration, and the U.S. place in globalization. This new moment requires a feminist rethinking of identity designation, intellectual grids, and disciplinary boundaries. In this introductory essay I will situate multicultural feminism in relation to diverse debates—about the canon, political correctness, identity politics, and affirmative action—and in relation to diverse "moments"—the move from anti-colonial to postcolonial critique, the "racing" and "queering" of hegemonic feminism, the commodification of difference by cultural institutions and transnational corporations; and the "new world order" of globalization, cyber-technologies, and cross-border displacements. At the same time, I will reflect on the relationships between the diverse interdisciplinary knowledges constituting multicultural feminist inquiry: gender and sexuality studies; ethnic and race studies; area, postcolonial and transnational studies. Throughout this essay I will return to these questions in order to contextualize the essays/images in the volume while also delineating the very project of multicultural feminism at this historical moment. To write this moment, I will argue, we have to move beyond a number of false dichotomies, double binds and catch 22s. This introductory essay aims to disentangle the various binarisms that construct color (black/white), gender (masculine/feminine), sexuality (lesbian/straight), discourse (authentic/artificial), temporality (tradition/modernity), space (local/global), academic rubrics (ethnic and area studies/gender and sexuality studies), and arenas of struggle (scholarship/activism or criticism/art).

The Mobilization of Difference

This book is not exactly about women of color. Nor is the term "women of color"—evocative of a determinate biological/social group into which one is born—equatable with multicultural feminism. But it is also no coincidence that most of the feminists represented here *are* women of color, since their experience at the intersection of oppressions has generated a multifaceted social critique. I do not mean to equate experience with politics, however; encounters with multiple marginalizations can bring a painful epistemological advantage but they do not necessarily generate a specific political affiliation, nor do they magically transform one into an activist for social change. Multicultural feminism as outlined here avoids the egocentric essentialism of "I am, therefore, I resist" (Chandra Talpade Mohanty). It attempts to remap the shape-shifting modalities of oppression and empowerment, recognizing that "oppression" and "empowerment" are themselves relational terms. Individuals can occupy more than one position, being empowered on one axis (class, say) but not on another (such as sexuality). Instead of a simple oppressor/oppressed dichotomy we find a wide spectrum of power relations among and within communities. Some women might be more empowered than some men; a female Wall Street executive is rather better off than an unemployed metal worker in the Rust Belt. At the extreme ends of the continuum are those empowered along all or most of the axes, versus those who are empowered along none or few of them. But even here there are no guarantees. Identities and identifications are not necessarily coterminous, and one's socially constructed identity

Ella Shohat

does not necessarily dictate one's politics: "It ain't where you're from, it's where you're at."[4] For example, Caren Kaplan's essay in this volume rearticulates Jewish whiteness by reflexively charting the multipositionality of a Euro-American Jewish woman, and elucidating multicultural feminism as a political process of affiliation, disaffiliation, and reaffiliation.

Talking Visions appears at a moment when the pedagogical debates about the canon and about curricula have been fueled by a radical critique of heteromasculinist Europe as the source of cultural value and meaning. Despite the interventions of multicultural feminists, most institutions base their educational and curatorial practices on an implicit heteromasculinist Eurocentric "norm." The "rest," meanwhile, are relegated to "special topics" courses and exhibitions. The by now axiomatic point that social stratifications shape both our conscious and our unconscious thinking has had only a superficial cosmetic effect on the ways most institutions go about their work. While putting racial "flavors of the month" on display, they fail to perceive that no one is above race, and that gender is not merely a woman's issue, nor is sexual orientation merely a gay/lesbian matter. Intellectual inertia, however, still turns multicultural feminism into something "they" do, rather than a social project that touches *all* communities, disciplines, and institutions. (The critical studies of whiteness, Eurocentrism, and hetromasculinism, in this sense form part of the multicultural feminist political project.)

That this volume is published by SoHo's New Museum of Contemporary Art and Cambridge's MIT Press is also not a coincidence: the decolonization of culture has impacted not only the public sphere of policy-making but also the academy, the museum, and the publishing house. And despite neoconservative hysteria, previously taboo questions have acquired a certain respectability. Yet *Talking Visions* also appears at a moment of saturation for the commodification of difference. The institutional-showcase approach to multicultural feminist work is now fading. What is "in" eventually goes "out": when what is displayed becomes passé, the displayers must offer something more "exciting." The thriller approach and the fetishizing of the "new" inevitably lead to fatigue, boredom, and a thirst for even more exotic adventures. The attacks on the liberal rationale for the expenditure of public funds have made alternative artists and cultural activists even more vulnerable. Thus the volume contains a variety of political moods from activist fervor to ironic skepticism. Shu Lea Cheang's fragmented account of eighties video activism ending up as TV's "funniest home videos" highlights hegemonic culture's power to transform subversive texts into exotic artifacts, whence the need to "coopt back," to perpetually reinvent forms of resistance.

Since institutions allow only for paradigmatic "niche" access to shrinking public funds, the multicultural feminist project confronts the false choice of either "letting a few in" or seeing none enter at all. Token gestures provide minuscule symbolic compensation for the history of dispossession on which much of this nation's wealth is based. (In fact, neither identity politics nor affirmative action can offer a fully adequate response to the dumb inertia of structures of domination.) The essentialism/antiessentialism debates also raise serious dilemmas for multicultural feminist practices. While poststructuralist feminist, queer, and postcolonial theories entail the rejection of essentialist articulations of identity and biologistic and transhistorical determinations of gender, race, and sexual identity, we theorists as political agents have at the same time supported "affirmative action," implicitly premised on the very categories elsewhere rejected as essentialist, leading to a paradoxical situation in which theory deconstructs totalizing myths while activism nourishes them. Given these complexities, an anti-essentialist multicultural feminist project is obliged to formulate identities as situated in geographical space and "riding" historical moment, to work through a politics whereby the decentering of identities, and the celebration of hybridities does not also mean that it is no longer possible to draw boundaries between privilege and disenfranchisement.

Talking Visions is conceived so as to avoid both falling into essentialist traps and the Hamlet-like political paralysis induced by certain deconstructionist formulations. It also avoids the "boxing in" logic by which diverse feminists of color have to wait their turn to speak. Rather than pit a rotating chain of oppositional communities against a white European dominant (a strategy that privileges whiteness, if only as constant antagonist), we must stress the links threading communities together in a conflictual network. Publications, exhibitions, and curricula on women of color that assume neat binarisms—black/white, Latina/white, Native American/white— ironically reposition whiteness as normative interlocutor. And all the other groups excluded by such analytical binarisms, are put on hold, fitting only as spectators or "extras" into such neatly dualistic categories. *Talking Visions* does not follow a color/racial schema whereby the diverse feminists of color stand in line to represent "their community." Such representations are always more complex than the straightjacket of identity politics might suggest. The multicultural feminist project places "minorities" (racial, sexual, religious) *in relation,* without ever suggesting their positionings are harmoniously identical, while also envisioning ways in which diverse histories and cultures parallel, intersect, and allegorize one another.

The multilayered, colonial history implicit in *Talking Visions* "exceeds" the misleadingly tidy five-part U.S. census categorization of "races." The census is in fact heterotopic, mingling issues of race (blacks), language (Hispanics), and geography (Asians) as if they were commensurate categories. "Asian-American," for example, is often applied only to East Asians, excluding Iranians, Pakistanis, Lebanese, or others from South and West Asia (the Middle East). "African-American," similarly, does not usually denote recent immigrants from Africa, or black immigrants from South America and the Caribbean. "Arab" is usually misconstrued as synonymous with Muslim, though some Arabs are Christian and others Jewish. Reductive categories like "Jew," "Arab," and "Latino/a," similarly, hide the racial variety of a chromatic spectrum that includes white, black, mestizo/a, and brown. In the U.S. many communities and individuals fit only awkwardly into the single-hyphen boxes, yet bureaucratic pluralism does not allow for the polysemy in the politics of color. The usual ways of talking about "minority" identities leave little room for the complexities of these categories, or for the porous borders between them (see Coco Fusco's "We Wear the Mask," Patricia Hoffbauer's "Are We Still Juggling Bananas?," and Adrian Piper's "Passing for White, Passing for Black" and "Political Self-Portrait #2 (Race)). The histories of Native Americans, African-Americans, Latino/as, and Asian-Americans may all have been shaped within U.S. colonialism, but the problematic nature of these categories becomes obvious when seen in relation to the parallel and inter-linked histories in the Americas.

The "hyphenated American," furthermore, is often assumed to sport only a single hyphen. But in fact the successive colonial and postcolonial displacements put too much pressure on the already stressful and overdetermined single hyphen. Each chain of hyphens implies a complicated history of accreting identity and fragmented belonging as multiple displacements generate distinct "distillations" of immigrant identity. But often the "host" country acknowledges only one link in the chain, and which link is stamped as "real" tells us less about the immigrant than about the geopolitical imaginary of the host. Even within a multicultural feminist space, identities can be misconstrued or misrecognized. A desire for a chimerical "authenticity" and officially inscribed "coloredness" and "sexuality" can lead to misapprehensions. A female bisexual of Indian-African origin, for example, may be pressured to conform to sexual orientation as defined by

U.S. norms, and may be accused of passing herself off as African, a charge carrying an implication of opportunism (see May Joseph's essay, "Transatlantic Inscriptions"). Yet the history of Indian-Tanzanian-Americans, which differs from that of both Africans and Indians who immigrated to the U.S. directly from their respective continents, need not be shorn of their Africaness.[5] To take another example, Jewish Moroccans who came to the U.S. after living in Israel are often labeled simply "Israelis." Whereas in the Indian-Tanzanian-American case what precedes the first hyphen is "frozen" to capture the essence of a dispersed identity, in the Moroccan-Israeli-American case it is the second term that is "frozen." What is it about such multiple displacements on the way to the U.S. that make the first part of the hyphenated label (Indian) essential in one case and the second part (Israeli) essential in the other? In the Indian-Tanzanian-American case, the African link becomes taboo because in the U.S. context "African" can only be equated with "real" black Africans, while in the case of the Moroccan-Israeli-American, Morocco is taboo because "Moroccan" is assumed to be only Arab (seen as an antonym to "Jewish") and Muslim, and because "Israeli" is associated with European Jews (when, in fact, the demographic majority of Israel is formed by relatively powerless black Jews of Asian and African origin).[6] Since racial definitions, ethnic hierarchies, gender identities and sexual belongings are situated and conjunctural, shifting and transmuting across histories and geographies, they explode and implode a unified narrative of what constitutes "racial," "national," and "sexual" identifications and affiliations.

Charting such multilayered displacements does not imply a politics of originary belonging. Multicultural feminism challenges salami-style identity politics with its infinite slicing of identity in a Zenon-like search for the minimal units of self-definition. Multicultural feminism, then, avoids the twin pitfalls of an atomized fracturing of units of the local "on whose behalf I truly speak," on the one hand, and a diffuse all-embracing cosmopolitan internationalism "which speaks for all of us," on the other. Instead, it shuttles back and forth between concentric circles of affiliation riven by power asymmetries. Feminists of color are not immune to trying to "speak for" sisters of the same race, especially when a First World platform offers privileged access to "global village" media. The critique of white feminists who speak for all women might be extrapolated to cases in which upper-middle class "Third World" women come to unilaterally represent "other" working class sisters, or to diasporic feminists operating within First World representational practices. Metropolitan feminists of color have to be aware

Ella Shohat

of these hierarchies, just as "Third World" feminists cannot ignore class or religious privileges when "speaking for our sisters."[7] The possibility of speaking for Third World sisters (even if of the same color) is rooted in global structural inequalities that generate such representational asymmetries, whereby some voices and some modes of speaking are amplified more than others. (See here Isabelle Gunning's discussion of the variety of legal and media discourses on "female genital surgeries,"[8] ranging from A. B. Rosenthal's op–ed pieces and Pat Schroeder's speeches to Oprah Winfrey's TV show and Alice Walker and Pratibha Parmar's film *Warrior's Marks*.) Even with the very best intentions, a fetishized focus on African female genital mutilation or on Asian foot-binding ends up as complicit with a Eurocentric victimology that reduces African or Asian cultures and women to such practices, while muting or marginalizing African or Asian agency and organizing. A multicultural feminist critique disrupts the narrative of center/periphery when talking "about" the "Third World," showing feminist resistant practices within a conflictual community, where opposition to such practices does not perpetuate the false dichotomy of savagery versus civilization or tradition versus modernity.

I am in no way suggesting that only those who have experienced clitoridectomy, sterilization, infanticide, or rape have the right to speak, but rather that we pay attention to narrative strategies and representational politics, especially given Eurocentric celebrations of such victimologies on the world stage. One challenge for first World feminists of color is how to avoid a Eurocentric rescue narrative that substitutes the First World woman of color for the white man (à la colonial narrative) or white woman (à la white feminism) rescuing a dark woman from a dark man. Questions of representation thus have consequences for the ways U.S.-based feminists of color do alliance work with those based in the "Third World" and vice versa. The point is not to speak in a way that paradigmatically replaces "our sisters," or to altogether hurtfully withdraw from speaking, or to speak only from the secure ground of a Cartesian "I," but rather to speak and act dialogically with, sharing the critique of hegemony and the burden of representation. Multicultural feminism is thus less concerned with identities as something one has than in identification as something one does. While rejecting fixed, essentialist and reductionist formulations of identity, it fosters a mutually enriching politics of intercommunity representation.

Talking Visions strives to transcend the narrow and often debilitating confines of identity politics in favor of a multicultural feminist politics of identification, affiliation, and social transformation. It even involves making representation less of a burden and more of a collective pleasure and responsibility. It is less about who can speak than about how the diverse constituencies of multicultural feminism can interweave resistant voices together; and about how to work from cacophony to effective political polyphony. Highlighting the shapeshifting nature of many communities of the hyphenated, *Talking Visions* suggests a desire for an open narrative of feminist terrains, making visible not only the fact of the multiply hyphenated identity, but also the dissonances among multiple political identifications. Power laden, hybridization is a historically nonfinalized process, shaped not only by common experiences but also by the political mobilization of difference.

After the Metanarratives of Liberation

Produced also in a moment of postmodern dissolution of metanarratives, *Talking Visions* offers neither grand salvations nor total revolutions. Indeed, the fact that the era of national liberation in the Third World has now ebbed is more or less obvious. In many regions, the powerful framework of nationalism, which once held such enormous liberationist promise, has begun to fall apart. Third Worldist euphoria has given way to the collapse of communism, the indefinite postponement of "tricontinental revolution," the realization that the "wretched of the earth" are not unanimously revolutionary, and the recognition that international geopolitics and the global economic system have forced even the "Second World" to be incorporated into transnational capitalism.[9] The slogans of nationalism, its mythos of hearth and home, are now trumpeted by national elites often repressive toward those who wanted to go beyond a purely nationalist revolution to restructure class, caste, gender, sexuality, religion, racial, and ethnic relations. The choice of the term "multicultural feminism" as opposed to "Third World feminism" in my title is not simply a matter of fashion; it signals a different historical moment and different set of discourses. The anticolonial struggle is echoed in contemporary efforts to decolonize Eurocentric culture; but the critique is now articulated within what I would call a "post-Third Worldist" perspective.[10] Moving beyond the ideology of Third Worldism, this perspective assumes the validity of antiracist and anticolonialist movements, but also interrogates the multiple fissures in the "Third World" nation and U.S. sixties national power movements. Contemporary postcolonial and diasporic writings testify to the difficulties of redefining and reestablishing a relationship to the icons, symbolic complexes, and discourses of anti-colonial and antiracist nationalism after the decline of its liberationist thrust.

The totalizing thrust of the women's movement, meanwhile, has been questioned from a different angle. In many national and international fora, "Third World" feminists and/or womanists have criticized the facile harmony of a Western-based global sisterhood that has on the whole been blind to the privileges it has derived from its comfortable station on the neoimperial pyramid. Debates about class, globalization, and sexual orientation have also led to interrogating the Eurocentrism, capitalism, and heterosexism underlying much of "mainstream" feminism. More recently, fissures in the utopian camaraderie of lesbian/gay liberation have also become visible, leading to mobilizing around the race/sexuality intersection, and to a mushrooming of gay/lesbian-of-color organizations. To put it differently, race *does* matter for an alternative politics of sexual identity, just as "globalization" matters for an analysis, such as Jacqui Alexander's here, that situates the "travel" of gay and lesbian desire within neoimperial formations of transnational capitalism. Such critiques challenge the liberal pluralist feminism which produces itself as "major" and others as "minor." Third World and First World-"minority" feminists have sought to shake the epistemological ground of the univocal understanding of "woman" upon which so much of the feminist intervention of the 1960s and 1970s was based. Gays and lesbians of color, similarly, have questioned a unified Western-centered understanding of sexual identity, and the heteronormative formulation of Third Worldist women's struggles. Interrogating the monocultural connotations of pseudo-universal terms like "woman," "womanhood," and even "feminism," "gayness," and "lesbianism," relational multicultural feminisms argue for linking specific intersecting modes of resistance in response to converging forms of oppression.

Multicultural feminism has had to address, then, both the Eurocentric assumptions of Western feminism and the (hetero)masculinist culture of nationalist movements. Historically, colonized women had been deeply involved in anticolonialist and antiracist movements, long before their dialogue with the "women's movement." (See Lillian Mulero's *Dolores* and *Wounds of Jesus*.) In fact, it was often their activism within anticolonialist and antiracist movements that led to their political engagement in feminism (even if this word was not used.) Not accidentally, anti-colonialist and antiracist discourses of national unity have often had to rely on the symbolic image of the (heterosexual) revolutionary woman to "carry" the allegory of the birth of the Nation, precisely because addressing women's demands for equality might have evoked a weak link—the fact of a fissured revolution in which unity, vis-à-vis the colonizer, does not preclude contradictions among the colonized. While inscribing gender and sexuality into the debates concerning nation and race, multicultural feminism also inscribes nation and race into feminist debates. These critiques perform a dismantling of patriarchal nationalist (even if anticolonial) historiography while also challenging the Eurocentric contours of "gender" and "sexuality" within feminist historiography. The disappointed hopes for women's empowerment within nationalist frameworks (including U.S. "minority" power movements) have shaped a fresh sense of community answerability. Navigating between being excommunicated by patriarchal nationalists as "traitors to the nation" or "betrayers of the race" and Western feminists' imperial fantasies of rescuing clitoridectomized and veiled women, post-Third Worldist multicultural feminists have not metamorphosed into Western-style feminists—even if Third World nationalists often accuse them of becoming "white" or "Westernized"; and even if white feminists embrace them as those who "finally learned their lesson."

What is often missed is that the long history of colonized/racialized women's commitment to gender equality has been practiced largely within the context of national/racial liberation. The strategies for achieving this equality, moreover, have changed dramatically in the post–Third Worldist era. That the criticism of the "brothers" is now more audible does not mean that the "sisters" had formerly been tongue-tied; it just means that dirty laundry is now being washed in public, no longer hidden for fear of "giving ammunition to the enemy." (See Reneé Cox's ironic recasting of classical representations of the Last Supper in her *Yo Mama's Last Supper*.) The end of Third Worldist euphoria, and skepticism about its liberationist promise for women, have allowed a public "outing" of what was previously whispered: the fact that the decolonization of the nation has not led to the decolonization of heterosexual women and gays and lesbians from patriarchy and homophobia. Furthermore, Third Worldist women's movements have generally become complicitous in a heteronormative discourse, sharing with patriarchal nationalists the vision of the fecund procreative nation. The simultaneous affirmation of struggles both against neocolonialism/racism and against patriarchy/heterosexism has led to controversial public stances; for example, the recent black-feminist critiques, visible in the media, of the Million Man March. *Talking Visions* thus looks at a historical moment of both rupture and continuity, when the macronarrative of women's liberation has ebbed yet sexism and heterosexism still prevail, and when the metanarratives of anticolonial revolution have long been eclipsed yet where issues of (neo-) colonialism and racism persist.

We have traveled a long road since the publication of such groundbreaking multi-racial feminist anthologies as Cherríe Moraga and Gloria Anzaldúa's *This Bridge Called My Back: Writings by Radical Women of Color.*[11] Using personal experience as a trampoline for an analysis of the social and historical forces shaping the consciousness of women of color, their anthologies filled important "gaps" both in the (white) feminist movement and in Third Worldist revolutions. By "giving name to the nameless" (Audre Lorde),[12] they transformed silence into speech. In fact, for feminists of color, language, voice, and writing have been key tropes articulated as "being silenced," "to be heard," "talking back," "speaking out," "gaining voice." It is not simply a case, as Aimé Césaire suggested in his rewriting of Shakespeare's *Tempest,* of using Prospero's language to curse him, but also, I would suggest, of hearing the voice of the absent dark woman, the missing "Calibana" of Césaire's anti-colonial text. Correcting a serious lacuna in the field of knowledge production, radical writings by feminists of color offered "theory in the flesh," (Moraga/Anzaldúa), and a search for an authentic expression beneath the alienating scars of colonialism and hetero/ sexism, which inspired many women of color. (See here images by Amalia Mesa-Bains, Marta Maria Perez Bravo, Dolores Zorreguieta, Maria Magdalena Campos-Pons, and Jossette Urso for more recent visual reworkings of the "biomythography" (Lorde) of bodily memory and counter spirituality.) Such works have reflected the fact that Third World feminists, and "minority" feminists in the First World, have found no cozy home in the communities of white First World feminism.[13] Their longing for a "home," or a bonding site free from oppression, was accompanied by concerns about how to create such a space of emotional knowledge and feminist language while doing away with the "master's tools" (Audre Lorde).

Anthologies by and about diverse women of color emerged out of a period when one could still speak of *the* movement, whether that movement was black power, *la raza,* the antiwar movement, or the women's movement; a period when one could still speak of "revolution" in the Leftist-Marxist, Third World, anticolonial sense. From the seventies the writing of women of color has been characterized by a complex and conflicted relation to the (Euro-American) women's liberation movement and to the diverse heteromasculinist race-based movements (Black Power, la raza). In the past decade meanwhile, one finds, even on the left, a self-reflexive and ironic distance from revolutionary rhetoric, eclipsed by an

Plate 3: *Counter/Quilt,* 1991
Fabric/mixed, handquilted, 74 × 65"
Josette Urso
Photo: Hallie Levine
Courtesy of the artist

idiom of "resistance"; Substantive nouns like "revolution" and "liberation" transmute into a largely adjectival opposition: "counter-hegemonic," and "resistant practices," indicative of a crisis of totalizing narratives and a shifting vision of what constitutes an emancipatory project. Recent multicultural feminist writings are very much indebted to the earlier texts, but they differ in their tone, in their modes of analysis, and in their ways of formulating transformative politics. The gradual shift from the revolutionary spirit characteristic of the early activism of feminists of color forms part of a more general eclipse of revolutionary projects. *A luta continua,* even in the late 1990s, then, but it *continuas* in a different way.

The shift from the unitary subject of "revolution" to a fragmented and dispersed scene of multiple resistances has also been evident in more recent volumes, such as *Scattered Hegemonies: Postmodernity and Transnational Feminist Practices,* edited by Inderpal Grewal and Caren Kaplan, and *Feminist Genealogies, Colonial Legacies and Democratic Futures,* edited by M. Jacqui Alexander and Chandra Talpade Mohanty, both of which articulate a complex theory and practice of feminism, unfolded within the realities of neocolonialism and transnationalism.[14] *Talking Visions* straddles this same postmodern fault line. It does not erase earlier writings by radical women of color; on the contrary, it draws nourishment from them, while at the same time recognizes that it has to formulate its vision within an altered theoretical and political framework that allows only for contingent forms of resistance. The volume, then, offers no single "safe house" but rather a makeshift network of dwellings, a mobile cohabitation of alliances. We may create a "safe house for difference" (here Audre Lorde's collective spatial metaphor has to be seen in contrast to Virginia Woolf's more individualist trope of "a room of one's own");[15] but even collective "houses" assembled from alliances will be constantly on the move in a world simultaneously undergoing globalization and fragmentation, a world where transnational corporations claim that "we're all connected" (to cite the New York Telephone ad) but where, at the same time, borders and passports are kept under thorough surveillance, a constant reminder that some have more "connections" than others. The goal of this book is to stage a shifting, multifronted constellation of struggles that can synergistically meet and mutually reinforce one another.

The Perils of Monoculturalism: Whose Feminism? Which Beginnings?

Multicultural feminism challenges a Eurocentric ordering of women's cultures, les/bi/gay identities, and feminist histories. It questions the benevolence of "allowing" other voices to add themselves to the "mainstream" of feminism by looking at feminism as *itself* a constitutively multi-voiced arena of struggle. The feminist work that has taken place within anticolonial and antiracist movements has often gone unrecognized by monocultural First World feminism. With some exceptions, the calls by feminists of color for white women to "listen up"[16] over the last two decades have not been adequately heeded. "Mainstream feminists" have accused "feminists of color" of endangering "our" movement by bringing up inconveniently divisive issues; the reassuring refrains of "I'm every woman" and "We are family" roll on.[17] (See Janet Henry's tales of NYC downtown feminist self-aggrandizing in relation to Asian-American or African-American feminist organizations, or Marina Alvarez's testimony on white feminists' supercilious charity toward working class Latina AIDS activists.) That the silence concerning the inequitable distribution of material and cultural resources among women itself generates fragmentation and tensions goes unacknowledged. (See Joyce J. Scott's *Nanny Gone Wrong* and Lynne Yamamoto's *Wrung*.)

In the academe, meanwhile, feminists of color working in ethnic studies and area studies have encountered a patronizing misrecognition—"So you do feminism too!"—an attitude that echoes the earlier dismissal of Third World work to empower women as "merely" nationalist and "not yet quite" feminist. Even in the 1990s, major cultural and educational institutions convey the notion of "Feminist Theory" (read non-racialized feminist theory) as normative, while the feminist work performed under the rubrics of "nation," "race," or "class" is politely ushered to the back seat. Recent debates over race, postcolonialism, and multiculturalism have led some white feminist scholars to integrate race in relation to gender and sexuality, but there is little participatory dialogue with "other" cultures and histories beyond token homage to a few star feminists of color.[18]

Tokenism "charitably" tacks on "other" cultures to a preexisting nucleus, reducing feminists of color to "native informants" whose contribution to feminism is limited to their authenticating report about their exotic forms of subalternity. In other words, the location of the "mainstream" in the white heterosexual First World is masked as universal, while all other contributions are regarded as relevant only to the remote provinces of feminism. Multicultural feminism questions the submerged epistemologies of Eurocentric studies of women, gender, and sexuality, thus asserting the active, generative participation of women/gays/bi/lesbians of color at the very core of a shared conflictual history. The longer history of activism at the race/gender crossroads has been generally elided by gender-specific feminism, creating the illusory impression of a meeting between equals at this multicultural, postcolonial moment when race may actually matter for "our" feminist inquiry. The intellectual energy devoted by feminists of color to analyzing life at the intersection is thus buried under a false threshold, as though "we" are all sharing equally in the exciting discovery of a hitherto untouched "virgin land." In this sense, feminist writing about race and postcolonialism is seen as something new, as some writers narcissistically confuse the contours of their own intellectual biography with the larger twists and turns of history. From a multicultural-feminist perspective, however, women and gays/lesbians of color, within and outside the U.S., have from the outset engaged the frictions of nation, race, class, gender and sexuality.

Such mutually shaping frictions, furthermore, still tend to be understood outside of colonial history, while diverse multicultural-feminist practices are comfortably subsumed as mere extensions of an all-embracing Feminist Theory. Old paradigms are extended onto new fetishized (dark) objects, torn from their content. "Feminist Theory" thus absorbs race into the homogenizing framework of the "shared critique of patriarchy" in a sponge approach that sees feminism's beginnings as always residing with "Western" theories and practices. An exclusive focus on gender and sexuality renders multicultural feminist blood and sweat invisible by failing to acknowledge the diverse ways of fighting for women's well-being as equally feminist, and by casting women obliged to address national and racial realities as "part-time" feminists. The concern of women of color for "their" nation or race is myopically seen as too local, too tribal almost, to qualify for the prestigiously theoretical realm of Feminist Theory, and, paradoxically, at the same time, too broad. These too-specific/too-broad preoccupations, it is implied, make women of color lose sight of feminism proper. But anti-patriarchal and anti-homophobic work within anti-colonial and anti-racist struggles will remain marginal to the feminist canon as long as Eurocentric feminism retains the power of naming. The dispute has to do with contested visions of which knowledges and struggles constitute a legitimate feminist "herstory," issues with serious consequences for how material resources are distributed, for how curricula are developed, and which social vision is projected into the future.

Although Eurocentric feminists have matronizingly misconstrued post–Third Worldist women of color as "latecomers" to feminism, many feminists of color have shunned mainstream feminist organizations (both

Plate 4: *Nanny Gone Wrong,* 1992
Beads, thread, leather; 20 × 8 × 8″
Joyce Scott
Photo: Kanji Takeno
Courtesy of the artist and Esther Saks Fine Art Limited

Ella Shohat

straight and lesbian) because of this ethnic/racial/national erasure. To counter Eurocentric narratives—the dark women who now "do the feminist thing"—multicultural feminist work must be re-narrativized also in relation to anticolonial and antiracist movements. U.S. women of color and Third World women's struggle over the past decades cannot conform to the orthodox sequence of "first waves" and "second waves," just as multicultural feminism cannot be viewed as simply a recent bandwagon phenomenon; it is a response to a five hundred-year history of gendered colonialist dispossession in the past and of massive postcolonial displacements in the present. In this sense the multicultural feminist project heightens our sensitivity to the resourceful ways women/gays/bi/lesbians have challenged the daily brutalities of the enmeshed systems of racist colonialism and hetero/sexist patriarchy. The dismissal of work on racism and colonialism as irrelevant for feminism has thus triggered ambivalence toward the feminist movement on the part of hetero/bi/lesbian women of color in and outside the U.S. Sometimes the very word "feminism" has provoked hostility, associated as it is with the privileging of single-issue struggle over the multi-axis struggles of "other" women, whence such coinages as "womanism." But rather than merely extend a preexisting Eurocentric feminism, as a certain notion of Euro-"diffusionism" would have it,[19] post–Third Worldist multicultural theories and practices shape a more flexible polycentric space for feminism, one open to historically contested racial, sexual, regional, and national imaginaries.

Although the battle over issues related to gender and sexuality is fought on many terrains, feminists of color have performed such work most often under the rubric of "community work," and in academia under the rubric of "ethnic studies" and "area studies." Thus, even if not necessarily rallying behind a feminist banner, Latina, African-American, or Arab-American women activists who work within their communities to make links between diverse forms of oppression can be seen or claimed as "objectively" feminist. (For example, see here Petra Allende and Rocio Aranda-Alvarado's "When Florida Isn't an Option," a testimony on aging and activism among diverse Latino/a communities in El Barrio, pointing to the links between local church-based organizing and national senior-citizens' militancy; and Marina Alvarez and Ginetta Candelario's "(Re)visiónes," a dialogue on AIDS activism and empowerment that discusses the alliance between grassroots organizers in the Bronx and the national and international AIDS movement activists; or Ellen Spiro's *DiAna's Hair Ego*). By deploying multi-axis analyses, multicultural feminism charts a non-finalized definition of feminism. It thus disinters stories of survival from the rubble of the master narratives of progress, while also contesting the Eurocentric rescue narrative that presents "modernization" and "development" as the keys to salvation.

Feminism often conceives itself as emerging out of Western modernity. Rather than project a linear stagist narrative in which women/gays/bi/lesbians of the "Third World" live "underdeveloped" realities carried out in another time-zone apart from the global system of the late capitalist world, time can more adequately be formulated as "scrambled and palimpsestic in all the Worlds, with the premodern, the modern, the postmodern and the paramodern coexisting globally."[20] In "supporting the agendas of modernity," Inderpal Grewal and Caren Kaplan point out, "feminists misrecognize and fail to resist Western hegemonies."[21] Echoing colonial discourse, hegemonic feminism has thus operated within the binarism of tradition versus modernity. Third World secular nationalism, including its feminist wing, meanwhile, have often adopted the modernizing agenda drawn from Eurocentric "progressive" discourses, venerating a modernity ironically made possible, as it were, on the backs of working class men and women.[22] The ideology of modernization has been crucial for assuring nationalist secular, even scientific notions of the "Nation," thriving on a binarist demarcation of opposing twin concepts—modernity/tradition, underdevelopment/development, science/superstition, technology/backwardness. Both bourgeois nationalists and marxist anticolonialists have seen "tradition" as dead weight to be transformed by the forward march of modernity. In Angola and Mozambique, for example, revolutionary progress also meant forbidding traditional healing practices (often performed by women) because they were viewed as non-scientific, mere superstition.

Feminists in the Third World, too, have often adopted this kind of binarist logic, also typical of "women and development" programs, which equates "tradition" with "backwardness" and "modernity" with "women's equality." Westernized indigenous nationalist elites have often absorbed the binaristic sexual norms of their colonizers, even in places like the Middle East/North Africa, where a kind of informal bisexuality had sometimes been tacitly accepted. The modernizing narrative thus stretches across geographic and national borders into the diverse "worlds." To take another example, it is seen not only in U.S. sterilization policies toward Native American and Puerto Rican women but also in similar policies of Third World nation-states themselves, often carried out in conjunction with U.N. "overpopulation" maps of the world. The Indira Gandhi population control program resulted, not unlike U.S. policies towards its internal female "others," in forced sterilization. Colonialist discourses of "progress" and "modernization," ironically, have thus found their heirs in postindependence Third Worldist development policies, at times carried out literally on the bodies of women, especially when their reproductive force is managed by the re/productive needs of the state-apparatus.

One might also question the relationships, as Maria Milagros Lopez does here, between production and reproduction, especially the feminist valorization of work. (See here Marina Gutierrez's *Isla del Encanto,* Nina Barnett's *At Casa Linda,* and Lynne Yamamoto's *Wrung.*) Puritanical, Marxist, and Third World nationalist ideologies share the hostile attitudes toward the subsistence cultures of indigenous "fourth world" peoples. They have portrayed subsistence economies as "leisure culture," presented as at odds with post/modernity and the brave new order of the "developing nation" in an earlier period and transnational corporations in a later period. In arguing that Marxism and capitalism share a productivist ideology of modernization in relation to work, body, land, and time, some Native American critics, for example, have challenged the Third Worldist marriage between Marxism and nationalism.[23] Feminists too, whether capitalist or socialist, whether First World or Third World, often share a productivist ideology that has clashed with other, non-productivist social visions. Therefore, a multicultural feminism looking through indigenist eyes might question the historical alliance between productivist ideologies and patriarchal cultures. But it has also to ask, within which social arrangements do we imagine a re-conceptualization of gender and sexual relations? And what are the consequences of challenging productivist ideology for feminists working within corporate culture, including within the publish-or-perish university?

For indigenous American feminists, it was an imposed "progress" that replaced the frequently matrilineal, matriarchal, or matrifocal social systems native to this hemisphere with the colonialist patriarchy of European settlers. Such "societies," writes Rayna Green, "were neither acceptable nor comprehensible to members of the European patriarchies who misunderstood Eastern tribes so profoundly that they sabotaged their own treaties regularly in making them with men who did not have the right to make such decisions."[24] Colonialism and neocolonialism have powerfully destabilized local social structures, including the economies of gender and sexuality. "Trickle-down patriarchy," as M. A. Jaimes ★ Guerrero argues here, subordinated Native American women to federally recognized male "progressive" leaders who were granted the power to override "traditional" male and female leaders. U.S. colonial discourse and federal policies—for example, the "blood quantum" definition of official "Indian" identity—have had a powerful impact on recodifying sexual norms, and on gendered distribution of power and material resources within contemporary reservation gender politics. Patriarchy-from-within has thus been symbiotically sustained by the Euro-patriarchy of the nation-state-from-without. Gender and sexual politics in Native American communities, in other words, are linked to state policy as well as to colonial history. A feminist analysis that takes as axiomatic an implicit "equality" of oppressions between *all* colonized women and colonizer women as similarly subordinated to patriarchy at the moment of the encounter, elides the fact that: (a) at the moment of "the encounter" not *all* colonized people were subjugated to heteromasculinist ideologies; (b) that colonialism played a role in encouraging or setting-up indigenous patriarchal structures and heterosexual codes subordinated to colonial power; and (c) that colonizing women, despite their own subordination, helped sustain these structures and nurture these ideologies.[25] Although some anticolonial rewritings of the past have displayed ahistorical essentialism about indigenous culture and spirituality, Indigenist feminist claims for the egalitarian nature of some precolonial societies cannot all be simply dismissed as romantic nostalgia. Such a blanket denial of indigenous American claims raises questions about the investment in the equalizing narrative of patriarchy and heterosexism on both sides of the colonial divide.

Rewriting the history of gender and sexuality, then, is thoroughly entangled within the rereading of colonial and racial histories. As multicultural feminism articulates its project, in other words, it rewrites the diverse neighboring discourses that have elided or subsumed it. Constructing resistant histories of women of color, as Chandra Talpade Mohanty puts it, "often requires reading against the grain of a number of intersecting progressive discourses (e.g., white feminist, Third World nationalist, and socialist), as well as the politically regressive racist, imperialist, sexist discourses of slavery, colonialism, and contemporary capitalism."[26] Complex relational study of varied gender and sexual histories can contribute to a polycentric feminist scholarship and to dialogical alliances.

The Situated Body

One arena of such relational study is highlighted by this volume concerns the imagining of the body. Lisa Jones's essay, "Hair Trade," speaks of the ways the production and consumption of hair is globally interwoven;

Shirin Neshat's image "Allegiance with Wakefulness," foregrounds the female flesh allowed by Muslim code to remain uncovered, while also "veiling" the exposed feet with Persian poetry written in the U.S. diaspora. The differentiated female body challenges the free-floating, ahistorical deployment of psychoanalytic categories such as "desire," "fetishism," and "castration," suggesting instead an analysis of the female body grounded in diverse women's experiences and agendas.[27] U.S. feminists of color have exposed monocultural feminism's "writing out" of these diverse experiences, raising such previously unaddressed issues as the political semiotics of the black female body, subjected to phallocentric erasure both from within and from outside the community. Thus, the feminist critique of the patriarchal family resonates differently for African-American feminists, for whom such a critique must take on board the memory of slavery, rape, castration, and lynching.

African-Americans were the only U.S. community expressly discouraged from establishing (heterosexual) families, a denial that went hand in hand with images of hypersexualization. The overwhelming connection between most interracial rape cases and lynching, as documented by Ida B. Wells-Barnett, was that "black women and children were raped prior to and during lynchings, as well as lynched with black males who assisted them in resisting or avenging rape by white males."[28] As spectacular orgies of hypocrisy, lynching can be seen as a disciplinary staging of forced confession and punishment. Lynching, along with other forms of perverse theatricality, such as the burning at the stake of heretics, witches, indigenous, Muslim, and Jewish infidels, was based on the construction of sexual, gender, racial and religious deviance, culminating in the excruciating *jouissance* of mass executions.

Images of black, Latin, or Arab women in "heat" versus virginal white women, meanwhile, have mythically elided the history of subordination of women of color by white men. The hot/frigid dichotomy implied three interdependent axioms within the sexual politics of colonial discourse: first, the sexual interaction of black men and white women could only involve rape (since white women cannot possibly desire black men); second, the sexual interaction of white men and black women could not involve rape (since black women are presumably in perpetual heat and desire the white master); and third, the interaction of black men and black women also could not involve rape, since both were presumably in perpetual heat. It was this heterosexist, racist *combinatoire* that generated the (largely unspoken) rationale for the castration and lynching of African-

American men, projected as a threat to white women, and the immunity of white men to punishment for the rape of African-American women. The denial of any erotic intercourse between whites and non-whites had the further advantage of maintaining the myth of the West's ethnic "purity." (This myth is challenged in Adrian Piper's work.)

Whether discussing issues of rape, sterilization (as in Maria Milagros Lopez's essay "No Body is an Island" and Juan Sanchez's image *Cultural, Racial, Genocidal Policy*), cosmetic eye surgery (Kathleen Zane's "Reflections on a Yellow Eye"; the image from Pam Tom's films *Two Lies*), or female genital surgery (Isabelle Gunning's "Cutting Through the Obfuscation"), *Talking Visions* attests to the multiple situatedness of the gendered and sexed body. Such feminist achievements as highlighting the inextricable links between public and private forms of violence to the female body acquires altered meaning when multicultural feminists protest transnational companies' discriminatory "dumping" of flawed birth-control technologies in Latin America or Africa. Pro-life activists terrorize abortion clinics, but they raise not even a silent scream concerning U.S. sterilization policies with regard to Native American and Puerto Rican women. What sense does it make, then, to examine the "abortion debate" without making such links? Whereas a white female body might merely undergo surveillance from the reproductive machine, the dark female body is subjected to what I would call a *disreproductive* apparatus programmed by a hidden, racially coded demographic agenda.[29]

The body, then, appears in *Talking Visions* as a site of contestation, seen within a long-term historicized perspective. The lineage of the representations of women of color in film, television, travel journals, and fashion magazines, for example, can be traced back to popular sideshows and fairs and to early pornographic ethnography, as well as to the tradition of exhibiting "real" human objects that goes back to Columbus's importation of "New World" natives to Europe for purposes of scientific study and courtly entertainment. Organizing the world as a spectacle, exhibitors paraded indigenous Americans, Africans, and Asians before the West's bemused anthropological/zoological eye as a variety of exotic "pathologies." In a context where "blacks" or "reds" were made invisible, since, for example, the right of U.S. citizenship was granted only to "free white persons,"[30] the only visibility allowed people of color was the hyperbolized pathological visibility of the auction block, the circus, and the popular scientific exposition. Taken together, Renée Green's *Sites of Genealogy—Loophole of Retreat,* Kara Walker's *The End of Uncle Tom and the Grand Allegorical*

Tableau of Eva in Heaven, the image from Walter Lima, Jr.'s film, *Chico Rei* and bell hooks's "Naked Without Shame," evoke the relation between contemporary body politics and the history of the imperial gaze.

The spectacularization of science is clearly exemplified in the case of the "Hottentot Venus," Saartje Bartman, an African woman, who was displayed on the entertainment circuit in nineteenth-century England and France. Although her protrusive buttocks were the main attraction, the rumored peculiarities of her genitalia also drew crowds, with her racial/sexual "anomaly" constantly being associated with animality.[31] After her death at the age of twenty-five, the zoologist and anatomist Georges Cuvier received permission to dissect her body, and produced a detailed description of her private parts. Her genitalia still rest on a public shelf in the Musée de l'Homme in Paris alongside the genitalia of *une negresse* and *une peruvienne*—monuments to a kind of imperial necrophilia. (The final placement of the female parts in the patriarchally designated Museum of Man provides a crowning irony.) Anthropological shows prolonged a museological project of gathering three-dimensional archaeological, ethnographic, botanical, and zoological objects in the metropolis, plunging spectators into savage territories, and transforming for them the obscure *mappa mundi* into a familiar, mastered world. Renée Green's image *Sites of Genealogy,* for example, makes this message of pathology boomerang against scientist "senders." Green turns the supposedly oxymoronic, actually aggressively Eurocentric, renaming of an African woman as the "Hottentot Venus" against its originators by juxtaposing a fragment of a nineteenth-century drawing of a white woman in a hoop skirt with another fragment showing the torso of the nude African. By fragmenting the black woman's buttocks, Green exaggerates what for the white scientists was already exaggerated; by highlighting the fact that the white woman's fashionable hooped skirt also shapes artificially outsized buttocks, she suggests that both the European and the African woman have been constructed for masculinist pleasures, one as the acme of coy virginal beauty, the other, imagined as naked exemplum of gross corporeality. Strategically manipulating Eurocentric representations of an African woman to reflect the colonial gaze back on itself, African-American visual work reframes ethnographic/pornographic spectacle as a kind of posthumous poetic justice.[32]

The existential life of the racialized/sexualized body has been harsh, subject not only to the indignities of the auction block but also to rape, branding, lynching, whipping, and other forms of abuse, as well as to the cultural erasure entailed in aesthetic stigmatization, and, more insidiously,

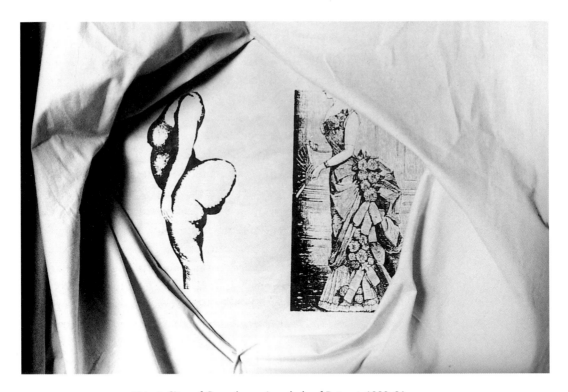

Plate 5: *Sites of Genealogy—Loophole of Retreat,* 1990–91
Detail from mixed media installation
P.S. 1 Museum, Long Island City, NY
Renée Green
Courtesy of the artist and Pat Hearn Gallery, New York

Ella Shohat

to an experience of shame. For the African-American female, as bell hooks shows here, nudity carries the shameful memory of the auction block's flesh market. The dominant media's long-term dissemination of the hegemonic white-is-beautiful aesthetic inherited from colonialist discourse have exiled women and men of color from their own bodies (see Tom Pam's *Two Lies* and Maria Hinojosa and Catherine Benamou's discussion of the racialized selection of female TV anchors in this volume). Anglo-American fashion journals, films, TV shows, and advertising have promoted a canonical notion of beauty, which dictates that only white heterosexual women and men are permitted entry into the public realm of legitimate images of desire. These media have extended a longstanding valorization of whiteness as aesthetic ideal. Nineteenth-century scientific and aesthetic writings on white pulchritude clearly ranked male brains over female beauty, but ultimately embraced white women for their membership in the family of (white) Man. It is only against the backdrop of this long history of fetishizing white "feminine" and "masculine" looks that one can appreciate the emotional force of the counter-expression "Black is beautiful." The contributions to *Talking Visions* transcend the normative gaze that has systematically devalued non-European appearance and aesthetics.[33]

Negotiating Looks

Colonial hierarchies have ramifications for the everyday negotiations of looks and identity. The hegemony of the Eurocentric gaze, spread by First as well as Third World media, explains why *morena* women in Puerto Rico and Mizrahi (African and Asian Jewish) women in Israel dye their hair blond; why Brazilian TV commercials are more suggestive of Scandinavia than of a country with a black majority; why Miss Universe contests around the world, even in North Africa, may elect blond "queens"; and why some Asian women undergo cosmetic surgery to appear more Western. The mythical norms of Eurocentric aesthetics come to invade even the intimacy of self-consciousness, leaving severe psychic wounds. A heteromasculinist patriarchal system contrived to generate neurotic self-dissatisfaction in *all* women (whence anorexia, bulimia, and other neuroses of appearance) becomes especially disturbing for women/lesbians of color attempting to recast themselves in the mechanical or electronic reproduction of fashionable selves. (See here Lorna Simpson's *Wigs*, Liliana Porter's *The Way Around,* and Pam Tom's *Two Lies.*) But while many writings have addressed the pain and shame caused by racism and hetero/sexism, few have spoken about the gaze that sisters of color impose on one another. bell hooks's essay here speaks of the internalized gaze toward the naked black female body resulting from a puritanical censorious regard directed at one's own black sisters; Tricia Rose's essay affirms the expressive staging of sexuality by female rappers. How can African, Asian, or Indigenous American feminists reclaim their bodies and sexualities, this volume asks, without reproducing the converse pathology of puritanical shame, which would hide the body as a corrective reaction to hypersexualization and to the mercantile exchange of "red," "yellow," "black," and "brown" flesh?

If anticolonial writers denounced the mimicry of colonized men, feminists of color have scored the complicity of women of color in the commodified display of their bodies. (See here Lorraine O'Grady's *Mlle Bourgeoise Noire Shouts Her Poem,* Maud Sulter's *Terpsichore,* and Adrian Piper's *Self Portrait: Class.*) Although women of color have experienced differing histories and sexual regimes, they have all lived under the sign of the exotic—as wiggling torsos balancing tutti frutti hats, as dark lascivious eyes peering from behind veils, as decorated feathered bodies slipping into trance to the accelerating rhythms of drums. In *Talking Visions,* Carmelita Tropicana, Ela Troyamo, Tiana (Thi Thanh Nga), Yolanda Andrade, Coco Fusco, Hahn Thi Pham, Annie Sprinkle, Maria Beatty, Jocelyn Taylor, Tricia Rose, Nicole Eisenman, Guerrilla Girls, Shu Lea Cheang, Patricia Hoffbauer, George Emilio Sanchez, and Peter Richards, for example, pleasurably re-appropriate the artifacts of exotic/erotic visual culture, reflexively foregrounding the artifice of ethnicity and femininity/masculinity. They undermine any expectation of sociologically "authentic" or ethnically "positive" representations. The skin and the mask become nearly indistinguishable.

The issue of "natural" versus "artificial" looks has complex implications for multicultural feminism. In anti-racist and anti-colonial contexts, men and women have often demonstrated loyalty to nation, class, and race through "authentic" looks, dress, or manner wielded as a response to a painful history of denial from without and self-rejection from within. The gendered construction of the authentic in the case of "Afro hair" or "Asian eyes" has demarcated specific looks as a kind of ethnic membership card. Yet one also may question the artificial/natural binary involved in self-remodeling. *Talking Visions* does not mold a new hierarchy of "natural" over "artificial."[34] While acknowledging the historically internalized colonization implicit in the prevalence of, for example, cosmetic eye surgery in the Asian community, it is also important to avoid essentialist fixations on originary looks. We can even discern a certain "agency" involved in such transformations, or invoke the possibilities opened up by self-hybridizations, while also examining the limits of the agency and hybridity exercised. Given the history of internalized colonization in relation to one's culture and body, cosmetic surgery has to be historicized, studied in different contexts: cosmetic surgery among Japanese-American women in the U.S., as Kathleen Zane's essay suggests, does not "signify" in the same way as it does in Japan. The challenge for multicultural feminism, then, is to criticize the visceral exile of Euro-"wannabees" while at the same time to seek a non-essentialist approach to looks and aesthetics, especially given the travel of images between the "Nation" and its diasporas.

Identity is often entangled in chromatically reductionist perceptions of color. A South Asian-Indian-Sudanese immigrant (Meena Alexander's "Alphabets of Flesh") may be misconstrued as "Latina" (even by Latinas themselves) in the streets of New York while a light-skinned African-American (Adrian Piper's "Passing For White, Passing for Black" and Political Self-Portrait #2 (race)) finds herself moving within the black/white divide as a "paleface" for blacks, or a "nonauthentic black" for whites. Meena Alexander's essay tells of negotiating New York City streets in a sari as opposed to negotiating them in jeans; and Caren Kaplan's "'Beyond the Pale'" recounts the vicissitude of identity (color, ethnicity, class, religion) when one is otherized as a dark-haired Euro-American Jewish girl in lily-white Maine (whose Native Americans are a mere submerged presence) but who in New York City's multi-racial streets experiences (Ashkenazi) Jewishness as a kind of norm. (See also Abbe Don's *We Make Memories*.)

Some postcolonial immigrant feminists, meanwhile, experienced class, caste, and ethnicity in their home countries as members of elites; they were not prepared for a painful, even surprising, racialization in the U.S. Whereas some immigrants to the U.S. suffered class and racial discrimination *before* their arrival to the U.S., elite Third World immigrants encounter such racialization only upon arrival in the U.S., *after* their psyches have been shaped. For the former, the U.S. might constitute a new form of racialization, even relative escape from the habitual racism to which they had been accustomed and which they had internalized (via shame of language, aesthetic self-rejection), while for the latter, the U.S. might bring a surprising and painful experience of subalternity for which they were not prepared. Those arriving from colonial-settler societies where race is central—such as Brazil and Israel—experience new forms of the gendered/raced oppression, this time in a new situation where the historical brunt of racism was largely borne by blacks, chicano/as, Puerto Ricans, and Native Americans. For myself, as an Iraqi raised in Israel, where my Mizrahi community was racialized as blacks by Euro-Israeli hegemony, the U.S. constituted a shift in register—no longer was I black but "only" a brown colored exotic with an accent. The sexualization and racialization one experiences, in other words, depend on the situation from which one has come, and how one is situated vis-à-vis "new" neighboring subaltern communities. Looks change with the angle of perception, with who is looking, and with how "we" look back at "them," and with what it is that "we" and "they" want to communicate with "our" looks. This differential perception of identity in shifting contexts calls for more situated articulations of the experiences of color.

Radical circles, too, are a fraught arena of negotiating looks. Butch and/or ethnic looks do not simply signify "natural" appearance; they enter into shifting configurations of meaning. A diasporic upperclass Palestinian wearing the traditional female peasant *gallabiya* stages the wearer's symbolic national allegiance, an allegiance mediated through a dispossessed class of women who actually worked the land before populating the refugee camps. Refashioning one's otherness across borders plays out a range of overlapping emotions from ambivalence about new geographies of belonging to claiming one's alterity as counter-cultural capital. Looks also take on their own life as cultural difference informs the performance of gay/lesbian/bi/transexuality. (See here Catherine Opie's *Dyke Deck* playing cards, Patricia Hoffbauer's *Carmenland, the Saga Continues,* Donna Han's *Flammable,* and Hanh Thi Pham's *Expatriot Consciousness, #9.*) Janet Henry's "WACtales: A Downtown Adventure" recounts the angry attempt by the Women's Action Coalition to eject a black man from one of their NYC meetings, only to discover that "he" was a black dyke. Queer politics has legitimized a woman's right publicly to enact masculine looks, and vice versa—whence the proliferation of male Carmen Mirandas (see Hoffbauer's *Carmenland, the Saga Continues*) and female Yentls (see Deborah Kass's *Triple Silver Yentl*). At the same time, cultural border-patrols police the flamboyant "femininity" of Latinas or Middle Easterner feminists wearing lipstick and long hair, finding them "in excess" of normative feminism/lesbianism. "All the problems and issues raised by feminism are valid and important," as Chrystos, suggests, but must one obey the lesbian dicta that "one must dress in a certain way or cut off one's hair to be real"?[35] Where one feminism scornfully sees the objectification of the female body, or heterosexualization of looks, the other sees an ingrained puritanism.

Communities of ethnic, racial, national, and sexual identity are not fixed, nor are all identities analyzable within an either/or (black/white, hetero/homo) binarism. Many Latina, Middle Eastern/North African, and Asian feminists, furthermore, complain of the restrictions on activism implicit in a black/white frame. Some even speak of being denied status as "women of color"; if they are not black, it is assumed, then they must be white.[36] We are reminded of Mirtha Quintanales's words:

> Ironically, when a Black American sister (or anyone for that matter) puts me, or other ethnic women of this society, in the same category with the socially dominant white American woman on the basis of lighter-than-black skin color, she is in fact denying my history, my culture, my identity, my very being, my pain and my struggle. . . . When she fails to recognize that the "social privileges" of lighter-than-black ethnic-minority lesbians in this society are almost totally dependent on our denial of who we are, on our *ethnic death,* she also falls prey to the racist mythology that color differences are the end-all indications of social inequality. That those who happen to have the "right" skin color are not only all alike but all hold the same social privileges. Yes lighter-than-black skin color may confer on some ethnic minority women the option of becoming "assimilated," "integrated" in mainstream American society. But is this really a privilege when it always means having to become invisible, ghostlike, identityless, communityless, totally alienated?[37]

Although not everyone moves within the spatial luxury of being able to go beyond such immediate lived dichotomies as black/white, Chicano/Anglo, and straight/gay, I have tried to organize these essays and visuals in such a way that the juxtapositions and contextualizations themselves at least implicitly deconstruct such dichotomies.

The multicultural feminist critique refuses the ahistorical articulation of sexual identities, tapping non-Western sexual histories and mythologies in order to envision non-dogmatic and non-binarist sexuality. (See May Joseph's evocation of Afro-Asian bisexual desire in diaspora, and M. A. Jaimes ★ Guerrero's account of the impact of colonialism on sexual roles in indigenous societies.) A few of the contributors here configure the raced and gendered body within sexually transgressive spaces. (See Han's *Flammable,* Opie's *Dyke Deck,* and Yolanda Andrade's *Big Tits Mendoza.*) Looks and identity, this volume suggests, are inscribed within the politics of visuality, but the politics of visuality also needs to be reinvoiced in relation to a rich polyphony of alliances.

Dissonant Polyphonies

Issues of gender, class, nation, race, religion, and sexuality all meet, and sometimes crash, at the intersection. In the U.S. as a constitutively multi-racial nation, with Indigenous Americans, African-Americans, and Euro-Americans standing at the core of a conflictual national formation, a constant process of synchresis has communities brush against and rub off on one another in a crowded ambivalent space of cultural interaction. Given the damage inflicted by colonialism, racism, and hetero/sexism, many feminists of color have drawn the contours of identity both around shared wounds and around the celebration of the "feminine principle of our cultures." Stories of solidarity and sacrifice have cemented the bonds among radical women of color. Tales of Indigenous American men and women helping black fugitives from slavery, or of black men and women joining Indigenous American resistance (in the Black Seminole maroon communities, say, or in the Afro-Brazilian maroon republic of Palmares), have inspired contemporary alliances. Many non African-American feminists acknowledge a strong debt to African-American political and intellectual interventions.[38] Maria Hinojosa and Catherine Benamou, for example, recollect here the influence of black activism and popular culture on Latino/a identity. Through "analogical structure of feelings"[39] minoritized communities identify with one another emotionally, culturally, and politically.[40] In a kind of oppositional syncretism Marina Alvarez and Ginetta Candelario, meanwhile, speak about Latina organizing around AIDS in the Bronx, collaborating with national organizations such as Act Up, while mixing Western science (AZT) with the healing powers of santeria, and Chinese medicine. Thus diverse communities can resonate together through strongly perceived or dimly felt affinities of historical experience and political perspective.

Such affinities as well as the shared critique of "mainstream" feminism have sometimes led to misleadingly homogenous paradigms of both "white women" and "women of color." *Talking Visions* does not, however, posit "women of color" as a uniform, univocal foil to the subjects of "white" or "mainstream" feminism. Multicultural feminism, acknowledges the palimpsestic complexity of these categories without erasing the stratifications within the imagined community of feminism. As anti-racist and

Ella Shohat

anti-homophobic feminists, we at times find ourselves speaking differently to different constituencies—"talking race" to white women, "speaking gender" to men from our own communities, and, yes, shouting, "Hetero-sexism!" to sisters of color. Despite this sliding positioning, however, we have not always creatively engaged our contradictions around such issues as class, sexuality, religion, immigration, and globalization. To forge alliances, we must face up to disparate sensibilities and contested histories, if only to better chart the terrain of shared struggles. Multicultural feminism is more than a politics of chromatic alliance. It addresses the shifting positionalities of women of color, not only in relation to white men, to white women, and to men of color, but also among women of color themselves, in a mul-tifaceted dialogue which includes not only commonalities but also fissures in the happy sisterhood of "women of color." The "women of color" category is not entirely false, of course; it corresponds to the need for a gen-eralizing articulation of common experiences that can enable political mobi-lization. But just as literal families can both liberate and oppress, the metaphorical "family" of multicultural feminists can cover cultural differ-ences and social contradictions

Yoshiko Shimada's installation *Look at Me/Look at You* sets up a dialec-tical relationship between the traditional Japanese "women of conformity" and that of the Korean "comfort women." The mirror in the exhibition room reflects a wedding dress with an apron tied over her pregnant-looking tummy. Across the room hangs a traditional Korean dress covered over a stained simple kimono. The bride/mother dress cannot "see" any-thing but her own reflection, while the Korean dress can see what she is not and that she is invisible. As a Japanese artist, Shimada questions the Japa-nese sense of victimization vis-à-vis the West, and also makes audible the si-lences of Korean women, subjugated under a Japanese imperial system that divided women's sexuality into two opposed national camps. Such works il-luminate the difficulty of establishing a dialogue when women's complicity with imperialism is overlooked.

Articulating the contradictions among multicultural feminists does not imply political immobility; rather, it suggests a more lucid and varie-gated coalition. Nor does the existence of tensions mean that we should draw detached chains of atomized communities and subaltern histories. A complexly articulated multicultural feminism needs to chart both the linked historical analogies and the diverse perspectives of disempowered groups. Often uneasy and painful, alliances are not conflict-free spaces. A multifaceted plurilog to restructure power relations has to both seize on the possible mutual identifications among minoritized communities while also acknowledging that those on the margins have sometimes had to survive at each others' expense. (It was an African Moor, Estevanico, who led Cortez's army in its colonial onslaught on the Pueblo Indians; some blacks participated in the conquest of the West, just as Indigenous Americans were at times induced to fight against blacks, and sometimes even employed as "slave catchers.") How do we then chart alliances without repressing conflictual histories and material realities while also moving in egalitarian directions?

The oppositional strategies of multicultural feminists can vary because they are grounded in different premises and histories. Feminists of color, for example, have often rejected liberal feminism's individualist philosophical premise of "women's rights" discourse. Yet, although both Native American and African-American women have fought the racialization of their identities, and the sexualization of their bodies, these fights have taken place in the context of distinct forms of colonial dispossession—one involving primarily the appropriation of land, and the other of labor. If civil rights discourse was crucial in obtaining a modicum of equality for African-Americans, for many Native Americans that same discourse has meant denial of sovereignty (see M. A. Jaimes ★ Guerrero's essay here). Nevertheless, the move from civil rights to human rights discourse was meaningful for both the Black Panthers and the American Indian Movement in their attempts to call attention to *collective* abuses taking place in a Western democracy. While effective as a political tool, "Rights" discourse also assumes the legitimacy of Western colonial-settler states. The recent slogan "women's rights equal human rights" has also provoked complex debates, some of which are played out here. While Mallika Dutt's essay deploys a human rights legal/activist discourse in service of a feminist human rights agenda, Inderpal Grewal's essay performs a transnational feminist critique of the universalist humanism underlying the "women's rights/human rights" discourse. Recent U.N. conferences contributed to an international recognition of violence towards women; but the discourse about violence privileges individually based violence, obscuring the role of the state in such violence (especially that of the internationally powerful nation-states), resulting in an emphasis on, for example, female infanticide in China but not on U.S. sterilization policies in Puerto Rico. The selection of women and issues for such conferences is embedded in the very problems of representation in general within the United Nations. Not all nation-states performing on the international stage of the U.N. are represented equally (certainly the contemporary global scene is dominated by a coterie of powerful nation-states, namely the U.S., Western Europe, Japan);[41] and that the United Nation's family members exclude many illegitimate minorities/majorities around the world: ethnic, racial, religious, and sexual nations-within-the-nation. These international gatherings of the "family of nations" form an alien nation for Native American Nations in the U.S., Kurdish nations in Iraq, Turkey, and Iran, and provide little home for the "queer nation."

Tensions within and between communities oblige us to go beyond a discourse of "common oppression" sisterhood. In the case of immigration, the divisive issues are many, making coalition work a challenge. Some immigrants to the U.S. bring with them racist attitudes, especially in relation to African-Americans. When immigrants got off the boat, Toni Morrison suggests, the "second word they learned was 'nigger.'"[42] Immigrants, including even black Africans, arrive to the U.S. already having been exposed to stereotypes transmitted by global media, for example the phobic hyper-sexualization of African-Americans, even if at the same time they have been induced to admire African-American musicians and athletes. (The same asymmetrical flow that disseminates African-American popular culture globally, also disseminates the hierarchical raced/gendered codes of the U.S. dominant society.) Immigrants of color, pressured by the reigning black/white binarism, may adopt ambivalent attitudes, identifying with fellow "minorities" but may also be tempted to affirm their precarious sense of American belonging by themselves rejecting blacks. We are all accountable not only to fight the discriminations of which we are victims but also the discriminations perpetrated by members of our own communities

That some lower-middle-class immigrants manage to achieve a simulacrum of the American dream reinforces a public discourse that indirectly blames African-Americans for their social plight. Media images of (black) welfare queens and gangs, on the one hand, and of "model minority" Asians on the other, obscures the traumatic violence done to the black family by slavery and segregation. Another related issue revolves around the ways in which immigrants from South Asia , West Asia (Middle East) or Africa fight against their own discrimination in the U.S., while simultaneously harassing community-based women's organizations on such issues as domestic violence; and while also remaining affiliated with the home country reactionary institutions that discriminate against their own religious or ethnic "minorities" (e.g., see here Meena Alexander's account of this contradictory positionality of U.S. Hindu fundamentalist immigrants' mobilization against Muslims). The feminist coalitionary work of postcolonial diasporas, addressed in this volume, for example, by Chandra Talpade Mohanty, rearticulates the experience of racism and heteropatriarchalism, not simply in the context of one immigrant community, but also in conjunction with other anti-racist feminist struggles, such as those of Latina and African-American women.

A multicultural feminist alliance confronts the limitations of a black/white framing of identities. The multiracial conflicts involving Koreans, African-Americans, and Latino/as in Los Angeles in 1992 speak volumes about these limitations. Although the black/white binarism is strongly inscribed in the material and ideological structures of the U.S., it is crucial for multicultural feminist alliances to examine the interplay of diverse communities—especially since the 1965 Immigration Act, by democratizing access to the U.S., has added even more "dark" layers to an already multilayered amalgam.[43] Yet recent waves of immigration by people of color are a result, not only of the inclusiveness of the 1965 Immigration Act, but also of U.S. imperial interventions, and of a globalized economic structure in which the U.S. has played a central role. In the context of rampant downsizing, recent Third World immigrants to the U.S. compete with people of color and white working class people over shrinking resources. Not only "Anglos" make up the marching troops of the "English-only" movement: they are sometimes joined ironically, by people of color who had themselves been brutally shorn of their own languages,[44] just as Proposition 187 in California has been applauded by some people of color who feel disadvantaged vis-à-vis recent immigrants. At the same time, the military remains one relatively secure avenue to a scaled-down version of the American Dream, promising a measure of racial and gender (but not yet sexual) equality within a neo-imperial nationalist framework.

A historical moment that features the global of transnationalism, on the one hand, and the local of identity politics on the other, inevitably has made issues of location and coalition a major concern for multicultural feminists.[45] The need to prioritize activist energies, meanwhile, has often generated dissonances in coalitionary politics. Teresa Carrillo's essay, for example, examines tensions between Mexicana activists who focus on issues of class and labor, and Chicana activists for whom issues of race and gender are paramount. The same First World feminists, white and black, who combat women's oppression in the Third World, Isabelle Gunning points out, end up fighting for laws that would punish the practitioners—largely immigrant African women—of clitoridectomy or "female genital surgery."

Within the hegemonic public sphere, however, only a Eurocentric narrative of the liberation of gays/lesbians and heterosexual women is permissible. Media depictions of Third World women/gay/lesbian immigrants as the victims of "savage traditions" like clitoridectomy and gay-killing, reincarnate the U.S. as the new millennium land of freedom. Thus, conceptual frameworks of civilization/barbarism and tradition/modernity, while facilitating the admission of immigrants, also elide (a) the U.S. support for such oppressive regimes (b) U.S. versions of homophobia and patriarchal fundamentalism and (c) the export of U.S. fundamentalisms to the Third World (e.g., American evangelical media). The point, then, is not to reverse the discourse about positive/negative geographical belongings, but to undo it altogether.

Liberal feminist discourse, studiously misses the links between U.S. policies and the torture and rape of indigenous people by U.S.-trained soldiers in El Salvador or Guatemala. A multicultural-feminist perspective rejects as absurd a posture of outrage directed exclusively toward clitoridectomy, because it is gender-specific, but which remains oblivious to torture and massacre (unless the atrocity involves rape). While drawing on indigenous, non-patriarchal traditions, multicultural feminism has to transcend the binarism that pits a liberal feminist, yet Eurocentric, discourse, on the one hand, against an anti-colonial, but hetero/sexist, discourse on the other.

A serious dilemma faced by multicultural feminists, then, is how to articulate opposition to such practices while also challenging Eurocentric feminist discourses. (Inderpal Grewal, Mallika Dutt, and Isabelle Gunning's essays here all reflect on these dilemmas.) Traditional patriarchal practice may raise highly sensitive transnational legal and cultural questions, as, for example, when Chinese immigrants seek asylum on the grounds that the Chinese government had subjected them to forced abortions, sterilizations, and persecution for defying the one-child-per-couple policy. For multicultural feminists, a cross-border dilemma is raised when immigrants from Africa or Asia themselves perform a Eurocentric interpretation of patriarchal and homophobic policies in their home countries because it is the only route to American citizenship.

"First Worldness," even when experienced from the bottom, brings certain privileges that must be considered as we reconceptualize a multicultural, transnational, cross-regional feminism. Living in the U.S. given the unequal global flow of economic, technological, and cultural production can generate certain advantages, such as a powerful currency and an opensesame passport. Struggles on behalf of African-American women and Latinas, for example, are not necessarily liberatory for women in Africa or Latin America, and vice versa. Being a U.S. feminist of color does not automatically guarantee a critical attitude toward the consequences of U.S. national interests for Third World women, whose cheap labor indirectly allows First World working-class women of color to consume products at lower prices. Multicultural feminism has to address these economic structures and the "structure of feeling" of Third World feminists toward U.S. power in the world. Applying globally the idea of "women of color" cannot paper over the asymmetries implicit in the gendered flow of capital and labor across nation-state borders.

Opposition to racism, sexism, and homophobia in the U.S., furthermore, has never guaranteed opposition to U.S. global hegemony. Mervat Hatem's and Wahneema Lubiano's essays offer gendered analyses of the global/local contradictions in relation to the Gulf War. For U.S. people of color the path to upward mobility has often passed through the obligatory display of patriotic devotion to the "American nation." Many people of color and gays/lesbians have fought as soldiers on the U.S.'s behalf in the last decade—in the Middle East, in Panama, in Somalia, in Haiti—occasionally alongside soldiers whose origins are in these countries. In times of national war efforts, hegemonic discourse transforms the usually black and Latino men from crack dealers and absent fathers into heroes in uniform, privileged, as Lubiano shows, in the hetero/masculinist narrative of the returning father soldier. The interwovenness of geopolitics and global economy suggests that our "hands are not clean." "Such an understanding," writes Lubiano, "disrupt[s] the tendency on the part of some black women to think that 'we' have a lock on the oppression sweepstakes and remind[s] us that the contempt that many of us direct toward something understood (or caricatured) as 'mainstream feminism' or 'a middle-class white feminist movement'—a contempt directed at white feminists for talking and behaving as though their particular oppression is absolutely primary—could in some measure be directed as ourselves." The essays in *Talking Visions,* then, try to account for precisely this relational web of contradictory positionalities.

Missing Links: Beyond National and Disciplinary Borders

Although nationalism is often seen as a specifically Third World malady, it is no less relevant to the labor, feminist, queer, and multicultural movements within the U.S. A submerged American nationalism often undergirds such practices and epistemologies, giving us a star-striped nationalism with a tan, a nationalism in drag, and rainbow nationalism. In my experience on various "diversity committees," I have found that educational institutions often glimpse multiculturalism, and feminist/gay/lesbian perspectives through a largely unconscious national-exceptionalist lens. And while I have no quarrel with the idea of U.S. uniqueness, I do quarrel with the idea that uniqueness is unique to the U.S. Every modern nation, I would suggest, has a palimpsestic uniqueness all its own. And along with that shared uniqueness we find historical parallels between different national formations. The implicit nationalism of many multicultural, feminist, and gay/lesbian agendas leads us to miss numerous opportunities for cross-disciplinary and transnational connection.

Focusing on national experiences outside the U.S., postcolonial studies, for example, often means overlooking race in the U.S., while ethnic studies often ignores areas outside the U.S. The diverse Area studies, for their part, ignore their connections to both postcolonial and ethnic studies, as well as the bonds between the various areas. Women's, gender, and sexuality curricula, meanwhile, often reproduce such divisions, where the single subject of women/gender/sexuality is apportioned out so that the West forms the "norm," while the "rest" is relegated to the "backyards" of area studies and ethnic studies.[46] In sum, "single ethnicity," "single nation," and "single region" institutional thinking risk impeding critical feminist and queer scholars, political organizers, and cultural programmers who wish to collaborate in ways that go beyond a confining nation-state and regional-geographic imaginary.

Women/gays/lesbians of color, meanwhile, have only intermittently critiqued the aporias of nationalist thinking in a transnational world. Race and sexuality within multiculturalism, feminism, and queer theory tend to be discussed in the U.S. as self-contained, ignoring not only this country's colonizing history but also its global presence and its impact on the rest of the world. Well-meaning curriculum committees and cultural programs applaud multiculturalism as the sum of the contributions of diverse ethnicities and races to the "development of the *American* Nation"—a formulation that incorporates a covert U.S. nationalist teleology. A corollary to this is the negative exceptionalism detectable in some work by ethnic studies feminists, which conveys a sense of the uniquely awful oppressiveness of the U.S. Ethnic nationalists offer a negative variation on the conservatives' "melting pot" exceptionalism, emphasizing instead "racist" exceptionalism, i.e., a view of the U.S. as uniquely racist, a position that ignores more general racialized colonial patterns common to many colonial-settler nations.

Area studies, for their part, are seen as located "elsewhere," as if the U.S. were not politically and economically implicated in other regions around the world, and as if people from those regions were not in the U.S. Women's studies programs often reproduce these ghettoizations through a division whereby required courses focus on "pure" issues of gender and sexuality, while optional courses focus on women of color and Third World women as "special topics." Within this approach, U.S. women of color are studied as sui generis, an entity unto themselves, while Third World women are seen as if living on another planet, in another time. Les/bi/gays in Africa, Asia, or Latin America tend to be further elided under the heterosexual frameworks of development studies, as well as under the binarist norms of heterosexuality. When ethnic studies courses, meanwhile, focus on women of color, they are severed from the gendered and colonial history of the regions from which they came, and there is little inquiry into their multilayered postcolonial displacements. And when area studies courses focus on Third World women they, too, are severed from the geopolitical interconnectedness of economies, histories, and cultural identities.[47]

Despite symptoms of irritation with the mantra of race, class, gender, and sexuality, many of those eager for a next wave Theory still lack a basic materialist understanding of colonial history and its aftermath. Students in my seminars are often well-versed in gender and sexual theories, but they often know little about anticolonial writings (Césaire, Memmi, Fanon), or about the history of imperialism and its relevance for feminist theorization, or about feminists such as Audre Lorde, Angela Davis, Gloria Anzaldua, Assia Dijebar, or Fatima Mernissi.[48] Those of us bringing postcoloniality and race into women's and gay/lesbian studies tend to work in an intellectual and institutional vacuum, just as those bringing gender and sexuality to ethnic and area studies face marginalization. Despite the attack on all forms of alternative study in academia, multicultural feminists are still faced with what Mitsuye Yamada has called the "loyalty oath"—a demand for exclusive allegiance either to women's studies or ethnic studies but not both.[49] U.S. multicultural feminists have had to walk a tightrope because of the institutional quarantine on their overlapping areas of activism and inquiry. Multicultural feminism exceeds the institutionalized academic boundaries of both ethnic studies and women's studies, asserting its relevance to all disciplines and fields of inquiry. Multicultural feminist pedagogy challenges the continued privileging of heteromasculinist Western cultural production within academic disciplines and cultural institutions, and suggests an altered vision of knowledge, aesthetics, and social relations. Striving for cross-fertilization, *Talking Visions* forges feminist links between usually compartmentalized interdisciplinary debates: on the one hand, the diverse ethnic studies, focusing on issues of "minorities," race, and multiculturalism (often within the U.S.), and, on the other, postcolonial theory associated with issues of colonial discourse, the imperial imaginary, and national narration (often outside the U.S.).

U.S. postcolonial theory, meanwhile, seldom dialogues with its U.S. context of production and reception. The innumerable postcolonial MLA papers elaborating abstract notions of "difference" and "alterity" rarely put these concepts into dialogue with "local" subalternities. The institutional embrace of a few third-world "postcolonials," largely by English and Comparative Literature Departments, is partially a response to U.S. civil rights and affirmative action struggles, yet the enthusiastic consumption of the theoretical aura of the "postcolonial" threatens to eclipse the less prestigious "ethnic studies" field.[50] Just as it is important to address the American nationalist tendencies of "ethnic studies"—and specifically its impact on gender and sexuality studies—it is also urgent to address the tendency of postcolonial studies to ignore U.S. racial politics. Needless to say, the embrace of postcolonial theory and study is welcome, indeed overdue, yet we also have to assess its institutional impact and politics of reception. Given the token space granted critical work in general, institutional hierarchies end up generating a fighting-for-crumbs syndrome. Institutions tend to see people of color paradigmatically, as a series of substitutable others, indirectly disallowing a wider constellation of historical perspectives. Thus some selected few academic speakers of poststructuralist-postcolonial discourses—even at times in spite of their radical politics—are seen as less threatening to university administrations than academics who are perceived as potentially linked to angry militant U.S. communities. Fundamentally conservative institutions, in this sense, get to do the "multiculti" thing without interrogating their own connection to contemporary U.S. racial politics. To ask this question is not to cast aspersion on specific intellectuals but rather to reflect on the ways in which postcolonial intellectuals, under the sign of "diversity," might be positioned as the "good academics" (much as the media construct "good ethnics") as opposed to those "vulgar militants," so as to recreate subtle stratifications and hierarchies, even on the margins. The point is not to minimize the racism and subtle prejudice that "postcolonials" also face, nor is it to assume that postcolonials cannot *also* be activists. The point, rather, is that we be lucid not only about the differences among feminists of color but also about how the institutional privileging of one discourse and field of inquiry at any particular historical moment might mean the blocking of other discourses and fields of inquiry, along with the sabotaging of possible alliances between discursive fields and the communities mediated by them.

At the same time, affirmative action is under attack and the presence of African-Americans, Chicano/as, Puerto Ricans, and Native Americans in the academy remains minuscule. Cultural and academic institutions may celebrate, and even produce, multicultural "stars," and may show an interest in the conceptual spaces opened up by postcolonial hybridity, but the marginalization both of U.S. "minorities" and of the non-English speaking world endures. The critique of orientalist discourse initiated by Edward Said, for example, has generated excitement in English and comparative literature faculties, but in its more fashion-conscious versions, including in some feminist scholarship, often focuses on orientalist discourse about "them," while "they" remain safely locked in Bantustans called "area studies" (orientalism with a vengeance!). The study of the postcolonial, one sometimes suspects, is relatively privileged in the U.S. precisely because of its convenient remoteness from this country's racial matters, often relegated to other historical eras and other geographies, in ways that also ignore U.S. global "implicatedness." The vibrant space opened up by "cutting edge" postcolonial theory for critical scholarship is also contested, particularly since, as we have seen, some practitioners of ethnic studies feel displaced by it. Since recognizing these tensions is crucial for multicultural feminists working toward effective alliances, this book attempts to dismantle the institutional barriers raised between postcolonial feminists and ethnic studies feminists.

Talking Visions, then, is edited so as to "relationalize" the academic corrals called "women's studies," "gender and sexuality studies," "postcolonial studies," "ethnic studies," and "area studies," and to show how they intersect with one another, intimately and, at times, abrasively. Although many of the feminists represented in *Talking Visions* work from within different institutional spaces, their work suggests a conscious commitment to working on multiple agendas. The book therefore hopes to show that it is possible, even vital, that immigrant feminists are respectful of those who endured before us at the intersection of oppressions; that it is incumbent on us to be aware of the historical perspectives of those who have long been inside the "belly of the beast;" just as all of us practicing feminism from within the U.S. are accountable to incorporate into our teaching and struggles the perspectives of those who suffer in their flesh the policies of the U.S. and its allies. We need to address the tensions precisely in order to construct alliances forged out of the complementarities of our differences. Friction, in this sense, can be a source energy. It is not a question of a pluralistic "adding on" of communities and fields of inquiry to an assumed core, but rather of working out the synergistic relationships among them. Hopefully, all these realms of struggle—ethnic studies, area studies, women's studies, postcolonial studies, gay, lesbian, and queer studies—would work in concert, without the narcissism of minor differences and the anxious competition for space and prestige.

The diverse interdisciplinary studies, furthermore, have different histories of institutional legitimization. Unlike ethnic studies, women's studies and gay/lesbian studies programs, which came about as a result of a 1960s bottom-up struggle among "minorities" to demand scholarly representation, the diverse area studies were instituted top-down by the U.S. defense department in the wake of the post–World War era. Governmental funding and university expansion of area studies have formed part of the cold war strategic cartographies of spheres-of-influence. Although the face(s) of area studies has dramatically changed over the years and many more voices have contributed to alternative scholarship, the feminist dialogue between area studies and ethnic studies scholars must further impact gender and sexuality studies. For one reason, covert taboos restrict which women/gays/lesbians of color can move, as subjects of inquiry, from area to ethnic studies. For example, although immigration from North Africa and the Middle East dates back to the end of the last century, and although its flow has increased since the sixties, Middle Easterners are seen as "forever foreign"; they are only seen as "from there."[51] (See here Jamelie Hassan's *Shame* and *For Tariq*, Mona Hatoum's *Measures of Distance,* Yong Soon Min's *Defining Moments,* and Diane Tani's *Forever Foreign.*) Chicano/as, to take another example, are treated by the media as ontologically, quintessentially alien ("from there"), although many did not cross the borders to the U.S.; it was the borders that moved around them. The first "illegal alien," Columbus,[52] is celebrated as a discoverer, while indigenous Mexicans are seen as "infiltrating" a barbed border, which in fact divides their former homeland. (See here Jaune Quick-to-See Smith's *Paper Dolls for a Post-Columbian World with Ensembles Contributed by U.S. Government* and Annie Nash's *Borderlands/Respect.*) Native Americans, similarly, are "from here," but for many Native American communities, such as the Cherokees, Nez Perce, and the Modoc, their geographical dispersal across scattered swaths of U.S. territory "hides," as it were, their "trails of tears" as internal refugees (see Quick-to-See Smith's *Big Myths Die Hard*). A nationalist multicultural map does not permit a narrative of refugees within the borders of the land of freedom, nor for displacements caused by devastating U.S. global policies.

Diversity discourses thus mask a series of coercions within and outside the "American nation." Multicultural feminism challenges the canonical patriarchal narrative of the birth of America: in the beginning was Columbus; in the middle the American Revolution and the Civil War; and in the end the "melting pot." But then the new immigrants pouring in "spoil" the already overcooked stew. Whereas the melting pot discourse celebrated the smelting down of differences as part of the forging of the nation's birth, neoconservatives see the birth as constantly being suspended, or even (horror of horrors!) aborted. The continually changing makeup of the U.S. forces "us" always to rethink the "we." The idea of a unitary "American Nation" benevolently receiving new waves of immigrants suggests that only the immigrants, rather than the nation itself, are being transformed, when in fact the nation is transformed by each new wave washing up on its shores. New immigrants stretch with their bodies the boundaries and definitions of Americanness.[53] But the country's openness is rarely conceived as multidirectional; the new immigrants ("they") are simply to be transformed into "us." The desire for a tidy closure fuels the anti-immigrant feeling expressed by Proposition 187. The proposed denial of schooling and medical care to new immigrants of color—the poorest of whom are women and children—can be seen as more than a simple cost-cutting device; it aims at disciplining this chaotic, open-ended notion of the "American Nation." Anti-immigrant hysteria can be seen as a phobic reaction to the disquieting perception that "the nation" might not be and never has been a fixed entity, a core of whiteness to which other "colors" were added later. The colors were there from the beginning. Indeed, over many millennia (Eurocentrically called "pre-Columbian," as if an entire hemisphere had been just waiting for Columbus to arrive), it was whiteness that was the absent color. All the waves of immigration to this country have stirred up nationalist anxiety, not only because of their obvious social implications but also because of more subtle questions about what "Americanness" is and about who belongs to the "American family." Third World immigrants in the U.S., especially anti-racist feminists with political demands, are often perceived as "ungrateful" to the "Nation of Nations." As a result activism against the abuse of women or gays/lesbians in immigrant communities is

Ella Shohat

Plate 6: *Defining Moments*, 1992
Detail, one of a six part photo ensemble, 20 × 16"
Yong Soon Min
Courtesy of the artist

often treated within the modernity/tradition paradigm: abuse is seen as a normal tradition that indicates that "they" haven't yet assimilated to the enlightened "mainstream." Yet the rampant abuse of women or gays/lesbians in the "mainstream" is seldom represented as possibly revealing something fundamental about gender and sexual inequality within "America."

By including recent immigrants in a U.S.-based multicultural analysis, *Talking Visions* calls attention to the U.S.'s continuing role in the lives of postcolonial immigrants even in the post-Third Worldist era, but also to the fact that there is no automatic, effortless solidarity among those labeled "Third World people." Feminists of color have a long history of struggle in the U.S.; for feminists new to this country, the challenge is to create a context for current struggles based both in the "theres" of the many original regions and continents and in the "heres" of the diverse communities in the U.S. Political geographies and state borders do not always coincide with "imaginary geographies" (Edward Said), whence the existence of internal emigrés, nostalgic rebels, people who may share the same passport but whose relations to the nation–state are conflicted and ambivalent. In the postcolonial environment of constant fluxes of populations, of houses on wheels as in Zarina's image, affiliation with the nation-state becomes highly partial and contingent. Furthermore, for women/gays/lesbians, whose bodies and sexualities are constructed as aberrations, and who can be easily excluded from their membership in their national family, such affiliation becomes especially ambivalent. Laura Aguilar, Yong Soon Min, and Tatiana Parcero's work evoke this entanglement of national territories and interior cartographies.

The Transnational Imaginary

Talking Visions is published at a post-Cold War moment when ethnic studies, area studies, gender and queer studies in the academy have to address the all-enveloping movements of people, capital, digital information, and ecological flow. The inert, static maps charted by ethnic studies, area studies, women's studies and gay/lesbian studies need to be mobilized to capture today's morphing, crisscrossing movements across regional and national borders. A relational analysis of co-implicated histories, cultures, and identities is crucial for institutional rethinking in the age of transnationalism. (Images such as Hung Liu's *Resident Alien*, Soo-Ja Kim's *Deductive Object*, Ernesto Pujol's *My Cuban Baggage*, Jamelie Hassan's *Shame* and *For Tariq*, Flo Oy Wong's *In 1930 Sue Shee Wong Came*, and Indu Krishnan's

Knowing her Place thematize displacement, suggesting its centrality to contemporary culture.) The global nature of the colonizing process, the global flow of transnational capital, and the global reach of contemporary communications technologies virtually oblige the multicultural feminist critic to move beyond the restrictive framework of the nation-state as a unit for analysis. An ideological construction of "here" and "there" obscures the innumerable ways that women's lives are imbricated in the forces of globalization. Although based in the U.S., *Talking Visions* reflects an awareness that globalization forces the feminist critic to surpass homogenizing conceptualizations that posit "nation" as well as "area" and "region" as coherent spaces of inquiry.

Although many First World feminists have not seen issues of "nation" as germane to feminism, for Third World feminists the critique of gender was always imbricated with national discourses. If First World feminists seem to float above petty nationalist concerns, it is because they take for granted the projection of a national power that has facilitated the dissemination of their "universal" feminism. African, Asian, or Latin American feminists, on the other hand, have not been able to assume a reassuring substratum of national power. In a Post-Third Worldist era, multicultural feminism is faced with the question of whether the nation is worth reclaiming as a site for struggle at a time when the primary function of the nation-state, besides granting citizenship, is as a terminal for the flows of transnational capital. Can we channel such flows? Will the rising tide lift all boats? Or will some be drowned by them? Or is it a question, as the Native American expression goes, of "access to the stream"?

Although this book takes the U.S. as its point of departure, it attempts to address multicultural feminism within a transnational framework that reflects an increasingly globalized economy. While explicitly critiquing any facile feminist internationalism, it delineates a complex relationality between the local and the global. How do we redefine "national interest" when the post-independence nation-state has become a vehicle for national elites increasingly integrated into the culture of transnationalism? How do we rethink the "postcolonial" nation as a site of identification and mobilization, as the "home" of critical consciousness, given its clear discriminatory history, its inability to mobilize men and women, heterosexuals and gays and lesbians, and ethnic/religious majorities and minorities on equal terms? And finally what has the Third World nation become in the era of globalization, and what are the implications of this new situation for U.S. based multicultural feminism?[54]

In critical discourse, the more dystopian view of "globalization" evokes an overpowering transnational economy that engenders the homogenization of culture, the feminization of poverty, the annihilation of political autonomy for the relatively disempowered, and, ultimately, ecological catastrophe, as an untenable consumerist model is spread around a globe that can ill afford it. In its more euphoric versions, in contrast, the term globalization evokes the mobilization of capital, the internationalization of trade, a salutary "competitiveness" on the part of labor, better job opportunities for poor women in developing countries, and the transformation of the world into a seamlessly wired global village. The term evokes a cybernetic dance of cultures, "one planet under a groove," the transcendence of rigid ideological and political divisions, and the world-wide availability of cultural products and information, whether it be CNN, IBM, world beat music, or American TV serials.[55]

In the era of globalization, some argue, the old imperial hegemonies have become "dispersed" (Arjun Appadurai), and "scattered" (Inderpal Grewal and Caren Kaplan). How do we negotiate these dispersed hegemonies, while also acknowledging that the historical thread or inertia of First World domination remains a powerful presence?[56] And what are the links between such hegemonies and the national and transnational regulation of the gendered and sexualized body? But "globalization," it is often forgotten, is not a new development; it must be seen as part of the much longer history of colonialism in which Europe attempted to submit the world to a single "universal" regime of truth and global institutional power.[57] As Robert Stam and I point out in *Unthinking Eurocentrism,* the 500-year colonial domination of indigenous peoples, the capitalist appropriation of resources, and the imperialist ordering of the world formed part of a massive world-historical globalizing movement that reached its apogee at the turn of the century. Globalization theory, in this sense, has its roots a "diffusionist" (J. M. Blaut) view of Europe's spreading its people, ideas, goods, and political systems around the world. Thus, patriarchal colonial diffusionism has undergone a series of metamorphoses: it transmuted into modernization theory in the late 1940s and 1950s, embracing the idea that Third World nations would achieve economic take-off by emulating the historical progress of the West; and it transmuted in the 1980s into globalization theory. Women of the "underdeveloped world," it was assumed, would have to be further modernized to "catch up."

From the early days of the "voyages of discovery," through the adventures on the imperial frontier, to the contemporary fiber-optimism of

"reach-out-and-touch-someone" circuitry, globalization has long been embedded in gender issues and sexual discourses. The "voyages of discovery"
initiated a process of massive movement of material resources and human labor across the Atlantic from the "Motherland" to the "virgin land" which
required fertilization and fecundation. That land also needed to be rescued
from its own libidinal savagery, a discourse continuous to the present-day
political-media metaphors of the "rape of Kuwait." In their eroticizing of
geography, the Voyagers "deflowered" virgin lands and tamed resistant
nature. And the project of latter-day imperialism was gendered from the
outset. While girls were domesticated as homemakers, deprived of what
Virginia Woolf called a "room of one's own," boys were raised to be aggran-
dized imperial subjects who imagined the future of the world as resting on
their shoulders.[58]

Contemporary cyber discourse, too, is rich in gendered imperial
tropes. It figures the early days of cyberspace as a kind of "Wild West," or
"hitherto-unimagined territory opening up for exploration." The Internet
can be a "tough territory to travel," given its "Khyber Passes," and the
"dangers of an uncontrolled cyber territory." Yet, according to cyber enthu-
siasts, the Net lacks "Banana republic-like center of authority."[59] The exciting, brave new world of cybernetics comes priorly textualized within a
tired rhetoric of gendered colonial metaphors. While cyberspace might
transcend the gravity of geographic location, the metaphors are definitely
grounded in the discourses constructed around specific Third World sites.
The image of Khyber Passes, associated with British colonialism in Asia,
evokes tough and dangerous roads while Banana Republics, associated with
unpredictable coups d'etat in Latin America, signify machoistic authoritarian take-over. As in imperial literature and film, the cyber frontier narrative
is focalized through the civilized explorer who gradually comes to master
the terrain of the mysterious, the savage, the despotic. Safety and freedom
of mobility in cyberspace are once again relayed in masculinist Eurocentric
terms, ironically as online ads promise a utopian world with "no genders,"
"no races," "no nations."

Cybernetic technology has created a kind of quick-to-settle, quick-
to-pack global production that can be profitably dispersed across the globe,
allowing mobile capital to surf freely, and making the nation-state only one
more liquid terminal for transnational flows. Not only do imperial ideologies travel, so do technologies and people. Border crossing can become an
act not only of economic survival but also of political transgression. After
all, the presumably open borders of the globalized world are constituted by

hierarchical economic power, and by the racialized, classed, and gendered flow of labor across unequal borders. Only those at the low end of the hierarchy are penalized for border-crossing. The crossing of U.S. corporations and executives into Mexico set up *maquiladoras,* which deprives working-class (North) Americans of jobs, is not stigmatized in the same way. National, racial, class, and gender hierarchies determine who can cross, in which direction, and on what terms. Laws discourage not only the literal crossings but also the metaphorical border-crossings of people of color, women, and gays/lesbians demanding their share of power.

Global economy and politics make cross-border movement a growth industry.[60] Although the globalization of the world economy can be traced to the beginnings of colonialism, recent years have seen an exponential surge in transnational capitalism. The U.S.'s neoimperial role, along with that of other G-7 states, is deeply linked to these movements across borders. As the G-7 move farther into the physical and cyber spaces of the Third and Second Worlds, those displaced from jobs, security, and political stability seek to escape into the relatively safer economic spaces of the First World. Cheap labor in places like Asia and the Caribbean, or in Silicon Valley (provided by largely Filipina and Mexicana migrant female workers), meanwhile, determines the production site of high tech electronic assembly; and purchasing power determines the targets for the packaging and marketing of these technologies as well as the target for dumping old technologies. In this sense transnational corporations still reproduce a world in which cyber privileges are constructed not so much on the backs but rather on the fingers and eyes of primarily female Third World workers who have little access to the finished digital products they themselves produce.

Multicultural feminism highlights the role of gender, sexuality, class and race in the new globalism. The transnational economy affects the fluidity of labor, not only from country to city but also globally. Eighty percent of this inexpensive labor is composed of Third World women. What has been called the "feminization of labor" epitomizes the economic-induced border-crossing of poverty-stricken women attempting to survive in the age of the IMF-generated debt crisis, leading to the exchange of surplus women's bodies as migratory cheap labor. At the same time, more traditional female labor has also become globalized to the point that, for example, transnational export of female domestic labor (including export to other Third World countries, such as those of the Persian Gulf) is an important generator of foreign currency in countries such as the Philippines and Sri Lanka. Within late imperial culture, women's bodies are exchanged transnationally. Performing identity and staging "looks" in the U.S. are themselves caught in the web of transnationalism. Lisa Jones's essay, for example, grounds the commodity fetishism of hair in a transnational context ranging from hair production in China and India, through Harlem's merchandizing of Afro hair extensions, to the wigs of Hasidic women in Brooklyn. Sexual transactions are also imbricated with these new transnational fluidities: the expanding business of mail-order brides cannot be imagined without the differential global flow of capital.[61] Or, to take another example, the sexual "free trade zone" at the U.S. Subic naval base in the Philippines means that there Filipina flesh is worth $7 US, whereas in the U.S. it's worth at least fifty.[62]

The neoimperial formations characteristic of the era of globalization also play a role in the transnational commodification of gay/lesbian desire. Vacation catalogues, as explored by Jacqui Alexander, offer exotic locales, such as Thailand, that cater to U.S. or Western European gay men in a global libidinal economy which allows for the unequal consumption of sex. (See here the cover of "the gay magazine and guide of Spain," *Mensual,* advertising vacations in Cuba.) And, albeit within a much smaller industry, organized tours for First World lesbians, I suggest, evoke nineteenth-century imperial female travel narratives. They echo the more recent nostalgia-for-empire imagery, such as Ralph Lauren's Safari ads, in which African locations appeal to a female colonial gaze of a "world without boundaries." Same-sex tourist brochures, similarly, place women of different generations and races in romantic exotic backgrounds, superimposed on fetishistic travel icons—diary fragments and a passport with an engraving of two female figures embracing each other—images of license for "unique vacations for women."[63] Same-sex exotica reflect the global positioning of First World upper-middle class lesbians, since as one brochure suggests, "It's never been so easy. . . ."[64] Globalization as a kind of late imperial travel culture means that racialized/sexualized bodies are commodified not only locally but also globally. A gendered, sexed, raced, and classed critique matters, as *Talking Visions* suggests, but it has also to matter across borders in relation to the processes of globalization.

Multicultural feminism navigates between the local and the global, without romanticizing either transnational globalism as a form of universalism or localism as salvation through the indigenous "particular." This caveat is particularly important when we get excited about boundary-less virtual communities, or when too much revolutionary hope is invested in the Zapatistas' Web Page or the Gynoanarchist e-mail group. The critical challenge is to negotiate between the forces of globalization and the resistant usages of the New Media online technologies. Neither the enclave nationalism of the "local" nor the subliminally nationalist internationalism of the "global" fully account for the unevenly developed, gendered, raced, and classed realities of the virtual access around the world.[65] Some of the texts/images in *Talking Visions* offer essayistic analyses or poetic ruminations on the complex relations between the local and the global. (See here works by Inderpal Grewal, Chandra Talpade Mohanty, Indu Krishnan, Ernesto Pujol, Laura Aguilar, Allan deSouza, Marina Gutierrez, Meena Alexander, M. Jacqui Alexander, Caren Kaplan, Wahneema Lubiano, and May Joseph.) In this perspective, immigration to the U.S., for example, cannot be discussed only from the "receiving" end—from the moment when female domestic workers cross into the space of "America" but also from the moment transnational economics generate such displacement. Here lies the difference between an implicitly nationalist feminism and a polycentric, multicultural feminism that privileges a multiply situated analysis. "Local" and "global" exist in relation to the ways "we" narrate "our" belongings and longings. Multicultural feminism asks us to reimagine a web of many such interrelated narratives as strategies for empowerment in given spatiotemporal conjunctures. This is not only a matter of "strategic essentialism" (Gayatri Chakravorty Spivak) but also of seeing the necessity of strategizing both locally and globally.

Just as multicultural feminism has to treat time palimpsestically, beyond the binarism of good modernism/bad tradition (or vice versa), it also does not have to choose between the false dichotomies of "good" local and "bad" global, (or vice versa.) A multicultural feminist critique asks more than "thinking globally, acting locally." It asks for a transnational imaginary that places in synergistic relations diverse narratives offering prospects of critical community affiliations. *Talking Visions* hopes to sustain the guerrilla-style energy of movement without proposing an improbable "total revolution." It practices multicultural feminism, not in the simple additive sense of many histories and geographies, but as a political and cultural project which mobilizes the polycentric relationality of a constantly moving world.

Notes

1. The definitions here of multiculturalism and Eurocentrism are taken from Ella Shohat/Robert Stam, *Unthinking Eurocentrism: Multiculturalism and the Media* (Lon-

don: Routledge, 1994). We contrast a critical polycentric with the liberal-pluralist multiculturalism. Within a polycentric vision the world has many dynamic cultural locations, many possible vantage points.

2. I am using such terms as "First World" or "Third World" in quotation marks as a way of suggesting their problematic nature as discussed in my collaborative work with Robert Stam in our book *Unthinking Eurocentrism*. These terms will be used throughout the introduction with quotation marks in mind, suggesting a contingent deployment of the terms.

3. The notion of polyphony is here adapted from the critic Mikhail Bakhtin, *Problems of Dostoevsky's Poetics,* Caryl Emerson, ed. and trans. (Minneapolis: University of Minnesota Press, 1984).

4. Quotation taken from Paul Gilroy, quoting the rap musician Rakim (W. Griffin). Gilroy uses Rakim's lyrics as the title of his essay on "The Dialectics of Diasporic Identification," *Third Text* 13 (Winter 1990–1991).

5. Africa itself has in any case always been culturally, religiously, and ethnically diverse.

6. In the long tradition of those variously called Asian/African Jews or Arab-Jews, those black Jews who have lived for millennia in North Africa, Libya, Sudan, Egypt, Ethiopia, Yemen, Palestine, Iraq, Iran, Afghanistan, China, and India, some of whom would be perceived as black in many contexts, and who within Israel have certainly been constructed as a racially black "other." Jews from Asia and Africa are distinct from those of European origins in culture, language, appearance. Third World nationalism has had complex implications for ethnic and religious minorities, especially when colonial partitions are involved. Arab-Jews have been displaced in the wake of the partition of Palestine. In the Arab-Muslim world Jews have not been constructed in terms of racial or even ethnic differences, but rather in terms of religion. In Israel, by contrast, Arab-Jews or Mizrahim were constructed racially; we have been considered black. The same kind of French sociological discourses about North Africans, that, for example, Frantz Fanon mentions in *Toward an African Revolution,* were directly applied to those North African Jews who ended up in Israel in this period of upheavals in North Africa in the fifties and sixties. In fact, a French diplomat and sociologist is cited in a well-known racist study on North African immigrants in Israel:

"You are making in Israel the same fatal mistake we French made. . . . You open your gates too wide to Africans . . . the immigration of a certain kind of human material will debase you and make you a levantine state, and then your fate will be sealed. You will deteriorate and be lost." (See Ella Shohat, "Sephardim in Israel: Zionism from the Standpoint of its Jewish Victims," *Social Text* 19 [Fall 1988], special issue on colonial discourse.) It was not an accident that one of our major liberation organizations, the *hapanterim hashhorim* (Black Panthers) was formed in the late 60's, and named itself in homage to the black American movement. The name Black Panthers also served as a jujitsu against the common Euro-Israeli Yiddish term for us "Schwartze Chaies" (black animals.) The common slogan was "dfukin veShhorim" (screwed and black.) The colonial and postcolonial displacements inscribed on my personal history across several geographies have led me ultimately to understand blackness as a situated identity and utterance. I speak as someone whose identity cannot easily be fixed within the national, racial, ethnic, and religious categories offered by both Eurocentric discourses on identity and reductionist nationalist imaginaries. We are neither simply the Asian, African, black, Jew, or Arab that Eurocentrism and nationalism designate, and yet all of these definitions have formed part of our experience. Whence my critique of the Eurocentric narrative of "Jewish History" in the singular. (See Ella Shohat, Mizrahim "Staging the Quincentenary: The Middle East and the Americas," *Third Text* 21 (Winter 1992–93). But the racial coding of Asian and African Jews in Israel as black undergoes a mutation in the U.S. Color-based identities like "blackness," therefore, are situated identities, especially within the context of the colonial and postcolonial displacements inscribed on Third World women immigrants and refugees to the U.S. The displacements prior to arrival in the U.S. cannot be erased or leveled as though all immigrant trajectories are the same, whence the predicament of the single hyphen.

7. For explorations of the complex issues of representation see Gayatri Chakravorty Spivak, "Can the Subaltern Speak?" *Marxism and the Interpretation of Culture,* Cary Nelson and Lawrence Grossberg, eds., Urbana: University of Illinois Press, 1988); and my reflections, "Can the non-Subaltern Speak?" in Roman de LaCampa, Michael Sprinker, and E. Ann Kaplan, eds., *Late Imperial Culture* (London and New York: Verso, 1995).

8. The term is Isabelle Gunning's. Her essay here explains her rationale for pluralizing it.

9. Fashioning their idea of the nation-state according to the European model, Third Worldists have remained ironically complicit with a Eurocentric Enlightenment narrative.

10. The move beyond Third Worldism is reflected in the terminological crisis swirling around the term "Third World" itself, now seen as an inconvenient relic of a more militant period. Three worlds theory not only flattens heterogeneities, masks contradictions, and elides differences, but also obscures similarities. (For example, the common presence of "Fourth World" [indigenous] peoples in both "Third World" and "First World" countries. Third World feminist critics such as Nawal El-Sadawi [Egypt], Vina Mazumdar [India], Kumari Jayawardena [Sri Lanka], and Fatima Mernissi [Morocco] have explored these differences and similarities in a feminist light, pointing to the gendered limitations of Third World nation-

alism. The term "post-colonial," as I have argued elsewhere, can ambiguously imply both a movement beyond anticolonial nationalist ideology and beyond a specific moment of colonial history, while Post-Third Worldism conveys a movement beyond a specific ideology, i.e., Third Worldist nationalism.) I am not suggesting "Post-Third Worldist" as a replacement for "postcolonial"; rather, I suggest that we need to use these terms contingently and in more precise ways. See Ella Shohat, "Notes on the Post-Colonial," *Social Text* 31–32 (Spring 1992), and "Post-Third Worldist Culture: Gender, Nation and the Cinema," in Jacqui M. Alexander and Chandra Talpade Mohanty, eds., *Feminist Genealogies, Colonial Legacies and Democratic Futures* (New York: Routledge, 1996).

11. Cherríe Moraga and Gloria Anzaldúa, eds., *This Bridge Called My Back: Writings by Radical Women of Color* (Watertown, MA: Persephone Press, 1981).

12. Audre Lorde, *Sister Outsider* (Trumansburg, NY: The Crossing Press, 1984).

13. See Chandra Mohanty and Biddy Martin, "Feminist Politics: What's Home Got to Do with It?" in Teresa de Lauretis, ed., *Feminist Studies/Critical Studies* (Bloomington: Indiana University Press, 1986), especially p. 192.

14. Inderpal Grewal and Caren Kaplan, eds. *Scattered Hegemonies: Postmodernity and Transnational Feminist Practices,* (Minneapolis: University of Minnesota Press, 1994), and *Feminist Genealogies, Colonial Legacies, Democratic Futures,* M. Jacqui Alexander and Chandra Talpade Mohanty, eds. (New York: Routledge, 1996).

15. For a postcolonial feminist critique of this metaphor, see Caren Kaplan's *Questions of Travel* (Durham, N.C.: Duke University Press, 1996).

16. Such a call was encapsulated, for example, in Hazel Carby, "White Women Listen! Black Feminism and the Boundaries of Sisterhood," in *The Empire Strikes Back: Race and Racism in 70s Britain,* Center for Contemporary Cultural Studies, eds, (London: Hutchinson, 1982); bell hooks, *Ain't I a Woman? Black Women and Feminism* (Boston: South End Press, 1981); Valerie Amos and Pratibha Parmar, "Challenging Imperial Feminism," *Feminist Review* 17 (Autumn 1984); and Chandra T. Mohanty, "Under Western Eyes: Feminist Scholarship and Colonial Discourses," *Feminist Review* 30 (Autumn 1988).

17. The process of preparing the "Cross Talk" conference on which *Talking Visions* is based, showed this. A few (white) artists called The New Museum to complain that they had heard the conference was going to exclude white women.

18. In this sense it is worth recalling Audre Lorde's lines written almost 20 years ago to a (white) feminist:

> So I wondered, why does not Mary [Daly] deal with Afrekete as an example [of old female power]? Why are her goddess-images only white, western-

european, judeo-christian? Where was Afrekete, Yemanje, Oyo and Mawulisa? Where are the warrior-goddess of the Vodun, the Dohoemeian Amazons and the warrior-women of Dan? . . . Then to realize that the only quotations from Black women's words were the ones you used to introduce your chapter on African genital mutilation, made me question why you needed to use them at all. For my part, I felt that you had in fact misused my words, utilized them only to testify against myself as a woman of color. . . . Did you ever read my words, or did you merely finger through them for quotations which you thought might valuably support an already-conceived idea concerning some old and distorted connection between us? . . . Have you read my work and the work of other black women, for what it could give you? Or did you hunt through only to find words that would legitimize your chapter on African genital mutilation in the eyes of other black women? Audre Lorde, "A Letter to Mary Daly," *This Bridge Called My Back,* 94–95, 96.

19. See J. M. Blaut, *The Colonizer's Model of the World: Geographical Diffusionism and Eurocentric History* (New York and London: Guilford Press, 1993).

20. Shohat/Stam, *Unthinking Eurocentrism,* 293.

21. Grewal and Kaplan, *Scattered Hegemonies,* 2.

22. We have to distinguish here between "modernity" as an epoch, "modernization" as an ideology, and "modernism" as an aesthetic.

23. See Ward Churchill, ed., *Marxism and Native Americans* (Boston: South End Press, 1983).

24. Rayna Green, *Native American Women: A Contextual Bibliography* (Bloomington: Indiana University Press, 1983).

25. See, for example, Helen Callaway, *Gender, Culture and Empire: European Women in Colonial Nigeria* (Chicago: University of Illinois Press, 1987); Cynthia H. Enloe, *Bananas, Beaches and Bases* (Henley-on-Thames: Pandora Press, 1989); Nupur Chaudhuri and Margaret Strobel, eds., *Western Women and Imperialism: Complicity and Resistance* (Bloomington: Indiana University Press, 1990); Margaret Strobel, *European Women in British Africa and Asia* (Bloomington: Indiana University Press, 1990); Ella Shohat, "Gender and the Culture of Empire: Toward a Feminist Ethnography of the Cinema," *Quarterly Review of Film & Video* 13.1-3 (1991); Ann Laura Stoller, "Carnal Knowledge and Imperial Power: Gender, Race and Morality in Colonial Asia," in Micaela di Leonardo, ed. *Gender and the Cross-Roads of Knowledge: Feminist Anthropology in the Postmodern Era* (Berkeley: University of California Press, 1991); Vron Ware, *Beyond the Pale: White Women, Racism and History* (London: Verso, 1992); Caren Kaplan, "Getting to Know You: The King and I," in *Late Imperial Culture.* Caren Kaplan, *Questions of Travel: Postmodern Discourses of Displacement* (Durham: Duke University Press, 1996); Inderpal Grewal, *Home and Harem:*

Nation, Gender, Empire, and the Cultures of Travel (Durham: Duke University Press, 1996).

26. Chandra T. Mohanty, "Cartographies of Struggle," in *Third World Women and the Politics of Feminism,* 4.

27. This is not a blanket argument against psychoanalysis, but a call for a more historicized deployment of its terms.

28. Joy James, *Transcending the Talented Tenth: Black Leaders and American Intellectuals* (New York: Routledge, 1997), 61.

29. See, for example, Angela Davis, *Women, Race, and Class* (New York: Random House, 1981); Angela Gilliam, "Women Equality and National Liberation," in *Third World Women and the Politics of Feminism;* Ella Shohat, "'Lasers for Ladies': Endo Discourse and the Inscription of Science," *Camera Obscura* 29 (Fall 1993); and Faye Ginsburg and Rayna Rapp, eds., *Conceiving the New World Order: the Global Politics of Reproduction* (Berkeley: University of California Press, 1995).

30. I have in mind, for example, the U.S. Naturalization Act of 1790.

31. The zoologist and anatomist George Cuvier studied Saartje Bartman intimately and presumably dispassionately, and compared her buttocks to those of "female mandrills, baboons . . . which assume at certain epochs of their life a truly monstrous development," Shohat/Stam, *Unthinking Euroculturism.* For further discussion of science and the racial/sexual body, see Stephen Jay Gould, *The Mismeasure of Man* (New York: W. W. Norton, 1981); Sander Gilman, *Difference and Pathology* (Ithaca, NY: Cornell University Press, 1985); and Donna Haraway, *Primate Visions* (New York: Routledge, 1989).

32. A similar artistic strategy can be seen in Renée Cox's image *Hot-enTot;* in Coco Fusco and Guillermo Gomez-Peña's performance, captured in Coco Fusco and Paula Heredia's video, *The Couple in the Cage: A Guantinaui Odyssey* (1993); and in Marlon Fuentes's film *Bontoc Eulogy* (1995).

33. See Cornel West, *Prophesy Deliverance: An Afro-American Revolutionary Christianity* (Philadelphia: TK, 1982); Clyde Taylor, "Black Cinema in the Post-Aesthetic Era," in Jim Pines and Paul Willemen, eds., *Questions of Third Cinema* (London: BFI, 1989); and bell hooks, *Black Looks: Race and Representation* (Boston: South End Press, 1992).

34. On the constructedness of Afro-diasporic hair, see Kobena Mercer, "Black Hair/Style Politics," *New Formations* 3 (Winter 1987).

35. Chrystos, "I Don't Understand Those Who Have Turned Away from Me," in *This Bridge Called My Back,* 68–69.

36. Mirtha Quintanales, "I Have Paid Very Hard for My Immigrant Ignorance," in *This Bridge Called My Back,* 153–154.

37. Ibid.

38. In my personal history, one of our major movements, the Black Panthers in Israel, was partially modeled on the African-American movement. (Charlie Biton, a Moroccan-Israeli Black Panther leader, named his daughter Angela after Angela Davis).

39. Amending Raymond Williams's "structure of feelings," Robert Stam and I argue in *Unthinking Eurocentrism* for an "analogical" *process* of structure of feelings; see p. 351.

40. Unlike "minorities," which assumes a hegemonic idea of who inhabits the "center" and who inhabits the "periphery," the term "minoritized," I suggest, calls attention to the political process by which some segments of society are generated as "major" and others as "minor."

41. This domination operates on several levels: economic ("the Group of Seven," the IMF, the World Bank, GATT), political (the five veto-holding members of the UN Security Council), military (the new "unipolar" NATO), and techno-informational-cultural (Hollywood, UPI, Reuters, CNN, IBM).

42. Toni Morrison, "The Pain of Being Black," *Time,* May 22, 1989.

43. Given earlier racist policies toward non-white U.S. populations and immigrants (e.g., in 1854, in *People v. Hall,* the California Supreme Court ruled inadmissible testimony against whites by Chinese, blacks, mulattos, and Native Americans), the inclusionary Immigration Act represents a major step in the population make-up of the U.S. Such liberalized change came in the wake of the Civil Rights movement, but the administration did not predict the degree to which such policy might influence the move across borders.

44. Shifting contexts also shape our speech, accent, dialect, intonation. *Talking Visions* is written in English, yet not all its contributors speak English as a first language. Educated in other languages, many of us are not completely comfortable in English, nor do we speak English in "correct" hegemonic mode. African-Americans, meanwhile, were historically dispossessed of their African languages; English for them became the only available code for expression. Along with other multicultural feminists, they decolonized English, reinvoiced it, subverted it, opened it up to polyphonic possibilities.

45. For a discussion of the "politics of location," see Chandra Talpade Mohanty, "Feminist Encounters: Locating the Politics of Experience," *Copyright* 1 (Fall 1987); Michele Wallace, "The Politics of Location: Cinema/Theory/Literature/Ethnicity/Sexuality/Me," *Framework,* no. 36 (1989); Lata Mani, "Multiple Mediations: Feminist Scholarship in the Age of Multinational Reception," *Inscriptions* 5 (1989); Inderpal Grewal, "Autobiographic Subjects and Diasporic Locations: *Meatless Days* and *Borderlands,*" and Caren Kaplan, "The Politics of Location as

Transnational feminist Practice," both in Grewal and Kaplan, eds., *Scattered Hegemonies.*

46. My claims here about the diverse interdisciplinary programs are perhaps somewhat general, and certainly there are exceptions to the rule. I don't mean to be categorical here, but rather strategically reductive. I am basing these claims on my experience at diverse institutions, as well as on that of informal conversations with some colleagues. I have also examined numerous catalogues and course offerings of American universities.

47. The well-equipped academic comes to the annual Asian Studies or Middle East Studies association meetings armed with a constituted discipline, a mapped region, and a circumscribed period, "from ____ to ____." The relatively sizable minority that attempts to break such routines is often disciplined by a withdrawal of the jobs, grants, and publications that the academic reward machine has to dispense.

48. I am pointing out a tendency rather than suggesting that *all* women's studies programs operate in this way (one exception, for example, is San Francisco State University's Women's Studies Program). Furthermore, individual scholars in diverse women's/gender/sexuality studies around the U.S. peruse such alternative scholarship, but they are often not in positions of power to reformulate such canons. Having been largely formulated by Euro-American feminists, women's/gender, and gay/lesbian studies programs have not yet seriously incorporated such scholarship into reformulating their curricula.

49. Mitsuye Yamada, "Asian Pacific American Women and Feminism," in *This Bridge Called My Back,* 73.

50. Essays that address the relations between the "postcolonial" and the "multicultural" include, Ella Shohat, "Notes on the Postcolonial," *Social Text* 31–32 (Spring 1992); Inderpal Grewal, "The Postcolonial, Ethnic Studies and the Diaspora," *Socialist Review;* and Ann DuCille, "Postcolonialism and Afrocentricity: Discourse and Dat Course," in *The Black Columbiad: Defining Moment in African-American Literature and Culture* edited by Werner Sollors and Maria Diedrich (Cambridge, Mass.: Harvard University Press, 1994.)

51. For some communities of color in the U.S., the status of being "of color" is uncertain. Despite a history of imperialist, racist, and sexist attitudes toward the Middle East and North Africa, for example, and despite that region's participation in Third World national struggles, "people of color" status has not usually been ascribed to Middle Easterners.

52. See, for example, "Green Card" art by Iñigo Manglano-Ovalle; Lourdes Portillo's video *Columbus on Trial;* and Culture Clash's performance on *Columbus—The Godfather.*

53. The discussion here of the non-finalized American Nation is partly based on "Ethnicities in Relation" in *Unthinking Eurocentrism.* I thank Margo Machida and May Joseph for inviting me to serve as a final commentator on "New Hybridities: Immigration and Asian Arts," where I presented some of this material at New York University, June 1995. I also thank Inderpal Grewal for sharing with me her work-in-progress, *Umrika,* which makes parallel arguments.

54. Some of these questions are taken from the introduction, coauthored by Aamir Mufti and myself, *Dangerous Liaisons,* coedited by Anne McClintock, Mufti, and myself. (Minneapolis: The University of Minnesota Press, 1997).

55. The theoretical challenge, however, is to avoid the twin pitfalls of both euphoria and melancholy. The globalization thesis, as a group of Australian analysts has recently put it, "often descends into teleological assumptions of global integration and uniformity or into uni-directional accounts of cultural imperialism and obliteration. There is a corresponding tendency among those who assert the primacy of the local to mythologize independence from international power structures and to romanticize indigenous cultural forms." See David Rowe, Geoffrey Lawrence, Toby Miller, and Jim McKay, "Global Sport? Core Concern and Peripheral Vision," *Media, Culture and Society* 16 (1994), 661–675. See also A. D. King, ed., *Culture, Globalization and the World System* (London: Macmillan, 1991); *Global/Local: Cultural Production and the Transnational Imaginary* Rob Wilson and Wimal Dissanayake, eds.,(Durham, N.C.: Duke University Press, 1996); and Arjun Appadurai, "Global Ethnoscapes," in Richard Fox, ed., *Recapturing Anthropology* (Sante Fe, NM: School of American Research, 1991); and Robert J. S. Ross and Kent C. Trachte, *Global Capitalism: The New Leviathan* (Albany: 1990).

56. See Heinz Dieterich, "Five Centuries of the New World Order," *Latin American Perspectives* 19, no. 3 (Summer 1992). Transnational globalization is enforced through deteriorating terms of trade and the "austerity programs" by which the World Bank and the IMF, often with the self-serving complicity of Third World elites, impose rules that First World countries would never tolerate. Although direct colonial rule has largely come to an end, much of the world remains entangled in a neocolonial conjuncture in which direct political and military control has given way to abstract, semi-indirect, largely economic forms of control whose linchpin is a close alliance between foreign capital and the local elite. These processes, however, have some ironic twists. The same multinational corporations that disseminate inane blockbusters and canned sitcoms also spread Afro-diasporic music such as reggae and rap around the globe. The problem lies, then not in the exchange but in the unequal terms on which the exchange take place.

57. Although colonization per se predates European colonialism, having been practiced by Greece, Rome, the Aztecs, and many other groups, what was new in Eu-

ropean colonialism was its planetary reach, its affiliation with global institutional power, and its imperative mode.

58. See Joseph Bristow, *Empire Boys: Adventures in a Man's World* (London: Harper Collins, 1991), 19.

59. "There are few *Khyber Passes on the* Internet . . . and there is no effective way to gain control of it. Unlike *Banana Republics,* it does not have a clear center of authority to take over in a coup. But *uncontrolled territory* has its dangers" (William J. Mitchell, *City of Bits: Space, Place and the Infobahn,* (Cambridge: MIT Press, 1995) (emphasis, ES); or, "The early days of cyberspace were like those of the *Western frontiers.* Parallel, breakneck development of the Internet and of consumer computing devices and software quickly created an astonishing new condition; a vast, *hitherto-unimagined territory began to open up for exploration.* Early computers had been like *isolated mountain valleys* ruled by programmer-*kings;* the archaic digital world was a far-flung range in which narrow, unreliable trail provided only tenuous connections. . . . An occasional floppy disk would migrate from one to the other, *bringing the makings of colonies.* . . . Cyberspace is still *tough territory to travel . . .* " (Mitchell, 109–110, in a section titled "Wild West/Electronic Frontier") (emphasis, ES); or, "Cyberspace is a *frontier region,* populated by a few hardy technologies who can tolerate the austerity of its *savage* computer interfaces" (Mitch Kapor and John Perry Barlow, in *"Across the Electronic Frontier,"* Electronic Frontier Foundation Washington, D.C., July 10, 1990) (emphasis, ES).

60. See Paul J. Smith, "Smuggling People into Rich Countries is a Growing Industry," *Herald Tribune,* June 28, 1996.

61. For more on mail order brides see Venny Villapando, "The Business of Selling Mail-Order Brides," in *Making Waves: An Anthology of Writings by and about Asian American Women,* Asian Women United of California, eds., (Boston: Beacon Press, 1989). U.S. heterosexual men's appetite for Asian women as mail-order brides, as Villapando suggests, is the complement to their fear of "strong," "feminist" U.S. women; their attraction is to the submissiveness stereotypically attributed to Asian "Cherry Blossoms" and "Lotus Blossoms." For their part, Asian women interested in these arranged marriages have less access to information than do American men, including men of color. Unlike the prospective grooms, these women must fill out a personality evaluation asking intimate questions about their lives and histories, which are then shared with the men. Some companies discourage their male clients from disclosing certain types of personal facts in their correspondence, including such potentially "negative" characteristics as being black, or having physical disabilities. In a white-dominated business one may argue, black men can be seen as an "inferior commodity." Yet their status as First Worlders to some degree "compensates" for their race. Latino and African-American men buying services from

Filipina women are similarly enjoying their position as First World men in the Third World, a status granted by the same state apparatus that continues to marginalize and oppress them at home.

62. See Chea Villanueva, "Factory Girls," in *Making Waves*. The Gabriella organization has been fighting this kind of U.S. presence in the Philippines; the issue was addressed by Ninochca Rosca at the Cross Talk conference, 1993.

63. I am quoting here from a brochure of "Olivia Cruises and Resorts: Unique Vacations for Women."

64. Ibid.

65. For more on this point, see Stuart Hall, "The Local and the Global: Globalization and Ethnicity" *Culture, Globalization, and the World System,* Anthony D. King, ed. (Binghamton: Department of Art History, State University of New York at Binghamton, 1991); Inderpal Grewal and Caren Kaplan's introduction to *Scattered Hegemonies;* and Ella Shohat and Robert Stam, "From the Imperial Family to the Transnational Imaginary: Media Spectatorship in the Age of Globalization," in *Global/Local: Cultural Production and the Transnational Imaginary.*

Plate 7: *Twister*, 1995
Ink on gessoed paper, 32 × 51"
Nicole Eisenman
Courtesy of the artist and Jack Tilton Gallery, New York

bell hooks

naked without shame: a counter-hegemonic body politic

> My talk will focus on representations of the naked black female body; the issue of how we can construct an affirming body politic within white supremacist capitalist patriarchy.
>
> —from the author's original description for the Cross Talk symposium, Saturday, June 5, 1993

preface

"Momma," I can hear them say, my sisters, voices dripping with scorn and hurt, "she stands naked in front of the mirror, just staring, as though she ain't got no shame! Anybody could be looking up and see her through the window."

Naked with shame on auction blocks, Black female slaves watched the world that was our body change. Nakedness that cannot be covered must be forgotten, shrouded in cloaks of modesty, Victorian Puritanism, religion without flesh. Signs that repeatedly say, "This Black female body is *not* on the block, not off the streets, not for sale, not without shame."

Ours is a history of shame. Written on the body we cannot erase. Imagine growing up with five sisters in two large attic bedrooms painted a dusky rose. Rooms with slanted roofs, huge windows from ceiling to floor. Six brown girls living in a private world no man can enter. You might imagine this world would be a place where we would forget all Puritanical notions about the body learned outside, and live in our flesh anew. That was not the way it was. When we climbed the stairs to the sanctuary, we moved all the more deeply into the heart of our repressions. We denied the presence of the body. Nakedness was forbidden. Nakedness hurt the eye like when Adam first looked at Eve. In these two rooms we wanted never to be caught looking. We refused to see one another's bodies. We worked hard to turn our eyes away, to dress in the dark, in half-light, to change when no [one] was there. To *always, always* wear gown or robe. To *never, never* be without panties, keeping underwear on even during sleep. We denied our bodies, our right to see and feel ourselves, to witness our bodies move gracefully through girlhood and beyond. We made no celebrations to herald budding breasts, moon flow, rounding hips. We lived to forget, to not remember our bodies naked, without shame. We dreaded our female flesh.

The Blackness of our bodies held no deep meanings. The range of shades and colors between us, so common as to be unworthy of note. More than Blackness we shared female being, felt the awesome power and presence of Woman becoming. That presence troubled us. We invented gestures of disregard, habits of being that allowed us to forget our bodies. We created closets where we stripped ourselves of flesh. We pretended to be invisible, that we could never be seen, not by any human eye. To be invisible hurts. To live in our bodies but always away from them was to live always alone in states of fierce and lonely abandonment.

As a Black girl in a house of woman-being I wanted to see myself. I longed to cherish mirrored reflections, to understand naked brown girl flesh becoming itself. At twelve I'm reading the book of *American Negro Poetry*, I learned these words by heart: "She does not know her beauty, she thinks her brown body has no glory." A poem called "No Images." If I understand the title, how can there be images if we insist on remaining invisible, lost to the flesh? In search of glory, I find my body. I search it out standing naked in front of mirrors, watching and giving my body sight—visibility. I'm looking at my Black-girl body, seeing it clearly, learning its trace, leaning to place myself outside history, re-inventing paradise, a garden of nakedness, a place where brown flesh can be known and loved. I search my body out in the dark, hands mapping familiar terrains. My skin is smooth—velvety soft—soft as marshmallows roasted over fire, the color of warm honey. When my tongue licks my arm I taste the sweetness there, warm honey. I fall asleep at night naked from the waist down, hands between my legs warm and wet, holding the memory of orgasm. Mountain peaks I climb alone; solitary, transcendent pleasure. I sleep deeply now, can lose myself in dreams, sure that my brown body is a haven, a home this spirit can come back to.

My sisters pull the covers back, try and capture my secrets. Brown hands between thighs, hands deep in pussy as sweet as warm honey.

"Why you got to use that word?" they say. "Ain't you got no shame?"

Their taunts seduce, fill me with the knowledge that to live as a

brown woman in my flesh, without shame, is pure rebellion. I am learning
. . . to let my body speak, to share its naked power. I celebrate freedom in
the flesh. They seek to silence.

"Ain't you got no shame?"

I touch lips with my tongue, biting the flesh with my small white
teeth, watch the fullness of their swelling blood coloring them earth-red.
Naked brown woman without shame. Refusing to keep her body hidden.
Refusing history.

★ ★ ★

Although black women have fiercely challenged white supremacy throughout our history in this society, we have not focused much attention on the
impact of this system of domination on the black female body. Rarely does
anyone call attention to the complex and diverse ways the body has been
foregrounded as a site of conquest in all efforts of colonization. Criticism of
white supremacist patriarchal constructions of black female images usually
highlight stereotypes—the fact that from slavery to the present day we are
likely to be portrayed as mammies, whores, or sluts. Rarely do we articulate a vision of resistance, of decoloniation that provides strategies for the
construction of a liberatory, black female body politics. Black female bodies
are almost always framed within a context of patriarchal, pornographic,
racialized sexualization. They are de-aestheticized and de-eroticized.
This process began during the colonization of this continent by white
Europeans.

The presence of a small minority of free black women who immigrated here of their own accord, or who were born free here, has never
been highlighted in anyway that counters the hegemonic representation of
enslaved black females, naked on the auction block, raped by white masters
and enslaved black men alike. Who among us, when remembering
eighteenth- and nineteenth-century representations of African-American
females, can call to mind any visual representation of the body of a free
black woman? The totality of our received body image, our inherited body
politics is always that of bondage—the body taken over, stripped of its own
agency and made to serve the will, desire, and needs of other.

White supremacy is not the only force inscribing negative stereotypes
on black female bodies. African-American internalization of sexist thinking, both in response to retentions from an African past wherein gendered
hierarchy was often the cultural norm and in response to acculturation in
the Americas, created a context of complicity. Racism and sexism combine
to make a world wherein black females are socialized to shape our body

Plate 8: *Appraisals of Slavery*
Image from Walter Lima, Jr.'s film *Chico Rei*, 1982
Courtesy of Museu de Arte Moderna, Rio de Janeiro

politics either via the embodiment of stereotypes or reaction against negative stereotypes. Nineteenth-century black female obsessions with bodily cleanliness, exaggerated displays of modesty, repression of the erotic, denial of sexual presence and desire, were all efforts made to counter notions that black females were inherently licentious, driven by animalistic sexual cravings which could not be controlled.

To justify breeding, the institutionalized sanctioning of ongoing rape of enslaved black females to produce future laborers, white supremacist patriarchs had to position the black female in the cultural imagination as always "sexually suspect." To make the black female body machine, vessel, was an act of dismemberment—a mutilation that ensured this group would always be seen as less than, as not really and truly worthy of desire. Black female bodies were forced to embody the sign of sexual ruin. Against this backdrop of devaluation and denigration black women in slavery and in freedom worked to regain status and value by embodying the norms of femininity set by the white colonizing imagination. White and black men exercised patriarchal privileges in relationship to black female bodies. Both groups could rape those bodies with relative impunity. Both groups could dare to fantasize and/or enact sexual acts deemed degrading with black female bodies since it was impossible to ruin that which was perceived as inherently unworthy, tainted and soiled.

Marked by shame, projected as inherent and therefore precluding any possibility of innocence, the black female body was beyond redemption. It is no wonder, then, that when slavery ended black females usually chose to follow the path of either obsessive representations of themselves as virtuous and therefore worthy of respect, or wantonly represented themselves as loose and licentious. The latter took pride in the racist/sexist stereotype that black females were more sexually free than their white counterparts. Individual black women who may have believed themselves to be always the losers in a world of sexist feminine competition based on beauty could see the realm of the sexual as the place where they triumph over white females. Absorbing the stereotypes, in part so as not to hold white men accountable for their sexual obsessions with black females often acted out in actual rape and sexual harassment, many white females were, and remain, eager to see black women as inherently more sexual.

This stereotypical racist/sexist image of black women as sexually licentious corresponds to that of the black male as rapist. Yet while contemporary black liberation struggles (the Civil Rights movement, the sixties movements for black power) consistently questioned the racist sexual stereotypes that were imposed on black males, the stereotypes imposed on black females converged with conventional sexist ways of thinking about female sexuality, particularly cultural representations and interpretations of any active female sexual agency. Contemporary movements for sexual liberation often praised black females and other ethnic groups like Latina women for being already "sexually free" so that they did not serve as sites of critical intervention. Since they focused exclusively on the liberation of white females from the confines of a racist/sexist notion of purity that had encouraged sexual repression, sexual liberation movements did not challenge degrading and limiting stereotypes imposed on black women and all women of color. As a consequence, those sexist/racist stereotypes continue to inform representations of black female sexuality in the cultural image as well as the ways many black women see themselves. Despite all the popular literature that suggests white women are more engaged with sexual liberation and more open in many ways about the body than their black female counterparts, many black women continue to believe that they are inherently more sexually desirable, more capable of attaining sexual fulfillment.

Within diverse black communities there is little discussion about the black female body. As popular music attests black males continue to place black females in the binary categories of madonnas or whores. Sexually active black women are most often portrayed in the mass media of the domination culture, and in those aspects of media that are black owned and operated, as inherently less moral. Their bodies are de-aestheticized, that is to say their sexuality [is] often portrayed as raw and uninhibited in vulgar ways. In other words, the naked black female body is made to appear grotesque, ugly—and all the more so if that body is actively sexual. These stereotypical representations were rampant in "black exploitation" films. When I first saw a screening of Melvin Van Peebles's film *Sweet Sweetback's Baadasssss Song* in the early seventies I was horrified by the ways black female bodies and our sexuality were portrayed. It was horrifying to me that no one in the audience that night found it problematic that an adult black female was sexually seducing a child. Rather than a violation and transgression, because the child was a young black male, the scene was viewed merely as an act of pleasurable sexual initiation. The black female was portrayed, like she would come to be portrayed in similar films from that time forth, as sexually voracious and out-of-control. De-eroticized as desirable female flesh, she was exoticized as raw meat, hot pussy. The vagina—the pussy—was evoked in black exploitation films (and in the works that came afterwards, which took their cues from these films) as the only way to tell black females from black males since we were, and still are, usually portrayed as just as mean, tough, strong, and angry as black men. Indeed, in many of these films it was only the possession of a vagina that marked the black adult woman as female, hence the graphic depiction of black female flesh by misogynist and/or sexist imaginations as grotesque and monstrous. The "pussy" in these films is potentially all consuming of male power. Hence it must be raped, violated, and tamed. Most films by black male filmmakers do not challenge in any way racist/sexist constructions of the black female body. Like their white counterparts they usually depict the madonna/whore dichotomy. Whereas black female bodies may be depicted in films by white filmmakers as whores and sluts to emphasize the purity of white female heroines, often black filmmakers rely on a skin color split to create the same binary opposition, with darker skinned women portrayed as more licentious and immoral than their fairer counterparts. Eddie Murphy's film *Boomerang* pitted black actress Robin Givens against bi-racial Halle Berry in a contest that aimed to show which female was more virtuous and worthy. Givens's character is powerful and sexually aggressive. Even though she has the conventional feminine look, the movie insists that this is only a mask, a front to entrap men. In reality, her character is hard, tough, and mean, a castrating bitch in direct contrast to the non-sexually assertive, subordinate, lighter skinned woman. Givens's character is only imitation femininity, Berry's character is the real thing.

Contemporary audiences are socialized to believe racist/sexist representations of the black female body as true and authentic. When a character is depicted in films in ways that challenge this interpretation, audiences resist these images. For example: when the film *Menace II Society* was first shot and shown to audiences, Ronnie, the redemptive young black single mother in the film is not actively sexual even though she is depicted as desirable, sensuous, and erotic. She is concerned with self-development. When viewers screened the film prior to its release they wanted to see this character engaged in sexual intercourse with the male hero. The public demanded that she be sexualized. And the way the film depicts her sexuality is that it is the means by which she is shown to be not as sincere and as devoted to her principles as earlier portrayals of her suggest. Since the way she is sexualized (she has sex in the midst of a party at her house) runs counter to her concern that her child be protected from adult party behavior, this scene is completely incongruent with the character the film has constructed. This righteous, courageous, politically conscious black woman is suddenly portrayed as disloyal to her own values, a representation that is completely in sync with patriarchal sexist/racist iconography of black women. Everyone who has written about this scene acknowledges that Ronnie's willingness to leave her guests and the care of her little boy to have sex during the party creates a pornographic voyeuristic moment. Everyone at the party knows she is having sex. This break with her character is enacted to fulfill the societal need to contain and control black womanhood and the black female body by always keeping us trapped in the prison-house of white supremacist, capitalist, patriarchal representations. Everyone in this culture, including black folks, are so accustomed to seeing black female bodies depicted as licentious, immoral, evil, consumed by hedonistic desire and monstrous longings for power, that there is little or no resistance to these images. Films that do not emphasize heterosexuality often depict black females in the same stereotypical ways. Black women characters in films by white lesbian filmmakers more often than not conform to the stereotype. Filmmakers like Lizzie Borden and Monika Treut are two examples. The black female characters in their films are always more aggressive, tough, and trashy than their white female counterparts.

In Sara Halprin's book *Look at my Ugly Face,* which examines links between appearance obsession in our culture and white supremacy, she analyzes the racism of white women who often "see" black women as more aggressive, as meaner, tougher, stronger. Commenting on her own experiences Halprin asserts: "It did not occur to me that when I went to the movies or watched television at home I never saw images of women or girls who were black like my friend, or Asian, or obviously Jewish." Her continued reflections are worth noting: "When I went to junior high school I had to take two buses from our housing project to get to school. I remember several black girls, older than I was, who rode the bus. Some of them had razors in their back pockets, and I heard them bragging about getting in fights and cutting each other. I was terrified. I did my best to be invisible, and never to get in anyone's way. But my own racism was invisible to me. There must have been tough white girls on that bus too, but I don't remember them. I just assumed that black girls were tougher than white girls, and I didn't look to see if there were any black girls who, like me, were terrified and trying to be invisible. I don't remember noticing that anyone was white, only that people were black. Whiteness was not something I ever noticed. It was easy to ignore. And it was easy to project qualities onto blackness that I didn't acknowledge in myself, for instance, toughness, or the ability to dance, or sexuality." There is a direct correlation between the qualities that groups who hold more power than black women and women of color assign to us and the fictive representations of our identity that bombard us in mass media. Concurrently, since so many black females have not decolonized their minds in ways that enable them to break with internalized racism and/or sexism, the representations they create may embody stereotypes. Let me give an example from my own experience. When a high powered mainstream fashion magazine did a story on me, I was called and asked for a photo to accompany the article that would be "fierce and aggressive." Were I not decolonized I might not question the desire of this magazine to represent me in this way. When I did, they willingly used another photo. However, the article itself, written by a black female, edited under the supervision of her white superiors, tended to emphasize that I was fierce and provocative but made little mention of the intellectual work that had led them to do the interview. Now in an earlier issue a Jewish white woman peer, another critic, had been featured. She was photographed in front of rows of books with a heading that indicated she was a major feminist thinker. Without in any way diminishing the power of her work, it is worthy of note that I have written many more books, that my work is used in classrooms all over this country in a way that hers [is] not. My point is to emphasize the stereotypes that are self-evident and operative here. It is very difficult for black women to assert more control over the ways we are represented in mainstream media, since so many folks who produce, market, and consume these images have not interrogated how racism and sexism inform the ways that they look at black females, the ways they see us.

Every day of our lives black females are assaulted by images of ourselves constructed by the white racist/sexist imagination. The "shame" that such images evoke in individual black women has yet to be fully named. That shame will never leave us until we begin to engage in collective resistance, which means that we must challenge the ways we are currently represented (that challenge may simply take the form of standing outside a movie with signs stating what we find problematic about the images folks are about to see). We must also decolonize our minds and imaginations in ways that empower us to create subversive and alternative images. To intervene critically in the existing ways our bodies are represented, black females must take the lead in defining a liberatory body politics that embraces us and our reality. The preface to this piece is meant to be just that—an act of critical intervention. Progressive black females who challenge racist and sexist representations are engaged in an ongoing struggle to reclaim our images—our naked black female bodies—so that we can construct an affirming body politic, so that we know our glory and revel in it.

Plate 9: *The End of Uncle Tom and the Grand Allegorical Tableau of Eva in Heaven*, 1995
Detail, Cut paper and adhesive on wall
Kara Walker
Courtesy of the artist and Wooster Gardens, New York, Collection Jeffrey Deitch.

Adrian Piper

Passing for White, Passing for Black

It was the new graduate student reception for my class, the first social event of my first semester in the best graduate department in my field in the country. I was full of myself, as we all were, full of pride at having made the final cut, full of arrogance at our newly recorded membership among the privileged few, the intellectual elite—this country's real aristocracy, my parents told me—full of confidence in our intellectual ability to prevail, to fashion original and powerful views about some topic we represented to ourselves only vaguely. I was a bit late and noticed that many turned to look at—no, scrutinize—me as I entered the room. I congratulated myself on having selected for wear my black velvet, bell-bottom pants suit (yes, it was that long ago) with the cream silk blouse and crimson vest. One of the secretaries who'd earlier helped me find an apartment came forward to greet me and proceeded to introduce me to various members of the faculty, eminent and honorable faculty, with names I knew from books I'd studied intensely and heard discussed with awe and reverence by my undergraduate teachers. To be in the presence of these men and attach faces to names was delirium enough. But actually to enter into casual social conversation with them took every bit of poise I had. As often happens in such situations, I went on automatic pilot. I don't remember what I said; I suppose I managed not to make a fool of myself. The most famous and highly respected member of the faculty observed me for awhile from a distance and then came forward. Without introduction or preamble he said to me with a triumphant smirk, "Miss Piper, you're about as black as I am."

One of the benefits of automatic pilot in social situations is that insults take longer to make themselves felt. The meaning of the words simply don't register right away, particularly if the person who utters them is smiling. You reflexively respond to the social context and the smile rather than to the words. And so I automatically returned the smile and said something like, "Really? I hadn't known that about you"—something that sounded both innocent and impertinent, even though that was not what I felt. What I felt was numb, and then shocked and terrified, disoriented, as though I'd been awakened from a sweet dream of unconditional support and approval and plunged into a nightmare of jeering contempt. Later those feelings turned into wrenching grief and anger that one of my intellectual heroes had sullied himself in my presence and destroyed my illusion that these privileged surroundings were benevolent and safe; then guilt and remorse at having provided him the occasion for doing so.

Finally, there was the groundless shame of the inadvertent impostor, exposed to public ridicule or accusation. For this kind of shame, you don't actually need to have done anything wrong. All you need to do is care about others' image of you, and fail in your actions to reinforce their positive image of themselves. Their ridicule and accusations then function to both disown and degrade you from their status, to mark you not as having *done* wrong but as *being* wrong. This turns you into something bogus relative to their criterion of worth, and false relative to their criterion of authenticity. Once exposed as a fraud of this kind, you can never regain your legitimacy. For the violated criterion of legitimacy implicitly presumes an absolute incompatibility between the person you appeared to be and the person you are now revealed to be; and no fraud has the authority to convince her accusers that they merely imagine an incompatibility where there is none in fact. The devaluation of status consequent on such exposure is, then, absolute, and the suspicion of fraudulence spreads to all areas of interaction.

> Mr. S. Looked sternly at Mrs. P., and with an imperious air said, "You a colored woman? You're no negro. Where did you come from? If you're a negro, where are your free papers to show it?" . . . As he went away he looked at Mr. Hill and said, "She's no negro."
> —The Rev. H. Mattison, *Louisa Picquet, The Octoroon Slave and Concubine: A Tale of Southern Slave Life*

The accusation was one I had heard before, but more typically from other blacks. My family was one of the very last middle-class, light-skinned black families left in our Harlem neighborhood after most had fled to the suburbs; visibly black working-class kids my age yanked my braids and called me "pale-face." Many of them thought I was white, and treated me accordingly. As an undergraduate in the late 1960s and early 1970s, I attended an

Adrian Piper

urban university to which I walked daily through a primarily black working-class neighborhood. Once a black teenage youth called to me, "Hey, white girl! Give me a quarter!" I was feeling strong that day, so I retorted, "I'm not white and I don't have a quarter!" He answered skeptically, "You sure look white! You sure act white!" And I have sometimes met blacks socially who, as a condition of social acceptance of me, require me to prove my blackness by passing the Suffering Test: They recount at length their recent experiences of racism and then wait expectantly, skeptically, for me to match theirs with mine. Mistaking these situations for a different one in which an exchange of shared experiences is part of the bonding process, I instinctively used to comply. But I stopped when I realized that I was in fact being put through a third degree. I would share some equally nightmarish experience along similar lines, and would then have it explained to me why that wasn't really so bad, why it wasn't the same thing at all, or why I was stupid for allowing it to happen to me. So the aim of these conversations clearly was not mutual support or commiseration. That came only after I managed to prove myself by passing the Suffering Test of blackness (if I did), usually by shouting down or destroying my acquaintance's objections with logic.

> The white kids would call me a Clorox coon baby and all kinds of names I don't want to repeat. And the black kids hated me. "Look at her," they'd say. "She think she white. She think she cute."
>
> —Elaine Perry, *Another Present Era*

These exchanges are extremely alienating and demoralizing, and make me feel humiliated to have presumed a sense of connectedness between us. They also give me insight into the way whites feel when they are made the circumstantial target of blacks' justified and deep-seated anger. Because the anger is justified, one instinctively feels guilty. But because the target is circumstantial and sometimes arbitrary, one's sense of fairness is violated. One feels both unjustly accused or harassed, and also remorseful and ashamed at having been the sort of person who could have provoked the accusation.

As is true for blacks' encounters with white racism, there are at least two directions in which one's reactions can take over here. One can react defensively and angrily, and distill the encounter into slow-burning fuel for one's racist stereotypes. Or one can detach oneself emotionally and distance oneself physically from the aggressors, from this perspective their personal flaws and failures of vision, insight, and sensitivity loom larger, making it easier to forgive them for their human imperfections but harder to relate to them as equals. Neither reaction is fully adequate to the situation, since the first projects exaggerated fantasies onto the aggressor, while the second diminishes his responsibility. I have experienced both, toward both blacks and whites. I believe that the perceptual and cognitive distortions that characterize any form of racism begin here, in the failure to see any act of racist aggression as a defensive response to one's own perceived attack on the aggressor's physical or psychological property, or conception of himself or of the world. Once you see this, you may feel helpless to be anything other than who you are, anything or anyone who could resolve the discord. But at least it restores a sense of balance and mutually flawed humanity to the interaction.

My maternal cousin, who resembles Michelle Pfeiffer, went through adolescence in the late 1960s and had a terrible time. She tried perming her hair into an Afro; it didn't prevent attacks and ridicule from her black peers for not being "black enough." She adopted a black working-class dialect that made her almost unintelligible to her very proper, very middle-class parents, and counted among her friends young people who criticized high scholastic achievers for "acting white." That is, she ran the same gantlet I did, but of a more intense variety and at a much younger age. But she emerged intact, with a sharp and practical intellect, an endearing attachment to stating difficult truths bluntly, a dry sense of humor, and little tolerance for those blacks who, she feels, forgo the hard work of self-improvement and initiative for the imagined benefits of victim status. Now married to a WASP musician from Iowa, she is one tough cookie, leavened by the rejection she experienced from those with whom she has always proudly identified.

In my experience, these rejections almost always occur with blacks of working-class background who do not have extended personal experience with the very wide range of variation in skin color, hair texture, and facial features that in fact has always existed among African-Americans, particularly in the middle class. Because light-skinned blacks often received some education or training apprenticeships during slavery, there tend to be more of us in the middle class now. Until my family moved out of Harlem when I was fourteen, my social contacts were almost exclusively with upper-middle-class white schoolmates and working-class black neighborhood playmates, both of whom made me feel equally alienated from both races. It wasn't until college and after that I re-encountered the middle- and upper-middle-class blacks who were as comfortable with my appearance as my family had been, and who made me feel as comfortable and accepted by them as my family had.

So Suffering Test exchanges almost never occur with middle-class blacks, who are more likely to protest, on the contrary, that "we always knew you were black!"—as though there were some mysterious and inchoate essence of blackness that only other blacks have the antennae to detect.

> "There are niggers who are as white as I am, but the taint of blood is there and we always exclude it."
> "How do you know it is there?" asked Dr. Gresham.
> "Oh, there are tricks of blood which always betray them. My eyes are more practiced than yours. I can always tell them."
> —Frances E. W. Harper, *Iola Leroy or Shadows Uplifted*

When made by other blacks, these remarks function on some occasions to reassure me of my acceptance within the black community, and on others to rebuke me for pretending to indistinguishability from whiteness. But in either case they wrongly presuppose, as did my eminent professor's accusation, an essentializing stereotype into which all blacks must fit. In fact no blacks, and particularly no African-American blacks, fit any such stereotype.

My eminent professor was one of only two whites I have ever met who questioned my designated racial identity to my face. The other was a white woman junior professor, relatively new to the department, who, when I went on the job market at the end of graduate school, summoned me to her office and grilled me as to why I identified myself as black and exactly what fraction of African ancestry I had. The implicit accusation behind both my professors' remarks was, of course, that I had fraudulently posed as black in order to take advantage of the department's commitment to affirmative action. It's an extraordinary idea when you think about it: as though someone would willingly shoulder the stigma of being black in a racist society for the sake of a little extra professional consideration that guarantees nothing but suspicions of foul play and accusations of cheating. But it demonstrates just how irrationally far the suspicion of fraudulence can extend.

In fact I had always identified myself as black (or "colored" as we said before 1967). But fully comprehending what it meant to be black took a long time. My acculturation into the white upper-middle class started with nursery school when I was four, and was largely uneventful. For my primary and secondary schooling my parents sent me to a progressive prep school,

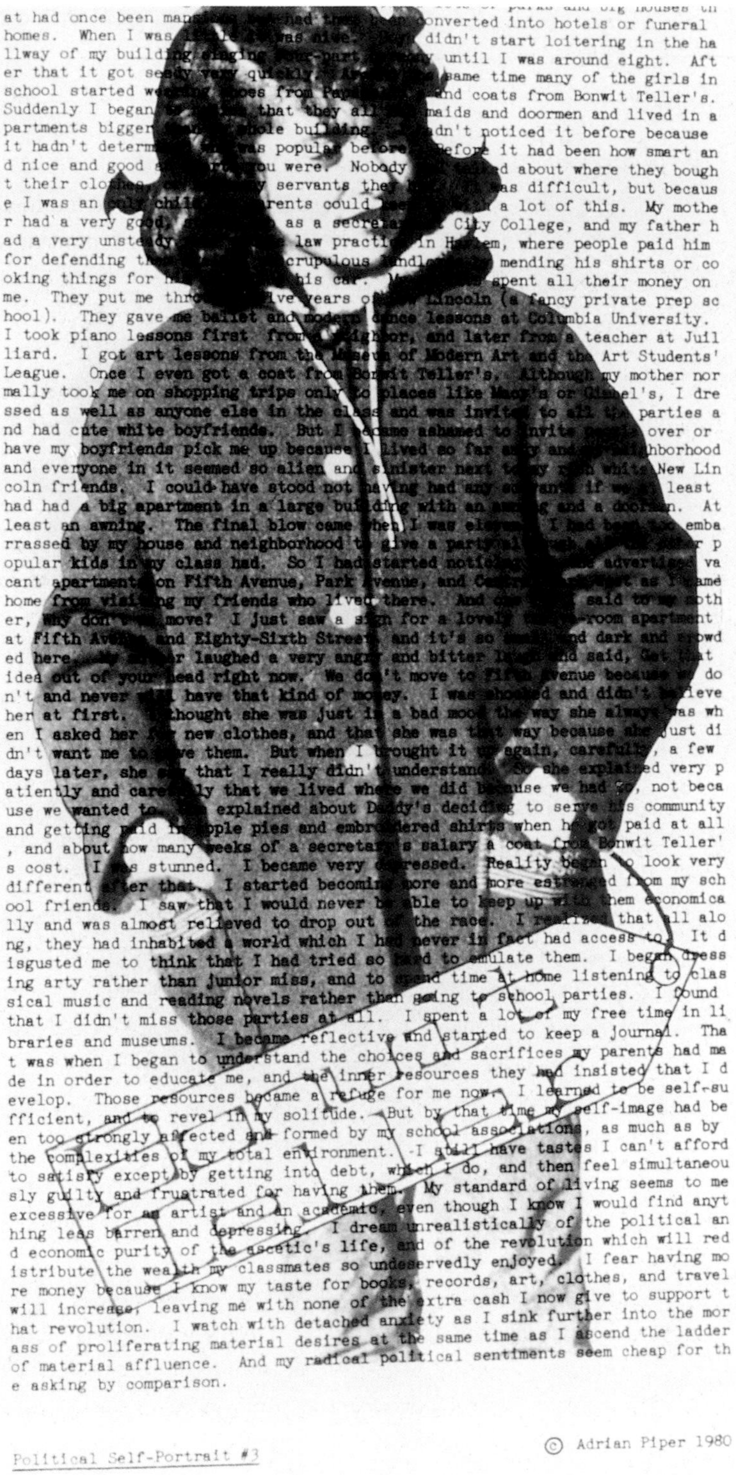

Plate 10: *Political Self-Portrait #3 (class)*, 1980
Poster 24 × 36"
Adrian Piper
Courtesy of the artist and John Weber Gallery, New York

one of the first to take the goal of integration seriously as more than an ideal. They gave me ballet lessons, piano lessons, art lessons, tennis lessons. In the 1950s and early 1960s they sent me to integrated summer camps where we sang "We Shall Overcome" around the campfire long before it became the theme song of the civil rights movement.

Of course there were occasional, usually veiled incidents, such as the time in preadolescence when the son of a prominent union leader (and my classmate) asked me to go steady and I began to receive phone calls from his mother, drunk, telling me how charming she thought it that her son was going out with a little colored girl. And the time the daughter of a well-known playwright, also a classmate, brought me home to her family and asked them to guess whether I was black or white, and shared a good laugh with them when they guessed wrong. But I was an only child in a family of four adults devoted to creating for me an environment in which my essential worth and competence never came into question. I used to think my parents sheltered me in this way because they believed, idealistically, that my education and achievements would then protect me from the effects of racism. I now know that they did so to provide me with an invincible armor of self-worth with which to fight it. It almost worked. I grew up not quite grasping the fact that my racial identity was a disadvantage. This lent heat to my emerging political conviction that of course it shouldn't be a disadvantage, for me or anyone else, and finally fueled my resolution not to allow it to be a disadvantage if I had anything at all to say about it.

> I will live down the prejudice, I will crush it out   the thoughts of the ignorant and prejudiced will not concern me. . . . I will show to the world that a man may spring from a race of slaves, yet far excel many of the boasted ruling race.
>
> —Charles Waddell Chesnutt, *Journals*

But the truth in my professor's accusations was that I had, in fact, resisted my parents' suggestion that, just this once, for admission to this most prestigious of graduate programs, I decline to identify my racial classification on the graduate admissions application, so that it could be said with certainty that I'd been admitted on the basis of merit alone. "But that would be passing," I protested. Although both of my parents had watched many of their relatives disappear permanently into the white community, passing for white was unthinkable within the branches of my father's and mother's families to which I belonged. That would have been a really, authentically shameful thing to do.

> "It seems as if the prejudice pursues us through every avenue of life, and assigns us the lowest places. . . . And yet I am determined," said Iola, "to win for myself a place in the fields of labor. I have heard of a place in New England, and I mean to try for it, even if I only stay a few months."
>
> "Well, if you will go, say nothing about your color."
>
> "Uncle Robert, I see no necessity for proclaiming that fact on the house-top. Yet I am resolved that nothing shall tempt me to deny it. The best blood in my veins is African blood, and I am not ashamed of it."
>
> —Harper, *Iola Leroy*

And besides, I reasoned to myself, to be admitted under the supposition that I was white would *not* be to be admitted on the basis of merit alone. Why undermine my chances of admission by sacrificing my one competitive advantage when I already lacked not only the traditionally acceptable race and gender attributes, but also alumni legacy status, an Ivy League undergraduate pedigree, the ability to pay full tuition or endow the university, war veteran status, professional sports potential, and a distinguished family name? I knew I could ace the program if I could just get my foot in the damn door.

Later, when I experienced the full force of the racism of the academy, one of my graduate advisors, who had remained a continuing source of support and advice after I took my first job, consoled me by informing me that the year I completed the program I had, in fact, tied one other student for the highest grade point average in my class. He was a private and dignified man of great integrity and subtle intellect, someone who I had always felt was quietly rooting for me. It was not until after his death that I began to appreciate what a compassionate and radical gesture he had made in telling me this. For by this time, I very much needed to be reminded that neither was I incompetent nor my work worthless, that I could achieve the potential I felt myself to have. My choice not to pass for white in order to gain entry to the academy, originally made out of naiveté, had resulted in more punishment than I would have imagined possible.

It wasn't only the overt sexual and racial harassment, each of which exacerbated the other, or the gratuitous snipes about my person, my lifestyle, or my work. What was even more insulting were the peculiar strategies deployed to make me feel accepted and understood despite the anomalies of my appearance, by individuals whose racism was so profound that this would have been an impossible task: the WASP colleague who attempted to establish rapport with me by making anti-Semitic jokes about the prevalence of Jews in the neighborhood of the university; the colleague who first inquired in detail into my marital status, and then attempted to demonstrate his understanding of my decision not to have children by speculating that I was probably concerned that they would turn out darker than I was; the colleague who consulted me on the analysis of envy and resentment, reasoning that since I was black I must know all about it; the colleague who, in my first department faculty meeting, made a speech to his colleagues discussing the research that proved that a person could be black without looking it.

These incidents and others like them had a peculiar cognitive feel to them, as though the individuals involved felt driven to make special efforts to situate me in their conceptual mapping of the world, not only by naming or indicating the niche in which they felt I belonged, but by seeking my verbal confirmation of it. I have learned to detect advance warnings that these incidents are imminent. The person looks at me with a fixed stare, her tension level visibly rising. Like a thermostat, when the tension reaches a certain level, the mechanism switches on: out comes some comment or action, often of an offensive personal nature, that attempts to locate me within the rigid confines of her stereotype of black people. I have not experienced this phenomenon outside the academic context. Perhaps it's a degenerate form of hypothesis testing, an unfortunate side effect of the quest for knowledge.

> She walked away. . . . The man followed her and tapped her shoulder.
> "Listen, I'd really like to get to know you," he said, smiling. He paused, as if expecting thanks from her. She didn't say anything. Flustered, he said, "A friend of mine says you're black. I told him I had to get a close-up look and see for myself."
> —Perry, *Another Present Era*

The irony was that I could have taken an easier entry route into this privileged world. In fact, on my graduate admissions application I could have claimed alumni legacy status and the distinguished family name of my paternal great uncle, who not only had attended that university and sent his sons there, but had endowed one of its buildings and was commemorated with an auditorium in his name. I did not because he belonged to a branch of the family from which we had been estranged for decades, even before my grandfather—his brother—divorced my grandmother, moved to another part of the country, and started another family. My father wanted nothing more to do with my grandfather or any of his relatives. He rejected his inheritance and never discussed them while he was alive. For me to have invoked his uncle's name in order to gain a professional advantage would have been out of the question. But it would have nullified my eminent professor's need to tell me who and what he thought I was.

Recently I saw my great uncle's portrait on an airmail stamp honoring him as a captain of industry. He looked so much like family photos of my grandfather and father that I went out and bought two sheets worth of these stamps. He had my father's and grandfather's aquiline nose and their determined set of the chin. Looking at his face made me want to recover my father's estranged family, particularly my grandfather, for my own. I had a special lead: A few years previously in the South, I'd included a photo-text work containing a fictionalized narrative about my father's family—a history chock-full of romance and psychopathology—in an exhibition of my work. After seeing the show, a white woman with blue eyes, my father's transparent rosy skin and auburn-brown hair, and that dominant family nose walked up to me and told me that we were related. The next day she brought photographs of her family, and information about a relative who kept extensive genealogical records on every family member he could locate. I was very moved, and also astounded that a white person would voluntarily acknowledge blood relation to a black. She was so free and unconflicted about this. I just couldn't fathom it. We corresponded and exchanged family photos. And when I was ready to start delving in earnest, I contacted the relative she had mentioned for information about my grandfather, and initiated correspondence or communication with kin I hadn't known existed and who hadn't known that I existed, or that they or any part of their family was black. I embarked on this with great trepidation, anticipating with anxiety their reaction to the racial identity of these long lost relatives, picturing in advance the withdrawal of warmth and interest, the quickly assumed impersonality and the suggestion that there must be some mistake.

The dread that I might lose her took possession of me each time I sought to speak, and rendered it impossible for me to do so.

That moral courage requires more than physical courage is no mere poetic fancy. I am sure I should have found it easier to take the place of a gladiator, no matter how fierce the Numidian lion, than to tell that slender girl that I had Negro blood in my veins.

—James Weldon Johnson, *The Autobiography of an Ex-Coloured Man*

These fears were not unfounded. My father's sister had, in her youth, been the first black woman at a Seven Sisters undergraduate college and the first at an Ivy League medical school; had married into a white family who became socially, politically, and academically prominent; and then, after taking some family mementos my grandmother had given my father for me, had proceeded to sever all connections with her brothers and their families, even when the death of each of her siblings was imminent. She raised her children (now equally prominent socially and politically) as though they had no maternal relatives at all. We had all been so very proud of her achievements that her repudiation of us was devastating. Yet I frequently encounter mutual friends and colleagues in the circles in which we both travel, and I dread the day we might find ourselves in the same room at the same time. To read or hear about or see on television her or any member of her immediate family is a source of personal pain for all of us. I did not want to subject myself to that again with yet another set of relatives.

Those who pass have a severe dilemma before they decide to do so, since a person must give up all family ties and loyalties to the black community in order to gain economic and other opportunities.

—F. James Davis, *Who Is Black? One Nation's Definition*

Trying to forgive and understand those of my relatives who have chosen to pass for white has been one of the most difficult ethical challenges of my life, and I don't consider myself to have made very much progress. At the most superficial level, this decision can be understood in terms of a cost-benefit analysis: Obviously, they believe they will be happier in the white community than in the black one, all things considered. For me to make sense of this requires that I understand—or at least accept—their conception of happiness as involving higher social status, entrenchment within the white community and corresponding isolation from the black one, and greater access to the rights, liberties, and privileges the white community takes for granted. What is harder for me to grasp is how they could want these things enough to sacrifice the history, wisdom, connectedness, and moral solidarity with their family and community in order to get them. It seems to require so much severing and forgetting, so much disowning and distancing, not simply from one's shared past, but from one's former self—as though one had cauterized one's long-term memory at the moment of entry into the white community.

But there is, I think, more to it than that. Once you realize what is denied you as an African-American simply because of your race, your sense of the unfairness of it may be so overwhelming that you may simply be incapable of accepting it. And if you are not inclined toward any form of overt political advocacy, passing in order to get the benefits you know you deserve may seem the only way to defy the system. Indeed, many of my more prominent relatives who are passing have chosen altruistic professions that benefit society on many fronts. They have chosen to use their assumed social status to make returns to the black community indirectly, in effect compensating for the personal advantages they have gained by rejecting their family.

Moreover, your sense of injustice may be compounded by the daily humiliation you experience as the result of identifying with those African-Americans who, for demanding their rights, are punished and degraded as a warning to others. In these cases, the decision to pass may be more than the rejection of a black identity. It may be the rejection of a black identification that brings too much pain to be tolerated.

> All the while I understood that it was not discouragement or fear or search for a larger field of action and opportunity that was driving me out of the Negro race. I knew that it was shame, unbearable shame. Shame at being identified with a people that could with impunity be treated worse than animals.
>
> —Johnson, *The Autobiography of an Ex-Coloured Man*

The oppressive treatment of African-Americans facilitates this distancing response by requiring every African-American to draw a sharp distinction between the person he is and the person society perceives him to be—that is, between who he is as an individual, and the way he is designated and treated by others.

> The Negro's only salvation from complete despair lies in his belief, the old belief of his forefathers, that these things are not directed against him personally, but against his race, his pigmentation. His

Adrian Piper

mother or aunt or teacher long ago carefully prepared him, explaining that he as an individual can live in dignity, even though he as a Negro cannot.

—John Howard Griffin, *Black Like Me*

This condition encourages a level of impersonality, a sense that white reactions to one have little or nothing to do with one as a person and an individual. Whites often mistake this impersonality for aloofness or unfriendliness. It is just one of the factors that make genuine intimacy between blacks and whites so difficult. Because I have occasionally encountered equally stereotypical treatment from other blacks and have felt compelled to draw the same distinction there between who I am and how I am perceived, my sense of impersonality pervades most social situations in which I find myself. Because I do not enjoy impersonal interactions with others, my solution is to limit my social interactions as far as possible to those in which this restraint is not required. So perhaps it is not entirely surprising that many white-looking individuals of African ancestry are able to jettison this doubly alienated and alienating social identity entirely, as irrelevant to the fully mature and complex individuals they know themselves to be. I take the fervent affirmation and embrace of black identity to be a countermeasure to, and thus evidence of, this alienation, rather than as incompatible with it. My family contains many instance of both attitudes.

There are no proper names mentioned in this account of my family. This is because in the African-American community, we do not "out" people who are passing as white in the European-American community. Publicly to expose the African ancestry of someone who claims to have none is not done. There are many reasons for this, and different individuals cite different ones. For one thing, there is the vicarious enjoyment of watching one of our own infiltrate and achieve in a context largely defined by institutionalized attempts to exclude blacks from it. Then there is the question of self-respect: if someone wants to exit the African-American community, there are few blacks who would consider it worth their while to prevent her. And then there is the possibility of retaliation: not merely the loss of credibility consequent on the denials by a putatively white person who, by virtue of his racial status, automatically has greater credibility than the black person who calls it into question, but perhaps more deliberate attempts to discredit or undermine the messenger of misfortune. There is also the instinctive impulse to protect the well-being of a fellow traveler embarked on a particularly dangerous and risky course. And finally—the most salient consideration for me, in thinking about those many members of my own family who have chosen to pass for white—a person who desires personal and social advantage and acceptance within the white community so much that she is willing to repudiate her family, her past, her history, and her personal connections within the African-American community in order to get them is someone who is already in so much pain that it's just not possible to do something that you know is going to cause her any more.

Many colored Creoles protect others who are trying to pass, to the point of feigning ignorance of certain branches of their families. Elicited genealogies often seem strangely skewed. In the case of one very good informant, a year passed before he confided in me that his own mother's sister and her children had passed into the white community. With tears in his eyes, he described the painful experience of learning about his aunt's death on the obituary page of the *New Orleans Times-Picayune*. His cousins failed to inform the abandoned side of the family of the death, for fear that they might show up at the wake or the funeral and thereby destroy the image of whiteness. Total separation was necessary for secrecy.

—Virginia R. Dominguez, *White by Definition: Social Classification in Creole Louisiana*

She said: "It's funny about 'passing.' We disapprove of it and at the same time condone it. It excites our contempt and yet we rather admire it. We shy away from it with an odd kind of revulsion, but we protect it."

"Instinct of the race to survive and expand."

"Rot! Everything can't be explained by some general biological phrase."

"Absolutely everything can. Look at the so-called whites, who've left bastards all over the known earth. Same thing in them. Instinct of the race to survive and expand."

—Nella Larsen, *Passing*

Those of my grandfather's estranged relatives who welcomed me into dialogue instead of freezing me out brought tears of gratitude and astonishment to my eyes. They seemed so kind and interested, so willing to help. At first I couldn't accept for what it was their easy acceptance and willingness to help me puzzle out where exactly we each were located in our sprawling family tree. It is an ongoing endeavor, full of guesswork, false leads, blank spots, and mysteries. For just as white Americans are largely ignorant of their African—usually maternal—ancestry, we blacks are often ignorant of our European—usually paternal—ancestry. That's the way our slave-master forebears wanted it, and that's the way it is. Our names are systematically missing from the genealogies and public records of most white families, and crucial information—for example, the family name or name of the child's father—is often missing from our black ancestors' birth certificates, when they exist at all.

> A realistic appreciation of the conditions which exist when women are the property of men makes the conclusion inevitable that there were many children born of mixed parentage.
>
> —Joe Gray Taylor, *Negro Slavery in Louisiana*

> Ownership of the female slave on the plantations generally came to include owning her sex life. Large numbers of white boys were socialized to associate physical and emotional pleasure with the black women who nursed and raised them, and then to deny any deep feelings for them. From other white males they learned to see black girls and women as legitimate objects of sexual desire. Rapes occurred, and many slave women were forced to submit regularly to white males or suffer harsh consequences. . . . As early as the time of the American Revolution there were plantation slaves who appeared to be completely white, as many of the founding fathers enslaved their own mixed children and grandchildren.
>
> Davis, *Who Is Black?*

So tracing the history of my family is detective work as well as historical research. To date, what I *think* I know is that our first European-American ancestor landed in Ipswich, Massachusetts, in 1620 from Sussex; another in Jamestown, Virginia, in 1675 from London; and another in Philadelphia, Pennsylvania, in 1751, from Hamburg. Yet another was the first in our family to graduate from my own graduate institution in 1778. My great-great-grandmother from Madagascar, by way of Louisiana, is the known African ancestor on my father's side, as my great-great grandfather from the Ibo of Nigeria is the known African ancestor on my mother's, whose family has resided in Jamaica for three centuries.

I relate these facts and it doesn't seem to bother my newly discovered relatives. At first I had to wonder whether this ease of acceptance was not predicated on their mentally bracketing the implications of these facts and restricting their own immediate family ancestry to the European side. But when they remarked unself-consciously on the family resemblances between us, I had to abandon that supposition. I still marvel at their enlightened and uncomplicated friendliness, and there is a part of me that still can't trust their acceptance of me. But that is a part of me I want neither to trust nor to accept in this context. I want to reserve my vigilance for its context of origin: the other white Americans I have encountered—even the bravest and most conscientious white scholars—for whom the suggestion that they might have significant African ancestry as the result of this country's long history of miscegenation is almost impossible to consider seriously.

> She's heard the arguments, most astonishingly that, statistically,
> . . . the average white American is 6 percent black. Or, put another
> way, 95 percent of white Americans are 5 to 80 percent black. Her
> Aunt Tyler has told her stories about these whites researching their
> roots in the National Archives and finding they've got an African-
> American or two in the family, some becoming so hysterical they
> have to be carried out by paramedics.
> —Perry, *Another Present Era*

> Estimates ranging up to 5 percent, and suggestions that up to
> one-fifth of the white population have some genes from black ances-
> tors, are probably far too high. If these last figures were correct, the
> majority of Americans with some black ancestry would be known
> and counted as whites!
> Davis, *Who is Black?*

The detailed biological and genetic data can be gleaned from a careful review of *Genetic Abstracts* from about 1950 on. In response to my request for information about this, a white biological anthropologist once performed detailed calculations on the African admixture of five different genes, comparing British whites, American whites, and American Blacks. The results ranged from 2 percent in one gene to 81.6 percent in another. About these results he commented, "I continue to believe five percent to be a reasonable estimate, but the matter is obviously complex. As you can see, it depends entirely on which genes you decide to use as racial 'markers' that are

Adrian Piper

supposedly subject to little or no relevant selective pressure." Clearly, white resistance to the idea that most American whites have a significant percentage of African ancestry increases with the percentage suggested.

> "Why, Doctor," said Dr. Latimer, "you Southerners began this absorption before the war. I understand that in one decade the mixed bloods rose from one-ninth to one-eighth of the population, and that as early as 1663 a law was passed in Maryland to prevent English women from intermarrying with slaves; and, even now, your laws against miscegenation presuppose that you apprehend danger from that source."
>
> —Harper, *Iola Leroy*

> (That legislators and judges paid increasing attention to the regulation and punishment of miscegenation at this time does not mean that interracial sex and marriage as social practices actually increased in frequency; the centrality of these practices to legal discourse was instead a sign that their relation to power was changing. The extent of uncoerced miscegenation before this period is a debated issue.)
>
> —Eva Saks, *"Representing Miscegenation Law," Raritan*

The fact is, however, that the longer a person's family has lived in this country, the higher the probable percentage of African ancestry that person's family is likely to have—bad news for the DAR, I'm afraid. And the proximity to the continent of Africa of the country of origin from which one's forebears emigrated, as well as the colonization of a part of Africa by that country, are two further variables that increase the probability of African ancestry within that family. It would appear that only the Lapps of Norway are safe.

In Jamaica, my mother tells me, that everyone is of mixed ancestry is taken for granted. There are a few who vociferously proclaim themselves to be "Jamaican whites" having no African ancestry at all, but no one among the old and respected families takes them seriously. Indeed, they are assumed to be a bit unbalanced, and are regarded with amusement. In this country, by contrast, the fact of African ancestry among whites ranks up there with family incest, murder, and suicide as one of the bitterest and most difficult pills for white Americans to swallow.

> "I had a friend who had two beautiful daughters whom he had educated in the North. They were cultured, and really belles in society. They were entirely ignorant of their lineage, but when their father

died it was discovered that their mother had been a slave. It was a fearful blow. They would have faced poverty, but the knowledge of their tainted blood was more than they could bear."

—Harper, *Iola Leroy*

There was much apprehension about the unknown amount of black ancestry in the white population of the South, and this was fanned into an unreasoning fear of invisible blackness. For instance, white laundries and cleaners would not accommodate blacks because whites were afraid they would be "contaminated" by the clothing of invisible blacks.

—Davis, *Who Is Black?*

Suspicion is part of everyday life in Louisiana. Whites often grow up afraid to know their own genealogies. Many admit that as children they often stared at the skin below their fingernails and through a mirror at the white of their eyes to see if there was any "touch of tarbrush." Not finding written records of birth, baptism, marriage, or death for any one ancestor exacerbates suspicions of foul play. Such a discovery brings glee to a political enemy or economic rival and may traumatize the individual concerned.

—Dominguez, *White by Definition*

A number of years ago I was doing research on a video installation on the subject of racial identity and miscegenation, and came across the Phipps case of Louisiana in the early 1980s. Susie Guillory Phipps had identified herself as white and, according to her own testimony (but not that of some of her black relatives), had believed that she was white, until she applied for a passport, when she discovered that she was identified on her birth records as black by virtue of having one thirty-second African ancestry. She brought suit against the state of Louisiana to have her racial classification changed. She lost the suit but effected the overthrow of the law identifying individuals as black if they had one thirty-second African ancestry, leaving on the books a prior law identifying an individual as black who had any African ancestry—the "one-drop" rule that uniquely characterizes the classification of blacks in the United States in fact even were no longer in law. So according to this longstanding convention of racial classification, a white who acknowledges any African ancestry implicitly acknowledges being black—a social condition, more than an identity, that no white person would voluntarily assume, even in imagination. This is one reason that whites, educated

Adrian Piper

and uneducated alike, are so resistant to considering the probable extent of racial miscegenation.

This "one-drop" convention of classification of blacks is unique not only relative to the treatment of blacks in other countries but also unique relative to the treatment of other ethnic groups in this country. It goes without saying that no one, either white or black, is identified as, for example, English by virtue of having some small fraction of English ancestry. Nor is anyone free, as a matter of social convention, to do so by virtue of that fraction, although many whites do. But even in the case of other disadvantaged groups in this country, the convention is different. Whereas any proportion of African ancestry is sufficient to identify a person as black, an individual must have at least one-eighth Native American ancestry in order to identify legally as Native American.

Why the asymmetry of treatment? Clearly, the reason is economic. A legally certifiable Native American is entitled to financial benefits from the government, so obtaining this certification is difficult. A legally certifiable black person is disentitled to financial, social and inheritance benefits from his white family of origin, so obtaining this certification is not just easy but automatic. Racial classification in this country functions to restrict the distribution of goods, entitlements, and status as narrowly as possible to those whose power is already entrenched. Of course this institutionalized disentitlement presupposes that two persons of different racial classifications cannot be biologically related, which is absurd.

> This [one-drop] definition of who is black was crucial to maintaining the social system of white domination in which widespread miscegenation, not racial purity, prevailed. White womanhood was the highly charged emotional symbol, but the system protected white economic, political, legal, education and other institutional advantages for whites. . . . American slave owners wanted to keep all racially mixed children born to slave women under their control, for economic and sexual gains. . . . It was intolerable for white women to have mixed children, so the one-drop rule favored the sexual freedom of white males, protecting the double standard of sexual morality as well as slavery. . . . By defining all mixed children as black and compelling them to live in the black community, the rule made possible the incredible myth among whites that miscegenation had not occurred, that the races had been kept pure in the South.
>
> —Davis, *Who Is Black?*

But the issues of family entitlements and inheritance rights are not uppermost in the minds of most white Americans, who wince at the mere suggestion that they might have some fraction of African ancestry and therefore be, according to this country's entrenched convention of racial classification, black. The primary issue for them is not what they might have to give away by admitting that they are in fact black, but rather what they have to lose. What they have to lose, of course, is social status—and, insofar as their self-esteem is based on their social status as whites, self-esteem as well.

> "I think," said Dr. Latrobe, proudly, "that we belong to the highest race on earth and the negro to the lowest."
>
> "And yet," said Dr. Latimer, "you have consorted with them till you have bleached their faces to the whiteness of your own. Your children nestle in their bosoms; they are around you as body servants, and yet if one of them should attempt to associate with you your bitterest scorn and indignation would be visited upon them."
>
> —Harper, *Iola Leroy*

No reflective and well-intentioned white person who is consciously concerned to end racism wants to admit to instinctively recoiling at the thought of being identified as black herself. But if you want to see such a white person do this, just peer at the person's facial features and tell her, in a complementary tone of voice, that she looks as though she might have some black ancestry, and watch her reaction. It's not a test I or any black person finds particularly pleasant to apply (that is, unless one dislikes the person and wants to inflict pain deliberately), and having once done so inadvertently, I will never do it again. The ultimate test of a person's repudiation of racism is not what she can contemplate *doing* for or on behalf of black people, but whether she herself can contemplate calmly the likelihood of *being* black. If racial hatred has not manifested itself in any other context, it will do so here if it exists, in hatred of the self as identified with the other—that is, as self-hatred projected onto the other.

> Since Harry had come North he had learned to feel profound pity for the slave. But there is difference between looking on a man as an object of pity and protecting him as such, and being identified with him and forced to share his lot.
>
> —Harper, *Iola Leroy*

> Let me tell you how I'd get those white devil convicts and the
> guards, too, to do anything I wanted. I'd whisper to them, "If you
> don't, I'll start a rumor that you're really a light Negro just passing as
> white." That shows you what the white devil thinks about the black
> man. He'd rather die than be thought a Negro!
>
> Malcolm X, *The Autobiography of Malcolm X*

When I was an undergraduate minoring in medieval and Renaissance musicology, I worked with a fellow music student—white—in the music library. I remember his reaction when I relayed to him an article I'd recently read arguing that Beethoven had African ancestry. Beethoven was one of his heroes, and his vehement derision was completely out of proportion to the scholarly worth of the hypothesis. But when I suggested that he wouldn't be so skeptical if the claim were that Beethoven had some Danish ancestry, he fell silent. In those days we were very conscious of covert racism, as our campus was exploding all around us because of it. More recently I premiered at a gallery a video installation exploring the issue of African ancestry among white Americans. A white male viewer commenced to kick the furniture, mutter audibly that he was white and was going to stay that way, and start a fistfight with my dealer. Either we are less conscious of covert racism twenty years later, or we care less to contain it.

Among politically committed and enlightened whites, the inability to acknowledge their probable African ancestry is the last outpost of racism. It is the litmus test that separates those who have the courage of their convictions from those who merely subscribe to them and that measures the depth of our dependence on a presumed superiority (of any kind, anything will do) to other human beings—anyone, anywhere—to bolster our fragile self-worth. Many blacks are equally unwilling to explore their white ancestry—approximately 25 percent on average for the majority of blacks—for this reason. For some, of course, acknowledgment of this fact evokes only bitter reminders of rape, disinheritance, enslavement, and exploitation, and their distaste is justifiable. But for others, it is the mere idea of blackness as an essentialized source of self-worth and self-affirmation that forecloses the acknowledgment of mixed ancestry. This, too, is understandable: having struggled so long and hard to carve a sense of wholeness and value for ourselves out of our ancient connection with Africa after having been actively denied any in America, many of us are extremely resistant to once again casting ourselves into the same chaos of ethnic and psychological ambiguity that our diaspora to this country originally inflicted on us.

Plate 11: *Mlle Bourgeoise Noire Shouts Out Her Poem*
First performed at Just Above Midtown Gallery, June 1980
Lorraine O'Grady
Photo: Coreen Simpson
Courtesy of the artist

Adrian Piper

In the early 80s, Mlle Bourgeoise Noire, wearing a gown of white gloves, attended gallery openings unannounced and shouted poems with punch lines such as "Black art must take more risks!" and "NOW is the time for an invasion," to make an equal-opportunity critique of the then still-separate white and black art worlds.

Thus blacks and whites alike seem to be unable to accord worth to others outside their in-group affiliations without feeling that they are taking it away from themselves. We may have the concept of intrinsic self-worth, but by and large we do not understand what it means. We need someone else whom we can regard as inferior, to whom we can compare ourselves favorably, and if no such individual or group exists, we invent one. For without this, we seem to have no basis, no standard of comparison, for conceiving of ourselves favorably at all. We seem, for example, truly unable to grasp or take seriously the alternative possibility of measuring ourselves or our performances against our own past novicehood at one end and our own future potential at the other. I think this is in part the result of our collective fear of memory as a nation, our profound unwillingness to confront the painful truths about our history and our origins, and in part the result of our individual fear of the memory of our own pasts not only of our individual origins and the traumas of socialization we each suffered before we could control what was done to us, but the pasts of our own adult behavior—the painful truths of our own derelictions, betrayals, and failures to respect our individual ideals and convictions.

When I turned forty a few years ago, I gave myself the present of re-reading the personal journals I have been keeping since age eleven. I was astounded at the chasm between my present conception of my own past, which is being continually revised and updated to suit present circumstances, and the actual past events, behavior, and emotions I recorded as faithfully as I could as they happened. My derelictions, mistakes, and failures of responsibility are much more evident in those journals than they are in my present, sanitized, and virtually blameless image of my past behavior. It was quite a shock to encounter in those pages the person I actually have been rather than the person I now conceive myself to have been. My memory is always under the control of the person I now want and strive to be, and so rarely under the control of the facts. If the personal facts of one's past are this difficult for other people to face too, then perhaps it is no wonder that we must cast about outside ourselves for someone to feel superior to, even though there are so many blunders and misdeeds in our own personal histories that might serve that function.

For whites to acknowledge their blackness is, then, much the same as for men to acknowledge their femininity and for Christians to acknowledge their Judaic heritage. It is to reinternalize the external scapegoat through attention to which they have sought to escape their own sense of inferiority.

> Now the white man leaned in the window, looking at the impenetrable face with its definite strain of white blood, the same blood which ran in his own veins, which had not only come to the negro through male descent while it had come to him from a woman, but had reached the negro a generation sooner—a face composed, inscrutable, even a little haughty, shaped even in expression in the pattern of his great-grandfather McCaslin's face. . . . He thought, and not for the first time: I am not only looking at a face older than mine and which has seen and winnowed more, but at a man most of whose blood was pure ten thousand years when my own anonymous beginnings became mixed enough to produce me.
> —William Faulkner, *Go Down, Moses.*

> I said . . . that the guilt of American whites included their knowledge that in hating Negroes, they were hating, they were rejecting, they were denying, their own blood.
> —*The Autobiography of Malcolm X*

It is to bring ourselves face to face with our obliterated collective past, and to confront the continuities of responsibility that link the criminal acts of extermination and enslavement committed by our forefathers with our own personal crimes of avoidance, neglect, disengagement, passive complicity, and active exploitation of the inherited injustices from which we have profited. Uppermost among these is that covert sense of superiority a white person feels over a black person which buttresses his enjoyment of those unjust benefits as being no more or less than he deserves. To be deprived of that sense of superiority to the extent that acknowledgment of common ancestry would effect is clearly difficult for most white people. But to lose the social regard and respect that accompanies it is practically unbearable. I know—not only because of what I have read and observed of the pathology of racism in white people, but because I have often experienced the withdrawal of that social regard firsthand.

For most of my life I did not understand that I needed to identify my racial identity publicly and that if I did not I would be inevitably mistaken for white. I simply didn't think about it. But since I also made no special effort to hide my racial identity, I often experienced the shocked and/or hostile reactions of whites who discovered it after the fact. I always knew when it had happened, even when the person declined to confront me directly: the startled look, the searching stare that would fix itself on my facial features, one by one, looking for the telltale "negroid" feature, the sudden, sometimes permanent withdrawal of good feeling or regular contact—all alerted me to what had transpired. Uh-oh, I would think to myself helplessly, and watch another blossoming friendship wilt.

> In thus traveling about through the country I was sometimes amused on arriving at some little railroad-station town to be taken for and treated as a white man, and six hours later, when it was learned that I was stopping at the house of the coloured preacher or school-teacher, to note the attitude of the whole town changed.

—Johnson, *The Autobiography of an Ex-Coloured Man*

Sometimes this revelation would elicit a response of the most twisted and punitive sort: for example, from the colleague who glared at me and hissed, "Oh, so you want to be black, do you? Good! Then we'll treat you like one!" The ensuing harassment had a furious, retaliatory quality that I find difficult to understand even now: as though I'd delivered a deliberate and crushing insult to her self-esteem by choosing not to identify with her racial group.

> You feel lost, sick at heart before such unmasked hatred, not so much because it threatens you as because it shows humans in such an inhuman light. You see a kind of insanity, something so obscene the very obscenity of it (rather than its threat) terrifies you.

—Griffin, *Black Like Me*

And I experienced that same groundless shame not only in response to those who accused me of passing for black, but also in response to those who accused me of passing for white. This was the shame caused by people who conveyed to me that I was underhanded or manipulative, trying to hide something, pretending to be something I was not by not telling them I was black—like the art critic in the early 1970s who had treated me with the respect she gave emerging white women artists in the early days of second-wave feminism until my work turned to issues of racial identity; she then

Hope. I had a friend named Karl who was sixteen and came from the boys' camp acr oss the lake. He played catch and volleyball with me and took care of me and I a dored him. I told someone that he was my big brother (I'm an only child) and she said But that's impossible; Karl's white and you're colored. She said Colored. I at he had blue eyes. A few years later my mom thought it was time I started goin g to and from school by myself instead of her taking me on the bus. The school w as far away because it was not a local public school but rather an expensive pro gressive prep school called New Lincoln where there were lots of rich mediocre w hite kids and a few poor smart white kids and even fewer, smarter b lack kids. But all I knew then was that there sure was a difference between wher e most of them lived (Fifth Avenue) and where I lived (Harlem). Anyway I started going to school by myself and the neighborhood kids would waylay me as I was wal king the two blocks from the bus stop to my house and would pull my braids and t ease me and call me Paleface. By then I knew what they meant. No one at school e ver called me Paleface. Once I was visiting one of my white classmates at her bi g fancy apartment house on Central Park West where there were four doors into th e house with a doorman standing at each and two separate elevators with an eleva tor man for each and only one apartment on a floor and a cook and a maid and a c leaning woman and a governess (!!). She said to her little brother I bet you can 't guess whether Adrian is white or colored. He looked at me for a long time and very searchingly and said White. And she said You lose, she's colored, isn't tha t a scream? I thought it was really a scream. I was afraid of the black kids on my block because they bullied me and I was afraid of the black kids at school be cause they made cutting remarks about my acting too white. But I wasn't afraid o f the white kids because they were so stupid. Later when I was in fifth grade an d getting sick alot and hating school I had a teacher named Nancy Modiano who re ally bullied me. Once we all went on a hike and I became very thirsty and she wo uldn't let me get any water. Then we went back to school and she forced me to fo llow her around the school for four hours while she did her errands but wouldn't let me stop at a water fountain for some water. When my mom came to pick me up I was almost fainting. In conference with my parents she once asked them Does Adri an know she's colored? I guess she must have thought I was too fresh and uppity for a little colored girl. My folks were very upset and wanted to transfer me in to another class but it was too near the end of the term. Nancy Modiano was one of the few whites who overtly bullied me because of my color. The only others we re white philosophy students later when I was in college who hated me and said Y ou don't have to worry about graduate school; a black woman can get in anywhere, even if she looks like you. But as I got older and prettier white people general ly got nicer and nicer, especially liberals. I was very relieved when my folks m oved out of Harlem when I was fourteen, and into a mixed neighborhood on Riversi de Drive because there weren't so conspicuous, and besides the boys in my old neighborhood were no longer pulling just my braids when I passed them on the str eet. In my new neighborhood I hung out with a Puerto Rican gang that accepted me pretty well and taught me to curse in Spanish. I didn't see New Lincoln people v ery much because they were turning into boring and neurotic people and were real ly getting into being rich. But I made other friends when I started going to the Art Students' League and Greenwich Village. I noticed that all my friends were w hite and that I didn't have much in common with the children of my parents' very light-skinned, middle class, well-to-do black friends. They seemed to have a ver y determined self-consciousness about being colored (they said Colored) that I d idn't share. They and many of my relatives thought it a scandal that I went out with white men. I felt just as alienated from whites as blacks, but whites made me feel good about my looks rather than apologetic. When someone asked me why I looked so exotic I would either say I'm West Indian (my mother's Jamaican) or if they looked really interested I would go on at length about my family tree: how my mother's family is English, Indian from India and African, and how there's a dispute about my father's family which my grandmother told me about before she d ied because there are now two branches of the Piper family, the rich ones who no w live in Chicago and founded the Piper Aircraft Company and the poor ones, i.e. us; how they were originally a single English family who settled in the South bu t at some point split up and disowned each other (i.e. the rich ones disinherite d the poor ones) because the poor ones publicly admitted to being partly descend ed from the slaves who worked on their plantation and the rich ones didn't want to acknowledge any African blood in the family; but how for the poor ones it was a matter of honor after the Civil War not to pass for white. But I would never s imply say Black because I felt silly, and as though I was coopting something, i.e. the Black Experience, which I hadn't had. I've had the Gray Experience. Also I felt guilty about unjustifiedly taking advantage of justified white liberal guil t. But I would never deny that I'm black because I understand how it can be a m atter of pride and honor for my folks to positively affirm their heritage and I don't want to deny a part of myself that I'm proud of. But sometimes I wonder wh y I should be caught in this bind in the first place; why I should have to feel dishonest regardless of whether I affirm or deny that I'm black; and whether I, my family, and all such hybrids aren't being victimized by a white racist ideolo gy that forces us to accept an essentially alien and alienating identity that ar bitrarily groups us in with the most oppressed and powerless segment of the society (black blacks) in order to avoid having that segment gradually infiltrate and ta ke over the sources of political and economic power from whites through the de f acto successful integration of which we hybrids are the products and the victims. When I think about that I realize that in reality I've been bullied by whites as well as blacks for the last three hundred years. And there is no end in sight

PALEFACE

Political Self-Portrait #2   © Adrian Piper   June 1978

Plate 12: **Political Self-Portrait #2 (race)**, 1978
Poster 24 × 36"
Adrian Piper
Courtesy of the artist and John Weber Gallery, New York

called me to verify that I was black, reproached me for not telling her, and finally disappeared from my professional life altogether. And there were the colleagues who discovered after hiring me for my first job that I was black, and revised their evaluations of my work accordingly. It was the groundless shame caused by people who, having discovered my racial identity, let me know that I was not comporting myself as befitted their conception of a black person: the grammar school teacher who called my parents to inquire whether I was aware that I was black, and made a special effort to put me in my place by restricting me from participating in certain class activities and assigning me to remedial classes in anticipation of low achievement; and the graduate school classmate who complimented me on my English; and the potential employer who, having offered me a tenure-track job in an outstanding graduate department (which I declined) when he thought I was white, called me back much later after I'd received tenure and he'd found out I was black to offer me a two-year visiting position teaching undergraduates only, explaining to a colleague of mine that he was being pressured by his university administration to integrate his department. And the art critic who made elaborate suggestions in print about the kind of art it would be appropriate for someone with my concerns to make; and the colleague who journeyed from another university and interviewed me for four and a half hours in order to ascertain that I was smart enough to hold the position I had, and actually congratulated me afterwards on my performance. And there was the colleague who, when I begged to differ with his views, shouted (in a crowded restaurant) that if I wasn't going to take his advice, why was I wasting his time?

> I looked up to see the frowns of disapproval that can speak so plainly and so loudly without words. The Negro learns this silent language fluently. He knows by the white man's look of disapproval and petulance that he is being told to get on his way, that he is "stepping out of line."
>
> —Griffin, *Black Like Me*

When such contacts occurred, the interaction had to follow a strict pattern of interracial etiquette. The white person had to be clearly in charge at all times, and the black person clearly subordinate, so that each kept his or her place. It was a master-servant etiquette, in which blacks had to act out their inferior social position, much the way slaves had done. The black had to be deferential in tone and body language, . . . and never bring up a delicate topic or contradict the white. . . . this master-servant ritual had to be acted out carefully lest the black person be accused of "getting" out of his or her subordinate "place." Especially for violations of the etiquette, but also for challenges to other aspects of the system, blacks were warned, threatened, and finally subjected to extralegal violence.

—Davis, *Who Is Black?*

In a way this abbreviated history of occasions on which whites have tried to "put me in my place" upon discovering my racial identity was the legacy of my father who, despite his own similar experiences as a youth, refused to submit to such treatment. He grew up in a Southern city where his family was well known and highly respected. When he was thirteen, he went to a movie theater and bought a seat in the orchestra section. In the middle of the feature, the projectionist stopped the film and turned up the lights. The manager strode onto the stage and, in front of the entire audience, called out my father's name, loudly reprimanded him for sitting in the orchestra, and ordered him up to the balcony, where he "belonged." My father fled the theater, and, not long after, the South. My grandmother then sent him to a private prep school up North, but it was no better. In his senior year of high school, after having distinguished himself academically and in sports, he invited a white girl classmate on a date. She refused, and her parents complained to the principal, who publicly rebuked him. He was ostracized by his classmates for the rest of the year and made no effort to speak to any of them.

My mother, being upper-middle-class Jamaican, had no experience of this kind of thing. When she first got a job in this country in the 1930s, she chastised her white supervisor for failing to say, "Thank you," after she'd graciously brought him back a soda from her lunch hour. He was properly apologetic. And when her brother first came to this country, he sat in a restaurant in Manhattan for an hour waiting to be served, it simply not occurring to him that he was being ignored because of his color, until a waitress came up to him and said, "I can see you're not from these parts. We don't serve colored people here." My father, who had plenty of experience of this sort, knew that I would have them, too. But he declined to accustom me to them in advance. He never hit me, disparaged me, or pulled rank in our frequent intellectual and philosophical disagreements. Trained as a Jesuit and a lawyer, he argued for the joy of it, and felt proud rather than insulted when I made my point well. "Fresh," he'd murmur to my mother

Adrian Piper

with mock annoyance, indicating me with his thumb, when I used his own assumptions to trounce him in argument. It is because of his refusal to prepare me for my subordinate role as a black woman in a racist and misogynistic society that my instinctive reaction to such insults is not resignation, depression, or passive aggression, but rather the disbelief, outrage, sense of injustice, and impulse to fight back actively that white males often exhibit as unexpected affronts to their dignity. Blacks who manifest these responses to white racism reveal their caregivers' generationally transmitted underground resistance to schooling them for victimhood.

A benefit and a disadvantage of looking white is that most people treat you as though you were white. And so, because of how you've been treated, you come to expect this sort of treatment, not perhaps, realizing that you're being treated this way because people think you're white, but rather falsely supposing that you're being treated this way because people think you are a valuable person. So, for example, you come to expect a certain level of respect, a certain degree of attention to your voice and opinions, certain liberties of action and self-expression to which you falsely suppose yourself to be entitled because your voice, your opinion, and your conduct are valuable in themselves. To those who in fact believe (even though they would never voice this belief to themselves) that black people are not entitled to this degree of respect, attention, and liberty, the sight of a black person behaving as though she were can, indeed, look very much like arrogance. It may not occur to them that she simply does not realize that her blackness should make any difference.

> Only one-sixteenth of her was black, and that sixteenth did not show. . . . Her complexion was very fair, with the rosy glow of vigorous health in the cheeks, . . . her eyes were brown and liquid, and she had a heavy suit of fine soft hair which was also brown. . . . She had an easy, independent carriage—when she was among her own caste—and a high and "sassy" way, withal; but of course she was meek and humble enough where white people were.
> —Mark Twain, *Pudd'nhead Wilson*

But there may be more involved than this. I've been thinking about Ida B. Wells, who had the temerity to suggest in print that white males who worried about preserving the purity of Southern white womanhood were really worried about the sexual attraction of Southern white womanhood to handsome and virile black men; and Rosa Parks, who refused to move to the back of the bus; and Eartha Kitt, who scolded President Lyndon Johnson about the Vietnam War when he received her at a White House dinner; and Mrs. Alice Frazier, who gave the queen of England a big hug and invited her to stay for lunch when the queen came to tour Mrs. Frazier's housing project on a recent visit to the United States; and Congresswoman Maxine Waters, who, after the L.A. rebellion, showed up at the White House uninvited, and gave George Bush her unsolicited recommendations as to how he should handle the plight of the inner cities. I've also been thinking about the legions of African-American women whose survival has depended on their submission to the intimate interpersonal roles, traditional for black women in this culture, of nursemaid, housekeeper, concubine, cleaning lady, cook; and what they have been required to witness of the whites they have served in those capacities. And I've been thinking about the many white people I've admired and respected, who have lost my admiration and respect by revealing in personal interactions a side of themselves that other whites rarely get a chance to see: the brand of racism that surfaces only in one-on-one or intimate interpersonal circumstances, the kind a white person lets you see because he doesn't care what you think and knows you are powerless to do anything about it.

> When we shined their shoes we talked. The whites, especially the tourists, had no reticence before us, and no shame since we were Negroes. Some wanted to know where they could find girls, wanted us to get Negro girls for them. . . . Though not all, by any means, were so open about their purposes, all of them showed us how they felt about the Negro, the idea that we were people of such low morality that nothing could offend us. . . . In these matters, the Negro has seen the backside of the white man too long to be shocked. He feels an indulgent superiority whenever he sees these evidences of the white man's frailty. This is one of the sources of his chafing at being considered inferior. He cannot understand how the white man can show the most demeaning aspects of his nature and at the same time delude himself into thinking he is inherently superior.
>
> —Griffin, *Black Like Me*

It may indeed be that we African-American women as a group have special difficulties in learning our place and observing the proprieties because of that particular side of white America to which, because of our traditional roles, we have had special access—a side of white America that

Adrian Piper

hardly commands one's respect and could not possibly command one's deference.

To someone like myself, who was raised to think that my racial identity was, in fact, irrelevant to the way I should be treated, there are few revelations more painful than the experience of social metamorphosis that transforms former friends, colleagues, or teachers who have extended their trust, good will, and support into accusers or strangers who withdraw them when they discover that I am black. To look visibly black, or always to announce in advance that one is black is, I submit, never to experience this kind of camaraderie with white people—the relaxed, unguarded, but respectful camaraderie that white people reserve for those whom they believe are like them—those who can be trusted, who are intrinsically worthy of value, respect, and attention. Eddie Murphy portrays this in comic form in a wonderful routine in which he disguises himself in whiteface, then boards a bus on which there is only one visibly black passenger. As long as that passenger is on the bus, all of them sit silently and impersonally ignoring one another. But as soon as the visibly black passenger gets off, the other passengers get up and turn to one another, engaging in friendly banter, and the driver breaks open a bottle of champagne for a party. A joke, perhaps, but not entirely. A visibly black person may, in time, experience something very much like this unguarded friendship with a white person, if the black person has proven herself trustworthy and worthy of respect, or has been a friend since long before either was taught that vigilance between the races was appropriate. But I have only rarely met adult whites who have extended this degree of trust and acceptance at the outset to a new acquaintance they knew to be black. And to have extended it to someone who then *turns out* to be black is instinctively felt as a betrayal, a violation. It is as though one had been seduced into dropping one's drawers in the presence of an enemy. So a white person who accused me of deceit for not having alerted her that I am black is not merely complaining that I have been hiding something about myself that is important for her to know. The complaint goes much deeper. It is that she has been lured under false pretenses into dropping her guard with me, into revealing certain intimacies and vulnerabilities that are simply unthinkable to expose in the presence of someone of another race (that's why it's important for her to know my race). She feels betrayed because I have failed to warn her to present the face she thinks she needs to present to someone who might choose to take advantage of the weaknesses that lie behind that public face. She may feel it merely a matter of luck that I have not taken advantage of those weaknesses already.

As the accused, I feel as though a trusted friend has just turned on me. I experience the social reality that previously defined our relationship as having metamorphosed into something ugly and threatening, in which the accusation is not that I have *done* something wrong, but that I *am* wrong for being who I am: for having aped the white person she thought I was, and for being the devalued black person she discovers I am. I feel a withdrawal of good will, a psychological distancing, a new wariness and suspicion, a care in choosing words, and—worst of all—a denial that anything has changed. This last injects an element of insensitivity—or bad faith—that makes our previous relationship extremely difficult to recapture. It forces me either to name unpleasant realities that the white person is clearly unable to confront or to comply with the fiction that there are no such realities, which renders our interactions systematically inauthentic. This is why I always feel discouraged when well-intentioned white people deny to me that a person's race makes any difference to them, even though I understand that this is part of the public face whites instinctively believe they need to present; I know, firsthand, how white people behave toward me when they believe racial difference is absent. And there are very few white people who are able to behave that way toward me once they know it is present.

But there are risks that accompany that unguarded camaraderie among whites who believe they are among themselves, and ultimately those risks proved too much for me. I have found that often a concomitant of that unguarded camaraderie is explicit and unadorned verbal racism of a kind that is violently at odds with the gentility and cultivation of the social setting, and that would never appear if that setting were visibly integrated.

> I will tell you that, without any question, the most bitter anti-white diatribes that I have ever heard have come from "passing" Negroes, living as whites, among whites, exposed every day to what white people say among themselves regarding Negroes—things that a recognized Negro never would hear. Why, if there was a racial showdown, these Negroes "passing" within white circles would become the black side's most valuable "spy" and ally.
>
> —*The Autobiography of Malcom X*

I have heard an educated white woman refer to her husband's black physical education student as a "big, black buck"; I have heard university professors refer to black working-class music as "jungle music"; and I have heard

Adrian Piper

a respected museum director refer to an actress as a "big, black momma." These remarks are different in kind from those uttered in expressions of black racism toward whites. When we are among ourselves we may vent our frustration by castigating whites as ignorant, stupid, dishonest, or vicious. That is, we deploy stereotyped white *attitudes* and *motives*. We do not, as these remarks do, dehumanize and animalize whites themselves. From these cases and others like them I have learned that the side of themselves some whites reveal when they believe themselves to be among themselves is just as demeaning as the side of themselves they reveal privately to blacks. This is, I suspect, the weakness whites rightly want concealed behind the public face; and the possibility that I might witness—or might have witnessed—it is the source of their anger at me for having "tricked" them. For part of the tragedy is that the racism I witness when their guard is down is often behavior they genuinely do not understand to be racist. So the revelation is not only of racism but of ignorance and insensitivity. The point of adopting the public face when whites are warned that a black person is among them is to suppress any nonneutral expression of the self that might be interpreted as racist.

Of course this brand of self-monitoring damage control cannot possibly work, since it cannot eliminate those very manifestations of racism that the person sees, rather, as neutral or innocuous. No one person can transcend the constraints of his own assumptions about what constitutes respectful behavior in order to identify and critique his own racism from an objective, "politically correct" standpoint when it appears. We need trusted others, before whom we can acknowledge our insufficiencies without fear of ridicule or retaliation, to do that for us, so as to genuinely extend our conceptions of ourselves and our understanding of what constitutes appropriate behavior toward another who is different. The fact of the matter is that if racism is present—which it is in *all* of us, black as well as white, who have been acculturated into this racist society—it will emerge despite our best efforts at concealment. The question should not be whether any individual is racist; that we all are to some extent should be a given. The question should be, rather, how we handle it once it appears. I believe our energy would be better spent on creating structured, personalized community forums for naming, confronting, owning, and resolving these feelings rather than trying to evade, deny, or suppress them. But there are many whites who believe that these matters are best left in silence, in the hope that they will die out of their own accord, and that we must focus on right actions, not the character or motivations behind them. To my way of thinking, this is a conceptual impossibility. But relative to this agenda, my involuntary snooping thwarts their good intentions.

My instinctive revulsion at these unsought revelations is undergirded by strong role modeling from my parents. I never heard my parents utter a prejudicial remark against any group. But my paternal grandmother was of that generation of very light-skinned, upper-middle-class blacks who believed themselves superior both to whites and to darker-skinned blacks. When I was young I wore my hair in two long braids, but I recall my mother once braiding it into three or four, in a simplified cornrow style. When my grandmother visited, she took one look at my new hairstyle and immediately began berating my mother for making me look like a "little nigger pickaninny." When my father heard her say these words he silently grasped her by the shoulders, picked her up, put her outside the front door, and closed it firmly in her face. Having passed for white during the Great Depression to get a job, and during World War II to see combat, his exposure to and intolerance for racist language was so complete that no benefits were worth the offense to his sensibilities, and he saw to it that he never knowingly placed himself in that situation again.

> "Doctor, were I your wife, . . . mistaken for a white woman, I should hear things alleged against the race at which my blood would boil. No, Doctor, I am not willing to live under a shadow of concealment which I thoroughly hate as if the blood in my veins were an undetected crime of my soul."
>
> —Harper, *Iola Leroy*

My father is a very tough act to follow. But ultimately I did, because I had to. I finally came to the same point of finding these sudden and unwanted revelations intolerable. Although I valued the unguarded camaraderie and closeness I'd experienced with whites, it was ultimately not worth the risk that racist behavior might surface. I seem to have become more thin-skinned about this with age. But for years I'd wrestled with different ways of forestalling these unwanted discoveries. When I was younger I was too flustered to say anything (which still sometimes happens when my guard is down), and would be left feeling compromised and cowardly for not standing up for myself. Or I'd express my objections in an abstract form, without making reference to my own racial identity, and watch the discussion degenerate into an academic squabble about the meaning of certain words, whether a certain epithet is really racist, the role of good intentions, whether to refer to someone as a "jungle bunny" might not be a back-handed compliment, and so forth. Or I'd express my objections in a personal form, using that most unfortunate moment to let the speaker know I was black, thus traumatizing myself and everyone else present and ruining the occasion. Finally I felt I had no choice but to do everything I could, either verbally or through trusted friends or through my work, to confront this matter head-on and issue advance warning to new white acquaintances, both actual and potential, that I identify myself as black—in effect, to "proclaim that fact from the house-top" (forgive me, Malcolm, for blowing my cover).

> "I tell Mr. Leroy," said Miss Delany, "that . . . he must put a label on himself, saying 'I am a colored man,' to prevent annoyance."
> —Harper, *Iola Leroy*

Of course this method is not foolproof. Among its benefits is that it puts the burden of vigilance on the white person rather than on me—the same vigilance she exercises in the presence of a visible black person (but even this doesn't always work: some whites simply can't take my avowed racial affiliation at face value, and react to what they see rather than what I say). And because my public avowal of my racial identity almost invariably elicits all the stereotypically racist behavior that black people always confront, some blacks feel less of a need to administer the Suffering Test of blackness. Among the cost is that I've lost other white friends who are antagonized by what they see as my manipulating their liberal guilt or good will, or turning my racial identity into an exploitable profession, or advertising myself in an unseemly manner, or making a big to-do about nothing. They are among those who would prefer to leave the whole matter of race—and, by implication, the racism of their own behavior—shrouded in silence.

But I've learned that there is no "right" way of managing the issue of my racial identity, no way that will not offend or alienate someone, because my designated racial identity itself exposes the very concept of racial classification as the offensive and irrational instrument of racism it is. We see this in the history of the classifying terms variously used to designate those brought as slaves to this country and their offspring: first "blacks," then "darkies," then "Negroes," then "colored people," then "blacks" again, then "Afro-Americans," then "people of color," now "African-Americans."

Why is it that we can't seem to get it right, once and for all? The reason, I think, is that it doesn't really matter what term we use to designate those who have inferior and disadvantaged status, because whatever term is used will eventually turn into a term of derision and disparagement by virtue of its reference to those who are derided and disparaged, and so will need to be discarded for an unsullied one. My personal favorite is "colored" because of its syntactical simplicity and aesthetic connotations. But cooking up new ways to classify those whom we degrade ultimately changes nothing but the vocabulary of degradation.

What joins me to other blacks, then, and other blacks to another, is not a set of shared physical characteristics, for there is none that all blacks share. Rather, it is the shared experience of being visually or cognitively *identified* as black by a white racist society, and the punitive and damaging effects of that identification. This is the shared experience the Suffering Test tries to, and often does, elicit.

But then, of course, I have white friends who fit the prevailing stereotype of a black person and have similar experiences, even though they insist they are "pure" white.

> It cannot be so embarrassing for a coloured man to be taken for white as for a white man to be taken for coloured; and I have heard of several cases of the latter kind.

—Johnson, *The Autobiography of an Ex-Coloured Man*

The fact is that the racial categories that purport to designate any of us are too rigid and oversimplified to fit anyone accurately. But then, accuracy was never their purpose. Since we are almost all in fact racial hybrids, the "one-drop" rule of black racial designation, if consistently applied, would either narrow the scope of ancestral legitimacy so far that it would exclude most of those so-called whites whose social power is most deeply entrenched, or widen it to include most of those who have been most severely disadvantaged by racism. Once we get clear about the subtleties of who in fact we are, we then may be better able to see just what our ancestral entitlements actually are, and whether or to what extent they may need to be supplemented with additional social and legal means for implementing a just distribution of rights and benefits for everyone. Not until that point, I think, when we have faced the full human and personal consequences of self-serving, historically entrenched social and legal conventions that in fact undermine the privileged interest they were designed to protect, will we be in a position to decide whether the very idea of racial classification is a viable one in the first place.

> She really thought everyone would be like her some day, neither black nor white, but something in between. It might take decades or even centuries, but it would happen. And sooner than that, racism and the concept of race itself would become completely obsolete.

—Perry, *Another Present Era*

> Yet it was not that Lucas made capital of his white or even his McCaslin blood, but the contrary. It was as if he were not only impervious to that blood, he was indifferent to it. He didn't even need to strive with it. He didn't even have to bother to defy it. He resisted it simply by being the composite of the two races which made him, simply by possessing it. Instead of being at once the battleground and victim of the two strains, he was a vessel, durable, ancestryless, nonconductive, in which the toxin and its anti stalemated one another, seetheless, unrumored in the outside air.

—Faulkner, *Go Down, Moses*

These are frightening suggestions for those whose self-worth depends on their racial and social status within the white community. But no more frightening, really, than the thought of welcoming long-lost relatives back into the family fold, and making adjustments for their well-being accordingly. One always has a choice as to whether to regard oneself as having lost something—status, if one's long-lost relatives are disreputable, or economic resources, if they are greedy; or as having gained something—status, if one's long-lost relatives are wise and interesting, or economic resources, if they are able-bodied and eager to work. Only for those whose self worth strictly requires the exclusion of others viewed as inferior will these psychologically and emotionally difficult choices be impossible. This, I think, is part of why some whites feel so uneasy in my presence: condescension or disregard seems inappropriate in light of my demeanor, whereas a hearty invitation into the exclusive inner circle seems equally inappropriate in light of my designated race. Someone who has no further social resources for dealing with other people besides condescension or disregard on the one hand and clubbish familiarity on the other is bound to feel at a loss when race provides no excuse for the former because of demeanor, whereas demeanor provides no excuse for the latter because of race. So no matter what I do or do not do about my racial identity, someone is bound to feel uncomfortable. But I have resolved that it is no longer going to be me.

Note

This essay was previously published in *Transition* 58 (1992) © W. E. B. DuBois Institute. Reprinted by permission of the author and Duke University Press.

Adrian Piper

Coco Fusco

We Wear the Mask

During a trip to Europe in 1993, I could not avoid taking note of resurgent hatred directed at foreigners in general, and Muslims in particular. It seemed as if Europeans reserved a special kind of malevolence for the last non-Christian people to have succeeded in conquering parts of their continent. In this climate of animosity, derisive comments about what was perceived as stubborn insistence on maintaining traditional connections between identity and appearance were common. More than a few Europeans reminded me of the legal battle involving the young Muslim girls and their chadors (veils), which the French state had sought to remove while they were in school. In many more conversations, I noted how even progressive Europeans equated "traditional" appearance with "oppressive" culture and minorities resistant to assimilation.

The European feminists I encountered were no exception. I heard too many horror stories about Muslim treatment of women that often began with comments about chadors, and led to assertions that "traditional" men didn't allow their women to be feminists (European style). But in Germany I was also told that the latest craze for middle-class European women trying to "get in touch with their bodies" was belly-dancing classes, which are even more popular than salsa workshops that have sprung up like weeds all over northern Europe. No one spoke of the simultaneous embrace of a culture and rejection of the people who originate it as a contradiction; in fact, some Germans even argued that their interest in Black culture, for example, was simply a by-product of an imperialist American culture industry. Exotic dance classes, herbal medicine and hair care, nose piercing, and world beat clothing, all acts of cross-cultural appropriation and identity displacement, were all among the latest defining markers of the transgressive northern European woman. As I have argued elsewhere in relation to my recent experiences masquerading as a "primitive" in a cage, Western culture continues to rely on stereotypical notions of otherness and non-Western identity to define itself; and Western feminism, together with other attempts to redefine, transform and broaden contemporary developed societies, also depend on those same reified notions of difference to delimit their transgressiveness.

The history of the Americas is rife with examples of transfers of appearance between privileged and subaltern women. One of my favorite cases is that of the *tapadas* of the sixteenth–century viceroyalty of Peru (and much of South America during the colonial period): libertine *criollas* used their shawls as chador-like veils, covering all but one eye to hide themselves and thus to be freer and less easy to identify in public places. This practice had originated in Spain where, after the expulsion of the Moors in 1492, Islamic veils were banned and Morisca slaves turned to shawls to cover their heads and faces. Catholic women quickly perceived in the use of this body covering the advantage of its allowing them more social mobility (downward) and privacy. They took on the practice with such gusto and success that the Spanish crown outlawed it soon thereafter. In South America in the 1580s, the Council on the Indies saw in *tapadas* potential damage to the empire, noting that their sexual behavior could not be controlled and that even men were using the shawls to engage in "sin and sacrilege." Despite frequent attempts to outlaw it, the practice continued into the eighteenth century, when Enlightenment ideas redirected privileged women's desire for more liberty to cerebral rather than sensual pursuits.

In my imagination, I envision *tapadas* as precursors to both commercialized and avant-garde "bad girls" such as Madonna and the thousands of non-Latin Frida look-alikes who roam the Southwest. They borrow from subaltern female and sex-trade stereotypes (and take belly-dancing and salsa classes), and in doing so miraculously transform signs of oppression into symbols of transgression. In the context of the current celebration of transferable identities, such acts of appropriation are posited as emblematic of the postmodern severing of traditional or natural unions of identity and appearance. Unfortunately, however, this celebratory position tends to depoliticize and equate all forms of identity twisting, reaching the point at times of assuming that women are what they wear. It collapses the historical, political and social influences in the construction of identity and appearance into a superficial reading of identity as appearance, complementing the impulses of a society that uses consumption as its model of cultural assimilation. Thus, the history among women of color of manipulating self-image

Plate 13: *The Way Around*, 1989
Liliana Porter
Courtesy of the artist

to negotiate sexist and racist realities (sometimes known as passing) becomes, at this moment, a kind of beacon for white feminists in the postmodern age in search of a positive relation to style. I take as an indicator of this phenomenon the current feminist film theory fad of teaching and writing about *Imitation of Life* more than just about any other films with African-Americans in them.

It is important to remember, however, that this was not always the mainstream feminist line on style, the body, and appearance. Much feminist art in the 1970s stressed the biological functions of the female body and ancient (or at least pre-capitalist) matriarchal mythologies. In the early 1970s, when white feminism established itself in the academy and within certain sectors of popular culture, "style" and other forms of attention to appearance were often written off, somewhat ethnocentrically, as capitulation to patriarchy. Implicit in this position was a puritanical rejection of adornment as a form of dissimulation. During this period, I recall being looked upon with skepticism by the director of the women's center at my college (always clad, by the way, in grays, brown, and tans), who could not understand how I could be a budding feminist theorist in fishnets, pink mini-skirts, and purple hair. My success strategy at that time at a very WASPy Ivy League university, was to deliver a paper at a conference at the women's center my senior year, dressed as a man, on Lit Crit goddess Virginia Woolf's only funny book, *Orlando*. I ended up winning the prize for the best women's studies thesis on the same subject a few weeks later. (And some people think I just started performing . . .) Two years later, I decided to drop the cultural drag, leave the academy and commit myself to less recherché pursuits.

It wasn't until I left school and tried to enter the work force that I grasped just how much of that past was still present, making the very idea I could escape an identity by altering my appearance patently absurd. While I had spent years nourishing my brain, identities I found reductive, unacceptable, and racist continued to be thrown my way. The best I could hope for in most cases was acknowledgment that my identity might be something different or more complicated than the expectations generated by my appearance. The cultural debates and resurgent racial tensions of recent years have only served to make those expectations more apparent, not to make them disappear. In the midst of this, I felt myself beginning to lose sense of the pleasure I might have found in delving into other cultures without sensing a connection to mine. There is nothing radical for people like me about trying to be somebody else—our problem is how to get others

Plate 14: *Terpsichore*, 1989
C-Print, Edition of 3, from the Zabat series, 60 × 48"
© Maud Sulter
Courtesy of Steinbaum Krauss Gallery, New York

We Wear the Mask

to see who we are. At some instinctual, or perhaps unconsciously political level of my psyche, I felt that the struggle to transform limiting notions of the self had to come from *within*, from inside the cultures that had socialized me, and began to excavate the language I had first learned to understand myself.

Was I sensitive to the relationship between identity and appearance because I was a feminist? I cannot answer that question without first asking what kind of feminist I am speaking of. Feminism as it was defined by institutions at the time I began to think of myself as an adult woman sent me very mixed signals about both my identity and appearance, and I negotiated those looks by parodying them. That strategy, however, was one I had learned from women who had never participated in a feminist movement, let alone called themselves feminists. They were my mother, my aunts, my maternal grandmother, and family friends, all masterful manipulators of appearance, as their being women of color in the highly stratified societies of the Caribbean had necessitated. Before I reached adolescence, my power to manipulate my appearance had been forcefully communicated to me. I had been taught how to lighten my skin, get rid of my freckles, narrow my nose, straighten my hair, walk like a Parisian, sit like a virgin, speak like a lady, and dress like someone wealthier than I was. I watched them all go in and out of that posing as the situation called for it, saving their feistier selves for private moments. To follow their example meant to look one way and be another—tough, self-reliant, and prepared to face off against a system that would block my success at every turn. When I was younger, I thought they were hypocritical, even silly. I resented their screams when I decided to wear an Afro in the seventies. I now see them as survivors, women who tried to shield me from the suffering that lives in their memories. In their suggestions that I feign weakness to avoid physical labor, I hear the weariness of women who never had the luxury to fight for the right to work, and who have never experienced the claustrophobia of being supported by a man because no man available to them could offer such security. Through their admonishments and masquerades, a past that binds me to them speaks to me.

Coco Fusco

The Hair Trade

In my personal stash of obsessions, hair rules (though Elvis as the Antichrist and chicken wings with Alaga syrup run close seconds). So when I say cracking the hair trade was on par with making that hajj to Mecca, you'll understand where I'm coming from. No offense meant, just my jones talking. Besides, the hair trade had all the Mecca prerequisites: mystery, an obstacle course, the sacred inner core. It was a pilgrimage bound to cover a solidly American hash of race, kitsch, and commerce. But to 'fess up, I had no theoretical master plan, I was just plain nosy. Who were these alchemists, and how did they turn bushels of straight hair nappy?

So I set out to find that factory. Such a factory, or so I imagined, was in Brooklyn, perhaps tucked away on a Flatbush side street, near the bustling Afro-Caribbean stretch of Church Avenue, and most certainly above a fruit stand that sells okra and salt beef. In this factory, "raw" hair would be magically, or not so magically, transformed from "Bone Straight" (straight out of the Liaoning province) to "French Refined Wavy" (a.k.a., African-American hair under the influence of a perm). Korean supervisors would keep watch over poor Haitian and Salvadoran women as they tended boiling vats of hair with long wooden sticks. Mecca would be a place that mocks nature and makes a pretty penny at it. Mecca would be a hair factory.

Of course, this took a minute because, so it goes, Mecca ain't about to come to you, you go in search of it. My odyssey carried me first to shops that sell the finished product, one hundred percent human hair for braiding and weaving, textured to match black hair types, untreated and permed. For looking too long and hard at labels, I was chased away, or shopkeepers would murmur things that made perfect sense, like, "We don't know where it comes from, we just sell it," and nudge me to the door. When the dependable creatures who work in hair salons were asked to direct me to . . . (having no name for it, I made one up) a hair factory, they ditched the subject quick. "Trust us," they said. "We provide the hair," which I translated as: something bad will happen if you step foot in such a place or, child, don't go stirring up no dirt, especially if it's gonna affect my personal livelihood, thank you.

The official information machine was of little help. The health departments, trade commissions, barbershop licensing offices, and regional customs bureaus of the world passed me back and forth. No one had clue one, and I became a quack for asking. Was this . . . (the name problem again) hair product a vegetable, mineral, or human appendage? Like a single strand of hair, it floated through the cracks.

The use of human hair extensions for weaving and braiding boomed in the seventies, yet it's a practice no doubt as ancient as Jerusalem. Herbert Feinberg's *All About Hair,* a short history of hair replacement, reports unequivocally, though without supporting detail, that hair weaving—the attachment of hairpieces to beget length and volume—was invented by black people a century ago. (I'd take it back another two.) The contemporary American trend seems to have piggybacked from the Motherland-inspired braid styles exhumed in the sixties. Ancient cornrow braids, often adorned with beads and cowrie shells, had their renaissance. By the next decade, braids were being elongated to Gidget-glam lengths with synthetic and human hair extensions. With the advent of buppiedom and *The Cosby Show*'s blow 'n' curl vision of America, permed tresses came back strong in the eighties. Weaving was an obvious next wave. Weaves are best done with human hair extensions called "wefts," so human stock, as opposed to the synthetics that flooded the market in the seventies, returned en masse to corner wig shops.

The importing and processing of human hair is a tiny, tight-lipped business. In this country, very few companies actually process hair—convert it from straight to curly/kinky textures. Most "raw hair," as the trade calls it, is processed abroad, in Korea primarily, and sold prepackaged here at Asian retail shops like Folipa International Imports on Fulton Street in downtown Brooklyn, a stretch known as "weave row." The smattering of American companies in the processing business, most in New York and California, have showrooms where they retail by the pound, though the bulk of their work is in supplying salons and shipping mail order around the globe.

Lisa Jones

A small hair world, it is. The processing companies—call them hair factories—are a closely tied, though intensely competitive, pack. These family outfits, Jewish and Italian, have intermarried employees and managers over the years. Old names in the business are the De Meo Brothers, the Tucciarones, the Rubins. (Alkinco Hair Company, run by the Rubins, has been in what the industry tags the "Afro side" of business for ages. Trade gossip has it that the name "Alkinco" is a polite version of "El Kinko," code for "he who processes kinky hair.") Several of these companies have been up and running for close to eighty-five years. Processing techniques have remained the same over time and are treated as family heirlooms. Employees outside the family take vows of silence. When asked about her processing methods, one company president would volunteer only this: "Does Sylvia tell you how she cooks her collard greens?" Case closed.

Even harder to track down than the hair factories are the import firms. Only a handful of companies do this end of the business full-time. No import license is needed to transport human hair Stateside, and, more and more, storefront businesses are shipping in their own product. (These days, hair arrives primarily by UPS and Federal Express.) Older hair factories express concern about a budding cottage industry in which shady retail operations process hair out of bathtubs and have the public convinced they're selling the same fussed-over hair goods.

Just as Korea came to dominate wig production worldwide in the late sixties, it has zeroed in on the braiding and weaving market. Americans once bought most of their raw product from China, Korea, and India; now Koreans buy from the same sources, process it themselves, and ship to their own retail networks in the States. The Jewish and Italian hair factories say Korean-made goods are mass produced and of cruder quality. (Quality is a big word in the hair business and is used in ways arcane and racially demeaning; but more on that soon.)

"Foreign" hair is imported to the States for two main uses: human hair for wigs and hairpieces, and animal hair—goat, pig, and horse—for paintbrushes and hairbrushes. The hair trade buys raw stock in bulk by the kilo. In most cases it's treated abroad first in an acid bath to kill bacteria. Processing companies "refine" the raw hair, a process that involves, among other things, removing the roots, as they mangle easily. Refined hair is then chemically or steam processed to hold curl. The end product is called "commercial hair." After all these conversions, commercial hair maintains a top and bottom and must be braided or attached accordingly. Treated and processed hair lives forever, making it congruous perhaps to an embalmed corpse. (If given the chance, however, silverfish and moths could devour an entire warehouse.)

The Census Bureau assigns every imported product a fixed description and commodity number, and you might be yearning to know that "human hair, dressed, thinned, bleached, or otherwise worked," is commodity number 6703.00.3000. Last year hair came from eleven countries, all in Asia and Europe. Top on the list were Korea and China; Indonesia, which the hair trade considers to be an "up and coming hair market," ranked third. Through the seventies, stock imported from Europe was the only hair product sold to what the industry calls the "Caucasian trade." Now that the European market is drying up, Asian hair goes to all races, in most cases, unless another type is specially ordered. When you buy human hair in lengths for weaving and braiding, for wigs, and as male hair-replacement products, what you buy nine times out of ten is Asian hair.

The trade also peddles animal hair, used mostly for braiding, as it can stand in for very tightly curled, "wooly" hair. (Often dreadlock extensions are made from animal hair. Animal stock is bleached and sold as human gray hair as well.) The animal of choice is yak, a long-haired wild or domesticated ox found in Tibet and central Asia. Yak hair is sometimes mixed with angora (from angora goats) to soften it. There are those who balk at mixing animal with human hair, yet it happens to be an old practice. In the sixteenth and seventeenth centuries, hairpieces were commonly made from animal and human hair. And until synthetic wigs became so common and cheap, the theatrical market always relied on animal hair, particularly yak wigs.

Many in the trade are worried that the seemingly abundant supply of raw hair from Asia could be on the wane. Most raw stock comes from China, though it's processed in Korea, and the concern is that the supply will dry up as China is gripped ever tighter by the long arm of the West. (Apparently beauty shops are sprouting up in China that promote ye ole magic Western elixir: the perm.) Adorable Hair-Do, in Manhattan's design district, has been importing Chinese hair since 1910 and isn't worried too much about the China supply. Despite westernization, Adorable believes population growth will zoom on, and the manes will be there to cut, especially in the rural provinces.

But what of the Italian story? Italian hair, once thought to be an ever plentiful source, has diminished to nearly a custom-order operation. Says one importer, every month he used to bring in twelve cases of Italian hair, weighing 110 pounds each. He can't even get a fifth of a case today, and the costs are out of bounds. (Adorable bills an item it advertises as "Italian First Quality Human Hair" for ninety-five dollars an ounce.) Another importer is convinced that the product known as Italian hair is no longer Italian. A good percentage of the hair processed in Italy, he says, is "cut" with raw hair from Spain and India.

Asking industry types where raw hair comes from, and how the business is organized abroad, is to knock up against a covenant of silence. From a dozen conversations you might end up with this: in China, hair is much like a crop. There are hair farms, where hair is collected and packaged for shipment abroad. In India, women cut their hair and offer it to the church as a sacrifice. Allegedly the church supplies exporters, who then ship raw goods to Korea or directly to the States. Factories in Italy that collect and process hair have been in business since the nineteenth century. Before the war, peddlers supplied these factories by crisscrossing the Italian countryside to buy hair from poor women. Ponytails were bartered along with "combings," from combs and brushes, which women stored in glass jars. With Italian hair now scarce, and white American buyers ever in search of Cortez's fountain (pure European stock), Russian hair has been flown in as a substitute. The fall of the communist bloc has paved the way for a busy black market in Russian hair.

An old rating system operates in the hair trade. Italian stock is the number one European hair import, despite how much the supply has declined. It's still referred to as "first quality" hair and is gobbled up by custom wig makers and the men's toupee market. Labeled "second quality" hair, Asian and Indian hair costs less and at one time was sold only to what old-timers in the business call the "colored trade." Among salons that specialize in weaving and cater to a black clientele, there's another rating system: "good hair" is human hair, period; "bad hair" is prepackaged hair that's been cut, or mixed, with synthetic or animal hair.

Asian retailers are adamant about not rating hair. They insist that all the hair they sell is "best quality," which of course is as much a feel-good strategy aimed at consumers as it is a reversal of the rating system's racial hierarchy. Still, the old rating system predominates. A throwback to nineteenth-century racial codes, the system is augmented symbolically by the industry's overall race schema. In this country, white and Asian-American men sell commercial hair for braiding and weaving, bought and worn primarily by black women. The only black company in the processing business in the New York area might very well be the only one in the entire country. A black salon owner who buys hair wholesale in

Plate 15: *Wrung, 1992*
Black and white reproduction
Washer part, synthetic hair, nails, 12 × 42 × 3"
Photo: Larry Lame
Lynne Yamamoto
Courtesy of the artist, Jeanette Ingberman and Papa Colo

Brooklyn sizes up the race dynamic like this: tensions between those who buy and those who sell aren't expressed overtly, yet resentments are bubbling near the surface. The owners of an established hair factory made sure to note several times during my visit that they sell to the Afro trade "by default, not by design," as over time the more lucrative side of the business has shifted from white to black. Meaning, one assumes, if they could pitch Ferraris to nouveau riche whites in Ramsey, New Jersey, they might feel better about their line of work.

After hiking much pavement and nosing my way into shops, I found two hair factories in the most obvious place, the Yellow Pages, under the banner of "hair replacement, goods and supplies," and, small wonder, they invited me down. It didn't matter that ten others slammed the phone in my ear, convinced I was out to steal their processing secrets. Mecca was near.

Hair factories might often attempt to camouflage themselves behind the more respectable label of "designer of hairpieces" or "supplier of hair." Their sales pitches, on the other hand, are a dead giveaway: "Manufacturers of 100% Human Hair," they boast, in phone book ads and on street signs. Lugo Hair Center in Brooklyn ranks among the boastful. (Lugo, it turns out, is in East Flatbush, though it's run by Hispanics, not Koreans.) The company claims to manufacture "First Quality Caucasian Hair in All Colors & Textures." This might translate as: we process straight hair to curly textures, but all our raw product is imported from Europe. Prepare: even before you step foot into a hair factory, you are required to suspend reality. They *make* human hair. This is not a grammatical error; this is a way of life.

Welcome to Harlem. Where 125th Street meets Fifth Avenue, look for the McDonald's billboard framed in a kente-cloth design, as it's a stone's throw from W. A. J. Wigs. In the hair business for thirty-one years, W. A. J. predates the nouveau-kente generation by a couple of decades. W. A. J.'s second-floor factory/showroom/salon shares space with a business called "The Miracles of Rev. James," which offers the services of a spiritualist who guarantees results in twenty-four hours. Jean Church, niece to company president Verlie Wyche, runs the showroom desk, where traffic never lets up. Women in search of the perfect match pull wefts of hair out of shoulder bags like dead rabbits, or juggle adjectives to describe the hair of their dreams. ("It's like black dirty blond that's a little nappier than French.")

The seventy-year-old Verlie B. Wyche and other Harlem salon owners will tell you that W. A. J. invented the Afro toupee and was the first hair company to process raw Asian hair into permanent kink. Other hair factories hotly dispute this, claiming they've made straight to kinky conversions since the forties. As a maker of custom-fitted Afro toupees, W. A. J. is well known nationally on the black salon circuit. And Mrs. Wyche did originate in the early seventies a widely used method of weaving. But the title of inventor of straight-to-kinky-weave stock remains up for grabs.

Adorable Hair-Do ("Human Hair Manufacturers Since 1910") inhabits a floor of an upscale office building in Chelsea. Like W. A. J., with its business based on word of mouth rather than advertising, Adorable ships its texturized hair product worldwide. Adorable's showroom is a shrine to celebrity clients, with posters and signed publicity shots plastered like wallpaper. En Vogue thanks Herbert generously, profusely, lavishly. Company president Herbert Teitelbaum, ensconced in his office, reaches his son Gary, the V.P., by intercom in the showroom. Mr. Herbert (so he's called in the company brochure) reports that Patti Labelle's stylist just called from the tour bus to say how pleased she was, really, absolutely, better-than-before pleased, with the hair Adorable sent overnight rush. Gary blushes. On the way to the factory itself we pass a fashion spread that includes the models Cindy Crawford and Naomi Campbell. Campbell wears a pout and an ankle-length weave. Adorable has taped its own legend on the photo: "Both women are beautiful, but only one is Adorable."

It's at Adorable that I first enter Mecca. Rhyme, reason, and order seem clear only to the initiated. After a month of searching the city, I find boxes of raw hair wide open before me. This hair, in lengths of roughly eighteen inches, is wrapped at the top in twine and fans out below like a whisk broom. It's as still as a movie prop, a scalped ponytail from a spaghetti western. And it's bone—as they say in the hair world—straight. (When I asked Mrs. Wyche of W. A. J. if "Bone Straight" was shorthand for "born with straight hair," she said quite earnestly, "No, 'straight as a bone.'") In another area of the factory, women, Salvadoran perhaps, uncoil hair product from dowels. It then joins a large pile of stiff coils for transfer to the next stage. Men, Dominican perhaps, pull the coils back and forth through upright stationary combs called "hackles." The hair comes out in a bushy mound, soft like a six-year-old's Afro puff before a lifetime of relaxers. Several more women, Honduran perhaps, take this crinkly hair and run it through a sewing machine, which attaches a thick seam on one edge. This seam, as you can learn in W. A. J.'s how-to-weave video, is used to anchor, with thread or glue, your living hair to the commercial hair.

I am led into the Kaaba, the sacred shrine, the inner sanctum, where straight is brewed kinky. I see dye buckets, shampooing machines, vats of

Lisa Jones

bleach labeled DANGER POISON. I leave the room dizzy from the fumes, as if I had spent the night at the old Paradise Garage riding the moon on poppers. Mecca at last, yet the mystery, like the smell, lingers.

Touring W. A. J. fills in gaps. Raw hair is washed, then wrapped on dowels. Dowel width determines kink. (In W. A. J.'s closet-sized "wrap room," two West African women wrap hair as methodically as metronomes while they chew gum and listen to Afro-pop on the radio.) This hair on dowels is dyed and processed chemically (smells like an industrial-strength version of a home perm). Processed hair goes through hackles to loosen curl and blend colors. Weft seams are made on a special machine that creates a stitch as intricate as an eyelash. Finally, lengths of commercial hair are sealed in small, clear plastic packs (dead ringer for bagged narcotics), then shipped in white gift boxes. During my tour, a Hasidic man delivers a large rectangular box. I ask President Wyche if there's raw hair in the box, and if so, if it's from China or India. She gives me one of those looks: Girl, you're far too grown for your age. Mrs. Wyche has quite deliberately evoked the archetypical black godmama with the eyebrows-raised legendary spirit. Quite a power move. Mecca was only letting me in so far.

Hair factories are a storehouse of kitsch beauty culture, but they can also hip us to that unwritten chapter of American social history, the hair trade.

In the 1970s, its prime, W. A. J. was a prominent Harlem institution. (The company sponsored two Miss Black Teenage America pageants. Actress Sheryl Lee Ralph, in an elegant short Afro, was a runner-up one year.) Wyche tells stories about traveling to hair shows in the South to demonstrate W. A. J. hair goods, and of the informal networks of salons run by black women, which, in the tradition of Madame C. J. Walker's beauty colleges, also functioned as community centers and counseling offices. As a memento of my tour, Mrs. Wyche and her sister, Ella "Terri" Dufau, the factory manager, present me with a copy of a W. A. J. flyer from the early sixties advertising "kinky wigs and toupees for the Negro woman and man." The flyer was autographed by Mrs. Martin Luther King, Sr., on a visit to W. A. J.'s showroom.

With a name as suffocatingly cute as its product line, Adorable Hair-Do was founded in 1910 by owner Herbert Teitelbaum's great-uncle, a Jew who emigrated from England. Until the seventies, the company maintained its original showroom above the Baby Grand Nightclub on 125th Street. (The Teitelbaums say "race riots" pushed them downtown.) Adorable claims to have done the original research on the machine-wefting process and has papers to prove it. (Before machines became standard in the late forties, hair was sewn into wefts by hand, strands at a time.) Gary the V.P. will also show you the company's 1942 catalogue, in which yellowed newsprint illustrates hair for weaving. "Crimpy hair transformations," as they were called, fit around the head with an elastic band, the whole apparatus resembling a theatrical beard. By Mr. Herbert's account, Adorable, called Howard Tresses at the time, began processing straight to nappy in the early forties, stewing hair in crocks on the roof of its Harlem showroom.

The Tucciarones are the most picturesque historians of the hair trade, no contest. That's Biagio ("Bill") Tucciarone of B. T. Hair Goods, established in 1969 (taking the name of his grandfather's company, founded in 1910), and his father, Joseph, now retired, of Accu-Hair International Consultants, opened in 1949. Joseph Tucciarone sold his business in the eighties to a woman who crafts sheitels, religious hairpieces, for the Hasidim. These days, B. T. Hair Goods is a small custom-order, sample-matching operation run out of Bill's mother's cellar in the Bronx, though at one time five generations of Tucciarones worked the Manhattan factory. Being a Tucciarone means you can name different "grades," really nationalities, of hair in the dark (e.g., Russian: "dead straight, but also tends to be lumpy"; Belgian: "more durable, better food"). The family has always sold "first quality" hair to the Caucasian market, and still upholds the old rating system. But Bill Tucciarone will assure you that "taking care of the colored trade" is not beneath him. "Don't get me wrong," he says, "if they want good hair, they can come to me. They just got to want it first." (Alas, if us coloreds would only aspire to "good hair," it would be within reach.)

The annotated and subjective chronicle of hair trade to the Americas as told by Tucciarones goes something like this: outside of medical and theatrical uses, early markets for commercial hair in this country were married Hasidic women and Chinese women (who, following ancient practice, embellished styles with add-on hair). During the Second World War the Italian connection dried up for a spell, sending American hair factories scurrying, like they are today, after black-market Russian hair. Supply from Italy has never returned to its original volume, as after the war Italian hair donors discovered two American imports: the beauty parlor and the haircut. "Second quality" hair goods have always been steered to Negro consumers. (Hair traders consider Asian hair to be a coarser stock that lends itself to curly conversions, Asians got rid of their middlemen).

It's clear that the manufacture of wigs and hairpieces for black women has been an active industry since at least the turn of the century. The business picked up steam during the war, an event that corresponds to the second great migration of African Americans to the urban North. Gary the V.P. from Adorable puts it this way: "More black people came to the cities to work in the forties, and therefore they needed hair for style." "Style" or social necessity, the manipulation of black hair has been key to the assimilation equation since square one.

And so ends the Tucciarones' saga, and so we peck at the surface of the hair trade as American social text.

Humanitarian spirit manifests itself in the oddest places: hair factories. Factories are often approached by people whose need for hair has little to do with lipstick vanity: burn victims of leukemia and alopecia (sudden, in some cases unexplained, loss of hair). Hairsmiths treasure these cases, especially when children are involved. It lends a certain largesse to what they do: not only do they manufacture human hair, they're in league with the tooth fairy. The elder Tucciarone has his story about the little leukemia victim who was able to go to school without shame wearing a wig he made from her own hair. She died nine months later. Mrs. Wyche has hers about the dog-bite victim so grateful for his Afro toupee he showed up at the factory with a Christmas present every year for twenty years straight.

In W. A. J.'s case the hair doctor/medical rescue worker role is supplemented by an even greater mission: race work. When Verlie Wyche talks about why she "invented" the Afro toupee it's with the righteous tone of one who has undertaken to uplift the race, despite how the world and the race may resist the effort. (Mrs. Wyche found it "ridiculous and demeaning" to see the black and hairless walking around with "Caucasian toupees.") Early photographs of Mrs. Wyche show a remarkable resemblance to the young Diana Ross. Not just looks: the aura of self-invention floats around both women like expensive perfume. Mrs. Wyche made kinky hair, those raised eyebrows are quick to remind you. What did you do for the race today?

With Mecca and my tour of the Kaaba behind me, I am feeling less wooed by the kitsch mystique of hair factories. I have my concerns. Given the hush-hush nature of the trade, do we know what we're getting? Commercial hair undergoes so many chemical processes, could it be caustic? And what of a particular rumor that dogs the trade like the smell of rotting flesh? If this rumor is true, should we pull the commercial hair from our heads right this moment and beg the higher power for quick forgiveness? Is cosmetic hair kosher product? You decide:

Plate 16: *Wigs (portfolio)*, 1994
Edition of 15. Waterless lithography on felt, 39 panels, 21 with photos and 18 with text,
6 × 13.54 feet overall
Lorna Simpson
Courtesy of the artist and Rhona Hoffman Gallery, Chicago

Poor labeling is rife. A common problem users encounter at the smaller retail outfits is that human hair is cut with synthetic. (Kanekalon, the synthetic that's made into wig and braiding stock, is the same fiber used for Barbie doll hair. Apparently Barbies exhaust more of it than the sum total of human wig wearers.) Although in some cases hairpiece makers combine human and synthetic hair for durability rather than for rip-off purposes, consumers feel that labeling should be required and monitored. Another typical complaint: yak is cut with human, which is something to watch for, given that allergic reactions to yak are not uncommon.

False advertising is business as usual. Retailers and hair factories routinely trump up an item they call "French Refined" hair. This is no special feature. All commercial hair has, by definition, been refined ("refined" merely refers to the chemical process that de-roots hair). The French component is also meaningless, along with being inaccurate. Very little hair is actually imported from France; that which is, according to several importers, is probably Spanish or Indian hair that was processed within French borders. The French angle is so widely exploited, though, that most hair factories and retailers carry "French Refined" as a standard hair texture. Adorable, for instance, advertises five standard textures, including "French Refined Wavy," "European Straight Look," and "Spanish Wavy" a "texture style" that they claim to have originated. All are made from Asian hair.

Human hair, the import, isn't governed by special regulations from any government agency, including customs. It's classified as a cosmetic (a product applied to the body to promote attractiveness), so it falls under the jurisdiction of the Food and Drug Administration. Customs and the FDA received my queries about the bacterial or health risks that might be associated with commercial hair with amused patience. "Not a high enforcement priority," customs compliance officers and FDA cosmetic specialists offered with a chuckle. (Did this response fall into the category of "We are sorry, your problem is not male enough or white enough to rate serious discussion"?) If customs opens boxes of raw hair they'd be looking for lice, but there's only a slim chance they would, because hair, I repeat, is not a PRIORITY.

The open-door policy on human hair is curious at first glance. Hair is human tissue, but dead cells. Of the body, bodylike, and, to quote shampoo ads, "full of body," yet not a body part, at least so says Western science. This doesn't stop hair from being an intimate and certainly sexual "personal object" that calls out for cleansing, grooming, vigilance. Hair product (embalmed hair), since it no longer grows, is classified as an inanimate object.

It's sold as "human" in the same way leather is sold as animal hide. What all this amounts to is that no one worries. Certainly customs and the FDA aren't losing any sleep.

The health concerns I have about cosmetic hair don't rate an international crisis, mind you. Nevertheless, mostly women make use of it—particularly women of color, particularly women who aren't heard from as consumers—so it's worth raising the questions. Hair factory queen bees told me about the mysterious acid baths hair receives abroad to kill bacteria. Okay, so what kind of acid? Does this acid go away when the hair is washed? Or does a wearer continually absorb it into her skin when she perspires? Raw hair is by routine bleached and dyed. Is the cosmetic hair wearer also absorbing bleach? Dyes, too? Allergic reactions to hair bleach are common. Certain coal-based dyes are toxic and no longer allowed in over-the-counter hair dye products. Could a storefront industry out to cut costs be using cheap, unapproved dyes?

Tucciarone, Jr., of B. T. Hair Goods, who's worked with hair since he was thirteen, believes the acid treatment performed on raw hair could be harmful to wearers if not washed out properly. He questions whether most hair factories bother to do a thorough job. Dr. Deborah Simmons, an attending dermatologist at Harlem Hospital, frequently sees patients with skin problems brought on by extensions. Most of these involve braids that are too tight (which can lead to alopecia) or scalp conditions from not washing braided hair adequately. Simmons hasn't come across an allergic reaction to processing chemicals, though she believes the potential is certainly there.

Which brings us to, what if? What if cosmetic hair was recognized one day as a bad-boy product? An unlikely event, but let's consider it. Would consumers rush to kick the habit? There's an expression in the salon world, relayed to me by stylist Brenda Davis: "I'll wear extensions until they cause cancer, or a bit longer." Like the breast implant ban, some users would go kicking and screaming, if they went at all. The most common anxieties clients have about commercial hair, according to stylists, don't involve health risks at all. They worry about the cost of hair and what will happen to it in the rain.

Fables of the hair trade could make a flamboyantly stereotypical, international spy thriller set in Milan, New Delhi, and "the Orient," starring Mata Hari's great-granddaughter as a British-raised, black Eurasian agent in the employ of Her Majesty's Secret Service. A black belt in Goju-Ryu Karate, Kenya Hari sets out to crack the hair trade, then is lovingly derailed by American hair-care scion Wesley Snipes. Legend has it, as passed down by the hair trade's more colorful historians, that in China before communism, hair was cut as an offering to the gods. This hair was then stored in caves for hundreds of years. At one time, caves in China were brimming with perfectly preserved hair, and for a good part of this century, hair traders made do on this back stock.

Another myth conjures up an underground market in American hair. During the war period, from 1941 to 1949, B. T. Hair Goods actually did process American hair. Founder Biagio Tucciarone solicited the hair by putting ads in newspapers across the grain belt. Tucciarone couldn't turn much of a profit on the slim pickings here (a length of hair must be at least eight inches long to process, and Americans weren't producing the length), so he went back to the import business.

Finally, there's that smelly rumor the hair trade can't shake: some in the salon world are convinced that raw hair comes primarily from cadavers. Factories and retailers deny this with great passion. How could it? they object. Raw hair must be in excellent shape to undergo processing. The Tucciarones, however, will tell you otherwise. When Bill Tucciarone was a teenager working at his grandfather's hair factory, he regularly saw pieces of scalp mixed in with the hair. His father Joseph will swear to you that at one time at least 85 percent of the hair was cut from dead folks.

Interestingly enough, from the FDA's point of view, the sale of cadaver hair, if it is taking place, isn't illegal. There are no medical warnings against it and no agency regulations currently forbid it. In the 1980s, anti-abortion groups were riled up about collagen-placenta beauty care products, which they thought were being concocted from aborted fetuses. These objections were never substantiated, yet there was no law on the books at the time that prohibited the use of "fetus-derived products." So fetuses or no fetuses, these products could have remained on the market.

All my gallows-humor illusions about the hair trade and the warehousing of "dead" hair were shattered by a very brief conversation with dermatologist Claudette Troyer of Harlem Hospital. Hair by definition is not exactly a bundle of life. "The thing is dead, medically speaking," says Troyer, "when it comes out of your head." Hair, like nails, is made from keratin. The growth activity happens below the skin. So, dead or alive, hair donors are created equal. Consumers can object to the sale of cadaver hair on spiritual grounds, but that's about it.

Enter a voice of lucidity: braid designer Ruth Sinclair. Sinclair tells me I've been crawling up the wrong tree. The hazard of cosmetic hair, she says, doesn't strike the body, it eats at the soul. Sinclair is of the new school of Afrocentric cosmetologists who surfaced in the mid-eighties at salons such as Tulani's Regal Movement in Brooklyn and Cornrows & Company in Washington, D.C. With partner Annu Prestonia, Sinclair owns the braiding salon chain Khamit Kinks, which has shops in Atlanta and Brooklyn. ("Khamit," an early name for Egypt, means "land of the blacks." By adding "Kinks," Sinclair explains, "we've taken a word perceived as bad and made it good.") Sinclair has been braiding hair for eighteen years, and to her, the real concern isn't the possibility of chemical emissions from commercial hair (no more a risk, she says, than perming one's own hair). It's a beauty industry especially oppressive to black women. Sinclair's rap is a familiar one. Although it neglects two vital points, women's personal agency and hair as a creative turf, it still has currency:

Black women are told that in order to be attractive and successful, we must emulate a European image of beauty. The damage this does to us subconsciously has never been studied. Just the daily pressure. Caucasian women will never have to live with the stress of taking their hair from straight to kinky on a daily basis just to be visually accepted in society.

We are told as black women to assume an image that goes against what most of us are born with. Basically, the industry is saying that there's something wrong with us. And that this something must be controlled with artificial means—with their help. The industry will continue feeding us this line because it makes money off of us. Of course, the industry is not about to give up the revenue that comes from [commercial] hair, chemicals, and rider products. If they could find a way to make more money off of natural hair, believe me, they'd be selling that.

Hair extensions were the black-hair coup of the eighties, even more than the short-lived, vilified Jheri curl. They are more "yours" than a wig, if only by virtue of being more securely attached. They sell convenience and cultural versatility. In April you can wear a weave, invent an entire mane of processed curls, and carry forth like Diana Ross. By May you can put in braids and make a statement of racial pride—or not make one. Hair is still corporeal, except now it isn't necessarily biologically determined. But the real social innovation is that, unlike costly wigs with few styling options, extensions have made hair affordably disposable. *Disposable hair*—the postmod answer to racial difference. Disposable skin can't be too far behind.

Which is not to suggest that the racial allegories of the hair trade are so cut-and-dried. If anything, the trade throws a curve ball at assumptions of racial difference. First look at the trade route. Hair is dispatched from Asia, processed in the States, and sent to points in the diaspora. (Take Paris, where hair for weaving and braiding is sold from kiosks in the Metro.) You have companies like W. A. J. Wigs, which buys hair from New Delhi, refines it in Harlem, and ships to, among other places, West Africa—a journey that suggests a gumbo of transcontinental influences.

In West Africa, braided extension and weaves are "huge," to quote a frequent traveler to the region. Older women even wear them, in elaborate, braided styles that resemble hats. For little girls in Nigeria, it's the rage to have your braided extensions curled in Shirley Temple ringlets, a style called "the darling." So while African-Americans are looking to Africa for cultural affirmation, Africans are hopping on the bandwagon of a "Europeanized" standard of beauty symbolized by wavy, loosely curled extensions. Or let's be more critically expansive, to advance the ideas of critic Kobena Mercer, and call it "New World": a syncretic beauty culture born in the diaspora.

If hair is the key racial signifier after skin, then the trade makes a fine mockery of it. Processed Asian hair passes as black hair. Italian stock is allegedly blended with hair from the Third World and this passes as European. The hair of yaks (the "black sheep" of the ox family) passes as nappy hair. As well it's worth remembering that most of what the hair trade sells is not dead straight hair, it's "texturized" hair, hair that is quite particularly African-American/African-diaspora hair, hair that is emulated in perms by European women worldwide. So, toward the close of the twentieth century, what we have is a whole industry devoted to selling black hair (or, let's not get too excited, a particular type of black hair). But black hair nonetheless: hair that was once demonized. Hair that was downcast. Hair that was "no good."

The Afrocentric braiders are on to something. They avoid the political swamp of extensions as European imitation by using synthetic stock. The likes of Khamit Kinks and Cornrows & Company design styles that are not simply hairdos; these are elaborate constructions, with hair piled high, woven with ornaments and shaped like fans, wedding cakes, hourglasses, and halos. Maybe they're crowns, maybe they're altars. Extensions here are not used to showcase length or "naturalness." This is hair as textile, fiber art, as nothing less than sculpture. What links the African-American/ Africa-diaspora cultural practice with African traditional cultures is not the naturalness of the braids, it's the idea of construction. Hair in both traditions suggests spectacle and pageantry. It's always handled and adorned; hair is never left "as is." Hair exists to be worked.

Those wise ones, the ancient Egyptians, played their own game with hair: They cut it all off. They thought it barbaric, scholars say, or maybe just too damn hot. Egyptian-designed hairpieces incorporated materials like palm leaves and wool that suggested hair, yet didn't try to duplicate it, allowing much room for creative play. (By the sixteenth and seventeenth centuries, Europe was hip to headpieces, and they were being worn there as tokens of class privilege.) Perhaps there's a cave full of Egyptian hair, perfectly preserved, waiting for us in the Nile Valley. Given the war of historical interpretation, it could be Nappy by Nature (to borrow the name of a hair salon just opened in downtown Brooklyn). Then again, it could be "Bone Straight." But ask Verlie Wyche. I bet she'd know.

Note

This essay was previously published in *Bulletproof Diva: Tales of Race, Sex, and Hair* by © Lisa Jones, 1994. Reprinted by permission of the author and Doubleday, a division of Bantam Dell Publishing Group, Inc.

Lisa Jones

Looking Good: A Performer's Perspective

I was born a woman, Catholic, Latina, with low self esteem genes. It's hard for me to speak in front of an audience. But if I put on some lipstick, pencil in a beauty mark, start singing . . . memories from the corners of my mind . . . I can do it!

Hello, people, you know me, I know you. I don't need no American Express Card. I am Carmelita Tropicana, Ms. Lower East Side Beauty Queen, famous nightclub entertainer, Head Priestess of the Carmelita Sisters of the Born Again Virgins. Don't worry if in the audience you are not a virgin. I make you one.

Let me describe to you my biggest orgasm. Oh. I am sorry. I forget where I am. I do so many conferences I had a déja vu, in Espanish is déja vi. I thought this was the LUST conference: Lesbians Undoing Sexual Taboos. I guess I was thinking of a great climax in my career when I won the Ms. Lower East Side Beauty Pageant. You look at me and say: dark, short, and chubby. What a beauty! That's right. But beauty alone doesn't win me the contest. You gotta have talent. I play Cuba's national instrument, *el sarten,* the frying pan. I play it with a wooden spoon. The competition was tough. This was 1984. Rita Redd was Miss Congeniality, Ethyl Eichelberger was the reigning queen. How we miss these beautiful biological boys who pranced in high heels. Both have died of AIDS.

Negotiating Looks. Are we talking about dressing for romance or work? Let's talk about work. I remember my acting days when I went to Circle in the Square for a workshop. The students were from all over the United States. The speech teacher came in one day and said the Puerto Rican Traveling Company needed actors and was having auditions. Everybody started to laugh. Like it was a joke. Like a Polish joke only a Puerto Rican one. I was the same as a Puerto Rican. Cuban. Same difference. I

Plate 17: *The Milk of Amnesia*, 1994
Black and white poster for performance by Carmelita Tropicana
Director: Ela Troyano
Photo: Paula Court
Poster design by Kukuli Velarde
Courtesy of Carmelita Tropicana

was not like Michele Pfeiffer, blonde with blue eyes. The ideal actress. Funny thing is that in Latin soap operas the leading actress is also blonde with blue eyes. Now it is also curious to me that when some Cubans see Carmelita they ask: Are you Puerto Rican? They don't see someone with a beautiful accent and multicolored clothes as a Cuban like themselves. Well, after the Circle in the Square experience, I took a hiatus from acting.

In 1982 I went to the WOW Festival and that began my journey back into the theater. This feminist women's Festival had theater, music, poetry. The best theater was a play called *Split Britches,* a girl's *Waiting for Godot.* And how appropriate to use the name of an outfit that gave pioneer women such freedom to do number one in the prairie. The great thing about this festival was the women spectators it attracted. What girls! There was not just battle fatigues, there was everything. Girls in dresses, suits, ties. In my bonding with girls who had such great dressing style and humor, I found something truly more long lasting than girls—theater.

It was in WOW that Holly Hughes asked me to be in her play *The Well of Horniness.* I was cast as Al Dente, Chief of Police and Georgette, Vicky's butch lover. Georgette was a big problem. I heard all those voices from the past coming to haunt me: don't talk so loud, that laugh is not lady-like, walk with grace. I was sent to charm school to correct my feminine deficiencies. And now here was Holly Hughes asking me to forget charm school, take my shirt off and flex my muscles. Be butch. I was scared. But when I did it the audience went, ooh, wow. So I think, hey, this is not so bad. It was at the WOW Cafe, which started after the Festival, that I learned about butch, femme, and ki ki.

In 1988 I went to Mexico and I visited the temples at Chichen Itza and Irma's Salon de Belleza. I recommend beauty parlors when you travel, a manicure, a pedicure. Hairstyling is a great way to talk to women and find out what their lives are about. One of my traveling companions to Mexico was supposed to be the sexual guru Bette Dodson. And because she couldn't come she gave me a scholarship to her sex workshop. I was excited thinking it was going to be an orgy. But no. It was like a tribal and ritual exploration into femaleness. One thing I learned is the connection there is between liking your body and the ability to get an orgasm. Here, too, my charm school demeanor went out the window. We were told to moan and groan very loud. I tell you people—all of you who like to go to The Drawing Center, to The New Museum—you girls should be looking down there because there is some beautiful stuff down there. You never

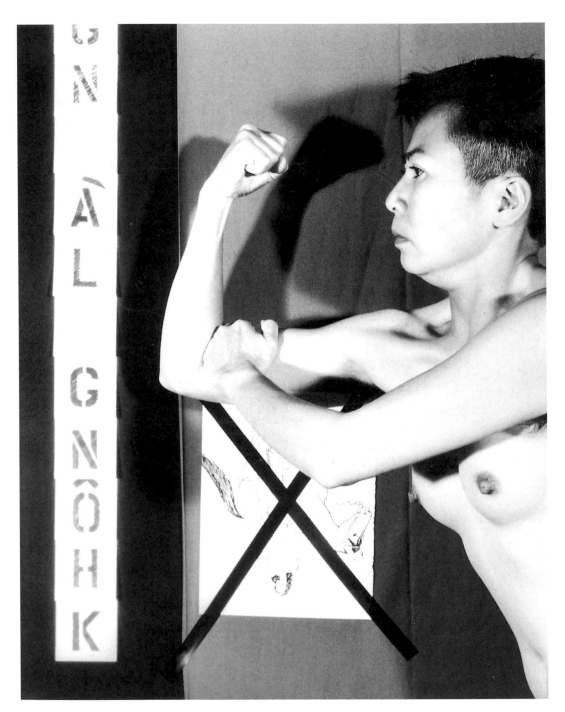

Plate 18: *Expatriot Consciousness, #9*, 1991–92
© Hanh Thi Pham
Words, composition, and photography
Courtesy of the artist

Carmelita Tropicana

know what you will discover, maybe some beautiful Moorish Alhambra design in purple. So check it out.

In the eighties is when I started to wear the fruit of my people. My outfits were designed by Ela Troyano and Uzi Parnes, my collaborators. With fruited boah and bustier I came on stage, and this was a problem for some. One was a girlfriend, very political, liberal, who after three months of being with me confessed she has a problem with fruit. It makes her cringe. She think it is Latina stereotype. I say she is not alone. A reporter I met before going on a show has the same problem. He says he sees the fruit and he thinks I am a stupid crazy woman. He hates me. But then he hears me talk and he likes what I say. Now that is a compliment. Enrique Fernandez, the columnist, wrote that I had dangerous fruits. But now I gotta change my outfit. It is the nineties. I have to think about politics and how to say it with an outfit. The new warrior woman considers and negotiates what to wear on stage. In the battle with AIDS I substitute charm school white gloves for sexy safe latex, and because I believe that women have got to have inner vision, to look deep within ourselves, I will be accessorizing with a beautiful speculum tiara.

A Boston critic once described my appearance: "She has horn rim glasses, orange hair with black roots showing and buck teeth." The one with the low self esteem genes, she cries; and I, Carmelita, I tell her she is great. Black roots, that's right, I'm proud of my African black roots. Buck teeth? Delicious overbite, à la Brigitte Bardot. And watch out, 'cause I bite. Grrr.

Meena Alexander

Alphabets of Flesh

I

There is something molten in me. I do not know how else to begin. To begin again, all over again, as if in each attempt something needs to be recast, rekindled, some bond, some compact between flesh, clothing, and words. There is something incendiary in me and it has to do with being female, here, now, in America. And those words, markers, of gender, of time, of site all have an extraordinary valency for me. When they brush up against each other, each of those markers—"female," "here," "now," "America"—there is something quite unstable in the atmosphere they set up. I do not have a steady, taken-for-granted compact with my body. Nor indeed with language. Yet it is only as my body enters into, coasts through, lives in language, that I can make sense.

II

I need to go backwards, to begin. Think of language and shame. As a child I used to hide out to write. This was in Khartoum where I spent many months of each year. My life was divided between that desert land and the tropical green of Kerala on the west coast of India where my mother would return with her children for the summer months. I hid behind the house under a sheltering neem tree, or by a cool wall. Sometimes I would find myself forced into the only room where I could close the door, the toilet. I gradually learned that the toilet was safer, no one would force the door open on me. There I could mind my own business and compose. I also learned to write in snatches. If someone knocked at the door, I stopped abruptly, hid my papers under my skirts, tucked my pen into the elastic band of my knickers and got up anxiously. Gradually, this enforced privacy—for I absorbed and perhaps in part even identified with my mother's disapproval of my poetic efforts—added an aura of something illicit, shameful, to my early sense of my scribblings. School work was seen in a totally different light. It was good to excel there, interpreting works that were part of a great literary past. The other writing, in one's own present, was to be tucked away, hidden. No wonder then that my entry into the realm of letters was fraught.

The facts of multilingualism added complexity to this split sense of writing in English. I was born in Allahabad and so Hindi washed over me in my earliest years. I chattered aloud in it to the children around. It was my first spoken language, though Malayalam, my mother tongue, has always been there with it, by its side, indeed alongside any other language I have cared to use: Hindi, English, French, Arabic. Malayalam is speech to me. Tightened, though, into the hold of privacy as I live here, it is closer to dream. Its curving syllables blossom for me in so many scripts: gawky, dazzling letters spray painted in fluorescent shades onto the metal sides of subway cars or the dark walls of inner tunnels, shifting, metamorphic. Sometimes I read letters in another script a man draws out laboriously in chalk on the sidewalks of Manhattan, spelling out the obvious as necessity so often compels: I AM HOMELESS, I NEED FOOD, SHELTER. A smattering of dimes and quarters lie near his bent knees. Those letters I read in the only script I know, make for a ferocious, almost consumptive edge to knowledge in me.

Never learning to read or write in Malayalam, I have turned into a truly postcolonial creature, one who has had to live in English. Though a special sort of English, I must say, for the version of the language I am comfortable with bends and sways to the shores of other territories, other tongues. First in Allahabad there was Hindi; then in my childhood months in Pune, Marathi; then in North Africa, French; and now in New York, there is Spanish. And always there has been Malayalam—that both heightens and undermines the course of my English. And necessarily so. Else, how would I be? Indeed, what would I be?

Yet the price of fluency in many places might well be the loss of the sheer intimacy that one has with "one's own" culture, a speech that holds its own sway, untouched by any other. But perhaps there is a dangerous simplicity here. And indeed how might such a mythic state be maintained at the tail end of the century? And it is a dangerous idea that animates such simplicity; small and bloody wars have been fought for such ideas.

Of course there are difficulties in the way of one who does not know how to read and write her mother tongue. For example, I would love to read the prose of the Lalithambika Antherjanam, the poetry of Balamani-amma and Ayyappa Paniker, rather than have them read to me. I would love to read Mahakavi K. V. Seemon's epic *Vedaviharam* rather than have it recited to me.

Or is there something in me that needs to draw on that old reliance, the voice of another reading, the sheer giveness of speech. After all, if it were just an issue of motherwit, I am sure I would be able to read and write Malayalam by now. Is there perhaps a deliberate dependency, revealing something of my childhood longings and fears, a community held in dream, a treasured orality? For the rhythms of the language first came to me, not just in lullabies or in the chatter of women in the kitchen or by the wellside, but in the measured cadences of oratory and poetry, and nightly recitations from the Bible and the epics.

Is there a fear that learning the script would force me to face the tradition with its hierarchies, the exclusionary nature of canonical language? And how, then, would I be restored to simplicity, freed of the pressures of counter-memory?

Sometimes all that has been forgotten wells up, and I use my English to let it surface. At the end of "Night-Scene, the Garden," is a vision of ancestors dancing free of the earth; allowing for the "ferocious alphabets of flesh."

"Alphabets of Flesh"

My back against barbed wire
snagged and coiled to belly height
on granite posts
glittering to the moon

No man's land
no woman's either

I stand in the middle
of my life.

I cannot see my mother
I cannot see my father
I cannot see my sister
or my brother

Out of earth's soft
and turbulent core
a drum sounds
summoning ancestors

They rise
through puffs of greyish dirt
scabbed skins slit
and drop from them

They dance
atop the broken spurts
of stone

They scuff
the drum skins
with their flighty heels.

Men dressed
in immaculate white
bearing spears, and reams
of peeling leaf

Minute inscriptions
of our blood and race

Stumbling behind
in feverish coils
I watch the women come,
eyes averted from the threads
of smoke that spiral
from my face.

Some prise
their stiffening knuckles
from the iron grip
of pots and pans
and kitchen knives

Bolts of unbleached
cloth, embroidery needles,
glitter and crash in heaps.

★★★★★

Slow accoutrements of habit
and of speech,
the lust of grief
the savagery of waste
flicker and burn
along the hedgerows
by the vine

The lost child lifts her eyes to mine.

★★★★★

Come ferocious alphabets of flesh
splinter and raze my page

That out of the dumb and bleeding part of me

I may claim
my heritage.

The green tree
battened on despair
cast free

The green roots kindled
to cacophony.

III

In my early days in Manhattan when my son was very little, I would take
him in a stroller down the subway. It was hard maneuvering down the steps.
Kindly folks would help now and then by carrying one end of the stroller.
Once it was a Latino man. He smiled at me, spoke to the baby in a warm
gush. I thanked him as he turned to me, right by the token booth. I heard
the melodious flow of words but did not understand the question. I shook
my head. I could tell he was offended. Why wasn't I replying.

Finally, in desperation I said "Indian, Indian!" and he nodded. At my
ignorance. He had taken me for a woman who could speak Spanish, a Latina. Other times I have gone down the streets, unaccompanied and been
asked, often by South Asians, "Where are you from? Guyana? Trinidad?
Fiji?" The jeans, the short hair meant that I might be from that elsewhere,
that shifting, diffuse South Asian Diaspora. Of course, when I wear a sari,
no one asks such questions. Those who might worry see it as a flag for

Plate 19: *Allegiance with Wakefulness*, 1994
Shirin Neshat
Courtesy of the artist

"Indianness. . . ." India, that strange land, far away. Land of maharajahs and snake charmers and poverty so desperate it ends in the plague.

"Hindu, they called me Hindu, then threw eggs at me. A group of skinheads in a car. I ran all the way home," one of my students told me. She was from a proud Muslim family, living at the edge of Queens. She was walking home late one night from a movie, this young woman who I shall call Rumana, though that's not her name. Her name does not matter, she might be you or I or she. What she went through matters terribly. Rumana had to figure out how to live her life after that episode, how to walk the streets, how to enter public space.

One is marked by one's body, but how is one marked?

"What wonderful English you speak," a young woman of South Asian origin is told. She is a woman in her twenties, utterly American, I would have thought. "Where are you from?" they ask her next. She wonders how she can speak of that small town outside Detroit she calls home. It is very common for young Asian Americans to be asked for their land of origin, whereas a young man or woman of European origin would never be asked such a question in quite that fashion. He or she would pass, unerringly. Though what such a person from Latvia or Ireland would feel deep down inside is another matter. After all, whatever the color of one's skin memories of dislocation can be deeply othering.

So what might it mean to pass in America? For an Asian-American to pass? For some of us it means making it in economic terms, assimilation translated into doing well, very well, not just making do. But the streets lined with gold are hard to walk and what happens with the heart can give one pause.

Once, in a small writing workshop for students at a prestigious Eastern University, there were twelve of us in a high room. I listened carefully as a young Korean-American student told me of the club his wealthy father took him to, how his father told him to behave impeccably, lifting up knife and fork just so, how coming home the father burst into rage at what he saw as the son's lack of culture. And all the while the student talked, his eyes red with the strain of remembering, I could see how he was so mad at being in the place he was. But what could I do?

Does passing mean being granted free passage? after fifteen years in this country I now have an American passport. It has a color photo of me clearly different from the black and white I had in my Indian passport, and the background to the image is a honeycomb pattern in sugary pink, blue and navy, quite a surprise. With this passport I can travel across borders, enter this country without visa or greencard. But what if I don't have the passport on me? And what difference will the passport make to my concern about walking on country roads where no other people of color are to be seen? And what of my fear of coming across men in army camouflage, toting rifles to kill deer, all the xenophobia of America sitting squarely on them, or bikers on Route 23 with big signs posted to their machines: "500 Years After Columbus Keep Out Foreign Scum!"

What does it mean to belong to America? In the city, I live close to Harlem. Sometimes when I walk up 125th Street I feel I am in another country—the shouts and cries, the passing figures, the small shop fronts in the old black neighborhood. I feel quite safe picking out a cap or a pair of overalls. There is no harm here in not being white. But I am not black either. "Indian?" a man in a khaki vest asks me. I nod. He passes me the clump of green plantains I have paid for. He smiles at me. I can pass here. But what does passing mean? For Asian-Americans, multiple ethnic borders are part of the shifting reality we inhabit.

The racial lines of black and white have been complicated by the layers of immigrants who have entered and are remaking this country. And we are part and parcel of a world of complex, often fluid allegiances. Ethnicity in such a world needs to be recast so that our moving selves can be acknowledged. Strolling through the streets of Jackson Heights, the El just behind me, blocking out part of the sky, I may feel quite at home—all the smells and sights of India, in fresh combinations—but I cannot live there either. The enticement of America lies quite precisely in its dazzling multiplicity.

But such shifting borders, particularly when radicalized, can be tormenting. Who am I? When am I? The questions that are asked in the street, of my identity: how do they mould me? Appearing in the flesh, I am cast afresh, a female of color—skin color, hair texture, clothing, speech, all marking me in ways that I could scarcely have conceived of. And there is a febrile edge to this knowledge, something that has always been with me, even in India, the country I "come from," a country where the issue of race never touched me. Years ago, living in Hyderabad, in my very early twenties, I wrote a poem. Somehow the thoughts and feelings return to me: the danger of being seen in the street, the danger of being a writing woman:

Meena Alexander

"Her Mother's Words"

If you sit in a dark room
no light behind you
no one passing in the street can see
my mother said to me.

I sit in a dark room
a small lamp beside me
how should I write these lines
without a light, how should I see?

I asked myself
not knowing that the street
had such a vision of my woman's soul
as I should scarcely understand.

Now I know
my hands grow cold and sight spills out of me.

Perhaps I should have said "body" instead of soul, I now think, but then
I correct myself. It is woman as prisoner of her sex that touched me, a
shocked awareness that led me to a study of the works of Mary Wollstone-
craft, writer, revolutionary, radical feminist.

But the borders here are different, the edges blurring. What knowledge can one draw on to live? I am Indian here, in a way I never was in the
subcontinent, in a way I never needed to be. And my femaleness is complicit in that radicalized awareness. Yet there is also the possibility of passing, of entering if only fitfully into multiple worlds.

But here I think of the darkness on which such a possibility is built:
Nella Larsen's world, female selves unraveling in the haste to "pass." Her
agile, anguished heroines come to mind: Helga Crane in *Quicksand,* Clare
Kendry in *Passing.* Invented almost seventy years ago, these fictional
women are torn apart by being African-American in a racist world. Larsen's vision is tragically divided: on the one hand is the crowd, the dark
thronging masses, the "hordes," one's own people rendered alien, a source
of pollution. On the other hand is a white world that might grant one exotic status. In Denmark one might be a bird of rare plumage, in America a
gypsy or an Italian. Multiple imagined ethnicities draw these women forward but blackness, borne deep inside, a fiery implosive, forces them to

their tragic fates. Passing in a racialised world offers no harbor and the self, site of so many invented identities, must perish. Though the tearing apart of the bonds of the past and the family might seem to allow for radical self-invention, Larsen was acutely aware of the quicksand of such an existence.

IV

I grew up in what might loosely be called the postcolonial Third World. I grew up both in India and in the Sudan. Multiple borders were part of my ordinary reality. In Khartoum as a young girl, I could sometimes pass for Sudanese, and this was always a comfort to me. But deep down inside, borne within me like contraband, was the knowledge that I was Indian, that my grandparents lived in Kerala, where both my parents were born and brought up—a land of ancient temples, churches, and paddy fields, quite unlike the stark lines of desert and sandstone that one found in Khartoum. In those heady days of Sudanese democracy my friends were experimenting with the tob. Some decided to wear the traditional covering, others found freedom outside it. Femaleness, then, at least in its external markers, could be negotiated. I understood, too, that what a woman chose to wear could be quite deceptive.

Assia Djebar writes of how the veil can allow women a subversive entry into public space. While Djebar's Algeria is far from this country, one can learn from her analysis of the danger of the moving body. Her vision, forged at the time of the anti-colonial struggles in Algeria, sharpened her sense of the multifarious, covert shapes a female body could take, and what contraband, literally explosive, could be hidden under female coverings. Drawing on her knowledge, one can reflect on a female body crossing the domestic border, entering public space. And indeed such crossings can have a truly communal valency. Here, now, in America we can reflect on such complexities, understanding that even as time and localities shift, there is very little we can take for granted as we etch ourselves into this culture, in complex palimpsests of knowledge and desire. Identity politics, in other words, or what commonly passes under that appellation, gains in power to the extent that it is anchored with multiple tie lines to a common, if shifting, social reality.

Several years ago, I gave a poetry reading at Tufts University with Marilyn Chin. I remember Marilyn reading her poem "The Barbarians Are Coming":

If you call me a horse, I must be a horse.
If you call me a bison, I am equally guilty.

I felt myself grow quiet as she read those lines. Then I read my poem "Ashtamudi Lake":

Arawac or Indian
the names confine
there is nothing for us
in the white man's burden . . .

In our different ways, both Marilyn and I were talking about living in America. Talking? Is that a good word to use for a poet's speech, that heightened, intimate vocalization? Why not? Surely poetry is as much speech as any other form of address. Defiant poems draw the hard power of naming, and of being framed as Other, into the veins of the present.

After the reading, as people milled about, helping themselves to sandwiches, a young woman came up to me. She beckoned, drawing me towards the window. When we were safely out of earshot of the others, she pointed at my sari.

"Can you really wear that here?"

"Why not?" Out of the corner of my eye I saw the window frame. Sunlight gleaming on the polished wood, but outside, in glittering heaps, soft as sugar, the snow.

"Not because of the cold, you mean?"

She shook her head. I shall see her still, this young woman with her hair cut straight across her face in bangs, her startled eyes. "They told my mother she couldn't."

"Your mother?"

She nodded. In the background a teacup fell to the ground. There were students milling about, sandwiches in hand.

"What does your mother do?"

"She's a doctor in Staten Island, she was told she'd have to wear a dress in the hospital. Can you wear that all the time?" she asked, touching the pallu of my sari.

"All the time I want. I guess I'm lucky where I work."

"The ethnic thing is not a fault?" I felt the sense of shame in her.

"No, no," I murmured, reduced almost to tears. And I put out my hand and touched her wrist. I wanted to draw off the six yards of silk I had draped over my body, wheaten colored silk, a gift from my mother in India. I wanted to show the young woman the glittering length of the sari, then let the fabric flutter out of the window, as a banner might, signifying some hidden, transient joy passersby could only guess at. Suddenly, the snow seemed ever so close, beautiful, blinding. And I wondered what it would be like to walk through the snow, all borders erased, skin tingling, eyes filled with blue skies of Somerville.

V

But the shining blue that exists in the imagination, a sheer and brilliant nothingness, forces us back onto the fraught compact between body and language in a world crisscrossed by violent borders. Sometimes it seems to me that it is only in the teeth of violence that we can speak the unstable truths of our bodies, our human lives. I think of Bensonhurst in Brooklyn, of Jersey City and the racist murders there. In Jersey City an Indian man was beaten to death, Indian women who wore saris or buttus were stoned by skinheads. I think of Hyderabad, Meerut, Delhi, Bhagalpur, and the communal riots and murders in those cities, as well as in the countryside of India. I think of the destruction of Babri Masjid in Ayodhya. And I feel that the habitations that language provides are always piecemeal, for we are haunted by the radical nature of dislocation, not singular, but multiple, given the world as it comes to us now—not just in the dailiness of our lives, waking up, walking down a winter street, setting down fifty cents for a newspaper—but in the manifold figurations of knowledge, through CNN, faxes, E-mail, the visible buying and selling of multinational corporations, the invisible telephone lines that link New York with Delhi or Tiruvella, which, with their rough oceanic sounds, threaten to obliterate beloved voices that sound a lifetime away.

In public spaces—and I am thinking now of Manhattan, the city where I normally live, walking down a crowded sidewalk, descending the subway—there is always one's body to mark one as Other. Ethnicity, we have learned, can draw violence, here and elsewhere. This, too, is part of the postcolonial terrain, part of the sorrow and knowledge of our senses.

And so the shelters the mind makes up are crisscrossed by borders, weighted down as a tent might be by multiple anchorages, ethnic solidarities, unselvings.

But having said this, I need to ponder a little further how these multiple anchorages of our feminism might work in the light of ethnic extrem-

Plate 20: **Image from Indu Krishnan's film *Knowing Her Place*, 1990
Courtesy of the filmmaker and Women Make Movies, Inc.**

Alphabets of Flesh

ism. I am thinking of the destruction of the Babri Masjid in India, on December 6, 1992, and the way in which Hindu extremism has coarsened the very fabric of the nation, the way in which tiny ripples from that violent eruption worked into the diasporic community here.

On a cold, damp day, I rode out with a group of other Indians to a small town across the Hudson river. After the choke hold of traffic in downtown Manhattan and the dim half-light of the Holland tunnel came the New Jersey turnpike and acres of industrial marshland, smoke stacks, and bits of old machinery, and the grayness of earth and sky, till suddenly we turned off and stopped in front of a small, low lying motel that housed the Akbar restaurant. The irony of the Bharatiya Janata Party meeting in a restaurant named after the great emperor Akbar, who espoused the idea of religious tolerance, was not lost on us. Inside the restaurant the BJP was hosting a Friends of India fundraiser. In the biting cold outside, protesters lined the muddy banks between road and parking lot, with raised placards reading "Hindu-Muslim Bhai-Bhai," "Rebuild Babri Masjid," and "Stop Funding Massacres in India." In the closed conference room of the restaurant, Sikander Bakht the BJP speaker who had come all the way from India especially for the occasion, spoke warmly of all the virtues of Hindutva, the cultural priority of Hindus, the indissoluble bond between Hindu identity and Indian nationalism. Cries of "Ram Rajya" raised by men, some of whom wore the red armbands of the RSS, echoed in the closed room. The speaker's plea to the listeners, not to forget their Indian identity, had not gone unheeded. Now an Indian identity seemed in that hot, closed room, to rest on the destruction of difference, on the excision of all others who were not Hindu. If the extremists had their way, the secular tradition, the rich, the multiethnic character would be expunged forever.

One of the members of the Mosque Committee told me how he was thrown out of the lobby outside the meeting room and threatened by the local police with handcuffs and the lockup if he resisted. While two carloads of police watched warily, some of the BJP group came out of the motel and the two sets of Indians confronted each other on American soil. The riots in Bombay and Surat were fresh in our minds. The blood letting of Partition was just behind us. Was India to revert to that again? Would mosques, temples, churches, houses, schools have to be destroyed at whim, just because there was a prior claim on the soil? The irony of the BJP speaker, inside the Akbar restaurant, invoking Mahatma Gandhi's name was not lost on us. How long did one have to live somewhere to make it one's home anyway? Was there no protection for minorities anywhere? It seemed quite appropriate to protest, to carry on this line of questioning on the democratic soil of New Jersey. The claims to identity that were made within the closed room of the Akbar restaurant were heard by men and women who in their daily lives were hardly members of a Hindu majority but lived rather as Asian immigrants, a clearly visible minority in America. Why could they not feel the predicament of minorities in their homeland? Why this terrible need to claim one cultural identity, singular and immovable for India?

One of the members of the protest group, shivering in the sudden wind, spoke of the 451 Palestinians expelled by Israel, living in makeshift tents in southern Lebanon. "It's cold there, too," she said, smiling bitterly as the cries of "Down, down BJP" grew louder and the cars, filled with party supporters, eased out of the parking lot. "What rights do we have anywhere?" she asked me. "How will you write this?" she continued. I smiled back at her wryly and stamped my feet, trying as best I could to free myself of the dampness. My toes were frozen and thoughts of writing were far from me.

Like many others, I had grown up at the borders of violent conflict. My mother's parents were Ghandians, believers in *satyagraha,* the way of non-violent resistance. But even as stories of peaceful resistance in the face of *lathi* charges and mass arrests filled my ears as a child, there were also mutterings about the INA, of women who armed themselves—of others, too, like Preetilata Wadekar, who threw bombs at the British. The struggle to decolonize took on a different hue in my years of growing up in Khartoum. There was a civil war raging in the south of the Sudan and university students who came from there would tell tales of torture and mutilation. As I left the Sudan to go to study in Britain I was well aware of the struggles for justice that raged on. In India, at the time there were students my age who joined the Naxalite movement, and many others were sympathizers in the cause of an armed struggle for justice. National independence was clearly only a very small first step and violence, in its multiple forms, would have to be confronted.

The struggle for women's rights flowed side by side with postcolonial struggles for freedom. The girlfriends I grew up with in Khartoum marched with men in the streets, demanding a solution to what was dubbed the "Southern Question"—the bitter civil war that was tearing the country apart. And those very voices, strengthened, were raised against the horrors of cliterodectomy. Then too, personal decisions were being made on how to dress, whether to use the tob or to discard it. In India where I returned in the early seventies, a powerful feminism that sought to rewrite the nation in terms of a viable existence for women was taking shape. Friends in Delhi organized against bride burning; friends in Hyderabad collected the stories of women who were active in the uprising of the Telengana movement. Within me, too, was the awareness that Gandhi, the apostle of nonviolence, in the course of his experiments in community living, both on Tolstoy Farm in South Africa and in Sabermati Ashram in Ahmedabad, had cut off the hair of young women he suspected of engaging in sexual misconduct. He wanted these young women to bear a mark on their bodies. What place did women have, I wondered, in this new world?

The complexities that underlie female existence need to be set in relation to the constraints of power, both patriarchal and colonial. It is against such constraints that the woman's voice pits itself, translating violence. In his essay "Representative Government" (1861) John Stuart Mill made the case for despotism. The natives of India were on his mind: "a vigorous despotism is in itself the best mode of government . . . to render them capable of higher civilization." The strictures of colonialism and patriarchy fuse in this belief in the necessary exercise of despotic power, an argument that I sometimes heard voiced in the postcolonial world I grew up in, fused though with a sense of the need to keep women in their place, teach them what to do. Although the details of the patriarchal argument were not voiced in the precise modalities of Victorian rationality (in India, after all, the elaboration of female sexuality is complex, woven into the fabric of a hierarchical society), a colonial sense of maintaining power, of keeping order, was critically present. And somewhere in there, as an undertone, was the grim feel of progress, a forward march into the new world. The regurgitation of Victorian rationality sat ill at ease, though, in a world where the bounding lines of behavior for both men and women were rapidly blurring. And there was a curious lack of fit between the corset-like constraints of dead British rule (one thinks of a garment shredded, shrunk, stays torn and visible but still held up to the living, growing body) and the nationalism that paradoxically permitted it to be voiced. Perhaps it is no accident, as Romila Thapar has pointed out, that the version of Indian history British colonialism established—indeed, required—for its legitimation is one that the Hindutva forces have used to build on: Golden Age of Hindu Rule; Barbaric Muslim Rule; Progressive British Rule. In each case, the Woman Question must be marshaled into line.

After the destruction of Babri Masjid and the riots that followed, one thinks: what the more extreme factions want is nothing less than the restoration of a mythic Golden Age, whatever the bloodshed involved. Women then stand in as the mothers of the nation state, or like the fierce female orators, Sadhvis Uma Bharati and Ritambara Devi, whose voices have been copied out onto countless tapes and distributed in households in India, cry out to raise the saffron flag on the Red Fort in Delhi, wipe clean the slate of history, a cry for a cleansing so pure that all the complexities of a multitudinous, multi-religious past are wiped out and history remade in the apocalypse of the mind.

What sense can the fraught reflections of a multicultural feminism offer us? If to be female is already to be Other to the dominant languages of the world, to the canonical rigors of the great classical literatures of Arabic or Sanskrit or Tamil, to be female and face conditions of violent upheaval—whether in an actual war zone or in communal riots—is to force the fragmentation both of the dominant, patriarchal mould and of the marginality of female existence. Indeed, such fragmentation can work powerfully into the knowledge necessary for a diasporic life, for the struggle for a multicultural existence in North America. Indian women's advocacy groups are working quite precisely against both the inherited patriarchal mould and the pressures of racism in the new world in which the immigrants have found themselves. And for feminism it is crucial to embrace the secular multiculturalism that is set at risk by political extremism. But how can the democratic struggles in India work into an understanding of multiculturalism in the United States? In the answer to that question lies part of my new praxis here, part of our exhilarating struggle for the future.

The possibilities, then, for female expressivity become multifarious, even verging on the explosive. My mind moves back to the tattered corset of Victorian rationality evoked earlier. It is as if one picked it up and tried to fit it over a female body, vital, magnificent, with as many arms as the goddess Saraswati, one of the arms, maimed from passage, still bleeding.

And how will our goddess speak?

In many tongues, in babble, too, I think, mimicking the broken words that surround her. Here, now, in America.

Kathleen Zane

Reflections on a Yellow Eye: Asian I(\Eye/)Cons and Cosmetic Surgery

I wish I had double eye.

. . .

I like go Honolulu
for get one double eye operation.
I no care if all bruise.

. . .

I take the operation any day.

—"Tita: Japs," from *Saturday Night at the Pahala Theatre* by Lois Ann
Yamanaka

When I was growing up in Hawaii, my parents and I were patients of the
ear, eye, nose, and throat clinic headed by two Chinese American doctors.
In their waiting room, I was always fascinated by the glass-encased display
of photographs and objects documenting the surgical recovery of foreign
matter (teeth, bottle caps, pins, marbles, jacks) from patients' ears, eyes,
noses, and throats. I don't recall exactly when these exhibits began to include "before and after" photographs of "double eyelid" surgeries, performed with no identifiable medical purpose. Despite the gruesome aspects
of this display, it was reassuring to know that if I were ever a victim of such
"matter out of place," I would receive competent medical care, and might
even become a star feature of the showcase. As for those eyelid surgeries, I
accepted them as normalizing procedures, in the sense both of practices
taken for granted by doctors and patients in this Honolulu clinic, and of restoration to a normal state.

At sixteen I decided I wanted contact lenses instead of the nerdy-
looking glasses I was embarrassed to wear. To my surprise, the doctor opposed my wearing contact lenses on the grounds that a foreign object in

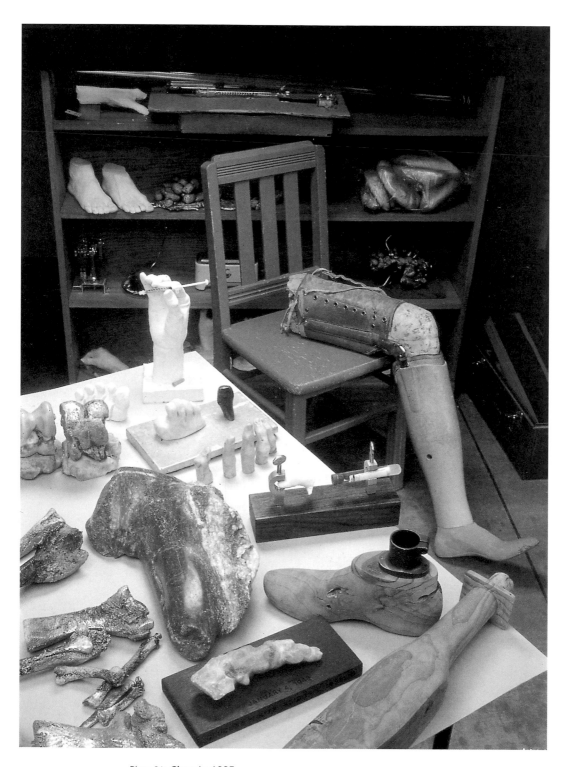

Plate 21: *Chronic*, 1995
Detail from installation, mixed media
Celia Rumsey
Courtesy of the artist and The Center for Curatorial Studies Museum, Bard College

direct contact with one's eye wasn't "natural." It was puzzling to hear this objection from a doctor whose services included the surgical alteration of patients' healthy eyelids for cosmetic purposes. However, his point of distinction between the artifice of a temporary device requiring daily insertion and the "natural" permanence of a surgically achieved eyelid was one I would remember many years later when my interest in body-sited constructions of gender and race led me to examine the dynamics of cosmetic eyelid surgery on ethnic Asians.[1]

This essay is formed in part by reflections on some of the responses I have received to my earlier research on the transgressive possibilities of diverse aesthetic interventions on the racialized body.[2] To re-think possible meanings of the optional double eyelid surgery for Asian women in relation to American racial histories, to feminist discourses about the body, and to ethnic pride politics, I have attempted a brief comparative review of some contexts for such surgeries. To chart meanings of agency in the context of historical and political settings, I question how cosmetic surgery functions differently for Asians (in the case of my research, the Japanese) than for Asian Americans; and how differently again for Asian Americans marginalized as minorities, as distinct from those constituting majority populations as in Hawaii.

Although I'm unable here to do more than merely sketch out some suggested directions for possible alternative readings of negotiative meanings, I want to emphasize the importance for multicultural feminism of dealing with our own discomfort with acknowledging variant forms of agency in cultural negotiations. This discomfort, or dis-"ease" often short-circuits Foucauldian views[3] by denying its own situation of identification with notions of property and propriety adherent to a Western hegemony, as when reverse mimicry or appropriation by mainstream culture links the ideas of originating culture and ethnic naturalness into a moral equation for authenticity. A by-product of this ambivalence has been described by Rey Chow as an "Orientalist melancholia."[4]

Such Asian(eyes)ing essentialism needs to take into account what the surgical subjects say, that is, to take them seriously on/in their own terms, without attempting to replace or "give" them their subjectivity, rushing to their defense, or reasserting their perspectives as singular truth.[5] Such alternative readings may open up ways we can begin to consider the place of hybridity among notions of authenticity and the natural as they function in ethnic pride politics or aesthetics of morality in the form of reconfigurations from Western "eye-cons."

A girls' high school in Okayama City caused a stir when it was found out last year that girls with natural brown hair were being made to dye their hair black to conform to the "uniform" regulations of the school.[6]

On the banning of colored contact lenses for its flight attendants by Singapore airlines, officials at Japan Air Lines and Malaysia Airlines concurred that the lenses were not suitable for "the Asian look": "How can an Asian girl have blue or green eyes?"[7]

. . . she had been relieved to see that her daughter had all her toes and fingers, and double eyelids as well. . . . Brenda was going to be an all-American girl.[8]

Some of the responses I have encountered when speaking about my research privately, as well as in feminist-organized venues, have confirmed the necessity, as well as the difficulty, of interrogating my location vis à vis my materials, my stake in academic feminism, and my own plausibility as a surgical candidate. The totalizing and dismissive assumption that Asian women who elect such surgery obviously desire to look/be Western has seemed too readily to essentialize Asians as degraded imitations and mimics. Labeling Asian surgical clients as mere victims of internalized racism resulting from their enthrallment with the patriarchal gaze of Western cultural imperialism seems to further a divide between enlightened or true feminists and these "other" less privileged "natives." Recounting that many Japanese involved as practitioners or patients have disputed the interpretation that the surgeries are intended to imitate a Caucasian appearance,[9] has tended to fuel dismissive mutterings about hegemony's efficacy in internalized racism. Such responses approach what Trinh T. Minh-Ha speaks of as a "form of legitimized (but unacknowledged as such) voyeurism and a subtle arrogance."[10]

Typical of these criticisms I encountered was the refusal to acknowledge what Asian/Asian American women who had been cosmetic eyelid surgery patients or had considered the prospect said, thought, or felt about the procedure.[11] Yet, many feminist discussions or critiques of *any form* of elective cosmetic surgery preemptively charged mutilation, self-hatred, and duping as givens, by conflating moral, aesthetic, and political judgments. Some of these critiques attribute certain ideal features to white, Western,

Kathleen Zane

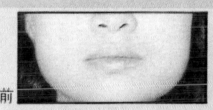
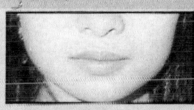

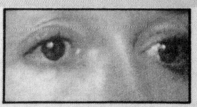
Plate 22: Advertisement for cosmetic surgery, *Sister's Pictorial* magazine, Hong Kong, February 1996

Anglo-Saxon bodies as property and propriety. This ignores the implicit idealization of white, Western, Anglo-Saxons, and denies the non-random and non-isolated occurrence of such features on the bodies of non-white, non-Western, non-Anglo-Saxon people.[12] Variety of hair type, skin texture and hue, facial structure, nose, lip, and eye shape within ethnic or racial groups is vast, but largely ignored among white feminists, as well as by feminists of color.[13]

The strong and specific repugnance with which eyelid surgeries on Asians is viewed insists on racially "authentic" meanings, which in turn elicit claims of proprietorship embedded in Western hegemonic culture. Medically termed a blapheroplasty, this eyelid surgery is also commonly performed on non-Asian women to combat their aging appearance.[14] In these cases, "heavy eyelids" are formulated as the problematic signs of age, indicators of the need for surgery. While the appearance they produce in non-Asians is interpreted as undesirable—lack of alertness, passivity, crankiness—these same indicators and appearance are deemed normal, "natural," and proper in an Asian's face.[15]

Consequently, the "problem" and the means of correction acquire legitimacy in the pre-determinacy of a racialized eye or face. An ethnic Asian's desire to "correct" what is culturally interpreted as undesirable, unattractive, abnormal, or problematic (out of place in a non-Asian face) is automatically construed as an inauthentic and inappropriate act, or purely symptomatic of internalized racial self-hatred. As a result, the ethnic Asian operatee's transgression of purported racial boundaries may be regarded as a moral issue—as denying her "natural" body, origins, and authenticity—in the manner of anti-miscegenation rhetoric, regarding it as trespassing on the law of the eye-con.

Like Michael Jackson, another purported "victim" of racial self-hatred and maven of cosmetic surgery,[16] Asian eyelid surgery clients must be located in the context of the imagery of the culture and sexuality they enact. Certainly, assumptions of the unnaturalness of these surgeries for Asians call into question received ideas about what Asians are supposed to look like. The collapse of Asian agency into a stereotype of the Asian mimic(wo)man, comes close at times to reiterating Orientalist discourse. Sources of this essentializing insistence on the mimetic nature of the Asian may be glimpsed through a further look at the representational systems producing the Asian eye-con.

Kathleen Zane

II. Eye-Conography: Reading in a Yellow Eye

In Western representational systems, the Asian eye has been iconized into the gestural abstraction of a slash: (\ /).[17] Like the "Oriental"-ized script used for representing Asianness in titles or signs, with its calligraphic reference or the suggestion of a bamboo graphic, the Asian eye (a slashed icon) is a racialized inscription identifying the Asian as Other. The operating dynamic of writing or cutting this eye-con on the blank face to signify "Asian" is an inscribing or branding by those with agency on those who are acted upon. While the "failure" by Japanese to represent themselves in Japanese *manga* (comics) with slanted "Asian" eyes is often noted with some amusement, perhaps the question needs to be reframed to uncover the expectations that predicate such a risible, seeming incongruity.

Commonly referred to as an "Oriental/Asian" eye and a "Western/Caucasian" eye, respectively, the so-called single eyelid expresses lack in the first instance while the double eyelid assumes presence in the second. Although many non–Caucasians, including Asians, have double eyelids, these purportedly "round eyes" are conventionally attributed to Westerners, who are presumed to be white. Echoing the inscriptive nature of Western representations of the Asian eye, the double eyelid is surgically produced by the cutting or slash in the eyelid. Paradoxically, fashioning a double eyelid, in what might be considered an augmentation or a creation of a previously non-existent part of facial anatomy in response to a lack, is achieved by removing the fat in the lid, which constitutes the lid itself (the epicanthic fold). The eyelid surgery's economy is suggestive of forms of genital or sexual surgical interventions also engendered in response to notions of presence and lack.

The process of symbolization in clitoridectomy, as discussed by Paula Bennett,[18] provokes insights into cosmetic surgery's racial discourse in relation to the epicanthic fold ("single lid"). Like the clitoris, the eyelid fat may be viewed as having no reason for being except as a marker; in the case of the clitoris, as Gayatri Spivak explains, its "pre-comprehended suppression or effacement . . . relates to every move to define [women] . . . with no recourse to a subject-function except . . . as "imitators" of men."[19] By reiterating predetermined definitions of mimicry as the sole means of subject-function for Asians, as for women, the epicanthic fold, like the clitoris, is defined as a suppressed/effaced excess. In a system based on the subordination and containment of "others," the autonomy represented by these entities of excess poses a threat to dominant rule generally. Where presence signifies impending lack, the Asian's practice of double eyelid surgery cuts into a Western iconic property to signal its transgression upon the seemingly stable marker of racial identity as well as its potential threat to the Western gaze. As a possible contestation of the Asianized eye-con, double eyelid surgery carves a racial construction into the body that reflexively reinscribes itself.[20]

That reinscription of eyelid fat as the Asian racial marker in an economy of presence/absence was maintained by Asian American activists as signifier of cultural pride and coded as authenticity. In the climate of Black Power and in emulation of ethnic pride movements, a relationship or equation between "roots/origins" and "natural looks" had been consolidated and validated among natives, appropriated into mainstream American aesthetics, and shifted into a moral sphere. While remaining a sign of foreignness,[21] the reification of the unexamined idea of the natural, the *idée fixe* on fixed eyelids sustained the eye-con as the version of the "natural" Asian eye throughout a system of aesthetic values.[22] In part, it subscribed to a preexisting notion of Asian beauty/ugliness that was both gender and class calibrated. The notion of an appropriately feminine beauty inherent in the exoticism of Asian looks functioned obliquely via Orientalist paradigms, like the "model minority" or the "China doll," by employing seemingly positive values to condescend or negate.[23] In contrast to its negative assessments of black looks, the cosmetic industry frequently advertised products offering formulas using "beauty secrets of the Orient" or in use traditionally by "ladies of the Orient." Similarly, the Asian beauty of reputedly slender and petite doll-like bodies was extolled in terms of soft skin and silky hair, and contrasted with images of repudiated and coarser African hair and skin.[24]

The actual beauty secrets or procedures used by some Asian women, such as glue, tape, tools for temporarily tucking a fold into the eyelid, and eyelid surgery, are discredited by Western liberal responses to such reshaping that parallel responses to black hairstraightening as unnatural and self-hating.[25] Nor have these "secrets" of Asian beauty culture been appropriated by a dominant culture that has taken to mimicking African–American identified, but de-politicized hair styles.[26] Aside from exoticized make-up styles, consistent with Western self-referential ideas of the Asian eye rather than emulations of actual make-up practices of ethnic Asian women, the mimicry is significantly unidirectional.

Several films by Asian American women are noteworthy in their attempts to offer valuable critiques of the pseudo-medical promotion of

Kathleen Zane

eyelid surgery and the racialized aesthetics of its beauty discourse. The critiques of the gaze presented in these films, however, are even further enmeshed in the sticky implications of visual politics. In a seemingly inescapable process of the visual, the women as subjects become at the same time objects of essentialism even as they speak. Caught within the politics of looking, the subject of a "fixed eye" is fixedly located outside the narrative, as another object of the gaze. Remaining within a white/other binary, the parameters of these critiques maintain the Western eye–con and ignore the possible usages of eyelid modifications as partial expressions of communalizing ritual, by articulating them only in terms of internalized racism. In voicing an opposition to the distortions of Eurocentric discourse upon the body of that other, it is pertinent to recall Rey Chow's point that a critique of orientalism "neither implies that only 'natives' of East Asian cultures are entitled to speaking about those cultures truthfully nor that 'natives' themselves are automatically innocent of Orientalism as a mode of discourse." [27]

Pam Tom's *Two Lies* (1989) is especially remarkable in complexly situating the inter-familial ramifications attendant on one woman's eyelid surgery and intersecting the issues of aging and racism. The film uses the event of an Asian American mother's eyelid surgery to explore the relationships between the mother and her two daughters. It places the "lies" of the mother's surgery against the hybridization of cultural artifacts, in particular the touristic imitation of a Native American lodge/resort where the family goes during the mother's recovery. The repetition of "lies" and contrived authenticities, as articulated by the more politically conscious daughter, serves as a critique of the false in cultural identity. The daughter's privileged perspective meshes with her role in familial and generational conflicts to detect the contradictions enacted by the mother. This critical strategy implicates the mother's desire in a moral imperative that deflects from her own motives and interpretation of her experience.

The film *Eyelid Surgery* by Tran T. Kim-Trung (1993), scrolls a Western medical treatise of historical lobotomy experiments on one side of the screen while a female, ethnic Asian client for eyelid surgery listens to a white male doctor recount the procedures and demonstrate his recommended modifications. The discourses of race, gender, and beauty implicit in this cosmetic surgical information are rendered as images of violent torture analogous to the butchering of brain lobes. The client's passivity mimics the body on which a white model of beauty will be imposed. Hence, the film's parody of scientific discourse upstages and effaces the patient's

Plate 23: Image from Pam Tom's film *Two Lies*, 1989
Courtesy of the filmmaker and Women Make Movies, Inc.

Kathleen Zane

desires and motives, while leaving the complexity of specific power relations unexamined.

Within the process of acknowledging institutional racism, the viewer is encouraged to see these others only as unwitting victims or as unenlightened collaborators who reproduce the system. The narrative scrutiny of the filmmakers' gazes serves to establish their own contrastive identities against those women who are seemingly unable to resist, interrogate, or control the manipulation of their desires by the eye-con. In dismissing these women as subjects and ignoring the power of a shared and historical racist experience, the gazes gloss an Asian American identity, but neglect to account for their own positions, in terms of class, educational, or occupational privilege. In consequence, they are able to do little to interrogate the positions of women who figure in their work as actual or possible surgical clients or to provide a dialogue with them. Occupying positions bonded with a privileged critical perspective, these purported confrontations of the very institutions that endow privilege instead operate in collusion with institutional power. The critiquing narrator is identified as exceptional, as successfully transformed, while locating those other(ed) women outside her critical production.

Fostering that "specialness," as Trinh T. Minh–Ha suggests, is founded on divisiveness and preserved at the expense of other women whose embodiment of the norm assists in maintaining one's exemplary status.[28] Although these could perhaps plausibly be read as narratives of the artist herself who might desire such surgeries but comes to see them in a different light, that is, read as in a sense autobiographical,[29] the disassociation of narrator from operatee seems effectively to reiterate a sense of self-hatred; and the attempted disassociation implies that the narrator's position is unambiguously transformed and in control. Thus the ambiguity that resides in racial self-contempt is foreclosed and its role in negotiating a hybrid-eyes-ed cultural position disenfranchised.

III. Cross-Secting Lids: Race for Beauty/Culture for Style

A former student at the University of Rochester, a Korean American, reported that her father had offered her as an unsolicited high school graduation gift the choice of either a car or a trip to Korea for eyelid surgery. She explained that this was a fairly common rite of passage for her Korean American peers and surmised it signified for her father a variety of relational meanings of his success in providing for his children.[30] The practice among many Korean Americans of sending adolescent offspring to South

Korea for summer courses in Korean language and culture highlights several aspects of their experience that is distinct from that of other Asian American communities. In regard to this example, the trip to Korea for cosmetic surgery that might have been performed in the U.S. could be viewed as an assertion of one's originary Korean cultural identity (gender and class), rather than its loss or denial.

In the Japanese setting, as in some Asian American communities, certain meanings of the "double lid surgery" are connected to social ritual, to family or community relationships, or to rites of passage. Not simply matters of personal self-esteem, facial alterations can mark changes of social status, such as graduation, coming of age, or first full-time employment. The eyelid surgery may be sanctioned as appropriate preparation for moving to the next stage of one's life among Japanese young women[31] within a culture whose highly codified markers of appearance correspond to specific age and gender status:

> A plastic surgery clinic in Tokyo's Minato Ward says that forty percent of its clients are female university students. . . . Over half of the young women cite their search for jobs as the main reason for visiting the clinic. . . . A twenty-one-year-old student with ambitious career goals says she had surgical adjustments made last fall to her eyes, nose, and chin. "I thought it was a drawback to look too serious."[32]

The interplay of power relations affecting meanings of the racialized eyelid is seen when we compare its cultural purposes and practices in movements across borders. As the reward and sign of economic agency, Japanese assume the prerogative of naming themselves "Western," or conversely, of naming the Western "Japanese," just as English (its fractured syntax a sign of appropriation rather than error) is used for Japanese purposes as a ubiquitous design element of T-shirts, toys, and shopping bags, or as cosmetic surgeons describe their achievement of a "Japanese eye."

The active appropriation of "Western" culture as agent rather than as passive recipient, as a means through which Japanese assume a "Western" prerogative and identity, especially vis à vis other Asian cultures, must also be considered. The ambivalence of Japan's self-identification as "Asian," as a consequence of this historical power dynamic with other countries of Asia, the contemporary export of its pop culture, and the economic cachet it enjoys in the region, also must be reiterated as background to a comparative cultural view of issues raised about eyelid surgery. Having been an active colonizer in Asia, Japan may be seen as maintaining its formerly imperialistic relationships through current labor, sex, immigration, tourist, or entertainment practices.

Under usual circumstances, the fat removal cannot be reversed, hence there cannot be a re-creation of a single lid, at least not with the same fat; nor is there much of a demand for such surgery.[33] However, the Japanese reinscription of "their" eye through their economic ascendance is reflected in the surgical creation of the single lid from an unconstructed double one to forge a visible Japanese identity for a number of Peruvians wishing to work in Japan. To "authenticate" their adoptions by Japanese or their purchase of false identity papers, these Latin Americans of would-be "Japanese" ethnicity have elected eyelid surgery to satisfy Japanese immigration authorities who have balked at admitting "so many 'Japanese' Peruvians [who] had such distinctly non-Asian features."[34]

By contrast, one team of Japanese cosmetic surgeons presenting a clinic workshop in the Philippines noted that the most advanced techniques for eyelid reconstruction were little appreciated by participants in a context in which ethnic Chinese were in positions of dominance.[35] Constituting the elite, professional, wealthy classes, and hence, the client pool for cosmetic surgery, Chinese in the Philippines wished to preserve the markers of their status that visually distinguished them from poorer indigenous groups whose eyes are "rounder." That is, power and status ascriptions both inscribe and prescribe the body as it is inflected by the dynamics of power relations, to reflect the positioning strategies of who sets the norm.

The effect on relationships of power is culturally relative in psychological, economic, and material ways. In contrast to the examples above, the single eyelid in the United States identifies one as Asian and constitutes a mark of the marginal despite the media touted images of Asian Americans as the model minority, whose economic and educational levels often surpass those of dominant white groups.[36] Long identified as ugly and inferior, distorted and weak, embodying perversion and vice, Asian looks as iconically focused on the slanted-eye graphic have been conventionally represented variously as indicating comic subordination, "inscrutable" deceit, or moral depravity.[37] Certainly, the power of the conventionally attractive in American culture cannot be dismissed as a potent factor in life experience only on the grounds of its being ideologically incorrect.

The destructive effect of racism on the self-image of people of color is well-documented and much bemoaned—especially among anti-racist whites. . . . Isn't it shocking that eye jobs creating a Western eyelid were popular among certain Vietnamese women during the war? . . . Yes. But at some level it is also profoundly reassuring to white women; we are, after all, the model. We do embody at least one element of the beauty formula. Our white Western lives are the stuff of global fantasy and demonstrably enviable.[38]

Yet, surgically transforming the eyelid is a far more complex cultural production than a simply imitative media-instructed practice that reasserts Western, white patriarchy as a remnant of cultural or political colonization. Cultural boundaries on aesthetics can be maintained within the seeming embrace of Western discourses of beauty, just as the cultural boundaries of otherness are maintained in the display and promotion of Western commodities in Japanese department stores as separate adjuncts to existing Japanese functions. By lending status or filling in a previously uncovered arena, they are thereby productive of meanings "consistent with the existing fabric of Japanese culture."[39]

Susan Bordo's work on anorexic reproductions of femininity offers several useful insights in this regard. Her view of the anorexic as embodying the intersection of traditional constructions of femininity with "the new requirement for women to embody the 'masculine' values of the public arena," such as self-control and mastery,[40] touches upon the ways in which Asian women's elective eyelid surgery can be motivated, not simply by the desire to simulate Caucasian looks, but rather as a response to the values of the new woman. It may be interesting to look at the surgeries in the light of escaping not simply from race but also from the traditionally limited options within a specific culture's gender-coded relationships. As an attempt to secure an aspect of male privilege within Japan's gendered economy, the surgery may engage resistance to traditional forms of femininity through "the illusion of meeting, through the body, the contradictory demands of the contemporary ideology of femininity."[41]

IV. Talking Lids: Hybrid-Eyed-Entities

An example of an Asian American literary production that enables an interrogation of hybrid aesthetics with colonialist appropriations as its subtext is offered by Lois Ann Yamanake's *Saturday Night at the Pahala Theatre*.[42] In her book of "poetic novellas," Yamanaka brings together hybrid racial constructs of the *hapa,* the vernacular voices of Pidgin,[43] and the hybrid eye (body) in relation to aesthetics and identity. Multiple positions and ongoing negotiations of colonialist re-sitings in the production of a "local" identity deploy polyvalent and simultaneous transgressions of racial, gender, ethnic, and class boundaries.[44] These transactions, as exemplified by the transgressive eyelid featured in cosmetic surgery,[45] are pertinent to the emergent idealization of the *hapa* (literally, "half" in reference to racial mix, often Eurasian) aesthetic within this hybridized landscape of Hawaii.[46] As a hybrid language carrier of political freight, Pidgin challenges boundaries as it performs and queries the multiple transgressions within its expressive sanctions. A communalizing form of expression that signals "local" identity, the use of Pidgin also enhances creative expressions by serving as a conduit of the particularity and fluidity of shifting hybrid identities.[47] Just as she can enact a "nice" standard English speaker at will, Yamanaka's protagonist, Tita, enacts the *hapa* through her active intervention and her "talk story"; "So what if not all true?"

> I get this guy wrap around my finger
> 'cause of the way I talk on the phone.
> I told him I get hazel eyes and I hapa—
> eh, I pass for hapa ever since I wen' Sun-In my hair.
> Lemon juice and peroxide too.
> Ass why all orange and gold.
> Plus when I glue my eyes and make um double,
> my eyes ain't slant no mo
> and I swear, everybody ask me,
> *Eh, you hapa?*[48]

Tita's unabashed engagement with double eyelid surgery as a signifier of problem and potential indicates the strategic momentum it provides her in shaping, negotiating, and crossing gender, racial, sexual, and class boundaries. The poem "Tita: Japs" (31–34) includes a three-stanza diatribe against the frustrating glue process she uses to create her double eyelid. After being pushed into the pool at a party, Tita fumes, "I had for do um *all over again.*/Took one hour for look normal again./I wish I had double eye" (33). With complete candor about her glue job, and appropriating a masculine demeanor, she has warned Lance not to throw her into the pool by threatening to exact for her loss of face the face-breaking vengeance of an eye for an eyelid: "*My damn glue going come off./Then I'm gonna have to break your face*" (32).

The importance of the tongue as locator of identity, especially in contrast to the instability of the single eyelid, is underscored by Tita's cherishing of Pidgin speech as fundamental to her "true self," while taking pride in the accomplishment of her manipulated appearance: ". . . I talk *real* nice to him./Tink I talk to him the way I talk to you?/You cannot let boys know your true self" (41). Whereas Tita can "put on" standard English as needed or when desirable, just as she puts on the double eyelid with glue, a permanent surgical transformation of her eyelids carries no sense of diminishment or loss of truth.

"Talking Pidgin" can be used as an oppositional strategy to send up and ridicule imported/external sources of authority, in part because of its association with working-class speech and its roots in plantation culture. Empowering Pidgin's intimate, communal and "localizing" features is its inherently subversive attitude in which the claims of genuine "real folks" (another expression for authenticity) are aligned in mocking the empty posturing, pomposity, and self-aggrandizement in the "proper" behavior associated with standard English, middle-class niceties and non-intimate public discourse. Like "English standard schools,"[49] such versions of the "correct" are associated with external colonizing authority.

Self-ironically, Pidgin slyly conceals its own bilingualism and covert competence in "correct" standards that enable a Pidgin speaker to play many parts, code-switching, as Tita does when speaking on the phone to a boy she wants to impress by acting *hapa*. It is in this respect a trickster's tongue.

Pidgin's resistance to the repression of local, intimate, communal, and "sincere" expression also extends to notions of racial and gender proprieties. Like Tita, the other women in *Saturday Night at the Pahala Theatre* interact from a centered yet subversive locality of identity in displacing and disowning the proper. They are not "good girls": they talk bad, in every sense—cursing, defiant, ungrammatical, impertinent, bawdy, loud, rude, speaking things or words expressly forbidden, talking about touching their bodies, obsessed with sexuality and bodily functions, revealing physical and emotional abuse and inflicting it on others.[50]

Through Pidgin, hybrid aesthetics, and double eyelid discourse, Tita rewrites the narrative of her body and of socially proper behavior. While acknowledging her own hybridized Japanese ethnicity, Tita defines herself in opposition to the models she perceives as meeting or aspiring to non-hybrid standards of propriety. Instead, Tita affirms an identity that disrupts the markers of class corresponding to a "proper" Hawaii-born Japanese

Plate 24: Image from Tiana (Thi Thanh Nga)'s film *From Hollywood to Hanoi*, 1993
Courtesy of the filmmaker and Indochina Film Arts Foundation

girl. "Their eyes mo slant than mine and yeah,/I one Jap, but not that kine,/the kine all good and smart and perfect/ . . . /That kine Jap is what I ain't" (31). Similarly, Tita transforms her own bodily difference into privilege by countering the stereotype of the petite and girlishly demure Asian female, subverting it not by denying her own "Jap"-ness but by valorizing her hybrid form's distinctions from the racial norm: "You jealous/'cause I one Jap with melons/and you one Jap with plywood board" ("The Bathroom," 29).

If we look at Tita's hand in this, it is the borrowed black nail polish she wears that broadcasts rebellion. Her disapproving teacher vaguely recognizes that motive, and asks Tita, "Why do you paint your fingernails black?" The constructedly "natural" female body, for whom red, pink, orange, or "clear" nails would not be a source of interrogation, but a mark of socially approved femininity, is being resisted and interrogated by Tita in her sullen nonchalance. Her claim of choice, "Cause I like. As why," voiced in an impertinent and nondeferential Pidgin response, manifests an aspect of Tita's collectively identified resistance to class constraints, the normalizing authority of "standards" of appropriate feminine grooming, and constructions of the natural—traces of which are present in her discourse on her double eyelid practices and plan for an eyelid operation. Just as in a coded punk rebellion, there is a simultaneous resistance and identification/compliance with some version of convention.

Tita repositions notions of artifice and the natural to depict the costs and pain of "acceptable" cosmetic commodities as indistinguishable from those of surgery. In her final assessment, she seems to prefer the temporary postoperative pain to her frustrating and humiliating experiences with non-invasive cosmetic intervention or other forms of lived pain. Her depiction of humiliation and emotional pain alludes to the racist and colonialist standards with which the alterations are deeply complicit, even, or especially, while they have been partially transmuted in the polycultural hybrid setting of Hawaii into the refined "local" consciousness of the unspoken gradations of comparative privilege.[51]

> I no care if all bruise
> like Donna's one for six months.
> Look Donna now, all nice her eyes,
> and she no need buy Duo glue
> or Scotch tape anymore
> for make double eye.
> I take the operation any day. (33)

I do not claim that Tita's jostlings of position are entirely optimistic resolutions nor free of residual and simultaneous complicities that can co-opt and covertly re-secure hegemony. Yet, anchoring instances of their seemingly offhanded or diffident resistance within a shifting history of colonization and colonizing can potentially expose ways in which, like Michael Jackson's, the surgically altered face of an Asian woman may more cogently be read as a surface of aesthetic and social inscription, rather than as manifesting personality traits or as what Mercer terms a "deracializing sellout and morbid symptom." Located within a network of affiliations and a climate of subversive irony forged in the solidarity and collective resistance of their local Pidgin-speaking community, these women are contenders. They recognize and contest the class, gender, sexual, and racial constraints of the colonial overlay while noisily negotiating them.

We have previously seen how narrative perspectives that present themselves as being outside a history of community struggle against racism promote the valorization of the anomalous and unaffiliated. Inderpal Grewal has pointed to the similar failure in other Asian American contexts to engage non-privileged classes of women in the critique, by making distinctions rather than affiliations among working classes and those not in privileged positions.[52] By rendering the hybrid (the hybrid eye and hybrid identity) as ordinary, and recalling a shared communal history of resistance, Yamanaka invites readings that recognize the variant forms of agency in multifaceted communal histories and that attempt to account for their own institutional investments, instead of ignoring or neglecting them through an absence which constitutes itself as social power.[53] By focusing on the dynamics of cultural hybrid contestations in this way, a more effective interrogation of the interplay of race, gender, and class constructions in relation to eyelid surgery can be accomplished.

To the extent that this intercultural beauty business interaction provokes a Pandora's box of possible readings, many questions still need to be asked. Because the epicanthic fold is overdetermined by dominant cultural norms as a sign of "correct" race, meanings of racial self-hatred often attached to its modification need to be interrogated. While avoiding crude and direct analogies, might eyelid surgeries be deracialized as the equivalent of having one's teeth straightened or capped, i.e., as modifications to appearance provoked and supported by adherence to a cultural, but not specifically racial, ideal? To these shifts of view, I would add the de-racialization of that so-called "Asian eye" to allow insights into its iconic status, that replace its being regarded as solely a biological entity with a consciousness of its operation as a signifier of power relations that shift within historical and national/geographical contexts related to an interplay of gender and class constructs. Understanding how, for non-privileged classes of women, forms of personal power or ways to manipulate disadvantageous social circumstances can be creatively engaged, we may confront the power and privilege that accrue from our espousal of our particular oppositional strategies. As multicultural feminists, in sum, we have to interrogate received notions of racialized and gendered subjects without conflating uses of power with issues of agency. From a less defensive posture, we may better see the power of an ethnic communality without regarding it as essentialist or essentially anti-feminist.[54]

As I see it, the eye-opening readings that most effectively encourage dialogue engage acts of speaking subjects as *their* subjects. Growing up in Hawaii as an English standard school student, aspiring to be, in Tita's words, "the kine all good and smart and perfect . . . [which] . . . I ain't," had kept me disconnected from girls like Tita, whom I feared and disdained in my isolation and envy. At a literary locale like Yamanaka's Pahala Theatre, I can meet anew the Titas I never knew, to be engaged by the hybridized discursive world of Pidgin, a dialect/language that I don't speak. Realizing that I need neither fear nor condescend to Tita, I may secure my own choices through remembering the privileges that enable such choices and indeed emanate from them. The recognition of hybridity's self-ironic communal and creative resistance reaffiliates me to "get it" when Tita foregrounds the issues of appropriation and complicity, subversion and colonization in her admonitory retort: "'cause when you accuse, you abuse/And I no use, I borrow." Seeing how, in those display cases of my childhood, what matters is not the sight of matter-out-of-place, but that it is place and sites that matter, I am enabled to enter a dialogue of multifaceted oppositional possibilities, even in (or especially in) places where I once could neither have imagined nor cited/sighted them.

Notes

1. I began thinking about representations of Asian women in American popular culture as a participant in the Seminar on Gender, Ethnicity, and Race as a Fellow at the Pembroke Center for Teaching and Research on Women at Brown University from 1987–1988. A subsequent focus on cosmetic surgery in Japan became part of my research as a Rockefeller Fellow at the Susan B. Anthony Center, University of Rochester, in 1992–1993. In January 1992 I was cordially provided full access to two cosmetic surgery clinics in Tokyo with the help of Doctors Sakata and Ishii.

Earlier assistance crucial to these and other contacts was generously given by Mr. Isamu Maruyama and the staff at International House, Tokyo, and Professor Hiroko Hara at the Institute for Gender Studies Center, Ochanamizu University.

2. Conference presentations of this research have included: the Asian American Studies Association, Honolulu, 1991; the American Studies Association, Costa Mesa, 1993; the New Museum of Contemporary Art, Crosstalk Conference, New York, 1993; and lectures or panels held in the U.S., Spain, and Japan between 1988 and 1995.

3. Susan Bordo clearly articulates the overly general application and misuse of Foucault in this context in her "'Material Girl': The Effacements of Postmodern Culture," *Michigan Quarterly Review* (Fall 1990): 653–677 although the value of other similar uses of Foucauldian notions of disciplinary power are not precluded.

4. Rey Chow, *Writing Diaspora: Tactics of Intervention in Contemporary Cultural Studies* (Bloomington: Indiana University Press, 1993), 4.

5. I am indebted to my friend and colleague, Karen Kosasa, who insisted in discussions that this work needed to be done, and who reminded me of the importance of not dismissing these voices, even while trying to negotiate around an awareness of the trap of representing and aspiring to the subjectivity of others.

6. Paul J. Buklarewicz, "The Me Generation," *Transpacific* (July–August 1990): 30–35.

7. Reported in the *International Herald Tribune,* via U.P.I. (n.d.).

8. Shawn Wong, *American Knees* (New York: Simon and Schuster, 1995), 96.

9. Examples of deferral include these statements: "It is looked upon by the Orientals [*sic*] as a method to enhance the beauty of the eyelids but not as an attempt to 'Westernize' their facial features. Various techniques . . . have long been used by ophthalmologists and nonophthalmologists in the Far East. Even nonsurgical means such as glue or tape have been tried. . . ." (Don Liu, M.D., Ph.D., "Oriental Eyelids," *Ophthalmic Plastic Reconstructive Surgery* 2 (2): 59, 1986); "Half of all Asians are born with a double eyelid. So you can still have a double eyelid and maintain your ethnic appearance" Edward Falces, M.D., quoted in Joanne Chen, "Before and After," *A Magazine: The Asian American Quarterly* 2, no. 1(1993): 15–18f.; "About 50 percent of Asians lack an upper eyelid crease, giving their eyes a sleepy look, Dr. Song said. The creation of this fold . . . if properly performed should not result in Caucasian-looking eyes" (Elizabeth Rosenthal, "Ethnic Ideals: Rethinking Plastic Surgery," *The New York Times,* September 25, 1991).

10. Trinh T. Minh Ha, *When the Moon Waxes Red: Representation, Gender and Cultural Politics* (New York: Routledge, 1991), 66.

11. Likewise, those who argue against straightening black people's hair, according to Kobena Mercer, "rarely actually listen to what people think and feel about it." ("Black Hair/Style Politics" reprinted in *Welcome to the Jungle* [New York: Routledge, 1994], 104). I do not imply that the operatee knows better; only that there is a total disregard for or lack of engagement with her version of the matter.

12. See Anne Balsamo, "On the Cutting Edge: Cosmetic Surgery and the Technological Production of the Gendered Body," *Camera Obscura: A Journal of Feminism and Film Theory* 28 (1992): 206–237; Kathryn Pauly Morgan, "Women and the Knife: Cosmetic Surgery and the Colonization of Women's Bodies," *Hypatia* 6, no. 3 (Fall 1991): 25–53; Diana Dull and Candace West, "Accounting for Cosmetic Surgery: The Accomplishment of Gender," *Social Problems* 38, no. 1 (1991): 54–65; Naomi Wolf, *The Beauty Myth: How Images of Beauty Are Used Against Women* (New York: William Morrow, 1991); and Susan Bordo, *Unbearable Weight: Feminism, Western Culture, and the Body* (Berkeley: University of California, 1993).

13. An accessible discussion of the denial in American racial constructions of physical variation among African peoples can be found in Jefferson M. Fish, "Mixed Blood," *Psychology Today* 28, no. 6 (November–December 1995): 55–61f.

14. Judith Newman reports that "it's a relatively easy, long-lasting and safe procedure for removing fatigue from your face," in her article, "Eye Hopes," *Mirabella* (May, 1993): 97–100.

15. I am aware that these "objective indicators for surgery" in both cases are what Don H. Zimmerman observes as "managed accomplishments or achievements of local processes"; but I am struck by how the interpretation of what the appearance of a heavy eyelid might possibly signify ("serious," "gloomy," "sleepy"), and its bearer's reasons for intervening in the ascription of such negative characteristics to her are dismissed as unwitting forms of racial self-hatred if she is an ethnic Asian. Don H. Zimmerman, "Ethnomethodology," *The American Sociologist* 13 (1978): 11 quoted in Dull and West, "Accounting for Cosmetic Surgery," 57.

16. Jackson's face and hairstyle are deconstructed by Kobena Mercer in ways pertinent to this study. See his "Monster Metaphors: Notes on Michael Jackson's Thriller," in *Welcome to the Jungle,* 33–52.

17. Barthes writes "The Written Face" of Japanese as an inscription and incision of "the strictly elongated slit of the eyes," describing how the blank mask onto which the ambiguity of the slash is inscribed produces the identity of the other as an inscrutability. Roland Barthes, *Empire of Signs,* trans. Richard Howard (New York: Hill and Wang, 1982), 89.

18. Paula Bennett, "Critical Clitoridectomy: Female Sexual Imagery and Feminist Psychoanalytic Theory," *Signs* (Winter 1993): 235–259.

19. Gayatri Chakrovorty Spivak, "French Feminism in an International Frame," *Yale French Studies* 62 (1981): 181, cited in Bennett, "Critical Clitoridectomy," 238.

20. Another thing to explore is how Barthes approaches inscriptions of the other and self-inscription to develop a way of understanding critiques of otherness, and how that critique is involved in one's own self-image; in effect, Barthes the inscriber performs his own *Bunraku,* being simultaneously present in his presentation of the presence of his puppet, and thus writing himself.

21. In the infamous article "How to Tell Your Friends from the Japs" that appeared in *Time* magazine, December 22, 1941, a distinction between friendly and enemy aliens fails in this singular and inescapably alien eye detail: "Although both have the typical epicanthic fold of the upper eyelid (which makes them look almond-eyed), Japanese eyes are usually set closer together." (33)

22. "Images of the small-eyed, round-faced Asian, so prevalent in cartoons and old movies, have been internalized to the point where even Asians believe that these features are essential, ignoring the reality that Asians have much more physical diversity than most people realize." Joanne Chen, "Before and After." *A Magazine: The Asian American Quarterly* 2 (1):15–18.

23. Chinese American writer and critic Frank Chin terms this "Racist Love," in *Seeing Through Shuck,* Richard Kostelanetz, ed. (New York: Ballantine, 1972).

24. Tired standards of Asian beauty continue to resurface as in the recent echo from William Prochnau, "The Boys of Saigon," excerpted from *Once Upon a Distant War* in *Vanity Fair* (November 1995): 234: "Women of exceptional Asian beauty— tiny, porcelain, ephemeral images of perfect grace . . . silken trails of their raven hair." Asian Americans have also been used historically as tools of control by the dominant culture, as contrasts against other less favored minorities, and as wedges to disrupt possibilities of affiliation or solidarity among minorities.

25. Mercer characterizes these responses as adjudgments of "wretched imitations," "a diseased state of black consciousness," and a "deracializing sellout and morbid symptom." "Black Hair/Style Politics," *Welcome to the Jungle,* 97–98.

26. These and other African American styles of hair fashioning are sometimes seen adorning young Japanese males and females during a few years of a brief stage in their lives before they assume, as expected, their first full time jobs.

27. Chow, *Writing Diaspora,* 7.

28. Trinh T. Minh-ha, *Woman Native Other* (Bloomington: Indiana University Press, 1989), 86–88.

29. This perspective was suggested to me by Ella Shohat.

30. Conversations with S. Kim, Rochester, NY, spring 1993.

31. Examples of the body/age focus of advertising that targets Japanese young women by offering a socially validated and identifiable image with clear group boundaries are presented in Rosenberger's analysis of fashion magazines. Nancy R. Rosenberger, "Fragile Resistance, Signs of Status: Women between State and Media in Japan," in *Re-Imaging Japanese Women,* Anne E. Imamura, ed. (Berkeley: University of California, 1996), 12–45.

32. Reported in the *Asahi Evening News,* April 14, 1993.

33. Reversals do occur, supposedly among the occasional repentant and enlightened victim of racism. In this sense, cosmetic eyelid surgery is distinct from face-lifts, which tend not to be reversed as a result of change of heart. People might regret the residual pain, or the imperfect outcome of a face-lift, but they do not elect to revert to the former state in which a face–lift was deemed desirable or necessary to begin with.

34. *Newsweek,* January 25, 1993, 39.

35. Japan is generally credited with developing these surgical techniques during the post–World War II period.

36. The ambiguous and converse value of the model minority appellation has been widely discussed, for example, by Ron Takaki, in *Strangers from a Different Shore: A History of Asian Americans* (New York: Penguin, 1989), in terms of its effacement of significant numbers of Asian–Americans trapped in poverty and violence, the constrictures of the label, and its use as a divisive tactic against other minority groups. See also Frank Chin, "Racist Love."

37. For examples of historical overviews of yellowface imagery, see John Kuo Wei Tchen, "Believing is Seeing: Transforming Orientalism and the Occidental Gaze," in *Asia/America: Identities in Contemporary Asian American Art* (exh. cat.) (New York: The Asia Society Galleries and The New Press, 1994); and Carla Zimmerman, "From Chop-Chop to Wu Cheng: The Evolution of the Chinese Character in Blackhawk Comic Books," in *Ethnic Images in the Comics* (exh. cat.) (Philadelphia: The Balch Institute for Ethnic Studies and the Anti-Defamation League of B'nai B'rith, 1986).

38. Wendy Chapkis, *Beauty Secrets: Women and the Politics of Appearance* (Boston: South End Press, 1986), 34.

39. Millie R. Creighton, "Maintaining Cultural Boundaries in Retailing: How Japanese Department Stores Domesticate 'Things Foreign,'" *Modern Asia Studies* 25, no. 4 (1991): 677.

40. Bordo, "The Body and the Reproduction of Femininity: A Feminist Appropriation of Foucault," in *Gender/Body/Knowledge: Feminist Reconstructions of Being and Knowing,* Alison Jaggar and Susan Bordo, eds. (New Brunswick: Rutgers University Press, 1989), 19.

41. Ibid., 19. See also Miriam Silverberg, "The Modern Girl as Militant," in *Recreating Japanese Women, 1600–1945,* Gail Lee Bernstein, ed. (Berkeley: University of California Press), 239–266.

42. Lois Ann Yamanaka, *Saturday Night at the Pahala Theatre* (Honolulu: Bamboo Ridge Press, 1993), 33.

43. "Pidgin" (Hawaii Pidgin English), although linguistically categorized as a creole, is the local term for popular speech in Hawaii, and I use the term Pidgin to refer to, and in accordance with, the entire cultural system of which speaking is a vital part.

44. In Hawaii the insider question, "What are you?" refers to ethnic antecedents, and the answer, "Japanese," most likely refers to a Hawaii-born American with Japanese immigrant antecedents, while Japanese nationals are denoted as "foreigners." Attempts at defining "local" or insider identity are frequent subjects of newspapers and magazines in Hawaii; "local" often references versions of authenticity. See Daryll Lum on "local" identity in "Local Literature and Lunch," *The Best of Bamboo Ridge: The Hawaii Writers' Quarterly* (Honolulu: Bamboo Ridge Press, 1986), 3–5.

45. "Double Eyelid Procedure Gives More Eurasian Look to Asian Eyes," reads the headline of a plastic surgery "advice" column/advertisement from *The Honolulu Advertiser,* May 22, 1995, B3.

46. The common use of the Hawaiian word *hapa* as a term extended to non-Hawaiian mixed ethnicity may be regarded by Hawaiians as another instance of the appropriation of Hawaiian culture and language without regard to its source.

47. Yamanaka claims Pidgin is "the heartspeak," and "part of our identity. It goes back to history. . . . If you're not born here you cannot talk like that." Quoted in Esme M. Infante, "A Dividing Line Between Locals, Non-Locals," *The Honolulu Advertiser,* May 14, 1995, F1.

48. Yamanaka, "Tita: Boyfriends," *Saturday Night at the Pahala Theatre,* 42.

49. English standard schools were officially established to counter the use of Hawaii Pidgin English after the replacement of Hawaiian by English in public schools following the overthrow of the monarchy in 1893, and were in operation from 1924 to 1948.

50. Tita's nickname alludes to this semi-tough attitude of resistance: "tita," the Hawaiian word for "sister," is colloquially used to connote a loose, slovenly, rude,

vulgar, streetwise female (not always without some degree of fondness). For a similar analysis of the power usages of "bad" attitudes see discussion of the Australian Aboriginal film *Nice Coloured Girls* in Ella Shohat and Robert Stam, *Unthinking Eurocentrism: Multiculturalism and the Media* (New York: Routledge, 1994), 326–327.

51. These complex class positionings in Tita's enactment of and aspiration to *hapa* looks also underlie the unspoken in the story "Hapa Haole Girl" from Hawaii writer Kathleen Tyau's novel, *A Little Too Much Is Enough* (New York: Farrar, Strauss and Giroux, 1995), 59–62; Tyau's narrator aspires to the *hapa* beauty of her classmate while pitying her for the particular illegitimate conditions of her marginal status.

52. Inderpal Grewal, "Reading and Writing the South Asian Diaspora: Feminism and Nationalism in North America," in *Our Feet Walk the Sky: Women of South Asian Diaspora,* ed. Women of South Asia Descent Collective (San Francisco: Aunt Lute Books, 1993), 226–236.

53. See Chow, 2–3.

54. See Haunani-Kay Trask, on the lateral struggle of solidarity in collective self-determination, in "Pacific Island Women and White Feminism," *From a Native Daughter: Colonialism and Sovereignty in Hawaii* (Monroe, Maine: Common Courage Press, 1993), 263–277.

Patricia Hoffbauer

Are We Still Juggling Bananas?
(Fill in the missing colors)

Plate 25: *Are We Still Juggling Bananas? (Fill in the missing colors)*, Patricia Hoffbauer

A map by which to read the geography of the text:

1-Science and Sanity-Alfred Korzybski, 1933

2-Wrote D. Pedro I in an echo of the Inconfidencia Mineira-eighteenth century Brazilian literary and political movement representing a national rupture with Portugal.

3-Dominican Friar, Frei Bartolomè de Las Casas, in his book *Brevìsima relacìon de la destruccìon de las Indias* (1552), estimates the number of the indigenous population killed between 1492 and 1542 at 15 million.

4-In 1556, when the "Black Legend" was already widespread through Christian Europe, the use of the terms *conquista* and *conquistadores* were prohibited and replaced by *descubrimiento* and *pobladores,* that is, *discovery* and *colonos*-colonist, settler. Dialética da Colonização, Alfredo Bosi.

5-"Ai, ai, ai, ai, ai I like you very much," song sung and recorded by Carmen Miranda in the movie *That Night in Rio.*

6-Macunaima and Iriqui-characters of Mario de Andrade's novel *Macunaima.*

7-Hamlet's dilemma becomes, in the words of Oswald de Andrade, an irreverent parody of Brazilian identity dilemma with regards to its indigenous Tupi history.

190   **Patricia Hoffbauer**

Plate 26: **From *Carmenland, The Saga Continues,* 1996**
Created and choreographed by Patricia Hoffbauer with George Emilio Sanchez
Photo: Paula Court
Float: Liz Prince
Performers: George Emilio Sanchez and Peter Richards
Performance series curator: Jeanette Vuocolo, The Whitney Museum of American Art at Philip Morris
Courtesy of Patricia Hoffbauer

María Milagros López

No Body Is an Island: Reproduction and Modernization in Puerto Rico

Contemporary postfeminist revisions seem to fall short when one approaches the area of the regulation of fertility as part of strategies for economic and political development. Older feelings of feminist outrage, now associated with the movement of the 1970s, come back in all their clarity. Puerto Ricans, at times a forgotten ethnic-national group for U.S. radicals who seem to have been more enticed by the Cuban, Chilean, or Nicaraguan revolutions than by their backyard colony, have been pretty much ignored. After all, are we not "legal aliens"?

I will argue that this status of "foreign but local," as the publicity of the Banco Popular in Manhattan claims, contains some of the most acute paradoxes of American capitalism and colonialism, a postmodern laboratory, if you will, for incomplete strategies of modernization where women's bodies have received the brunt of failed promises. Again, a sense of orthodox militancy of the past two decades that I can hardly recognize within myself, clutches!

After the Second World War and until the present, strategies of modernization were put into place that depended on some major colonial pillars: (1) export-led forms of industrialization (as opposed to more indigenous developmentalist approaches) were meant to entice American capitalism to invest in Puerto Rico through tax exemption offers and lower labor costs; (2) expansion of the government sector as Puerto Rico's major employer; (3) government stimulated migration; (4) direct consumption subsidies for 60 to 70 percent of the population; and (5) population control strategies. Perhaps Puerto Rico precolonized in the fifties the contemporary internationalization of the social division of labor. The last area included a massive program of public sterilization services, the development of extended family planning services, experimentation with contraceptive

Plate 27: *Cultural, Racial, Genocidal Policy,* 1983
Black and white reproduction from color slide
Oil, mixed medium on canvas. 60 × 96"
Juan Sanchez
Courtesy of the artist and Guariquen, Inc., New York

pills on sample groups of Puerto Rican women, and, more recently and more obliquely, the widespread use of cesarean operations in public and private hospitals on the island.

If this sounds like a paranoid fantasy, let me proceed with some quantitative data. To summarize, Puerto Rico has the highest percent of women (in the world) in their reproductive years who are sterile. Thirty-five percent of women in their reproductive years have been sterilized. This has been increasingly the case since the 1950s when the publicly financed sterilization programs began. "Sterilization as option" as a contraceptive practice/discourse can now be said to have become generalized as an unquestioned premise of cultural consciousness and is not seen as a government initiative, nor is it seen as undesirable. In conjunction, these efforts have, in fact, resulted in lowered fertility rates, which resemble those of "advanced industrial countries." For comparative purposes, while Japan and the United States had around a 5 percent sterilization rate, Puerto Rico had a 34 to 35 percent rate for the year 1968. In urban areas, this rate went up to 39 percent. Ninety-two percent had been sterilized by age 35 and the prevalence of sterilization was significantly higher among women whose formal education ended before the eighth grade.[1] *La Operación,* a film about sterilization practices in Puerto Rico by Ana María García, documents these patterns. The film highlights the procedures of inducement into sterilization and the power given to the women's mates in authorizing the practices with only dubious knowledge by both partners. At the time, many women thought that they were submitting to a temporary birth control process. While the offer for vasectomies was also made it had no impact on the male population. The great majority of the women came from the poorer sectors of the country while they were also subjected to experimental birth control pills whose dosage, at the time, were very potent compared to contemporary dosages.

More recently, a growing concern among Puerto Rican feminists has been the widespread practice of cesarean sections on the island. José Vázquez Calzada[2] documents the fact that Puerto Rico holds the record for the highest number of births by cesarean operations in the world. In 1989, according to the Department of Health, 30 percent of all births were subject to this surgical procedure. Urban women had higher rates (32.9 percent) and women who were assisted in private hospitals higher still (48 percent). Interestingly, women with more adequate prenatal care, higher educational achievements, and those with professional husbands had a fifty percent rate. The justification provided in the medical records was that the would-be mothers did not have adequate pelvic measurements to insure safe vaginal births. Paradoxically, young, less educated, poorer women, single mothers, and adolescent mothers who gave birth at public hospitals had lower C-operation rates. The expected tendency is for these sectors to have higher risk pregnancies, poorer prenatal care, and complicated births that may justify surgical procedures. The conclusion seems to point to the interests of the medical profession as the overriding consideration, and not to any variables pertaining to health needs themselves. An update of these data in 1995 confirms previous results and finds them to be on the increase.

The response of organized groups during these times was non-existent. More recently, after the late 1970s, responses have been articulated within the framework of feminism and later within the renewed efforts against anti-abortion groups. At present, however, questions around reproductive issues have caused organized feminist groups to coalesce. The history of these regulatory practices has come under clear focus. In the name of progress, so characteristic of Operation Bootstrap,[3] the merits of controlling the reproductive habits of the poor under so-called conditions of overpopulation on the island went unquestioned. The demographic argument—fewer children, more prosperity—had a common sense aura about it not linked to any overt political strategy, and seemed intended to raise the living standards of the general population. Class considerations were not part of the analysis. On the contrary, influenced by the work of anthropologists like Oscar Lewis in his classical study *La Vida,* the urban poor in the slum were seen as in need of supervision, given their proclivity for immediate gratification and their inability to plan for the future. The discourse of the subculture of poverty of the sixties made a perfect fit with the legitimation of interventionist practices and the expansion of the "helping" professions. This enabled a bypassing of the discourse of choice, or actually made choice irrelevant. The functional role of these sectors (which has appeared more recently, as these scandals have been exposed) has coincided with the cultural acceptance of sterilization among large numbers of women across classes. Sterilization is currently a practice most Puerto Rican women find acceptable, in spite of widespread Catholicism, which has vividly protested the public and private intervention.

Presently, "middle-class women" also shoulder the weight of private interests. Again, the impact on overall fertility rates is the same. Women who undergo C-operations tend to have fewer children, or none at all, after having had one C-section. The transversality of the cultural adoption of these contraceptive practices makes us rethink the feminist(s) binary

Maria Milagros López

between choice or no choice. The statistics also show that poor women in public hospitals who have undergone one C-operation tend to have at least one future vaginal birth, contrary to all expected probabilities.

If, since the 1950s, through publicly financed policies, sterilization has been the way to control the fertility of poor women, and migration the way to expel a significant portion of the Puerto Rican working-class population, in the 1980s, cesarean sections served the same purpose of controlling fertility for better-off women. Likewise, it has been documented that better educated Puerto Ricans have, for the last 25 years, constituted an important part of the migratory flux. "Middle-class" Puerto Rican women have been the object of the same regulatory policies while they, themselves, have financed it and convinced themselves of the merits of technological innovation and the flight from medical backwardness. In that sense, the international crises of capital since the 1970s have perversely democratized the technologies of non-reproduction. I want to argue the contemporary transversality of these regulatory practices and to emphasize that, despite our efforts, they are not a thing of the past or of distant places. The failure of modernization strategies has cut across social classes, although not so much across gender and racial lines. It has been displaced upwardly, for the last 25 years, as the collapse of the wage structure has left up to 70 percent of the population expelled or disqualified from the formal economy.

I also want to underline the encounter or reencounter of premodern cultural semantic basins with the postmodern requisites of State and Capital. If the lack of family planning is associated with premodernity, along with a present oriented disposition towards life, sterilization promises the same carefree attitude towards reproduction and the alteration of bodily capacities in the name of greater comfort. Surgically mediated bodies propose gender indifferentiation and permanent readiness for time and spatial dislocations under contemporary labor conditions and the disassembly of the Welfare State. More precisely, the carefree attitudes toward contraception that are usually associated with pre industrial times find a parallel in the technological dislocations that have resulted from modern and postmodern innovations. The premodern reencounters the postmodern in unexpected ways!

It is accurate, at least at this time in Puerto Rico, to say that most women want to have fewer children. In contrast to previous times, they don't think they have to have all the children they can. It is also probable that sterilization has become cultural second nature in the face of this recent consciousness—a revised common sense—and that soon C-sections will seem a natural way of giving birth. (It may even become associated with a more hygienic, predictable form of giving birth, complete with class overtones!) In these paradoxical ways, women effectively or phantasmagorically negotiate their subjection to reproductive mandates. Similarly, we are constantly reminded that agency is not acquired by the power of numbers.

Another source of regulatory reproductive practices for Puerto Rican women, particularly in the context of the United States (and which we share with African-American, other Latinas, and poorer women, and Native American women) is the tense relationship with the Welfare State. The notion of "behavioral technologies"[4] has been coined to describe practices such as wedfare, learnfare, and workfare. They are forms of regulation achieved mostly by reducing payments or making entitlements contingent on good behavior, such as working, attending job skills courses, not having more children (as in the case of the recent New Jersey legislation), marrying, living with one's mother, surveilling children's school attendance, demonstrating eagerness to learn English, and integrating into the American mainstream. In general, these regulations strive to recycle the work ethic under conditions of the structural impossibility of obtaining salaried work. The requests of the increasing conservative and punitive discourses against "welfare mothers" are that poor women have to train, retrain, integrate and do whatever necessary to stop depending. Some women, at least, have countered with the argument that their "middle-class" counterparts are not stigmatized for depending on their "middle-class" providers in order to stay home and take care of their children. Why is private patriarchy acceptable and public patriarchy considered repugnant in the age of the return of family values? Welfare recipients have come to feel "entitled" to receive subsidies from the public patriarch—the State. Hopefully, this sense of entitlement, which renders them disagreeable and ungrateful (clients with "an attitude," at least from the point of view of caseworkers), will not subside in the era of shrinking entitlements and will become sedimented as a contestatory gesture.

The questions for organized feminists are: Are we guilty of having shared in the common sense assumption that salaried work is the moral arbiter of a person's worth and insertion in the wage structure is the way out of subordination? If not, how can we render an account of the historical absence of the women's movement in welfare rights struggles? Does the majority of the feminist movement also feel repulsion for women who do not have salaried jobs or do not want them? Is it time to reconsider this alliance between welfare rights struggles and the feminist movement? Are we able,

Maria Milagros López

Plate 28: *Isla del Encanto*, 1986
Marina Gutierrez
Courtesy of Museo del Barrio and the artist

as we once claimed, to recognize and valorize labor outside of the wage structure?

The prospects for feminist alliances have matured within the context of the transversal class deterioration of labor conditions. The segmentation and fractionalization of tasks, the displacement of jobs towards the service sector, the loss of benefits for the employed working class, the amplification of subemployment and part-time jobs, and the reduced need for human labor threaten the ensemble of the population. Yet, unemployment and state dependence come to be seen increasingly as choice or moral turpitude.

I would argue that only after rethinking these questions can we address the violence of modernization strategies as they have made their claims on women's bodies and their reproductive rights and needs. As Nancy Fraser has suggested, we have to redefine the notions of needs and rights and demand the extension of the social wage.[5] Eventually, we may be able to redefine the notions of citizenship, reproductive needs, and consumption rights.

In Puerto Rico, feeding on the fertile ground of Catholicism, the struggle against anti-abortion groups has also started. Being pro-choice is presented by nationalist conservatives as being a pro-American woman whose loose morals constitute the dark, insidious side of American imperialism. Anti-choice officials position themselves as anti-American, pro-Puerto Rican nationhooders. As we can see, the issue of having choices becomes even more complex in this context of development strategies, women's bodies, and national colonial contradictions. The question of national identity and the survival of Puertoricanness has served both as a resistance, by separatists, to the use of women's bodies in the interest of colonial development strategies, as well as the recycling of the patriotic impulse that the responsibility to reproduce the nation under siege rests on women's shoulders.

In the transition toward the postmodern, the state's policy tends toward disentangling itself from costly public policies to allow groups in civil society to fight it out through their own means. The crises of modernizing strategies and population policies have left a vacuum that becomes filled with so-called personal choices—those dictated by micro-communities of interpretation—or the crudeness of private interests that we have witnessed with the C-operations.

The goal of reducing birth rates has been achieved and constitutes a part of contemporary common sense, as in earlier periods. Higher birth rates are now found among communities that have immigrated to Puerto Rico, as in the case of poor Dominicans. For them, the tightening of immigration policies, and the eventual loss of public health, social, and educational services are expected to serve as deterrents. So far, the organizational weakness of these groups and their fears of deportation have prevented mobilizations in the direction of asserting civil rights.

In conclusion, I would like to underscore the complexity of the personal and political issues that intersect with policies and private choices. Having declared that anatomy is not destiny our analysis and activisms must move in the direction of the understanding of temporal and spatial specificities. The contemporary discourses of personal reproductive freedom, of women's insertion in the labor force as an emancipatory gesture, and notions of rights, needs, and entitlements require a reassessment based on the changing nature of capital's and states' restructurings. Some feminisms have, in fact, come to admit that women's bodies are not just equal in their readiness to their subsumption to labor, but that perhaps we need to claim a space where there are needs that pertain to our role in reproduction. Rather than ignore them or minimize their importance we can reclaim them if only the metaphysics of labor can be questioned. Similarly, our positions in macro-politics and development strategies should guide our understanding and practices of contemporary ideologies of reproduction. While we need to hang on to notions of choice, choices need to be further problematized, as the Puerto Rican experience demonstrates. The terms of the debate have been transformed; at this moment choice has become, at best, a double-edged sword.

Notes

1. José L. Vázquez Calzada, "La Esterilización femenina en Puerto Rico," *Revista de Ciencias Sociales* 17, no. 3 (September 1973): 281–308.

2. Vázquez Calzada, *Las Incógnitas de los partos por cesárea en Puerto Rico* (unpublished manuscript, Escuela de Salud Pública, Recinto de Ciencias Médicas, University of Puerto Rico, 1991).

3. "Operation Bootstrap" was the name given to a development strategy put forth by the popular democratic party in 1952.

4. M. Abramovitz, "The New Paternalism," *The Nation* (October 5, 1992): 368–372.

5. Nancy Fraser, "The Struggle over Needs: Outline of a Socialist Feminist Critical Theory of Late Capitalist Political Culture," in L. Gordon, ed., *Women, the State and Welfare* (Madison: University of Wisconsin Press, 1990), 199–225.

Isabelle R. Gunning

Cutting through the Obfuscation:
Female Genital Surgeries in Neoimperial Culture

In recent years several films and television programs have "discovered" female genital surgeries (FGS),[1] making them more of a topic than before for American news editorials and feminist discussion. In an editorial column for the *New York Times,* A. M. Rosenthal proposes a Tarzan-like plan to "bring about the end of a system of torture" common in about thirty African countries.[2] Such a rescue operation, according to Rosenthal, can be easily realized because "all it demands is the will of the American people and their Congress," which need only allocate money and create a commission to eradicate the problem. Dominant discourse on FGS has suffered, not surprisingly, from an "arrogant perception"[3] that aggrandizes Western culture while ignoring its own patriarchal practices, which have had devastating consequences for women both in the United States and abroad. FGS discourse also tends to denigrate all other cultures, typically African, virtually in their entirety.

As feminists of color we have little expectation of mainstream representations of ourselves and our sisters. But how an issue like FGS is talked about by feminists of color in the First World and how it affects our relationship with African and Third World immigrant women present opportunities to re-examine and problematize our "Westernness." When I characterize myself as a "Western" feminist, I am engaged in a struggle of "coming to terms with terms," i.e., the complexity of being a "woman of color" in a "First World" nation-state. We all have inherited certain historically constructed categories within which we may fit with a greater or lesser degree of comfort. Like many U.S. born and raised African-Americans, I have felt both a personal and political alienation from the United States and from eurocentric political and cultural perspectives while I also identify with the struggles of people of color, especially those of the

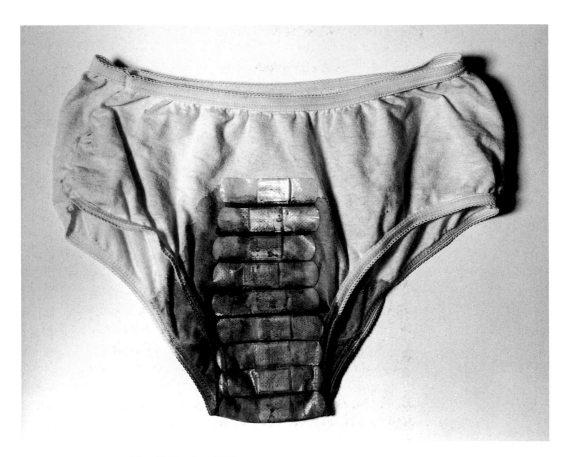

Plate 29: *Panties*, 1994
Black and white reproduction of color slide
Band-aids, acrylic, fabric, 9½ × 10″
Dolores Zorreguieta
Courtesy of the artist

Isabelle R. Gunning

working class, both in the United States and internationally. Thus, while I see, claim, and struggle for an identification with African feminists and other feminists of color, I continue in this context to describe myself as "First World" out of a recognition that as a First World feminist of color, despite racism, I cannot eradicate all the historical and class formations that tie me to imperial culture. Identification and alliance among feminists of color, however, takes place within specific discursive frameworks that have significant implications for specific arenas of struggle. In this paper I will focus on the links between the cultural debate on FGS and their impact on domestic law against FGS in the U.S. The problem can be explored by comparing the representation discourses of "liberal" feminists of color to the discourses of "progressive" feminists of color.

Alice Walker[4] and Pratibha Parmar's *Warrior Marks*,[5] in both film and book form, has received serious publicity, contributing to the increasing visibility of FGS in this country. Although *Warrior Marks* focuses on the conflicted agony of circumcised African mothers who carry on the tradition, and includes a few determined women who oppose it, Alice Walker is privileged by the narrative. Walker's "starring" in the film has been a point of controversy. Some see her analogy between female genital mutilation and her own partial blindness, the result of an accident caused by her brother, as self-aggrandizing.[6] Why not let the true women warriors, the African women involved, be portrayed as the heroes of their own lives and "star" in the film? Surely a major thrust of all feminist (or womanist[7]) work is to undermine eurocentric patriarchal notions of the concept of women, especially African women. By silencing FGS activists, Walker and Parmar reproduce eurocentric film imagery rather than "reintroduc[ing] the African into history . . . since for approximately four centuries Africans have been expelled from its domain by capitalism, colonialism and imperialism."[8]

These are serious criticisms. I do see in Walker, an African-American woman, and Parmar, an Indian-Kenyan-British woman, a rejection of the racism, colonialism, imperialism, sexism, and homophobia of First World culture, as First World diaspora women who identify personally and politically with Africa and the Third World generally. But Parmar and Walker cannot fairly represent a critique of the oppression of African women without challenging the discourse integral to that oppression. In starring in *Warrior Marks,* Walker not only silences the voices of African women,[9] she also reinvigorates the familiar and negative representations of African people. Walker's analogy between female genital mutilation and her own blinding does have the virtue of evoking the general societal violence perpetrated, "formally" or "informally," against women by people who love us. However, since her own injury takes place in another context, the film fails to contextualize FGS within their own cultures as well as within the various misogynistic global cultures.

Beyond Walker's prominent appearance in the film and book, African feminists in the U.S., Britain, and on the Continent have been concerned with the film's representations of the people involved with the surgery. Parmar and Walker's representation of diverse African cultures is reduced to the image of the female circumciser,[10] who is described as being in "complicity"—the epitome of all mothers and grandparents. The description mocks the circumciser's status within her culture by discussing her crown of authority in quotation marks, focussing on the "gunk" under her fingernails and dismissing the gold jewelry, apparent marks of her stature, as "very cheap." Walker and Parmar later suggest that the only "real link" that African women have with their Egyptian heritage is the surgeries, implying there is nothing else of value in African/Egyptian culture. Given this discourse, it hardly comes as a surprise that even African feminists who vigorously oppose FGS and who support legitimate critiques of *some* practices of their culture, have been enraged by this criticism wrapped in apparent disdain for all that they value. First World women of color, in such instances, can sound dangerously like the old and still vital imperialist: what we have is great, or at least defensible, while what you have is worthless.

Two African feminist immigrants to the U.S., Seble Dawit, a human rights lawyer in New York City, and Salem Mekuria, a filmmaker and teacher at Wellesley College, wrote an article published in the *New York Times* on behalf of several African feminists long active in the fight to abolish the surgeries. The authors took "great exception to the recent Western focus on female genital mutilation in Africa, most notably by the novelist, Alice Walker."[11] Criticizing Walker and Parmar for representing Africans in a monolithic way, "common in Western depictions," they take issue with the portrayal of African women and girls as lacking personality or autonomy; all they can do is wait for Walker, the "heroine-savior," to rescue them from the circumciser who has been transformed by the film into a "slit-eyed murderer." Parmar and Walker's isolation of the surgeries as "the gender oppression to end all gender oppressions" is viewed by Mekuria and Dawit as a reduction of the surgeries to one symbolic example among numerous gender oppressions that transforms them into an "emotive lens through which to view personal pain," as well as "a gauge by which to measure distance between the West and the rest of humanity." They end by raising the problematic of so identifying with the "similarities" or ties that do connect us as women that we lose sight of our own perspectives and necessary distances and overwhelm the voice of those "others." "Neither Alice Walker nor any of us here can speak for them [hundreds of African women on the continent who are working to eradicate the surgeries]; but if we have the power and the resources, we can create room for them to speak, and to speak with us as well."

Despite Walker's and Parmar's good intentions, which resulted in good deeds,[12] the discourse they employ in *Warrior Marks* is embedded in eurocentric representation. By deploying the monolithic, static images of Africa and her peoples in an effort to reach First World audiences, Parmar and Walker's critique of FGS simultaneously reinvigorates those very destructive myths. In breathing more life into the myths, Third World feminists are further constrained in their attempts to represent themselves and their struggles in the First World in complex ways. In contrast to Walker and Parmar's *Warrior Marks,* the documentary film *Fire Eyes,* directed by Soraya Mire, a young, circumcised Somalian-American filmmaker, offers a different perspective on FGS.[13] A highly contextualized film, both locally and globally, *Fire Eyes* tells Mire's story of enduring FGS, later followed by her decision to undertake reconstructive surgery. The film emphasizes the positive dimensions of Somalian culture. It does not attempt to show abstract, exotic, or savage Africa; it is culturally specific, unique, detailed, and beautiful. It also does not present the static, single-perspective view of Africa. Mire interviews a broad range of Somalians, from men and a few women who continue to cling to the surgeries to the women and men who oppose them. Mire's intimate knowledge of Somalian culture enables her to show its contradictions and tensions. The women interviewees who endured the surgeries describe how alone they felt before they had "that piece of flesh removed" and how loved and accepted they felt afterwards. The feminists *Fire Eyes* profiles are men and women who would not characterize Somalian grandmothers, mothers, and daughters as acting in "complicity;" they are too aware of their diverse cultural practices as well as the socio-economic forces that affect Somalians. They love and respect their culture, their elders, while still being critical of this particular aspect of it and of them.

Significantly, *Fire Eyes* also places the surgery in a global context of patriarchal control over the female body and sexuality. Rather than single out African traditions, the film, overall, makes clear that every culture has a way of mutilating women. The surgeries continue to be performed in the

United States—and not just on immigrant Third World women, as the dominant mythology suggests. Mire interviews a white American woman whose parents had her clitoris removed when she was one and a half years old because they thought her external genitalia were "too large."[14] A group of African-American women also discuss the fact that the surgeries have been performed in the U.S. in cases where parents felt that their daughters "masturbated excessively." The documentary's narrator, furthermore, underscores the point that FGS constitute but one example of global violence against women, as the camera flashes images of women from various countries around the world, including the United States, Thailand, and China.

This contextualized approach is shared by many African feminists whose voices have been heard at times in mainstream U.S. media. The ABC news program *Day One* ran a show on the surgeries in 1993 featuring interviews with several African feminists.[15] Two of the women, Safia Singeteh and Efua Dorkenoo, activists in women's health organizations, did not target FGS as the "gender oppression to end all gender oppression." Rather, they situated FGS within the context of a panoply of women's health issues requiring educational efforts. Singeteh clarified the cultural context—the fears and the courage—while Dr. Nahid Toubia, a Sudanese obstetrician, long active against the surgeries, made quite clear that breast implantation is an analogue to FGS because mutilating our bodies is a cross-cultural phenomenon that involves "comply[ing] with a certain social definition of being a woman."

Articulating a multicultural feminist perspective within the public sphere, however, poses serious challenges. Even when a Toubia speaks or a Mire crafts a film that conveys the complexity of African feminists' positions on FGS, there is always the danger their statements will be understood and used in reductive stereotypical ways by the dominant media. When Mire, for example, appeared on the *Oprah Winfrey Show* (September 14, 1995), she had to address a set of eurocentric questions posed, ironically, by an African-American women who has fought for women's rights. Despite Mire's insistent attempts to contextualize her personal pain and her continuing love of her family and culture, her passionate remarks were disrupted by Winfrey's questions, which largely revolved around the inability of "us" Americans to understand how "you other" women could put up with such things. Yet, even First World feminists of color who work within alternative organizations face the danger of simplification. We could view Mire through that "emotive lens." Her articulation of her pain seems so like our own, or like what we imagine our pain to be like, that we assume too much about our ties and connectedness with her or any other woman who has endured the surgeries. Now that we "have" her, we could begin to think that we can speak for all women combatting the surgeries and ignore the more critical voices, like those of Dawit or Merkuria, who demand much more of us in recognizing both ties and distance.

Both the *Oprah Winfrey Show* and *Warrior Marks* show that First World feminists of color can project a eurocentric perspective. Given the ties with imperial cultures, we have more access to the media, which privilege our voices over those of Third World feminists, especially when we allow our voices to recycle and reinvigorate eurocentric discourse. We must first acknowledge such power relations among people of color. While FGS make headlines, the voices of feminists such as Toubia and Mire are marginalized. Struggling to eradicate these vestiges of eurocentrism is an integral part of the building of relationships and connections between First and Third World feminists. Moreover, how First World feminists, especially those of us of color, represent FGS in the public sphere has consequences in other political arenas. If our representations mimic those of the dominant media, then those same simplistic and demeaning representations will provide the framework for the kinds of solutions that are proposed around the eradication of the surgeries. The increasingly high profile of the FGS debates in the United States has led to the proposal of legal solutions to combat the surgeries. Assuming a eurocentric perspective and a self-righteous approach, the American neo-imperial myth reemerges: that with little research or guidance from Third World feminists, "we" could pass American laws; and that, through the simple criminalization of the surgeries in this country, "we" could have a positive effect on the reduction of the practice in the U.S. A more complex, contextualized approach would have been enlightened by unsuccessful colonial attempts to outlaw FGS[16] and from current Third World feminists battling FGS in order to craft solutions that acknowledge the interrelationships between law and other aspects of people's lives.

In late 1993 Representative Patricia Schroeder (D-Colorado) introduced the Federal Prohibition of Female Genital Mutilation Act of 1994 on the floor of the United States House of Representatives.[17] A companion bill on the Senate side was also introduced.[18] The law was finally enacted in 1996.[19] The Federal Female Genital Mutilation (FGM) Act makes the performance of the surgeries on a minor a felonious crime, punishable by a fine or imprisonment for up to five years. No violation would occur if the procedure were "necessary for the health" of the patient *and* "performed by medical professionals." Specifically, the Act notes no violation would occur if the surgeries were "performed on a person [*sic*] in labor or just giving birth." The Act also makes it a misdemeanor to deny medical treatment to anyone who has had the surgeries done or who has requested that the surgeries be performed on another. The Act further directs the secretary of Health and Human Services to compile data on the numbers of women who have had the surgeries done, both in the U.S. and abroad, with a particular focus on children; and to identify the communities that practice FGS in the U.S., such that educational activities to inform people of the health risks would be designed and implemented. The proposed educational efforts are to be done in collaboration with "representatives of ethnic groups and representatives of organizations which have expertise in prevention of FGM."

The text of the Act focuses on children, girls under the age of eighteen, who might undergo the surgeries. Indeed, in the remarks made during the introduction of the Act, the surgeries are described as "a horrific form of child abuse as well as a human rights violation." [20] The imagery here is not that of conflicted parents, although mention is made of the great societal pressures to perform the ritual.

What is the impact of having such a federal crime enacted? Not all the ramifications can be predicted, but some results may not come about as the congressional sponsors intended. As one senator recounts the story of the Egyptian men who held down and spread the legs of a little girl so that a cable news crew could film her surgery, one gets the impression that the Act's sponsors envision these men as the likely criminals to be targeted. Or when Senator Reid notes that a constituent wrote him to say that her gynecologist told her "that a colleague of his in Los Angeles regularly performed this ritual legally," [21] one imagines that Reid sees unscrupulous medical personnel as the likely targets. However, given that the majority of traditional circumcisers comprises women, it is likely that it will be immigrant African and Middle Eastern women who will be arrested and prosecuted. This prospect of trying and imprisoning women in the name of liberating women from a patriarchal practice raises serious dilemmas for feminists.

French feminists have faced a similar conflict in recent years. The criminalization of the surgeries or "excisions" has involved a polarized debate between "universalism" and "cultural relativism" that has largely lost sight of the intricate and concrete reality of the lives of immigrant women—the subjects of the debate. [22] The controversy around the criminalization law has painfully divided both the progressive community in general and the feminist community in particular. The pro-trial feminists want to use the legal system to pressure those who practice the surgeries to stop. However, their justifications have often been couched in questionable terms or interpreted as wholesale attacks on African culture. Additionally, the targets of the prosecutions have largely been circumcisers and parents, particularly mothers. Anti-trial feminists, who work on grassroots organizing and educating of immigrant women, have viewed criminalization as victimizing the victim and, consequently, they see it as inappropriate and insensitive to the complex realities of immigrant women's lives.

Some of the problems and tensions identified in France seem very likely to emerge in the American context since the surgeries have been criminalized. Fundamentally, the American legal system is included in the French feminist criticism of the criminalization law. Within this analysis, "western legal systems, based as they are on a concept of the individual that not only excludes women's specific reality as women but also fails to account for differences in social, cultural and economic conditions that will affect how the system operates, can at the very best provide only a partial solution to what is fundamentally a political and cultural problem."[23] U.S. legal scholars, of course, have made similar criticisms about the U.S. legal system. The U.S. has its own history of racialized representations of the "simple native" or "noble savage." Since patriarchal discourse continues to dichotomize life into "public" and "private" spheres, leaving issues regarding the safety of women and children inadequately protected, one can easily imagine that criminalization of the surgeries in this country could well produce an American version of the cultural relativism versus universalism debate.

That debate has already appeared in conjunction with the various uses of the cultural defense arguments that have been employed in American courts with varying degrees of success. The types of cases range from one involving a Japanese mother charged with the murder of her children (the cultural defense involved the assertion of a different worldview of handling shame through parent-child suicide) to a case involving a Laotian refugee man charged with the stabbing murder of his wife following a phone call from a former boyfriend (the cultural defense here also involved a different worldview on handling shame that triggered an excusable loss of self control).[24] In these cases, the cultural defense was raised in an effort to excuse behavior that would be considered criminal activity under U.S. law by showing that the same behavior would be considered acceptable in a different culture. FGS could constitute maiming or child abuse and,

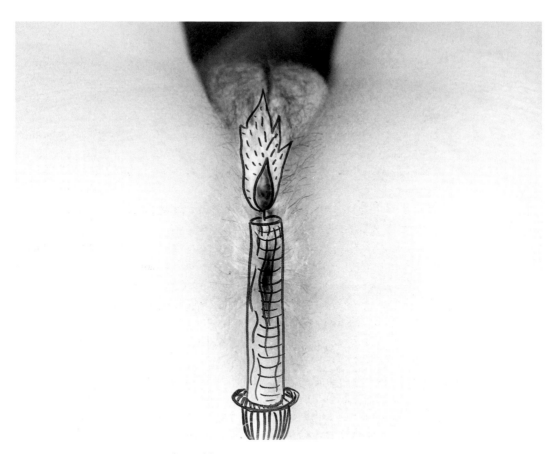

Plate 30: *Flammable*, 1995
Black and white photograph and black ink
Donna Han
Courtesy of the artist

arguably, the cultural defense could be raised to ensure that the surgeries could be performed in this country without sanction. The problem confronting (and possibly dividing) progressives and multicultural feminists is already emerging and would surely erupt around the FGS here as it did in France. "Minority" cultures, Third World cultures, are entitled to receive respect. Yet some practices of different cultures may be as patriarchal and repressive as any "homegrown" variant that feminists and progressives would ordinarily combat. How do progressives and multicultural feminists make distinctions between "good" and "bad" practices, whether within their own communities or in other communities and, more problematic, how can the legal system be entrusted to understand and effectuate such distinctions?

The federal bill assumes culturally sensitive education as a major part of the bill. The contours of the reality of the educational component could be all important. However, the political-cultural perspectives of the chosen "representatives of ethnic groups and representatives of organizations which have expertise in the prevention of FGM," and the nature of the funding for such educational efforts, are crucial. My concerns regarding the "representatives" focus again on First World feminists interested in the eradication of FGS. Which ones will be selected? By whom? And through what process? Most significantly, which discourses on FGS will they represent and present? In France an underfunded educational campaign had preceded and currently accompanies the criminalization of the surgeries. French pro-trial feminists seem to exhibit either an indifference to the educational component or an oversimplification of what such an educational campaign involves. The isolation Third World immigrant women experience as a result of their separation from family, neighbors, and the community's familiar cultural fabric is not addressed by white French or U.S. women. Isolation suggests more than just an inability to speak French or English or to find a doctor who could explain the necessity of not performing the surgeries on one's daughter in one's language. It suggests the absence of intimate others, friends, relatives, neighbors, who understand one's situation and reaffirm one's sense of self and value. Exacerbated by displacement this need that we all have may be underestimated by First World feminists, including women of color, whose own cultural experience emphasizes "rugged" individualism. This unquestioned individualism is one eurocentric cultural aspect that may not be shared by the more communitarian ethnic communities in which organizations find themselves providing educational support.[25] It is certainly not the only difference. It is an example of any number of presumptions and cultural perspectives that must be unmasked in order to make concrete connections with women from different cultural contexts. As for the federal bill, the ability of First World feminists involved in the eradication of the surgeries to recognize both similarities and differences in the way patriarchy affects women will likely mark the success or failure of any educational effort.

The other concern with the federal bill is funding. My fear is that this issue could become analogous to the current move to prosecute drug addicted mothers for child abuse.[26] There was a time over ten years ago, for example, when I practiced as a public defender, when criminal statutes were invoked against addicts for drug possession; but there was some understanding in the law and legal system of the physical and psychological aspects of addiction and, to a lesser extent, the social and economic conditions, such as poverty, that affect drug addicts. It was not unusual for convictions to result in placements in drug rehabilitation programs. As the political climate has changed, dwindling funds remain for such programs. Our "war on drugs," rather than focus on major drug distributors at home and abroad, has armed and aimed its big guns on poor addicts, largely those of color, and prison is seen as the singular solution.[27] It is in this changed political climate that addict mothers, who never had much access to rehabilitation programs anyway since most programs specifically excluded pregnant women,[28] find themselves under attack. And still, resources are not allocated to get at the root of the problem. At a time when the dominant political discourse of well-off white Americans can only be characterized as "hateful" towards other "fellow" Americans, I fear that there will be little sensitivity or compassion afforded "foreigners." We are already in the grips of virulent anti-immigrant sentiments recycled and reaffirmed through the media. The representation of Third World immigrants—especially, but far from exclusively, undocumented—or "illegals" as dangers to and stains upon the national culture already exists. The bill could, through underfunding, produce too few results in an unrealistically short period of time and then the shift might be towards prosecution through the federal bill and perhaps through state child abuse statutes, as the sole solution.

The criminalization of the surgeries could have other effects, namely deportation problems. The Immigration and Naturalization Act (INA) makes an alien deportable if s/he has been convicted of certain types of crimes.[29] An immigrant convicted of a crime of moral turpitude is deportable if the crime was committed within five years after his/her date of entry and the sentence suspended or imposed is greater than one year; if

Isabelle R. Gunning

more than one crime involving moral turpitude is committed, no limitations on the period of time one has lived in the country or the amount of prison time imposed are observed. Whether the proposed federal bill outlines a crime of "moral turpitude" is an open question. The issue of what constitutes a crime of moral turpitude and whether the immigration statutes invoking this language are unconstitutional because of the "void for vagueness" doctrine have plagued the courts and immigration classes for years.[30] There is no satisfactory definition of crime of moral turpitude, although the Supreme Court has resolved the constitutional question in the immigration context, in part, by noting that the "void for vagueness" doctrine is used to warn individuals of the *criminal* consequences of particular acts they commit.[31] Courts struggling with the definition focus on the inherent nature of the act or the extent to which "the violations are generally considered essentially immoral [by moral standards prevailing in contemporary society]."[32] Will an act that has been characterized as a "horrific form of child abuse and a human rights violation" be a crime of moral turpitude? If the answer turns out to be "yes" then traditional immigrant circumcisers and parents, mothers perhaps most particularly, will be subject, not only to criminal prosecution and imprisonment, but also to banishment from the country. Conceivably, this could occur even if there were no conviction. If the commission of the surgeries is considered a crime of moral turpitude, then "admitting having committed" the crime would make one excludable, i.e., one who could be prevented from entering the country.[33] Even if one made a successful entry, the deportation statutes make "any alien who at the time of entry . . . was within one or more of the classes of aliens excludable by law . . . deportable."[34] Thus, an admission that one has committed a crime of moral turpitude means one should never have been allowed to enter the country in the first place; and one's original "inadmissibility" is itself grounds for deportation now.

The INA also makes deportable any alien convicted of an "aggravated felony." Originally, language on "aggravated felons" was designed to reach drug traffickers as part of the "war on drugs" but has since expanded to include a range of serious crimes, including "crimes of violence."[35] The statutory definition of a crime of violence is "an offense that has as an element the use, attempted use or threatened use of physical force against the person or property of another. . . ."[36] Thus the performance of the surgeries, as a crime, could easily fit into the category of aggravated felonies and thereby subject convicted Third World immigrant women to deportation, largely without the benefit of any of the typical forms of relief from deportation.[37]

The specific statutory interpretation accorded the language in the federal bill and related immigration statutes will likely follow the rise or (hopeful) fall of anti-immigrant sentiment in this country. But even the more sympathetic interpretations of current laws, in the immigration context, involve the original problem that I have been exploring. The laws employ a certain racialized, imperial rhetoric and framework and thereby make it difficult to articulate the needs and circumstances of Third World immigrant women without employing the very terms one wants to combat. How can multicultural feminists, then, fight patriarchy without entering another patriarchal and racist framework? The terms of the FGS public and legal debate assume simplistically a victimizer and a victimized. With such discursive framework, legal practice forces women who oppose FGS to denounce everything about their culture and to be rescued by the A. M. Rosenthals, at worst, or the Walkers, Parmars, and Winfreys, at best.

The highly publicized immigration/refugee case of Lydia Oluloro, a Nigerian woman, exemplifies some of the issues at stake. Requesting suspension of deportation or asylum because of Oluloro's fear that if she returned to Nigeria her two young, U.S. citizen daughters would be forced to endure the surgeries,[38] Oluloro's lawyer, Tilman Hasche, mounted a vigorous and successful defense to her deportation, but, in doing so, relied upon a reductionist, racialized representation of FGS and Nigerian-Yoruba culture.[39] Although the surgeries are somewhat more accurately contextualized when Hasche underscores that they are performed "*out of love for their children*,"[40] the main and initial characterization is totally consistent with the civilized-barbaric oppositional imagery: FGS are described as "a brutal, gruesome ritual that violates the most fundamental notions of decency and civilization at the heart of this Republic."[41] This distance between "us" in the civilized West and "them" in barbaric Africa is emphasized at several points, in tortured ways. Hasche notes that while the situation in Nigeria is improving, women in Nigeria are still "forced to endure second class citizenship and are subject to myriad legal, social and economic disabilities. . . . [T]o this date Nigerian law and society . . . discriminate against women with respect to divorce, inheritance, widowhood rights, and reproductive rights; and tolerate domestic violence against women."[42] To be sure, there are differences between the U.S. and Nigeria—for example, in the continued existence of laws allowing child marriage and polygamy, which are outlawed in the U.S. But the great distance between "us" and "them" seems quite tortured when one is well aware that in the U.S. sexism, racism, patriarchy, rape, and other violence plague U.S. women; or

Isabelle R. Gunning

when one understands that U.S. women tend to become impoverished through divorce; see, increasingly, our reproductive rights eroded; and continue to battle against the indifference of American police forces and society when it comes to domestic violence.

The immigration judge, Kendall Warren, rejected Oluloro's plea for asylum but did grant her withholding of deportation. Operating within a eurocentric discursive framework, Judge Warren accepted the FGS representations and described them, without any irony, as procedures used "in some cultures," notably in "male dominated patriarchal societies to repress women's status and sexuality."[43] He did not appear to be aware that the U.S. was one such culture that has practiced the surgeries, nor did he acknowledge that we, too, constitute a "male-dominated patriarchal society." Judge Warren did not wholly buy into the notion of a unidimensional ignorant native woman, remarking that Oluloro was not as innocent as her lawyer portrayed her when she committed various fraudulent acts in order to stay in the country, that "she is an educated and intelligent woman and seemed to have a clear understanding of all the issues in this case and was very articulate in expressing her feelings and thoughts."[44] However, her humanity, individuality, and strength are wiped out, according to the judge, because she is "a member of the Yoruba tribe where the husband is boss. . . ."[45] The judge's analysis of why Oluloro might have felt pressured to lie did not rest upon her unfamiliarity with U.S. customs and laws, her social isolation in a new and different culture and country, her financial dependence upon her husband, or her fear of the physical and sexual violence that her husband perpetrated upon her.[46] Although these circumstances could pressure any woman, or person, regardless of race or culture, to take extreme measures to protect herself and her children, the judge, instead, focused on "tribalism." It is as if the violence of a Yoruba husband is somehow greater than that of a John Fedders.[47] The former is treated as norm, the latter as an aberration.

The "othering" of this form of the patriarchal practice of male domination of women allows the judge to "forgive" Oluloro her fraudulent behavior, which might otherwise have prevented her from being granted relief. It is actually hard to imagine how a judge could honestly contextualize and represent the situation of a woman like Oluloro and still "bend" the law in a way that would help her by allowing her to stay in the country. After all, to acknowledge the similarities and connections between the two patriarchal cultures, American and Nigerian, Judge Warren would have had to focus, not on any particular patriarchal practice like FGS or specific ethnic methods of expressing misogyny, but rather on the broader question of domestic violence and male domination. Were he to do that it is not clear whether he could then characterize returning to Nigeria as constituting an "extreme hardship," as immigration law requires. The racialized, oppositional representation was an essential aspect of the legal discourse involved in Oluloro's case. Neither her attorney nor the judge had much room to break free of the discursive parameters—not if she were to be allowed to have her own wishes granted, i.e., to stay in the United States.

The explicit use of eurocentric language in the introduction of the federal FGM Act, as well as the continuing vitality of the stereotypical imagery used to marshal public opinion against the surgeries, have raised concerns about the possible impact of the federal FGM Act on the ways immigrant women might use current immigration laws. The very fact that the FGM Act simultaneously criminalizes the surgeries and initiates research on the extent of the problem criminalized suggests that the motivations are largely symbolic. How can one know what the appropriate solution to a problem is without having studied it thoroughly beforehand? The "solutions" proposed are, consequently, problematic.

I would have preferred that the federal FGM Act had been passed *only* in terms of its research component, i.e., the compilation of data on the numbers of women and children in the U.S. who have had the surgeries performed, the identification of the communities that practice FGS in the U.S., and the creation of anti-FGS educational activities and materials. As the Act proposes, these efforts should be shared with "representatives of ethnic groups and . . . organizations which have expertise in the prevention of FGM." The experts the legal system has to turn to are those African feminists who have long experience in combatting the surgeries both in African and Middle Eastern countries as well as in the First World. While the Act's language suggests that the educational effort would revolve around informing people of the health risks attendant to FGS, more than information on health risks needs to be part of the campaign. A more fundamental question will be how are *any* of the health needs of the women and children in the identified communities being met? And if they are not being met, how will they be serviced? More than just health needs will have to be a part of this educational effort if it has any chance of being successful. How are immigrant women and children connecting linguistically, educationally, economically, and socially with each other and with other "indigenous" American communities? A serious anti-FGM campaign cannot isolate itself from the other aspects of the lives of the people in the targeted communities. Such a comprehensive research and educational approach needs to precede criminalization legislation, which risks penalizing, again, the very women the legal system and the media claim to want to help.

First World feminists of color, in particular, need to be ever vigilante in the discourses we use to represent and combat FGS. While we as feminists ought not become paralyzed in the face of the need to combat and eradicate FGS and all culturally dictated mutilations of women, it does become essential that we be mindful of the context within which we battle and engage, as well as of the tools we use to reach our goals. We need to search for and create imagery and language that contexutalize and empower rather than cling uncritically to the familiar. Such a struggle has to take place in conjunction with that of Third World feminists who have organized around FGS. Such a dialogue would have to involve a critique of our own historical context of imperialism and racism as well as the specific, complex cultural contexts in which Third World feminists both battle and love.[48]

Our representations of FGS become important as we face practical battles to connect and support immigrant Third World women in legal forums. The law is more than a powerful referent in our lives, it exerts power over our lives. But we need always be mindful of its limitations. The categorizations and definitions that the legal system may require us to use to improve the life of one particular woman, like Oluloro, can never become the defining categories of our analyses. They are fictions that we may be forced to use. But our larger struggle around FGS must be articulated as part of the culturally diverse violences committed against women's bodies by racially diverse patriarchies. Our struggle to eradicate all forms of patriarchal violence, therefore, must be located within the multifaceted realities that inform diverse feminist struggles.

Notes

1. I have wrestled with the problem of what term to characterize the surgeries: mutilation? circumcision? clitoridectomy? I felt keenly the concern that some activists and scholars have raised, which is that some African feminists are rightly insulted by the term "mutilation." My own view was that "circumcision," which may well accurately describe the *sunna* form of the surgeries and overstate the case of symbolic prickings, still conveys a false sense of parity with male circumcision. While the symbolism and ritual may be intended to do exactly that, both the *sunna* and infibulation forms of the surgeries are more physically invasive of the female genitalia

than the male circumcision is of the male genitals. "Clitoridectomy," too, is an accurate description of some forms of the surgeries, but not all. Consequently, I most often use the term "female genital surgeries." Surgeries, in the plural, conveys the sense that there is a range of procedures involved. Moreover, the term "surgeries" is meant to remind the reader that the cutting and manipulation of the female body is a multicultural phenomenon; in First World countries these procedures are given "scientific" status through the medical community and called "surgery" (as in breast implant surgery or breast reduction surgery), but serve similar controlling functions as FGS.

2. A. M. Rosenthal, "On My Mind: The Possible Dream," *New York Times,* June 13, 1995, A25. Mr. Rosenthal has written a number of editorials denouncing the surgeries. Other American columnists have joined him in editorializing about the surgeries. See, for example, William Raspberry, "Women and a Brutal 'Tradition,'" *Washington Post,* November 8, 1993, A21; and Judy Mann, "Women Launching Effort to Halt Barbaric Mutilation Ritual," *Rocky Mountain News,* January 31, 1994, A26.

3. Refer to Isabelle R. Gunning, "Arrogant Perception, World-Travelling and Multicultural Feminism: The Case of Female Genital Surgeries," *Columbia Human Rights Law Review* 23: 189 (1992).

4. Alice Walker is a well-known, Pulitzer Prize winning author who has written, among other works, an intense fictionalized account of a woman who has the surgeries performed upon her. Alice Walker, *Possessing the Secret of Joy.* (Harcourt Brace1992).

5. Alice Walker and Pratibha Parmar, *Warrior Marks: Female Genital Mutilation and the Sexual Blinding of Women* (Harcourt Brace, 1993).

6. This point was flagged for me by several participants, notably Inderpal Grewal and Caren Kaplan, at the conference *Questions of Women, Culture and Difference,* sponsored by the University of Washington, Seattle, May 17–18, 1995.

7. *Alice Walker, In Search of our Mother's Gardens* (Harcourt Brace, 1984), xi. Walker defines the "womanist" as a "black feminist or feminist of color."

8. Kagendo Murungi, "Get Away from My Genitals!: A Commentary on Warrior Marks," *Interstices* 2 (11): 13 (Spring, 1994) (quoting Ntongela Masilela). On eurocentric film history see Ella Shohat and Robert Stam, *Unthinking Eurocentrism: Multiculturalism and the Media,* (Routledge, 1994).

9. Some feminists have defended Walker by noting that it was not easy to get African women to speak about FGS on camera. While there is some truth to that (after all, breaking social taboos is typically a dangerous venture for women), the Walker-Parmar crew had few prior connections or contacts with the women they at-

tempted to interview or the ones who ultimately agreed to be interviewed. The project was not the result of some longstanding collaborative feminist project that could establish trust and understanding between and among all the women warriors involved. Indeed, since it was not clear until later which particular African country they would be able to film in, the crew members knew little about the language, history, or politics of the parts of Gambia in which they spent their two weeks filming. See Caren Kaplan, *Remarks Before the Society for Cinema Studies Conference: March 3, 1995* at 4–6. (copy on file with author).

10. Alice Walker, "A Legacy of Betrayal," *Ms. Magazine,* (November–December 1993), 55. This article is an excerpt from the film script and underscores the representational problem.

11. Seble Dawit and Salem Merkuria, "The West Just Doesn't Get It; Let Africans Fight Genital Mutilation," *New York Times,* December 7, 1993, A27.

12. Some African feminists who are long time combatants against the surgeries were consulted for the movie/book and other groups have lauded Walker's work. The Inter-African Committee Against Harmful Traditional Practices congratulated her efforts at the movie's Washington, D.C., premiere. Moreover, Walker has used funds from the screenings to provide support and room for the unsung heroes to work and speak.

13. Mire produced *Fire Eyes* with the financial assistance of philanthropist Laurence Rockefeller, Kodak, singer Michael Jackson, and Alice Walker. See Renee Tawa, "Shattering the Silence," *Los Angeles Times* March 12, 1995, F1

14. This woman's experience is but one example of the routine use of genital surgeries to construct socially acceptable genitalia and genders in hermaphrodite or intersexed infants and children. See Suzanne Kessler, "The Medical Construction of Gender: Case Management of Intersexed Infants," *Signs* 16: 3 (Autumn 1990)

15. ABC, *Day One,* September 20, 1993 (transcript obtained through LEXIS/NEXIS).

16. Gunning, "Arrogant Perception," 227–229. The earliest attempts to prohibit FGS in an African country occurred in Kenya in 1906 by the Church of Scotland. Allison Slack, "Female Circumcision: A Critical Appraisal," *Human Rights Quarterly* 10: 437, 477 (1988). Similar efforts were made by Christian missionaries in Senegal, the Gambia, and Egypt. In Kenya, the indigenous people were largely unsupportive of the anti-FGS legislation. Indeed, under the postcolonial presidency of Jomo Kenyatta, the government expressed pride and approval in the practice. Slack, Female Circumcision: A Critical Appraisal, at 447. President Kenyatta remarked that "[t]he overwhelming majority of [the local people] believe that it is the secret aim of those who attack this country's old custom to disintegrate their social order and thereby hasten their Europeanization" (Jomo Kenyatta, *Facing Mt.*

Kenya: The Tribal Life of the Kikuyu, (Random House, 1953) 133. In 1946, the Sudan passed a law prohibiting the most popular and radical of the surgeries, the pharaonic type or infibulation, although the law still allowed for the removal of the "free and projecting parts of the clitoris" (Slack, 477). The law and the anti-FGS campaign which accompanied it came in response to pressure from the British colonial authorities. The law was rarely enforced, and while it did lead to an increased use of the milder *sunna* form, infibulations are still widespread in the Sudan (Slack, 478, n. 169).

17. H.R. 7546, 103rd Cong., 1st sess. (1993).

18. S. 2501, 103rd Cong., 2d. sess. (1994).

19. Illegal Immigration Reform and Immigration Responsibility Act of 1996 Section 645, 8 U.S.C.A. S1375 (1996).

20. 140th Cong. Rec. S14242–44 (1994) (statement of Sen. Wellstone).

21. 104 Cong. Rec. S14242–3 (1994) (statement of Sen. Reid).

22. Bronwyn Winter, "Women, the Law and Cultural Relativism in France: The Case of Excision," *Signs* 19: 93 (Summer 1994).

23. Ibid., 962.

24. Alison Dundes Renteln, "A Justification of the Cultural Defense As Partial Excuse," 2 Southern California Law Review (Spring 1993):pp#.

25. For a discussion of the communitarian tradition in Africa as well as the tensions created between this tradition and Western liberal notions of individualism, see Adrien Katherine Wing, "Communitarianism vs. Individualism: Constitutionalism in Namibia and South Africa," Wisconsin International Law Journal 11: 295 (1993).

26. See Dorothy Roberts, "Punishing Drug Addicts Who Have Babies: Women of Color, Equality and the Right of Privacy," *Harvard Law Review* 104 (1991), 1419.; Lynn Paltrow, "When Becoming Pregnant Is A Crime," Criminal Journal of Ethics 9:41 (1990); and Dwight Greene, "Abusive Prosecutors: Gender, Race and Class Discretion and the Prosecution of Drug-Addicted Mothers," Buffalo Law Review 39:737 (1991).

27. See Myrna Raeder, "Gender And Sentencing: Single Moms, Battered Women and Other Sex-Based Anomalies in the Gender Free World of the Federal Sentencing Guidelines," Pepperdine Law Review 20:905. Professor Raeder explores the impact of the federal sentencing guidelines on women and notes that increased prison time for drug offenses, especially, has affected primarily poor, minority women.

28. Roberts, "Punishing Drug Addicts Who Have Babies," 1448 and n. 147.

29. Immigration and Naturalization Act Sec. 241 (2), 8 U.S.C.A. Sec. 1251 (1990).

30. Thomas Aleinikoff, David Martin, and Hiroshi Motomura, *Immigration: Process and Policy,* 3d. ed. (pub info, 1995), 549–559.

31. *Jordan v. De George,* 342 U.S. 223 (1951). Void for vagueness doctrine focuses on the unfairness of punishing someone for conduct when the criminal statute in question is unclear or "vague" as to what conduct is actually prohibited. American courts cling to the notion that deportation is *not* punishment and therefore immigration laws are not *criminal* laws.

32. Ibid., p. #.

33. Immigration and Naturalization Act, Sec. 212 (2) (A) (I), 8 U.S.C.A Sec. 1182 (1990).

34. Immigration and Naturalization Act Sec 241(a) (1) (A), 8 U.S.C.A. Sec 1251 (1990).

35. Aleinikoff, et al, *Immigration: Process and Policy,* 559–561.

36. Ibid., 560.

37. Ibid.

38. Timothy Egan, "An Ancient Ritual and a Mother's Asylum Plea," *New York Times,* March 4, 1994, A25.

39. In the Matter of Lydia Omowunmi Oluloro, (File No. A72 147 491) Respondent's Summation At Close Of Hearing, U.S. Dept. of Justice, EOIR (March 3, 1994) (on file with author).

40. Ibid., 5. Emphasis in text.

41. Ibid., 1.

42. Ibid., 4.

43. In the Matter of Lydia Omowunmi Oluloro, (File No. A72 147 491), U.S. Dept of Justice EOIR, Oral Decision of the Immigration Judge, (March 23, 1994) at 2–3.

44. Ibid., 19.

45. Ibid., 20.

46. Respondent's Summation at Close of Hearing, 8–10.

47. John Fedders was the Securities and Exchange Commission enforcement director during the Reagan administration who admitted to beating his wife during

their marriage. Jerry Knight and Victoria Churchville, "SEC Enforcement Chief Beat Wife Repeatedly, Court Told," *Washington Post,* February 26, 1985, A1. Although Fedders received support from his boss and then president Reagan, Fedders did resign from his position as a result of these revelations. Robert L. Jackson and Zack Nauth, "Fedders Resigns As SEC Chief of Enforcement, Apologizes to Agency," *Los Angeles Times,* February 27, 1985, D1.

48. I am summarizing here a three-part approach I outlined in an earlier work on FGS that involves (1) understanding one's own historical context; (2) appreciating how the "other" women might perceive you as regards the colonial/imperial heritage that First World women, of all colors, have inherited; and (3) recognizing the complexities of the life and circumstances of the "other" women in her particular context. See Gunning, "Arrogant Perception."

Mallika Dutt

Reclaiming a Human Rights Culture: Feminism of Difference and Alliance

The 1995 UN Fourth World Conference on Women in Beijing once again underscored the existence of a powerful global women's movement with women firmly positioning themselves in the global policy arena. The collective efforts of women from around the world defeated the attempts of religious fundamentalist forces, such as the Vatican, to hold sway over the contents of the Platform for Action, forced governments to acknowledge the negative effect of structural adjustment programs and economic restructuring on them, and, among other things, demanded government action to prevent violence against women in all its forms. One strategy that women have successfully used to place their concerns on the world agenda has been to insist that "Women's Rights are Human Rights," a slogan that was first used at the UN World Conference on Human Rights in Vienna in 1993. This paper examines the potential use of the human rights paradigm by women of color/immigrant women/Third World women based in the United States.[1]

The human rights paradigm can be used as both a system of values and a tool to examine power relations in society in our efforts to create a just world order. Its power lies in our ability to transform human rights from being either a set of international legal principles or a foreign policy weapon used by the United States to further its narrow economic and political objectives. The notion of human rights has political resonance as an international ethical vision and can be used to hold states and other actors accountable for actions and omissions that violate these rights. Women around the world have begun to infuse human rights discourse with their own agendas and have forced the United Nations system not only to gain acknowledgment of our many human rights violations but also to obtain specific commitments to advance women's equality.[2] Gains at the international level have been critical for women; however, the potential for human rights discourse to transform power relations at the local and national levels is only now beginning to be explored.

In order to demonstrate the transformational potential of the human rights paradigm, I will begin with a short overview of the political, social, and economic climate globally and in the United States. I will then describe my vision of the human rights paradigm and its relationship to culture and politics. The paper will conclude with concrete examples of how human rights might be used in local organizing.[3] My aim is not to recommend a totalizing ideology that subsumes difference, but rather to suggest a framework of principles that enables women to challenge locations of power. My hope is that we can develop a human rights language that is able to incorporate difference in a positive and empowering way while we forge an alternative global vision.

The world is undergoing significant transformations that provide both new opportunities and pose serious challenges to the creation of a just world order. The politics internal to most countries around the world occur against the backdrop of some common global trends.[4] For example, with the break-up of the Soviet Union, the force of socialism as an alternative to capitalism has been seriously undermined with the free market system now regarded as the only viable economic system. This trend towards the free market model of economics, combined with technological innovation and increasingly fluid capital, has resulted in the creation of an international global economy. Such emphasis on the "market" as the answer to all economic problems, in conjunction with unfettered capital mobility, has led to the growing power of transnational corporations and a corresponding decline in the role of the state. Recent international economic accords, such as the North American Free Trade Agreement (NAFTA) and the General Agreement on Tariffs and Trade (GATT), have further consolidated the power of transnational corporations and eviscerated state sovereignty.[5]

Parallel to the trend toward the globalization of the economy has come an increase in religious fundamentalism in social and political organization. Although there are important differences in how it has manifested itself in different regions, religious fundamentalism, whether it be Christian, Jewish, Hindu, or Muslim, has incited public debate on many issues through an organized and concerted focus on definitions of the family and the state. Religious fundamentalism places great emphasis on the role of culture and religion in society, and in particular on the role of the family.[6] Since women are held responsible for the well-being of the family and are often considered to be the site of the preservation of tradition and culture, the growing power of religious fundamentalism reinforces patriarchal notions of appropriate roles for women both within the home and without. Restrictive prescriptions about dress, public mobility, and sexuality have surfaced worldwide, accompanied by an increase in violence against women who break these rules. Gains that have been made in some countries in the areas of reproductive control, sexual choice, divorce, child support, and access to the work force are now often under attack.

In the United States the economic globalization process, in conjunction with the Reagan-Bush legacy, has spurred a decrease in real wages, a rise in contingent or temporary work, the loss of jobs, and a continuing growth in homelessness and poverty.[7] As the very basis of democracy, the electoral process in the United States faces a predicament as fewer and fewer citizens vote and people become increasingly cynical about representational politics. The religious and political right, through organizations like the Christian Coalition, has used issues like abortion and lesbian and gay rights to capitalize on people's uncertainties created by economic transformations to increase its power in policy-making and in setting social agendas.[8] It has also fomented the currents of racism prevalent throughout the U.S. by using initiatives like Proposition 187, with the result that anti-immigrant sentiment is on the rise and people of color are being scapegoated for the country's problems.

At the same time that women all over the world grapple with these contemporary political processes, they continue to contend with pervasive, day-to-day violence. Women experience female foeticide, selective malnourishment, domestic violence, and rape and torture on a mass scale in times of peace and war, in refugee communities, at home, and in the workplace. In addition, the problems of unequal wages, unpaid labor, land ownership, and access to resources like water and firewood continue to pose serious obstacles to women's full participation in civil society.

Women have struggled against these difficulties at multiple levels, including the family, society, the state, and international systems. A deeper understanding of the roles that class, race, sexuality, culture, and geography play in defining women's experiences has developed through these struggles. Despite the very real differences that exist among women, vibrant communities of women combatting a myriad forms of injustice can be found all over the world. These forms of struggle are influenced by the local, national and global forces that women are subjected to in their different locations. The many agendas overlap, conflict, and conflate; however, they are connected by a common thread of women in the leadership of progressive change.

Plate 31: *Prostitution Trafficking: A Global Human Rights Crisis*
From the NGO Forum on Women, Huairou, September 1995
Reproduction of poster image
Photo: Anne S. Walker (IWTC)
Courtesy of International Women's Tribune Center

For women in the United States, this state of flux provides us with an opportunity to advance our many agendas. However, a movement in this direction requires an understanding of the interconnectedness of women's oppression across identity and social or political lines; it also requires a political analysis that connects local organizing to global trends and movements.

Why Human Rights?

Many layers of human rights intersect to create a dynamic process of change. Human rights can be understood as a system of values which provide a moral underpinning to ideas about how social mores should be exercised. In this version, human rights arise from a fundamental notion of people's humanity. These rights are considered inherent and inalienable to the very essence of being human.[9] Another perspective on human rights views rights as including social, political, cultural, economic, and civil rights, which have often been defined through the struggles that people undertake to ensure the conditions for a just social and economic order. As Charlotte Bunch puts it, "The concept of human rights, like all vibrant visions, is not static or the property of one group; rather, its meaning expands as people reconceptualize their needs and hopes in relation to it."[10] This understanding of human rights makes the paradigm a tool through which individuals and groups can understand the power structures in their societies.

Another approach to human rights bases its utility in the existence of international treaties and legal obligations that are codified at the level of the United Nations or in regional bodies. Advocates using this approach use state obligations under international law to bring pressure to bear on violators through public opinion, sanctions, reports on violations, and legal cases. International organizations like Amnesty International and Human Rights Watch best represent this strand of human rights organizing.[11]

The most effective use of the human rights paradigm would incorporate all these levels into organizing, depending on the goals of the group invoking the paradigm at any given historical moment. Philip Harvey captures the normative and strategic utility of using human rights when he notes:

Few weapons are as powerful in the struggle for social justice as a popular human rights claim. The existence of such a claim can galvanize support for a progressive movement, demoralize the opposition, and alter the terms of public debate concerning the movement's goals. To counter a credible human rights claim it is not enough to argue that the policies needed to secure the right lack public support. A human right is an entitlement that even democratically elected majorities cannot infringe. This is what gives human rights claims their bite—even in democratically governed societies—and causes public discussion to transcend the normal boundaries of political debate.[12]

One question that often gets raised with respect to using a human rights framework is why we should use the language of "rights," especially given our experiences with its limitations in this country.[13] Rights language has been criticized because it places too much emphasis on the individual at the expense of the community. Further, a reliance upon a discourse of rights often means that disenfranchised groups become reliant on the state to grant them their rights. The very legal definition of rights also limits the kinds of demands that may possibly be placed on the state. These limitations can lead popular movements to define their goals only in relation to state-defined parameters. Another criticism is that the language of rights fosters the creation of rights that potentially conflict with one another and which then have to be balanced *against* one another. This problem of competing claims finds an expression in the demands of the religious right in the United States for recognition of the rights of the foetus over those of the mother; it has also surfaced in the demands of father's rights activists for custody of children in situations of divorce, which has created particular difficulties for battered women.

While these criticisms are valid, they do not undermine the important role that the assertion of rights has played in significant social movements in this country as a critical tool for empowerment. As Patricia Williams points out, "the [black] experience of rights-assertion has been one of both solidarity and freedom, of empowerment of an *in*ternal and very personal sort; it has been the process of finding the self."[14] When one moves to define rights as fundamental human rights, one claims the notion of a self in relation to others, a claim which, for historically disempowered groups of people, is an important step in declaring their humanity.

Any attempt at advocating a metanarrative (like the human rights paradigm) that defines itself as universal, indivisible, and inalienable will be met by skepticism in an age when universalisms of any sort are suspect. Universalisms such as human rights are criticized either because all individual experience is said to be contingent on the location of the person involved and/or because cultural and other differences between people need to be respected.

While these reservations need to be taken into consideration when articulating any universal frameworks for progressive social transformation, the fact that almost all social change movements that women, indigenous peoples, minority groups, and other oppressed peoples have engaged in around the world have relied on such frameworks must be acknowledged. For example, as Upendra Baxi explains, criticism of metanarratives cannot be allowed to "deflect the endeavor of the Beijing World Conference on Women; only metanarratives of women's exploitational repression can challenge the obscene patriarchal constructions of the modern world."[15] Baxi argues that understanding human rights as the *right to be human* underscores the fact that the paradigm is not a language game but a mechanism through which we understand that we cannot take *rights* seriously without taking human *suffering* seriously.[16]

The issue of cultural and/or religious differences and their relationship to a universal notion of human rights has been particularly thorny for women. Various forms of inequality, discrimination and oppression that are experienced by women are often justified in the name of culture and/or religion. Some groups thus argue that certain practices like the veil and female genital mutilation, and other cultural or religious mores that oppress women, should not fall within the purview of human rights monitoring. Still others argue that universal human rights are not respectful of differences among women, and that they should not be used as a standard for critical evaluation.

In order to be effective, therefore, a women's human rights framework must address these competing ideas about culture and religion. Some women's groups have approached the problem by separating those oppressive practices based in culture from those that are based in religion by demonstrating how these can differ among countries and within regions of the same country that claim the same culture and/or religion. By exposing these differences, women have demonstrated that none of these practices can claim universal moral legitimacy and that they are not inherent to any culture or religion.[17]

Feminists have also pointed out that culture is not a static, unchanging norm but is constantly renegotiated by all of the constituencies that make up a social unit. Men's dual attitude toward culture is reflected in how they apply cultural norms to their own lives. The changing nature of culture is one that men in all societies incorporate in their day-to-day lives to justify their deviation from rituals, dress, or other cultural norms. It is no coincidence that culture assumes its rigid prescribed nature only when those aspects of it that oppress women are challenged. Many calls for human rights campaigns to be sensitive to culture protect the interests of those parts of the state or religious forces that benefit from women's oppression.[18]

In the United States, women from marginalized communities have often used culture as a means of resistance to the hegemony of dominant groups by insisting on the recognition of diversity. This position has evolved as a reaction to the imposition of ideas of universality based on views of reality shaped by white, Western, male, heterosexual, upper-class, Christian norms. Because of the power imbalances between dominant and minority groups, such impositions have had devastating consequences for people of color, immigrant communities, lesbian and gay people, poor people, and other oppressed groups.

Yet, while the use of culture has been an important process of empowerment for marginalized groups, women in these constituencies have often found themselves in a double bind. The assertion of culture or religion has often been made in such a way as to consolidate the patterns of oppression within that particular community. Thus, women who raise their voices against domestic violence and rape within their communities are often silenced because their struggle is perceived as threatening to the men of the community or the entire community itself. At the same time, batterers have successfully invoked a "cultural defense" in court as justification for killing their female partners by arguing that they should receive a lighter sentence because in their (Chinese, Indian, Arab, etc.) culture, it is acceptable for men to kill women in their families under certain circumstances. Or, when lesbian and gay groups attempt to march in ethnic parades, they are banned for not representing true (e.g., Indian/Irish) culture. Thus, for women of color/immigrant women/Third World women, it is necessary to engage with culture in a multi-dimensional way such that we simultaneously acknowledge its liberating and oppressive aspects.

For women of color/immigrant women/Third World women, the issue of culture is further complicated in the context of women's organizing. The tendency of many white women who are part of the dominant culture and/or religion not to recognize the patterns of oppression fostered within their own culture makes it difficult for women of color/immigrant women/

Third World women to work in solidarity with them. This difficulty is exacerbated when white women perceive the oppression of women in minority communities as an inevitable aspect of those minority cultures or religions, which are then labeled as inferior to their own Western/Christian context. However, to reject the paradigm of human rights because it is perceived as racist or disrespectful of cultural differences can lead to the misleading conclusion that this paradigm can only be legitimately claimed by white women, because somehow Western/Christian culture is better suited to accepting equality between the sexes. Or, if one were to begin to interrogate Western/Christian culture in the same manner as Islam or Hinduism, one would reach the conclusion that the call for equal rights for Western white women is equally suspect because many elements within that culture denounce full equality for women.[19] A recent example is the attempts of the Vatican to prevent the inclusion of women's human rights language—particularly in relation to reproduction and sexuality—in UN World Conferences.

The difficulties raised by the imposition of racist and (hetero)sexist universal norms do not necessarily imply that the principles that define the human rights framework—which can be based on an understanding of differences and power relations—inevitably lead to a biased and coercive universality. There need not be a contradiction in the assertion that human rights are universal and that they recognize difference. In fact, a legitimate movement against a coercive universality should not dismiss the power of a set of universal principles that demand a just world order. This is especially so where demands for respect for difference that are expressed in terms of the protection of culture and/or religion serve to oppress women.

The notion of human rights as normative, as distinguished from legal, can provide a value-based challenge to the religious and political Right's rhetoric around morality. Human rights rest on respect for the human dignity of all and should inform the values on which we construct our families, communities, and states. Ethics, values, and morality are far too critical to our existence to be left to the religious and political right; we must reclaim this terrain and human rights can provide the means by underpinning our definitions of ethics and morality. If understood as a political and oppositional framework that allows women to question different locations of power, human rights become a powerful mobilizing tool. In staking our claim to humanity, women move human rights discourse out of the limited legal paradigm of specialized international instruments and bureaucracies into the realm of subversive political action.

If we approach the human rights paradigm as one that can provide a system of values as well as the tools to interrogate power structures in society, we can begin to unravel the limitations placed on our political power by strict issue and identity based organizing.[20] Women's position in society is the result of a confluence of factors, yet organizing tends to be "single-issue" oriented. Such "single-issue" political organizing in the U.S. has resulted in fragmented women's movements: domestic violence activists have little to do with advocates for homeless women, even though battered women constitute a large percentage of the homeless population. Childcare workers who work in day care centers do not often organize with domestic workers, even though the wages of both are kept low by forces in society that benefit from their lack of unity. There is also very little strategic interaction between welfare organizers and reproductive rights activists, even though women on welfare have been the targets of repressive reproductive policies. A human rights framework, which brings a holistic perspective to the needs and rights of each individual, enables women to bring together the wealth of knowledge of organizing around specific issues to create shared agendas at local, national, and international levels without detracting from their specific area of organizing.

The human rights framework also enables women to work across differences of race, class, culture, ethnicity, religion, and sexual orientation, and to build on the strengths of identity-based organizing while moving beyond its limitations. Organizing around identity lines has been important for marginalized groups in society to empower themselves and develop strategies to counter their oppression.[21] However, the focus on diversity and identity politics has led to several problems. In many instances the struggle has focused on who sits at the table. Thus, activists have limited ourselves to focusing on whether there is appropriate representation of women of color, lesbians, disabled women, etc., at the table with no regard for what power actually exists between the individuals and/or institutions at the table. Also, identity politics "suffers from failing to acknowledge that the same multiplicity of oppressions, a similar imbalance of power, exists within identity groups as within the larger society."[22] In this way, a South Asian immigrant group will find racism, sexism, homophobia, and class oppression within its ranks even as it experiences racism and xenophobia in the larger society. The concept of human rights requires an articulation of basic fundamental rights to which all human beings are entitled. Framing an agenda that is based on a vision of what society might be moves us from

Mallika Dutt

a reactive position to understanding the interconnectedness of oppression with a view towards transforming society. Thus, the creation of a human rights agenda that is meaningful for all women requires that we better understand the ways in which gender is mediated by race, class, and other factors.

Using Human Rights

Articulating our concerns as issues of human rights enables us to challenge the current political discourse that dismisses the claims of all marginalized groups as "special interests" by insisting that these claims are based on internationally recognized normative and legal principles. At present, popular domestic perception regards human rights violations as phenomena external to the United States in which the United States plays a key policing role. This perception makes human rights violations effectively invisible in the domestic arena, and also allows the U.S. to act with impunity in the rest of the world. Women in the United States and the world over often bear the brunt of violations of human rights condoned or committed by U.S. players in such matters as arms sales, "rest and recreation" for soldiers, and exploited labor in free trade zones or the garment industry. As women in this country organize within a human rights framework, they need to demand that the U.S. incorporate respect for human rights in its policies and actions overseas and at home.

There are many ways in which the human rights framework could be used to organize and mobilize women around the United States. In practice, methods will emerge from a process of discussion that should involve women from diverse segments of society, including churches, block associations, the labor movement, the environmental justice movement, and women's movements. It is important to move beyond narrowly constructed definitions of what constitute "women's issues" while retaining women at the center of the discussion. The goal is to create a human rights agenda that connects women across identities and concerns and that builds stronger strategies for action that will ultimately work to transform the existing world order. Organizing methods could include popular education, hearings and tribunals, national and international campaigns, electronic communication and other technology, strategic media coverage, conferences, and litigation formulated to further a women's human rights agenda. A few examples follow.

Plate 32: *Forever Foreign*, 1989
Diane Tani
Text by Kimiko Hahn
Courtesy of the artist

Popular Education

Popular education can involve women in an empowerment process that leads to the definition and claiming of their fundamental human rights. It is only when people feel a sense of entitlement that political action to claim that right follows. The workshop could identify human rights violations by examining the difficulties women face in their day-to-day lives and by connecting those violations to other issues at the national and international levels.[23] A sample series of workshops could begin with a discussion of popular notions of human rights that focuses on how discrimination or exploitation experienced by women constitutes a human rights violation, and follow with an exploration of the ways in which such an approach can be useful to local organizing. Participants would be encouraged to see the connections between different forms of oppression and exploitation, and to develop an understanding of their lives in the context of national and global events. A presentation of the formal human rights system, including a description of treaties, the U.N. system, and enforceability and accountability issues, could follow. Participants would explore the utility and the limitations of the existing human rights framework, and then be invited to articulate their own human rights agenda. Audiovisual tools such as the video of the Global Tribunal on the Violations of Women's Human Rights, held at the Human Rights Conference in Vienna, could be used to generate discussion.

The basic format outlined above could be modified according to the needs of the group. For example, if one were to engage in such a workshop with an immigrant women's organization focused on domestic workers, the discussion could begin with what human rights are at issue. In such workshops, women have identified exploitation within the workplace, violence within the family, and immigration-related concerns, as some of the difficulties they face. Reasons that led to *their migration*, such as civil war or poverty in their home country, have been brought out to demonstrate the connections between global forces and immigrant women's presence in the United States. Discussions have moved to the attempt to identify what human rights are being violated in each of these scenarios: the rights to life, to security of person, and to livelihood, for example, have emerged as some of the human rights at stake. The next step would be to identify who was violating these rights. The intimate partner, in the case of domestic violence, the employer, in the case of workplace exploitation, and the government, in the case of immigration persecution, have emerged as violators. The discussion could then identify which rights had already been recognized by the government in either national laws or international treaties. In this example, relevant local and national laws, along with the *"International Convention on Economic, Social and Cultural Rights,"*[24] the *"Convention Relating to the Status of Refugees,"*[25] or the *"Convention on the Elimination of All Forms of Discrimination Against Women,"*[26] could be highlighted. The workshop could then move to the creation of a campaign that highlighted human rights violations experienced by domestic workers to demand accountability by employers and/or the government.

The fundamental principles of self-definition and empowerment are already being used by women around the country as they work for change. Adding the human rights lens enables women to connect this work to national and international processes and movements, effectively linking the local with the global.

Economic and Social Rights

The human rights framework could be used to counter the scapegoating of women on welfare; to demand well-paying jobs and benefits; to insist on safe working conditions for women, which includes the elimination of sexual harassment; and to ensure that women's needs are included in all discussions about trade, financial, and economic policies. Movements addressing each of these components individually have, of course, accomplished a great deal in individual areas, but a human rights framework would add a cohesive element to a campaign for action.

The *Universal Declaration of Human Rights*[27] provides a powerful tool around which to organize and highlight the fact that economic problems, particularly those of economic justice, are inseparable from social and political concerns. There are several provisions in this document that call for just and favorable work conditions; protection against unemployment; the right to a standard of living adequate for the health and well-being of the individual and family, which includes food, clothing, housing, medical care, and social services; and the right to security in the event of unemployment, sickness, and old age. These kinds of provisions could be identified and used to buttress the demands of the economic justice agenda.

Putting an economic justice agenda within the framework of human rights moves the demands beyond the status of "women's issues" to a normative plane that demands the creation of a just economic system, not as a matter of special dispensation, but rather as a matter of human rights. To frame the discussion in human rights terms also connects women struggling for economic justice in this country with women around the world. For example, in the trade strategies that are currently being pursued by the U.S., the exploitation of women's work provides a key ingredient for success. A human rights strategy would help to prevent women in the U.S. who join forces with women in other countries from being manipulated against one another in the process of exploitation. Given the role that the United States plays at the global level, women in the United States should be integrally involved in the creation of a just international trade structure which has at its base respect for human rights everywhere. Women in the U.S. could devise strategies to counter the global exploitation of women workers by transnational corporations in this country, as in other parts of the world, by developing a human rights agenda that demands international standards of accountability for corporate behavior.

Human rights treaties and customary law provide mechanisms to counter the increasing exploitation of women because they create international systems of accountability for governments, corporations, and other multilateral institutions.[28] For example, to counter some of the adverse effects of NAFTA, women from Canada, the United States, and Mexico can cite the *American Convention on Human Rights*[29] to demand guarantees for human rights.[30] This regional convention already has enforcement mechanisms and structures, but campaigns within both Canada and the United States are necessary for its ratification. Similarly, women can also look to International Labor Organization conventions to address economic globalization issues. As with all law, enforcement will depend on a vigilant and organized constituency of women here and in other countries. Women could also create a Charter for Human Rights Accountability for transnational corporations and other employers who do not fall directly within the purview of international conventions and push for the Charter's incorporation into the newly forming World Trade Organization.

The Copenhagen Hearing on Economic Justice and Women's Human Rights, convened at the World Summit on Social Development in 1995, provides a recent example of how women in the United States have attempted to forge human rights agendas with women from other parts of the world. The Hearing, convened by the Center for Women's Global Leadership and DAWN (Development Alternatives with Women for a New Era), brought together five testifiers from the United States and five testifiers from other countries to describe human rights violations perpetrated by the United States government. The hearing spotlighted the connections between the abuse of women on welfare in Vermont and the impact of structural adjustment policies on women in Tanzania; it showed the links between Chinese immigrant workers in California and Mexican workers in the *maquiladoras;* and highlighted the intersections of racism in the lives of African-American women in Georgia and Filipina women exploited as sex-workers on U.S. military bases. By demonstrating the power of women's voices that insisted on the indivisibility of human rights in a global context, where the role of the United States was made visible, the hearing sent a powerful message to the World Summit. Demands from the testifiers were then presented to the United States delegation to the conference.

Violence Against Women

In the United States, violence against women is a problem of staggering proportions: women are battered every fifteen seconds; one out of every five women will be raped in her lifetime; and almost half of all female homicides will be committed by the victim's male partner.[31] For immigrant women, the violence in their lives can often lead to deportation if their abusers are their sponsors; for African-American women, the racism of the legal system complicates their ability to access law enforcement agencies for protection; for lesbians, there is often nowhere to go. Women are also at greater risk of HIV/AIDS because of violence and women in prison experience severe abuse at the hands of guards and wardens.

Identifying the complex violence that pervades women's lives as a human rights issue enables women to confront violators within their own communities as well as institutional and state actors. Naming the violence that Latin American women experience at the hands of border immigrant guards as a human rights issue places accountability at the hands of the government. Naming domestic violence as a human rights issue places responsibility at the hands of community groups, religious organizations, law enforcement agencies, and government officials. Similarly, identifying the sexual abuse of women by U.S. armed forces on military bases around the world as a human rights issue exposes U.S. culpability for this violation.

Violence against women infringes on a range of women's human rights including their rights to life, equality, health, and personal freedom and security. Women have successfully invoked the human rights paradigm in the international arena with the result that the prevention of violence has catapulted to the forefront of the UN agenda as well the national programs of many governments. For example, the Vienna Declaration on Human Rights recognizes violence against women as a human rights issue and calls for measures for the eradication of such violence. Women's efforts at this conference led to the appointment of a UN Special Rapporteur on Violence Against Women and the adoption of a General Assembly Declaration on the Elimination of Violence Against Women.[32] The United States government has been a key player in these developments; unfortunately, because the domestic women's movement has not been engaged in organizing in the international arena, few efforts have been made to bring pressure to bear on our government to implement these measures at home.

Health and Reproductive Rights

Control over reproduction and access to the health care that is essential to this control are at the core of efforts to empower women to realize their agency in society. In setting reproduction and health concerns within the framework of human rights, women are able to counter their abuse from the standpoint of promoting human dignity and social justice.[33] In making this move, it is critical for women to link reproductive rights to civil and political rights as well as to social, economic, and cultural rights.

Women encounter barriers to the full enjoyment of their reproductive rights from a variety of sources. The family, cultural and social mores, religious fundamentalism, family planning services, employers, lack of basic health care services, international donors, pharmaceutical companies, government population policies, and UN policies all directly affect women's reproductive health. A human rights approach allows women to address the political, economic, social, and cultural dimensions of abuses of women's right to reproductive health. Various provisions of international conventions provide the basis for demanding access to health care. For example, Article 12 of the *Economic Convention* recognizes the right to enjoyment of the "highest attainable standard of physical and mental health." *CEDAW* includes language that ensures access to information and advice on family planning, the right to decide freely the number and spacing of children, along with the means to exercise this right. The fight for recognition of women's human rights in the area of reproductive health has been most recently apparent at the International Conference on Population and Development (ICPD) held in Cairo in September 1994, and at the Fourth World Conference on Women held in Beijing in 1995. At the ICPD women's global organizing led to the adoption by governments of a Programme of Action that aids women in demanding the protection and promotion of their reproductive health and rights.[34] The language adopted at this conference has been reaffirmed in the *Beijing Platform for Action*.

The U.S. government, along with others, has recognized women's empowerment, reproductive health, and human rights to be of central importance in population and development policies. Women must hold U.S. population policies accountable to the words of the *Cairo Programme of Action* for its internal and external policies. The Programme of Action can be invoked to challenge coercive contraception policies, inadequate funding for reproductive health, racist immigration policies, and oppressive welfare policies.[35] Women could challenge as well the population control policies of USAID around the world. Aspects of the *Cairo Programme of Action* and the *Beijing Platform for Action* that can be used strategically include:

• *The recognition of development as a fundamental human right with particular attention to be given to the socio-economic improvement of poor women in developed and developing countries.* This recognition could be used by women's movements to counter attacks on poor women and women on welfare that take the form of unsafe contraception, penalties for numbers of children, and scapegoating for flawed economic and social government policies.

• *The recognition that documented and undocumented migrants should be protected against racism, ethnocentrism, and xenophobia.* Women could challenge the population policies of the U.S. government as they relate to anti-immigrant measures that are being introduced at both the state and federal level (including in health care plans).

In both Cairo and Beijing, women battled the religious and political right to insist on recognition of their fundamental human rights. In the United States, Christian fundamentalism and the political right have fostered anti-abortion terrorism and promoted "family values" that are racist, homophobic, and inimical to women's reproductive self-determination. The struggles that have taken place in the international arena provide women in the U.S. with an opportunity to build stronger links with women internationally in a common struggle for the protection and promotion of fundamental human rights.

Conclusion

Given the present political climate, many have asked why I see potential in the human rights paradigm when so many of our attempts at social transformation have failed. My desire to explore this paradigm as a political tool rests in my belief that there are three fundamental shifts that we must make in our political organizing to achieve change. First, we must move beyond single-issue and identity-based politics to create a holistic vision of society that defines our direction, rather than a reactive and limited response to the assault of the right and other forces. Second, we must reclaim the domain of ethics, values, culture, and religion from the religious and political right. And third, we must connect our experiences and organizing with people in other parts of the world to better counter the economic, social, and political forces at play in our region as well as to shape the role U.S. institutions play around the world. The human rights framework provides the potential for enabling these shifts in our political organizing, and it is in this potential that I see hope.

Notes

1. I have been struggling with the issue of how to define "women" in ways that are more inclusive. Ideally, I would like to be able to refer to "women" and understand the term to include women in all their diversity. Although I am referring to women of color/immigrant women/Third World women in this article, my argument really targets *all* women. Because we have not yet created a common language that addresses this concern over terminology, for the purposes of this article I would like the reader to assume that I use the word "woman" in its broadest sense. However, I will continue to refer to women of color/immigrant women/Third World women as the primary audience for this article.

2. For a lengthy discussion on the gains made at the international level through the use of human rights, see Charlotte Bunch and Niamh Reilly, *Demanding Accountability: The Global Campaign and Vienna Tribunal for Women's Human Rights* (Center for Women's Global Leadership and UNIFEM, 1994).

3. This paper is an edited version of a longer pamphlet that includes greater detail of all the points made in this paper. See Mallika Dutt, *With Liberty and Justice for All: Women's Human Rights in the United States* (New Brunswick, NJ: Center for Women's Global Leadership, 1994)

4. For an excellent and lengthy discussion of some of these issues, read Rajni Kothari, *Growing Amnesia: An Essay on Poverty and the Human Consciousness* (New York: Viking Press, 1993).

5. Jeremy Brecher, "After NAFTA: Global Village or Global Pillage," *The Nation* (December 6, 1993): 000–000. See also Richard J. Barnet and John Cavanagh, *Global Dreams: Imperial Corporations and the New World Order* (New York: Touchstone, 1994).

6. See Helen Hardacre, "The Impact of Fundamentalisms on Women, the Family and Interpersonal Relations," in Martin E. Marty, and R. Scott Appleby, eds., *Fundamentalisms and Society* (Chicago: University of Chicago Press, 1993).

7. Alternative Women in Development (Alt-WID), *Reaganomics and Women: Structural Adjustment U.S. Style, 1980–1992* (Washington, D.C.: Center of Concerns, 1992).

8. For specific examples of how the Right has used social issues to advance its agendas, see Dutt, "God's Guerillas," *The New Internationalist,* no. 270 (August 1995).

9. A detailed description of different understandings of human rights can be found in Ayesha Ely-Yamin, "Empowering Visions: Toward a Dialectical Pedagogy of Human Rights," *Human Rights Quarterly* 15 (1993): 640–685.

10. Charlotte Bunch, "Women's Rights as Human Rights: Toward a Re-vision of Human Rights," *Human Rights Quarterly* 12 (1990).

11. I will not explore the international legal framework of human rights in this paper. For further details see Dutt, *With Liberty and Justice for All.*

12. Philip Harvey, "Unemployment as a Human Rights Issue," *Peace & Democracy News* (Winter 1992–1993): 41.

13. For a more detailed discussion of the rights debate see Elizabeth Schneider, "The Dialectic of Rights and Politics: Perspectives from the Women's Movement," *NYU Law Review,* no. 61 (1986): 589; and Patricia Williams, "Alchemical Notes: Reconstructed Ideals from Deconstructed Rights," *Harvard Civil Rights Civil Liberties Law Review,* no. 22 (1987): 401.

14. Williams, 414.

15. Upendra Baxi, *Inhuman Wrongs and Human Rights: Unconventional Essays* (New Delhi: Har-Anand Press, 1994), ix.

16. Ibid.

17. Marie Aimée Hélie-Lucas, "Women Living Under Muslim Laws," in Johanna Kerr, ed., *Ours By Right: Women's Rights as Human Rights,* (Atlantic Highlands, NJ: Zed Books/Washington, D.C.: The North South Institute, 1993).

18. Arati Rao, "Politics of Gender and Culture in International Human Rights," in Julia Peters and Andrea Wolper, eds., *Women's Rights Human Rights* (New York: Routledge, 1995).

19. Ann Elizabeth Mayer, "Cultural Particularism as a Bar to Women's Rights: Reflections on the Middle Eastern Experience," in *Women's Rights Human Rights.*

20. See Ely-Yamin, "Empowering Visions."

21. For a fuller discussion see Suzanne Pharr, "Multi-Issue Politics," *Transformations* 9, no. 1 (January/February 1994).

22. Ibid., 2.

23. See Maria Suarez and Roxana Arroyo, "Tough Challenge for Women's Rights Educators," *Human Rights Education: The Fourth R.* 3, no. 3 (Fall 1993): 000–000. See also Julie Mertus with Mallika Dutt and Nancy Flowers, *Local Action Global Change* (Center for Women's Global Leadership and NY: UNIFEM, forthcoming 1998).

24. United Nations, *International Covenant on Economic, Social and Cultural Rights,* RES 2200/A/xxi. December 16, 1966.

25. United Nations, *Convention Relating to the Status of Refugees.* RES 429 V, December 14, 1950.

26. United Nations, *Convention on the Elimination of All Forms of Discrimination Against Women,* RES 34/180, December 18, 1979.

27. United Nations, *Universal Declaration of Human Rights,* RES 217/A/III, December 10, 1948.

28. Harry Browne and Beth Sims, *Runaway America: U.S. Jobs and Factories on the Move* (Albuquerque, NM: Resource Center Press, 1993). See also New Brunswick, NJ: Center for Women's Global Leadership, *Copenhagen Hearing on Economic Justice and Women's Human Rights,* 1995.

29. Organization of American States, *American Convention on Human Rights,* OEA/Ser.A/16, November 22, 1969.

30. Minnesota Advocates for Human Rights: "No Double Standards in International Law: Linkage of NAFTA with hemispheric system of human rights enforcement is needed—Canada, Mexico & the United States must become full partners in the Inter-American System of Human Rights." December 1992.

31. Lori Heise, with Jacqueline Pitanguy and Adrienne Germain, "Violence Against Women: The Hidden Burden," in World Bank Discussion Papers published by the World Bank in Washington, D.C. (1994).

32. For a comprehensive overview of women's organizing around violence as a human rights issue, see Bunch and Reilly, *Demanding Accountability.*

33. For a fuller discussion, see Sonia Correa and Rosalind Petchesky, "Reproductive and Sexual Rights in Feminist Perspective," in G. Sen, A. Germain, and L. Chen, eds., *Population Policies Reconsidered: Health, Development, and Human Rights* (Cambridge, MA: Harvard University Press, 1994).

34. United Nations, *Programme of Action of the International Conference on Population and Development,* A/CONF. 171.13, October 18, 1994.

35. For a discussion of these issues as they relate to the U.S., see *Statement on Poverty, Development and Population Activities* prepared by the U.S. Women of Color Delegation to the International Conference on Population and Development (September 1994).

Marina Alvarez and Ginetta Candelario

(Re)visiónes: A Dialogue Through the Eyes of AIDS, Activism, and Empowerment

Latina/os[1] and African-Americans comprise a disproportionate share of AIDS cases reported since 1981.[2] Women of color constitute the majority of AIDS cases reported among adolescent and adult women.[3] Clearly, our communities are faced with a crisis. However, as Latinas, feminists, activists, and academics, we believe that there are many ways of seeing our communities' responses to that crisis. This re-viewing allows for an alternative vision of what constitutes activism, particularly where feminism is concerned, and what facilitates empowerment.

MA: My first experience with organized activism came through ACT UP,[4] the AIDS activist organization. When I first started going to ACT UP meetings in 1991, I was the only Latina and one of the few women of color there. At first I was afraid to be part of the group because of its reputation of members getting arrested and what not. But I found that there were other ways to be involved. ACT UP made it easy for women of color to be involved in demonstrations. They provided child care, lodging, food, and transportation. They facilitated participation. By giving financial support, they set the stage for connections to be made and they provided a forum for people who wouldn't otherwise speak. It was my first opportunity to meet other women with AIDS from around the country, to experience the camaraderie and fellowship of activism. As a white organization, it has the means and political clout to do that. A Bronx-based or Latina/o ACT UP would not be as protected.

GC: We have to ask ourselves why that's the case. While ACT UP was helpful, that activists of color need a go-between to provide a forum for them speaks to the continued roles of gender, race, and class in structuring political experiences, even as regards a problem that is commonly, if mistakenly, identified with groups marginalized because of sexual orientation or

Plate 33: *No Sufre en la Soledad* (She Doesn't Suffer in Solitude), 1992
Gelatin Silver Print
© Marta Maria Perez Bravo
Courtesy of Throckmorton Fine Art, Inc., New York

drug use. I think, in part, this is so because of a systemic willingness to privilege some issues at the expense of others. White feminists are willing to challenge gender exploitation but unwilling to challenge hierarchies based on race and class; heterosexual men of color are willing to fight racism but unwilling to explore sexism, heterosexism, and homophobia; and heterosexual women of color are fighting racism, sexism, and classism but accepting heterosexism, homophobia, and imperialism. None of these folks is seeking to call into question a *system* of privilege, but rather where they and their concerns are positioned within that system. In essence, they are all seeking approval and validation from the norms that exclude them.

MA: That's probably true, but the fact remains that ACT UP helped to empower the community, it didn't overwhelm it. That's very different from what upper-middle-class white women's agencies want to do for us, crippling us in the process, creating dependence rather than empowerment and independent spaces.

GC: It's interesting that you make that comparison. In the last decade, White feminists *have* been more intent on "reaching out" to women of color and on "addressing their concerns." Yet often, their efforts are met by rejection from the same people they're trying to reach. The problem is that because they are rooted in the experiences of white, heterosexual, middle-class women, U.S. feminist discourses and politics traditionally have developed paradigms and platforms that elide the unique and various race and class positions of other groups of women. That elision ultimately fosters the continued invisibility and subjugation of women of color. It's also why a multicultural approach remains relevant.

MA: If you continue to care for me, I will never have the opportunity to care for myself. That's the difference. We deserve the respect and we deserve the opportunity to be able to care for ourselves. There's a basic lack of trust in us, of knowledge about us and sensitivity to us on the part of many of the outsiders who come into Latina/o communities to "help us." What they should do is enhance women's own survival skills rather than care for them and create dependence. They should facilitate. Women inside the community facilitate each other's survival, even in terms of family support for one another—for example, taking care of each other's children so we can work. Because we often have low educational levels, have to deal with drugs in the community, and violence all around us, we learn survival skills, we learn to overcome barriers. That's something we can build on as activists and leaders.

GC: Instead of trying to make a community fit into some predetermined model of what constitutes activism, or for that matter feminism, notions of activism and feminism should be culturally attuned. Traditionally, when we think of activism we envision protest marches, sit-ins, and more formal lobbying activities. If we limit ourselves to that definition, we fail to recognize the kind of quiet, often familial activism that takes place in Latina/o communities. Resistance to oppression and oppressive conditions occurs in many forms. Failure to recognize that is in itself oppressive, not to mention misguided.

MA: Yes, exactly. Among Latina/os, the family itself often becomes part of the care of HIV-positive family members. This is a form of activism because there is a group of people involved in care, not just the patient and a doctor. Also, there's an implicit challenge to community denial of the existence of AIDS through caregiving activities. For example, when we have to go through a process of education about the disease, its manifestations, its treatments in order to take care of our loved ones, we are implicitly acknowledging that there is a crisis.

GC: Let's address the issue of denial in our community. When it comes to AIDS, I think the denial centers on a real difficulty in accepting the fact that there are gay and lesbian Latina/os. Sometimes when people are diagnosed, they have to disclose to their families not only that they're HIV-positive, but that they're gay, too. So, AIDS is forcing our community to confront issues of sexuality in the context of a health crisis, which adds to the homophobic currents in our community. On the other hand, the general reality of AIDS has forced us to re-evaluate how we think about sex and sexuality.

The whole issue of what it means to be gay is culturally embedded. For example, among many Latinos, having sex with another man doesn't necessarily make you gay. You're not gay unless you're being penetrated by another man. Consequently, when AIDS education targets "gay men," a whole group of Latinos who are not exclusively "gay" in terms of their self-conception, their being-in-the-world, exempt themselves from the discussion. The question is how sexual behavior is labeled in a given cultural context, and not so much denial of the behavior itself. In some ways, the imposition of a bilateral perspective on sexuality by non-Latino AIDS activists and researchers—if you are having or have had sex with someone of the same sex, then you must be homosexual—is a lot like the "one drop of blood" rule of racial composition, meaning that if you have one African ancestor, then you must be black. Just as a dichotomous paradigm of race doesn't obtain among Latinos, neither does it work with reference to sexuality. That discursive imposition only serves to occlude actual behaviors, which is after all what AIDS education seeks to address. Which is not to say that Latina/os aren't still in denial when it comes to homosexuality as such, as well as to female sexuality in general; just that "denial" needs to be contextualized and interrogated.

MA: Our community *is* in denial about a lot of things. Oftentimes, denial is a survival skill. If we're dealing with poverty, racism, sexism, sexual abuse, drug addiction, homophobia, etc., sometimes in order for us to survive we have to shield ourselves from these realities until we can get to a place where we can confront those issues. Empowerment is about helping each other get to that place.

GC: That's why educating the community about AIDS should refer not only to the particulars of the disease, but also to knowledge of the institutions one confronts daily—hospitals, government agencies, schools, etc. Education should generate knowledge of sexuality and knowledge of related social issues, such as racism, classism, and homophobia. For example, although Latina/os historically have been constructed as hyper-heterosexual, south-of-the-border sizzlers, with devastating political and human consequences, it often happens that our own community leaders and activists continue to privilege hetero-normative politics when it comes to AIDS, rather than confront issues of drug use, bisexuality, homosexuality, female heterosexuality, and lesbianism. In the process, we perpetuate silences that are deadly in the context of AIDS.

MA: It's not just AIDS. We're looking at the issues of empowerment and education through the eyes of AIDS. I think education is successful when it's grounded in the context of people's lives, their surroundings, their day-to-day existence. What do they have that we can work with? What are their needs? Oftentimes you have to care for seemingly unrelated things— health care, housing, nutrition, emotional and psychological well-being, finances, etc.—in order to confront the "real" problem. As community educators, we have to make it possible for others to confront their issues. For example, telling people to "Just Say No" to drugs is ridiculous. If we want to get people off drugs, or to stop them from getting on drugs, we have to help them in concrete ways. Do they have train fare to get to rehab sessions? Is there someone to take care of their kids? Do they have enough to eat? Do they have access to decent work? These things are crucial.

Maria Magdelena Campos-Pons

Plate 34: *The Seven Powers Come by the Sea*
Maria Magdalena Campos-Pons
Installation/Performance, Boston 1992
Mixed media (wood, glass, photos, African beads, metal, soil, 45-minute performance,
18′ × 12′ × 7′)
Commissioned by ICA Boston
Photo: Melissa Shook
Courtesy of the artist

GC: So it's not enough to tell people that they have a problem, or that they're being oppressed. We also have to give them the tools with which to confront those realities themselves. And yet, providing information that would not otherwise be available is something of a subversive endeavor in and of itself. As my mother often says, "Knowledge is power." On the other hand, what constitutes valuable information is determined by the powerful. When it comes to activism, to multicultural feminism, to empowerment of the disenfranchised, "knowledge is power" in traditional forms of activism—lobbying, protesting, voting—but the eventual mainstream adaptation of marginalized knowledge and methods belies that dictum. So, for example, despite extensive campaigns to "modernize" (i.e., Westernize) medical methods in Africa, Asia, and the Americas, traditional, natural healing methods continue to flourish. Ultimately, those same "advanced" Western scientists and polemicists have come to realize that methods they considered primitive and backward were as successful, if not more so, than their own. Now, there's an embracing of "primitive" methods, to extent of their current near co-optation. One could say that the way Latina/o communities approaches AIDS treatment itself has subverted the "knowledge is power" paradigm, particularly since there's a gender dimension to the issue, in that it's generally women who seek out and employ alternative methods.

MA: Middle-class white women bring their knowledge of Western medicines and access to mainstream political power to the AIDS-care table. Women of color bring alternative therapies discovered in their communities along with the kind of political power implied by educating the community, giving out information, and employing alternative treatments in addition to Western ones. There's a certain faith in the use of herbs and holistic medications passed down through generations and through word-of-mouth in the community. There's a parallel in the relationship between Western medicine and alternative medicines and the relationship between Catholicism and Santería. AZT and other medicines are used, but not alone. They're used in combination with alternatives: for example, Chinese traditions such as acupuncture and Zen meditation. In the same way, Santería works with Catholicism. The *santero* is both a spiritual and a medical resource. The community feels that Santería helps the Western treatment of AIDS, it lifts the spirits. And *santeros* are becoming acknowledged outside the community. For example, *santeros* were invited and incorporated into the spiritual workshops at the "AIDS, Medicine and Miracles" national retreat for HIV-positive people and their care providers.

GC: Santería itself could be considered subversive resistance to dominant institutions because it arose partly as a response to the violent institutionalization of Catholicism in Latin America and the Caribbean. Santería, as you know, is rooted in West African cosmologies which survived the mid-Atlantic slave trade. The followers of Santería were able to syncretize traditional African beliefs in deities with the Catholic belief in saints. Santería has acted alternately as a complement to and a subversion of Catholicism among Latina/os. Today, since the Church as an institution has been so regressive in its policy and discourse around sex and sexuality, Santería provides a spiritual venue that is in many ways much more rooted in the lives of flesh-and-blood people.

Where in Catholicism faith requires a certain amount of spiritual passivity—we pray to God and our saints and hope for the best—Santería is very active: we consult *santeros,* we follow their prescriptions, we light our candles, and we recite our orations. There's a sense that you're doing something tangible to affect your situation. Not to mention the fact that Santería also offers treatment alternatives, which the Church doesn't. And, as you point out, Santería is becoming a venue for inter-communal discourse and links, which provide an additional sense of activeness. So there are many new and diverse kinds of connections being made within and outside the community as it confronts its problems.

MA: Absolutely. For example, relationships are being established among diverse women as a result of HIV. Drug users, gay, lesbian, poor, middle-class, Latina/os, African-Americans, Native Americans, and Asians have forged connections which each other through activism. We meet at rallies, support groups, demonstrations, healing ceremonies, and memorials. There is the creation of a community out of a "tragedy." We're sharing our diversities in an effort to support each other. We're overcoming the barriers of politics, economics and culture through our survival skills and positive action.

I think that's one of the reasons women of color are surviving AIDS longer than men of color. We are more linked to community supports, we have a strong belief in the role of spirituality. Also, politically, we seem more willing to consider the ways in which we're connected instead of simply focusing on how we've hurt one another. When we were documenting the experiences of two HIV-positive Native Americans for *Positive: Life With HIV,* the PBS documentary for which I was content director, we were invited to attend a healing ceremony but we were not allowed to film the rituals. I can understand that because making connections doesn't mean that you can violate someone's privacy.

The goal was to make PBS programming more sensitive to diverse community concerns. The series was intended as a vehicle and a forum for people with HIV to represent themselves within the specificity of their experiences as members of different groups. Consequently, the participants were African-American, Latina/o, Southeast Asian, Native American, homeless, gay, lesbian, etc. Stations in some parts of the country wouldn't air the series or segments of it because they found the frankness of the content troubling. The question is, of course, how does one talk about AIDS without discussing sexuality and drugs?

GC: Well, AIDS discourse has been rife with misrepresentation and omissions when it comes to sexuality and drug use. On the one hand, AIDS has been and continues to be constructed as the gay disease, the drug addict's disease, and, therefore, not the concern of "normal" citizens who are magically exempted from contracting it. On the other hand, there's also been enormous fear that mere social contact with HIV-positive people leads to AIDS contraction. So there's a really uneasy balance that needs to be struck between acknowledging the facts of AIDS transmission without distorting its widespread impact.

The impact of AIDS is doubled by virtue of the wall of silence built around HIV-positive Latinas by their families. Because only with rare exceptions is AIDS contracted in any way but through needle-sharing or sexual activity. Latinas who get AIDS are forced and force those around them to acknowledge them as sexual subjects, and not just as sexual objects. If the problem of sexuality for Latinos is one of how their behavior is culturally defined, for Latinas the issue is one of existence as self-aware and publicly acknowledged sexual beings. Among Latinos, Latina lesbianism is *inconceivable*, literally not even conceptualized, because it operates entirely outside the realm of Latino subjectivity, as does the self-determined hetero Latina. We're there, but not there. We're (in)visible. The title of your documentary, *(In)Visible Women* points to that tension.

MA: *(In)visible Women* came out of my participation in a demonstration held by ACT UP in Atlanta in front of the Center for Disease Control for its exclusion of women from the current definitions of AIDS-related illnesses. The CDC revised the clinical definition of AIDS in January 1993 to include cervical cancer as a potentially HIV related condition. Nonetheless, there are still many diseases and infections that afflict women who are

Plate 35: **Image from Ellen Spiro's video *DiAna's Hair Ego: AIDS Info Up Front*, 1990 Courtesy of the videomaker and Women Make Movies, Inc.**

Marina Alvarez and Ginetta Candelario

HIV-positive that are not within the CDC's definition. Because gynecological diseases are excluded, women are not getting recognition, health benefits, and medications. That exclusion, that disappearing of thousands of women, is devastating to women with AIDS, both physically and politically.

GC: To say that women have been "disappeared" in AIDS discourse really highlights the political import of their exclusion. It's like the disappearing of political dissidents in Latin America: making dissidents go away physically doesn't erase the fact that there is a pressing political conflict, nor does it erase the conditions that lead to unrest. Instead, disappearing dissidents only compounds the problem in the long term because the *desaparecidos* always leave someone behind to speak for them. I mean, *Las Madres de la Plaza*[5] rose up because their children weren't allowed to rise up. In the end, *Las Madres* were an even more formidable force than their children. Similarly, disappearing women with AIDS has political ramifications.

MA: That's also the irony of AIDS and activism. In essence, because of having HIV, I met these wonderful people and got involved in activism and working with my community, which I might not have done otherwise. I've been doing training of service providers in the community, of AIDS educators, on how to use video to educate the community. Videos are a wonderful teaching tool.

Independent media allows you a certain freedom of expression because your constituents are different. Videos allow us to present and represent ourselves. When I was little, I wanted to be Patty Duke. But when I turned off the television, my household wasn't Patty Duke's. It was a totally different reality. It's that different reality that's usually overlooked in mainstream media. When you do independent media, there's an empathy for the marginalized audience, they're seeing themselves, they can identify. That's empowering.

GC: I agree that video making and video use is another form of activism. Nancy López and I found that documenting the experiences of Dominican women on welfare was powerful for the women themselves, for viewers inside the community, and for outside viewers, all of whom hold many of the same damaging misconceptions about welfare use among Dominicans. As clichéd as it may sound, video documentary puts a human face on an issue in a unique and widely accessible way. This alone constitutes multicultural feminism because it defies the ease with which welfare politics are used as a proxy for race politics, or, in your arena, with which AIDS politics are used as a proxy for hetero-normative politics, by re-casting the problem in a counterhegemonic way.

MA: By making videos and showing them, and by speaking at AIDS conferences, the exposure one gets becomes an indirect form of lobbying. You're getting your message across without actually lobbying. Being able to reach out to other women with AIDS is very effective. It's like being a voice for the voiceless, the barred, the excluded.

For example, although I was nervous, I was thrilled to be the keynote speaker at the World AIDS Conference in Amsterdam because I was the first HIV-positive person to do it. Generally speaking, those conferences are research conferences. They are considered a forum for the presentation of scientific and medical findings, not a vehicle for activism. Activists protested, and finally the 1993 conference was opened up to us. In thinking about how I should use the opportunity to speak, I decided to talk about my own life story because I can never represent everyone with HIV. We all come from different places.

GC: During that address you spoke about your personal experiences as an HIV-positive mother, former drug user, and in prison. Very often, women of color get caught in the conundrum of addressing public issues from the perspective of their life experiences, of trying to politicize what might otherwise be brushed off as personal, without having their experiences and perspective ghettoized. For example, as undergraduate civil rights activists, my peers and I were conscious that both the media and the administration would attempt to draw us into the old patterns of discussing racism and oppression, so we developed detailed strategies for confronting those attempts. When a reporter would ask one of us "Have you *personally* experienced racism on campus?" we, regardless of race or ethnicity, would respond something along the lines of "*Everyone* who lives within a system of institutionalized racism experiences racism." When asked to recount racist incidents on campus, we would respond that the issue was not the incidents, but the environment that fostered them.

MA: How can you identify with oppression and survival if you haven't experienced it? So often those who haven't had those experiences prefer to see you as a victim rather than as a cause for celebration, rather than as an example of strength and survival. So I speak, and my philosophy is that it's up to the listener to draw the appropriate message. I'm not sure what needs to happen for people to celebrate you instead of pitying you. On the other hand, I understand that people often don't have the relevant frame of reference. They don't know how to celebrate your strengths.

GC: Celebrating our strengths as Latinas, and more broadly as women of color, as survivors of so many attempts on our emotional, spiritual, intellectual, and even physical lives, is perhaps the most powerful form of feminism. I found that my life experiences as a poor, urban, Latina daughter of a single immigrant mother became the foundation of my later intellectual and political development. Indeed, there's a certain sense of empowerment that comes from knowing that you're moving in circles you weren't expected to infiltrate, that as Miss Celie says in *The Color Purple,* you may be black, poor, and ugly, but you're still here. Ultimately, I think that's what feminism is about. Declaring that we're here and won't be *desaparecida* that easily.

MA: I became an activist because my own personal health was at stake, as well as that of my family members, friends, and peers in the community That reality was a catalyst for me to act as an advocate for us. It empowered me and, ultimately, my activism has made me survive longer. My experience has been that I'm not a victim, even though I was a drug addict for twenty years, even though I have been HIV-positive for twelve years, even though I live in the South Bronx, even though I'm poor, because in spite of all that, I'm here talking to you. There was a time when I felt intimidated. But now I feel that my life experience qualifies me to speak. Who I am today, and what it took to get me here, comes through. I am not a victim. As I see it, having survived drugs, twenty years on the street, and being a Latina woman raising her kids alone in the South Bronx, indicates survival skills, it indicates strength, a strength that people who haven't confronted those barriers don't understand.

GC: Activism, then, is about looking inside the community for those places where strength is evidenced by the ability to survive otherwise devastating realities. At the risk of being repetitive, take the example of Dominicans on welfare again. Here is a group which is often portrayed in the media as being over-represented on the welfare rolls when, in fact, given the extraordinary rates of poverty despite high labor force participation rates, there is an underutilization of public assistance relative to need. In other words, Dominicans are surviving, indeed thriving, in many ways, despite conditions which would otherwise be devastating.

MA: There are things that activists can do to ease the transition from devastation to empowerment. Just going in there and "fixing it" for others is not helpful in the long run. In my own experience, for example, I believe that out of this process of getting help for my drug addiction, of learning more about HIV, of finding out what it does to women, of finding out what it does to women of color, of having to write a living will for my children, all these things that happened helped me to grow, I was empowered. As a result of that learning and growth process, I was able to share my experiences with other women who in turn helped someone else. Ultimately, that process creates a community of people intent on empowering and helping each other. That's been essential to me, to my family and to my community.

GC: The bottom line is that empowerment doesn't have to come through organized activism. The everyday activities of women of color are activism, a sort of organic feminism. Taking care of ourselves and our families, fighting epidemics, confronting violence, overcoming barriers in education and employment, just making it through the day sometimes, are political acts because they take place in the context of systemic violence, exclusion, and/ or indifference. Consequently, empowerment occurs in a myriad of different forms and arenas. Ultimately, that's what multicultural feminism is about: challenging rigid, dichotomized categories of thought, envisioning a more fluid reality, one in which race might be lived on a continuum, where sexuality might be a practice and/or an identity, in short, where different visions are possible.

Notes

1. Although we use "Latinos" for the sake of conversational ease, it must be born in mind that the term occludes a vast diversity of cultures, geographies, political economies, and histories.

2. Office of Communications, National Institute of Allergy and Infectious Disease, "Minorities and HIV Infection," U.S. Department of Health and Human Services, March 1995.

3. Office of Communications, National Institute of Allergy and Infectious Disease, "Women and HIV Infection," U.S. Department of Health and Human Services, February 1995.

4. ACT UP stands for "AIDS Coalition To Unleash Power."

5. Mothers of men, women, and children who were disappeared by the Argentinean military government for their political activities and affiliations.

Janet Henry

WACtales: A Downtown Adventure

As a high scorer on the multicultural feminist index, my view of the New York downtown art scene is, you can safely say, atypical. I'm an East Harlem born African–American of working class Antiguan and Panamanian parentage. I'm female, omni-romantic, and partially educated. I'm a drum-banging, community minded, intellectually curious visual artist, art instructor, and former art administrator.

However, if you erased the previous paragraph, how I recollect Women's Action Coalition (WAC) would still be unusual because I haven't adopted the "put-the-best-spin-on-us-girls" mindset characteristic of many former members. WAC was an impressive, though short-lived burst of feminist activism in the early nineties in New York City. WAC's membership was an extension of Manhattan's downtown coterie of educated, accomplished, and financially independent women, most of whom were visual artists or lawyers. It brought a level of inventiveness and humor to feminist politics that hadn't been seen before and hasn't been seen since. It even inspired white women in other cities to start up their own chapters. Some of the women who began WAC were veterans of ACT UP, and had, in fact, patterned WAC's modus operandi on that organization. But, as organizations go, WAC wasn't one: it was a process, an accumulation of procedures and rituals loosely based on Robert's Rules of Order. "We will take visible action" was in WAC's mission statement, and the enormous amount of publicity, from the *New York Times* to *Sassy* magazine, was testament to that fact. It wasn't one, but a bunch of good stories; and the WAC members, who knew the PR ropes, promoted it for all it was worth.

WAC's visibility made it look like media attention was *the* only means to address issues of gender and racial exclusion in feminism. But this wasn't

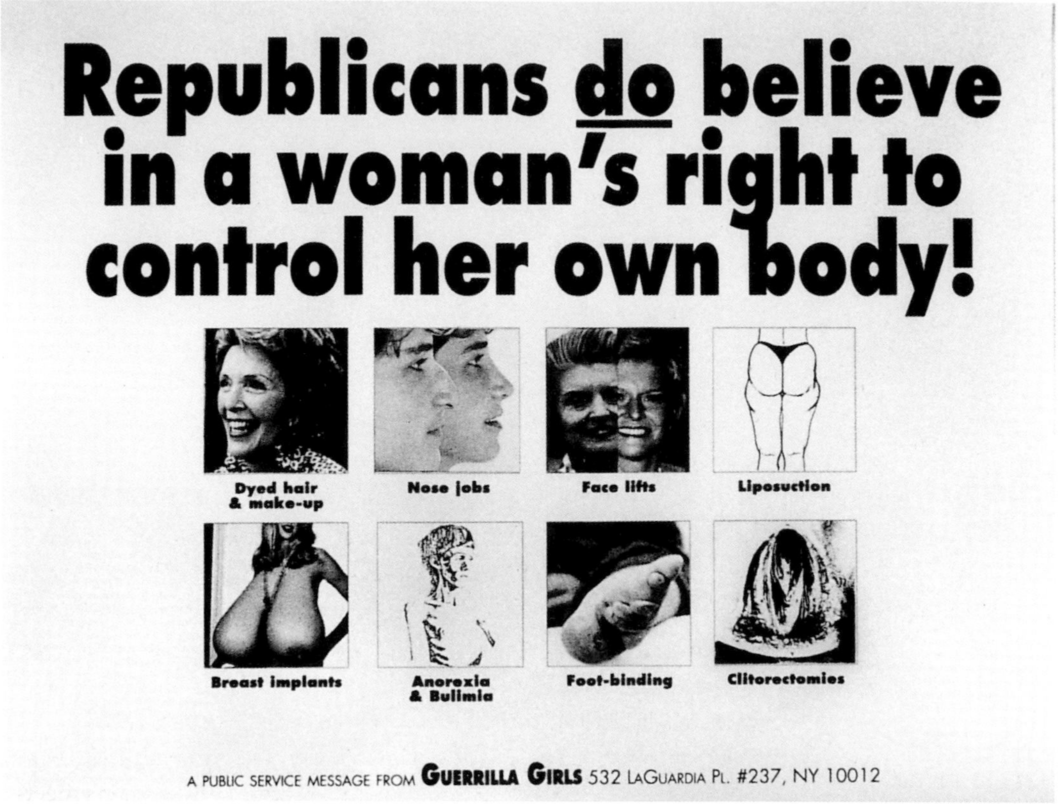

Republicans do believe in a woman's right to control her own body!

Dyed hair & make-up   Nose jobs   Face lifts   Liposuction

Breast implants   Anorexia & Bulimia   Foot-binding   Clitorectomies

A PUBLIC SERVICE MESSAGE FROM GUERRILLA GIRLS 532 LaGuardia Pl. #237, NY 10012

Plate 36: *Republicans Do Believe in a Woman's Right to Control Her Own Body*, 1992
Guerrilla Girls
Courtesy of the Guerrilla Girls

true at all. Organizations, established by visual artists of color, had been doing the feminist *and* the multiculti tango all along: Coast to Coast, a group that produces large-scale traveling exhibitions of work by women of color; Vistas Latinas, which consists of Latina visual artists doing essentially the same thing as Coast to Coast; and Where We At, a collective of black women artists who ran workshops in addition to organizing exhibitions. (Of the three, Where We At is the oldest by a decade or more.) Women Asian-American artists had Godzilla, which published newsletters and mounted exhibitions, but it was co-ed. They also took on the "We're what's shaking, baby" mantle of the Whitney's 1993 biennial, questioning the abysmally low number of Asians included; and WADIDO (Women of African Descent in Defense of Ourselves) drew in women of color from a range of professions, not just the creative areas. WADIDO, also a short-lived organization, came into existence the week after the Anita Hill/Clarence Thomas debacle. The full page advertisement, placed in papers all over the country, declaring, "a black woman's right to defend herself," was its most memorable act. Although I became a member of WADIDO, I was more active in WAC (how could you not be if you didn't want to be invisible and on the side lines, again?).

I was one of the few black women who joined WAC, and one of the minuscule number to have stuck it out. A cab ride shared with colleagues prompted an invitation from one to come to an interesting women's meeting. It happened that the next of these "interesting women's meetings" coincided with the monthly session of the Fantastic Coalition of Women, an interracial reading group. Since other Fantastic members were curious about these "interesting women's meetings" as well, we trooped across town to the Drawing Center in SoHo as soon as our meeting was over. When we walked in the door we single-handedly increased the "colored" membership by 500%. Even in WAC's infancy there were never more than ten, maybe fifteen, women of color in attendance at meetings at any one time: three or four African-American women, about five Asians, and some Latinas. There might have been more Latinas but some women blended in so well that it wasn't until they spoke to each other in Spanish that you found out.

On top of the ingrained racism in this society, there's the effect of the Republican onslaught which has seen to it that the gains previously made in civil and human rights were reversed, and the country re-segregated. So much so that white women living in New York City could say that they only knew a "few women of color superficially," and therefore "couldn't broach the subject of bringing them to WAC meetings." Then there are the interpersonal lessons of the last twelve years, which have influenced a lot of us, regardless of the politics we espouse. "Hey, you don't make friends with people unless they can do something for you." The lack of exposure and indifference to other sensibilities led to women in WAC making incredibly ignorant, insulting statements. I walked into my second WAC meeting as a young black woman was storming out. She stopped just long enough to warn me that I was going into a racist hornet's nest. WAC was discussing how to react to the Mike Tyson case. But by the time I got into it, more reasonable voices had suggested that WAC review all the rape cases of 1991–92 together, making it clear that the rich white boy, William Kennedy Smith, got off, while the poor, black, semi-socialized boxing celebrity went to jail.

These early meetings served to identify those who wanted to grope on "from within" and those who wanted to see if WAC could shape up, "on its own." Those who chose to grope on within WAC, were also recruiting. The responses of women of color to our outreach fell into three categories: 1) I've been burned before and don't want to subject myself to that kind of abuse again; 2) Isn't WAC that white women's group? If I'm going to work with other women, I prefer to work with women of color; and 3) Feminism—feh! I'm not a feminist. For my part, as someone who has grown to see feminism as more than self-assertion, I understand it as taking on the power structure and actively challenging the accepted place of women in society. I tried to tough it out in WAC. Besides, I and another black woman who joined WAC observed that we both had "missed" the previous wave of feminism, and as a result were not as gun-shy as other women of color who had run that gauntlet. WAC was, at its best, a damn sight more interesting and stimulating than the grim determination and dead seriousness that some sisters in African-American women's groups adopted in response to everything. I also felt determined to make the feminists in WAC understand that race is inevitably on any woman of color's agenda. "When I walk into a room," "the first thing people see is my color; so my priority has to be race."[2] This pronouncement was a revelation to the white women I told it to.

I will never forget the time a very butch black woman strolled into one of the early, humongous general meetings— you would have thought a bear had invaded a campsite. The women in attendance didn't scream and run but they came mighty close. Even though "the intruder" had achieved a certain perfection—she was immaculately turned out with her clean

shaven head, her dapper grey pinstriped suit and her wing-tipped shoes—
they saw a black face in men's clothes and panicked. Men weren't allowed
at WAC meetings and here one was—why was no one kicking him out?
By the time they looked up again for their fifteenth furtive glance and anxious whispering about the true nature of her gender she had sauntered out
again.

The Committee on Diversity and Inclusion (CODAI), WAC's intended vehicle to address diversity issues and "do coalition"—except we
didn't. With the exception of the march in support of the Civilian Complaint Review Board in New York City and the "Save Our Cities, Save
Our Children" march in Washington, D.C., it was mostly individual WAC
members who took it on themselves to work with women of color on specific issues. An unfortunate misunderstanding that eliminated a Latina
filmmaker from a general meeting agenda provided the impetus to start the
Minority Caucus. But that name was jettisoned at our first meeting in favor
of the Multi-Cultural Caucus, since we didn't see ourselves as a minority of
anything. The first two meetings in the Drawing Center's basement extended into the general WAC meeting time. On the surface this was an
"up yours" gesture, but it had to be. We had things to say to each other
and we had things to say about WAC. The organization wasn't two months
old, and some of us were smarting from the patently insensitive things we
were hearing from the floor. By the time the Multi-Cultural Caucus became CODAI, it included middle-aged, young, African-American, Irish,
Latina, Italian, Asian, Anglo Saxon-Protestant, Jewish, lesbian, straight, bisexual, working-class, poor, middle-class, rich, educated, professional, and
unemployed women. We all agreed that we wanted to work with a diverse
group of women either because we couldn't imagine doing otherwise or
because we wanted to learn how. We realized we couldn't bring in new
women of color without working first on WAC, so we did "Words of the
Week"; we did "How to Plan Actions"; and we did diversity training and
organized a retreat. It barely made a dent. CODAI even lost its umbrella
status when the younger (white) lesbians in WAC started their own caucus,
because they refused to be a subset of anything else. They felt that their
concerns always got short shrift in groups that also addressed racial issues.
Unlike the lesbo-phobia attitudes of Second Wave feminism, (white) lesbians were very welcome in WAC and constituted a large percentage of the
membership. They provided such a welter of role models (WAC's finest
public speakers were lesbians), sartorial influences (heavy black boots
were de rigueur), and heart throbs (some of the best looking, hands-down

attractive women in WAC were the dykes), that after a while you couldn't tell the queers from their supporters, from the wannabees.

It became apparent to me that most white feminists (straight and lesbian) we were trying to work with see class and race as subcategories of feminism. The perceptive ones do acknowledge that if feminism isn't diverse then it's misrepresenting women's issues, and can't be as effective as it needs to be. These (white) women usually got disgusted and left WAC. On the other hand, the gung-ho naive ones felt that those of us who persisted on raising the "race" issue should stop jabbering about the lack of diversity and decorate the room already. Talk about role reversal! These women, even with a sea of "white" faces staring back at them, would, in all seriousness, describe WAC's membership as diverse. Square business—they felt that the meetings stood as models of heterogeneity, and would point to stuff like the different physiques, sexual preference, styles of dress, and the length or color of hair as evidence. Racial diversity was an issue all the way through the life of WAC. From the very beginning some white women realized that WAC should be inclusive, and wanted to delay starting until the group was diverse. But the rage released by the Thomas hearings turned the ignition on and WAC roared off to take "visible action." WAC's founding mothers assumed that women of color, the differently-abled, and working-class women were similarly aroused, and would join forces to beat back the common oppressor once it was known that WAC existed. An Outreach Committee was formed almost immediately, and just as quickly fizzled. Identifying women with whom to work in coalition is a laborious process. It doesn't just happen because it should. You-have-to-work-at-it! It requires doggedness, patience, and a high tolerance for frustration. And then you also have to deal with the open mistrust of white feminists among women of color.

I once overheard a WAC member say: "It used to be that most of us in [a committee that will remain nameless] knew each other, because we shared a summer house. But since there had been such an influx of new faces into WAC it isn't true anymore." This group evaporated as soon as the "girls" from the other side of the tracks started horning in. I think their commitment only extended to spending time with their friends in new, exciting settings that had the thrill of instantaneous political activity. As the difficult questions and hard choices became more prevalent, as the chances to cruise and vent diminished, they lost interest and split. Although the previously method of disassembly was particular to the aforementioned committee, without an overview the rest of WAC ended up in the same condition. See, groups like WAC don't stabilize and grow. They head for every point on the compass and disintegrate, because, in the struggle to set the direction, the cliques and interests groups that make up the larger organization cancel each other out as they vie for acceptance (at first), recognition and resources (next), and (lastly, and most lethal) primacy. As a result of my involvement in WAC, I've come to the unshakable conclusion that socio-economic status trumps everything else in this culture. I also found that political activism involves bringing together the dissimilar. The first thing these congregations have to work out is power (you know, who calls the shots). The ones who understand warfare go for it; the ones who feel that by breeding and circumstances they should naturally assume control, alight on it; and the rest wonder what the hell is going on. They might try to make sense out of what they're undergoing, but lack of resources limits what the "rest" can accomplish.

Issues of privilege and affluence also influenced the shape of WAC's political activism, generating serious conflicts. Take, for example Women Ignite, the name given to WAC's parallel activity during the 1992 Republican Convention in Houston, Texas. The organizers assured "the floor" that money for this action could be raised outside of WAC so that the WAC treasury wouldn't be drained. Women Ignite spent approximately $42,000 on flying nearly 50 women to Houston, on an elaborately produced slide show projected on a drive-in movie sized screen at nightly speak-outs, on the rental of an ice cream truck for the drum corps "Dessert Storm" daytime action, and on the production of a video tape, plus the requisite promotion, banners, posters, and flyers. Feminists who had taken part in the Women Ignite Houston action were later befuddled, hurt, and angry because they couldn't understand why anyone would oppose an action that directly confronted the religious right, got press, affected hundreds of women, and energized WAC in Houston. But the low-tech dime-squeezers, who were used to producing posters, flyers, banners, and the like for next to nothing, thought that an action of this scope was a product of class privilege. This faction of feminists also felt that the Houston action played into careerism; participation in Women Ignite did give new luster to a fair number of résumés.

When the right wing detritus finally gained control I discovered what most of the feminists of color who wouldn't "join" WAC must have known already. Many WAC members, in spite of their efforts to overcome racial prejudices, class biases, and cultural isolationism, reverted to what they were familiar with. The Lani Guinier dust-up taught me how race and

Plate 37: *WAC/Guerrilla Girls Protest Guggenheim SoHo Opening*, June 25, 1992
© Teri Slotkin
Courtesy of the photographer

gender get played out in New York City's cultural/activist milieu and served as a test for their progressive resolve. As it became clear to us that another black woman was being trashed by the media and abandoned by the Clinton administration, a member of CODAI came up with an idea for action. The idea, inspired by WADIDO, was to place an ad in the *New York Times,* but this time on the editorial page, where it would take on a different kind of significance. It was a chance to bring about the kind of coalition that had been the unrealized promise of WAC. An Iranian lawyer, a Jewish photographer, and I were trying to update WAC about this action at the weekly meeting when a particularly disagreeable segment of WAC's conservatives revved up. We hadn't gotten half way through our presentation when they lit into us. Some thought the copy wasn't feminist enough, and tried to rewrite it on the spot, while others called us the "real racists," because we wouldn't accept the reverse discrimination argument they wanted to foist on us. Given the Guinier case, and given the goal of coalition with black women's organizations, the assault was astonishing. Although our action came in response to a political decision directly affecting an African-American woman, and an effort to change "the continued devaluation and vilification of African-American women," some of WAC's white women couldn't tolerate the idea that WADIDO would have the final approval of the advertisement's copy. Most items on meeting agendas never took more than ten minutes total, including questions and a vote, yet this farce went on for more than half an hour. But the pièce de résistance took place the following week when I was told that even if I had been called a "Nigger" I had no business responding, as I had done in writing, to what we had been subjected to.

The behavior of most WAC members in response to the Guinier incident made me understand that having decision-making authority is a novelty for a lot of white women, and they will reflexively eliminate anything that interferes with exercising this hard-won agency. The reasoning goes something like: "If you're a real feminist you do not impede your sisters' use of their power, even if it clearly puts you at a disadvantage." That's why some of them will go to their graves still wondering why we darker sisters took visible (yada, yada) and pulled the infamous watermelon action. We got ourselves on the agenda of a subsequent weekly meeting in 1993 and ceremoniously cut up watermelons with *clear plexiglass knives* when anyone got up to say something we interpreted as unsupportive during our ten minutes addressing the group. Oh, you'll love this: there were hockey pucks that swore we used *black-handled butcher knives* and that the violent overtones of our presentation instigated the tussle between one of the white women in our group and a corporate lawyer who was trying to win support for an antediluvian comment she made about this woman even though this happened later in the meeting. To assuage their conscience, I've become "the too angry black woman." This addled perception of power and authority affected everything; as WAC activity started generating less media attention, the remaining members insisted on credit and recognition even when it was inappropriate. The Guinier-WADIDO incident wasn't the only one. When WAC got involved by organizing a fundraiser and donating money to the Silver Palace Restaurant Women Workers strike that took place in sub-freezing weather, WAC placed its name before everyone else's, even before that of the union organizers and local Chinese groups. In another incident, even though men were not allowed at meetings "the floor" was willing to waive this prohibition to allow German cameraMEN to shoot a meeting.

Two pieces came out of my WAC experience: a narrative lariat entitled *WACtales* and a life-sized, multiple image chronological series of portraits of myself. If I hadn't done this work I probably would have ended up booby trapping tampons. Being thoroughly vilified to serve other people's agenda is like the proverbial slap in the face with a simultaneous kick in the ass. As a result, my first reaction to *all* doctrinaire feminists is suspicion and not a little contempt. Their espousal of prescribed dogma rather than the exercise of feminist principles just burns my butt. I tried to approach my nominally multicultural feminist activism with a certain level of equanimity (we're all fallible), but it got tiresome to be always accommodating and ready to inform, especially when it wasn't reciprocated. Makes ya mean after a while—"You gonna be a dummy? Here—boom—take that!" But I wanted to be effective more than I needed to act out so I tempered my behavior to an extent that those "girls" will never know. Besides, what sense does it make to alienate the very people you should be working with on what you've identified as your issues? As politically and socially inept as they can be, and as bound up in personal concerns that you don't understand, much less care about, you probably look the same way to them. In this arena, especially in the age of Uncle Pecker Head, Bush, and Newt, you can't point your finger without also turning it back on yourself sometimes.

If spontaneity and fractiousness are your idea of organizational structure you've condemned your group to the periphery of social change and an absence of institutional memory. If a perceived variety of physical characteristics is the only thing holding your organization together envision your existence in terms of months not years. If, like some WAC members, you revel in the knowledge that you have at your "disposal" a confluence of feminists with outstanding skills and ample resources, to what advantage are you using this? More often than not novel approaches to bringing attention to important issues *need* the back-up of unheralded scut work and follow-up. And it's naive to think that the tissue of race or gender or sexual preference can effectively embrace all the other segments of a person's life, let alone that those three in combination will create diversity. What I'm saying here isn't another case of "Tell ya something you don't know," it's more, "Illustrate things that can be applied." The creation and development of alternative organizations intrigues me, that's one of the reasons I get involved with them; but it wasn't inevitable that WAC crash and burn on me, among others. Especially in light of the fact that those testosterone driven, self-obsessed, overbearing louts we're always on about can create large, long-lived associations. As a feminist of color, who tried to work with everyone including white feminists, I'm very conscious of how powerful the voice of feminism is when it's strengthened by diversity. When policy is based on the articulated needs, concerns and desires of the different communities we represent that's taking . . . "visible action."

Petra Allende as told to Rocío Aranda-Alvarado

When Florida Isn't an Option: Testimonio on Growing Older in El Barrio

Petra Allende, an important activist involved in the Puerto Rican Community Development Project of the 1960s and 1970s, has dedicated her life to the struggle of unprivileged senior citizens, members of her community. Through her work she has become a legend in the community of El Barrio. Her warm spirit and generous energy characterize her fight for the rights of the 20,000 senior citizens who live in El Barrio as well as her advocacy on behalf of seniors in upper Manhattan. A symbol of hope for many, Petra's testimony here, however, is not that of one woman's struggle, but of a joint struggle among all aging women in the U.S. urban landscape.

Una Joven Puertorriqueña

I was a young woman when I arrived in this country from Puerto Rico in 1949. I remember how I had to struggle to survive then. I had originally been promised a job upon my arrival, but something happened and the job was no longer available. I had to look for a job on my own for the first two weeks I was here. I found my first job in a clothing factory. When I was asked if I had any experience in sewing, I lied and said that I did. Working from sunrise until after dark, I earned twelve dollars a week and lived in an apartment without heat. I worked in different factories until 1966 when I began working for the city.

Now, in my old age, I find I am still struggling to survive. Not all seniors winter in Florida. Hundreds of thousands of racial minority seniors are preoccupied with subsistence. Growing older as a Latina or African-American female senior in New York City is very challenging. The ways in which we deal with the problems of aging and the ways in which we organize for change are central to our existence. I can tell you a lot about it because, as the saying goes: "Más sabe el Diablo por viejo que por Diablo" (The Devil knows more because he's old, not because he's the Devil).

Plate 38: *Descanso de Marina Mesa*, 1994–95
Mixed media, 14 × 14 × 13"
© Amalia Mesa-Bains
Courtesy of the artist and Steinbaum Krauss Gallery, New York

Some people have no idea what it is like to be old, poor, and sick, especially with language and cultural barriers in an English-speaking country. They do not know what it means to be denied equal access to benefits and services, which many others take for granted. Finding adequate, affordable housing is something to which most upper-middle class Euro-American senior citizens feel entitled. For economically deprived senior citizens, it is a constant battle. Because many seniors of color were previously employed in low-occupational, low-wage jobs, a large percentage of minority seniors receive Social Security payments of $635 a month, which to a large degree represents their only income. Those who receive Social Security and a pension have combined incomes of $10,000 or less a year. Even supplemental Social Security Income payments (SSI) are only $532 a month. Rentals of apartments in new or rehabilitated housing are predicated upon incomes of $12,000 or more. Furthermore, out-of-pocket health costs have increased faster than Social Security. Rising prices, falling interest, and cuts in Medicare and Medicaid all work to reduce the condition of poor seniors. Poverty among seniors, especially among senior women, is rising rapidly. The Latino/a and other minority seniors in or near poverty are having difficulty making ends meet. They must maintain their strength, their will, their hope, and try to make the most out of what life has given them. Do you think that poor seniors can simply have a wonderful life? Can you have a wonderful life when you're surviving on one meal a day?

What is desperately needed is universal health care to ensure that economically deprived people can receive the care they deserve but can hardly afford. The social services cuts made by the city, state, and federal governments must be reinstated. These funds are critical to maintaining current (if substandard) levels of income and support. Currently, state subsidized beds in nursing homes for seniors are offered to those who are less sick than others, because this is cost-effective for the State. Current proposed cuts in Medicare will eliminate home-care programs, which are vital to the aging community. We have been waging battles against this on the Advisory Committee of the Department of the Aging of both New York State and New York City.

Una Mujer Fuerte

Despite these conditions, we are not completely helpless. There are several strategies we use to meet these economic obstacles. Lobbying has been a fundamental instrument in combatting such inhumane policies. As a woman without formal education or even full knowledge of English, I learned the

Washington, D.C. path to empowerment. I learned to lobby during the 1970s with a group of African-American women, the Manhattan Political Caucus. Through this work with other women of color, I was introduced to a lifetime of cooperation across communities. At that time we were lobbying for better public day care facilities for children of working mothers. Today, the African-American and Puerto Rican communities continue to work together on projects such as the Renaissance Health Care Center Network, which provides affordable health care in Manhattan to those without medical insurance. Lobbying for such enterprises is what the Manhattan Political Caucus taught me most. I realized that going to Albany to lobby the state legislature requires a great deal of work, particularly in the compiling of lists of constituents as proof that changes need to be made because the community is dissatisfied. I also learned that the registration of voters is equally essential, and absolutely complementary to lobbying. Voter registration is therefore one of the most vital things we do at the Gaylord Senior Citizens Center. We get not only the senior citizens registered to vote, but we also encourage members of the surrounding community to register. I first became aware of the importance of voting when I had to take my literacy test in order to vote in the United States. It was then that I began to work in voter registration. The people in power have the capacity to destroy our lives, which is why voting and lobbying are crucial.

Recently, I went to Washington, D.C., to represent the State of New York at a conference on aging. There were 2,569 delegates from all over the United States. Together we developed the Senior Citizens Act. Numerous resolutions were signed at the conference and a nationwide policy for the aging was proposed. Through the Hispanic Senior Action Council, we're currently in the process of lobbying congress against the proposed cuts in Medicare and Medicaid. The health of seniors, women, and children should not be jeopardized, especially when there is a budget large enough for military spending and for subsidizing large corporations. This is, in essence, what the government is doing, and this is what we're fighting at the Hispanic Senior Action Council. Our struggle is vital because we represent the people who are most likely to be hurt by the drastic budget cuts. We're currently waging a battle against the "living with others" code, which tends to affect principally women. If an elderly woman lives with her son or daughter, for example, she receives less in Social Security benefits than if she lives by herself. This is because the government takes into account the income of others living in the same household and thus limits the amount given to the senior citizen who does not live alone.

But along with lobbying in Albany and Washington, D.C., it is important to continue our work in our communities. During the week some of us volunteer at the East Harlem Interagency and at the Gaylord Senior Citizens Center, where health services are provided to seniors. Healthcare providers from the area, particularly from the Mount Sinai Medical Center, donate their time in order to offer free services, such as mammograms, and special services for those with disabilities. We visit those who are sick in hospitals and nursing homes.

One of the major health issues being addressed in the senior community now is the AIDS epidemic. This is usually because the seniors have family members who are infected with the virus. Because of the way the disease has affected the family structure, we now have a group of grandparents, and especially grandmothers, who are raising their grandchildren. There are also people in the senior community who are infected with the virus. This issue is rarely addressed in a public way; this is probably a result of the fact that the Latino/a senior population is generally ignored by the media. Among the cases of AIDS reported for 1993, 11 percent were of people aged 50 to 69 and 3 percent were of people aged over 70. While some cases were contracted through blood transfusion, in many cases, the virus was contracted through unprotected sexual contact or through intravenous drug use. Some older men and women seek the company of younger men and women and may contract the virus through unprotected sex with these younger partners. Do you think safe-sex education is not needed for seniors? Those who didn't practice safe sex when they were younger need to be educated now.

La Cultura de la Tercera Edad

A major aspect of our community work is integrating our culture with our advocacy. Music and dancing are a central part of our lives and are central to our work at the Gaylord Senior Citizens Center. We invite groups of musicians and Spanish-language singers and have dancing and festivities. *Plenas, danzas,* and *boleros* are favorites among the seniors at the Center. We also play bingo in the basement of a local church. Most of the players are senior women and it gives us all a great sense of community; we entertain ourselves this way, we laugh, scream, curse, play, and relive the stories that are our lives. This is one of the few places where mostly women get together. It allows us to bond, and discuss issues affecting our lives as aging women, from government policy to the most intimate concerns of our personal lives.

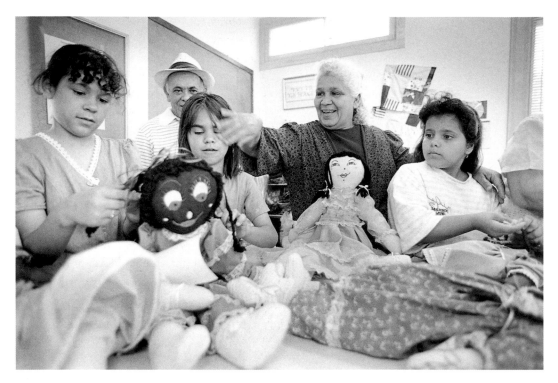

Plate 39: *At Casa Linda: Senior Citizens from the Otonal Housing Project Teaching Children to Make Dolls*, 1994
Black and White photo
© **Nina Barnett**
Courtesy of the photographer

We come together as women because, in fact, many of us are alone. Some have relatives nearby, but many have family that are far away—whether in the U.S., Puerto Rico, Cuba, Dominican Republic, Mexico, or elsewhere—and others have no family except their friends at the Senior Center. In some ways, it seems that our cultural socialization has allowed us to remain alone because of the fact that men are *de la calle* (of the street) and women are *de la casa* (of the home). That is, men do their business, socialize, and live outside of the home while women make their lives on the inside. Once friends and neighbors and relatives of the same age also pass away, the women remain alone. Part of what we generate at the Center is a coming together. As older women, we gravitate toward each other; we rely on places like the Center to provide us with a place to come and see familiar faces. We provide counseling to seniors who are alone, those who may be victims of abuse, and help integrate them into the community of aging people. The problem of senior abuse is a serious one for older women. At the Center we counsel women and help them to see that they have a support system. Being without close family members, or ones you can trust, does not mean you have to be alone.

Our community work is about trying to change negative situations by empowering ourselves. We work towards changes not only in public institutions but also in terms of our own cultural heritage. Working towards the empowerment of aging women means making many fundamental yet slow and difficult changes. It is something for which we constantly work. We don't want our sisters to be "La Pobre Melania" of Carmen Valle's poem:

tu marido hacia planes	*your husband was planning what he would do*
con tu herencia	*with your inheritance*
y se emborrachaba	*and he drank*
hasta estrellarse	*until he got stoned*
. . .	*. . .*
tu hija reprimía	*your daughter held herself back*
para que los demás	*so that people*
no hablaran otra vez	*would not talk*
de la familia;	*about the family again;*
y todos dirigian y actuaban	*and they all directed and acted in*
esa pelicula, en la cual	*that movie, in which*
te fueron llegando	*your wrinkles*

las arrugas,	*started to appear,*
el pelo ralo	*your hair began to thin*
y esa manera de mirar	*and you got that look*
que te dió el titulo	*that gave you the title*
"La pobre Melania,	*"Poor Melania,*
tan buena ella."	*such a good woman."* [1]

As Latina women, we have all heard many times this expression, "tan buena ella." It is always said with a rueful and resigned expression, as though there is nothing to be done for this "pobre mujer," as though her lot in life is one she will live with forever. We can accept wrinkles and thinning hair. We can't accept the war waged against our bodies, in terms of food, medication, and shelter. We cannot allow ourselves this kind of resignation. We all know that we have the privilege of helping to form young lives through our children and that in this process we can forge necessary changes. The struggle for fair treatment of the aging in the United States is equally a struggle for our lives as for the future of the younger generations and the quality of their lives as they age.

Note

1. Carmen Valle, *Glenn Miller y varias vidas después,* (Mexico City: Primera Editora, 1983), 49.

M. Jacqui Alexander

Imperial Desire/Sexual Utopias:
White Gay Capital and Transnational Tourism

> Sexualized, gendered, cross-cultural bodies . . . have histories of pro-
> duction in the United States at the nexus of academic and non-
> academic discourses. These histories are histories of tourism and ex-
> ploitation. They are histories that simultaneously seek and produce
> commodities as queered fetishes, feminized fetishes and nativized
> fetishes.
>
> —Gita Patel, "Sleight(s) of Hand in Mirror Houses"[1]

The development of a transnational gay political economy of desire anchored within white gay tourism raises some profoundly disturbing questions at this moment in our history. I say disturbing because in my earlier
work on the practices of the neocolonial state in the Caribbean, I had assumed that the processes of ideological and material exploitation of which
Gita Patel speaks in the epigraph above followed a trajectory that was intrinsic to heterosexualized tourism and the operation of nationalist states alone.
Central in my formulation was the state's sexualization and commodification of black women's bodies, and the mechanisms it deployed to recolo-
nize and renativize the population, more than three decades after flag
independence. The state relied on tourism to boost its allegiance to multinational capital and to make capitalism appear as integral to the "natural"
order of things, as "natural" even as heterosexuality. I had found that these
states tended to position tourism as economically central when in fact tourism was responsible for exacerbating the economic precariousness of the nation and compromising its sovereignty as a result. The state, I had argued,
consistently attempted to mask these processes by eroticizing the dissolution of the nation and by blaming lesbians, gay men, prostitutes, and
people infected with HIV for promoting nonprocreative, presumably

nonproductive sexual behavior. Such behavior ostensibly contradicted the very dictates of orderly nation building. Tourism, then, in the contemporary Caribbean, and perhaps elsewhere, came to be imbricated not only within the ongoing reproduction of heterosexuality but also in the commodification of the bodies of black women, whom Gita Patel argues are simultaneously, contradictorily even, transnationalized and nativized—positioned within systems of transnationalized labor at the same time that they are imagined by the "West" back into their "native" (read colonial) contexts. My assumption was that these processes of recolonization and renativization were necessary for the neocolonial state to offer up, as it were, a loyal heterosexualized citizenry to pay the debt which a crisis-prone capitalism perennially demanded: a putative heterosexual family to act as its ideological anchor and secular savior. I had not imagined a systematized interdependent relationship between heterosexual capital and gay capital, nor had I considered that capitalist competition might push these two systems to draw from the same epistemic frameworks, to consume from the same site, as it were, in much the same way in which black capitalism has been called upon to do a similar kind of work as/for white capital.[2]

In one sense, I had only narrowly engaged the question of the organization and production of gay tourism. Yet it was evident that white gay tourists had also become the subject of neocolonial state surveillance. Arriving at Negril Beach in Jamaica after having driven past Hedonism 11 on Norman Manley Boulevard, I had witnessed the covert racial trade in illicit sex of which everyone was aware (including the police) but about which everyone was reluctant to speak. It pertained as much to heterosexual practice as it did to same sex desire among men. The transactions seemed to carry that same valence of silent knowing that Shyam Selvadurai described on a beach in Sri Lanka, in his coming of age novel *Funny Boy*.

> The sun was setting, and the beach was quite crowded with foreigners and local villagers. We sat in silence, watching the sky change color at the horizon. Then Jegan leaned forward in his chair and looked keenly at something on the beach. My father regarded him, curious. Jegan turned to him and said, "Is what is happening what I think is happening?"
>
> I turned to look down the beach now, wondering what Jegan had seen. There was nothing out of the ordinary. As was usual at this time, there were many foreign men around. A lot of them were talking to young boys from the village.
>
> "Yes," my father said.

"And they come back to the hotel?"

My father shrugged. "Sometimes."

"You don't mind?"

"What am I to do? They have paid for the rooms. Besides if I tried to stop it, they'd simply go to another hotel on the front."

"But isn't it illegal?"

My father chuckled. "I don't see any police out there, do you?" He poured himself another drink. "It's not just our luscious beaches that keep the tourist industry going, you know. We have other natural resources as well."[3] Racialized bodies as natural resources are privileged in other texts such as cards produced and marketed by New Market Investment Company, the same company that produces a certain hypercommercialized generic white femininity, poised to feel "Hot, Hot, Hot in the Bahamas." It also produces cards of topless and almost bottom less black and white men together, with the same invitation, "Hot, Hot, Hot," luring women? Men? Or both? to Jamaica.[4]

So as not to reinforce the ordinariness, or normalization of these processes, I was prompted to foreground the imperial and to tentatively inquire whether the erotic consumptive patterns of white gay tourism followed the trajectory of white heterosexual capital. From the legend of Ernest Hemingway's "discovery" of Bimini—and as the irony of imperial history would have it, twenty miles from San Salvador, the site of the origin of "New World" colonization —way after nineteenth-century tourism had taken its hold in the Bahamas, and the use of the legend by state managers to market its attractiveness to "Western," primarily American tourists, I had posed an indirect question about whether Hemingway's (presumed) homosexuality had made a difference to the kind of narratives he crafted about the Caribbean. It could have been the case that Bahamian state managers had deployed the discourse of imperial discovery to enhance and advance *their* own first claim to inheritance, which might not have been at all what Hemingway had invented. An examination of *Islands in the Stream,* Hemingway's acclaimed work on the Caribbean demonstrates, however, that his stories are firmly structured within the sensibilities of imperial travel narratives whose origins clearly predate him or any of his contemporaries. Bimini was the place where Hemingway fashioned narratives in which he commanded the presence of black people and erased them. It was there that he perfected the practice of having black people anticipate the desires of white people, even before whites gave them voice. It was there that he developed the trope of serviceability of black people, the serviceability on which tourism is anchored. And it was there that Hemingway developed his prowess for shooting sharks and fish (the basis of contemporary tournaments and competitions), recirculating the tradition of white predatory, roguish masculinity, daring and powerful enough to dominate nature. In his faithfulness to white (hetero) masculinity as rogue and pirate, Hemingway had not only inherited the legacy of the imperial, he had become complicit as well in reproducing and advancing it.[5]

White gay tourism need not of course be built upon Hemingway and his discursive inventions. First, Hemingway's own gayness can be disputed and tossed aside. Also, he writes before the widespread formation of gay identity communities in the United States. Yet, I introduce him here to point to the manner in which discursive, which is to say ideological production can and does serve as the basis for certain consumptive practices, in this case accumulation within tourism. And if we were to generously conclude that Hemingway were gay, we would have to ask, at the very least, how and why his narratives of travel so closely resemble heterosexual travel narratives. But it is not only the case of a single resemblance that is crucial here, even with a figure who occupies as important a place in the psyche of the American nation as Hemingway. When one examines the generative scripts of heterosexual tourism and those of gay tourism, one sees that they traverse a similar imperial geography and draw upon similar epistemic frames to service an imagined "Western" tourist. The similarity requires our analytic and political attention for it suggests that material and ideological gestures of recolonization and renativization may not be the province of heterosexual capital alone. Rather, certain interdependencies and strategies of competition are configured in these processes. I see this as a disturbing development, for if we invoke a common experience of sexual queerness as the ground upon which we are to establish global solidarity communities, what is to be the position of the "queer native" colonized as "native" within the discourses of Anthropology, fetishized as sexual other at the inauguration of imperialism, and now colonized yet again by white gay capital whose economies of the erotic had been forced underground by white heterosexual capital, but function now above ground borrowing from the very tropes of sexual serviceability of this fetishized "native" to invent and imagine itself. What does one make of the similarity between regressive homophobic state gestures and the practices of white gay capital? Does capitalism inevitably commodify and fetishize, despite whose face it wears? What is to be the relationship between gay capitalism and gay political praxis? What is the content of "gay"? What kinds of solidarity communities do we wish to construct and what kinds of geographies of desire and pleasure are possible

M. Jacqui Alexander

and necessary in the face of a hegemonic global heterosexual capitalism that has perhaps intentionally conflated the erotic with the exotic? What are to be the politics of the erotic under the increasingly fragmented and alientating conditions created by the operations of capitalism itself? What critical political stances are required when the oppositional begins to assume the shape of the hegemonic and when the hegemonic simultaneously continues to insinuate itself into the oppositional in aggressive and destructive ways.[6]

These are not easy questions to undertake at this moment when attempts at deep self reflexivity within marginalized communities run the risk of perverse appropriation and distortion by right-wing movements whose secular and religious arms are unrelenting in their desire to mobilize homoerotics as a pretext to refuse citizenship. The myth of the gay consumer as a prosperous, perhaps undeserving elite, is now so prevalent as to be politically dangerous. As Amy Gluckman and Betsy Reed have argued, in order "to bolster antigay campaigns in Colorado, Oregon, and Maine, right-wing groups have seized on the legal advances that lesbian and gay men have won, arguing that homosexuals are now a privileged minority and that antidiscrimination statutes are unnecessary 'special rights.'"[7] Some of these campaigns have been waged with the full support of conservative segments within the black church. Deep fissures and contradictions around continued male privilege, class hierarchy and nationalism exist within a fractured gay community in which there is little consensus about the terms upon which a mass movement could be constructed. Many predominantly white gay organizations in the United States refuse to confront racism or the unequal effects of the very processes of globalization in which they are imbricated and continue to reproduce. They refuse to see that "First World" citizenship is linked to consumption and that the "Third World" enables the standard of living and the unequal consumptive patterns of the "First World" overall, providing cheapened labor that makes it possible for lesbian and gay consumers living in the U.S. and other "First World" metropoles to enjoy a certain way of life. Further, the consumation of an early marriage between queer theorizing and the dominant methodologies of post-structuralism in the United States academy, have almost emptied these disciplines of any attention to the histories of colonialism and of race, which could point the way to a radical activist scholarship anchored in a sexual politic of anti-colonial and anti-racist feminism.

The more specific purpose of this paper, therefore, is to present the outlines of a genealogy of interdependence and competition between heterosexual capital and gay capital and to elaborate the gay imperial

Plate 40: **Cover image of** Mensual—The Gay Magazine and Guide of Spain, No. 70 (July 1996), a special issue devoted to vacations in Havana

production of sexual utopias undertaken in the "West" (within organizations such as The International Gay Travel Association and in travel brochures such as the Spartacus International Gay Guide) in order to illustrate this interdependence. I argue that these guides have become formative ideological tools in the arsenal of the transnational tourist trade. Again, I foreground the imperial not only because the unequal dichotomies between consumer and producer, and producer and audience follow a "First World/Third World" hierarchy, but also because implied within this nexus of sexual transaction is the production of a "queer fetishized native" who is made to remain quietly within his local economy in order to be appropriately consumed.[8] It seems that in order to satisfy the terms of the imperial contract, this fetish cannot live and breathe for purposes other than the sexual, nor is he allowed to travel elsewhere. Nor can he be his own sexual agent for that would contravene one of the basic tenets of the imperial script. I say *he*, because the subject/agent/producer/citizen within this gay tourist economy is almost always imagined as a white, able-bodied and upwardly mobile man who lives in the "West." There are presumably no cultures of whiteness in the "Third World," not according to these guides. This man assumes his rightful place in the competition between these two segments of capital. He is the same agent/citizen that white heterosexual capital has produced as the quintessential gay consumer, and brings with him the potential to develop new and perennially changing needs and desires that capitalism alone can satisfy. Although citizenship based in political rights gets forfeited, they do not disappear. Instead, they get reconfigured and restored under the rubric of consumer at this moment in late twentieth-century capitalism. For heterosexual capital would make it appear as though the only gay people are consuming people and the only gay consuming people are white and male. I argue that whiteness and masculinity operate together through a process of normalization that simultaneously erases lesbians, working class gay men, and lesbians and gay men of color of any class in order to produce this above average homosexual consuming citizen.

I begin such an examination by first outlining what is at stake for heterosexual capital in creating what is now known as "the gay marketing moment." Inspite of claims to the contrary, heterosexual capital's gesture of rolling out the "welcome mat" has less to do with hospitality than with the creation of a new consumer and a new market both of which must be colonized. But what does gay capitalism do with the gay consumer who is the construct of the heterosexual imaginary? In the section that follows, I use the specific example of gay tourism and its ideological production of gay travel guides to demonstrate that gay capital mobilizes the same identity and operates through a similar set of assumptions as heterosexual capital. These systems not only mutually construct each other, but also simultaneously compete for a market each is willing to colonize. Both segments are engaged in nativizing and colonizing moves that I had assumed earlier were generated by processes of heterosexualization alone. I end by suggesting that if we are to build effective solidarity movements that embody pleasure while not simply reifying it, we need to understand and confront the orientalizing discourses and practices of travel and their effects on urban metropolitan racisms and interrupt, at the same time, the colonial fantasy of the silent "native."

Manufacturing the Contemporary Gay Consumer: U.S. Heterosexual Capital Rolls out the "Welcome Mat"[9]

Despite the widespread deployment of "Woman" and the marketing of white middle-class "Western" femininity as central ideological tropes of white heterosexual capitalism, the quintessential homosexual consumer within the contemporary racialized, gendered political economy of the United States is invented and imagined as male and white. This often masculine man (akin to, although somewhat different from the ["real"] Marlboro man), is well educated, and on that basis correspondingly well paid. The one glitch is that he "happens" to be homosexual.[10] This corporate construction of his homosexuality as coincidence and perhaps incidental to the (buying) point creates a context in which gay operates as potential spoiler in the "mainstream" heterosexual market. He can be invoked—that is, summoned—to consume through advertising, yet be made hidden, which means that his sexuality does not have to be the subject of his consumption. In 1992, for instance, an article entitled, "Tapping the Homosexual Market," which appeared in the *New York Times* announced that "for the first time advertisers [were] vying for homosexuals' buying power, though they [worried] about offending mainstream consumers."[11] The significance of that buying power lay in the apparent statistical fact that it outstripped that of the very "mainstream" consumer who presumably took offense at homosexuality. The statistical weight for such a conclusion came from a survey conducted by Overlooked Opinions of Chicago in that same year which found that the average household income for "lesbians was $45,827 in 1992, while for gay men it was $51,325, well above the average annual household income in the United States which stood at $36,520.[12] In addition, those

M. Jacqui Alexander

who customarily alert capitalists to the consumptive proclivities of the affluent announced that gay men spent two out of every three "queer" dollars; 80 percent of them dine out more than five times in any month; 48 percent of them are homeowners; and together 43 percent of lesbians and gay men took more than 162 million trips in 1991 alone.[13] These statistics appear with vigorous frequency, particularly now in the gay press where they operate with the power of myth, in the sense that they no longer require either explanation or context from which to derive legitimacy. As tainted as it appears, no potential market would escape capital's logic to transform it into an arena of competition and a site for potential profits.

There has been an acceleration over the last five years in the commercial interest investigating "gay and lesbian niche marketing," some of it spurred by white gay men themselves who work in the corporate sector. An amorphous "Wall Street" is now poised to recruit lesbians and gay men to help roll out, not the proverbial red carpet, but the "welcome mat" for gay investors, believing that gay corporate executives are best suited to engage "gay" clients. One mutual fund in California, Sheppard and Meyers, specifically guides gay investors toward "gay friendly" companies of which it believes there are 375 in the United States.[14] But perhaps the most frequently referenced guide was one that promised to point the way toward "untold millions" and advise businesses about how they might position themselves for the impending "gay and lesbian consumer revolution." The text, written by "America's leading authority on marketing to gay and lesbian consumers," argued that as companies across America battled for increase market share, many of them had ignored the vast untapped market segments of consumers, ready and waiting to throw their economic weight behind those companies that acknowledged who they [were] and what they want[ed]." Lesbians and gay men were a new "defined consumer segment," an attractive "niche" with the ability to "bolster corporate image, its market savvy and its competitive advantage."[15] All areas of consumption were targeted: alcohol, drugs (complicated in the age of worsening HIV infection), clothing, film, cigarettes, and travel as arenas where the struggle for this new defined segment would take place.

Finance capital, which includes investment and mutual funds, retirement estates, credit and insurance companies and the viatical services they provide, have also discovered the well-off gay consumer. Yet it differs significantly from its counterparts in the economy of travel. While the latter rely upon well-off, living, able bodies who travel well, these segments of finance capital are organized to underscore the spectre of vulnerability and death.[16] Of course death is rarely directly invoked. The euphemistic use of viatic, which the dictionary defines as "supplies for a journey as in traveling provisions," both masks the "Western" anxiety about death at the same time that it underscores it. The provisions or supplies necessary for the journey of those people living with AIDS are advertised on the same pages (often quite literally) with those presumed to be able-bodied travelers. In mainstream gay magazines such as *Out* and *The Advocate,* as well as regional newspaper/publications such as *New York, Homo-Xtra, Metro-Source* and *Gay and Lesbian New York,* advertisements for gay travel options seem to live comfortably with agencies offering cash in exchange for life insurance policies. Such hyperawareness of the "needs" of the dying at once script people with AIDS as dying rather than living with disease, and as people who are expected to die soon. Although this narrative clearly contradicts the model of the imagined-ideal traveler—dead bodies do not travel—it stands uncontested, not even discussed.

Despite the manufacture of a particular gay consumer and the faith in his potential to generate "untold millions," the gay market gets constantly mediated by heterosexual capital's putative preoccupation with its own self-representation and with how that gay consumer is to be (re)presented. In its pursuit of "gay" dollars, heterosexual capital has worried aloud about how it might pursue those tainted dollars without "offending mainstream consumers." Homophobia, then, is positioned as a threat to profits. Yet, in this instance, concern is focused not on corporate homophobia, but on the homophobia of the mainstream consumer. Capitalism is able to position itself as being more progressive than the "mainstream," progressive enough to "sell" to homosexuals, and even in some instances to hold out the promise of befriending them, as depicted, for example, in an advertisement by General Motors in Chicago, "where customers become friends."[17] Certain factions of capital have moved to utilize heterosexism as a competitive wedge in their war for the gay consumer. In its financial advice, American Express found it necessary to remind "unwed" gay men and lesbians "who [could not] count on the protections that married couples [took] for granted," that "unlike married couples, [they could not] pass to each other assets of more than $10,000 a year without exhausting the $600,000 gift and estate tax exclusion [they] might want at death."[18] The struggle for this consumer then, alive or dead, is so fierce that heterosexual capital feels entirely compelled to use the perversity of heterosexism to discipline lesbian and gay men into well-behaved consumers.

Of course, this is not the only instance in which capitalism has been caught between its own market imperatives and the ideological casing

M. Jacqui Alexander

around the identities of its potential buyers, caught in the contradiction, to use Bessie Smith's words, "of wooing an audience for whom it feels contempt." In this instance, contempt can be read through the violence of erasure, what heterosexual capitalists call a dual marketing strategy, in which the advertisements directed at an ostensibly heterosexual audience are emptied of the full force of their gay content. In a sexualized market, such advertisements could only be refracted through the sexual—the very trope through which all homosexuals are imagined. With this strategy, capital creates images that presumably elude the heterosexual consumer, but are suggestive enough so that the homosexual consumer—who consumes more avidly than his heterosexual counterpart—gets the point that it is he, too, for whom these ads are intended.

The same strategy manifests itself in the singular line of advertising directed toward the lesbian and gay community, seemingly constructed to reassure lesbians and gay men that while gay erasure is necessary for the functioning of heterosexual capitalism, there is an appropriate place for visibility: the lesbian and gay press.[19] Within these pages, American Airlines announces a "new partnership" in "gay travel value." "Seaspirit, the only ship designed specifically for gay travelers," offers the promise of "a positive gay experience you will never forget." It is within the pages of the gay press we learn that Detours Travel Guides ("for those who don't necessarily travel the straight and narrow") has teamed up with USAir to save money "for you and your 'traveling *companion*.'" Subaru, advertising in the *Windy City Times,* the Chicago Gay and Lesbian weekly, secures its legitimacy by making itself "the proud founding sponsor of the Rainbow Endowment," with an ad that featured two white men on their way to the ski slopes in a Subaru sports car. Similarly, the Private Water Corporation announces itself in the same publication as the proud sponsor of the Gay Games in 1995. These ads are never to be found in the mainstream press, the *New York Times,* nor in advertisements for AT&T, Time Warner, or the Disney Corporation, the very companies that are said to provide some medical benefits to domestic partners or have been named as gay friendly firms and, therefore, safe for gay investments. It is indeed a paradox that more than two decades after the gay movement deployed pride in identity to destabilize the shame produced by heterosexism, heterosexual capital now moves to redeploy gay identity in the service of legitimizing its own heterosexual pride.

Transnational corporations that have successfully established themselves as gay friendly in the United States, and perhaps in other "First World" metropoles, have not been similarly successful, however, in establishing corporate policy that uphold the dignity of those who labor in the "Third World." The Haiti Justice Campaign has shown, for instance, that the Disney Corporation exploits its workers in Haiti by paying them abysmally low wages of 28 cents an hour.[20] No doubt, winning access to health and other benefits as domestic partners is a considerable, albeit tenuous victory, given the intent of the membership of the Baptist Convention, the largest Protestant denomination in the U.S., to undermine it. If solidarity politics were not so narrowly grounded in the sexual, however, one could conceive of an alliance between U.S. based employees who have fought for domestic partner benefits and those who mobilize with the Haiti Justice campaign against the Disney Corporation and its subcontractors who have coralled mostly female labor into export processing/producing zones. But if gay capitalists continue to believe that "American businesses do not have to become the forum where lesbian and gay political battles are fought," and perhaps by extension political battles of any kind, then such alliances are indeed hard to imagine.[21] Since only a few of us are willing to problematize the production of "the gay marketing moment," we need to ask ourselves whether an unwitting trade in silence is the price we want to pay in order to provide a few of us with a ticket to walk on the welcome mat.[22]

More than a decade after this consumer revolution, we know little about the earning and owning power of different racialized groups in the face of the hypervisibility of whiteness and a normalizing process that makes a linear, positivist link between earning power and consumption. The marriage between white gay citizenship and white gay consumption has been efficiently sealed. While the obligatory lesbian gets appended to gay as a descriptor to consumer, lesbians, as Danae Clarke has argued, "have never been targeted as a separate consumer group within the dominant configuration of capitalism, either directly through the mechanism of advertising, or indirectly through media representation." Lesbian visibility, however, has prompted the commodification of what she calls "a fashionable form of androgny."[23] The overriding messages of these ads codify gay as white, able-bodied and mobile, certainly perennially upwardly mobile; whiteness becomes a proxy for both production and consumption. White gay men are positioned as trendsetters in a leisure economy, or are followers of style, not agents of politics, and with the capacity to consume more than "ordinary" consumers gay people can be pressed into spending the income that presumably stands higher than these ordinary consumers. But perhaps there is a certain historical trajectory operating here, for it is not the case that capitalism permanently shies away from creating markets where none existed before, or from boosting existing ones, from finding, in other words, new areas to colonize. There was indeed a time when heterosexual capital wanted nothing to do with the gay consumer. Now it seems that the very crises that have come about as a result of aggressive transnationalization and expansion, have forced heterosexual capital to consume on the same site, as it were, with homosexual capital, a fraught arrangement indeed. The ideological scaffolding of that arrangement is the topic to which I turn in the following section.

White Gay Tourism and the Construction of Sexual Utopias

John D'Emilio argued more than two decades ago that capitalism was indispensable in the creation of gay identity. It freed the individual from kinship and family-based economies, thus enabling women and men to enter a paid labor force in which production was socialized. "Only when individuals began to make their living through wage labour instead of as parts of an independent family unit, was it possible for homosexual desire to coalesce into a personal identity—an identity based on the ability to remain outside the heterosexual family and construct a personal life based on attraction to one's own sex."[24] But if, as D'Emilio maintains, capitalism created the conditions for the emergence of a gay identity, it has also been able to appropriate that identity in that the right to consume and even the right to produce are believed to constitute that very identity. Given how consumer colonization functions, this consuming gay individual is only virtually free however, for heterosexism ensures that gay dollars, though dollars they may be, are tainted dollars. Since they cannot be bleached of that taint, they must at times be kept hidden.[25] I am not for a moment arguing that this colonization has been enabled by quiescent lesbian and gay communities, and I recognize the oppositional deployment of what Danae Clark has called selective strategies of "(re)appropriation, resistance and subversion" by lesbian communities in particular.[26] Nevertheless, I want to suggest that no matter their source, processes of reification draw little from the real lives of pulsing, vibrant, contradictory, provisionally-organized communities of any kind. For gay capital, queer dollars are clearly not tainted dollars. They need not be bleached of anything before they are spent. But they *do* need to be spent and it is this imperative that provides the uneasy meeting ground for gay and heterosexual capitalists who have reified the same consuming subject in their struggle for profits.

Stonewall marked a watershed in the emergence of gay commercial enterprises and in the kinds of strategies that would be used to address an outlaw pariah status. Pre-Stonewall bars, the visible underground sexual economy of bathhouses and mail-order businesses have given way over the last two decades to a range of enterprises that straddle a thin line between the political and the commercial. By 1995, the same year that lesbian and gay consumers were believed to be source of "untold millions," and three years after the *New York Times* had announced that advertisers were vying for homosexual buying power, *Out,* published by Warner Books of the Time Warner Company, announced in its publication that business had come out of the closet and that gay liberation had spurred a new development of commercial enterprises: bookstores, counseling services, porn-shops, newspapers and magazines, and clothing boutiques. Yet market opportunities still existed. While the growth of lesbian and gay businesses in the late '80s and '90s meant that more queer dollars were being spent within the lesbian and gay communities than before, the article asserted that most queer dollars still ended up in the coffers of straight businesses. Gay capital has emerged in this conjuncture to reduce this perceived gap, working out of the assumption that gay providers know best how and what to provide as gay services to gay consumers. More important, gay providers assume, and perhaps rightly so, that they are best able to organize a sexual economy of desire and pleasure for gay people. Gay tourism has been premised and perfected on these same assumptions, so much so that it now occupies the place as the greatest commercial area of gay growth.[27]

Sexual consumption within gay tourism, as perhaps with heterosexual tourism more generally, is a transnational event. It traverses different national borders, oftentimes the same geographies that were established during the earlier phases of imperialism. Travel guides comprise one of its primary ideological anchors and their discursive expression elaborate a certain historically intransigent colonial relationship in which a previously scripted colonial cartography of ownership and production, consumption and distribution all conform to a "First World/Third World" division in which "Third World" gay men get positioned as the objects of sexual consumption, rather than as agents in a sexual exchange. If colonialism fetishized, racialized and sexualized the "native," and tourism, as the epigraph by Patel suggests, produces commodities as nativized fetishes, then in this instance white gay tourism becomes simultaneously co-implicated in the elaboration of these very processes of nativization and recolonization of which heterosexual tourism is the originator. This form of tourism, orga-

M. Jacqui Alexander

nized as it is on sexual consumption in the "Third World," has also become complicit in recirculating an earlier colonial myth that attempted to replace subjectivity with the sexualized "native" body, for in this sexual narrative of consumption those providing service are never positioned as agents.

White gay tourism's transnational structure is perhaps best embodied in the International Gay Travel Association, which represents itself as a travel resource, a clearing house for gay travel information. Based in the United States with a corporate companion in Germany, the association has grown from a charter group of 25 members in 1983, to over 1,200 enterprises of lesbian and gay-owned and "gay-supportive" businesses within the travel industry in different parts of the world. It continues to assemble a growing network of hoteliers, resort owners, travel agents, tour operators, airline and cruise line representatives, as well as "ancillary" businesses such as advertising agencies, car rental firms, video producers and distributors, travel clubs and associations, and travel and travel accommodation guide publishers. (I shall return to this designation of "ancillary" later). Still, the primary flow of the Association's resources is directed at travelers in the United States and Europe where the bulk of the membership is based. The 'West' usually functions as a tourist generator, while the 'Third World' functions as receiver. The getaway place is located elsewhere, outside the 'West,' envisioned as having something that can be used, however temporarily. This elsewhere can be coveted, then, for its use value, its serviceability (a strip of beach, a hotel, a club, a much-needed place for cruising). Different segments of the industry—highly integrated in terms of finance, management, research and development, as well as marketing and advertising—are also located in the "West."

It is difficult to ascertain precisely how this market operates primarily because paid membership and informal networks of "who is who" seem to be the sole paths to belonging. I can only suspect, for instance, that tour operators, the producers and retailers of travel and tourist products, are crucial here because of the predominance of all-inclusive package tours organized by gay-friendly travel agents on gay-friendly airlines with gay-friendly people. A class-based computer technology fuels transnationalization in the sense that one need only enter the "Rainbow Mall" on the World Wide Web to receive a "personal invitation" to join the membership of "the largest growing and dynamic organization: the International Gay Travel Association." The IGTA's designation of travel and travel guide accommodation publishers as "ancillary" service needs to be reconceptualized. The

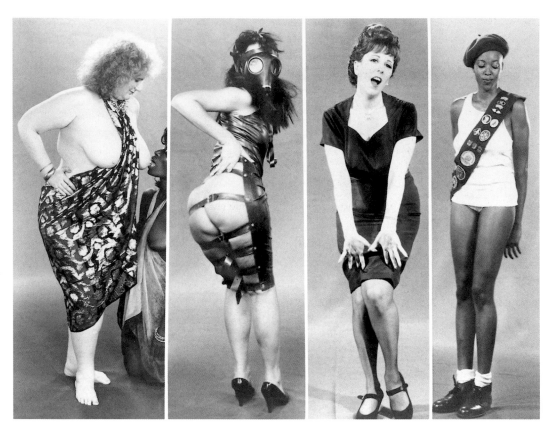

Plate 41: **Image from Annie Sprinkle and Maria Beatty's video** *The Sluts and Goddesses Video Workshop or How to be a Sex Goddess in 101 Easy Steps*, 1992
Photo of Scarlot Harlot, Barbara Carrellas, Annie Sprinkle, and Jocelyn Taylor by Tracy Mostovoy
Courtesy of the videomakers

M. Jacqui Alexander

designation may pertain more to the kind of market edge such services occupy relative to airlines, cruise liners, and tour operators in the changing hierarchy of competition. However, I see this segment of the industry as ideologically formative in fashioning and articulating desires, tastes, and satisfaction among producer and consumer primarily because of the quasi-underground character of the transnational sale of gay sex, its location somewhere between the illegal and the immoral, and also because in most instances the threat of homophobic violence can express itself swiftly and with grave consequences. The kind of pleasure that is sold, who sells and consumes it, the conditions under which it is sold, the ambiance, the mystery, the "friendliness" of the people (which needs to be more intimate and personable than the friendliness of even the most gay-friendly corporations in the United States) are both elusive and real enough that they require codification; they need to conform to certain standards to which certain people (in the "West") are accustomed. It may actually be the case that homophobia operates in a way that lesbian and gay travelers, to a much more significant degree than heterosexual folk, need to have the "unknown," in this case the "foreign," made intelligible to them. Traveling gay bodies rely heavily upon national and international gay guides to provide the signs, symbols, and terms through which leisure is to be understood, experienced, and interpreted. So, rather than ancillary, these enterprises are crucial in the ideological arsenal upon which other segments of the industry rely, upon which the gay tourist relies. They are also crucial in the production of the identity of those who produce and those who consume gay tourist services.

The market in gay travel guides has experienced a major shift from the earlier periodic homespun, mimeographed sheets that circulated underground before the 1950s, to a well-established economy over which heterosexual and gay capital compete. Well-established publishing houses such as Fodor (a division of Random House) or Ferrari International Publishers contend with *Bob Damron's Address Book* or the *Spartacus International Gay Guide* to establish the signs and symbols by which gay people ought to travel. The market caters to local (San Francisco, Amsterdam), national (*Thai Scene Gay Guide,* the *Philipine Diary* or Time Out which publishes a series of national guides), as well as international economies. It aims to satisfy particular economic circumstances: rough guides for bargain hunters published by Rough Guides of London; specific tastes for those, for instance, who wish nudity and seclusion, such as Lee Baxandall's *World Guide to Nude Beaches and Resorts,* or those who desire more cosy, home experiences such as the ones offered through Mi Casa Su Casa: International Home Exchange and Hospitality Network; specific communities such as *Gaia's Guide* for Lesbians and Ferrari which keeps lesbian hidden under its *Worldwide Women's Guide*. In most instances, these publishing houses are located in major metropolitan centers in the 'West,' from which distribution logically occurs. No other guide has achieved the status, scope, or overall market edge, however, than the *Spartacus International Gay Guide*, so it is for this reason that it deserves our close attention.

The *Guide*, published by the Spartacus organization, is a hefty 1000+ page compendium encompassing close to 900 countries, mapping a wide geography from Albania to Zimbabwe in a fairly standardized way, including demographics and climate, the legal status of homosexuality, the location of bars, clubs, cruising areas, religious organizations, health service organizations and AIDS organizations. The guide has described itself as "the world's best and most famous gay guide;" "a guide compiled by gay men for gay men." Its popularity is confirmed by its numerous appearances on best seller lists; it receives over 12,000 letters annually from "friends" around the world; it was reprinted three times in 1987; it appears in four of the major colonizing languages: English, German, Spanish, and French.

Within its pages the colonial is produced and maintained through four simultaneous discursive moves. The first, which I mentioned earlier, occurs through the reproduction of the boundaries of colonial geography. For instance, countries colonized by France, such as Martinique or Guadeloupe, are listed as pertaining to or belonging to France, while the colonial relations of seizure and possession go unmarked. France itself is similarly unmarked, and therefore made to be white. Lest the white gay tourist be confused about the racial configuration of Guadeloupe and confuse it with a white France, the *Guide* is quick to clarify that the majority of the inhabitants in this country that pertains to France are of African descent. Second, the writer, imagined reader/potential tourist consumer are all positioned as white and western, familiar to one another, within each other's cultural proximity and milieu. It is elsewhere, the unfamiliar "Third World" that needs to be made intelligible. This intelligibility is achieved by deploying a language in which the presumed audience is already white. "Be among the first to experience the South Pacific's most exclusive all-gay resort"; or as the *Guide* wrote about Burundi in 1988, "*We* (emphasis mine) know little about this little Central African agricultural country between Lake Tanganyika and Lake Victoria . . ." Third, the *Guide* resorts to a nativist discourse that pretends to construct the 'character' of 'Third World' people.

"Friendly" is the most frequently invoked descriptor here, a trait that is indispensable for the comfort of the foreigner and the pivotal nub upon which tourism can successfully operate. This "character" cannot be guaranteed the tourist, of course, but it at least needs to be invoked, for without it the ambiance upon which tourism is based will flounder. The construction of Thai character is almost singular here for it makes for a certain specialness that simply put, makes Thailand "nirvana," "a single slice of paradise." Finally, the *Guide* reproduces and maintains the colonial through a mode of elaborating and narrating geography that places it squarely within the genre of colonial travel literature. Nature is wild, untamed, sometimes disappointing. Countries suffer from "severe drought." Cruising in Barbados, for instance, can occur in "lots of bushes;" in Cuba one can go into "the small forest," whereas in France one goes into the jardin/garden or behind the castle, that symbol of European royal pedigree. Nature can also conspire sympathetically in providing the erotic frame for the meeting of these white bodies with nativized bodies: "The junction of the Amazon with the Rio Negro," we are told, "provides a spectacular natural wonder where one side of the river carries the typical orange hue while the other half retains the black color of the Rio Negro."[28] This description is evocative of a more vivid moment in the *Men of South Africa 11,* a South African gay porn video, in which images of black people are interpellated with wild animals, providing what Ian Bernard has called an "exociting frame for white sex performers."[29]

The colonial narrative, when combined with the reification of the sexual, can produce some particularly bizarre elaborations of "primitivism." We learn that Burundi, the same little country of which *we* know little, was a country that practiced "African Nature Religions." This obscure but important ideological detail cannot in fact be explained since no such thing as "African Nature Religions" exists. More than this, it does not require explanation, for *we* all presumably know that these "nature religions" do not conform to civilized practices. The obscurity can be made palatable for white gay "Westerners" only within the context of homosexuality: "*We* know little . . . but what *we* have heard sounds interesting: The country is governed by the Tutsi tribe for whom bisexuality is the norm."[30] Bisexuality within primitivism is exotic indeed. By the time reports of civil war in Burundi began to be given global attention in 1996, and the bisexual Tutsi "tribe" which controlled the state apparatus massacred Hutu civilians in large numbers, Burundi was disappeared from the exotic geography of white gay desire without a trace of explanation of the kind accorded the global shifts in right-wing homophobia, or the experience and politics of HIV infection, accounts of which are known to distinguish Spartacus from other gay guides, such as *Damron's Address Book,* for instance.[31]

The disproportionate attention given to Germany and the United States implies that traveling gay bodies travel in search of white on white sexual pleasure. Yet, somehow those who provide sexual service in the "Third World" are not presumed to be the travelers. Fetishes are not supposed to circulate in the reverse. That constructed "Third World" fetish is somehow not expected to journey from home simply in search of sexual pleasure in the "First World"; he is to be encountered in the authentic local geography, imagined back into the "native" context in order to conform to and complete the terms of this colonialist fantasy. He can perhaps journey from countries "with poor literacy rates and living standards" for labor and economic gain; and he surely journeys to enjoy democratic freedoms in "interesting, modern and enlightened" metropoles like Canada, fleeing from his own country that is inherently repressive, tradition-bound and poor. The nativized fetish, as constructed, must not only remain at home in "spectacular natural wonder," he must also remain silent, the same ideological requirement imposed upon lesbians and gay men for whom heterosexual capital has rolled out the welcome mat. Unlike *Gaia's Guide* for lesbian travel in which one finds lesbians characterizing the nature of their own lives in different countries, the *Spartacus Guide* grants the authority to speak to the editor/writer who journeys for first-hand knowledge. Authority is even granted the German Embassy in different "Third World" countries, but never the "native" who is made not to speak even the terms of his own sex.

Speech is costly; what the "queer native" has to say might indeed be dangerous. When nativized fetishes traverse the bounded sexual geographies assigned to them, and move to the metropoles which is the home of the returned tourist, not only are they not in their assigned place (elsewhere), they are not what the travel scripts imagined them to be. Having refused the colonizing scripts assigned to them, they are political and politicized subjects inhabiting a highly contested racial geography. The learned nativist discourses of tourism no longer apply. But nativist ideologies produced about the elsewhere simply do not disappear. Rather, they circulate at home as well, weaving themselves into the existing discourses and practices of urban racism, complicating a merely dichotomous relation between indigenous black and white, in the U.S., for example. In order to make coalition politics irresistible, we would have, at this moment, to take account of

M. Jacqui Alexander

the fact that travelling bodies return home and they return accompanied, or
at the very least, influenced by the colonialist travel narratives that prepared
them for travel. Tourist behaviors get reproduced at home, and sustain
themselves by finding resonances that reside deep within culture. But there
are also choices one can make. The reason that we must be deeply suspicious of reification and unrelenting in our desire to root it out, is that it produces ontological distortions and paradoxes that have nothing to do with
personhood. In the same way that a person could never be chattel, move-
able property, so too sexual consumption cannot stand in for who we are.
It takes a great deal of work to figure out who we are and who we wish to
be for each other. Actively refusing racism is a necessary beginning, but we
would need to build politicized spaces in which Orientalism (broadly defined and understood) is actively refused as well. Speech is indeed dangerous, for the homogenized queer 'native' can and will speak back in *his* new
home, out of the specificity of rage and bitterness such nativist practices
have produced. As this poem, "Game Boy," by Regie Cabico implies, refusing Orientalism is an absolute necessity in any mutual struggle for a loving
freedom.[32]

Game Boy

he buys me a glass of bass draft & asks if i am japanese/
his remarks/
you are the perfect combination of boy& man/

are you the hip, hot, hung 9 inches of fun/seeking the slim
smooth, smiling, authentically thai tasting, geish-guy
on-the-side macho dancer/looking for his lord-&-master?

i am not a korean dragon lady/running down avenue "a" with a
teapot
between my legs/shoutin'/where's my tip?/gimme my trophy!/you
wanna play
with me?/

you can/just quit orientalizin'/cause i ain't
gonna change my cotton-knit calvins for you or my mother/
if i lose

i ain't gonna fry you an emperor's meal or throw you eurasia/
or butterfly you an opera/
i'm thru givin sex tours of unicef countries/3rd world is for hunger/
& fat sally struthers

i've long been the "it" in a "rice queen phenomenon"/
that's burned faster than gin bottles/thrown at the black
of my skillet/
games so old as jason & hercules/men fucking my body like fresh-
golden fleeces/they ride my boyhood on bikes in the woods/
then rape/n' kill it/with leashes/spit words
in personal ads/
those clever written puzzles

for fun/they blood-brother baptise my emotions/then martyr
my sisters in the back room basements

I am beyond being poker-faced/mysterious/submissive/wanted-by-
you
or a being who's glossy & "g.q."-queen gorgeous

you wanna play freeze-tag?/i'm frozen already
touch me you'll swear i'm the ice-man's ice monkey
hit me/& watch where the mah-jongg chips land

play with me then/if you think/
the sweet that's left to the taste in my tongue is enough & not bitter/
love me for this/i forfeit the game/remove my makeup/
& call you the winner

Acknowledgments

I am enormously grateful that we are still able, at this moment of profound political challenge and increasing community fragmentation, to build neighborhoods of different kinds, including intellectual ones. Plenty thanks to Gloria I. Joseph, Jerma Jackson, Gita Patel, Gary Lemons, Barbara Herbert, Linda Carty, Kerry McNeil, Saradhamanidevi Boopathi, Heather Sibley, Aleyamma Mathew, Colin Robinson and the Audre Lorde Project, Brooklyn, New York.

Notes

1. Gita Patel, "Sleight(s) of Hand in Mirror Houses," Paper delivered at Conference, *Queer Theory on Location,* New York University, April 1996.

2. See in particular, M. Jacqui Alexander, "Not Just (Any) *Body* Can be a Citizen: The Politics of Law, Sexuality and Postcoloniality in Trinidad and Tobago and the

M. Jacqui Alexander

Bahamas," *Feminist Review,* No. 48 (1994), 5–23; also, "Erotic Autonomy as a Politics of Decolonization: An Anatomy of Feminist and State Practice in the Bahamas Tourist Economy," in M. Jacqui Alexander and Chandra Talpade Mohanty, eds., *Feminist Genealogies, Colonial Legacies, Democratic Futures* (New York: Routledge, 1997), 63–100. For a discussion of the operation of Black capitalism see, E. Franklin Frazier, *Black Bourgeoisie* (Glencoe, Illinois: Free Press, 1957).

3. Shyam Selvadurai, *Funny Boy* (New York: Harcourt Brace and Co. 1994), 162–67.

4. The frame represents the body of a gym-enhanced black man flanked by two slender, playful-looking white men on a sandy beach that could actually be anywhere. The faces of the white men are made to look back at the camera, while the black man on the other hand, his head slightly bent, is made to stare ahead so that to viewers he remains faceless. Black manliness need not wear a particular face.

5. A fuller analysis is presented in Alexander, "Erotic Autonomy," (93). See also Toni Morrison, *Playing in the Dark* (New York: Vintage, 1992) for an analysis of Hemingway's *To Have and Have Not* and *The Garden of Eden,* and an incisive illustration of what she calls "American Africanism." See chapter entitled "Disturbing Nurses and the Kindness of Sharks."

6. This incursion of the hegemonic into the oppositional can be found in neocolonial structures as well.

7. Amy Gluckman and Betsy Reed, eds., *Homo Economics: Capitalism, Community, and Lesbian and Gay Life* (New York: Routledge, 1997), xii, Introduction.

8. I have been influenced here by three related analyses: David T. Evans, *Sexual Citizenship: The Material Construction of Sexualities* (London: Routledge, 1993), 89–116; Ian Bernard, "The Men of South Africa: Constructing Gay Whiteness," Paper delivered at Conference of the Lesbian and Gay Studies Association, Iowa City U.S.A., November 1994; and bell hooks, "Eating the Other," in *Black Looks: Race and Representation* (Boston: South End Press, 1992), 21–39.

9. Reed Abelson, "Welcome Mat is Out for Gay Investors—They Have Cash, and Distinct Needs," *New York Times* (September 1, 1996), 1, 7.

10. As the irony of heterosexism would have it, this thoroughly heterosexualized masculine Marlboro man who was gay died early in the AIDS epidemic.

11. Karen Stabiner, "Tapping the Homosexual Market," *New York Times Magazine* (May 2, 1992), 34–35; 74.

12. These statistics are now frequently invoked, but this citation comes from a discussion about Homoeconomics that appeared in *OUT in all Directions: The Almanac of Gay and Lesbian America,* Lynn Witt et al., eds. (New York, 1995), 574–575. For an excellent discussion of the biased assumptions embedded in these data, see

M. V. Lee Badgett, "Beyond Biased Samples: Challenging the Myths on the Economic Status of Lesbians and Gay Men," Gluckman and Reed, 65–72.

13. These were prepared by Affluent Marketers Alert. There is as well a significant growth of these instruments of the information industry. They come from both gay and straight marketers, including the Strub Media Group, Simmons Market Research Bureau, Over-Looked Opinions and others.

14. Reed Abelson, "Gay Friendly Fund Has Blue Chip Focus," *New York Times* (Sept. 1996), 7. Meyers, who manages the Meyers Sheppard Pride Fund, seeks companies whose portfolio of stocks return a good investment. She is not "hamstrung" on the social objective of the fund. She defines "gay-friendly" as corporations who are explicit in anti-discriminatory language against sexual orientation and those with health and other benefits for same-sex partners.

15. Grant Lukenbill, *Untold Millions: Positioning Your Business for the Gay and Lesbian Consumer Revolution* (New York: Harper Business, 1995).

16. There are some in the lesbian and gay community who believe that heterosexism has necessitated these services and that viatics are in some instances underdeveloped, while in others they evidence a premature disinterest on the part of capital. See Deborah Stone in *Homo Economics* for a discussion of "AIDS and the Moral Economy of Insurance."

17. *Windy City Times* (October 31, 1996), 61.

18. See "Welcome Mat," 7.

19. See Gluckman and Reed, "The Gay Marketing Moment," in *Homo Economics,* 3–10. See as well, Dan Baker, "A History in Ads: The Growth of the Gay and Lesbian Market," Ibid.

20. The Disney/Haiti Justice Campaign, "Fact Sheet Update," (November 12, 1996). For a discussion of the problematics of the union-based gay rights movement, see "Laboring For Gay Rights: An Interview with Susan Moir," in *Homo Economics,* op. cit.

21. Lukenbill, 182.

22. Gluckman and Reed offered one of the earliest analyses critical of the terms of this discursive formation. Their essay, "The Gay Marketing Moment," first appeared in *Dollars and Sense,* No. 190 (November/December, 1993), 16–19.

23. See Danae Clark's excellent discussion of "Commodity Lesbianism" in Henry Abelove, Aina Barale and David M. Halperin, *The Lesbian and Gay Studies Reader* (New York: Routledge, 1993), 186–201. There have been significant representational shifts both in print and television media regarding lesbians and a great deal of pleasure in our own reception. I have not yet met a lesbian who has not seen *Ellen,* now no longer being televised.

24. See John D'Emilio, "Capitalism and Gay Identity," in Ann Snitow et al., eds., *Powers of Desire: The Politics of Sexuality* (New York: Monthly Review Press, 1983), 144.

25. I borrow this metaphor of the taint from Toni Morrison in her analysis of the American state and media's positioning of Anita Hill during the Senate confirmation hearings in which Hill accused the then Supreme Court nominee, Clarence Thomas, of sexually harassing her. See the essay, "Friday on the Potomac" in Morrison's, *Race-ing Justice, En-gendering Power: Essays on Anita Hill, Clarence Thomas and the Social Construction of Reality* (New York: Pantheon Books, 1992), vii–xxx, especially pp. xvi–xviii.

26. See Clark, "Commodity Lesbianism," 199.

27. See Evans, "Homosexual Citizenship: Economic Rights," 108.

28. This specific reference comes from *The Guide* (1995), 82. I consulted most of editions of the Guide, published since 1970, in order to do this analysis.

29. See Bernard, ibid., 4.

30. The *Guide,* 1988, 129–130. There is an important caveat which Gloria Wekker has offered in the case of Suriname regarding this metropolitan facility in naming practices it does not understand according to terms set up in the "West." See Gloria Wekker, "One Finger Does Not Drink Ochra Soup: Afro-Surinamese Women and Critical Agency," in Alexander and Mohanty, ibid., 330–352.

31. "U.N. Reports Burundi Army Slew Civilians by Thousands," *New York Times* (August 4, 1996), 4.

32. This poem was passionately read and received at the First Anniversary celebration of The Audre Lorde Project (November 8, 1997), the only national organization in the United States working within lesbian, gay, bisexual, transgender, twospirit people of color communities. See Regie Cabico, "Game Boy," in Miguel Alagrín and Bob Holman, eds., *Aloud: Voices from the Nuyorican Poets Cafe* (New York: Henry Holt, 1994), 48–49.

There is a more extensive piece of work to be done here on the specificities of homosexual Orientalism, which can draw upon the work of Edward Said. Thailand stands out here because the cultural and sexual practices of men are pedestalized in the erotic geography of white gay tourism. Cabico's poem is not accidental, given the excessive ideological production of "Asia." See Thanh-Dam Truong for a careful argument on the institutionalization of exploitative sexual practices in Thailand and the ways in which the Thai state benefits disproportionately from the accumulation which the labor of prostitutes generates. Thanh-Dam Truong, *Sex, Money and Morality* (London: Zed Press, 1990).

Shu Lea Cheang

Don't want my orgasm simulated

never

never held

You've never held

my demilitarized desire

remain narcissistically in love

Because he is white

never never held

POKE ROLL

I wanted to look

into your eyes when you came

double erotic fuck gift genes

never what

MASH SMACK

cross out cross out cross out

Because he is white

plain vanilla no jimmies

no syrup

STIR MIX BEAT

x-rated yearning zone

Those Fluttering Objects of Desire
Exit Act, 1992
Biennial Exhibition, Whitney Museum of American Art, 1993
Shu Lea Cheang with collaborating artists in a coin-operated porno joint
installation

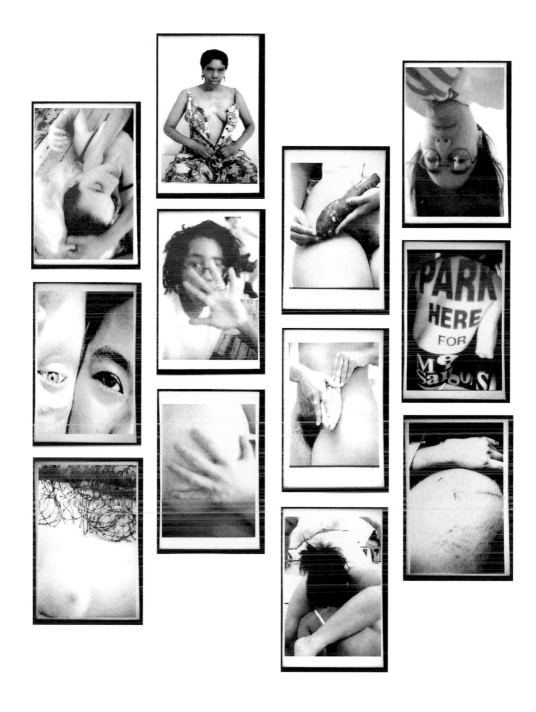

Plate 42: *STRIP/STRIPPED*
videostrips from collaborating artists
Shu Lea Cheang
Courtesy of the artist

Don't Want My Orgasm Simulated

Baby, I love you to want me
The way that I want you
the way it should be

I am institutionally legitimized. I am in.
The guard at the Whitney Biennial greeted me,
"It's so nice to meet you in person, a living artist in the museum.

I check myself in.
I want to be institutionalized, in the museum.
I want to have many TV sets on loan by Sony.
Can I also bring my people? twelve for the last supper.
Sorry, did we just close the chapter of multiculturalism?
Are we still negotiating or the deal is closed?

My installation is a site of cross-cultural collaboration in an attempt to make political alliance. My work is about "break ins." Break in as a form of intervention. High concept penetration with no strap on. Thrusting, am I in? Can you feel it?

I make coin-operated installation. In COLOR SCHEMES (1990), I put televisions inside the washing machines. The viewers insert quarters and cycle through the mumble jumble of racial wash. In THOSE FLUTTERING OBJECTS OF DESIRE (1992–1993), I device my own 25 cent peep show with red phones as channel switching apparatus. Exposed body parts stripped down the hanging TV sets, disembodied desire reconfigured by 25 participating woman artists. The piece ended up in 1993 Whitney Biennial and I was framed a "petite lesbian enterpreneur."

"FADE FROM WHITE, the Whitney Biennial gives center stage to women, gays and artists of color", *Newsweek*'s Peter Plagens reviews the Biennial. he cites Fluttering Objects as, "a video installation about lesbian eroticism within racial minorities within a hostile America."

Keep them closeted and let them eat meat.
Lesbian chic is storming in.

ON SALE.
Our collective desire and sexuality are of public domain, stripped naked. Image for consumption, emotion for trade.

I came out as *Newsweek* demanded.
Yes. You too can be lesbian. *POWER TO THE PUSSY.*

"The museum should be about quiet time. . . . Weary of hectoring
voices and blinking lights, I longed for the sepulchral silence of the
Rothko Chapel." *Art Forum*'s David Rimanelli writes. Are we making
too much noise?
Coming, coming to terms with the missionary position.
Coming, screaming, Am I too loud?

Faking orgasm can be the ultimate art form.

"The sex was good for Soon-Yi". Mia quotes Woody.

"At the Whitney, sound, Fury and Not Much else." *New York Times'*
Michael Kimmelman claims. "To succeed, the art of minority artists
and women must be closely tied to their personal situation, preferably
to their sense of victimization." another *New York Times* art critic
sums up a generation of women, color and queers.

Bend over and keep your ass up.
Feminists reclaim sexual pleasure.
and I refuse, refuse to be victimized. . . . .

The 90's was over in 1989. The 80s' was spent with video camcorder
in one hand and another hand desparately seeking orgasm. Video activism turned America's most funnist video, frozen gaze locked behind the lens.

done multi-cutics
been crosstalkingcrossculturalcrossbordercrossgender
verbal masturbation as a required language
the colonized uprooted
left to surf a dystopian cyber landscape

Call it eco-cybernoia or not quite lesbian, my current feature film
project FRESH KILL crawls out of the wreckage of a channel switching culture. Global toxic logic meets omni-national mediapoly; raw
fish lips utter disjointed words; black mom white daughter go heart
to heart and South Asian lesbian knocks down Native American
ex-cop father; red tinted New York sky opens up and snows soap
flakes. . . . .Strategy invented and reinvented, my attempt to tackle an
unresolved narrative based on conspiracy theory. Kiss the fish, kill
your television and don't cut my phone lines.

The yellow tide for my ride never arrives,
the cybership is coming to take me home.

> —at the cross talk panel, 1993

Summer, 1995—An airy bubble rises off my burnt finger, penetrated by a toothpick, alien genes flow out of the shrinking bubble and got away inside my fish tank. Got a tank full of baby aliens, green grLowing. At night, the cybership will arrive at the frontstep on Bowery. . . . .taking a hi-tech aborigine tripping—walkabout on the WWWeb in the long gone 90's.

1995, the year I accidentally swallow my camera.
Caught in my throat, the camera is dis-framed.
Spit out the camera, I split my legs.
Legs wide open at the end of the bowling lane,
the ball runs toward me. . . . .

Bowling Alley, a cybernetic installation set to negotiate public and private as commissioned by Walker Art Center, bears two cyber warning signs.

Shu Lea Cheang

Plate 43: from *Dyke Deck Playing Cards*
Functional. Artists multiple.
Catherine Opie
Courtesy of the artist and the Museum of Contemporary Art, Los Angeles
Computer design: Brad Verebay

Tricia Rose

"Two Inches or A Yard": Silencing Black Women's Sexual Expression

In these times, matters of cultural censorship are serious business. Prominent figures from across the race, gender, and political spectrum have been able to rally support and invaluable media coverage by railing against popular cultural examples of "degraded values" as expressed in vulgar sexism and non-state sanctioned violence. Senator Bob Dole, Reverend Calvin Butts, activist C. Delores Tucker, Senator Carol Moseley-Braun, and R&B singer Dione Warwick, among others, have in various ways and to different degrees called for the censorship of popular music and culture, especially the highly visible and ubiquitous sound for black youth, rap music.

Even though I disagree with the responses among some prominent leaders to angry and abusive expressions by black youth, I can empathize with the concern regarding the degradation of women that sometimes underwrites such leaders' frequently misdirected efforts. To confuse matters even further, recent public, media-driven discussions on the relationships between images and behavior tell us very little about the roots of sexism and violence and obscure important distinctions between positions taken by these political and community leaders. Overall, these high-pitched, excessively reductive attacks on black popular culture tacitly support and sometimes evade the larger issue of structural patriarchy in the name of protecting black women. Instead of exposing relationships between "civilized" and "vulgar" patriarchy, too many episodes in the public censorship debates thrive on the most highly transgressive and often deeply disturbing images and narratives as a way to facilitate a broader attack on popular expression.

This strategy denies widely-felt tangled pleasures associated with various transgressions and, more importantly, it encourages two repressive, non-dialogic responses: abstract defenses of free speech and/or impassioned

Plate 44: **Image from Jocelyn Taylor's video** *24 Hours a Day,* **1993**
Courtesy of the videomaker

protectionist calls for respecting and protecting women. Free speech defenses sometimes evade the complexity of cultural complicity in reproducing sexual oppression of women within acceptable legal parameters and protectionists often drain women's sexual agency through advocating restrictive and oppressive narratives of sexual purity, modesty, and feminine vulnerability. Neither position in this debate emphasizes black women's rights as expressive actors, even though both sides suggest that they are operating either directly or indirectly on black women's behalf. Instead, both positions clatter over the acts and behaviors of men (a move that centers and affirms their authority) in lieu of directly challenging the cultural, ideological, and economic oppression of black women or the ways in which *black women's* sexual expressions are censored.

In response to this hole in the public debates, I would like to explore a brief, but important instance of the sexual censorship of visibly progressive, young black women by taking a brief look at TLC, a high-profile, very popular black and Latina R&B/Hip Hop group that emerged on the black music scene in 1992 with its hit song, "Ain't 2 Proud 2 Beg."[1] How this group was pressured sheds light on how the seemingly pro-women censorship crusade can actually work against female sexual agency and self-definition; and, more specific to the arena of black popular culture, how anti-rap morality crusades have contributed to an environment in which the rare and potentially liberating instances of black feminist sexual self-possession/resistance in popular culture are gathered up into the same net as ubiquitous traditional male acts of the sexual objectification of women.

"Ain't 2 Proud 2 Beg" introduced TLC to America's youth as a fun loving, playfully aggressive group of women in their early twenties dressed in surreal, oversized b-boy clothes—a style perhaps best dubbed a rap/R&B version of Pee Wee Herman's Playhouse characters. Not only does "Ain't 2 Proud 2 Beg" speak about shameless female desire for sexual gratification from a male lover ("If I need it in the morning, or the middle of the night, I ain't 2 proud 2 beg"), but they sang and danced this chorus in brightly colored baggy pants, suspenders, tops, and oversized hats with condoms—real and comically "enormous" ones—conspicuously attached to them.

These condoms were "safety pinned" to their pants and tops, and in the case of member Lisa "Left Eye" Lopes, her left eyeglass lens was frequently covered by a condom. An openly pro-safe sex group, TLC's carnivalesque image coupled with the lyrics and anthem-like beat and chorus of "Ain't 2 Proud 2 Beg" brought young black women's sexual agency and sexual free play to the fore of black popular culture. In passages such as: "screamin' loud and holdin' sheets, scared that you'll be called a freak, gotta let it go while you can," the song places black female desire and pleasure in the forefront while acknowledging society's stigmas against female sexual agency and desire. Here, black female heterosexual sexual fulfillment is considered equal to male pleasure; and one partner's pleasure is not achieved at the expense of the other. At the same time, a more familiar pattern of male possession of women is playfully turned on its head in the song's chorus, where the male body and the penis (in any condition, size, or shape) is "possessed." If any one section of the song caused the censors to choke, this last one was most certainly it.

"Ain't 2 Proud 2 Beg's" lyrics—especially the chorus, "2 inches or a yard, rock hard or if it's saggin', I ain't 2 proud 2 beg"—coupled with TLC's openly safe-sex position and condom-wear became not only a thrilling anthem for many young black women but also a target for media censorship. Rather than understand their lyrics as an exciting moment when young black women turn the tables on female sexual passivity and redirect objectification, television censors seemed to view this anthem as though it were a potential battle cry for soon-to-be teenaged mothers. TLC's youthful appearance and sexually direct pleasure was fearfully considered a potential call for sexual irresponsibility and, therefore, necessarily censored in at least two contexts.

Probably the most important and sustained mode of censorship against TLC's hit song was constituted by the pressures they faced to change the penis references in the chorus. In the radio version of the song and in a revised version of the music video (the original lyrics slipped by until the song gained a bit of steam) the lyrics "2 inches or a yard, rock hard or if it's saggin" were changed to "my hat's to the back and my pants are surely saggin" in order to satisfy music video outlet censors, most importantly, I imagine, MTV. This substitution not only destroys the chorus's thematic continuity, but it erases the deliberately transgressive (albeit visually and lyrically indirect) claiming and mocking of the penis—which is the centerpiece of the song. And, in the face of the sustained sexism on various music video outlets, this substitution by demand is outrageously hypocritical.

After the song began climbing the R&B and pop music charts, TLC was invited to appear on the then popular, black youth oriented, Hip-Hop inflected comedy show, *In Living Color.* Once the show's censors got wind of TLC's lyrics and their trademark safe sex accessories, they requested that both be dropped from the on-air performance. Their reason: these women, they felt, didn't look old enough to be having sex. According to TLC's publicists the incident took place this way:

> Due to the demands of Fox network censors Hip Hoppers TLC's appearance on the fabulously raunchy *In Living Color* has been canceled. Initially scheduled for a January 31st (1992) taping, the group was rescheduled to allow censors at the show, whose recent episodes have included gerbil jokes, and a skit involving a gluteus-phallic family called the ButtMans, an opportunity to evaluate the lyrical comments of TLC's hit called "Ain't 2 Proud 2 Beg." The streetwise group was rescheduled for February. Though only if they, the censors asked, would substitute acceptable language for some of the racier lyrics. "We wanted to be accommodating," TLC said, but they felt that their requests were too extreme. Although they look much younger, TLC is comprised of three 20 and 21 year old girls who address adult issues. While the group would be delighted to perform another song on the show we wanted their first live television performance to enhance the group's image and not compromise it.[2]

In their negotiations with censors, TLC offered to wear T-shirts with large print displaying their respective ages, to diffuse concerns about under-age sex. This offer was refused. In the final analysis, TLC refused to appear on either episode of *In Living Color* and a few months later went on to appear on the Arsenio Hall show and performed another, less sexually direct hit single.[3]

There are a number of perplexing contradictions here: 1) the Fox television network owes its financial success to youth oriented, highly sexually irreverent material. Early evening shows such as *Married with Children* and *In Living Color* are extremely risqué in content and in visual representation. The mother and *adolescent daughter* on *Married with Children* wear extremely sexual, revealing clothing, while adult burlesque celebration/spoofs of extremely sexist, male-centered themes drive the show's entire structure; 2) the network drew and continues to draw a great deal of energy and identity from Hip Hop youth culture, and has done little to redirect Hip Hop's sexism. Instead, executives felt moral disease (and pressure?) in the face of black female, non-sexist, Hip Hop inflected sexual desire; 3) finally, Fox, the first network to air condom advertisements, became squeamish in the face of a moment of safe sex popular culture.

It is likely that censors were responding anxiously to an increasingly powerful reactionary and pro-censorship lobby, especially given their emphasis on black teen culture's narratives of sex and violence. At the same time, there is a larger and related context within which I think we should interpret their anxiety. TLC's brand of young black female sexual agency is unsettling for at least a few reasons. First, it displaces masculine privilege—black, white, and beyond—drawing energy away from a male-empowered sexual space toward a female centered and empowered one. Second, it de-objectifies black female sexuality without repressing it, which, again, troubles the entrenched notion that explicit female desire is itself vulgar. This is partly because of lingering Victorian notions of female sexuality and also because explicit female desire (not male fantasies of it) are less familiar and, therefore, more shocking than the ubiquitous male exploitation of women's sexuality. TLC's brand of young black female sexual agency also displaces the white female sexual subject (and object) in a racist culture that reveres white female sexuality (as much as any female-narrated sexuality is openly revered) at the direct expense of public affirmation of black female sexuality.

Given this potentiality, what were the effects of TLC's refusal to perform on *In Living Color?* Is this an effective form of resistance? What happens when this sort of refusal takes place? I mean, how can this strategic refusal be made public and rendered more powerful? TLC could have compromised its sexual politics for national coverage, with the hopes that record buyers would be more greatly influenced by the album content. But what are the political effects of this move? They might, too, have attempted to slip in subversive content, which often results in last minute censure and possible loss of future media access. These sorts of behind the scenes censure happen a great deal, not only to artists without commercial clout who are never considered, but to those whose commercial power is diluted because of marginal politics or values. How then should access to this treacherous and yet crucial medium be negotiated? How can we engage—attempt to speak through—powerful media outlets without either being erased, compromised to the point of non-recognizability, or completely silenced? Simultaneously, what are the consequences of refusing to politically engage this arena at all?

In my view, the sustained and multidirectional erasures/distortions of black female sexual subjectivity in American culture call for the *creation and support of more black female-narrated and controlled, sexually empowering and, if so desired, sexually explicit materials.* Silence and complaint in the face of this history is not enough. Black women must also reinscribe their image in the very spaces that have done them the most harm. I am painfully aware that fighting sexual myths, stereotypes, and the plethora of abusive, objectifying images and stories with openly feminist or womanist sexual stories and narratives is dangerous territory; it is especially dangerous for black women whose supposed "sexual deviance" has been market fodder since the founding of this nation. Simply articulating one's own sexual truths or politics continues to have dire consequences for black women across class, age, and political perspectives (remember: Tawana Brawley, Anita Hill, and, to a lesser extent, ex–Surgeon General Jocelyn Elders). Crafting and publicizing sexually explicit yet black womanist/anti-sexist images and tales may place oneself at even greater risk. The fact that in this highly mediated environment black women have limited access to and virtually no control over the media's capacity to re-contain, re-direct, and refuse radical ways of seeing and interpreting the world only makes matters worse.

In response to the history of sexual oppression (and in support of women's own sexually-oppressive training) black women sometimes adopt themes of super sexual control and restraint; they re-invent the sexually and morally "pure" black women that racist and sexist America has refused to acknowledge. I think many sisters may hope that sexual silences and conformity will diffuse and perhaps counter the historical legacy of black women as so-called sexual deviants. Strategic silences can be powerful, they can help us dodge short-term bullets and divert attention away from an exploitative arena. At the same time, space for politically informed, open sexual expression by women must be forged and defended as a way of transforming this powerful and all too objectifying arena. Sexual silence, on its own, will not counter systemic modes of sexual domination in a patriarchal society. More to the point: *refusing to make desires, pleasures and terms of intimacy known will not reduce sexually objectifying, male-empowering representations and treatment of women.*

Unfortunately, publicly empowered black female narratives, by themselves, are not likely to prevent abusive or exploitative relations between men and women. This fact is poignantly illustrated in the personal life of TLC member Lisa "Left Eye" Lopes. About two years after TLC's debut on the popular cultural scene, Lopes, who contributes many of the group's lyrics, made headlines in the press for setting her pro-football player boyfriend Andre Rison's house on fire. Little explanation (beyond her being "wild") was given for this enraged response, even though she claims to have evidence of his physical abuse of her.[4]

Tricia Rose

Plate 45: *Yo Mama's Last Supper,* 1996
Renée Cox
Courtesy of the artist

Publicly acknowledging the wide range of loving, irreverent, conflicted, and angry sexual expressions and feelings that black women have—especially those that respond to a complex history of sexual/racial oppression—is dangerous but vital work in a racist and patriarchal society. It is work that, at its best, is careful, mature, and sustained by a diverse community of supporters who understand the risks and the meaning of the struggle at hand. Still, too, we should support and nurture youthful and less complex attempts, such as the one I've attended to here, that might contribute to the cultivation of more trenchant expressions.

All of these expressions will be as contradictory, potentially manipulated, and as contested as the collectivity of black women. But, perhaps, too, narratives of sexual self-possession and self-love can be as empowering as that which takes place in the context of intimate sharing. To some degree, the former can help lead some of us to the latter. Without a sustained effort to craft and support the full range of black women's expressive capacity and need for self-definition, black female sexual silence and prudery—especially in the world as we know it—serve patriarchy, not sexual equality and mutuality.

Notes

1. TLC, "Ain't 2 Proud 2 Beg," *Oooooooohhh . . . On the TLC Tip* (Arista, 1992).

2. Arista Records press release following the incident.

3. As the tone of the Arista press release illustrates, the record label executives are taking advantage of the situation to promote their group and perhaps are only marginally concerned with the matter of censorship in general.

4. Joan Morgan, "The Fire This Time," *Vibe* (November, 1994): 62-?.

Catherine Benamou

Those Earrings, That Accent, That Hair:
A Dialogue with Maria Hinojosa on Latino/as and the Media

> I've always said that in this business, you've got to think like a man,
> act like a lady, and work like a dog; and that *still* hasn't changed.
>
> —Martha G. "The Queen" McQueen, WJLB and WQVH Radio,
> Detroit[1]

*Maria Hinojosa is one of the most prominent Latinas working in the U.S. communi-
cations media today. Her frequent audibility on National Public Radio, both as a
regular correspondent and as host of the English language news program,* Latino,
U.S.A., *transformed Hinojosa into a household name for millions of listeners nationwide. She has also made regular appearances on local network and public television,
hosting NBC's weekly magazine on the Latino experience,* Visiones; *and participating in* Informed Sources, *a journalists' roundtable on political and social issues
affecting New Yorkers, produced and narrowcast by WNET/Channel 13. Since
May 1997, she has worked as a correspondent for the New York bureau of CNN
television.*

*Notwithstanding this exposure, Maria has maintained a firm commitment to
both "grass-roots" reporting and the mentoring of young Latino/a college students
pursuing media studies. Her steady concern for urban youth is expressed in "Kids
and Guns,"[2] a radio report on teen armament and urban violence; and in "Crews," a
radio documentary transformed into what she describes as a "Studs Terkel-type" book
about crew (as opposed to "gang") members from various ethnic (Afro-American,
white, Latino) communities in New York City. At CNN, she has continued to work
with community-based reporting, using the long story format.*

*In 1995, as a follow-up to the conference and at Ella Shohat's request, Maria
and I began to exchange views on another arena of struggle, one that is rarely within
reach of the public eye: the professional, personal, and political challenges encountered
by Latinas working in the mainstream media today. We focused more on the processes*

and ideologies shaping their media participation, than on the impact of the media on the Latino/a community, although in many ways, the two concerns are intertwined.

Latina media professionals currently face the challenge of whether to work in the Spanish language media, which remain under the "threat" of stylistic influence by the English language media and are equally controlled by corporate interests, but which offer more latitude in the coverage of Latino issues; or, whether to try their luck at penetrating the English language media, thereby bringing marginalized community experiences to the attention of the general public, as Maria has done. There, the standards for what one is able to communicate, and how, are almost always determined with hegemonic identities and interests in mind; there, other timeworn, gendered, sexualized, and ethnic image fabrications help set the parameters not only for a Latina's appearance and performance, but for the specific tasks she can perform, the power she is granted behind the scenes. On the film and television screen, the Latina image derives its potency not from the referencing of culturally-specific traits or its proven general popularity, but from the accumulated years of usage. From the screen personae of Carmen Miranda and Dolores del Rio to Lupe Vélez and Rita Moreno and Marisa Tomei, this sexualized image has generally been forged from the creative manipulation of phenotype in the form of "brownface" and its obverse, "passing," thus linking and at the same time distinguishing Latino/a representation from that of other racialized groups, notably Afro- and Native Americans. This image has been forged together with the modulation of spoken accent (whereby Latinas have figured as an eminently "foreign" presence), and pronounced bodily gestures and girations (to convey a smouldering, at times insatiable sexuality). Reaching fully bloomed proportions on the film screen, the Latina image has appeared mainly as a source of excess or rupture in the flow of the narrative—and thus affords slim possibilities for the actress to represent the broader concerns of the Latino/a community. On television and radio, meanwhile, flamboyant uses of sexualized Latina imagery are far more erratic. In news programming, such images must make way for a protocol of uniformity in appearance and delivery (from program to program, station to station), not to mention the iron-clad hierarchy of modes of address and camera styles assigned by category of professional involvement (anchor versus reporter, "expert" versus witness).[3] Further, the newscaster is expected at all times to serve as much as a conduit of information—capable of "representing" a wide array of issues—as an audiovisual object of attention.

In the midst of this high-pressure gloss of "neutrality," a woman of color's capacity to represent both herself and beyond herself forms a constantly contended and ambiguous terrain. Recycled stereotypes, working gingerly in conjunction with models of uniformity (both catering to the self-image and tastes of the socio-economic groups in national power), define the "permissible" forms of expression, while the "permissible" spaces for that expression are often transitory, "token," and marginal. Ulti-

Catherine Benamou

mately, who owns *and* controls *the direction taken by the organization, and who* decides *what does or does not get on the air carry more weight in a Latina media professional's career than any mitigating or binding ideology of democracy and fairness (formulated and enforced by the FCC and Congress) that might have led to her hiring as a representative of a homogeneously-defined "community" (or, more rarely, as part of a "minority" constituency within the growing pool of women media professionals).[4] Maria clues us into the hidden complexities of working within these strictures, and imparts some of the many stances she has taken to improve the representation of Latinos and Latinas in the U.S. media.*

The Linguistic Border and the Perils of Media Enfranchisement

CB: Recently, there's been an apparent expansion of Spanish language media directed at the Latino community, and in New York City specifically: we now have *El Daily News,* published along with the *Daily News;* Lite FM has a Suave FM twin on the radio dial; and I just noticed there is Spanish programming for Showtime on cable television. I say *apparent* because there are still hierarchies and debates inside this media, and one might question whether it has had a "spillover" effect in terms of English language, mainstream media.

MH: I think it's interesting that despite an increasing anti-immigrant fervor on a national scale, you do have this recognition that there are people here who speak Spanish, are looking for access to the media, and who want to see media that reflects themselves. But, you're right: whether Spanish-speaking media actually reflect the community here is debatable. I could watch Spanish language television, read Spanish language newspapers, and listen to Spanish language radio and create a world vision from here in New York that is going be very different from what you would get if you watched Channel 7, read the *New York Times,* and listened to CBS News Radio 88. This is not to say that to have a separate world vision is necessarily good or bad, but we need to recognize that there's not enough overlapping going on. Too often, the stories that are really important to the Latino community still consistently will be completely invisible within the mainstream media. These are big stories and debates in terms of what's going on with political organizations, leaders, or community groups, and they're completely insulated.

I'm still concerned about that, because learning Spanish is not a requirement when you become part of the news media in this city or in the rest of this country. Yet we need to recognize that there is a whole part of our country that moves within this language. I always say that if there were one language that I would learn, right now it would be Korean. Why Korean? Because there's a huge Korean immigrant community in New York, and I, as a good reporter, should be having access to that community, and the best way to do that is to learn the language. We know this other media exists: you flip past it when you're channel surfing. Most people go right through it: "This is not me, this has nothing to do with me, I don't care." And the fact is, it *is* part of you, it *does* have something to do with you. To just zip through it is damaging to your own psychic image of what this country is really about.

CB: You're referring to a general process of ghettoization, of balkanization, rather than of translation. In other words, there isn't enough support for talking across cultural, racial, and ethnic communities. The most the "immigrant media" can do is try to conquer, with their own capital, their own little space on the airwaves. . . . But you are also making a methodological observation: how people who are journalists, such as yourself, regardless of your own backgrounds, should be trying to get stories and offer coverage of events on the communities' own terms.

MH: It's crucial, because my experience as a Latina growing up in this country—which I've finally come to understand—has been a very painful process. Anyone who has had a bicultural experience has gone through feeling that you never really believe that your experience is a legitimate one, that how you see the world around you isn't "the right way." There's somebody else who's had the "real" American experience, but yours isn't it. It's been a long process toward being able to say, "No, my experience is as real, as American, as Walter Cronkite's."

We simply see our America differently, and I always try to talk about the fact that it's not just race and ethnicity, it's a question of class difference. So, for example, how Korean immigrants see this world of theirs, yes, it's going to be very different from how I see it, or from how another reporter who has no immigrant experience sees it. My goal as a reporter is to try to place us where we see the world through those people's eyes, whoever they may be, whether they're young people in jail, or vendors on the street, or wealthy business men. We need to see the world through those different eyes.

CB: But this genuine sharing of experiences is very different from what I think presently exists within the framework of the cardinal rules of American media. One of these rules, that "in a democracy, everyone has equal access to the media," has led to a kind of multicultural tokenism. When you watch the evening news, you notice there's only one white anchor person, or maybe two: one Anglo and perhaps an Ashkenazic (white) Jewish person; and then you've got your Afro-American, and your occasional Asian American and Latino/a. It gives the media a gloss of diversity, but is it really diverse? Your criteria for approaching diversity seem to be very different.

MH: I think that first of all, this belief that it's a democracy and everybody has access to the media is not true. We have to remember who is making the decision about what is or is not news, what should or should not get on the air. You have to start from there because the effects of those decisions are apparent on all kinds of levels. For example, an African-American or a Latino reporter is usually still responding to an editor who is a white male, and who probably lives in the suburbs. This means that, unless he's a wonderful journalist, his decisions about what is or is not news will be based on editors' comments   such as I've heard—like: "That's not interesting to me," or "Who really cares about that?" or "That's not really news," or "Well, we've heard too many of those kinds of stories." "Those stories," then, don't get beyond that point.

Our role as journalists of color, or as journalists who understand the need to be representative in the media, is to fight consistently with those editors, those bosses. It's a *fight*, it's not like *play*, it gets heavy a lot of the time. One of the things that I say that some other people may find controversial is that it has been very safe for directors of news media—newspapers, television stations—to get around this diversity issue by hiring someone who's brown, or black, to put them in front of the camera and say, "we have diversity." I'm very leery of that. . . . [She pauses and asks] . . . Who's going to be reading this?

CB: Probably feminists, mostly of color, and people who are interested in these issues: semi-scholarly, semi-political people who have a real interest in improving the situation. Given the strongly alternative viewpoints it contains, I doubt that the anthology will make the bestseller list of the *New York Times*. [I hope she feels safer to speak now, in this circle of allies.]

MH: There are situations whereby a news director will hire somebody who looks the part, but only looks the part: somebody who historically has not been tied to that community that they "represent." And this can get very uncomfortable, because who are we to judge somebody else about what their ties are? What I would ask is, what kind of a journalist are you?

Are you a journalist who, regardless of your skin color, regardless of your ethnicity, is a journalist who can cover any number of communities? Who knows something about the community that you're supposed to represent? Or, even assuming that you don't know everything about it, are you willing to dig and go into sources and talk to people in that community: in the African-American, Chinese, lesbian, or academic communities? That's the mark of a good journalist. But simply to put somebody with the right color of skin in front of the camera and say, "Well, we've resolved our diversity problem," is very dangerous and it worries me. This call on the part of a lot of minority journalist organizations, "Just hire more of us"—what does that mean? I say, hire more of us who are good journalists, who have a commitment to true diversity in the media in terms of representing a variety of voices, who have a true commitment in terms of representing class perspectives. But a lot of news media directors, people in power, don't necessarily want that.

CB: For some immigrant groups, and particularly for Afro-Americans, there has been an overall progression from media segregation—a black press, all-black casts in films, and segregated theaters—to "assimilation" and "integration" of various types. Yet, history has also shown that often this means assuming a new position of marginality within the mainstream,[5] and "integration" is also contingent upon one's willingness to conform to the standards and codes that have already been set within mainstream media. Do you see this happening with Latino/a journalists?

MH: We definitely have to conform. But there is still segregation, and that has to do with where Latino/as stand in terms of still having to prove ourselves, because if you do anything that shows your ties to your community, media organizations immediately assume that you're not a good reporter because you've got a "Latino agenda." Just because I pronounce my name the way I do, people all the time say that I have this "Latino agenda," and I always say I have a journalist's agenda. People who listen to public radio, for example, immediately assume that I only do Latino stories, which I don't.

What happens to Latino/a journalists is very complicated: you hope they're hiring you because you're a good reporter, but on the other hand, they're hiring you because they want you to do these Latino stories. Then, once you're there and you want to do the Latino stories, they're telling you, "No, we don't want you to do those stories because you're pigeonholing yourself." When I do Latino stories, I'm doing them not because I have a "Latino agenda," but because they're important stories that involve an incredibly large community in the U.S. that remains invisible. Ultimately, the people who come out losing are the people who listen to public radio, because they're not hearing these stories about the Latino community that they *should* be hearing.

CB: Isn't this type of "segregation" guided by the apprehension that if Latino media professionals are permitted to maintain ties to the community they "represent" on the job, it could lead to the formation of an autonomous power base for Latinos?

MH: When you have this type of power relationship in the media, this way of writing history continues. The only reporters allowed to show any level of sensitivity or commitment to a story are white men. It's safe for them to look like they're caring toward a certain person in the story; but if I show that, then I'm not a professional, I have an "agenda," I'm not a good reporter.

CB: Segregation is often the flip side of conflation: decision makers in the mainstream media also seem to have trouble recognizing that there may be different "agendas" *within* a given community. For example, when a neighborhood like Washington Heights[6] becomes home to drug dealing and violence, there's an assumption of complicity on the part of *all* community members. The Latinos who live there become the target of discriminatory practices and stereotypes. The notion of "incomprehensibility," attached to the fact of language difference, also goes hand in hand with a lack of differentiation: there is a group apart and, from an outside viewpoint, it is easy to dismiss, or at least difficult to distinguish the "significance" of events affecting that group.

MH: When you have most of the mainstream media not hearing or reading what is being said, those stories are not considered consequential. The one person who was able to cross that line, crossed it in tragedy. That was Manuel de Dios,[7] a prominent Latino journalist who was assassinated. You had some coverage—not a lot—in the mainstream press about his killing. It may have had something to do with the fact that he was from New York, and had reported on the drug cartels; but the fact is that maybe up to fifteen U.S.-based journalists have been killed in the United States in the past 10 years. Most people don't know that because these journalists were writing for immigrant publications. If they had been twelve reporters from the *Kansas City Star,* the *New York Times,* or even the *Brownsville Journal,* you can be sure this would have been a "good story." There would have been a tag on this story because the victims were journalists, and drugs were involved. But coming from this immigrant press, such stories just aren't so important.

I would say that the basic issue is that as journalists, we have been consistently part of the struggle to get our community covered: insisting that what's happening in our community is important. How many stories will they let us do about Latino issues? At what point will our editors start getting worried because they will want to pigeonhole us, when we really don't want to be pigeonholed, but feel these are important stories?

CB: Language, then, can also effect a division, to the point that the mainstream media might say it's not necessary to cover stories of relevance to the Latino community, since the Spanish language media will presumably "take care of all that." Your mention of Manuel de Dios reminds me of how in mainstream fiction films, "dangerous" events in Third World settings are often mediated through a foreign, First World journalist whose life is at risk. These mediators provide the "safe" distance that is needed to ensure a measure of ideological balance. It seems that all producers, and certainly news editors, are wary of the problem of "balance"—indeed, that's a big part of *their* job. Even on public television, "wrap around" commentaries are created for documentaries that are deemed too controversial.[8] In your experience, has the need for "balance" affected the development of some news stories?

MH: I have a story about the issue of balance that I always think about, and it gets back to the problem of trusting people's voices, who they are, and how they see the world around them as being a legitimate expression of their experience. About a year and a half ago, I went and spent some time with people who live in Washington Heights to do a story about living in a community where there is a tremendous amount of violence. Along with the violence of the street, there is the violence of simply living in an abandoned community. Violence can be expressed in any number of ways: it can be constituted by just having huge amounts of garbage that needs to be picked up; it can be noise that is excessive, streets that are clogged, etc. So what does that do to a person's psyche? As part of the story, a woman took me on a tour of her street. We walked by some police officers, and she later said to me: "You see those police officers? You see what they were doing? They were talking to those drug dealers right there." I asked, "What do you mean?" And she replied, "Well, you know, because they're friends, they hang out, they're on the take. I live a block away from the police precinct, but I can't do anything about this. I can't talk to the police about it, because they see *me* as the problem when I complain about the drug dealers, because *they're* having a relationship with the dealers."

Now, to me, the fact that this woman felt that, although living one block away from the police precinct, she was not protected, was a very important part of the story. When I later told this to my editor, he said, "Well, no, we can't use that, because we need to get the perspective of the police who can deny. . . ." And I said, "This is not a story about the police, this is a story about her vision of the community. Sure, I can make a phone call and I'm certain the police will say this is not true. But that's not the central point." Well, it was not included in the piece. Lo and behold, six months later, there is huge corruption scandal in a police precinct in New York City. Where was that precinct? A half a block away from this woman's home. She was right! She had been experiencing living under a corrupt, scandal-ridden, police precinct, but, because of the impression that the police give on a general level—certainly in the eyes of my editor who lives in the suburbs—"Well, no, police aren't like that, so we can't accuse them." It was so telling: we omitted that part of the story, and by including it we would have been ahead of the story.

CB: Isn't there also a gender bias there? The idea that women can't speak with authority and that we need to have a male voice present at all times? Cops certainly convey an impression of tremendous male authority. . . .

MH: I am inclined to agree with you, but I would say that in this story, even if it had been a man who complained it would have been worse, because if he's a Latino male, he's seen as a criminal or as someone who has something against the police. So he's less of a legitimate spokesperson. I really see this as a question of not being able to accept another version of reality.

CB: We *do* see an increasing tendency to "criminalize" Latino men in news reports, and even in Hollywood films, regardless of genre (the Willie López character in the film *Ghost,* a combination melodrama/romantic comedy, is a good example). This is contributing to a growing "culture of fear" in this country. Criminalization has already been directed in the American media at male members of other ethnic groups, such as Asian-Americans, African-Americans, and even—without the racial component—at Irish and Italian Americans. But why the current focus on Latino males?

MH: It's easy: we're the fastest growing "minority" group. And certainly in California they've been able to criminalize the entire Latino community and blame it for what's going on in California, since it's growing. And what's worse is we speak another language; we're proud to speak it, and this is considered a threat. In effect, the media have inflamed the situation so much that it really begins to feel like a threat. Instead of wanting to learn about these communities that are going to be a part of society, you create this otherness, which is much easier for people outside to contend with. What's changed is the composition of American society, and what's *not* changing is the composition of American media to keep pace with what's happening in American society.

CB: In addition to the linguistic and demographic "threat," there is the issue of fitting newcomers comfortably within the prevailing system of social classification. For example, when Puerto Ricans came to this country, they were "assimilated" as a *racial* category, instead of being placed in another social or national category.[9] You could see this early on in the use of "brown face," or making actors up to "look" Puerto Rican on the screen, regardless of their national origin or natural skin color: in *West Side Story,* both Rita Moreno and Natalie Wood are made up to "look like" recent Puerto Rican immigrants. But I've also seen it in a new stereotype emerging both on television (*NYPD Blue*), and in Hollywood films (*Mambo Kings*) in the form of voodoo, "black magic," the casting of spells by urban Latino/as. Potentially, the reference to African based religious beliefs could be a source of bonding with the Afro-American community, since it points to African roots *within* the Latino community; but it is such a confused and mystifying representation (especially for those of us who know or have had contact with Santería)[10] that it ends up exoticizing Latino/as further, placing them outside the bounds of "proper social conduct" and rational logic. Rather than serve as cultural affirmation, these representations stress the malevolent manipulation of "innocent" victims through the (ab)use of one's psychic powers.

MH: I think it's really interesting that in New York these days, there are ads on the buses for—I'm not sure what drink it is—but it's called "voodoo for your mouth," and I always thought, what are they trying to say? I can think of a couple of things in response to that.

Recently in New York, they found the carcass of a bear that had been dissected in a park. Within the first line of a *New York Times* piece on the story, it said, "Authorities are assuming that this is connected to the Afro-Cuban practice of santería." They went on to talk about animal sacrifice, Santería, and all kinds of [occult] stuff and how the animal was found. Then, at the very end of the article, it said, "Oh, and by the way, there is traffic in animal organs in Chinese medicine [I think they said it was Chinese medicine]; also, the sacrifice of bears is rarely known in the Santería tradition." The whole article was about how this animal death was Santería oriented, when in fact, more than likely it had nothing to do with Santería. This was an article from 1995; we could pull out articles on Santería from five, ten, twenty years ago to show they're still talking in the same language. People still see Santería as something that is so dangerous when, my god, in New York, if you're in any neighborhood of color, or where there are immigrants, you're going to see a *botánica*.[11] You're going to see all kinds of people from the neighborhood going in and out of there, and it's not a dangerous place. Even mainstream books have talked about elements of Santería: there are women's books that place it within the context of just another form of spiritual worship.

Looking and Sounding "Latina," Compared to What?

CB: It is well known that the mainstream U.S. media have traditionally "set the tone" for the format and style of news programming in Latin America. How do you see the influence of U.S. mainstream media on the Spanish language media inside the U.S.? Has there been any effect where the treatment of gender is concerned?

MH: Spanish language media in many ways are shaping themselves after the English language media. They recently went to a two-person news-team, a man and a woman,[12] probably following what mainstream TV has done to attract women audiences. In Spanish network television there is professionalism, but also a level of familiarity allowed on the part of both men and women newscasters. The newscasters talk to you like they're part of your family. You don't see that level of affection on the part of anchors or reporters in U.S. media. With Maria Elena Salinas,[13] there's something she exudes, there's a warmth the producers want her to exude; they want that in her style.

CB: Yet, do you think that the self-conscious attempt on the part of both Spanish language and English language media to have a gender balance (i.e., by increasing the number of women anchors and reporters) has helped Latinas at all in getting more of a voice in the media?

MH: Well, it's hard to generalize and say that since we have more white women it means that it's going to be good for Latinas, or African-American women, or such. We already know that having a woman in a position of power does not necessarily mean that she is going to be interested in covering women's issues. Those are all parameters that you have to look at. I think that having more women out there has inspired younger women to think, "Maybe this is something that I can do," and that's probably one of the things that I take most seriously in terms of my work. I can say, "Hey, look at me, I don't look that much different from you, I talk the same way you do, we can hang on the same level and, check it out, this is where I'm at." It's not impossible, and the more Latinas we have out there feeling like part of their role is not just to be there and conquer their own space, but also to be opening up the doors, the better. I see myself as carrying this big Santa Claus bundle on my back and saying, "Come on, let's go, open up not only for me, open up for a lot of other women." At the same time, I think that we have our own series of battles to confront—for Latinas, specifically. If you want to talk about being on camera, there's any number of issues for Latinas.

CB: For example?

MH: Well, I think there is tremendous pressure on Latinas to look like everybody else. Thank god, my primary job is in radio, because most people don't have to see what I look like, and that way I can continue to keep my persona intact. My experience in television has been very much one of "the image is key," and "you've got to do something about that hair."

I was upstate giving a lecture to a predominantly white middle–class audience that knew New York, so these people had seen me on television. The lecture was on a very serious topic, and I had my hair pulled back in a braid because it was summer. Usually, I have my hair pretty wild and just the way it is. A number of people came up to me and said, "You know, you look so much better with your hair pulled back like that. Why don't you wear it like that all the time?" Kind of like, "You look more clean cut, you look more acceptable to us." People will say to me, "Do something about that hair, get rid of those earrings, tone down that necklace." It's really interesting that people feel that it's within their realm to say these things to me.

My first television experience was one in which I was being really remodeled, curlers in the hair and the whole bit. My husband would tell me that I looked like I was coming out of a Talbot's catalogue. And I was working with people of color, I did not have a white boss in that case. It was very hard, because it was my first television experience and I didn't have a lot of say in it. It was a learning experience, but I wouldn't let it happen again. Now, I'm in a situation where whenever I do something on camera, I am who I am, but I think that it has closed doors. There are certain people who say, "We just can't have that," and you begin to ask the question, "What should I be sacrificing?" or "How much should they be sacrificing?" But I'm content where I am.

When I think of the image of Latinas, many, many Latina journalists on television are very good journalists, but they're also stunning, very good-looking Latinas, and that's weird. I remember the first time I wanted to go on the air with my hair loose, people said, "You're going to look too sexy, and we just can't have that." At the same time, I think there's something about being a Latina that prompts the comment, "Well, we also want you to look sexy, that's kind of who you're supposed to be." So you're getting conflicting instructions.

CB: Given the overall stress on the uniformity of the image of news professionals on television, what, specifically, does it mean for Latino/as to "look like everybody else"?

MH: To assimilate; depending on how you look at it, and depending on what your political stance is in relationship to mainstream American culture. There are many Latino/as who look like they can pass, and they are happy to pass as white people. There are others who cannot, and they have no interest in "passing." On television, what they often want is to have somebody with a Spanish last name, but who looks white, or who does not pose any visual challenges to the viewer.

Side-comment: Insofar as they are symptomatic of the social marginality of most Latino/as, the twin strategies of "passing" and "brown-face" are analogous in U.S. media to the practice known as "black-face" in relation to the Afro-American community; yet, as a mode of performance that is positioned halfway between transvestitism and minstrelsy, "brown-face" is in a way more insidious than "black-face," in that it relies upon naturalism, rather than reflexivity (in the form of caricature) to "succeed." As such, "brown-face" facilitates the naturalization of racialized stereotypes of Latino/as, to the point that the deconstruction and resignification of these stereotypes in oppositional texts or performances becomes unwieldy: there is still a considerable risk that viewers will lapse into unwitting complacency or complicity with the dominant interpretation.[14]

CB: Were the demands that you "whiten" your appearance subtly insinuated, or were they made explicit?

Plate 46: *La Cabrona Anacaona,* Coco Fusco
From *The Year of the White Bear,* 1992
Created by Coco Fusco and Guillermo Gómez-Peña
Photo: Glen Halvorsen
Courtesy of Coco Fusco and The Walker Art Center

MH: It was pretty unsubtle. The word was, we need to put some suits on you, change your earrings, your hair; you need to look like Barbara Walters because that is the image of a good woman journalist who looks respectable. I think they're much more leery of appearance when you're Latina, because it's O.K. for Diane Sawyer to look sexy; it's problematic for a Latina journalist to look sexy and be a news reporter.

CB: Is there an unspoken fear that a Latina's sexual attractiveness (however that is defined!) would subvert her objectiveness in delivering the news?

MH: There is some uncomfortableness toward a Latina who is challenging mainstream notions of what is or is not acceptable.

CB: Couldn't one say that there is, then, an en-gendering of criminality around Latino/as in a *double* sense, with the feminine version taking the form of erotic suggestion and sexual aggressivity? Isn't this a component of the Latina "threat"?

MH: It means a loss of control: it's problematic to have white men attracted to Latinas, it means we're going to have all these mixed race babies, and that right there is the downfall of American society as we know it! It completely plays into the notion that the media has perpetuated, which is the Marisa Tomei *Pérez Family*[15] caricature of Latinas, namely that we basically want to have sex with anything that moves, and that's a problem for white women and white men.

CB: Aside from preferences for and against specific images of Latinas in film and on television, there is the issue of the Latina voice and whether it is deemed to carry enough authority. What is often invoked in defense of certain forms of exclusion is the cost involved in making a film or television "statement," and what decisions are needed to ensure that the money invested will be recuperated when the product is shown. You might recall my own frustrations working to find a voice-over narrator for the documentary *It's All True* that was to be shown in commercial movie theaters. I was told by the key producers that it probably wouldn't be given to a woman, and absolutely not to a woman such as yourself, who, regardless of professional achievements, was not a recognized white actress. The resistance to trying a serious alternative was a result, allegedly, of box-office "paranoia" on the part of the studio: the feeling was that people would not be drawn to a Latina as a spokesperson for a nationally distributed documentary.

MH: Actually, I think that a lot of people would be accepting. There's always this dual reality that we face in this country. On the one hand, you have this backlash that is very real. On the other hand, there are a lot of people out there who are genuinely open and accepting, and who may come from places like Kalamazoo, Michigan, where they may not have a lot of experience with diversity, but are incredibly open to it. But again at the top, there's a perspective of, "Well, no, it will never fly, so we won't even try it." I think a good example of that is Selena [the late Chicana singer]. *People* magazine came out with a divided cover: they did not feel that having Selena on their cover would sell across the country. And you know, I think they lost. I think it was a bad marketing decision. Apparently, when they did their commemorative issue on Selena, it had one of the highest selling rates of *People* magazine in its history. They had never conceptualized that and, of course, they continue to see Selena as this non-American performer, when Selena was born in Texas, and her primary language was English—she learned Spanish to sing in Spanish; but her experience is still not considered an American experience. What does that do to ourselves as a country when we can't see her as part of the American experience?

CB: It seems that bilingualism—the mastery of a second language to communicate effectively—is not enough: one's dominance in Spanish, even one's pronunciation in English, can also act as a barrier to media access for Latino/as.

MH: Indeed. There recently have been reporters who have had problems getting on the air because they have a Latino accent. It's not a problem if you have a British accent. I would say that NPR has been better than most about accents. There is a reporter, Chitra Ragavan, who has a slight accent, and NPR has let her on the air. But people have written very nasty letters. Somebody wrote a letter regarding me, Chitra Ragavan, and Suni Kalid (Sylvia Pagioli was not mentioned): "Who are these people and why do we have to hear them? Why do we have to hear their accents?" NPR is better than most stations, but it still has problems.

CB: As someone who has worked in both television and radio, you have had the chance to experience different pressures or standards with regard to the development of your media persona. How would you compare these media in terms of the "image" you are able to project?

MH: When people who know my work—but don't know me—meet me they always say: "But you're so small, and the voice that comes over the

Catherine Benamou

radio is so big." They have this image of this big Amazon-like woman, or a real revolutionary, like the women known as Adelitas, who fought with Zapata in Mexico. Then they see this petite woman, and they think this doesn't jibe with the kinds of stories I do, with the way I say my name. Some people are always so shocked to see I am small, so I think there is an image thing that goes beyond TV. People assume I am tall, just from what they hear me say on the radio.

The Differences Within, the Ties Beyond

CB: Clearly, Latinas must face—as you have faced—many challenges in trying to break through the "ice" of the Anglo-centric power dynamics and styles of presentation in the English language media. At the same time, the intense competition for racialized "minority" professionals to get decent jobs, as well as the ambiguities surrounding the representation of Latino/as in those media, can also produce conflicts where one would least expect to find them—among members of one's own community. Do you want to talk about your experience with the NBC public affairs program *Visiones?*

MH: For the first time, the network hired a Latina to be the executive producer, and it turned out that this Latina was not interested in having me continue as part of the show. There was this notion that we were supposed to be sisters, but we need to be realistic about what really draws Latino/as together; I think a primary part is how we see the world around us. It doesn't exactly matter what color you are, but what kind of a world view you have; that's what can draw you together. To make these alliances solely based on ethnicity can backfire on you, and it's very nasty when it does. I also think we need to recognize that as more Latino/as are brought into the media, that that means there's going to be more competition among Latino/as. And not just for Latino/as: it's a very competitive field, period. Then there's this assumption that as Latino/as, we're all brothers and sisters in this, that we all share the same agenda, and frankly we can't: we have different experiences.

So, with *Visiones,* I always knew that my time there was limited. Why? Because it was just a very strange set of circumstances that landed me at that show. In Spanish, the term would have been *que me colé.*[16] It's not that I was subversive, but somehow I was able to get into a place where I shouldn't have been, even given all the limitations of a show like that: you have no resources, and it's a "ghetto" program that nobody gives a damn about. But I still felt that I was doing things that were political, or that I was raising a different kind of awareness around issues like homosexuality, feminism, or spirituality in the Latino community, incorporating Santería, for example. I had kind of maneuvered my way into this role in a strange place: here I was on local NBC, it wasn't national. So although I had been told by the higher-ups that things were great with the show and they loved my work, as things go with TV, they found somebody else that fit their agenda better. Even though I had been in that job for three years, and I had had three different Afro-American bosses, I ended up being fired by a Latina. As Latino/as, we have to prepare ourselves for confronting this competition among ourselves, and the least we should learn how to do is to treat each other with a certain degree of respect and professionalism. This experience made me question again this notion of "Latino community," and of sisterhood, not just among Latinas, but among women in general. I think that she saw me as too progressive, as too questioning of authority, as too critical, as too much of an intellectual, perhaps too much of a feminist.

CB: It's most distressing when these tensions are silenced. In some ways, this would have been an opportunity to open a debate and productively expose the key differences in viewpoint between two Latinas who work in television.

MH: It would have been the perfect opportunity if she had been willing to work together. I said to her that it was really unfortunate that we couldn't show diversity in front of the cameras. In Spanish language television and newspapers, they do. They have, for example, leftist and right-wing commentators on some networks and papers, and that's good, but it would be nice if we could also see Latino/a diversity in the mainstream media.

CB: While there may be more ideological pluralism in the Spanish language media (or rather, more open acknowledgment of political differences), there are also persistent hierarchies in terms of ethnicity and nationality: most studio professionals are middle-class Mexicans, South Americans (Argentinians, Colombians), or Cubans. Even in the category of local reporters, you almost never find Dominicans, Puerto Ricans, or people who visibly exhibit indigenous or African roots. You spoke earlier of your sensing that people wanted to whiten you on television in the English speaking media, but is this also not happening in the Spanish language media?

MH: Yes, sure. Network television is still predominantly white, and the whiter you are, the better. There is maybe one woman of color who's dark-skinned, who's in front of the camera. But overwhelmingly, the women are all white, and the men are all white. You have one or two mulattoes, but you don't have any that have dark skin.

CB: This is interesting: on the one hand, there is the pressure for Latino/as to pass as "white" announcers on the television screen, yet increasingly it seems that Latino youth, picking up on their own racialization by the dominant society—and straying away from the Spanish language enclaves that may have worked to keep their parents' sense of nationality intact—are actively choosing to become "syncretizers with synthesizers": they share music, dance forms, dress, and even slang and pronunciation with Afro-American youth. I've noticed this especially among the young Latina women I've had contact with, regardless of their phenotypical appearance.

MH: Well, it happened to me. This is not to minimize my experience, but the first person who made me feel like I was part of this country was Martin Luther King. He was saying something that I felt touched me. I was very young back then, but he was saying "I'm different, you're different, but we're O.K." Growing up, what I would watch on television were a lot of those programs—the few that were out there—that were geared to the African-American community because we didn't have comparable prime time programs. I do think this is a source of tension, particularly among young people and in terms of whether or not these young people are recent immigrants. Recent [Latin American] immigrants don't necessarily identify with black culture, whereas those who have grown up here do, because it's cool, it's powerful, it's attractive, because it's very strong. When I was in high school I only danced to African-American music—I wasn't dancing to salsa—because it's a part of American culture, a part that I think feels more natural. But it is still a source of tension. Latino kids, for example, will say: "He sold out, he went to their side," speaking of the African-American side. You hear that a lot. On the other hand, many Latinos have been raised to negate their African roots, so when they can in fact embrace them, I think that it's a positive step.

CB: Do you think that we are developing emergent identities that go beyond "Latino" because of continued immigration? It seems to be breaking down into other kinds of identities: it's no longer sheerly a question of nationality. In Brooklyn, there is a strong immigration wave from Mexico that is very indigenous. Definitely, they identify themselves as Mexicans, but as they begin to negotiate their way here, what is that going to bring?

MH: I think that it's completely wide open, and I watch with a tremendous amount of fascination when I see Mexican *campesinos,* or peasants, for example. I know that they're peasants, that their primary language is not Spanish. I see them soon after they've arrived, and they're in this shock of being in New York. Seven months later, I see them again and they're wearing walkmans and headphones, and they may be rollerblading with an earring in their ear. It's like, wow, what does this portend for the future of New York and for the future of their towns back there? These young men and women—because I've seen it with women, too—are in for that same negotiation that so many of us are involved in on a day-to-day basis, which asks: where am I from? Hopefully, many of them will be able to find a certain level of comfort with who they are. Maybe New York and other cities like it in this country, where you have a tremendous amount of diversity, can afford them that place of being a part of everyone. Somebody once said to me that this whole multiculturalism trend is very interesting because I, we, embody multiculturalism in this country. I'm part Mexican, I'm part Jewish, I'm part Dominican, I'm part African-American, part Puerto Rican, part Catholic, part *santera,* I'm any number of combinations of things and they're all right here embodied in one person. I think many of us have that experience, so how can we fear what we embody inside of us, how can we fear ourselves?

Strategizing Beyond Token Multiculturalism and Mainstream Feminism

CB: What do you think people in your position can do to try to combat the stereotyping, criminalization, and exoticization—the "culture of fear" and censorship—that these forms of segregation help to produce?

MH: First, we have to continue to be strong, because it can really wear you down to have to continue to sing this song of, "This is an important story, it's not just a Latino story, it's not just an immigrant story, it's an important story for all of us." You have to have a lot of strength and resolve, you have to trust your instincts. What happens with a lot of reporters is that they get tired of the fight. They begin to believe that maybe their editors are right when they tell them that it's not such an important story, after all. So you have to work hard when you're a person of color in the news media, one who's out on the front lines of doing the reporting. You have to remember to trust your voice and your instinct, and continue to push. The other thing that we have to do is to keep our eyes open, to be very aware of what's happening in our countries and our cities, of the kinds of divisions that we're experiencing. I remember the times I've been to Brazil, people have always said to me, "Whatever you do, don't go to the *favelas,* don't get near them, don't set foot in them." So the *favelas* have always been a place where I cannot go. It's a territory which is unknown to me.

I parallel that statement with how people, journalists and reporters, often see certain areas of our city: "Don't go to that neighborhood, that place is off limits, it's not for you." And reporters begin to believe this, that these are places where they should not go. They assume that what's happening there is not that important and their lives are in danger if they go. To me, that is just the crystallization of the huge gap between the haves and have nots in our city and in our society, along with the damage that we are suffering, because now we've gotten to the point where it's like a *favela:* you just don't set foot in there, what happens there is entirely its own little world and we don't care. I think this is dangerous, because if we're reporters and we're not going there, then we're not being good reporters.

CB: What of the possibility of a strategic alliance between Afro-Americans and Latinos around the issues of marginalization, stereotyping, and tokenism? If the two groups were to join together, they would represent a tremendous force.

MH: I don't know whether Quincy Jones and Afro-American journalists would come out in support of Latino television. Is that their priority? Is that their agenda? What's in it for them? I don't think it should be limited to only a coalition between Afro-Americans and Latinos, because the assumption that we are all brothers and sisters in these communities . . . I don't know. I think there are brothers and sisters in different communities: in the Asian community, in the gay and lesbian communities, the white community. The fact that we [Afro-Americans and Latino/as] are the most visible minority groups doesn't tie us; what ties us is what kind of country we are struggling for: it's beyond ethnic coalition, it's more ideological.

CB: Another area of challenge is the problem of how differences *within* the Latino community can be represented without dissolving the issues into hermetic little debates that nobody can understand outside the community. How do you avoid developing a pseudo-homogenized Latino identity that erases difference? How do you encourage people to understand that Latinos come from different countries, that they have different experiences, and they certainly belong to different classes?

MH: Well, I think that a program like *Latino, U.S.A.* on National Public Radio is a step in the right direction, because it's a program that is covering

Plate 47: *Dolores,* 1994
Detail
Lillian Mulero
New York State Museum
Courtesy of the artist

"March 2, 1954, a woman named Lolita Lebrón led a suicide squadron of three gunmen into the U.S. House of Representatives. They opened fire from the visitor's gallery, wounding five of the astonished legislators. Lebrón shouted, 'I want freedom for my country. My country is Puerto Rico.'"—Gloria Waldman

Catherine Benamou

the truly American Latino experience in the sense that we're talking about what's happening with Dominicans in New York, or Cubans in Miami, or Mexicans in Miami, or Salvadorans in L.A., or Puerto Ricans in Chicago. While we're covering the communities that are kind of representative of whatever a city might be, we are also breaking the mold: we're informing other Latinos about the Latino experience, and hopefully, in the process, also informing the general public. But this kind of program doesn't exist on television, nor in the mainstream mass media, which is unfortunate. When you have a medium like *Latino, U.S.A.*, it means that you can begin to understand what's happening with the Cuban American community in Miami. It may not be your issue, but you can understand it. You might ask, "What do I share with them besides language?" Maybe not much, but that's O.K.

I also think we need to be less freaked out about our own diversity. I think they try to reflect the level of diversity in the Latino population in the Spanish network news, but they aren't doing a good enough job because they don't have a lot of time for national news. A lot of what they're doing is international news, and that's fine, because the only place where you're going to hear about what's happening in Latin America is on those programs. That's good for informing other Latinos about the situation, but it doesn't do much in terms of the general public. Again, there's this sense that nobody would be interested in it—that a *Latino, U.S.A.* could not exist on TV, because nobody would care, and I strongly disagree.

On the other hand, perhaps the greatest challenge that we as Latino/as have to confront and don't do a good enough job of is the question of race. It's right out there for us. In a city with recent Mexican immigrants like New York, I'm sure it must be very interesting for them to come into a city like this and see such a huge black population that speaks Spanish, because when you're in Mexico, you imagine a black population as being from the United States. I think we need to recognize that we have very big problems in Latin America on the question of race. Either you're black, or you're Indian, or you're white, or mulatto, but it's not something that we have resolved at all. So we need to confront it, and we need to confront it in terms of the images that we're putting out there.

CB: It seems that issues around gender and sexual orientation are also coming to be seen in a different light. Could you speak a little about your ad hoc group of Latina journalists? What kinds of patterns do you see developing? What issues do you feel that women are most concerned about right now?

MH: The one thing that keeps this ad hoc group together is a sense of a tremendous amount of friendship and respect. We all realize we're in the same boat because of the similarity of being Latinas and being journalists in New York City. Just knowing that there are a few of us out there gives us the strength to know that we can call on each other: "I have this situation, and I don't exactly know how to handle it."

Before I had this group, I didn't necessarily have anybody to turn to. Now I can call on women who understand where I'm coming from, and they will say, "Well, this is what I would do." I can't tell you that we've all sat around and talked about questions of sexism, in the sense that this is the predominant issue. No. Each of us has stories, but it's not as if that is the overwhelming issue. Maybe in a way we've all had to confront it now for so long—many of us have been in the business for ten years or so—that you just learn to do a *jogo de cintura*[17] about it: you just know that it's there and how you are going to work around it. One of the special things that has happened is that we have learned so much from each other, learned to see other Latinas who have had the strength and the resolve to confront difficult situations. It's very special to have a place to tell stories, to share our experiences of working as media professionals.

CB: Why have you limited your group to Latina journalists?

MH: It's almost like you wanted to get to that first step of going over some of those hurdles. You don't just form this group: there is tension, competition, strong-headed women, things that need to be resolved in the group, and they *have* been. It's important to get through the difficulties in a group that is somewhat homogeneous.

There are women in the group who don't speak Spanish, we have different political perspectives, and different sexual orientations. Yet there is some similarity: we say, let's try to work it out here, just for this commonality of experience. So there hasn't been much dialogue about expanding it to other women of color, although that would be great. It's partly logistical, just meeting once a month is a feat. All it is for me is simply a group of women who share my vision of my role as a Latina journalist. It's not that there are ten rules to which you must adhere, it's just a sense of commitment to the Latino/a community that is expressed in terms of how you see yourself first and foremost as a journalist who doesn't limit herself only to being a good journalist when covering the Latino/a community, but a good journalist when covering the Asian community, or people with AIDS.

When I first became involved with the group, I had really hoped that we would have lots of people with different perspectives, engage in political debates. It didn't turn out that way. But we have been able to have a dialogue in terms of differences. For example, when the "Rainbow Curriculum"[18] was being debated, we were able to disagree and move on. That's great when you can share the space and dialogue about it. So I suppose maybe the key component is being able to respect a difference of opinion.

CB: One of the issues that came up at the conference that *Talking Visions* came out of, was that feminism as it's been published and circulated in this country has been useful and inspirational to women of color to some extent, but it really has been deficient in addressing some concerns, and it's taken white feminists a long time to be able to reckon with this. One of the real deficiencies of the feminist ideology that came out of the whole movement of the sixties and seventies was its individualist tinge. There was a sense not of responsibility to a larger community that involved men and women, young and old, sick and healthy, etc., but really responsibility to oneself as a woman. This has led to the corporate woman phenomenon we're seeing today, where it's really a matter of competition, not a matter of solidarity. And it can cut either way. Many feminists of color have said that they just can't keep within that boundary—or at least the ones who are more critical and insightful say, "You know, I just really can't forget the political struggles that my community has experienced to side only with women."

MH: As you're talking my sense is that the feminist movement became— I don't think it started out this way—but it became centered on issues of success: how successful can I be? It's about me, it's about my success. It's not about how I will bring these sisters along, and, not only that, but will I be prepared to bring along women who don't look anything like me in this success? I think there are women in the feminist movement who maintain a perspective of likemindedness in our society, which I continue to refer to as ultimately where you *are* able to build bonds. But it's interesting, because I do not hang out with "white" feminists, it just happens that way. I still feel that for them to recognize my concerns they have to go someplace: they really have to get to another level to be able to see them, as opposed to simply understanding that we may have differences. My issues are as legitimate as theirs.

Recently in New York there was the case of an abortion doctor who basically murdered a Latina Honduran immigrant, and the feminist movement in this country, in New York, did not say a lot about this. What would have happened if that woman had been the daughter of Gloria Steinem? My god, what kinds of demonstrations would we have seen, if the woman who was allowed to bleed to death had been Gloria Steinem's daughter! The feminist movement needs to understand that it represents but one voice of the woman's community, that there are women who are very diverse from them who have other voices, and other problems and perspectives. It really means being able to sacrifice your own perspective enough to see the validity of other people's perspectives, and it means work on the part of feminist organizations. It means that those who have got a structure, who have money, who have mailing lists, who have got the organizational base, who have got the networking down, who understand all that lingo, it means saying, "We're going to go into other communities now and find out what the women who represent those communities are saying"—not to come in there and say, "Hi, accept this now."

No; go in and find out who's voicing the concerns of women in those communities, and establish dialogues with them. Just deal with each other as a matter of equals, the same way they've been able to develop their whole political structure here. And ultimately, it's a responsibility, because we are always looking on the outside: we who live in minority communities, in poorer neighborhoods, we are always looking on the outside, we see how everybody else lives. Same relationship between the United States and Mexico, you know Mexico always knows what the United States is doing, but the United States doesn't necessarily have to know what Mexico is doing. It's the same thing in this situation: privileged "white" feminists have got to make the effort to look and study and work.

CB: There is something I meant to bring up earlier—and which I think you raised—in that the situation got very uncomfortable for you once you had become more prominent. That is a lesson that I think is to be learned from Sor Juana Inéz de la Cruz and Trinh T. Minh-ha alike: that a position of apparent marginality allows you sometimes to see things and to do things that you couldn't do if you were always at the center. It pushes you both into an awareness of your own position, and into a more comprehensive analysis of the relevant power structures, so as to reveal your full range of options. Sometimes, in a form that people may not recognize as significant, you can say very significant things.

MH: I've always felt that my experience of growing up and being very aware of the fact that I was the "other" in this country has led me to where I am now, because I am therefore always interested in what the "other" has to say. And the "other" in this case is whoever it is that may not necessarily be part of the mainstream. That otherness that I have experienced and continue to live with and which will be a part of my life forever is what has given me that ability to see the otherness in any situation; and to imagine that what has got to happen in this country is that we've all got to recognize the "other" in ourselves, because we are all the "other." There is this notion that "I am it"—no, you're not.

To recognize that otherness in ourselves can be very liberating. But it means letting go of "I know more than you, I am better than you, I am more advanced than you." It means letting go of all of those things, which is very humbling, to put yourself in a position where you can learn to identify with the other, wherever you may be. And particularly in a city like New York, that means being able to identify with another right when you step out on your doorstep and you come across a Mexican who probably does not speak Spanish, and probably is speaking Nahuatl, who is bringing with him a tradition of centuries, from a culture of centuries, but you bump into him because he is delivering your pizza.

CB: What of the prospects for establishing alliances with other women of color in your field?

MH: The camaraderie I look for in other women of color journalists usually comes from the political perspective that we share: we see the world and our role as journalists in similar ways. Many of them have probably gone through similar experiences, maybe they have been overlooked for a position by someone who belonged to their same racial and ethnic background, but was more willing to play by the rules. But at this point, beyond the conversations that I have had with women of color journalists with whom I can share the experience, no, there has been no formation of a group, we're not at that level yet. Being able to have a group in which you can talk about difference—I don't know how many academics are able to do that, how many politicians do that. When there is a commonality of experience that results from how we view our role as journalists in a society, *there* is where you can have a sense of sisterhood and "work your way through it" in supporting each other.

Post-Reflections

Feminist Latina critics have urged us to consider the many facets or "voices" of Latina subjectivity as it has come to be shaped by women's historical experiences in different socio-cultural contexts.[19] *This multidimensionality is not only crucial to reaching a deeper cultural understanding of the positions from which Latinas are speaking, but provides a broader field of possibilities across which Latinas can "tactically" forge a new, more psychosocially fulfilling sense of identity for themselves.[20] Indeed, the very word "Latina," as we have seen, evokes the way that this gendered subjectivity is constituted across racial, ethnic, class, and sexual categories of experience, and historically has been bound up with the primarily ethnic and racial categorization of people (of diverse languages and nations) into a singular "community." An important corollary to the recognition of the complexity of self-definition is the notion of feminism as an* ethos, *as well as an ideology guiding one's personal/political praxis. For many Latinas, feminism is not restricted to a woman's individual rights, desires, and responsibilities but is a function of one's assumption of responsibility towards a larger social community(ies). Within the framework of the individual-collective dialectic, where the fate and well-being of the community take a high priority, the collectivity can itself be redefined to embrace women's other "vectors of identification," i.e., beyond the national-linguistic criteria that have traditionally defined Latinos as an "ethnic" community. For some Latinas, ties to a lesbian/queer community or to a professional community can assume an importance equal to that of ethnicity, while for others, blackness or indigenous identity becomes a source of strength to confront the mainstream society, not a stigma.*

A discussion of the professional experience of Latinas in the media thus has to take into account: 1) the historical elements—the tightening of international borders; the intensification of interracial tensions; the export of industrial jobs to Third World labor markets—currently affecting the social construction of Latinos in the U.S.; 2) the competing cultural and political agendas (including feminism) within the heterogeneously-constituted Latino community; and 3) the powerful political and economic interests, which, working in tandem with media industry protocols, set the terms by which subaltern groups, such as Latinos, can publicly express themselves.

Maria Hinojosa's observations also urge us to reflect on the distinction between several modalities of Latino/a visibility via the media within the national public sphere. These are: 1) "vertical visibility," or the upwardly mobile process whereby one allows oneself to be "made visible" according to prevailing industry ideologies, power structures, and practices: here, quotas of social diversity are met by hiring token Latino/as; 2) "diagonal visibility," a form Maria herself has promoted, which involves the making visible of community perspectives within the national media, by conquering brief "windows" for people to speak in their own voices, while adhering to industry formats of editing and delivery; 3) "horizontal visibility," or community-to-community communication, in which the "horizon" is usually found locally on alternative radio (local public or non-profit stations) or cable channels, free of many of the constraints and protocols imposed by hegemonic media—this is still the most impor-

tant venue for Latino/a expression; and 4) "rhizomatic visibility," in which Spanish language provides both the ticket to a linguistically homogeneous market, and a barrier with respect to the English language market.

Within each of these categories, and bearing in mind the parallel ways in which "audibility" as well as "visibility" on the air are shaped by the power dynamics inside media organizations, one might also ask the following questions: 1) How do Latinos and Latinas get to "speak" as well as be "seen": is it as interview subjects, or as unidentified bystanders? As reporters or as anchors? On national or local networks? Using the Spanish or the English language? 2) To whom do they speak? To other, "anonymous" subjects? To a reporter? To a "white" male anchor? In direct address to a cross section of viewers "out there"? And 3) to what extent is their mode of expression conditioned by a concern with the composition of the audience? Are they allowed to speak in what they choose to be their own "voice"?

Maria Hinojosa's consistently defiant stance in favor of crosscultural communications and community-based reporting (whether over the radio waves or on television, whether at the local or the national level of transmission) eloquently illustrates how one's resolve against established power structures, one's own attention to professional ethics, and one's broad definition of community and resourcefulness in relating to others outside one's own ethnic constituency can work to improve the terms governing the audibility and visibility of women of color in today's media.

Notes

1. As heard on *Black Radio, Telling It Like It Was,* hosted by Lou Rawls, produced by Public Radio International, and broadcast on WBGO-FM-Newark, February 15, 1996. One of the nation's first Afro-American woman disc jockeys, "The Queen" was heard over the airwaves in Detroit from the 1950s onward.

2. The report was first produced for NPR in July 1992, then released in a half-hour version via *Soundprint,* at WJHU, Baltimore.

3. John Ellis and Robert Stam have both remarked on how the restricted use of direct address in combination with close-up for newscasters and politicians works to sustain social power relations both on and off the screen. See John Ellis, *Visible Fictions/Cinema: Television: Video* (London: Routledge, 1992), 139–143; and Robert Stam, "Television News and Its Spectator," in E. Ann Kaplan, ed., *Regarding Television: Critical Approaches: An Anthology* (Frederick, MD: University Publications of America, 1983), 27–28, 38. For the stress on uniformity, see Margaret Morse, "The Television News Personality and Credibility: Reflections on the News in Transition," in Tania Modleski, ed., *Studies in Entertainment: Critical Approaches to Mass Culture* (Bloomington: Indiana University Press, 1986), 64–65; 74–76.

4. A *New York Times* survey conducted in 1994 revealed that only 2.7 percent of all television and radio stations in the United States are "minority-owned" (i.e., owned by Afro-Americans, Latinos, Asian-Americans, and Native Americans). Latinos take second place, after Afro-Americans, with 92 stations, the vast majority of which were radio stations (*New York Times,* May 31, 1994). It is anticipated that the recent lifting of FCC regulations on radio monopolies will reduce further the number of "minority-owned" radio stations (heard on *Black Radio: Telling It Like It Was,* hosted by Lou Rawls, produced by Public Radio International, and aired on WBGO FM-Newark, February 29, 1996).

5. Indeed, Cuba Gooding, Jr.'s nomination and receipt of the 1997 Academy Award for Best Supporting Actor was considered (and represented as) an industry breakthrough. Moreover, an article in *People* magazine revealed how only one out of 166 nominees for the 1996 Academy Awards was an African-American, and in 1995 (as compared with 1992 through 1994), there were *no* African-Americans among the 25 nominees in the most significant Oscar categories. See Pam Lambert, et al., "What's Wrong with this Picture?" *People* (March 18, 1996), 44 and 47, respectively. The numbers are unquestionably *much* lower for Latino film professionals.

6. This is a neighborhood located in the Northern-most section of Manhattan, and is inhabited predominantly by Dominican immigrants, mixed in with older Eastern European Jewish and Irish populations. In recent years, it has become a visible site of both community organizing and inter-ethnic tensions, especially in the areas of housing and police-resident relations.

7. Manuel de Dios, an investigative reporter for the Spanish language newspaper *El Diario,* took great risks in exposing links in the international drug trade to New York City. On March 11, 1992, he was ambushed and shot to death in a Queens restaurant by gunmen who apparently were hired by a drug cartel.

8. Such compensatory measures, as well as the general concern with balance, stem directly from the FCC's "Fairness Doctrine," in force at least since the sixties, which instructs the broadcast media to "afford reasonable opportunity for the discussion of conflicting views on issues of public importance." See Robert C. Allen and Douglas Gomery, *Film History: Theory and Practice* (New York: Alfred A. Knopf, 1985), 230–231. Ironically, this doctrine is applied most religiously to "public affairs" programming, which provides precisely the air space within which alternative perspectives, such as those expressed by and for Latino/as, are most likely to be transmitted.

9. Perhaps nowhere are categories of race, ethnicity, and nationality more confounded than on census and affirmative action forms: Puerto Ricans are separate from "Hispanics," and only non-Hispanic whites (and Jews) can claim to be truly

Catherine Benamou

"white." Hispanics of Native American or African descent must choose between linguistic, ethnic, and phenotypical categories of identity.

10. Santería is an Afro-Cuban religion that combines the Yoruba worship of deities who are linked to nature (*orishas*) with aspects of Catholicism. It is practiced throughout much of the Spanish-speaking Caribbean, and although ceremonies incorporate ritual possession, music, singing, and dancing, it is quite distinct from *vodun* (or voodoo), which is practiced mostly in Haiti and combines influences from the Fon (Dahomey) and Kongo cultures, as well as Catholicism.

11. A familiar part of the urban landscape in New York's Caribbean immigrant neighborhoods, *botánicas* are small shops that sell amulets, statues, and other paraphernalia used in connection with the worship of Santería, spiritism, and other African based religions.

12. Previously, most Spanish language networks in the U.S. had single male anchors, with special male announcers (sports, weather) on the side.

13. Salinas is Jorge Ramos's co-anchor on Univision's international newscast, which follows a half-hour of local news.

14. Examples of the reworking of "brown-face" imagery in contemporary performance include the video and live work of the performance collective Culture Clash; Coco Fusco and Guillermo Gómez-Peña's quincentennial anti-commemorative performance/installation *The Couple in the Cage,* staged in museums and public spaces internationally; and John Leguisamo's televised impersonations of ethnic types (Asians and Latinos). Of course, these examples represent a wide range of strategies and ideological positionings vis-à-vis the "mainstream."

15. *The Pérez Family,* a feature-length film, directed by Mira Nair, 1994.

16. The figurative English translation of this phrase is: "I managed to sneak in through the back door."

17. In Portuguese this is literally "a twist of the waist." In colloquial Brazilian usage, it means the ability to negotiate oneself in a non-conflictual manner out of a particularly uncomfortable or confrontational situation.

18. Between 1992 and 1993, a 300–400 page document known as the "Rainbow Curriculum" was circulated to teachers in the New York City public school system. Commissioned by the Central Board of Education, then under the chancellorship of Joseph Fernández, its primary purpose was to help teachers teach tolerance towards different ethnic and racial groups, and towards children of gay parents. According to Billy Tashman, who was writing on educational issues for the *Village Voice* at the time, even though the curriculum was *not* mandatory for teachers to adopt (like countless other curricula developed and circulated each year), Mary

Cummins, President of the all-white District School Board #24 in an ethnically diverse community in Queens Borough, pushed for the outright banning of the document, citing a few pages which she claimed promoted sodomy as "normal" sexual behavior. The ensuing city-wide controversy led to Chancellor Fernández's being voted out of office by the mostly conservative central advisory board. This apparently was the "real" objective for Cummins, whom then U.S. Vice President Dan Quayle named "Conservative of the Year."

19. I am referring primarily to the formulations of Norma Alarcón, Rosalinda Fregoso, and Chela Sandoval, as they are quoted and commented upon in Rosalinda Fregoso, *The Bronze Screen* (Minneapolis: University of Minnesota Press, 1993), 92, 97, 105.

20. See Fregoso, 98, 101.

May Joseph

Transatlantic Inscriptions: Desire, Diaspora, and Cultural Citizenship

Cultural citizenship is a nomadic and performative realm of self-invention. The struggle for cultural citizenship under participatory politics of a liberal democracy, and the limits of hybridity embedded in the secular rhetoric of the modern Western nation-state, shape much creative work situated at the crossroads of minority, immigrant, progressive, and emancipatory expressions of life in the United States. Cultural citizenship is a contingent process, a state of becoming that is strategic in its solidarities with multiple publics as they negotiate simultaneous identifications within various political communities.[1] It privileges the importance of the self in performing identifications with social identities in public ways, such as being Asian-American, queer South Asian, etc. However, what the performance of cultural citizenship in the United States overlooks are the competing histories of self through which identities such as those of South Asian bisexuals must reinvent themselves to participate as cultural citizens.

Political visibility is a performative act. It is historically specific in its transnational resonances and pedagogical processes that produce the citizen as a cultural subject. Political visibility makes it possible to stake claims for cultural legitimacy because it operates on a sense of belonging within the state. It deploys strategic identities in the interest of cultural citizenship. The forging of communities, alliances, and discrete identities, such as queer Asian-American, is one such tenuous arrangement through which the pedagogical performance of cultural citizenship is realized. But the narrative of coming out, an enactment of political visibility, is neither transparent nor the only avenue through which complex identities express themselves as citizens. On the contrary, such a performance of visibility hinges on very North American notions of self and its relation to the social.

Many cultural producers have addressed the dilemma of cultural legitimacy in relation to dominant and minority notions of self in the United States. For those with histories of travel and residence in numerous countries before arrival in the United States, the process of cultural citizenship is elusive and troubling, though necessary. It produces a host of concerns around the politics of representation that are essentially different from concerns of legal citizenship.[2]

Acquiring political visibility is neither immediately available nor easily occupiable for new social identities. For many bisexual South Asians, political visibility involves struggling between the legal and the unofficial, between the intertwining categories of identities like Asian-American and queer, and the arenas of ambiguity and disaffiliation generated around sexuality, nationality, and belonging.[3] This is further complicated if one comes from a relatively obscure diaspora, such as East African Asians in the United States who foreground those diasporic communities that have had to migrate three or four times across different national boundaries such as Uganda, Tanzania, Britain, Canada, India, the UAE, and the U.S. Cultural citizenship for a queer South Asian from East Africa might mean identifying simultaneously with the affiliations "Asian-American," "black," "South Asian" "East African Asian," "Afroasian," "queer," thereby complicating any easy allegiance with a single political identity.

Foregrounding certain aspects of belonging for political visibility results in selective and partial identifications as various South Asian organizations like Sakhi for South Asian Women, the Lease Drivers' Coalition at the Committee Against Asian American Violence, the South Asian Youth Action, the Nav Nirman/Queens Child Guidance Center, the Forum of Indian Leftists, the South Asian Women's Creative Collective and Manavi, an organization for South Asian women demonstrate through their respective interactions with South Asians in New York. Yaar, a South Asian civil rights organization based in New York city was an activist organization involved until 1995 in educational, anti-racist work countering violence affecting youth in South Asian communities in the Tri-State area, while the South Asian Lesbian and Gay Association continues to work as a support group with activist concerns in the face of conservative, homophobic, and rabidly nationalist sentiments within the South Asian diasporic communities in the region.

For multiply migrated communities such as the various South Asian communities, the lines of desire and participatory politics are tenuous at best. Emerging into political consciousness out of such nomadic histories involves the contradicting spheres of lived reality, conflict between desire and political allegiances, between the demarcated public spheres of political engagement and the messier realms of pleasurable, mutable desire. Both Yaar and SALGA cast a large umbrella to include diasporic constituencies of different South Asian nationalities from Pakistan, Bangladesh, Myanmar, Sri lanka, India, and the Caribbean, African, Latin American, and British diaspora, with differing levels of success. These organizations raise the question of what it means to participate in transnational visibility politics with such a fractured and discontinuous sense of context and political investment.

The relationship between nomadic histories, immigration, political desire, and activist allegiances are partial and traumatic. The elaborate process that precedes that first encounter with the bleary-eyed immigration officer with your armament of passports, visas, innoculations, bank statements, medical tests, permission to stay, and addresses of contacts delineates the tensions of legal citizenship. But the struggle to participate in cultural citizenship is a performance between the seamless discourse of clear political affiliations and the reality of partial, cynical, hopeful, and passionate sympathies within the public sphere.

Coming to cultural citizenship is a process compressed between the blurr of available political identifications, whether legal, sexual, cultural, mythological, or identitarian. The complexity of constituency percolates in its coagulated forms—Asian-American, Latina/Chicana, white, black, Native-American—contingent and in relation to each other. If one has lived in hazy ethno-self-absorption in previous lifetimes, the flight into the night brings with it the harsh light of identity politics and communities in formation. For immigrant queers of color, these lines of affiliation and belonging are drawn against the easy parochialities of masculinist ethno-nationalisms, heterosexual tribal enclaves, the normative premises of immigrant rights discourse, and petit bourgeois dreams of the American nuclear family. The phrase "immigrant queers of color" is loaded with the bodies, passports, histories, languages, tastes, voices, and movements of different women from the various diasporas in the United States. Francophone, Anglophone, Lusophone, Iberian, the stories of displaced memories and devoured pasts merge into the tumultuous and hostile anti-immigration public rhetorics of the late 1990s.[5] Iranian-American, Iraqi-Israeli, Filipino-Chinese, Afro-Asian, Indo-Trinidadian, the myriad nuances of ethnicities contend for cultural citizenship. Immigrant queers of color struggle between the interstices of patriarchy, state policies, coerced identities and

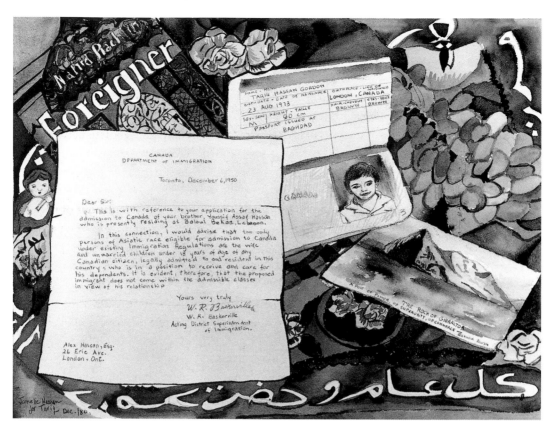

Plate 48: *For Tariq,* 1980
From the series *Common Knowledge,* detail from installation, watercolor on paper
Jamelie Hassan
Photo: John Tamblyn
Courtesy of the artist

tenuously formed affiliations as political citizens within the state. They grapple with former traditions and new-found avenues to enact their citizenship. Often on the outer peripheries of legal and cultural citizenship, as youths, workers, single women, mothers, wives, daughters, lesbians, and students, immigrant queers of color live within multiple, informal circles of same-sex kinship systems, extended same-sex families.

For bisexual South Asians, normativity implies elaborate networks of comrades in struggle, surrogate sister-friends, activists of discontent, paramours in cyberspace, inventors of new urban warriors, women lovers, irreverent violators of masculinist logic, passionate innovators of forbidden pleasures, enervated domestics of errant chores. The circulations of fractured mythologies become ways to narrate the multiple layers of memory and myth through which a coming out as a cultural citizen is possible. Hovering between new orthodoxies, old allegiances, emergent hegemonic formations and counter-hegemonic communities, immigrant women of color struggle for a place from which to shout, to lucidly write, to boldly rebel, to playful partake in self-invention. Between shifting ground and gasping air, the fluctuating histories of the various diasporas of the United States complicate identities in relation to legal categories.[6]

The rising politicized visibility of queer South Asians in the United States over the last decade is one site of contention and pleasure where the ambivalence and possibilities for transnational political identities in the United States have been played out. The practices of lived relations for women of South Asian descent and other immigrant queers of color, raise the question of the layers of normativity through which regulative logics operate outside the realm of the state. The differing histories of immigration of South Asians to the United States from the Caribbean, Africa, Latin America, and Britain has condensed and imploded the kinds of racial and sexual histories narrativized through these migrations. For many of these diasporic communities in the United States, same-sex relations have been the most powerful and meaningful modes of erotic and political desire. Often structured as binary and segregated informal communities of men's and women's social and psychic spaces, many of these diasporic South Asian communities include women who exist along interdependent same-sex affiliations. Muslim, Hindu, Jain, Ismaili, Zoarashtrian, Christian, and Buddhist South Asian women of the different diasporas historically have looked for support and sustained themselves through these openly anti-patriarchal modes, while coexisting within the oppressive regulative regimes of tradition, religion, and nationalism.

Plate 49: *My Cuban Baggage*, 1994
Black and white reproduction
Ernesto Pujol
Courtesy of Linda Kirkland Gallery and the artist

May Joseph

afro asians and the politics of blackness

> you are not black!
> how come you consider yourself black?
> you are black
> but not black enough
> you are black
> but not threateningly so
> you are a person of color

but not black
if you are indian, how come you come from africa?
which side of your family is african?

"there is no essential black subject"

you are a sister
you can never be a sister
you may be a person of color and a minority

> but not a recognizable one in the U.S., you understand?
> because you are not a citizen
> because you are neither black
> nor an established asianamerican community
> are south asians/asianamerican/are they black?

depends which side of the atlantic you are on the question.

what does it mean for afro south asians to claim blackness
in britain, in the caribbean, in east and south africa, . . .
in the U.S.?
coolies, slaves, indentured servants
bondsmen, middle-men, nomadic entrepreneurs,
dingos from east africa, fiji, seychelles, mauritius,
hybrids from guyana, trinidad, jamaica, barbados
mongrels playing bhangra, salsa, the rhumba, chimurenga
syncretics playing ngoma, soca, juju, and zouk

if you have long hair—how come you're a dyke?
if you're bi, you're not queer,
being bi, lesbian or queer
in the diaspora, struggling for coherence
pourtugesesouthasians, francophonesouthasians,
germansouthasians,

anglosouthasians
muslimshindusbudhistsjains
christianszoarashtrianssikhsjews
sweetloving ardhnareshwara[7]
halfwomangod
travelling many bodies, multiple nations
her blackness tenuously wrapped around her

Cultural collisions in the chance encounter of a glance, a face, a fragrance, a caress, a sound. The street a panoply of contestation of ethnicities, languages, communities, sexualities and classes. The corporeality of life shatters the legal frames of identity and belonging. Writing, etching, inscribing, performing—the hegemony of visuality is splintered across cultural fissures. Sight is not the only text deciphered. New sounds, polylingual sensations, seductive aromas, tantalizing textures. Political specificity keeps vigil over post-everything deferral. The struggles of multicultural heterogeneity erode the hydra head of myopic cultural singularity. Outside the hermetic frame of race and gender lie the sliding and interlocking realms of unstable visual categories, emergent aural paradigms, disconcerting spectatorial sensations, migrant lascivious desires. Trans-pacific, trans-atlantic, trans-american landscapes of desire bombard multi-lingual visual culture. Women from the north, the south, from newborn nations and dissolved territories shock, lure, tear apart, and compose passionate experimentations in cultural citizenship.

Ardhnareshwara, halfwomanman, poised in movement, between many worlds
Ardhnareshwara, the foraging for an epistemological underground,
the simultaneity of different imaginative realms of the erotic,
Ardhnareshwara, the embodiment of *khush,*[8]
in transit through mutable desires
Ardhnareshwara, bisexual deity transexual being
transnational spirit
Ardhnareshwara, halfwomanman
poised between strangleholds,
in transit, between here and there.

Cultural citizenship—the struggle for recognition, legitimacy, and cultural capital—comes with its hoops and obstacles of passports, borders,

May Joseph

visas, greencards, garments of citizenship, gesticulations of legality. Living between the official and informal spaces of cultural citizenship, immigrant queers of color traverse the parabolic spectrums of sexuality in the nation of citizenship, living between the pasts and presents of other nations traversed, caught between the disappearing present of languages in tension, tongues of rupture. This transforming space of displaced gods, mutant geographies, protean psyches, and emergent identities, envelops the surreptitious sexualities of hybrid selves.

she whispers saris on the subway
crossing the waters of colonialism's histories
lanka many times forged:
ame-irike
says the *chai kade* wallah to columbus's *jamaa*
before history, so the saying goes, is the *banyani*
selling *chai* to global nomads.

many have passed here, *amme, irica,* have some tea, the
journey's just begun.
if one must speak of origins let it be the atlantic
africacaribbeaenglaaanammerica,
crossing the waters of slavery and indentured servitude
kampala, entebe, nairobi, dar es sulaam
havens of peace; promises of the made and madly begotten,
lies from lies, true gods from true gods,
through the cartographer's lense all nations made

i n d i a a f r i c a a r a b i a c h i n a

the lemming all but erased
whose histories to be accounted for? whose histories
forgotten?
afro-asian, afro-mestizo, chino-latino, indo-anglo,
karapan, mzungu, creolio, dingo
must the naming be the accounting?
what new maps? what new territories, does this post-national
unmapping call for?[9]

if we must tell of origins, let it be the pacific
whose histories accounted for? whose histories forgotten?
Ravana had a thousand heads before Vasco da gama's siting of

the Indies

sugar islands, spice islands

islands of memory and forgetting

migrations by boat, journeys by air,

travels by water, passages by night

arrivals by shock, departures of terror,

ghosts of a thousand histories, unspoken and unsaid

sycorax—halfwomanman

Notes

1. The work of feminist scholars such as Norma Alarcon, Inderpal Grewal, Lisa Lowe, Gloria Anzaldúa, Caren Kaplan, Ella Shohat, and Gayatri Spivak have been crucial to this process. I would like to thank Ella Shohat for her skilful editing and support in writing this piece. To Radhika Subramanium and Meena Alexander I owe much as well for their continuing audience and encouragement.

2. "Dimensions of Desire," *Amerasia Journal* (UCLA Asian American Studies Center) 20, no. 1 (1994): pp. 000; Russell Leong, ed., *Asian American Sexualities* (New York: Routledge, 1996); Women of South Asian Descent Collective, eds., *Our Feet Walk the Sky* (San Francisco: Aunt Lute Books, 1993); Andrew Parker, Mary Russo, Doris Sommer, and Patricia Yaeger, eds., *Nationalisms and Sexualities* (New York: Routledge, 1992). These anthologies address some of the ambivalences around the politics of representation more broadly and, more specifically, the relation of self to cultural citizenship in terms of incomplete, partial, or strategic identities.

3. See Chandra Mohanty, "Defining Genealogies: Feminist Reflections on Being South Asian in North America," in *Our Feet Walk the Sky,* pp.

5. Proposition 187 and the phasing out of Affirmative Action Legislations in California are two examples of the anti-immigration policies that have altered the psychic landscapes of cultural life in some states.

6. The work of critical race theorists Kimberle Crenshaw, Neil Gotanda, Mari Matsuda, and Kendall Thomas has been indispensable in demonstrating these slippages within U.S. legal discourse.

7. Ardhnareshwara, a hindu deity that is literally half man and half woman in form. The deity has gained currency among diasporic South Asians as an image signifying, among other things, queerness with different epistemological baggage. Visual artist Allan D'Souza has popularized this image further through his work.

8. *Khush,* a Sanskrit word meaning joy, happiness, ecstasy. The word gained popularity in North America with Pratibha Parmar's film *Khush,* and has been appropriated for South Asian queer signification.

9. Glossary of foreign words: *ame,* Malayalam word for mother; *irike,* Malayalam for sit; *chai,* Swahili for tea; *kade,* Tamil for shop; *jamaa,* Swahili for relatives; *banyani,* Swahili derogatory slang for Asians of Indian origin, from *banyan; karapan,* Malayalam for black; *mzungu,* Swahili for white.

Mervat F. Hatem

The Invisible American Half: Arab American[1] Hybridity and Feminist Discourses in the 1990s

In the middle of the Gulf War, Bob David, a Michigan Republican congressman used Arab women to offer an anti-Iraqi joke. He asked: "What is the difference between a catfish and Iraqi women?" In answer, he replied: one was a fish and the other had whiskers and smells bad. Activist Arab American women reacted very quickly to David's offensive joke by holding a press conference the next day with a crate of catfish which they held up to photographers to correct what the congressman knew about both catfish and Arab women.[2]

The joke showed the intersection of sexism and racism in U.S. attitudes toward Arab culture and/or Arab women. The quick and assertive reaction by Arab American women showed that in 1991 a new generation of Arab American feminists understood the reciprocal effects of the devaluation of women and the racist denigration of Arab culture. In this short essay, I want to trace briefly the history of Arab American feminism prior to the Gulf War. Next, I want to show how racism and sexism during the war and its aftermath left their imprints on the agendas of the community leading to post war reassertion of Arab American feminism. Finally, I want to examine these different discourses. Conscious of the impact that racism and sexism had on women, they developed a double critique of their "Arabness" and "Americaness." This position placed Arab American women firmly, but uneasily within the camp of "women of color."

Arab American Consciousness and Arab American Feminism

Up until 1990, Arab American[3] political consciousness had been shaped by the history of the Arab-Israeli conflict and its different wars. During and after the 1967 war, overwhelming U.S. support of the Israeli military effort against Egypt, Syria, and Jordan galvanized the Arab American middle class and pushed its organizational effort. First, the Association of Arab American University Graduates (AAUG) was formed in 1967 to speak for the group and to educate the U.S. public about the Arab world.[4] In 1972, the National Association for Arab Americans (NAAA) emerged as a political lobbying group.[5] The American–Arab Anti Discrimination Committee (ADC) followed in 1980 to fight against the prevalent public defamation of Arab Americans in the United States.[6]

U.S. support of the Israeli invasion of Lebanon in 1982 unsettled the oldest and most established Lebanese American community and challenged their belief in a common Christian bond as a means of assimilation into the American mainstream. For Lebanese Americans, both Christian and Muslim women, who were becoming active in the U.S. women's movement, the attempt to mobilize opposition against the war brought a rude awakening. In 1982, they asked the Third World caucus of the National Women's Studies Association to condemn the Israeli invasion of Lebanon. The caucus unanimously recommended such a resolution to its overwhelmingly white delegates, who rejected it.[7] Subsequently, an article written by a prominent[8] Euro-Jewish-American[9] member of the feminist establishment for *Ms.* magazine accused Arab and Arab American women, along with other critics of Israel, of being anti-Semitic. Despite many responses by Arab American women to the article, the magazine, which served as a voice of the white mainstream, did not acknowledge or publish any of their reactions.[10]

These encounters with different institutional representatives of the women's movement persuaded Arab American women of the racist tendencies within the feminist establishment. As one of them suggested, Arab American women were treated as an inferior "other." Their right to express a different view of Israel and of U.S. foreign policy towards the region was denied. In discussions of the Middle East, Euro-American feminists imposed on Arab and Arab American women an emphasis on the veil and cliterodectemy. These issues were forced on Arab and Arab American women by Euro-American women who also lectured them on the oppressiveness of their culture, establishing American women's authority on how the liberation of women should proceed.[11]

The frustration and rejection felt by Arab American women were behind the creation of the Feminist Arab-American Network in 1983. It represented a loosely organized group of Arab American academics and activists who were committed to increase public awareness of issues affect-

Mervat F. Hatem

ing Arab American feminists, to eliminate negative stereotypes of Arabs particularly within the American feminist community and to work in a coalition with our sisters in Arab countries and to share resources and support among ourselves.[12] The Network also debated how it could carve a space for itself within the American feminist community. According to the founder of the Network lack of funding and clerical support were behind its demise.[13]

Without discounting the importance of the reasons listed above for the demise of the Network, its statement of purpose suggested others. With the negative reaction of the U.S. feminist establishment, the Network was unable to consider working with other women's groups that were similarly marginalized. Other than educating the American public and the feminist community about Arabs and Arab American feminists, the only coalitions that it considered were with women in Arab countries. While in and of itself this was a worthy goal, it shifted practical attention from the specific experiences of Arab American women in the U.S. to the experiences of women in the Arab world whose social and political conditions were different and distinct.

The rejection and lack of recognition experienced by Arab American feminists were collectively felt by the larger community during the 1984 presidential campaign. The Democratic contender, Walter Mondale, returned campaign contributions from Arab Americans.[14] His democratic rival, Gary Hart, repaid a loan from a Washington, D.C., bank that had Arab financial interests to dispel any connections to the group. These experiences led to the creation in 1985 of the Arab American Institute whose goal was to work towards greater Arab American participation in the U.S. political system.[15] In its search for support of the Arab American agendas at the local and national levels, the Institute found in African American political figures and organizations, such as the Reverend Jesse Jackson and the Congressional Black Caucus, valuable allies during the 1988 elections. At a time when no one within either major political party would support the principle of a Palestinian state as a solution to the Arab–Israeli conflict, Reverend Jackson's Rainbow Coalition put that issue on the agenda of the Democratic party.[16]

It gave Arab Americans visible positions in its campaign. In exchange, the community raised $700,000 for the campaign and delivered the votes of 50 delegates.[17] Finally, the alliance between the Jackson campaign and the Arab American constituency placed the community for the first time within the rainbow of colors that included other "minorities." This was where the community and its feminists stood when the Gulf crisis and then the War broke out.

Race and the Gulf War

Setting aside the Palestinian-Israeli question, the Gulf War concerns provided an opportunity to focus attention on the troubled relations between Arab Americans and the hegemonic culture and its political institutions. The Gulf War[18] was the first regional war that did not involve a military confrontation between Israel and other Arab states. The war pitted the U.S., backed by an international alliance that included Arab states like Egypt, Syria, Saudi Arabia, and Morocco, against Iraq following its invasion of Kuwait. In this sense, the war was an American-Arab war: it pitted the U.S. against an Arab country (Iraq), but cemented the alliance of some Arab states with the U.S. American policymakers viewed the Iraqi occupation of Kuwait as a threat to the security of the Arabian Gulf's oil resources and their control by friendly Arab states. The U.S. led international alliance successfully liberated Kuwait from Iraqi occupation and reduced an industrial Iraq to preindustrial status.[19] It also dramatically displayed the United States' political and military strength as the world's only superpower. In the aftermath of the war, an unstable Pax Americana was set up in the region.[20] It was supported by unpopular and undemocratic Arab governments whose legitimacy was contested by their Islamist opponents. This new level of U.S. military and political involvement in the affairs of the region had ominous political consequences for Arab Americans.

At the outset of the Gulf crisis, the public discourse that mobilized the American public for war initially focused on the past and present horrific record of the Iraqi regime. The anti-Iraqi political discourse very quickly deteriorated, however, into a broad anti-Arab one. The daily reporting, analysis, and discussion of the crisis denigrated Arab culture, history, politics, and character. The new anti-Arab discourse was both old and new. It tapped into an existing latent reservoir of prejudice against Arabs (as treacherous, warlike and cruel to women and children)[21] to describe the Iraqi regime as an enemy, thus reasserting the public belief in the unflattering views of the entire region and its people.[22] The fact that the governments of Egypt, Syria, Morocco, and Saudi Arabia condemned Iraqi actions and supported U.S. war against Iraq did not yield differentiated views of the region and its people. The "Arabs" continued to be homogeneously represented as a cultural and political "other."

Nowhere was the U.S. public's repudiation of the Arab "other" clearer than in the way it asked Arab Americans to respond to the war. According to one radio commentator, "In war there are no hyphenated Americans, just Americans and non-Americans."[23] Given this view, it was not coincidental that the media only sought "Arab protestors . . . to voice opposition to war."[24] In either case, Arab Americans' questionable loyalties were highlighted. Arab Americans could not define themselves in nuanced or complicated terms reflecting their greater familiarity with and sensitivity to the reality of U.S.-Arab relations. Only crude choices and definitions were available. One could support the war and in this way prove one's nationalist credentials as an American. Or, one could oppose the war and be identified as un-American/traitor/enemy/Iraqi/Arab. There was no place for the many Arab Americans who simultaneously disapproved of the Iraqi invasion of Kuwait and the U.S. military plans for its reversal. Those who wanted the liberation of Kuwait through political negotiations were considered at best foolish or, at worst, unwitting agents of the Iraqi enemy. These views indicated the deeply held belief that being both Arab and American was an oxymoran to the mainstream: one negated the other.

The only groups to break with this public discourse on the war were activist people of color. Due to the diminishing opportunities for advancement available to this segment of the population, "many women as well as Blacks, Asians, Latinos and Native Americans opted for the military as a road for professional advancement and education."[25] As a result these communities were over-represented in the U.S. army in comparison to the rest of the population. For example, thirty percent of troops serving in the Gulf war were African American and eleven percent were women nearly half of which were black.[26] For the major representatives of these groups and their kin, the political views of Arab Americans, which favored a political settlement of the conflict made social and national sense.

Unfortunately, the premium put on nationalist reactions to the war prevailed. It contributed to the dramatic increase in the number of hate crimes against Arab-Americans. According to the Arab-American Anti-Discrimination Committee (ADC), there were five violent attacks against Arab Americans during the period from January to August of 1990.[27] This number rose to forty from August to December; it escalated to sixty incidents during January and February of 1991 when the fighting broke out.[28] Equally significant was the FBI's decision, before the war, to interview/interrogate two hundred Arab American business and community leaders across the country. The stated purpose was to offer members of the group

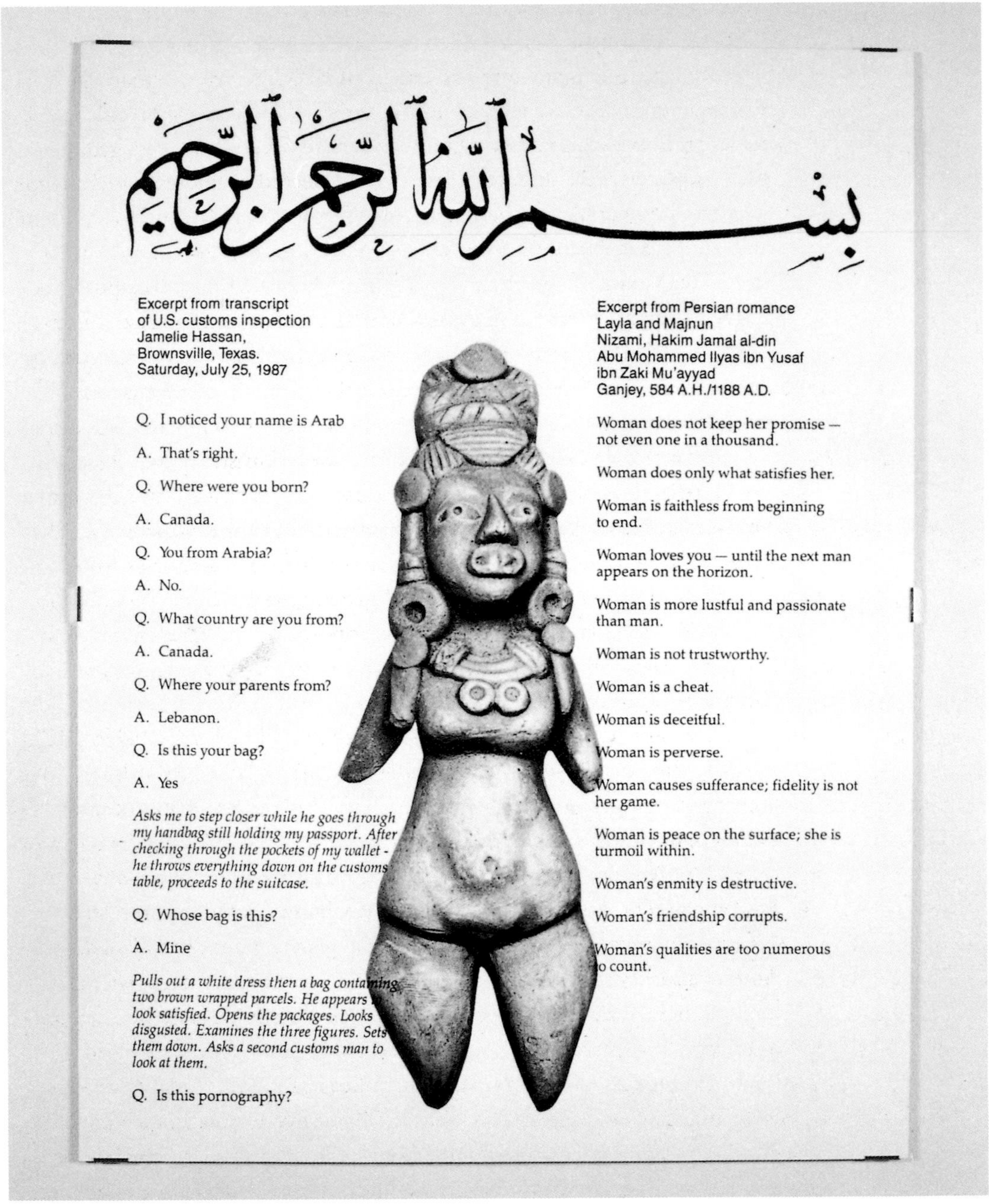

Plate 50: *Shame (from The Trilogy)*, 1990
Detail from mixed media installation
Jamelie Hassan
Photo: Patricia Holdsworth
Courtesy of the artist

protection and to also ask them if they personally knew any terrorists! Here, the stereotype of "Arabs as terrorists" became the basis of the FBI's interviews. The political views and beliefs of individual Arab Americans were no longer private matters protected by the law. The leadership and other members of the community were suspect as representatives of a group whose loyalties were suspect. They were suspected of knowing recruits for "terrorist" operations by the opponents of the U.S. and/or of giving them support. In either case, Arab Americans were a national security concern.

This discourse continued to define Arab Americans in the post-war period. Islamist attacks on the Arab states that supported the Pax Americana in the Middle East led to the suspicion that Arab Americans could become surrogates of these new international enemies. The group was misrepresented as homogeneously Muslim and anti-American. This disregarded the fact that many Arab Americans were Christian (e.g., Egyptian Copts, Lebanese Christians, and Iraqi Caldians) and that many American Muslims were not Arab (e.g., African Americans, Asian Indians, and Pakistanis) and that many who were opposed the Islamists. The arrest of Arab American Muslims of Palestinian and Egyptian origins in the 1993 bombing of the World Trade Center in New York seemed to lend credence to the U.S.'s suspicious and narrowly defined views of Arab Americans as American Muslims and as internal enemies.

Two years later, the investigation of the bombing of the federal building in Oklahoma City showed how these deep suspicions contributed to the very precarious political standing of Arab Americans. Without much evidence to support their claims, the early reports by the U.S. media and a variety of local and national public figures blamed Middle Eastern terrorists for the incident. Some in the American public suggested putting Arab Americans in internment camps, just as the government did to Japanese Americans in World War II.[29] A Palestinian American computer programmer was held as a suspect, freed, then reapprehended because he happened to be traveling from Oklahoma City to Jordan on the day of the bombing.[30] The homes of Arab American families in the Oklahoma City area were attacked. Arab American school children were taunted by classmates who told them to go back to where they came from.[31] Even after the arrest of white Americans with no links to Muslims, some callers to a radio talk show in the area refused to believe that Muslims were not responsible![32] Not only did this indicate the depth of American suspicions of Arab Americans and American Muslims, but it also showed how these suspicions persisted even when contradicted by the facts.

An American Muslim summed up the dilemmas facing the community in the following way: "Thank God it was not a Middle Eastern person this time, but even if it had been that does not mean that we are all terrorists anymore than violence by members of the Irish Republican Army makes all Catholics dangerous."[33] Unfortunately, discrimination against Arab Americans and American Muslims in the U.S. worked by setting Arabs and/or Muslims apart as different from the rest of us. In this way, one could make statements about them that would be considered ridiculous or slanderous had they been made about any other groups. In short, the Gulf War and political developments that followed it showed the proliferation of old and new forms of racism against Arab Americans in the United States.

Gender and the Gulf War

Anti-Arab racism camouflaged sexism as another important component of the contempt Americans feel for Arab culture. It made it difficult for Arab American women to begin the exploration of the difference gender made in the position one had in the community and the formulation of its agenda. The politically precarious position of the Arab American community during the war led to feelings of anxiety, fear, and danger among its members. In response, the community relied on group solidarity and the privileging of collective concerns as defense mechanisms. Racism was the defined as the primary problem while there was silence around the sexism with which the hegemonic culture and its institutions viewed and treated Arab American women, or the way men and women were given very gendered roles in the defense of the community. The result, conscious or unconscious, was continued patriarchal control of Arab American institutions and definitions of the group's agenda, problems, and strategies.[34]

The Gulf War presented members of the community with a major ethnic dilemma. It pitted their Arab and American identities against one another. Arab American men and women reacted to this development in simultaneously shared and distinct ways. While most disapproved of the Iraqi regime and its policies, they were divided about what the U.S. should do about it. Some supported U.S. military intervention against this repressive regime, putting American interests ahead of any ethnic sentiments. Most were opposed, however, to U.S. military intervention and stressed the potentially devastating military and human costs of the war.[35] For Iraqi Americans, in particular, the prospect of having relatives fighting in both the Iraqi and the U.S. armed forces constituted a form of fratricide that provoked unbearable anxiety.[36] Many in the larger community voiced fear over how the

Mervat F. Hatem

war would precipitate a backlash against Arab Americans in the United States. For some, this was a question of personal safety; for others, the primary concern was the safety of their small businesses.[37]

The FBI's "interviews" of Arab Americans before the war broke out reinforced the group's sense of danger. In media discussions of this event, which underlined the implication this action had for the civil rights of the group, there was silence on why the FBI agents chose to interview Arab American business and community leaders along with their wives. It could be said that the FBI considered Arab American men and women to be equally suspect. In most of the cases, the wives were not politically active. As both Arab and/or American women, they were considered by the FBI as extensions of their husbands. Only in one case was the wife the president of a local chapter of the Arab-American Discrimination Committee and could be considered a separate source of information.[38] What is clear is that these Arab and American women were questioned because of their relation to these men. The FBI did not treat these Arab and American wives as separate individuals. The American social construct of wife, which guided the FBI's behavior does not accord a woman separate legal standing but assumes that she is an extension of her husband. By not acknowledging such sexist connotations, the U.S. media seemed silently to accept them.

Arab American civil rights organizations did not question this assumption or action either. Like similar U.S. organizations, the Arab American ones largely had men as their official spokesmen. They assumed the important patriarchal role of public protectors of the rights of the community.[39] The Arab American men in charge of these organizations took on the tricky task of pressuring the patriarchs of the majority to uniformly respect the definition of the rights of citizenship. With the FBI, the policing arm of the state, they protested the use of ethnicity to deny members of their groups their right to privacy and the presumption of innocence until guilt was established. With the larger public, they argued cultural differences should not be used to undermine these legal rights. Yet, it was clear that cultural difference was the reason why minority patriarchs, as protectors of the community, were less able to defend their community against the attacks of the majority. As minority patriarchs, they had a subordinate status to white, Anglo-Saxon patriarchs who set the cultural standards of masculinity and who were able to provide better protection to members of their community.

The dilemma for these Arab American spokesmen/patriarchs, which was presented as that of the community as a whole, lay in how they could reconcile their minority status with the majority cultural (patriarchal) views and roles. As a second generation Yemeni American factory worker at General Motors in Michigan put it: "We are looking out of two windows. We love our people here, but we love our people there too. We are existing in two worlds, but one of the things that hurts the most is how little people in our world here really know about the world there."[40] In this statement, a hybrid masculine perspective of the problem is offered—a product of male experiences in two cultures. Clearly, there was equal identification with and comfort in these two cultural/patriarchal worlds even in the midst of the Gulf crisis. Despite their difference, Arab American men felt at home in both. The threat to this doubly privileged masculine existence came from the devaluation of one by the other. The goal was to eliminate the sources of misunderstanding and tension to preserve the privileged masculine gaze that these windows offered. Although this problem was described as a collective one, the interests of Arab American women would not be satisfactorily attended to through a simple elimination of cultural misunderstandings. Because they occupied subordinate positions in both cultures, their problems required the critique of these cultural systems of meaning, and then effective change.

For some Arab American Christian men, whose families had immigrated to the U.S. at the turn of the century, the solution to the above problems facing Arab Americans was assimilation. The patriarchal anxiety that resulted from the negotiations of different cultural definitions of masculinity was eliminated by emphasizing Christianity as the common bond with the hegemonic American culture and accepting the U.S. view of Arabness as synonymous with an alien and antagonistic Islam. For example, a prominent lawyer declared his full support of President Bush and, as proof of his cultural assimilation, reiterated the U.S. view of Saddam Hussein as an international thug.[41] A similar reaction came from a car salesman who, in addition to declaring his love of the U.S., volunteered the following assessment of the problems facing Arab Americans: "If there is a misperception of Arab, I think it is our fault. It is not the WASP's fault. I think it is the *Arab Americans of today,* who some of them can be awfully obnoxious. I do not even like them and they are my people."[42]

For many Arab Americans, the condemnation of Saddam Hussein's repressive regime was not particularly problematic. The demonization of Hussein as a Hitler or an international thug was. It evoked the stereotypical image of Arabs and/or Muslims as outlaws or terrorists. These were problematic views that many were not very interested in reinforcing in the imagination of the U.S. public. For many older immigrants, who were

Mervat F. Hatem

Christian, assimilation into WASP culture was desirable. It was the historical strategy used by that generation. It was not workable for Muslim Arab Americans for whom assimilation was hard or not desirable. The hegemonic views of the Muslim Arab Americans as responsible for their own victimization was used by some Christian Arab Americans to differentiate themselves from this hated group. It revealed the cultural and the generational divisions within the community and how some Christian Arab American men used the hegemonic definition of Arabness to devalue their Muslim counterparts. By setting themselves apart, they hoped to be treated differently. Unfortunately, the cost of this form of assimilation was alienation from other Arabs and the diverse Arab cultural heritage.

For Arab American women, a different set of dilemmas shaped their response to the war and the attacks against the community. Many women experienced both conflicts through the effects that they had on their families, neighborhoods, and communities. While many Arab American men negotiated with the majority groups and the government on behalf of the community or debated the regional and international politics of the war, most Arab American women placed their energies at the service of families that were traumatized by these events. In some cases, the war took parents away from their children and pressured other women to act as surrogates for the absent caretakers.[43] In other instances, women experienced the war as the personal trauma of sending daughters, sisters, sons and/or husbands to fight in the Gulf.[44] The possible loss of sons, husbands, and now female kin, along with the disruption of their lives and the doubling of their family responsibilities took their toll. At the same time, adults needed to be available to younger children who were feeling the disruption just as intensely.

On the home front, many Arab American professional women provided specialized care to the community as psychologists or physicians. Academics and community activists chronicled the way the community was reacting to events connected to the war. They reported and explained the feelings of anger, fear, hurt, and despair that made the war and its aftermath part of their durational collective memory.[45] They also defended the culture against numerous attacks. Community activists were particularly sensitive to the hostility shown to Arab American women by the American public. One reported how some of her women relatives in Michigan, who adhered to an Islamic mode of dress, feared that their appearance in public places during the war would provoke male violence against them as women and as visible symbols of their culture.[46] These Muslim women's fears clearly

Plate 51: **Image from Mona Hatoum's video *Measures of Distance*, 1988**
Courtesy of the artist and Women Make Movies, Inc.

indicated that male violence against women in the U.S., combined with cultural prejudice was a problem that was specific to them as Arab Americans. Once the war was over, Arab American women called for healing the divisions within the community.[47] In all the above ways, they emerged as an important voice for the community during its hour of need.

In short, the war and the anti-Arab attacks against the community that accompanied it made it possible for U.S. and Arab American institutions not to acknowledge or to react to sexist actions and views that affected Arab American women. The problems that were specific to women went largely unacknowledged, unreported, and unaddressed. The war also reinforced the gendered roles that Arab American men and women played in serving the community. During the crisis, most of the energies of Arab American women have been devoted to taking care of traumatized families and communities. While this delivered important emotional and social resources needed to survive the Gulf crisis, it also contributed to enhanced patriarchal control of community agendas. With women busy taking care of families, neighborhoods, and communities, the men and their organizations proceeded to define the problems facing the group. In claiming to speak for a community that was not differentiated by gender, they unconsciously as well as consciously maintained existing gendered relations of power. U.S. reporting of the FBI's interrogation of Arab American wives as extensions of their husbands did not question its sexist assumptions. In the discussion of nation or international crises, the reporting of and commentary on the sexist behavior of the security apparatus of the state took a back seat. While the war highlighted the conflict of interest between the majority (Anglo) patriarchs and their Arab American counterparts, cultural nationalism reinforced the patriarchal control that both maintained of their community agendas.

Hybridity and the Quest for New Directions: Arab American Feminist Discourses in the 1990s

Following the end of the war, there were numerous attempts by Arab American women to examine how the war had influenced their self definition, the analysis of their problems, and possible strategies of social change. In this debate, generational, cultural, and political differences contributed distinct discourses on what Arab-American feminism stood for. The earliest feminist attempt to analyze the way the war influenced Arab American women's definition of themselves came from the older and more established segment. It offered a U.S. nationalist perspective on what it means to be Arab American. Elmaz Abinader, a self-proclaimed feminist who traces her family history to Lebanese Christian immigrants who came to the U.S. before the Second World War, presented her own experience as a paradigm.[48] While she noted how an Arab surname and complexion led to harassment by the authorities at U.S. airports, she highlighted her identity as a native-born American. The Arab part in Arab American signified being knowledgeable about the region and having sympathy for the woes of its women. She resented, however, the way other Americans treated Arab Americans as Arabs who were not different from those in the old world. She took pride in how other Arabs identified her as an American. As an Arab American woman, she set itself apart from that of other Arab and/or Muslim women.[49] Their traditions, religion and patriarchal culture were not hers. She considers American-born Christian women of Arab ancestry as more liberated than those who were born in Arab countries, including many recent Muslim immigrants. This school of Arab-American feminism internalizes U.S. views of Arab culture as patriarchal/restrictive and of Arab women as its submissive victims and legitimate objects of U.S. criticism and attack. Assimilation into U.S. society has been seen as a means of combatting Arab sexism and of claiming for Arab American women the privileged status of Western feminists.[50]

In contrast to this older, but nevertheless still current definition of American feminism as the solution to the problems of Arab women, the anthology of Arab American and Arab Canadian feminist writings titled *Food for Our Grandmothers* (1994) offers the novel perspectives of a new generation of women, including many Christians. It questions the feasibility of assimilation or passing for white.[51] Many of the contributors recognize that in a race-conscious American society, Arab Americans are always identified and treated like people of color and that some of their struggles with the hegemonic culture that has devalued them are similar to the experiences of other minorities.[52] This self-conscious definition of Arab Americans and Arab American women as members of an ethnic minority represents a break with older attitudes and strategies. It represents a new emphasis on their hybrid cultural character as at once Arab and American. The Arab component is not only shaped by the past and present history of their countries of origin, their diverse ethnic/cultural traditions, but also by the history of Arabs' immigration to the U.S. and the positions they occupy here. The American component is largely shaped by widespread intercultural marriage, the experience of being a cultural and a religious minority, and the treatment of Arabs and/or Arab Americans by the hegemonic culture as a cultural "other."

Because of this distinct history and position, Arab American feminism has not sat comfortably within either of these cultures. It offers a hybrid perspective with all that this adjective signifies: the ambiguous cultural character, the multiple cultural mutations, and the equally diverse politics. As such, it promises a conscious double critique of both the Arab and the American determinants of women's experience/identity. By focusing on the analysis of the "conflicted interaction of Arab and American cultures"[53] and the particular forms of intersection between sexism and anti-Arab racism, *Food for Our Grandmothers* promises a new agenda.

This new discourse on what it is to be Arab American highlighted the rewarding potential of forming alliances between Arab Americans and other people of color, especially with African-Americans. This will not be an easy alliance because of historical and cultural factors.[54] Many African-Americans associate Arabs with the East African trade in slaves and view them as participating in the historical exploitation of Africa and its people. Some Arabs have been equally shaped by the existence of white and black slaves in their pre modern societies into very race-conscious individuals. For those who are more conservative on race- and class-conscious, an alliance with other minorities is hard to accept in their quest for mobility. On the question of Islam, there are bases for both alliance and conflict: since approximately fifty percent of Muslims in the U.S. are African-American, Islam represents a common bond between two communities; yet many African-Americans share the American stereotypes about Islam and its treatment of women. Some African-American nationalists consider Islam not to be an African religion. It is instead the religion of the Arabs who are outsiders to the continent. In a similar vein, many Arab Muslims are puzzled by the racial views and positions taken by the Nation of Islam. In short, while American racism and sexism might provide the basis for strong alliances with other people of color, there are many historical, cultural, and political considerations that make sympathy more difficult than one might think.

Finally, a naive liberal feminism, in the name of celebrating cultural diversity, has attempted to romanticize the Arab American experience, including its history of racism and cultural stereotyping. In *Arabian Jazz,*[55] the author Diana Abu-Jaber revelled in a fictional account of the imperfections of Arab American experiences including the celebration of the hegemonic cultural stereotypes of the groups and its racist portrayal.[56] In using many of the cliched representations of Arabs, Arab Americans and/or Muslims as aspects of their reality that have entertainment value,[57] she claimed that these fictional accounts celebrated cultural diversity. She also claimed to follow in the footsteps of Toni Morrison and Alice Walker in offering different perspectives on the community and its experiences.[58] In invoking Morrison and Walker as literary models, she was significantly silent on how their fictional works also offered powerful critiques of racism in the U.S. Not only is this critique absent from her accounts of the Arab American experience, but she viewed the attempt by one critic to refocus attention on racism[59] as an appeal to political correctness i.e. "to prescribe on specific approved tale".[60] Instead, she offered Arab American critics the liberal promise "of celebrating the many ways that people can open up and write their lives".[61]

While the discussion of racism does not preclude the opening up of a community for internal critique, laughing at its imperfections or giving its members agency, all are necessary for a complex appreciation of a collective social experience. The idea of individuals freely writing their lives without reference to the social relations of power that shape their experiences is at best naive and at worst a defence of the hegemonic liberal ideology and its strategy of domination.

In a review she offered of the feminist anthology *Food for Our Grandmothers,* she offered another problematic liberal position designed to contain the subversive and critical insights of the new discourse which defines Arab American women relation to "whiteness" and its system of power relations. In discussing the political dilemma faced by Arab American feminists who are asked to align themselves with "white women" vs. "women of color," Diana Abu-Jaber observes: "No one points out that such categories are social constructs, the kind that form the underpinnings of prejudice. In other words, thinking in terms of race may be inherently racist. The challenge . . . is how to celebrate heritage without participating in the same form of classification and racial otherness."[62] In this view of liberal society, it is possible to treat the category of "white women" and that of "women of color" as equally racist. Relations of power captured by these categories are lost in this equation. More seriously, Abu-Jaber's view entertains the possibility that it is possible in U.S. liberal and racist society to escape thinking in racial terms. In fact, the fight against racism requires one to critically uncover the relations of power implicit in the dominant categories as part of the effort to challenge them. For liberal feminism, the question of power is skirted by upholding the illusion that individual choices can transcend problematic categories and realities.[63]

Conclusion

During the last ten years, the Arab American community and its women have begun to move in new political and intellectual directions. Through the Rainbow coalition in the 1988 presidential elections, politically minded Arab American formed successful alliances with other people of color and through them were able to further their community's agenda. Two years later, the Gulf Crisis then the War served to highlight the common interests and views that Arab Americans shared with other minority groups. Despite the participation of large numbers of African American and Latino soldiers in the war, these groups were also significantly represented among the anti-war activists who underlined the human costs of the war and the disproportionate share of these costs their communities were asked to shoulder. Following the war, a new generation of Arab American feminists, who pondered the impact that the war had on their community and other communities of color, began to develop a new discourse that theorizes the similarities and differences that they shared with women of color.

This is a development that some segments within the community and its women do not view with favor. The advocates of a liberal feminist discourse have already tried to disarm this new discourse with the claim that the identification with women of color perpetuates racial thinking and politics. There is also evidence that Arab American men have used the racist attitudes within the community to discredit the mobilizing effort of this new feminist group.[64] If you add to this the fact that some women of color are reluctant to acknowledge Arab American women as members of a distinct minority with its own concerns,[65] then one can have a clear appreciation of the difficult struggle ahead. This is a struggle that is nevertheless worthwhile. The discourse that defines Arab American women as women of color gives a new impetus for the discussion of racism not just as a problem facing the community, but also as a problem within the community. The fight against the racist attitude and practices within opens the door to the discussion of homophobia and the hostility some members of the community show towards Arab American gay men and Lesbian women. These problems which are internal to the community undermines its ability to mobilize against the racism of the hegemonic culture and to build successful coalitions with other groups and communities with the U.S. political system.

The fight against these problems provide important levers for overcoming the "partitioned"[66] and "ghettoized"[67] existence that have dissipated the collective and intellectual energies of Arab Americans as people of color in the U.S. The attempt to establish historical and representational connections without ignoring the differences that make each singular promises to enhance the ability of the group to effectively develop new discourses and alliances capable of challenging the hegemonic culture and forces they face in the U.S.

Notes

1. I have consciously not used a hyphen in Arab American to underline the existing tension between these two cultural sources of their identity. One of the goals of this article is to develop an appreciation for this tension. Then, one can proceed to examine the existence and the implications of this hyphenated identity. If the hyphen implies a well-formulated and/or a single synthesis of the Arab and American identities, then nothing can be further from the complex cultural realities of the community where endless permutations are developed. Religion (including the different denominations of Islam, Christianity, and Judaism), geographic roots (both in the Arab world and in the U.S.), sexuality (heterosexual men, heterosexual women, gays, and lesbians) and language (Arabic, English, Berber) are only some of the factors that will determine these different articulations of Arab-Americaness.

2. The incident was reported by Zana Macki, who took part in it, as part of her contribution to an Arab American feminist anthology. See Zana Macki, "Pulled," in Joanna Kadi, ed., *Food for Our Grandmothers: Writings by Arab-American and Arab-Canadian Feminists* (Boston: South End Press, 1994), 212.

3. When Arab immigrants arrived in the U.S. in the last quarter of the nineteenth century, the Arab world was a culturally diverse region inhabited by Muslim, Christians, and Jews. Underlining this religious and ethnic diversity further, Arab "Muslims," "Christians," and "Jews" were differentiated by religious denomination and culture into complex groups. For example, while Islam was the religion of the majority, Arab Muslims were divided into Sunnis, Shìa, Druze, and Alawites. Arab Christians belonged to indigenous and non-indigenous denominations including the Maronite, Chaldean, Coptic, Greek Orthodox, Armenian, Protestant, and Catholic churches. Arab Jews added to the complex religious fabric of the region in Morocco, Tunisia, Egypt, Syria, Lebanon, Palestine, Iraq, and Yemen. Finally, the indigenous African religions of Southern Sudan were part of the religious map of the region.

While Arabic was the dominant language of these different religious groups, there were many linguistic minorities within Arab societies like the Kurds, the

Turkmen, the Kabayle and the African populations of Southern Sudan. The literature that discusses the ethnic (religious and linguistic) characteristics of "Arab Americans" simplifies the above cultural diversity by relying on the generic categories of "Christian" and "Muslim" to explain the cultural makeup of the community. An equally serious distortion involved dropping any reference to Arab Jews as part of the past and present of the region and its immigrant communities. For a discussion of this Eurocentric view and disciplinary approach to the history of Arab Jews, see Ella Shohat, "Sephardim in Israel: Zionism from the Standpoint of Its Jewish Victims," *Social Text* 19/20 (Fall 1988), 1–35; Shohat, "Dislocated Identities: Reflections of an Arab Jew," in *Movement Research: Performance Journal* 5 (Fall-Winter, 1992), 8; and Amitav Ghosh, *In an Antique Land* (New York: Vintage Books, 1994), chapter 10.

The reader is asked to keep the limitations of this literature in mind. Whenever possible the author has attempted to include these differentiations into the discussion of the community.

4. Michael Suleiman and Baha Abu-Luban, "Introduction," in *Arab Americans: Continuity and Change* (Belmont, Mass.: Association of Arab-American University Graduates, 1989), 6.

5. Ibid.

6. Ibid.

7. Carol Haddad, "In Search of Home," 220; and Azizah al-Hibri, "Tear Off Your Western Veil," 163, both in *Food For Our Grandmothers*.

8. See Letty Cottin Progrebin, *MS.* (June 1982).

9. As Ella Shohat points out, within an American context only a single (European/Ashkenazi) Jewish memory exists and/or is allowed. Not only is the Middle Eastern/Arab/Sephardic history (and memory) repressed, but the hegemonic discourse presented it as an oxymoron. Yet it is important to make such a distinction for an understanding of the distinct perspectives that exist within the U.S. Jewish community. See Shohat, "Dislocated Identities: Reflections of an Arab Jew," op. cit.

10. Haddad, 221.

11. Al-Hibri, 162.

12. "Statement of Purpose," *Feminist Arab-American Network News*, 1.

13. Haddad, 221, 223.

14. Nabeel Abraham, "The Arab-American Marginality: Mythos and Praxis," in *Arab Americans: Continuity and Change*, 19.

15. Ibid.

16. The Arab American Institute, *Ending the Deadly Silence* (Washington, D.C.: Arab American Institute, n.d.), 9, 11.

17. Ibid., 12–13.

18. Even though the Gulf War was identified in the U.S. as simply the Gulf War, it was more accurate to describe it as the second Gulf War. The first Gulf War was between Iraq and Iran. It lasted for nine years (1979–1988) without a clear winner. The second Gulf War took place in January 1991 to liberate Kuwait from the Iraqi invasion and occupation that began in August 1990.

19. Tom Wicker, *New York Times,* April 3, 1991, p. 1.

20. Roger Owen, "Reflections on the Meaning and Consequences of the Gulf Crisis," in Dan Tschirgi, ed., *The Arab World Today* (Boulder, CO: Lynne Rienner, 1994), 16–17; Hosam El-Tawil, "The United States and the Arab World After the Gulf Crisis," in *The Arab World Today,* 231–232.

21. Owen, "Reflections on the Meaning and Consequences of the Gulf Crisis," 16–17.

22. These were also the most widely held American views of Arabs as an ethnic group. See Shelly Slade, "The Image of the Arab in America: Analysis of a Poll on American Attitudes," *The Middle East Journal* 35, no. 2 (Spring 1981): 149.

23. Quoted in Lisa Suhair Majaj, "Boundaries Arab/American," in *Food for Our Grandmothers,* 82.

24. L. J. Mahoul, "Battling Nationalisms to Salvage Her History," in *Food for Our Grandmothers,* 24.

25. Church Women United, *Women and the Gulf War* (New York: Church Women United, 1991), 5.

26. Ibid, 6.

27. Lisa Belkin, "Inquiries on Arab Americans by the F.B.I. Raise Concern," *New York Times,* January 12, 1991, 10.

28. Peter Applebome, "Arab Americans Fear a Land War's Backlash," *New York Times* February 20, 1991, A14.

29. Melinda Henneberger, "Bias Attacks: Muslims Continue to Feel Apprehensive," *New York Times,* April 24, 1995, B10.

30. William Booth, "A Nightmare of a Stopover in London," *Washington Post,* April 24, 1995, A12.

31. Henneberger, B10.

32. Ibid.

33. Ibid.

34. In this part of the discussion, I will provide nuanced descriptions of the diverse views held by Arab Americans, which were shaped by class, religion, gender, and generation. In developing an understanding of these different views, I have relied on the numerous articles that appeared in the *Washington Post* and the *New York Times* on how Arab Americans and/or American Muslims were dealing with the war and its aftermath.

35. Jay Mathews and Jill Walker, "For Iraqi Americans, Crisis is Emotional Mix of Dread, Disgust and Exasperation," *Washington Post,* August 25, 1990, A9.

36. Tim Golden, "For America's Jews and Arabs, the Pain of Divided Emotions," *New York Times,* January 19, 1991, A13.

37. Mathews and Walker, A9.

38. Belkin, 10.

39. Ibid.; Mathews and Walker, A9; Golden, 13.

40. Quoted in Peter Applebome, "Arabs in the U.S. Feel Separated by Other Gulfs," *New York Times,* February 10, 1991, p. A1.

41. Applebome, "Arab-Americans Fear a Land War's Backlash," A14.

42. Ibid., A14.

43. Applebome, "Arabs in U.S. Feel Separated by Other Gulfs," 30.

44. Golden, 13.

45. Ibid.; Applebome "Arab-Americans Fear a Land War's Backlash," A14; Sanchez, B1, B7.

46. Applebome, "Arab-American's Fear a Land's War Backlash," A14.

47. Ruben Castaneda, "Muslims Hoping for Healing: Ramadan Expected to Mend War's Rifts," *Washington Post,* March 16, 1991, D11.

48. Elmaz Abinader, *Children of the Roojme, A Family's Journey* (New York: W. W. Norton & Company, 1990).

49. Elmaz Abinader, "Here, I Am an Arab; There an American," *New York Times,* May 9, 1991, A25.

50. Ibid.

51. See, in particular, Michelle Sharif, "Global Sisterhood: Where Do We Fit In?," 151; L. J. Mahoul, "Battling Nationalisms to Salvage Her History," 24; and Lisa

Suhair Majaj, "Boundaries: Arab/American," 80, all in *Food For Our Grandmothers*.

52. Joanna Kadi, "Introduction," xvi; Therese Saliba, "Sittee (or Phantom Appearances of a Lebanese Grandmother)," 8; Majaj, "Boundaries," 66, in *Food for our Grandmothers*.

53. Majaj, "Boundaries," 80.

54. I base the discussion in this section on my own experiences and the numerous exchanges I have had as an Egyptian-American professor of political science with students and faculty at Howard University, one of the leading historically black colleges, where I have taught for the last fifteen years.

55. Diana Abu-Jaber, *Arabian Jazz* (New York: Harcourt Brace, 1993).

56. See the review by Elaine Hagopian, *AMEWS Newsletter* 9, 3 (September 1994): 1–3.

57. Ibid., 2.

58. Diana Abu-Jaber, "The Untitled and Hogtied," *AMEWS Newsletter* 8, 3 (October 1993): 7. To follow the debate, see Diana Abu-Jaber, "The Honeymooners, Growing Up Half Muslim in America," *AMEWS Newsletter* 8, 2 (May 1993): 7–9; also Mervat Hatem, "The 'Invisible' American Half in Arab American," *AMEWS Newsletter* (October 1993): 4–5.

59. Ibid.

60. Abu-Jaber, "The Untitled and Hogtied," 7.

61. Ibid.

62. Diana Abu-Jaber, review of *Food For Our Grandmothers, Middle East Studies Association Bulletin* 29, no. 1 (July 1995): 103–104.

63. See Abu-Jaber, "The Untitled and Hogtied," 6–7.

64. L. J. Mahoul, 28.

65. Kadi, xx.

66. Ghosh, 340.

67. Ella Shohat, "Staging the Quincentenary: The Middle East and the Americas," *Third Text* (Winter 1992–93): 98.

Teresa Carrillo

Cross-Border Talk: Transnational Perspectives on Labor, Race, and Sexuality

The *frontera* between the United States and Mexico is one of the world's most fluid international boundaries. A constant flow of people, goods, and services traverses that two thousand mile border and links the two countries of my birth: Mexico and the United States of America. Yet, in many ways, Mexico remains separate from the United States; the border demarcates a divide between rich and poor, English and Spanish speakers, Mexican and "American." As Chicanas, our lives straddle the border and are embedded in the crisscross of communities. We are therefore uniquely positioned to create channels of communication and collaboration with women in Mexico. As regional integration fosters economic homogeneity and reinforces capitalist hegemony, it is imperative that we do so.

This is an essay about *mujeres* talking to *mujeres*: Chicana/Latina women North of the border, and Mexicana women to the South. In this era of economic restructuring, trade agreements like the NAFTA and GATT raise expectations that increased trade and investment will bring an increase in transnational communication and network-building, not only among business leaders but also among North American citizens. Progressive visionaries have predicted that transnational networks at the grass roots will have a hand in shaping economic and political outcomes in the Americas. *Cross Border Links,* an alternative, grass-roots directory of North American organizations, for example, opens with these words: "From grassroots groups in border towns to labor union headquarters in New York, Toronto, and Mexico City, people are sharing experiences and ideas, fostering mutual understanding, and developing strategies to advance their interests. These social contacts are helping to shape the new economic structures being built on the continent."[1] This and other sources offer an optimistic view of the possibilities for a global society in which citizens, grass-roots

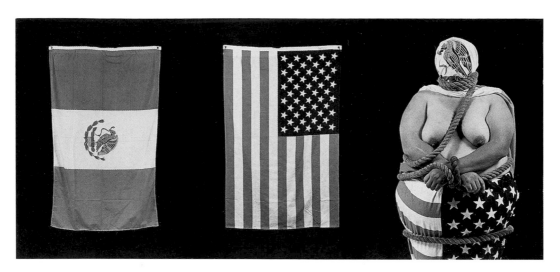

Plate 52: *3 Eagles Flying*, 1990
Laura Aguilar
Courtesy of the artist

movements, and nongovernmental organizations (NGOs) communicate and build networks across borders in response to an increase in shared interests and concerns.[2] But can we, as workers and women keep pace with the changes brought about by regional economic integration? While capital is eliminating tariffs and knocking down barriers to international trade, investors are positioning themselves in an extremely advantageous position in relation to labor and the communities providing human and natural resources for their investments. It is often low-cost female labor that attracts foreign investors to Mexico. How can we, as women activists, gain access to transnational networks so that we can come up with our own response to economic restructuring? How is economic restructuring affecting women on both sides of the border and what is standing in the way of building a collaborative response to these changes? These are some of the questions framing this discussion of contemporary transnational organizing among Chicana/Latina and Mexican women in a post-cold war context.

Between Chicanas and Mexicanas

When an organized tour of Mexicana garment workers visited the garment district in Los Angeles and San Francisco, they were amazed to find that the conditions were similar to those in Mexico City, leading to a radically altered perspective of the U.S. garment industry. "Conditions in Los Angeles," said one of the tour members, "were worse than here in Mexico [D.F.]. Garment workers there have to deal with being undocumented on top of everything else. There are women from all over the world, from Asia, Mexico, Central America, trying to make their living in the garment district. It seems like clothes can be sewn anywhere and the [industry] owners are just looking for the cheapest labor. . . . Seeing all this for myself helped me to realize that making our own little union is not enough, we need to go beyond a national union and figure out how to get together with other garment workers who, like us, are trying to make a living by sewing clothes whether they work in Los Angeles, the Philippines, or Mexico."[3] Rafaela, another tour participant, commented, "At least at home we can't get deported."[4] Rafaela and her colleagues often discuss the forces of globalization and their place within that process. Their tour through Los Angeles, Watsonville, and San Francisco eroded the lines dividing Mexican and U.S. workers and the Mexicana women returned to Mexico with a new determination to organize across borders. U.S. workers who met with the Mexican garment workers were likewise inspired and determined.

They talked about the futility of striking for higher wages and better working conditions if a victory would eventually lead to plant closures and relocation across a border so that management could exploit other women. They reaffirmed their commitment to transnational organizing with Mexican and Canadian workers.

Little happened, however, after the tour. The contact dropped off to almost nothing, the flow of information ceased, and the joint actions that had been discussed never took place. This pattern is not uncommon in attempts to build transnational links among women of the Americas. There have been numerous attempts to create transnational links between U.S. Latinas and other women of the Americas. In some cases, women have attempted collaborative actions such as drafting statements of women's rights in the UN-sponsored International Covenant of Human Rights and the 1995 Women's Conference in Beijing, or participating in labor protests and international boycotts of products (e.g., Gallo wine, Nestlé, Levi Strauss). But the majority of contacts across the border have not yet reached a point of collaborative action, remaining instead in a beginning step of establishing contact and discussing common ground. While U.S. Latinas readily express a need and a desire to establish transnational networks at the grassroots level, they, as individuals and organizations, have experienced substantial roadblocks, largely because of a lack of resources as well as differences in the central focus and agenda. Part of the daunting nature of the enormity of the task of transnational organizing is that Mexicanas and Latinas have distinct ways of defining their agendas. Chicanas and Latinas in the United States have focused on questions of race and ethnicity while Mexicanas have focused on class issues and survival. Adding to these differences is a widespread perception that the interests of U.S. workers are at odds with the interests of workers in Mexico. (Ross Perot's imagery during the 1992 presidential debates perpetuated this idea when he warned of the "large sucking sound" of jobs going to Mexico).

Combing through the various attempts to build alliances among Latinas, a two-sided problematic emerges. North of the border, the "multicultural women's movement" tends to privilege race, ethnicity, culture, and national origin, arguing that women of color experience a four-way intersection of oppressions based on race, class, gender, and sexual orientation; given the centrality of racism in the experience of women of color, the multicultural women's movement privileges above all the discussion of racial difference. South of the border, the popular women's movement focuses on family survival. A broad-based popular women's movement

Teresa Carrillo

emerged in Mexico after the 1985 earthquake and defined what has been called a "popular" women's agenda centered around issues that have a great effect on "women's work" within a traditional division of labor, such as housing, basic nutritional needs, and public services.[5] Residentially-based organizations such as neighborhood groups and renters unions constitute the bulk of the popular women's movement, formed to survive the "lost decade" of the 1980s. The losses have continued during the first half of the 1990s with Mexicans experiencing a constant erosion of their buying power, standard of living, and employment opportunities. Compounding these losses is a climate of political instability and violence punctuated by a string of political assassinations, rebellion in Chiapas, and a collapse of the economy. Within this setting, women have organized around issues of survival and their domestic responsibilities of caring for their homes and families—around what has been called "feminine consciousness" or "militant motherhood."[6]

To Mexican activists, the most immediate needs of housing, food, and services are not adequately addressed in the U.S. multicultural women's movement. When they have searched for counterpart organizations in the United States, Mexican women have found organizations not readily identified in the United States as "women's" groups, but rather as serving the poor: homeless shelters, welfare rights groups, labor groups, and church communities. To U.S. Latinas, meanwhile, the popular women's movement in Mexico appears to be confined to a domestic or private sphere with little attention specifically directed to what is perceived to be the central problem: the interplay of race and ethnicity with gender. U.S. Latinas find hardly a mention of race, ethnicity, or colonialism among Mexicana women activists in the popular urban movements. The color/culture line, an essential starting point for "women of color" in the United States, is seemingly ignored by the Mexican popular women's movement. Race and ethnic differences exist between upper-middle-class and educated feminists, and poor, working-class women in the popular movements, but the topic is largely skirted, as is the related topic of domestic service. Although Mexico is racially stratified, women activists disregard racial hierarchies among themselves, falling back on the revolutionary ideology of *mestizaje*—that all Mexicans are of mixed race.[7]

On a number of occasions, the centrality of race and ethnicity for U.S. Latinas has become an issue for Mexican women in various transnational forums. In one international exchange, for example, Mexicanas voiced a concern that too much attention to racial and ethnic difference was going to derail the alliance discussion, while U.S. Latinas demonstrated impatience with having to argue, yet again, that race indeed matters. Neither U.S. Latinas nor Mexicanas found comparable developments in women's organizing in the two countries, making it difficult for the movements to identify with counterpart groups and thus reach out to them across the border.[8] Despite these obstacles to establishing transnational alliances and collaborative actions between U.S. Latinas and Mexican women, there are many examples of positive connections between women of color across the Americas. And in spite of the divisive spin of the NAFTA debate, women have been quick to realize that the benefactors of neoliberal economic reform are neither women nor workers on either side of the border, but investors and employers on all sides. While there are many points of contradicting interests in the short term, Chicana, Latina, and Mexicana women have voiced an interest in creating cross-border links around their increasingly shared interests as women, workers, and community activists. Some of the most effective links between Chicana and Mexicana women have emerged around the very issue that has been at the heart of popular women's organizing in Mexico: community survival. Alliances between women in border communities, for example, have resulted in transnational coalitions within the environmental justice movement. Even women separated by thousands of kilometers are beginning to define a type of politics that is residentially or domestically based, but globally linked.

Differential Survival

From within a very traditional gendered division of labor, Mexicana and Chicana/Latina women have organized around their responsibilities of maintaining the home and family. While this focus may do little to alter the gendered division of labor, it highlights the importance of the home, the neighborhood, and the politics of everyday life. Transnational alliance-building has been limited in this realm of women's organizing, partly because it is inherently tied to a spatially continuous geographical location. Within the borderlands, where both Mexican and U.S. communities occupy the same geographical location, there are numerous examples of transnational alliance-building among Chicanas and Mexicanas around community issues such as water, health, environmental toxins, and access to public services. Women make up the bulk of the membership in organizations confronting the issues of community survival on both sides of the border. One example of an effective transnational network is the Southwest Network for Environmental and Economic Justice (SNEEJ). The SNEEJ includes working class and poor people of color fighting for economic and environmental justice, encompassing groups as diverse as the Asian Immigrant Women's Advocates,[9] the West County Toxics Coalition,[10] Mothers of East Los Angeles, and Fuerza Unida, an organization of Chicana and Mexicana garment workers who were laid off when Levi Strauss closed its plant in San Antonio, Texas, and moved production to Costa Rica.[11] The network has organized in small border towns in Mexico where Mexican communities have been fighting toxic waste and health hazards that result from the practices of corporations attracted to the border for its lax labor, environmental, and health regulations.

In Nogales, Arizona, and Nogales, Sonora (Mexico), women activists have pursued a class action suit against various manufacturers and agencies that dump Trichloroethylene (TCE), a toxic cleaning agent, into river water that runs in a northerly direction from Sonora to Arizona. Along the Arizona portion of the border alone, there are at least ten binational organizations engaged in coalitional activism around issues of environmental justice.[12] Although women rarely head these organizations, they constitute the majority of the active membership. Women's labor organizations such as Mujer Obrera in El Paso, TX; the San Antonio chapter of the Amalgamated Clothing and Textile Workers Union (ACTWU); and Fuerza Unida in San Antonio, have all been active in a wide range of arenas, including the environmental justice movement and the Texas Network for Fair Trade and Clean Environment. In example after example of community organizing, women are a driving force, and when the community is spread out over an international border, women are engaging in transborder struggles for community survival.

By contrast, in communities whose difference is compounded by spatial separation and distance, it has been harder to create transnational alliances around the politics of community survival. Even if women are aware of the relationship between conditions in their own neighborhood and international agreements, political action is usually focused upon local government and business. A Mexican activist may be attempting to bring potable water and bus service to her street while a Chicana activist may be resisting the elimination of after-school child care in the local schools. Both are attempting to hold their respective state to its role in providing public services that alleviate the burden of domestic work and child care for families, but the specific terms of survival differ in diverse contexts and the connection between the movements, therefore, is more tenuous than if the communities share at least a geographical location.

The bulk of the popular women's movement in Mexico is organized around residentially based survival concerns in organizations for poor and working-class women, such as neighborhood groups or renters unions.[13] These organizations often address the problem of the double day of labor for women, attempting to alleviate the burden of a long work day both in and out of paid labor by, for example, securing access to health services, public transportation, or public utilities such as water or electricity.[14] The *Tendencia Feminista* (Feminist Tendency), one of the principal components of the Mexican feminist movement, is made up of feminist groups seeking expression of a new form of feminism grounded in the problems of the popular sectors of Latin America.[15] Together with activist women in diverse popular organizations, they form a mass-based women's movement dedicated to the concerns of women in the popular sectors, and have developed feminist projects in response to those concerns.[16]

Because neighborhood associations and renters' unions focus on issues of housing and homelessness, Mexican activists have looked to U.S. advocates of the homeless for transnational alliances. In 1986, women from CONAMUP, an umbrella organization of Mexican neighborhood groups, became involved in planning the International Year of the Homeless caravan to the United Nations. They sent three members of the Women's Regional Council to take part in the caravan, which made its way north through Mexico, Texas, and the Eastern states, ending up at the United Nations in mid-1987. Since Mexican and Latina participants were not satisfied with the treatment of gender issues during the caravan, they organized a second women's caravan back to Mexico City in 1988. While the second caravan paled in comparison to the scope and visibility of the first, it allowed women involved in solving housing problems to exchange information and experiences with fellow community activists as they explored the gender implications of the problems of housing and homelessness. For example, women discussed the correlation of domestic abuse and homelessness among women. However, once the caravans ended, cross-border contacts dwindled. As the Mexican representative explained: "You don't really have neighborhood associations in the U.S. like we have here in the D.F. and in other Mexican cities. Here, lots of neighborhoods were built by what you call 'squatters,' people who claim their land, build their houses, and refuse to move when authorities come to evict them. Later,

Teresa Carrillo

women marched for paved streets and schools and services and now they have neighborhoods. Everything in the popular neighborhoods is there because of the struggles of the people who live there and the women are very important to that struggle. We didn't find the same thing in the U.S."[17] Indeed, neighborhood activists exist in the United States, but their struggles are not readily linked to feminist struggles.

Labor organizations have been more successful than other types of Chicana/Latina and Mexicana groups at identifying counterpart groups across borders. Garment workers in particular have been especially aware of the need to organize beyond national borders. Before 1990, the independent "19th of September" Garment Workers Union represented the only predominantly female sector of the Mexican industrial work force which had managed to establish substantial transnational links. Since its dramatic inception in the aftermath of the 1985 earthquake, this union has attracted international attention from feminist, labor, and church groups, resulting in a fruitful exchange that included a number of sponsored international tours and some funding for union projects and programs. In 1988, internal divisions put into question the legitimacy of the union's leadership and many supporters abroad suspended their support until the union could present a more united front. Nonetheless, Chicana and Latina organizations have maintained relations throughout the union's ten year history.

The Garment Workers Union, with the help of Mujer a Mujer and other advocacy organizations in the United States, sent various delegations of women on international tours to compare living and working conditions and to exchange materials and experiences with other women garment workers. They spoke at events and showed the documentary film, *No Les Pedimos Un Viaje a la Luna* (*We Aren't Asking For the Moon*), which is about the movement that gave birth to their union.[18] From 1987 through 1989, the union and its International Commission produced and distributed an international newsletter to approximately three hundred individuals and organizations in the United States, Canada, and Europe.[19]

Chicana and Latina garment workers in Fuerza Unida, Mujer Obrera, and the two biggest garment worker unions in the United States, the International Ladies Garment Workers Union (ILGWU) and the ACTWU, have pursued a relationship with Mexican garment workers in the "19th of September" union. Irene Reyna, a leader of Fuerza Unida, described the relationship between her organization and the "19th of September" union as "good." "They are aware of what is going on with us and we are aware of what is going on with them. While attending a conference on

Plate 53: **Image from Maria del Carmen de Lara's film**
We Aren't Asking for the Moon, 1987
Courtesy of the filmmaker and First Run Icarus Films

Teresa Carrillo

NAFTA, I stayed with women from the '19th of September' union and they have visited us here in San Antonio." She went on to explain that "it has been hard to keep communication going . . . [because] the phone bills are expensive . . . [and] so are plane tickets. . . . [S]o we keep in touch by phone, but not very often." [20]

Despite the accomplishments of the international tours and occasional exchanges, even garment workers have not been able to maintain ongoing exchange and communication or longer-term coordinated action. Transnational mutual solidarity remains a wish that has never become a sustainable daily practice, largely because of lack of resources. This sector that comprises garment workers has maintained a high level of awareness of the global nature of its industry, and has made the most of the transnational contacts it has managed. Foundations and individuals interested in building links between Chicanas, Latinas, and Mexicanas would do well to focus on garment workers.

Beyond the Cosmic Race

During the international tour of the Mexican garment workers there were moments that highlighted a difference in approach to issues of race and ethnicity between Mexican and Latina activists. The first took place in the San Francisco office of the ILGWU when the union leadership mentioned the racial divisions between Asian-American, African American and Latina garment workers. At that time, the San Francisco office was run by Asian women but the union's elected leadership was made up predominantly of African-American women. Latina garment workers had their own organization within the larger union and had sponsored a separate reception for the Mexican garment workers. This was very confusing for the Mexican garment workers, who felt the tension in the office but persisted in asking question after question about the racial dynamics of the ILGWU. They could not comprehend the divisions based on race and kept returning to this point until finally the ILGWU's local president, an African-American woman, abruptly ended the meeting and referred the visiting delegation to the union's Latina organization. Later, when we met with Latina garment workers, the relevance of race, ethnicity, and national origin was clarified in the numerous references to immigration status and discriminatory practices in the industry. It was a crash course on U.S. race relations for Mexican garment workers.

The *desencuentro* at the International Lesbian Conference in 1987 provides another illustration of how the treatment of racial dynamics is another fundamental difference between Chicana/Latina and Mexican women's movements. In 1987, Mujer a Mujer, a collective of Mexican and U.S. feminists dedicated to promoting communication and exchange among activist women in Canada, the United States, and Mexico, helped to organize and fund a binational lesbian conference in Mexico. Putting a high priority on the connection between Chicana/Latina lesbians from the United States and lesbians from Mexico, they made funds available to Latinas in the United States and fifteen Chicana/Latina women attended. During the conference the U.S. Latina contingent requested a closed session limited to women of color to talk about racism. The Mexican women rejected the request for a closed space. They were offended by the request and defended the rights of their white, middle- and upper-class friends to remain in the room and be a part of the discussion rather than separating with the "strangers" from the United States. This incident, combined with language barriers and stereotypes, made the meeting a disaster—what was called a *desencuentro total,* a total mis-encounter.[21]

Just as the U.S. Latina women's movement has been reluctant to frame women's issues in terms of community survival and a traditional gendered division of labor, Mexican women's groups have shied away from issues of race and ethnicity. Mexican women's groups are often made up of women of like ethnic and racial background but they rarely put forth race or ethnicity as a basis for their collective identity. Even organizations of predominantly indigenous women made scant reference to issues of race and ethnicity or to a collective identity based on race or ethnicity. Given the racial stratification and segregation within the various tiers of the Mexican women's movement, the absence of racial discourse is glaring. There is a marked predominance of indigenous and *mestiza* women in the popular women's groups organized around community survival while the white or light-skinned women form feminist groups focused more explicitly on gender-based issues. Some of the white feminist activists work with women of color in the popular women's movement on issues of labor and community survival but none of the groups emphasizes race or racial hierarchies. The silence of white women is easy to understand; they enjoy racial privilege and depend upon women of color to perform burdensome daily tasks in the home, such as cleaning, buying and preparing food, and caring for children and elderly family members. Much like upper-class women in the United States, their emancipation from housework and childcare

Teresa Carrillo

comes at the expense of women of color who work for low wages as domestic servants and care-givers. If racial inequities were addressed, women
enjoying racial privilege would put at risk their freedom from domestic
duties.

It is harder to understand the silence around racial issues on the part
of Mexican women of color. Perhaps it is related to the general tendency in
Mexico to elide issues of race. Since early revolutionary writers such as José
Vasconcelos, in his book *The Cosmic Race,* advanced theories of *mestizaje*
and promoted the idea that the majority of Mexicans are of mixed racial
heritage, the concepts of *indigenismo, mestizaje,* and the Mexican as *mestizo*
have diverted the discourse on race and racism, resulting in a reluctance to
discuss racism and assign racial meanings.[22] But Mexico is a country deeply
stratified by race and there is a great need to address issues of race and racism in the women's movement as well as in other progressive movements.
While women of color in the United States tend to define their collective
identity equally around gender and race/ethnicity, Mexican women's
groups focus more on gender and class, often without elaborating a formal
position on race and ethnicity. This is a shortcoming on the part of the
Mexican women's groups much like the failure of the movement of
women of color in the United States to adequately address issue of class
and community survival.

Despite these difficulties, transnational network building is an important and consequential part of the women's movement in Mexico and
among U.S. Latinas and feminists in general. More than any other function, transnational contact helps activist women on both sides of the border
place themselves and their collective actions within a global context and understand how citizenship is not gender neutral. Transnational networks facilitate the exchange of information, materials, and experiences *between*
groups, which allows women to make connections, both in theory and
practice, between local issues, gendered citizenship, and processes of globalization. Transnational networks also serve to link otherwise isolated groups
with organizations that can offer support and mutual solidarity from other
areas of the world.

Comunidades in Cyberspace

One of the groups that succeeded in establishing a substantial and extended
network of communication and exchange between women was the School
for International Organizers developed by Mujer a Mujer in Mexico.[23]

Plate 54: *Wounds of Jesus,* 1995
Black and white reproduction of color slide
Lillian Mulero
Courtesy of the artist

During 1992, twenty Mexican women from the labor and popular urban movements participated in a weekly training seminar that examined the process of regional economic integration and its effects on U.S. Latinas and Mexican women. Each participant went on at least one international tour to the United States and gained firsthand knowledge of women's organizations in the United States. Another of the group's accomplishments was to establish communication with Latina women in the United States via electronic mail over the Internet. Participants in the school, especially those already familiar with computers in their workplaces, learned how to use the Internet system and the World Wide Web and established electronic addresses on PeaceNet.

> We use electronic mail to exchange ideas and information, plan things, and to access a wide international public. During the Trinational Encuentro of Working Women, we were able to instantly disseminate the results of the conference in Spanish and English, to electronic addresses on our mailing list. Within days we were receiving responses and making new contacts. We got over that old feeling that the conferences we organized were like a tree falling in the woods with no one around to hear it. Now we have a way to send information about what we are doing and receive immediate responses from women in this and other continents.[24]

In September, 1995, daily summaries of the International Women's Conferences in Huairou and Beijing, China, were instantly disseminated in Mexico and the United States by a joint team of Mexican and U.S. activists.

Instant and widespread dissemination of information via electronic mail was extremely important in the case of the 1994 Zapatista rebellion in Chiapas, Mexico. Sub-commandante Marcos communicated with the world via his laptop computer and modem. His communiqués gained popular support for the rebels and helped to pressure the Mexican government into a cease-fire, temporary amnesty for rebel leaders, and peace negotiations. For women, access to a public via electronic mail will diminish the problems of isolation and silence. With the capability of instantly and affordably spreading information and analysis, women gain the protection offered by vigilant eyes and ears in the international community. This vigilance has helped to limit army abuses in Chiapas, environmental abuses in the borderlands, and sexual abuse by government agents, most notably by Drug Enforcement agents in Mexico City. Although access to electronic communication is still extremely limited among U.S. Latinas and Mexicanas, there are some Raza women cruising the Internet, creating a transnational sense of *communidad* in cyberspace.

A transnational level of organization is more likely to be built around some issues than others. Neighborhood and housing issues, for example, are more difficult to frame within a global context than environmental, labor, or trade issues. Many Latina and Mexicana women active in popular movements are involved in these localized concerns have had a difficult time addressing them through regional and global networks. One Mexican feminist faulted her organization's lack of resolve to create transnational channels of communication: "We haven't laid out a clear objective to establish transnational links. Projects have been determined by the necessities of the moment . . . and although we know it's important in the long run, in the short run, we don't have the energy to carry through on a project like that. . . . With the Free Trade Agreement comes a more urgent need for communication and more concrete initiatives."[25]

Women have been most effective in building networks around specific regional or single-issue causes . Women in the *maquiladoras,* for example, are part of the Coalition for Justice in the Maquiladoras and the Tri-National Commission for Justice in the Maquiladoras. Women's labor groups have collaborated in a number of trade related bi- and tri-national coalitions, including the Mexican Free Trade Action Network, the U.S.-Mexico-Canada Labor Solidarity Network, and Common Frontiers. Transnational collaboration among women in specific industries have been organized by Fuerza Unida in San Antonio; La Mujer Obrera of El Paso; Trabajadoras Desplazadas (a committee of Mexicana workers laid off by Green Giant in Watsonville, California, when the company shifted production to Irapuato, Mexico); and Mujeres en Acción Sindical and the Frente Auténtico de Trabajo in Mexico D.F.[26] Mujer a Mujer in Mexico D.F. has been especially active and successful in facilitating transnational exchange among women through *encuentros,* conferences, tours, and correspondence. They have greatly expanded their work in connecting activist women in the region through various networks, including an electronic mail network (via Peacenet) and participation in bi- and tri-national coalitions. Once women gain the facility to communicate across borders, they are faced with the challenge of addressing the many contradictions and conflicts of interests, real or perceived, that exist between women—Chicanas/Latinas and Mexicanas, white women, and women of color. Whether the conflicts arise from distinctions based on race, national origin, immigration status, or culture, they present formidable obstacles to alliance building between women.

One activist comments that "globalization has started to erase the barrier of disinterest" in other women.[27] Time and time again women showed a strong interest in making connections and taking a more active role in establishing the rules and regulations of the process of regional integration. The frustration voiced by both Chicana/Latina and Mexicana women was that no one knew exactly how to take the next step in transnational network building after establishing initial contact. Women's movements lack a unifying focus or initiative around which groups can find common ground and take collaborative action. On every front, the move from communication and contact to collaborative action was not clearly defined.

The in-between step of increasing mutual awareness and understanding between U.S. Latinas and Mexican women has been one of the most consequential aspects of transnational communication and exchange. Exposure to the vibrant and multi-faceted women's movements of Latin America has offered U.S. Latinas a valuable lesson in examining the gendered nature of citizenship and broadening the basis of support for our own movements. Sonia Alvarez writes, "We in the U.S. have much to learn about how to promote and reinforce the process of empowerment and gender consciousness among low-income and minority women who are involved in welfare rights struggles, in our own growing numbers of *comedores populares* and collective survival strategies, in our own government make-work programs, and permanent 'emergency' relief programs."[28] The extensive engagement between popular women's groups and feminist advocacy groups in Mexico, and in Latin America in general, has advanced our consciousness and analysis of how class and gender issues are intertwined. In the United States, the connection between gender, race, and class consciousness needs to be established within the mainstream feminist movement, especially now that congress is legislating welfare reform and retreating from affirmative action. Organizations formed by U.S. women of color have come into the forefront of feminism in the United States, demonstrating how issues of race and ethnicity are integral to women's empowerment. During the 1970s and 1980s, Latin American feminists drew on a rich and abundant source of criticism and analysis from feminists in the industrialized countries of Europe and North America. But in the 1990s, Latin American women's movements may capture the attention of U.S. feminists in search of a mass base of support for both gender issues and problems of community survival. In the past few years, collaboration and exchange between U.S. Latina and Mexican women has become a busy, two-way street.

Note

1. From Ricardo Hernandez and Edith Sanchez, eds., *Cross-Border Links* (Albuquerque, NM: Inter-Hemispheric Education Resource Center, 1992). See also: Milton H. Jamail and Margo Gutiérrez, *The Border Guide: Institutions and Organizations of the United States-Mexico Borderlands,* 2d ed. (Austin, TX: CMAS Books, 1992). Both guides provide comprehensive listings of organizations and agencies that seek to create links and promote collaborative action between peoples and communities of Mexico and the United States.

2. Cathryn L. Thorup examines the link between free trade and the need for coalition-building in her article, "The Politics of Free Trade and the Dynamics of Cross-Border Coalitions in U.S.-Mexican Relations," *Columbia Journal of World Business* 26, no. 2 (Summer 1991): 12–26.

3. Octavia Lara, Secretary of External Relations of the "19th of September" Garment Workers Union, interview by author, March 25, 1989, San Francisco.

4. Rafaela Dominguez, Secretary of Sports and Culture of the "19th of September" Garment Workers Union, interview by author, March 25, 1989, San Francisco.

5. See Marta Lamas, Alicia Martínez, Maria Luisa Tarrés, and Esperanza Tuñón, "Junctures and Disjunctures: The Women's Movement in México, 1970–1993" (unpublished paper, sponsored by the Ford Foundation, Mexico).

6. Temma Kaplan argues that in line with a traditional sexual division of labor, women accept the responsibility for "preserving life" and act on what she calls "female consciousness," forming mass mobilizations in defense of their right and obligation to maintain a home and provide the basic needs for their families. See Temma Kaplan, "Female Consciousness and Collective Action," *Signs: Journal of Women in Culture and Society* 7, no. 1: 55–76. For a related discussion of "militant motherhood," see Sonia Alvarez, *Engendering Democracy in Brazil: Women's Movements in Transition Politics* (Princeton, NJ: Princeton University Press, 1990).

7. See Alan Knight, "Racism, Revolution and Indigenismo in Mexico," in Richard Graham, ed., *The Idea of Race in Latin America* (Austin: University of Texas Press, 1990).

8. The groundbreaking text on feminism among women of color in the U.S. is Cherríe Moraga and Gloria Anzaldúa, eds., *This Bridge Called My Back* (Watertown, MA: Persephone Press, 1981). A more recent collection, *Making Face, Making Soul/*

Haciendo Caras, edited by Anzaldúa, was published in 1990 (San Francisco: Aunt Lute Books). For a discussion of the differences in women's agendas across national boundaries, see Chandra Mohanty's "Introduction" and "Under Western Eyes," in Mohanty, et al, *Third World Women and the Politics of Feminism* (Bloomington: Indiana University Press, 1991).

9. The Asian Immigrant Women's Advocates (AIWA) is a group of Asian and Asian-American women in the electronics, hotel, and garment industries working to improve their own working and living conditions. AIWA has pursued a varied agenda, ranging from leadership training and literacy campaigns to improving health and safety regulation and enforcement in the workplace. Asian garment workers organized a boycott of Jessica McClintock garments and their major retailer, Macy's, in order to pressure the company for back pay owed to workers that had been laid off. AIWA's agenda is described in the newsletter *Race, Poverty and the Environment* 3, no. 1 (Spring 1992): 12.

10. The West County Toxics Coalition is made up of residents of an area in Richmond, California, known as the "petrochemical corridor" where Chevron, Ortho, Whitco Chemicals, and other petrochemical firms generate and process hazardous waste on-site. Coalition activists, predominantly African-American women, have opposed expansion of the industry and pushed for more stringent control of toxins. In 1995 they reached a compromise with Chevron for a new health center as a condition of expansion. For more on the West County Toxics Coalition, see Robert D. Bullard, *Confronting Environmental Racism* (Boston: South End Press, 1993), 29.

11. For more on Fuerza Unida, see Kara A. Zugman, "Rising from the Ashes: Raza Labor in the Global Economy," César E. Chavez Institute for Public Policy Working Paper Series, San Francisco State University, 1996.

12. Some of the binational environmental organizations include: The Health Council for Northeast Sonora and Cochise County in Agua Prieta, Sonora, Ecological Link in Agua Prieta, Sonora, and Douglas, AZ; Arizona Toxics Information in Bisbee, AZ; the Border Ecology Project in Naco, AZ; Grupo Dignidad in Nogales, AZ; Grupo Ecológico los Campitos in Cananea, Sonora; Proyecto Fronterizo de Educación Ambiental; the Coalition for Justice in the Maquiladoras in San Antonio; Alert Citizens for Environmental Safety in El Paso; and the TCE Information Center in Tucson, AZ.

13. See Julio Moguel, "Caminos del movimiento urbano popular en los ochenta," *El Cotidiano* 50 (September 1992): 221–226.

14. For an excellent analysis of Mexican women's survival strategies against ecological and environmental impoverishment, see Lynn Stephen, "Women in Mexico's Popular Movements: Survival Strategies Against Ecological and Economic Impoverishment," *Latin American Perspectives* 19, no. 1, (Winter 1992): 73–96.

15. Norma Mogrovejo Aquise, "Feminismo popular en México: analisis del surgimiento, desarrollo y conflictos en la relacion entre la tendencia feminista y la regional de mujeres de la CONAMUP" (Masters Thesis, Dept. of Social Science, U.N.A.M., Mexico D.F., 1990).

16. Marta Lamas and other Mexican feminist analysts have pointed out that the feminist movement and the broader based women's movement in Mexico are not synonymous. Lamas describes the "movimiento amplio de mujeres" as a loose coalition of *campesinas,* women from popular urban organizations, women wage-earners, and feminists, in Marta Lamas, "El movimiento feminista en Mexico: una interpretación" (unpublished paper, 1995). Lamas cites a preliminary attempt to classify women's democratic struggles in the second wave of feminism in 1970, in an article by Acevedo, Lamas, and Liguori published in the feminist journal, *FEM,* no. 13 (1978).

17. Vicki Villanueva, Regional de Mujeres de la CONAMUP, interview by author, May 6, 1992, Mexico D.F.

18. *No Les Pedimos Un Viaje a la Luna,* Mari Carmen de Lara, prod. and dir., 1 hr. (New York: First Run/Icarus Films, 1987).

19. For more on the Mexican Garment Workers Union, see Teresa Carrillo, "Women, Trade Unions, and New Social Movements: The Case of the '19th of September' Garment Workers Union in Mexico" (Ph.D. diss., Dept. of Political Science, Stanford University, Stanford, CA., 1990).

20. Irene Reyna, Fuerza Unida, interview by Kara Ann Zugman, September 13, 1995, San Francisco.

21. Elaine Burns, Mujer a Mujer, interviews by author, July 20, 1992, and August 25, 1992, Mexico D.F.

22. José Vasconcelos, *La Raza Cósmica* (Paris: Agencia Mundial de Librerias, 1925). For more on racism in Mexico see Knight "Racism, Revolution, and Indigenismo in Mexico."

23. For more on this and other programs of Mujer a Mujer, see *Correspondencia,* a bilingual newsletter containing information and analysis about the impact of globalization and economic restructuring on women's lives and struggles. It is published three times a year by Mujer a Mujer, AP 24–553, Colonia Roma 06701, Mexico D.F.

24. Elaine Burns, Mujer a Mujer interview by author, August 25, 1992, Mexico D.F.

25. Itziar Lozano, CIDHAL, a feminist service organization, interview by author, June 30, 1992, Mexico D.F.

26. For more information on these and other cross-border networks, see Hernandez and Sanchez, eds., *Cross-Border Links*.

27. Elaine Burns, August 25, 1992.

28. Sonia Alvarez, "Redibujando el Feminismo en las Americas and 'Redrawing' the Parameters of Gender Struggle" (paper presented at the conference *Learning from Latin America: Women's Struggles for Livelihood,* University of California, Los Angeles, February 28, 1992), TMs, p. 8.

M. A. Jaimes * Guerrero

Savage Hegemony: From "Endangered Species" to Feminist Indiginism

Chronologies of Native Definition

1887: The Dawes Allotment Act: The first time "blood quantum" criteria was put into legislation was in this Act. Its purpose was to make a distinction between the "full-bloods" and "mixed-bloods" among the targeted Cherokees and related tribal groups. It was used in order to determine who was to be "eligible" for allotment lands as a result of the 1887 Act, and which resulted in many "mixed-bloods" being "disqualified" if they could not meet "half-blood" status. This was said by federal authorities to protect Indian "full-bloods," but in actuality it managed to manipulate the process that led to most Indian lands falling into the hands of non-Indian and government authorities while exploiting the "eligible" "full-blooded" allottees.

1924: The Indian Citizenship Act: As a "clean-up measure," this Act was passed to pick up all those missed or excluded by the General Allotment Act—the law which unilaterally conferred U.S. citizenship on "all non-citizen Indians born within the territorial limits of the [U.S.]."[1] A number of indigenous peoples, notably among the Hopi and Onondaga, have informally refused to acknowledge the Citizenship Act as in any way binding upon them, and continue to engage in such expressions of sovereignty as issuing their own passports.

1934: The Indian Reorganization Act: The IRA was imposed by the U.S. to supplant traditional forms of indigenous governance in favor of a tribal council structure modeled after corporate boards.[2] In order to put a "democratic face" on the maneuver, it was stipulated that each native nation be reorganized and agree to the process by referendum. The referenda were then systematically rigged by the then Commissioner of Indian

Affairs, John Collier. One result of the Act has been a deep division between "traditionals" and "progressives" (the latter endorse the IRA form of government) on many reservations to this day.

1968: The Indian Civil Rights Act: While it negated many of the worst potentialities of termination policy, this Act served to bind the forms assumed by indigenous governments even more tightly to federal preferences than had the IRA. In effect, it made native governments a functional part of the federal system itself. Such incorporations, however, only afforded Indian peoples constraints upon their sovereignty rather than any of the constitutional protections of basic rights and other benefits supposedly accruing to members of the U.S. polity.[3]

1990: The Indian Arts and Crafts Act: As an amendment to a "foreign commerce and international exports" law, the Act states that it is meant to "promote the development" of Native American art. In order to sell Indian art, a person must be a member of an Indian tribe or have certification as an Indian artist by a tribe. Most tribes in more modern times, themselves, have also mandated to have official recognition (called "federal recognition") from the U.S. government in order to be able to grant this "legitimacy" to an Indian artist. The Indian Arts and Crafts Board has been given power to "establish standards and regulations" for government-owned trademarks and the ability to register these trademarks with the U.S. Patent and Trademark Office. "It is unlawful to offer or display [art] for sale . . . ,with or without a Government trademark, in a manner that falsely suggests it is Indian produced, or the product of a particular Indian or Indian tribe or Indian arts and crafts organization, resident within the United States." "Indian" in this Act is defined as "any individual who is a member of an Indian tribe or . . . is certified as an Indian artist by an Indian tribe." A "tribe" is defined as: "(A) Any Indian tribe, band, nation, Alaskan Native village, or other organized group or community which is recognized as eligible for the special programs and services provided by the (U.S.) to Indians because of their status as Indian; or (B) any Indian group that has been formally recognized as an Indian tribe by a State legislature or by a State commission or similar organization legislatively vested with State tribal recognition authority." The amendment also establishes criminal penalties which can now be imposed upon anyone convicted of "ethnic fraud" and of "misrepresenting" a product as "Indian produced."[4]

Plate 55: *Big Myths Die Hard*, 1995
Charcoal, collage on paper, 30 × 22″
© Jaune Quick-to-See Smith
Photo: George Hirose
Collection of Marilyn Stewart
Courtesy of Steinbaum Krauss Gallery, New York

Civil Rights versus Sovereignty

The congressional and judicial illustrations noted above show that American Indians have been disenfranchised and dispossessed legally and democratically in the U.S. After centuries of colonial destruction of community, culture, and ecology, the 1924 Indian Citizenship Act was a U.S. imposed "blanket policy" on the identity of all American Indians. Consequently, we became refugees in our own homelands. In no other societal arena has the impact been more devastating than in jurisprudence, both criminal and civil. Prior to Euro-American hegemony, Indian tribal societies had no concept of civil rights because every member of the society was related, by kinship and clan responsibilities, to every other member. Indians understood fully that injury is personal. Hence, historically and at least in theory, Indian tribes derived their basic powers from that primordial contract era when they enjoyed "perfect political freedom."[5] The erosion of Native North American traditional egalitarian cultures, since the onset of European colonization, has had the corollary of disempowering Native women who historically participated in matrilineal societies and matrifocal spheres of women-centered power-bases, handed down to the younger female generations. Lack of autonomy has had even harsher consequences for Native American women, who, along with their offspring, have lost their tribal status, whether because they have left the reservation or married outside their own tribe. Since the 1934 Reorganization Act, in particular, the process of a "trickle-down patriarchy"[6] has been reinforced. Within this "trickle-down patriarchy" Indian women have often found themselves subjugated as Native women in a racist and sexist society that has established a male-controlled tribal group. Many Native American women today, often single parents without traditional extended family support, live in impoverished and disadvantaged conditions, in urban or rural ghettos, marginal even to the reservation.

Among many, if not most tribes, it is apparent that there is a clash of two societal systems that has created legal and cultural conflict. Federal reorganization has resulted in complex jurisdictional problems, such that a tribe's male authority might clash with the civil rights of women. In these scenarios, Native women and their offspring are more likely to be pitted against a predominantly male tribal government leadership that asserts "sovereignty" over their "civil rights" grievances. The 1934 Indian Reorganization Act created tribal governments as extensions of U.S. patriarchy, that had the legal power to determine the right of an Indian woman's children to membership in the tribe. Questioning women's identity today raises major contradictions and dilemmas for the offspring of intertribal marital unions.

The two Martinez decisions (1957, 1978), as legal cases-in-point, illustrate the socio-political problems in these legal scenarios. The first modern case of a civil rights nature was the 1957 *Martinez v. Southern Ute Tribe,* which challenged the power of a tribe to determine its own membership over the power of individual Native Americans. There is no indication that the Martinez woman in the 1957 case actually lost to the pueblo council, which more likely means there was some kind of settlement out of court. A much later case, the 1978 *Martinez v. Santa Clara Pueblo* also involved a Native woman (not related to the first Martinez), as a former member of the pueblo whose residence status on the reservation was being threatened, while her offspring's tribal membership was denied because she married another Indian outside of the tribe.[7] In the 1978 case, the Martinez woman was suing the male-controlled pueblo council, predicated on her civil rights grievance that also involved her children's non-status. What complicated this particular case further, and what is still confusing today, is that the pueblo governance and its court system had been reorganized by the IRA as an extension of the federal government. Prior to that time, however, the Santa Clara Pueblo's traditional society had been a *matrilineal* society, of which an ethnologist provided evidence in court. Pre-IRA, this case would not have concerned a legal issue if the traditional matrilineal kinship social system had been legally recognized. Furthermore, since Martinez had married an Indian man from a tribe that opposed the IRA, the Navajo (Dineh), and that still practiced its matrilineal customs, this particular case was deeply entangled in sovereignty confusion and jurisdictional violations. Martinez was told and even pressured by tribal council members to move her family to the Navajo Reservation. Therefore, her case clearly illustrates a three-sided triangle that resulted in the denial of her Pueblo and Navajo matrilineal rights as well as her U.S. civil rights, while at the same time the denial of her children's tribal membership in both the Santa Clara Pueblo and Navajo (Dineh) societies.[8] There are other more contemporary tribal court cases pending regarding these affairs that negate Native women's rights.

A comparison between the U.S. and Canadian government systems reveals variations in Federal Indian/Aboriginal policy in North America. The Canadian government ruled in favor of tribal reinstatement of a New Brunswick Tobique Reserve woman and her young son. The Sandra (Sappier) Lovelace case argued that her civil rights had been violated

(predicated on the existing Canadian Indian Act) when the male-dominated Tobique council took away her Reserve status after she married
outside of the tribe and left the community. She and her son eventually
returned, after leaving her spouse. Even though she still had relatives on the
reserve, the leadership denied her housing and other services she once had
with her previous membership. The Lovelace case went all the way to the
United Nations (in 1977), with support from a Native women's group that
eventually arrested the attention of the Canadian women's movement. This
women's alliance pressured the Canadian government to amend the Indian
Act of 1985 in order to protect women and their offspring who found
themselves in a similar predicament; subjected to the predominantly male
tribal leadership that has the power to offer employment, housing, and
other services on the reserve, as well as to determine the Indian status of
women and their children. The Lovelace case resulted in a male tribal leadership that cried foul in the preemption of its "sovereignty" by both the Canadian government and the United Nations.[9] The Canadian case and the
two respective Martinez cases in the U.S. illustrate the philosophical, ideological, and cultural contradictions generated by the federal "blanket policy." This situation seems to have escalated, given the growing degree of
federal intervention into the internal affairs of tribes.[10]

It is at this juncture that the significance of the conceptual meaning
and understanding of "sovereignty," as it is derived from the "divine right
of kings" in monarchy, should be addressed. It also behooves theorists to
study how sovereignty historically has been placed in the service of an ideology of nationalism and constructed under patriarchal colonial imperialism.
Although tribal leaders in the U.S. often refer to "tribal sovereignty" as a
form of "cultural nationalism," this sovereignty is the product of colonial
history and eurocentric culture, which includes chauvinism and misogyny.
These tribes are still mandated by the federal government to "spell out"
civil rights codes that have to be incorporated into the respective tribes'
IRA constitutions.[11] Under these circumstances, Indian women activists engaged in land and life struggles have especially suffered when their Indian
and tribal rights come into conflict with the "civil rights" of non-Indians.
The case of Ramona Bennett, an Indian (Puyallup) woman activist in the
Northwest, brings to light the complexity of the "duel-citizenry" status
claimed by many Indians of both genders. Bennett, exercising both her
U.S. civil rights and her tribal status, was arrested by state authorities for
representing her tribe as a tribal council member in an Indian fishing
rights demonstration under the state and national guidelines of "civil dis-

obedience." She describes how and why she and other demonstrators had been arrested:

> They [the police] came right on the reservation. . . . They gassed us, they clubbed people around, [and] they laid a $125,000 bail on us. At that time I was a member of the Puyallup Tribal Council, and I was spokes(person) for the camp [of local fishing rights activists]. And I told them what [our] policy was, that we were there to protect our Indian fishermen. And because I used a voice-gun, I'm charged with inciting a riot. I'm now faced with an eight year sentence.[12]

This was happening while Indian fishermen were being threatened for practicing their traditional fishing methods, as stipulated in Indian treaty rights of tribal members. The then pregnant Bennett was eventually acquitted after being shot and wounded by "white vigilantes."

This case illustrates the constraints that many traditionally-oriented women leaders in grass-roots movements experience when their assertion of Indian/tribal rights is undermined by the federal government's anti-Indian standard—especially whenever the tribes and individual members stand in the way of non-Indian self-interests.[13] Many Native women, meanwhile, have been struggling to survive while simultaneously engaging in conflicts over land, working in their own communities, and being activists in regional, national, and international liberation struggles. The contradictions between civil rights and sovereignty have, then, resulted in Native women's concerns being subordinated to those of tribal and federal patriarchies.

The relative power bestowed upon the "good Indians" results in direct correlation to their cooperation with the federal government, which ironically bestows civil rights as a form of contradicting sovereignty. This legal and cultural conflict between the concepts of civil rights and sovereignty has resulted in situations like the 1973 U.S. para-military operations at Wounded Knee, as well as in the 1978 Martinez case. These incidents have raised complex and divisive socio-political and legal questions about federal intervention in Native communities. The most explosive event focused on Indians was the occupation and resultant siege known as the Wounded Knee Occupation of 1973, on the Pine Ridge Indian Reservation in South Dakota. "As tensions built up on . . . Pine Ridge . . . the tribal government was consistently used by one group of Indians to harass and oppress another group of Indians. When violence (finally) erupted, there was no role for the tribal court except to echo the sentiments of one side of the intratribal dispute."[14] The American Indian Movement (AIM) had been brought into the disturbance by the request from traditionally oriented reservation residents. They were protesting the civil rights abuses of their IRA-imposed government, and they were backed by Lakota elders, many of whom were women, such as Gladys Bissonette. These tribal members made harsh accusations that the tribal council—headed by a tyrannical tribal chair, the infamous Dickie Wilson—was an oppressive creation of the eurocentric patriarchal colonialist.

"Civil rights," as Vine Deloria and Clifford Lytle state, "depend first of all upon a social contract theory of government, which Indian tribes do not espouse, but they do rely on a kind of government that allocates sovereign powers to branches, and then separates the branches of government to act as a check-and-balance protection for the citizenry."[15] According to these co-authors, the real effect of the Indian Civil Rights Act (ICRA) of 1968, ". . . was to require one aspect of tribal government—the tribal court—to become a formal institution more completely resembling the federal judiciary than the tribal government itself resembled. . . . The informality of Indian life that had been the repository of cultural traditions and customs was suddenly abolished. . . . The ICRA basically distorted reservation life . . . [with] impositions of rules and procedures. . . . In philosophical terms, traditional Indian society understood itself as a complex of responsibilities and duties [to its members]. . . . The ICRA merely transposed this belief into a society based on rights against government and eliminated any sense of responsibility. . . . People did not have to confront one another before their community [to] resolve their problems; they had only to file suit in tribal court."[17] This analysis, however, does not make a gender-specific contrast, since these traditional indigenous nations were egalitarian in recognizing matrifocal and patrifocal spheres of authority. Their *egalitarianism* entitled each member to the support of her/his family and clan as well as engendered egalitarian group positions. Hence, this traditional jurisdiction was able to resolve any gender-specific conflicts that might arise within these indigenous systems.

Echoing these senior scholars, Ward Churchill and Glenn Morris describe the consequences of the 1968 ICRA as a "clean-up" measure: "While it negated many of the worst potentialities [of destructive federal Indian policy, most significantly], . . . the 1950s termination policy that terminated targeted Indian communities (i.e., Menominee of Wisconsin and Klamath in Oregon), this "blanket policy" as a legislative Act . . . served to bind the forms assumed by (indigenous) governments . . . [as] a functional part of the federal system itself. Such incorporation, however, afforded Indian peoples only constraints upon their sovereignty rather than any of the constitutional protections of basic rights and other benefits supposedly accruing to members of the U.S. polity."[17] What the 1968 Act wrought, therefore, was that land and resource negotiations would be conducted between "American citizens" rather than between representatives of separate nations. This is a context in which federal and corporate arguments for "the greater good" could be predicted to prevail in the courts as well as the government, and, among Indians, as plaintiffs *or* defendants. In either case, the Native litigants continue to get the short stick of "justice" in the legal arena.

Who Is an Indian?

From early colonialist practices followed by Federal Indian Policy, judicial decisions and executive and congressional orders have all led to a contemporary state of statistical erasure of Native peoples. It was in the 1830s that Chief Justice Marshall of the Supreme Court made the determination that Indian tribes in the U.S. were "domestic dependent nations." In *The Cherokee Cases* (1831–1832), Chief Justice Marshall argued that American Indian peoples constituted nations domestic to and dependent upon the U.S.[18] According to his perspective, they occupied a status of "quasi sovereignty," being sovereign enough to engage in treaty-making with the U.S. for purposes of conveying legal title to their lands, but not sovereign enough to manage their other affairs as fully independent political entities. "Quasi-sovereignty" laid the groundwork for the Plenary Power Doctrine, ensuring that the federal government would hold full and inherent power over Indian affairs, and a concomitant "trust responsibility" over all Indian assets.[19] Such democratically instituted legal decisions meant that land and water resources could be diverted off Indian lands for U.S. populations and states. In this major Supreme Court decision, the original *bilateral* relationship between tribes as nations and the U.S. government in the form of treaties, were reverted to a *unilateral* relationship, keeping Indian peoples in perpetual subordination and leaving Native women more disempowered, congressionally and judicially, than Native men.[20]

Under the paternalistic guise of the "trust responsibility" or "guardianship" of Indian populations as "wards" of the U.S. government, this legal discourse has also been implemented in the name of "national interest," "for the common good," and "in the best interests" of Native peoples.[21] U.S. "national interest" has always been accommodated at the expense of the original inhabitants, as autochthonous peoples in their indigenous homelands. Within the current historical moment of U.S. colonialism, Native people have partially succumbed to a *racialized* experience under the various federally constructed classifications of the dispossessed and disenfranchised—for example, "relocated Indians," and "federally recognized" or "federally constructed" tribes. When colonialism is deeply internalized, these "subcultural" groups, rather than assert their nationhood, advocate the perceived advantages of referring to themselves as a disadvantaged "ethnic minority" population. Although this re-definition of indigenous identity might bring monetary and economic gain in the short run, through the category of "ethnic minority" under Affirmative Action, more often it establishes federal dependancy, which thwarts the more long-term sociopolitical goals of self-determination and self-sufficiency.

Within this system of domination and dependency, the identity and situation of Native American women are highly embattled. Presently, Native women, whether they marry non-"Indian" men or other Indians, seem to fare worse than men who intermarry outside of the tribe, in that they lose their tribal Indian status. Marrying a white male and giving up one's Indian identity and tribal membership is one way of climbing up the racial ladder in mainstream American society. But in general, Native American women's positions depend on who and what families have control of the tribal politics on the reservations, as well as what "federally recognized" tribe or Indian individual has access to the political apparatus of the U.S. governance system, from the White House on down. This is a system of federal and tribal partisan politics that has little to do with the essence of being "Indian" or the reality, truth, or justice in the liberation struggles of indigenous peoples. Rather, it is the result of a contemporary version of Euro-American colonialism that by now has become deeply enmeshed in a kind of trickle-down patriarchy.

Within this patriarchal-colonial hierarchy, many, if not most, Native women become dislocated "Third World" women, who, because of their land and cultural dispossession, find themselves as single parents with children and elders to take care of. They no longer have the support of extended family networks and kinship structures. This is especially so among those that have left the reservation community and married outside of the tribe. Although about fifty percent of Native American men and women intermarry, Indian men, especially those in leadership positions, do not suffer the same community dislocation and loss of the traditional support system. The male-dominated tribal council leadership, which has prevailed since the 1934 Reorganization Act, is, in fact, primarily made up of Indian men who have married non-Indian women. The leadership has, as a result, disempowered Native women's spheres of authority and rights. This convoluted situation has created "duel citizenry" status (in theory if not in practice) between diverse tribal nations and the U.S., which has posed domestic and international legal questions about the national identity of U.S. indigenous peoples vis-à-vis the U.S. as a nation-state.

The federal government, furthermore, has a long history of legislating criteria to determine who is "Indian." The U.S. government has been involved in the determination of "Who is an Indian?" ever since it first corralled Native peoples onto reservations. However, the more formal legislative history, in what is called Federal-Indian policy, began with 1887 Dawes Allotment Act that first stipulated "half-blood-quantum" criteria in order for Indian individuals to be "eligible" for land allotments, which splintered the communal landholdings of the tribes. Later came the establishment of the Bureau of Indian Affairs (BIA), an agency under the Department of the Interior (its proto-agency was established in the Office of War, when American Indians were overtly perceived as "savage" and "primitive"). The BIA interpreted from the 1928 Snyder Act, a formulation of how to determine "who is an Indian," which included a "quarter blood-quantum" criteria for education program services. This Act was established under what was called the Johnson-O'Malley Indian Education programs, administered under the BIA in the mid-1980s. A racial and gendered policy of "blood quantum" formula was implemented by the BIA, leading to a process of "statistical extermination," or "statistical genocide" in government census taking.[22] U.S. racialized codifications of Native Americans clearly contradict the traditions of indigenous societies, which did *not* previously hold to a "race" construct to determine tribal membership.[23] The federal stamping of Indian identity has generated major conflicts among Native Americans. In the arena of these racialized and genderized "Indian politics" regarding "who is an Indian," official carriers of Indian "identity" have the power to marginalize Native Americans who are not certified by the BIA. Often these certification are not granted for a myriad reasons — not least for political positions that have nothing to do with cultural determination or integrity, or political accountability over who can or cannot legitimately claim to be Indian.

Plate 56: *Borderlands/Respect (Clearcut)*, 1993
Black and white reproduction of color slide
Acrylic and mixed media on canvas, 30 × 30"
Annie Nash
Courtesy of the artist

Indian Identity and Censorship

The 1990 amendment of the BIA Indian Arts and Crafts Act was the culmination of the earlier 1930s Act, and was meant to protect Native artists from foreign appropriation. It was directed especially against Taiwan, China, and other Asian producers and distributors of "imitations of American Indian arts and crafts."[24] This latest restriction of indigenous sovereignty not only perpetuates "Indian" stereotypes, but also has punitive legal restraints that promote censorship in the arts and other arenas. Since the BIA Certification Act as a "blanket policy" imposes "blood quantum" as part of the U.S. government's determination of "who is American Indian," it criminalizes any "non-certified" Indian or art gallery that sells "Indian" art, subjecting either or both to penalty for fraud. This congressional legislation, which has support from the political leadership of some "federally recognized" groups of Indians/tribes, has resulted in denying many "non-federally recognized Indians" access to this federal stamp of identity via the BIA, under the Department of Interior. This restrictive policy, signed by former President Bush, has marginalized "non-federally recognized" Native artists, many of whom are political activists, for whom defining their history, culture, and art as American Indian is essential. Today, an "uncertified" Native artist who sells his or her work as an "Indian" can be fined, arrested, and imprisoned for "impersonating an Indian." This Act, a blatant case of politically motivated and racialized censorship in the arts, also threatens art galleries, shops, etc., with fines and even bankruptcy for the same reasons. This very controversial issue continues to pit Indians who are "federally recognized" against those who are not. Such divisive tactics also threaten other spheres of Native American representation, in education and academe, in literary careers, and so on.[25] Native writers and artists, both federally and non-federally recognized, have been challenging this Act and its implications in their work, referring to themselves as "uncolonized" Natives. (The context of the legislation also raises questions regarding what is a "federally recognized" and/or a "federally constructed" tribe.)

The "blood quantum" criterion still operates under a racialized category of "who is an Indian?" and assumes that all "Indians," "whites," or "blacks" are genealogically "pure." It is often overlooked that Native peoples have been intermarrying with non-Indians since long before the onset and establishment of Euro-American colonialism and patriarchy. This would not *traditionally* have been a problem in an indigenous society that based its membership on kinship systems (what anthropologists call moieties) and cultural criteria, including "naturalization" of non-Indians by way of intermarriage, adoption, and other means.[26] It was not unusual for Native societies to practice exogamy as customary law. Sandy Gonzales's contemporary comparative findings reveal that approximately fifty percent (48.0, wife's race; 48.3, husband's race) of American Indian and Alaska Native males and females marry "whites" compared to other non-Indian categories, such as black, Asian, other. This percentage is also about ten percent higher (46.3, wife's race; 47.6, husband's race) than the number of Natives who marry other Natives of both genders.[27] While Gonzales concludes that "interracial" intermarriage inevitably leads to assimilation, I would in turn argue that there are many assimilative forces at work in more modern times that do not solely depend on intermarriage. In addition, there are controversial cases in which non-Indian spouses and their offspring have gotten on the tribal rolls through intermarriage; for example, the "Dawes Rolls" of 1887 among the Cherokee, who do not hold to a "blood-quantum" criterion for this very reason.[28]

Among Native societies, the interdynamics of gender relationships traditionally took place in the context of elaborate kinship systems with clan structures. In matrilineal societies "clan mothers" determined kinship relations within the extended families and the communal society as a whole. In Lakota society, women who were taken in from other Native nations could only be considered a Lakota member once they learned the adoptive language and traditions. However, their children would be considered Lakota by birth regardless of "mixed-blood" biology.[29] The practice by custom and law of intermarriage outside the nation necessitated raiding other Native nations of women and children, particularly when a nation needed to increase its tribal membership for survival. Such practice has a different moral connotation today than it did among precolonial societies. Navajos, meanwhile, being matrilineal, traditionally belonged to the clans of their mothers, but they were also considered "born for" the clans of their fathers. Clan exogamy prevented them from marrying into either their mother's or their father's clan. Today, however, the "mixed-blood" controversy has become critical, and is a ruthlessly divisive, political tool of the federal government adopted by Indians themselves. There is even now tribal leadership that advocates calling for the prohibition of marriage outside of the tribe, particularly if one wants to continue to hold tribal leadership. As is apparent, this agenda could have dire consequences, not the least among them the breaking of incest taboos that violate the clan structures within

M. A. Jaimes * Guerrero

traditional kinship systems, which were meant to avoid these very situations of inbreeding.

The dominant authorities in North American Native societies in line with the U.S. hegemony hold to restrictive "race" categories that reject "interracial" categories of "mixed-blood" offspring as products of this traditional exogamy. Therefore, I agree with Jack Forbes when he asserts that the reality among Native peoples, as *mestizos,* mulattos, and *metis,* is that they are not well represented in these "race" categories, especially since the Census Bureau discourages, if it does not actually prohibit, any "mixed-blood" categories among the federally constructed racial categories—as *American Indians* or *Native Americans.*[30] Historically, Euro-American men participated in the generation of "mixed blood" when they took Native women as their "squaws,"[31] many without legal license or tribal sanction, and often mistreating them as subservient women under their authoritative domination.[32] And although historically Native societies did not define tribal-national identity by blood or race, today the BIA stamp excludes "mixed-bloods" from being defined as fully Native.[33]

From Blood Quantum to New Order Eugenics?

The statistical genocide implicit in "blood quantum" policy has conceptually prepared the grounds for what I call a "New Order Eugenics." Genocide, ethnocide, and ecocide have affected an increasingly growing list of "endangered species" on the planet, including, alongside plants and animals, indigenous peoples and their traditional cultures. Recent federal and academic projects have, under the guise of protecting endangered people, targeted Indigenous people for genetic engineering. The Human Genome Diversity Project (HGDP) has been designated to determine which indigenous groups are "threatened" peoples worldwide. While the Human Genome Project (HGP) is government sponsored to sample human genes for a DNA bank among all human populations globally, the HGDP, as the "Diversity Project," is being sponsored by mega-corporations, with nation state collaboration, to test the human genome for a genetic DNA bank which specifically targets selected indigenous groups. International in scope, both projects are well under way in sampling the human population in order to establish genetic data banks. The Diversity Project is backed by leading research institutes, such as Stanford University, and has as well the endorsement of private and corporate interests with federal and state political support. These "threatened" groups, specifically indigenous peoples and cultures, are being perceived as becoming "extinct" because their economic and industrial *underdevelopment* prevents them from keeping up with hypermodernization. There are over seven hundred among these targeted indigenous groups, more than seventy of them located in the U.S. and Canada.[34] Concerned non-governmental organizations, which continue to send delegations before the United Nations with little success, are calling the practice the "Vampire Project," because it samples DNA by testing blood, hair, and skin scrapings. Given the genocidal history toward the indigenous people of the Americas, it is difficult not to discern within this project a hidden demographic agenda, especially in terms of how such data will be used in the long run.

Indigenous women and their organizations challenge the work of the HGDP for its exploitation of the natural world and appropriation of the Earth, our mother host, and also for its clandestine "New Order Eugenics" that violates their basic human and cultural rights. Activism against the Diversity Project raises serious questions: if the target groups are so "threatened," by biological, ecological, and cultural forces, why, then, is nothing being done to assist them in surviving the onslaught of predatory and parasitic modernization? Why can the profit motive of transnational corporations hold even state governments "hostage" to their financial control? What are private mega-corporate interests in terms of a covert agenda of transnational industrial competition for DNA technology? Activists have also criticized the HGDP in terms of "intellectual property" issues among indigenous peoples. Why should profit-driven corporations hold a monopoly on indigenous spheres of knowledge? Science presumes to offer answers concerning the origins and migrations of indigenous populations, without engaging in a dialogue with Native people's cultural beliefs regarding their own origins. As ambassadorial representatives of their respective families, communities, and Native nations, and as members of distinct peoples and cultures, Native women activists are raising these issues in international fora, such as the recently convened International Women's Conference, in Beijing, China.[35]

Sexuality, Spirituality, and Cross-Gender Practices

Eurocentric representation of indigenous sexuality, especially in the context of female sexuality, emphasizes its unconstrained savagery as exotic erotica. The fifteenth-century Italian navigator, Amerigo Vespucci (after whom two continents were named), remarked that "New World" women were so "lustful and promiscuous," they made "eunuchs" of their male counterparts.[36] In colonial representation, Indian women are "beasts of burden," or "squaws" marked as possessions of their non-Indian male keepers. Along with the image of licentious seductress arose the equally pathetic "Cherokee princess" syndrome, seen in recent cinema in Disney's animated *Pocahontas,* as the "new" Indian Barbie doll. Little, however, is said about Native American women's tradition of control over their bodies in terms of sexuality, reproduction, and gender identity, and about the role colonialism has played in destabilizing the largely balanced gender relations. In what was likely the closest state of egalitarianism in human history, socio-cultural communal structures of many indigenous societies were designed to balance out any internal conflicts, including gender-based conflicts among the membership. The Native North American woman has a long and life-sustaining legacy of respect and empowerment within traditional indigenous societies. *Tradition* here, as elsewhere, is meant in the context of long-term and life-sustaining indigenous values and belief systems, versus the word's eurocentric connotation of "being in the past" and therefore "backwards," an obstacle to Euroamerican ideas of "progress." Traditionally, then, gender equality is not a new phenomenon since Native women have always held important and influential positions in their communal societies. Among these tribal nations are the Creek and Cherokee Nations, and the Haudenosaunee's Iroquois Confederacy in New York state; the latter is called the "longhouse" form of government with Clan Mothers who select male council leaders. Others include the Narragansett of Rhode Island and the Delawares, among the Algonquin peoples along the Atlantic coast, who in the past generically referred to themselves as "women," which was meant to be supremely complimentary.[37] This same government tradition, albeit in varied forms, can also be found among the Southwest tribal peoples, such as the Navajos (Dineh) and Pueblos, and among the Great Plains nations as well as the Northwest tribal peoples. Traditional Native women also tended—unless provoked to defend themselves and those kin relations they were responsible for—to be noncombatant to a greater degree than the men. There was the other side of this scenario, as well: Lakota women of the Great Plains, for instance, traditionally maintained at least four warrior societies of their own.[38] Dr. Beatrice Medicine, an influential Lakota scholar and anthropologist, has written extensively on Native women's experiences and perspectives and conceptualizes "Warrior Women" in the context of "sex role alternatives for Plains Indian Women."[39] She illustrates the fluidity of gender among the Great Plains cultures as

indigenous egalitarian societies. Plains gender relations were not dichtom-
ized into the passive "feminine" and active "masculinity," and even though
coded gender roles were encouraged, there was respect for the fluidity of
sexual boundaries among both women and men.

It is well documented that the disempowerment of our ancestral
Native women within their cultural nations was among the first goals of
European colonizers eager to weaken and destabilize indigenous societies.
According to Theda Perdue, traditional Cherokee culture was both matrilineal and matrifocal, marked by substantial personal freedom as well as economic and political power. Women held the land, raised the crops, and
controlled most of the family food supply. Colonial government officials,
teachers, and missionaries, however, did their best to upset traditional
Cherokee sex roles, and by the Removal era of the 1830s (male) tribal
leaders had adopted non-tribal ideas about the role of women in their
society.[40]

Similarly, colonialism has played a crucial role in the erosion of cross-
gender practices. Early anthropologists documented the *berdache* (originally
a French term used to refer to the tradition among some indigenous cultures. It was a form of transvestism adopted by Native males who would
take on exaggerated female expressions.[41] Among the Great Plains cultures,
the Lakota, as Dr. Medicine points out, called such men *winktes,* a lyrical
term meaning to be "captured by the moon." The Navajo (Dineh) and Ya-
qui were other Native cultures whose members sometimes practiced the *berdache* tradition. These individuals would sometimes become second wives
in a polygamous marriage, and were highly valued by spouses of both gender, as well as by the community. There is even evidence that a *berdache*
could have been either gay or bisexual in his intimate relations, but it was
usually the latter; some were even celebrated in certain periods of their life.
If not married, they lived with other *berdaches* in a special sphere with sacred rituals. But this did not have to represent the fixed status of one's lifetime, since one might decide to reenter the more conventional,
heterosexual society at large. There is less information on the female counterpart to the *berdache* tradition. Yet there are accounts of Native women, often referred to as "warrior women," who chose to dress like men and go
with them on the hunt.[42] These were women who did not want to conform to the more female conventional roles in the general society, including motherhood. But there is also some indication that these women never
withdrew from the matrifocal spheres among their people, and therefore
did not separate from the heterosexual women even though they established their own sexual identities in unconventional modes. These cross-

M. A. Jaimes * Guerrero

gender practices, however, went underground with colonization and patriarchy, because of the harsh criticism, punishment, and moralistic judgments advanced by Europeans against the Native societies and their "abominating" practices.

There has always been a strong resistance to European encroachment, with Native women activists in the vanguard of indigenous liberations struggles in North America. Our ancestors formed the backbone of traditional indigenous nations in the northern hemisphere. In recent decades, Native women have also been at the very core of their respective people's protests against Euro-American moral and social hegemony. Today, this tradition is continuing with the reemergence of Native women serving as tribal chairwomen of their respective Native nations. Native women both in the U.S. and Canada have occupied other, not so visible leadership positions throughout the twentieth century, for example, in the areas of Indian education and community development, as well as land and resource reclamation and restoration. Although more Native American women have become involved in Indian politics, winning elections as tribal chairs of governance, they do so within an established colonialist patriarchy and a chauvinistic tribal system. Despite "trickle-down patriarchy," however, North American indigenous women have established organizations, such as the Women of All Red Nations (WARN) and the Indigenous Women's Network in the U.S. The latter was well represented at the 1995 Beijing Conference, even though it has not taken a public position on the "blood quantum" issue in Indian identity politics, it has supported many non-federally constructed Native and "mixed-blood" groups in the U.S. The group also advocates Third World women's and indigenous peoples' rights to self determination in their sociocultural membership. The same can be said of WARN, a smaller Native women's organization, which has focused on grass roots struggles and the urban plight of Native American women, who count among their population a high number of "mixed-bloods." These Native women's organizations continue to focus on family, community, kinship, and nationhood, while at the same time they have a woman-centered agenda that opposes the trickle-down patriarchy that prevails among non-traditional tribal communities.

In Canada, Native women's organizations have put forth statements for "gender equality," among them the Native Women's Association of Canada as well as the Women of the Metis Nations, in Alberta province. At this time in Canada, Native women organizations are protesting their lack of access to the Canadian constitutional process currently under way, attempting to amend this document in such a way that it guarantees

"Aboriginal rights" throughout Canada. The Women of the Metis Nation have expressed distrust over the definition of "gender equality" in this legislative process for revised Canadian Aboriginal policy, because they consider it a dangerous precedent that pits Native women's equity rights against men's collective rights for the Canadian common good. It is in the context of colonialism, then, that struggles over "civil rights *versus* sovereignty" and "Feminism *or* Indigenism" become apparent. Native women activists have argued that the priorities and socio-political agendas of the predominantly white women's movement are not necessarily constitutive of the same liberation agenda for Native women in their indigenous struggles for decolonization. As community-based women, Native women cannot afford to participate in what often appears to them to be an individually oriented Euro-American middle class women's sociopolitical agenda. Women's organizations usually advocate for individually based interests that must be articulated within a hegemonic perspective that does not address Indian/ tribal rights within the existing eurocentric paradigm, much less acknowledge the backlash from white, male-led, anti-Indian supremacist groups.

Despite their opposition to the patriarchal politics of federally approved tribal leaders, Native American women have had limited involvement in the mainstream women's movement. Native women perceive this liberation from U.S. hegemony in the context of human rights, since we are traditionally communal peoples. The fact of human rights needs to be addressed in any socio-political agenda or movement for Native women's liberation and empowerment. This is what some of us are referring to as an *Indigenism* movement.[43] Indigenism means to be literally born of a place, a "bioregion." In its broader connotation, it also means for an auchthonous people to derive a sense of identity through a sense of place, as an indigenous homeland. It concerns where a peoples' ancestors have been buried and where their children are born. It is also related to Native American culture's derivation from the land, and that includes a spiritual relationship to the Earth, manifested in indigenous worldviews and cosmologies, as in other land-based cultures. Female, male, and androgynous entities form the principles in these geomythologies, which can might be considered "ecocultures." Among what can be conceptualized as spiritual energy configurations for procreative and regenerative symbolism, deities were often depicted as indigenous women and linked with agranomics (economics derived from nature and agrarianism). "Female organic archetypes" include Corn Daughter (Hopi); Changing Woman (Navajo/Dineh); First Woman (Abanaki); Sky Woman (Iroquois); Spider Woman (Navajo/Dineh and Hopi); Thought Woman (Laguna); White Buffalo Calf Woman (Lakota,

Dakota); and, in a more secular sphere, the traditional Cherokee had Beloved Woman of the Nation.

Native North American women are at the forefront of protest and resistance in our movement for Indigenism, which focuses on the rights of Nature and our human relationship with the Earth. We see feminist struggle today as part of our life and land struggles, which we are confronting globally, locally, bioregionally, and transnationally. Among us, our mothers are teaching our children of both genders to respect "The Female Principle" that is connected to the earth as our Mother. Our elders and Clan Mothers have taught us to be exemplars of Indigenism according to our precolonial traditions and values, which espouse greater gender egalitarianism. Indigenism is a broad, inclusive movement that involves transnational feminisms that recognize women's shared condition of subjugation, as a result of patriarchal colonialism. At the same time, Indigenism challenges our advanced stage of Native imperialism by Euro-America, which includes "Our Mother's Sons."

Notes

1. ch. 233, 43 *Stat.* 25.

2. ch. 576, 48 *Stat.* 948, now codified at 25 U.S.C. 461–279; also known as the Wheeler-Howard Act.

3. Ward Churchill and Glenn Morris, "Table: Key Indian Laws and Cases," in M. Am. Jaimes, ed., 13–17. *The State of Native America: Genocide, Colonization and Resistance* (Boston: South End Press, 1992), P.L. 90–284; 82 *Stat.* 77, codified in part at 25 U.S.C. 1301 *et seq.* The Act was then amended in 1986, under provisions of the federal Anti-Drug Abuse Act (P.L. 99–570, 100 Stat. 3207) to allow tribal courts greater powers of penalization on certain types of criminal offenses

4. *Statutes at Large*, 104, sec. 102, 4662. An artist so convicted can be fined up to $250,000 and/or be imprisoned up to five years; a gallery or a museum can be fined up to $1,000,000; if a person is convicted of subsequent violations, he or she can be fined up to $1,000,000 and/or imprisoned for up to fifteen years, while a museum or gallery can be fined up to $5,000,000.

5. M. A. Jaimes with Theresa Halsey, "American Indian Women: At the Center of Indigenous Resistance in Contemporary North America," in *The State of Native America,* 311–344.

6. The term "trickle-down patriarchy" was coined by a reviewer of *The State of Native America;* see Elliot, "Once Upon a Conquest: The Legacy of Five Hundred Years of Survival and Resistance," *Labyrinth* (October 1992): 2–3.

7. 151F., Supp. 476, 1957. *Martinez v. Santa Clara Pueblo case* (436 U.S. 49).

8. See Jaimes and Halsey, "American Indian Women," 341, n. 101; and Churchill and Morris, "Table: Key Indian Laws and Cases," 16. Churchill and Morris cite the 1978 Martinez case, stating that it also involved *habeas corpus* interpreted as "relief" in the federal decision.

9. For more on the 1981 Sandra Lovelace (Sappier) case, see Jaimes and Halsey, "American Indian Women," 330–331.

10. Vine Deloria, Jr., "Implications of 1968 Civil Rights Act in Tribal Autonomy," *The Indian Historian,* (1977). Deloria, a Lakota scholar, wrote in 1977, "I don't think tribal governments today fully understand what rights they have within the 1968 Indian Civil Rights law. . . . The U.S. government [actually] has two principle concepts of what a tribe is. . . . By the same token I don't think any federal agencies understand what has happened, as far as federal-Indian relationships are concerned." See also references to Deloria in Jaimes, *Federal Indian Identification Policy for Eligibility of Educational Service Programs,* Ph.D. Dissertation, Arizona State University, 1990, p. 183–5 (fn#43). Deloria highlights the case of *U.S. v. Sandoval* (231, U.S. 31 at 45–47, 1913) as a precedent that was imposed on all American Indian groups as a federal "blanket policy."

11. Twila Martin Kakabeh, "Native American Women in Tribal Leadership," (tape-recorded presentation, Law School Seminar, Cornell University, Ithaca, NY., November 12, 1991). Kakabeh, a former tribal chairwoman, also stated, in her keynote presentation on same topic at the Great Plains Program *Subaltern Terrain* conference (University of Lincoln, Nebraska, July 23, 1992), that the first barrier she had to overcome in tribal council politics was sexism among the predominantly male members, who expected to have her fetch their coffee. Kakabeh had a productive two year term as the Tribal Chair of the North Dakota Turtle Mountain Band in that state, but she has since lost her second election to her opponent (whom she had previously unseated). She was reelected later on, but only to find herself in trouble again with those who opposed her. Such are the highs and lows of a precarious leadership, particularly for Native women in patriarchal tribal politics. Kakabeh is an examplar of Native women's fortitude in tribal partisan politics.

12. Quoted in Jaimes and Halsey, "American Indian Women," 311–312. Since the Bennett episode Indian men have been imprisoned, among them the elder David Sohappy, who died soon after his release from prison. He had been imprisoned for his leadership in the fish-in protests that took place in Washington state.

13. R. L. Robbins, "Self-Determination and Subordination: The Past, Present, and Future of American Indian Governance," in *The State of Native America,* 87–121. See, in addition, "In Usual and Accustomed Places: Contemporary American Indian Fishing Rights Struggles," by The Institute for Natural Progress, in *The*

State of Native America, 217–239. Both works address "white hate" groups that tar get Native peoples and land rights.

14. On the Wounded Knee Occupation of 1973, see Vine Deloria Jr. and Clifford M. Lytle, *The Nations Within: The Past and Present of American Indian Sovereignty,* N.Y.: Pantheon Books, 1984, 213–214.

15. Ibid., 212–213 (on the Indian Civil Rights Act of 1968).

16. Jaimes, *State,* 13–21.

17. Ward Churchill and Glenn Morris, "Table: Key Indian Law Cases." Both teams of Indian scholars cited are also alluding to the overall impact of a legislative and jurisdictional record by the federal government in the systemic intervention and colonization of American Indians, as groups and individuals, since treaty-making years up to the present. Most notable among them is the precursor to the 1968 ICRA, the mandated Indian Citizenship Act of 1924 (itself preceded by key Indian legislative acts and congressional laws systematically preempting tribal sovereignty).

18. In *Cherokee Nation v. Georgia* (30 U.S.) (5 Petition) 1 (1831)) and *Worcester v. Georgia* (31 U.S.) (6 Petition) 551 (1832)).

19. Churchill and Morris, "Table: Key Indian Law Cases,".

20. On the legislation and judicial decisions that have "developed" within the U.S. government, and the Indian/Tribal "relationship" to the U.S. as a "settler state," see Ward Churchill, "Perversions of Justice: Examining the Doctrine of U.S. Rights to Occupancy in North America," in *Struggle for the Land,* Common Courage Press, 1993 33 83. Churchill quotes Robert Stock's earlier article, "The Settler State and the American Left," *New Studies on the Left,* "Work and Society" special issue, 154, no. 3 (Winter, 1990–1991): 72 78; he also notes that the first time the term "Tribe," as used in a legal context, was in *Lonewolf v. Hitchcock* (1903), which preempted the use of "nation" in "domestic dependent nations" that Supreme Court Chief Justice Marshall coined in his milestone decisions of the 1830s *(Worcester v. Georgia* [1831] and *Cherokee v. Georgia* [1834]).

Deloria, meanwhile, provides a legal context for dominant/subordinant relations, in an article titled "The Application of the *U.S. Constitution* to American Indians," in Oren Lyons, John Mohawk et al., eds., *Exiled in the Land of the Free: Democracy, Indian Nations, and the U.S. Constitution* (Santa Fe, NM: Clear Light Publishers, 1992), 282 315. In citing the court decision on *Native American Church v. Navajo Tribal Council* (272 F. 2nd 131 [1959]), Deloria stated it thus: "[A]lthough tribes are comparable to states, they have a higher status than states because they are dependent domestic nations, not the originators of the constitutional social contract or creatures of the national government. The principle announced by the Senate Judiciary Committee in 1870, in finding that Indian nations were excluded from the operation of the [Fourteenth] Amendment, was that it would be unfair and unjust to subject them to a rule or law to which they had not consented. Consent, the basis of modern Western social contract theory, can only be found in the Indian treaty relationship with the [U.S.]" (314–315). Deloria predicates this analysis on his earlier work, co-authored with Lytle, in *The Nations Within*. He does not, however, address the relevant political position some non-treaty (as well as non-ratified) Indian groups hold, among them the Abenaki of Vermont. Since these groups never signed a treaty with the U.S. authorities in the first place, they still hold title and its attendant sovereignty to their traditional lands and control their own internal affairs. In this scenario, the Abenaki of Vermont have asserted their claim of a significant proportion of that particular state. With regard to Native American women and their involvement in traditional indigenous governance, it should be noted that Lyons and Mohawk's volume, *Exiled in the Land of the Free,* in which Deloria figures among other notable Native male contributors, bears a conspicuous absence of Native women contributors. The book also down plays, albeit without entirely ignoring, the importance of the societies of the matrifocal Clan Mothers among the Six Nations in the Iroquois Confederacy.

21. For legal analysis of what I refer to as the "Dominant/Subordinant Construction" in U.S. government and Indian "relations," as predicated by the mid-1800s "Marshall Decisions" in the Cherokee cases, see Deloria and Lytle, *The Nations Within;* and Deloria and Lytle, *American Indians, American Justice,* Austin: University of Texas Press, 1983. Regarding the federal authorities' handling of Indian affairs, and tribal water rights and federal diversion projects, see M. A. Jaimes * Guerrero, in *The State of Native America.*

22. I refer to this federal process as a form of "statistical genocide" in "Federal Indian Identification Policy," in *The State of Native America,* Dr. Susan Lobo, who calls it "statistical extermination," is with Intertribal Friendship House, Oakland, CA. She is quoted in John Anner, "To the U.S. Census Bureau, Native Americans are Practically Invisible," in Donna Nicolono, ed., *1492–1992: Commemorating 500 Years of Indigenous Resistance: A Community Reader* (Santa Cruz, CA: Resource Center for Nonviolence, with Santa Cruz Resistance 500 and the Central Coast Quincentennial Indigenous Council, 1992), 143–146. In addition, refer to Jack Forbes's essay on the subject, "Undercounting Native Americans: The 1980 Census and the Manipulation of Racial Identity in the (U.S.)," *Wicazo Sa Review,* 4, no. 1 (Spring 1990): 2–26.

23. This race construct is a basic point of comparison between Europeans and cultures indigenous to the Americas; see Jaimes, "American Racism: The Impact on American Identity," Rutgers University Press, 1995).

24. P.L. 101–644–104 *Stat.* 4662.

25. See Nannette Gross Hanks, "Who's An Indian? The Arts and Crafts Act Is No Help," *Colors* (January-February 1993): 16–19; and Walkin-in-stik-man-alone, statement titled "Request for an Injunction Against or Revision of (P.L.) 101–644 Indian Arts and Crafts Act of 1990." In addition, see Ward Churchill, "Nobody's Pet Poodle," *Z Magazine* on the case of artist Jimmie Durham (1992).

26. Jaimes, "American Indian International Perspective," and "Findings and Recommendations," My current research indicates that clan societies in traditional kinship systems were also set up to establish taboos that prohibited incestuous practices, in order to protect against biological and physiological disabilities. Offending individuals would be punished by illness, insanity, or the birth of deformed children (at one time, however, there was a ceremony to counteract these effects of incest). The exogamic taboo is strong even today . . . Navajo kinship nomenclature emphasizes grouping by clan. . . . It is a classificatory system (according to Murdock as "Normal Iroquois"), at some points merging lineal and also collateral relatives. At certain points the unity of the unilineal group is expressed in the over-riding of generations. (citing Aberle, 1961: 172,183). Kinship terms are extended to members of one's own and one's father's clan. However, kin terms may be extended out of politeness to non-relatives. . . . Linked, grouped, or affiliated clans are clans that are considered to be related either as a result of the division of a larger clan or by the attachment of one clan to another. There is no agreement on just which clans are linked. . . . Theoretically, marriage is prohibited into clans linked to one's own or to one's father's clan, but in practice some distinction is made between those which are closely related and those which are distantly related" (35–36). The traditional Navajos are unique in that they also created the "Mexican Clan," called *Nakai,* when a number of their members intermarried with Mexican Indians near the U.S. southwestern border in proximity to Mexico. From Mary Shepardson, "Navajo Ways in Government: A Study in Political Process," *American Anthropologist, Memoir 96* 65, no. 3 (Part 2) (June 1963).

27 Sandy Gonzales, "Intermarriage and Assimilation: The Beginning or the End?" *Wicazo Sa Review* 8, no. 2 (Fall 1992): 48–52. The "mixed-blood" experience among Native women is poignantly illustrated in the historical fiction of Louise Erdrich, a Turtle Mountain Chippewa *métis* (*Love Medicine* [1984], *Tracks* [1988]). See also the historical literature of Linda Hogan (*Mean Spirit* [1991]), in which she describes the predicament of allotment years for "full-blood" Indians who were determined "incompetent" to hold land and "mixed-blood" Indians who were declared "unqualified" for their allotments. In Canada, there is also the autobiography of Marie Campbell (*Halfbreed* [1973]), a Canadian *métis,* which highlights the marginalization of "mixed-bloods" both on and off the reservations.

28. Current Cherokee enrollment statement, submitted by the Cherokee Nation, Talauqua Oklahoma, regarding "Dawes Rolls" and a policy of "no blood quantum" criteria.

29. J. R. Walker, *Lakota Society* (Lincoln: University of Nebraska Press, 1982). My thanks to Ed Valandra (Lakota) for calling this citation to my attention.

30. See Forbes, "Undercounting Native Americans"; and Forbes's seminal book, *Black Africans and Native Americans: Color, Race, and Caste in the Evolution of Red-Black Peoples* (Oxford and London: Basil Blackwell 1988). Related essays can be found in E. T. Price, "A Geographic Analysis of White–Negro–Indian Racial Mixtures in Eastern (U.S.)," *Association of American Geographers Annals* 43 (June 1953): 138–155; and Rayna Green, "Traditional Roles," in *Women in American Indian Society,* Indians of North America series (New York: Chelsea Publishers, 1992).

31. Paula Gunn Allen writes that the origins of "squaw" is an Arabic word meaning "sex slave boy," but she doesn't reference her source (see "title," in *Ms.* magazine 3, no. 2 [November 1992]: 22–26).

32. Jack Weatherford, "Women (and a Few Men) who Led the Way," *Native Roots: How the Indians Enriched America* (New York: Fawcett Columbine, 1991). See also, Green, op. cit.

33. Relevant to this intermarriage phenomenon among Indian peoples in more modern times is the exodus of Indian males from the reservations, generally as draftees during the war years as well as because of high unemployment. Many of them returned from the world wars suffering from "post-traumatic stress syndrome," and had to undergo special ceremonies to heal themselves with the help of their communities. See Tom Holm's work in this area, "Patriots and Pawns: State Use of American Indians in the Military and the Process of Nativism in the (U.S.)," in *The State of Native America,* 345–370. I would add to Holm's discussion of this trend that many of these returnees intermarried with non-Indians and drifted to the urban metropoles, which exacerbated their traumatized condition. Indian women on reservations took over the functions of the communities that suffered the paucity of Indian males during the war years, which were then followed by the relocation of many Indian families in the 1940s and the termination of some tribes in the 1950s.

34. On the Human Genome Diversity Project (HGDP), Stanford University issued a "Summary of Planning Workshop 3(B)," regarding the "Ethical and Human Rights Implications" of the project, and addressing the methods of sampling (cover letter dated May 17, 1994, signed by Jean Dobie, Assistant Director, Morrison Institute for Populations and Resources Studies, who was involved in the selected dissemination of report). This summation comprises more than thirty pages with a tentative list of more than seven hundred indigenous groups targeted for DNA sampling worldwide, and about seventy in North America, the U.S., and Canada. The report also lists thirteen participants at this session who are among the leading "genetic experts," several of whom are affiliated with the National Institutes of Health.

35. See Debra Harry, "The Human Genome Diversity Project and Its Implications for Indigenous Peoples," *Indigenous Women,* a publication of Indigenous Women's Network, 2, no. 2 (date): 30–33. The article reprints a "Declaration of Indigenous Peoples of the Western World Regarding the (HGDP)."

36. Amerigo Vespucci, *Mundes Novas* (1504–1505).

37. Jaimes and Halsey, "American Indian Women," 311–319.

38. Ibid.

39. Beatrice Medicine and Patricia Albers, *The Hidden Half: Studies of Plains Indian Women* (University Press of America, 1983), 267–280.

40. Theda Perdue, "Cherokee Women and the Trail of Tears," in R. L. Nichols, *The American Indian: Past and Present,* ed., 4th ed. (New York: McGraw-Hill, Inc., 1992), 151–161. It should also be noted that the Cherokee were not atypical compared to other traditional matrilineal Indian societies, for example, the Navajo (Dineh) Nation and Iroquois Confederacy, among others. As another post-conquest illustration, M. C. Wright researches the successful actions of the Indian women of the Pacific Northwest during the early decades of the fur trade. She indicates, for example, that although the coming of the fur trade weakened traditional tribal cultures, it strengthened the position of "prominent Indian women" within their villages. This was the result of to early fur traders' demand for the women's mediation (and translation) skills as tribal representatives. However, Wright concludes that the women's role in the growing cash economy failed itself to grow, so they found themselves pushed farther out of public life and tribal affairs.

41. Pierrette Desy, "How Can One Be A Woman? The Paradox of the Berdache," *Radical Therapy: New Studies on the Left,* 13, nos. 3–4 (Summer-Fall, 1988): 60–64.

42. Paula Gunn Allen, "Sky Woman and Her Sisters," *Ms.* 3, no. 2 (September/October, 1992): 22–26.

43. See Ward Churchill, "I am an Indigenist: Notes on the Ideology of the Fourth World," *Struggle for the Land: Indigenous Resistance to Genocide, Ecocide, and Expropriation in Contemporary America* (Monroe, ME: Common Courage Press, 1993); and M. A. Jaimes, "Native American Identity as Indigenism for Environmental Ethics in Economic Development" (unpublished treatise, 1994).

Wahneema Lubiano

Talking about the State and Imagining Alliances

Talking across the difficulties that inhere in the project I'm trying to give account of here make me careful about claims for any kind of success. But the labor is useful even when the occasion provides yet another gloss on the productiveness of failure. I come to this project with, of course, the dirty hands of someone who can't inhabit a clear, clean position.

This work comes out of my interest in the ways a corporate capitalist, racist, misogynistic, and imperialist state's world-making makes itself present in the thinking and language of people who know (in some ways) themselves to be oppressed by it. Or, in fewer words, I'm asking, how does state hegemony work? I'm going to address that question by talking about the obstacles to "imagining alliances" that present themselves within a particular group. I pull here some examples from discussions I've had with community groups, church groups, and community college student groups.

There are two consistent difficulties that are part of the dynamic of this work:

(1) As an academic, particularly as one who teaches in an Ivy League university and who talks about her research interests when asked, I have positive and negative valences within the groups of which I've been a part. Because I bear credentials from the academy, I'm asked to address particular groups and to do certain kinds of work. But those same credentials provide these groups with an occasion to register their own anger and contempt for the intellectual realm generally, and for my specific place in it.

(2) State interests are often unexamined and uncritically internalized among many of us—whether or not the "us" is made up of people marginalized by the overlapping social realities of racism, classism, and sexism, or those who think of themselves as existing within the comforting parameters of the "mainstream"; therefore, in my encounters I have first to present

ideas that can be recognized as foreign and/or domestic sites of domination, a presentation which generally makes people even angrier once they recognize their own complicity in those sites.

What my presence sometimes offers is a highly fungible political position that members of the group reject, coopt, reform, rearticulate, or in some way manipulate in order to advance and often settle arguments that were part of the group before I was invited into it. I often find that my political positions are characterized by the audience in the room as conservative, based on their assumptions that anyone who is obviously middle class is conservative; this happens despite the fact that my political analysis is considerably to the left of most of the audience. Watching the way my position gets labeled, relabeled, and then used by various members to advance particular agendas has been educational. And, finally, what I say about myself is the least interesting event over the course of such an occasion; what is important is what happens to the political understandings of the group. I am invited because there's something about my existence in the academy as well as my social identifications that intrigues the groups inviting me; I show up because I want to figure out what people are thinking and because I want to speak to that thinking.

What I describe below is part of a larger project of mine that looks at black nationalism and the U.S. state through the prism of a black feminist critique. My essay has two focii that serve as illustrations of the difficulties of imagining grounds for alliances: (1) an examination and criticism of U.S. power and/or privilege shared, albeit differentially, among all U.S. women—with black women as my specific example—despite black women's lack of influence on state policy; and (2) an examination of within-the-group exclusions, with reference to discussions among some black women during and after the Gulf War. These two focii are the ground on which I talk about the willingness of many black women, even within class stratifications, to both reproduce and oppose some of the narrow exclusions that they condemn in "mainstream" or "white, middle-class," feminism. I talk about those exclusions and the language in which those exclusions are opposed in order to point to the difficulties and possibilities of bridging even larger connections: those between feminists of different racial groups in the U.S. "Imagining alliances"—this conference's most explicitly stated project—requires that we look carefully at the difficulties, at the obstacles to alliances; otherwise, the powerful attractiveness of alliance possibilities will hide the very pitfalls that frequently disrupt those alliance possibilities.

My general concern is to consider where black women—feminist and non-feminist, poor and privileged, young and old—are implicated in

Plate 57: *George & Co. (After Peto, 1879)*, 1996
C-Print
Allan deSouza
Courtesy of the artist

Talking About the State and Imagining Alliances 443

the work of the U.S. state. As part of this consideration, my first (and brief) example is the use that I've made of a song often performed in concert and recorded by Sweet Honey in the Rock. I brought a cassette to a group of working women, some of whom have children in the judicial system. The women worked for the most part in lower-rung clerical jobs, in grocery stores, fast food restaurants, or in domestic work; others relied on AFDC as their primary means of support. I was invited to the group because, as is often the case, they called the Program in African-American Studies and asked for either Cornel West or Toni Morrison, and were offered me. I was there to talk about what it was a black intellectual did at a place like Princeton.

The lyrics of the song that I played as part of my presentation are important. The song, "Are My Hands Clean,"[1] from Sweet Honey in the Rock, is based on Bernice Johnson Reagon's adaptation of an article by John Cavanagh (a fellow at the Institute for Policy Studies, a Left think tank) which demonstrates the unequal relation of power between First World and Third World countries through a description of the relationship between labor and production. The song charts—through the production of a blouse—the movement of global capital, international labor exploitation, and U.S. consumer culture. (One could call her adaptation of Cavanagh's work an example of an alliance, even if momentary, informal, non-organizational—which helps us consider the range of activities that we call alliances.) The song documents a chain of labor beginning in a cotton field in Central America amidst a war where cotton is picked for two dollars a day. The cotton crosses the sea to a factory in the United States where the cotton is weaved into fabric and shipped to another Third World country in the Caribbean where workers are paid three dollars a day to turn the fabric into a blouse. After this chain of exploitation, the blouse is sold in the United States for a twenty percent discount at a large retail department store with relatively low prices, at which many black women who are not middle class shop.

The encounter was problematic, of course. There were individuals, powerfully articulate and accustomed to having their opinions and analyses respected, who resisted being called to account by others of the group— equally articulate and accustomed to being heard—and who knew much of what I was talking about. Some of those in the know were working in sweat shop-like conditions and were happy to have an opportunity to use my presence and the discussion to push further an analysis they had begun often before. Previous group dynamics played themselves out in our encounter, previous battles were recounted, older hurts over name-calling re-surfaced. Nonetheless, the song itself was interesting and beautiful enough (we played it several times) that my bringing it to the group added some-thing pleasurable both to the politics of that evening and that group, as well as to our political discussion, which in turn meant that people continued to talk past the moments of rage and confusion.

The song articulates the connection *across* class lines of international labor exploitation to a U.S. black female consuming public—an especially vexed site because Sears (to which the song refers) is where many working-class and lower-middle-class black people shop. While the song reminded the women with whom I talked of their already critical understanding of exploitative labor practices, it also taught many of them something they didn't know: international labor wage scale differences. The song pushed them to consider their own implication in the movement of global capital-ism, their own implication in U.S. consumerist desires and needs. For many of them, it was the first time that they had considered that as poor as many black women are, we are still "consuming" other poor people inter-nationally. Such an understanding disrupted the tendency on the part of some black women to think that "we" have a lock on the oppression sweepstakes and reminded us that the contempt that many of us direct to-ward something understood (or caricatured) as "mainstream feminism" or "a middle-class white feminist movement"—a contempt directed at white feminists for talking and behaving as though their particular oppression is absolutely primary—could in some measure be directed at ourselves.

My second example is the use to which I've put a photograph of a re-turning black Gulf War veteran. This photograph was produced as a full-page ad "welcoming back" the soldiers from the Gulf War. It ran during the hysteria of U.S. post-war celebrations. On the occasion that I talked about this photograph, I was asked to talk about black history to a women's church group during Black History Month. I was invited to this particular church, whose membership is largely, but not entirely working-class, be-cause the facilitator of this particular group had been part of a university-community alliance opposing the Gulf War; I had met her under those circumstances.

Before I talk about this photograph, however, and its position in our present moment, I want to remind us (as I reminded the group) of earlier aspects of black history. I offered these reminders then because they help make the point I've tried to make in my encounters with black people who

Plate 58: *Sgt. Richard Muse Welcomed Home by Daughter,* June 12, 1991
Photo: Michael J. Okoniewski
Courtesy of *New York Times* Pictures

Wahneema Lubiano

want to talk about black Americans in the nation and in the world: that the positioning of black Americans is vexed, and that examining the grounds of those vexations means encountering our complicities with the operations of the U.S. state. I began with the participation of black people in the construction and maintenance of the eighteenth and nineteenth centuries' U.S. "western frontier." In short, I talked about what blacks' connection to that "frontier" had meant:

It meant escape from murderous white supremacy, especially in the South; it meant some alliances with Native peoples, it meant some intermarriage with Native peoples; but it also meant much black participation in the U.S. state's genocidal policy and actions against the Native peoples—it meant the complicity of many blacks in state-ordained Native American genocide.

Now, to the photograph: this representation points up what is obvious (black participation in the military) as well as what is not always so obvious by extension (black participation in U.S. policing and disciplining of the rest of the world, especially the "Third World"). It is, of course, no news to most of the people who invite me to talk about black history that blacks are disproportionately represented in the military, although it might be news that black women are even more disproportionately represented in that military than black men are. But what came out in discussion is how incredibly interesting and attractive that photograph's representation of the black male soldier was among the women—those who described themselves as feminist and non-feminist alike—for two different but overlapping reasons: (1) not *because* of his military status, but because they were aware of the racism in the U S that has produced the military as an attractive economic labor site for black people (for example, some of the women were teary-eyed when they looked at the photo because they both opposed the Gulf War and understood why "he" and other black men and women were a part of it); and (2) because he is standing with his arms around his daughter. That photo and that pose evoke the "black family" in all of its distorted and pathos-inflected narrative glory. There he stands: the "missing" black father aesthetically and sentimentally inscribed on the full page of the *New York Times* with his child, and more importantly, *with his female child*. He thus steps into both patriarchal and warrior glory, and shows, by hugging example, how a black male ought to treat a black female.

This is the U.S. state at its ugliest and most subtle: the Gulf War and the military's exploitation of a racially, economically, and politically oppressed group is costumed into a black father's doing his duty for his country and his daughter. This representation was especially poignant to the groups with whom I talked about it because years of "underclass" and "culture of poverty" discourse in the corporate media has trained much of the U.S. public, including blacks, to think of the poor black family as pathological, the mother as a monstrous breeder, and the father as missing and irresponsible. This photo was an incredibly powerful counter-narrative—especially interesting given what Moynihan's Report on the black family had to say about the military's ability to teach black males how to be men.

After we talked about that photo and similar images all over the media, the discussion of that war, its effects, and its massacres turned into a discussion, first, of returning black vets, many of whom were black women; then a discussion of black families; and finally, perhaps predictably, a discussion of welfare. Many of the women I talked with, including those who identified themselves as some kind of feminist or womanist, are welfare recipients, or are themselves workers but know someone (often a family member) on AFDC and/or food stamps. I listened to both non-welfare and welfare recipients alike blast poor women and welfare mothers for being lazy, irresponsible, and a "problem" for black people.

The fervor with which welfare mothers were denounced reproduced the U.S. public discourse language about individuality, the sanctity of paid labor, disdain for poor people; their language was full of the virtue of toughness, the need for people to get out and take care of themselves, and the reasons why "those women" should make "those men" take care of them and their babies. What I heard, in short, reproduced all the language that pushes poor, state aid-dependent women outside of the space inhabited by "good," "hard-working," people. "Poor women" became the people with whom imagining alliances was extremely difficult. Not everyone talked or felt this way, but many did. The ones who were critical of that marginalizing, however, were articulate in their contempt for those who, based on their arguments, seemed willing and ready to jettison the poor. The articulation of those who staked out a space of solidarity pulled me back into the discussion; they needed my support because I presented an opportunity for their criticism to mean more, something that was especially important to them given their minority status within the group.

I pointed out that in these discussions, many of them were literally drawing themselves away from poor black women, that they were performing the kind of exclusions that they had criticized and condemned in the "middle-class white women's feminism." I reminded them of things

Wahneema Lubiano

that they had said about white feminists: that white feminists don't care about black women; that white feminists don't care about poor women; that white feminists just wanted to be in the same position as white middle-class men, etc. We were silent thereafter for a few minutes. As a result of confronting that silence and coming to terms with what that silence meant, however, we began addressing what we had to undo in order to figure out what to do.

I've described those encounters and discussions in order to illustrate some of the necessary work of imagining alliances. If "we" who are feminists of color can engage *within* our circumstances in the self-criticism that recognizes not only where we are different from the more powerful group, but where we actually replicate their misunderstandings, their blind spots, and their exclusions, then "we" who are feminists of color, after beginning the work of self-criticism among our groups and in our communities, can use the insights gained from that work to promote alliances *within* the group. And from that work itself we can make possible the "imagining of alliances" between communities within the U.S.—as well as outside its borders. Such work might require picking our way through binary oppositions instead of simply dismissing them as unproductive; for such oppositions help make up the political imaginary of communities. And whether or not groups recognize the same vocabularies, political work rests on imagining strategies for one's own politics.

Note

1. "Are My Hands Clean?" Composed by Bernice Johnson Reagon, Songtalk Publishing, 1985. Performed by Sweet Honey in the Rock. Live at Carnegie Hall. Flying Fish Records, 1988.

Caren Kaplan

"Beyond the Pale": Rearticulating U.S. Jewish Whiteness

> Why do we have such an absurd need for a solid, deep-rooted, ro-
> bust, and pink-cheeked identity, a peasant identity anchored for cen-
> turies to the same land? Why not embrace an empty self? What is so
> awful about emptiness once you get used to it? I have no roots. It's a
> fact. . . . I am a crowd, a one-woman march, procession, parade, mas-
> querade. . . . To be a crowd, what a marvelous gift!
> —Alicia Dujovne Ortiz[1]

Some years ago—probably in the late 1980s—I attended a feminist conference and heard several papers on diaspora and Jewish feminist topics. One
speaker argued that the use of the term "diaspora" by African-Americans
and by post-colonial scholars made the historical phenomenon of Jewish
dispersion less concrete. The speaker suggested that the term should be employed in its more generic sense to avoid erasing Jewish cultural specificity.
Another speaker spoke about the Holocaust in terms that separated the
events in Western Europe from other imaginable contexts. At the end of
that paper I asked how we might reposition our thinking about Jewish diaspora and genocide to see commonalities or similarities with other instances
of genocide and displacement in this century. I was thinking about mass
murders in numerous places around the globe and the circulation of certain
peoples who become stateless and homeless in contemporary times. I certainly did not mean that all locations and times could be made to be equal
or reduced to the same. But the rhetoric of singularity with which "the"
Jewish experience was being referred to that day, while overwhelmingly
familiar, seemed so insufficient for any analysis of atrocities and violence
globally. The speaker, a Holocaust survivor, was deeply offended by my
question and responded angrily. I can no longer remember her exact

words. I do remember that I began shaking and that I cried as I drove home, feeling both defiant and deeply shamed. Just as my question must have threatened her fragile sense of safety by questioning the distinct qualities of her particular horror, her anger towards me was a reminder of how ex-centric I am to the conventions of Jewish feminism in the United States. With my inappropriate feelings and questions, I felt like a bad Jew. And in that context, a bad Jew was a bad feminist. I was, in fact, beyond the Pale.

Internalized anti-semitism? Insufficient ethnic identification? Classism? Racism? The list of possible crimes against "my people" is as long as my propensity for self-flagellation can support. Betrayal is at the end of the road for such a journey away from home base. But what is "home base" in the current climate of identity politics in the United States, when so many subjects express contradictory, ambivalent, or multiple affiliations? Between the demand for singular adherence to a modern identity script and the homogenization of assimilation there lies a zone that could be described as "beyond the Pale." The literal meaning of *pale* is a stake driven into the ground to mark a boundary. The word also connotes a limit or restriction. Thus, to be *beyond the pale* suggests a transgression, a movement beyond the boundaries of civilization, beyond the reach of a community or collective sense of values and identities. Historically, the term refers to a "district within determined bounds, or subject to a particular jurisdiction."[2] In this sense, the phrase resonates for me with the displacement of the Jewish population of what was once czarist Russia into the "Pale"—a region along the edges of the nation.[3] Such removals and restrictions marked a time of changing territories and shifting certainties. In this sense, "beyond the Pale" signifies migration, displacements on a global scale, beyond the imaginary confines of one nation to meet the unimaginable future on new shores in any number of other nations. This diasporic moment in time sent my own family from sites across the Russian Pale to South Africa, South America, the United States, and Palestine. But I want to stretch the metaphor even further—beyond the whiteness or paleness that signals the Euro-American centrality of Jewish cultural articulation in the United States, beyond my allusion to Eastern European Jewry alone in my recourse to the phrase itself, and beyond the romanticized conventions of immigration and displacement. That is, I want to begin with what I know best—the hegemonic cultural dominance of Eastern European Jewish history and identity—and deconstruct that highly mystified narrative of migration, race, and class through the lens of transnational feminist cultural studies.

In examining my sense of situation "beyond the Pale" on any number of registers, however, I do not want to celebrate or romanticize a border or marginal position. I want to get that old chip off my shoulder, as it were, in order to investigate the compelling investments in mobility, positionality, and power that are conferred by certain historical configurations. I have borrowed more than the title of Vron Ware's book on white women and racism in considering the cultural valences of "beyond the Pale." I am indebted to her project of deconstructing ideologies of whiteness, especially those that surround and construct Euro-American white women, to recognize that "to be white and female is to occupy a social category that is inescapably racialized as well as gendered."[4] But in this essay I am interested in moving to a more specific aspect of the ideology of whiteness in the United States—the ascription of whiteness to Jews of European backgrounds—and the complex interplay between power and marginality that this history puts into play, particularly in its gendered articulations.

No one is free of the burden of definition in a political society that operates through rights claims that assert an intrinsic quality or identity. This aspect of the liberal, democratic state plagues the feminist theorist who adheres both to post-structuralist concepts of the social construction of categories and to activist agendas for social change. But some categories are less marked by ambiguity or angst for me than others and that can't be accidental. Rather, such certainties and uncertainties can be read as maps of power, privilege, and discrimination inscribed on the body as each person's social text. In my own case, it is my understanding of myself as a Jew that tends to throw the limits of identity politics into sharp relief. More specifically, my uncomfortable and complex relationship to my ethnicity/religion provides me with an opportunity to investigate the construction of whiteness in an historically detailed way. I have experienced the cognitive, if not political, dissonance of access to the privileges of whiteness accompanied by the threat of racist violence and discrimination expressed as anti-semitism. It's confusing but instructive. Such points of complication can serve as sites of investigation: they are the signs of ideology at work. As critics, our job is to come to understand those signs, to deconstruct and rearticulate them.

In calling attention to the cognitive dissonance of whites experiencing racism directed against them I am not claiming that anti-semitism, even when it is expressed in unremittingly biological or essentialized terms, renders Jews of European origin non-white. When Michael Lerner published a piece in 1993 called "Jews Are Not White," he homogenized the term

"Jew" into a singular category of victims with no cultural, national, class, or gender distinctions.[5] Rejecting "whiteness," Lerner urged North American Jews to stop trying to pass as white in a society that has always viewed them as biologically "other" and expendable. Yet Lerner admitted to no class *or* ethnic privilege, no ambiguity, and only reinforced rather than destabilized the binary between white and non-white. The notion that European Jews who emigrated to the United States became white through the very processes of immigration and assimilation does not necessarily entail the privilege of reversal when it is politically convenient. As James Baldwin points out in his essay, "On Being 'White' . . . And Other Lies," for European Jews the "price of the ticket" of admission to the United States was "becoming white."[6] Baldwin rightly laments that this "opting" to be white prevents a full alliance with those of African origin who came to the same land as slaves. Thus there is no simple rejection of an identity and set of benefits that took several generations and a "vast amount of coercion" to consolidate.[7] The ascription of whiteness for Jews of European origin has required a series of costs and benefits that are most often shrouded in misty romanticism or stirring sentiment. Unlike Sephardic, Asian, and African Jews who are linked to nationalities or ethnicities of color, Jews of European origin in the United States are incontrovertibly "white" in the legal and social context of the nineties.

Thus, rather than argue that Jews of European origin are not *really* white by virtue of a history of anti-semitism, and therefore always already available for anti-racist alliances, I am arguing that regardless of the nature of one's relationship to the term "Jew," it is possible to use that term as a point of entry into a complicated history of race, gender, sexuality, and class, among other categories. Richard Dyer has written that the representational power of whiteness is based on its normalizing properties, its ability to appear to be "everything and nothing."[8] Or, as Ruth Frankenberg terms it, whites in the United States practice both "color evasion" and "power evasion" as white supremacy enables the privilege of actively universalizing white experiences and viewpoints.[9] Examining the construction of Jews of European origin as "white" in the history of the United States necessitates a destabilization of both ethnicity and race.[10] The homogenizing and normalizing powers of representations generated by and about Jews of European origin in the United States can be demystified by histories attentive to diasporic links across transnational circuits of immigration in modernity as well as to those social relations in the United States that form and reform ethnicities out of such diverse factors as class, nationality, and citizenship.

Thus, the term "Jew" has to be contextualized not only in terms of time and place but in a myriad ways. What is the history of its use, who has the power to influence and determine this usage, and what is lost or elided through such usage?

In this essay, although I cannot attempt a comprehensive response to the questions that I have just raised, I would like to begin to explore my sense of cognitive dissonance, my confusion, and my learned ignorance about the links between Jews of European origin, whiteness, and national agendas of racialization through class and property relations. As a feminist I am curious about the gendered versions of these histories and I have a heightened awareness of how easily a substitution effect limits the arithmetic of identity in my culture. When I write about ethnicity, considerations of gender and class can fall away. When I turn my attention to gender, the universalizing force of the conventions of Western feminist analysis can suppress considerations of race, ethnicity, and class. Just as distressing, all these categories seem to love to dwell in the United States, as if an entire world is too distant and ex-centric to the crucible of race and class to count in any meaningful way. The ascription of a single, primary identity as the locus of selfhood, pride, and agency arises in the midst of agitation against discrimination and oppression, yet our lives are never determined solely by one quality. Gender always mediates ethnicity and race, just as sexual practices differentiate the multiples of identity. Economic class and ethnicity invariably have an impact on categories of gender and sexuality. Citizenship and nationality, as well as access to state benefits, to housing and employment, and to a family system, affect people's identities and cultures in profound ways. All these elements of social relations are produced and not simply found. This is the methodological imperative that faces any feminist inquiry into the construction of subjects and their locations in postmodernity—articulating the conditions of production as well as reception of cultural identities.

Meanwhile, as I write, a lifetime of ambivalence—identification with as well as resistance toward my ethnic/religious affiliation—threatens to obstruct my inquiries. Writing about Jewishness and whiteness makes me feel extremely vulnerable to old ghosts of recrimination and rejection. But it seems to be the best way to disturb and examine a nexus of entangled and mystified subjects. After giving a lot of thought to my reservations about confessional autobiography, I keep coming back to the instances in my own life that convince *me,* that lead me in the process of deconstructing ideological constructions but this, too, makes me nervous.[11] I may gain personal insight sifting through my own experience but, living in California in the nineties, this information means little if it doesn't help me to understand the virulent anti-immigration efforts that mark state and now national politics as part of a continuum of racist, sexist, and homophobic discrimination. Exploring my own ethnic and racial construction seems useful only if I can use it to learn more about what motivates legislation such as Proposition 187, anti-affirmative action initiatives, and other attacks on education, jobs, and health care in the context of globalized and segmented markets under transnational conditions. The project of deconstructing identity politics and rearticulating identities has to be collaborative, multilayered, and not simply personal.

As Evelyn Nakano Glenn has argued in her study of the social construction of racialized gender, experiential testimony of diversity is not enough. Such a conception ignores the "systematic connections between the lives and experiences of different groups of women."[12] My aim is not to recapitulate guilt or blame but to make more complicated the terms of Jewish identity in the United States in the current moment and to work to elucidate those structural connections that cultural mystifications often mask. Within the process of racialization and the construction of ethnicity in the United States, how does "Jewish whiteness" come about? That is, when and where do some Jews and not others become "white" in the specific context of U.S. white supremacy as it interacts with Euro-American anti-semitism? What is the relationship between whiteness and Jewishness across histories of immigration, geopolitics, economies, as well as genders and sexualities? How does U.S. nationalism produce racialized and gendered as well as sexualized categories of citizenship and practices of property rights? How do these histories subvert or consolidate contemporary identities and affiliations? How do I rearticulate my own shifting and complex sense of Euro-American, Jewish, female, whiteness in the face of these histories? Revealing the historical ties between oppression, modernity, and the mystification of identities makes rearticulations of "Jewish whiteness" possible as acts of progressive affiliation with other identities and subjects.

Immigration, Anti-Semitism, and the Construction of Jewish "Whiteness"

In my family there is good-humored but pointed joking about who is "really" Jewish—Jacklyn Smith (one of the Charlie's Angels of seventies TV fame), and Kathy Lee Gifford (who sings Christian gospel music and stars in TV Christmas specials) are among our favorite stars to "out" with knowing glee. Celebrities are revealed to embody this secret, unacceptable ethnicity with surprising regularity. An older relative is really expert, almost preternatural, in this activity. She scours the obituaries, noting the particular cemetery of burial (Jewish or other affiliation), and can list lots of big stars and famous people who have tried to hide their Jewish origins. Each innocuous, brief, bland, Americanized (Anglicized?) name signifies a history of betrayal or renunciation that is supposed to warn the rest of us, You can change your name but you can't hide from Molky Smoodin! Her method for ferreting this information out makes me wonder: do you *have* to be buried in a Jewish cemetery if you were "born" Jewish? Are there modes of policing this? More seriously, these name changes and elisions of ethnic identity are markers of a second order, more nuanced anti-semitism. No one wants to be Jewish; or, no one can afford to be?

I know that Jews are despised in the United States as I know my own, unchanged name. My knowledge stems from day to day experience; I have been subjected to anti-semitic attacks and slurs, I endure the hegemony of Christian holidays and cultural attitudes in a supposedly secular state, and I am pained by the marginalization and caricaturization of Jewish ethnicity/religion and diversity in mass culture (Jackie Mason is not my kind of guy while Fran Drescher skirts that dangerous terrain of the beloved but racist stereotype).[13] Cultural examples of a vexed relationship to U.S. citizenship abound in my life yet I am not aware of a specific situation when I have faced *legal* discrimination as a Jew. That my parents' generation suffered anti-semitic oppression is indisputable. Late nineteenth- and early twentieth-century immigrants from eastern and southern Europe, including many Jews, were the subjects of eugenic rhetoric and racist science. For example, as Nancy Ordover's research has documented, a 1920 congressional hearing on the "Biological Aspects of Immigration" heard testimony that claimed that such immigrants were prone to "insanity, feeble-mindedness, moral turpitude, or shiftlessness."[14] Throughout the 1920s, universities such as Harvard, Columbia, and New York University sought to limit Jewish enrollment through legal and informal methods while membership in private associations and access to housing and certain occupations (especially the upper echelons of corporations) remained limited and discriminatory.[15] During the twenties and thirties, Jewish students were denied admission to medical, dental, engineering, pharmacy, veterinary, and law schools based on criteria such as "overcrowding," newly instituted geographic distribution requirements, and the results of "character tests."[16] Thus, anti-semitism flourished throughout the early decades of this century and was articulated through contested but consistent discourses of biological racial inferiority, social restrictions, and attacks on immigration.[17]

Yet, in my immediate family's case, such discrimination did not prevent most of them from reaching the middle and even (in the case of those who entered manufacturing or entrepreneurial occupations) the upper class: if my paternal grandfather was a car mechanic, his son was a Ph.D. in psychology; if my maternal great-grandfather worked the immigration miracle of moving from peddling to manufacturing, his sons became wealthy entrepreneurs. However, gender often made a difference.[18] My maternal grandmother did not become a rich manufacturer or entrepreneur like her brothers, she lived in relative poverty following early widowhood and a lack of formal education. And her daughter, my mother, got her educational degrees with no small amount of struggle and sacrifice. Regardless of gender, members of my family would tell me that they arrived in this country "with nothing" and worked their way "up."

Through marriage, through education, and through the proverbial "hard work" that contributes to the immigrant mythology of assimilation and assumption of citizenship, my family had firmly entered the middle class once and for all by the time I was born in 1955.[19] From their passionate testimony, I know that despite their class position members of my family felt marked and ex-centric to a Christian majority in North America. Their distrust of Christian tolerance and their fear of Christian fundamentalist violence communicated itself to me in a million spoken and unspoken ways and was reinforced by my own experiences of anti-semitism. Yet, my extended family prospered materially through their immigration. If they felt discriminated against, they also felt entitled to due process and to inclusion in the social contract that underlies the idea of democracy in part because, as their class position became consolidated and more secure, their racial classification became more and more allied with the group that enjoyed the most power. How did a group that many believed to be a hygienic and moral danger to the nation by virtue of *racial* characteristics at the turn of the century arrive at the status of "white" by mid-century? How did European Jewish immigrants' whiteness become consolidated during this time period?

Stated in its baldest terms, the myth of Jewish immigration to the United States concerns the large numbers that emigrated from Europe—particularly from the Russian Pale of settlement—in the later years of the nineteenth century and the early decades of the twentieth. According to the narrative conventions of the myth, poverty and religious persecution drove Jews to leave a tradition-bound life as peasants or small urban traders

Plate 59: From *We Make Memories*, 1995
© Abbe Don
Courtesy of the artist

behind and to enter modernity in the metropoles of the United States and Canada. The myth further dictates that once eastern European Jews arrived in the United States, cultural values that stressed education (for males) and a work ethic ensured material success and ethnic survival. Inherent to the myth is the belief that other immigrant groups could achieve as much in as short a period of time if they adhered to the same values and cultural beliefs. Questioning the mystified notion of a teleological development from a level playing field among immigrants to Jewish assimilation and "success," John Bodnar's research on European immigration argues that Jewish immigrants during this period were neither the poorest nor the wealthiest of their communities and that their travels were complicated, motivated not simply through a desire to change countries and citizenship to escape antisemitism but through rational attempts to improve the lives of family members. Bodnar argues that these immigrants did not leave tradition-bound "preindustrial worlds" for the modernity of metropolitan locations. Rather, they left "worlds which were already encountering capitalism and experimenting with ways to deal with its realities."[20]

While many Jews were, indeed, poor in their European countries of origin and while they may have been prohibited from owning property in the Pale of settlement, their displacements and strategies for survival created conditions that would prove useful in immigration. In his spirited debunking of the myth of the "Jewish Horatio Alger," Stephen Steinberg argues that Jews of European origin experienced greater social and economic mobility than most other immigrant groups during the same time period because they had more resources and skills that enabled them to make use of the opportunities of immigration.[21] That is, most Jews who immigrated in the later part of the nineteenth and early twentieth centuries were workers with industrial or entrepreneurial skills that were needed in the expanding economy of the United States. High rates of literacy and knowledge of the textile and garment industries greatly aided immigrants who settled in the greater metropolitan New York area, for example.[22] Steinberg also cites the rapid growth of a scientific and industrial managerial class coincidental to the entrance of large numbers of Jews of European origin in higher education in the first several decades of the twentieth century.[23] Andrew Heinz argues that eastern European Jews "sought important elements of American identity more quickly and thoroughly than other groups of newcomers" through acts as consumers; women, in particular, "assumed a new power over the social adjustment of their families," and as entrepreneurs, eastern European Jews could become "magnates in the province of mass consumption."[24]

Thus, my grandparents' and parents' generations were able to make good use of a variety of skills, knowledges, and values that they brought with them to the United States. That these resources met specific needs upon their arrival accounts for their gradual shift in class but the question of their racialization remains. In her essay "How Did Jews Become White Folks?" Karen Sacks challenges the myth that Jews from Europe simply "pulled themselves up by their own bootstraps." Sacks makes her argument by tracing the changes in U.S. social policy and national politics that contributed to a shift in racialization of Jews of European origin in the periods during and after World War II. Referring to this shift as "the biggest and best affirmative action program in the history of our nation" in its consequences for "Euromales," Sacks argues that benefits such as the GI Bill and government sponsored home loans were differentially allocated in ways that distinctly favored European ethnics including large numbers of Jews of eastern and western European origins over and against groups such as African-Americans.[25] Making a related argument in his essay "The Possessive Investment in Whiteness," George Lipsitz points out that the absolute value of being white in the United States has only risen throughout the century as structured benefits in loan policies, tax "reforms," local and federal government contracts, and other ways of "helping" the middle and upper class to continue to favor particular groups over others, enabling and constructing "whiteness."[26]

If the greatest culprit in this form of institutionalized racism remains the U.S. government, with so many tangible benefits linked to social and legal practices based on "blood" laws and other racist discourses, the majority of European immigrants, including Jews, embraced the property rights of whiteness, in effect viewing whiteness as a quality of "American" citizenship that had been obstructed by anti-semitism but was now more fully restored.[27] As Cheryl Harris has so powerfully demonstrated in her essay "Whiteness as Property," whites have come to "expect and rely on these benefits, and over time these expectations have been affirmed, legitimated, and protected by the law."[28] The upward mobility of some immigrants and not others, of some people of color and not others, has resulted in what Sacks refers to as "racially skewed gains" that have been "passed across the generations so that racial inequality seems to maintain itself 'naturally' even after legal segregation ended."[29]

Contributing to a shift in public discourse and perception, after World War II the rhetoric of anti-semitism became less fashionable and less overt. As David Gerber points out, while in Europe Jews were traditionally "the least protected group in society," in the United States anti-semites had not managed to consolidate attacks on Jews exclusively and racists were divided in their biases against numerous groups.[30] Further, the economic gains made by Jews of European origin during this period reinforced the property rights of whiteness even as growing official support for the zionist state of Israel cemented the impression that Jews were now part of Western "civilization," protected by the geopolitical alliances formed during World War II and defined against an "Arab" threat (thereby erasing Arab Jews from the discourses of Judaism and the "modern" Middle East).[31] As a growing civil rights movement intensified the politics of anti-racist activism in the United States and laws set limits on non-white immigration, the construction of "whiteness" in the U.S. appeared to embrace the nation's Jews, very much to their benefit.[32] Thus, Sacks writes, "By the time I was an adolescent, Jews were just as white as the next white person."[33] This metropolitan phenomenon of ethnicized "whiteness" had to be seen as a form of triumph by many people who remembered harsher forms of discrimination as well as the very real threat of genocide. Yet, it also signifies a shift from the marginal and contested status of outsider to a new nativism that celebrated nationalism and claimed whiteness over and against newer, non-European immigrants and people of color. As Harris writes, "[W]hiteness and property share a common premise—a conceptual nucleus—of a right to exclude."[34]

Yet, the experience of whiteness as it is imbricated in the experience of Jews of European origin in the United States is more complex than some of these accounts might indicate. While this complexity does not obviate the property and cultural privileges of whiteness, different or contrasting experiences can lead us to construct more nuanced social histories. My childhood in rural North America—relatively far from the majoritarian versions of ethnic whiteness in urban centers such as New York or Chicago—provided me with a less homogeneous or even experience of whiteness. In fact, I spent most of my youth *feeling* simultaneously not-white-enough and not-Jewish-enough. This gives me a view at a tangent, as it were, from the centricity of whiteness even though the experience of disjunction from majoritarian U.S. Jewish experience alone has not rendered me any less white legally, or even socially in many contexts. It does mean that my sense of myself as Jewish is different from my parents' or from that of my cousins who grew up in the city and had similar experiences to those Sacks recounts or to those of a younger generation (who may have experienced a lessening of urban/rural distinctions through wider access to mass culture).

From a young age, my experience of whiteness and Jewishness as both linked but discontinuous or uneven made me skeptical of claims about any intrinsic qualities of race and ethnicity—first, on an intuitive level and, later, on a more analytical plane. My experience as a Jew of my particular generation in the United States, then, is complicated: I was extremely privileged by class, race, and nation as well as marginal, distrusted, and sometimes despised. My uneasiness is only increased by my academic training and interests; as a feminist in colonial discourse studies in the United States at the present moment, it is not possible for me to embrace a holistic Jewish cultural identity based on territorial and cultural imperialism. That is, like many Jews around the world, I cannot support Israeli zionist policies and projects. In addition, as a secular Jew in the United States (where Ashkenazi or eastern European Jews dominate the ethnic discourse of Judaism), if I do not participate in religious culture and if I cannot promote Ashkenazi superiority over those Jews who are not white or of European backgrounds, it does not leave me many options to identify myself with other U.S. Jews. This very situation begs the question of identity yet it used to render me silent on the subject of being a Jew. I felt profoundly confused, displaced, and trapped between unattractive options.[35] However, if I neither "disavow" nor "impugn" Jewishness, to borrow George Yudice's phrasing, I may find that I can rearticulate one aspect of whiteness in the United States.

In an essay on whiteness and the limits of identity politics, Yudice argues that it is in the interests of whites as well as non-whites to "transform the ethnoracial order."[36] Whites do not have to collude in the reproduction of whiteness' centrality but the tendency for many white people in the United States has been either disavowal (Yudice points to Michael Lerner's declaration that Jews are "not white" as a recent example) or impugning (the interesting but problematic journal *Race Traitor* illustrates the latter).[37] Yudice argues that "declaring nonwhiteness" is not really an option for many whites who are poor, unemployed, or disenfranchised. In addition, explorations of identities such as "Latino" and "Jew" in the context of U.S. immigration and social history underscore the contingent and constructed nature of "whiteness." Drawing on Diana Jeater's work on the possibilities of oppositional practices of whiteness, Yudice calls for a "rearticulation of whiteness."[38]

Rearticulating whiteness can mean a number of things in current times. Rearticulating whiteness deconstructs not only the primacy or supremacy of a racial categorization but calls into question the ontological status of the categories themselves to reveal the political stakes in these constructions. That is, rearticulating whiteness queries the conventions of ethnic studies as well as racist critical practices. Rather than focus on the history of discrete terms of identity, rearticulating whiteness can problematize the erasure of the state in discussions of identity. Thus, Jewish identity can no longer be divorced from the history of other immigrations and diasporas or from U.S. foreign policy, First World geopolitics, or transnational market restructuring. Once such erasures or mystifications are addressed, the collusion between globalizing economies, nation-state formations, and various other interests can be seen to be linked. Yudice warns that when identity politics do not allow for a look at the "larger picture," the "relationship between identity groups and institutions—e.g., the academy and business institutions, the relationship between these institutions, the state—the military and welfare bureaucracy—and the economy, and the articulation of all these relationships in a global context" are all suppressed.[39]

My inquiry into the rearticulation of whiteness brings me back to the place and time that produced many of my own myths of ethnicity. It is in that location that I can find the ways that a knowledge of global as well as local conditions were suppressed in favor of specific sentiments and prejudices.

The Politics of Location in the Articulation of Euro-American Jewish Whiteness

"I'm going to Jew you down!"
"You're a dirty, stinking Jew!"
"Where's your tail? Where're your horns?"
My grandmother taught me a curse in Yiddish to holler back at the kids who yelled at me and kicked me all the way home from school. I wish I could remember the words but they are long gone. . . . I know they meant something like "Drop down dead you disgusting creep!" Although I knew that my grandmother and my parents would try to protect me, most of the time I had to face this kind of attack alone. I was the only Jew in my year at school and one of only four in the entire school (it was just my little brother, two sisters from another family, and me). How did everyone know what I was? How could they tell? It was easy—I was marked in a million ways. My parents would not allow me to say the Lord's Prayer at school (before the law was changed and relieved me from this daily torture of open, principled resistance). My parents also forbade me from saying the Christian prayer that opened the Brownie and Girl Scout meetings. Most crushingly and, to me, most obviously, I was the only person in my ballet

Caren Kaplan

school who could not participate in the December performance—a Christmas "Cortege." How I wanted to play the part of Mary! . . . Even a shepherd would have been fine. But my parents were adamant about the appearance of assimilation. Our house had no Christmas tree or holiday decorations. Beyond the realm of such acts, I was marked most overtly by my physical characteristics—my dark hair and eyes, what I thought was a prominent nose—it seemed immense and not at all right for a "girl." I felt certain that my dark hair and unfeminine nose caused me to lose the parts in plays I wanted; I was cast as the villain, the older woman, or the mother, but never the princess or the ingenue. "You're beautiful. You're smart," my parents said. "You're ugly. You're a Jew," my town said; and it had the power of mainstream culture behind its views. When the librarian confused my name regularly with that of one of the other two jewish girls in school, a girl who did not resemble me in height or facial characteristics, she was saying, in effect, "You're only a Jew to me." "You're a dirty Jew," the bully whispered in my ear at school or yelled from the path through the field to our homes. "Dirty, dirty, dirty." "What does that make you?" I yelled back, trying not to cry. "What does that make you?"

It's tempting to remain fascinated by the narrative of ethnicity and race. Those of us who have faced its ugliness, its vile and demeaning nature, can find a recuperative balm in the telling. The power of witness, of testifying to the vicious inhumanity of discrimination, reinforces the belief that one can not only survive this system but change it. Although there is almost no other possible response to racism or to any other form of hate-filled expression than fighting back, our strategies invariably mirror the terms of our oppression. Thus, identity politics can engender a response that naturalizes and homogenizes the categories of resistance. In the scenario of my "hometown," for example, I find it challenging to understand my experience of anti-semitism beyond the familiar terms of ethnicity and race. If I heard or was hailed by racist epithets as a child, what did that *make* me? That is, how did I construct an identity over and against such information? I was told that my family emigrated to escape anti-semitic persecution in eastern Europe, a historical phenomenon that was underscored by the loss of contact with anyone who did not immigrate. In addition to the catastrophic disappearance of family left behind several generations ago, I knew that the German state had enacted a systematic genocide against its Jewish citizens only a little more than a decade before I was born. The European Jewish Holocaust was a constant leitmotif against which I evaluated my rural hometown experiences. I was very conscious of the fact that people could be singled out and killed in modern times *because* they were Jews. To not assert my Jewishness—and not assert it proudly and loudly—was to collude with those I was taught to see as enemies not only of Jews but all darker peoples (in my childhood Jews were *always* "dark" and always from eastern Europe—I had no other frame of reference). Anything else, I was instructed by my family, was a kind of treason. And every small act of principle mattered.

I grew up in a small university town in central Maine during the sixties and seventies. My parents were Jewish academics from New York City, the children of immigrants from the Russian Pale. In migrating to Maine and leaving the metropolitan center of U.S. Jewish subculture behind, my parents were beyond a different "pale." In my town, as in thousands of others in the United States, it was best to be considered white, heterosexual, Anglo-Saxon, Protestant, and middle-class. In addition to the "town-gown" divisions inherent to most small university towns, ethnic, racial, and class divides (very often articulated as religious ones) sharply demarcated this locale. Catholics, especially French-Canadians, were treated with disdain and a French-Canadian surname insured discrimination and name-calling.[40] South Asians and Middle Easterners met with problems similar to ours (and if their skin tones happened to be darker, it ensured more abuse). The Native Americans who were the earliest inhabitants of the land we occupied had been relegated by the government to a reservation about three miles away. It is almost impossible to describe the virulent climate of bias against this population; generally living in extreme poverty, the object of invectives and insults, Native Americans were at the very bottom of the hierarchy of discrimination in the locale I called "home."[41] As for other Jews, there was a Jewish community of significant size that sponsored a conservative synagogue in the neighboring small city of Bangor (and a smaller congregation in nearby Old Town). Because my family was not religiously observant, we didn't make any long-term, meaningful ties to these families—although my beloved pediatrician came from one of these old, established Jewish families in Bangor.[42] The longevity of the Native American population's struggle to survive and the long-standing nature of Jewish communities in other Maine municipalities notwithstanding, any marginality in this general site seemed extremely fraught to me. That Maine has a long history of anti-semitic and anti-Catholic movements came as no surprise to me when I was doing research in the University of Maine library for a high school assignment and discovered that the state's enrollments in the Ku Klux Klan during the twenties rivaled anything found in Alabama or

Mississippi.[43] As a child, I found it a frightening and generally unwelcoming place to live.[44]

Thus, I grew up feeling preoccupied by my own marginalization and I took for granted many of the considerable privileges I enjoyed as the middle-class child of cosmopolitan parents who valued education and travel. But I was always looking for allies or searching for subjects with whom I felt an affinity. Although I deeply desired the bright, light hair of the most popular girls in my school, in my make-believe play I always chose the dramatic roles of people I associated with dark skin or hair. I pretended that I was the Indian princess Morningstar (inspired by a TV show I liked) and I conspired against the cowboys and soldiers. I dug up my backyard looking for clamshell heaps and other evidence of Indian settlement. I pretended that I was Anne Frank and I climbed way up high in the pine trees to hide from the Germans. When I heard a rumor about the existence of a stop on the pre-Civil War era "underground railroad" along the riverbank of my town, I pretended to be Harriet Tubman. Running through the woods, fingering the bark to find the mossy north side of trees after the sun went down, I imagined that I was helping escaped slaves on their way to Canada. I knew I was never going to be blonde or Christian so I tried to ally myself in my imagination to people who looked more like me or to those who had been the underdog in mismatched fights.

Yet, these romanticized, imaginary alliances never brought me to recognize just what kinds of differences and similarities might have existed between myself and "others." For example, the Penobscot Indian residents of the neighboring reservation, people who lived in extreme poverty and who experienced tremendous discrimination were not the "noble savages" of my half-baked imagination (heavily influenced by racist children's books and mainstream TV shows). Long-neglected by the state and categorically discriminated against both economically and culturally, the Native Americans in central Maine might as well have lived on another planet as far as my little, narrow daily life was concerned.[45] Along with the larger Passmaquoddy nation, the Penobscots had begun the legal procedure to reclaim their land while I was growing up in the same region—a process that was ultimately successful and that set important precedents.[46] Somehow I never dreamed about taking land claims to the Supreme Court or Congress! And I never thought carefully about how Native American alterity in my community made me "white": if not white enough then whiter than others.[47]

At that time I was not able to understand that my sympathies and imagination were not palliatives for structural inequities. My own deeply rooted, child-like essentialism used lightness and darkness as symbols of something real rather than as signs of ideology at work. And in a kind of complicity that signals privilege (in this location it was a privilege of race and class), I came to depend upon my sense of otherness: it made me distinct and it gave me something around which to organize my sense of self. My "darkness" was something I could learn to use and cherish instead of only regretting and resenting. But I did not know how to demystify my imaginary alliances and I was often guilty of appropriating the signs of other people's cultures and assuming similarity when there was no historical or structural basis for it.

Yet, no matter how "white" my various positions made me, in the public spaces of Maine I felt profoundly and uneasily marked by ethnic customs and physical traits. If I think more carefully about this situation, I know it is only a small part of the story—that I was hampered by a child's lack of a broader frame of reference even as I was encouraged to ethnicize my point of view both by bigots and by well-meaning "liberals." As an adult, I can try to determine other relevant factors in the construction of that locale and its sets of meanings and practices. For example, as a senior administrator at the state university, my father was responsible for instituting affirmative action policies and significant changes in student life, such as liberalized dorm curfews and relaxed drinking regulations. During this period, protests against the war in Indo-China interrupted classes and a small but dedicated chapter of SDS made the headlines regularly. Outreach programs to enroll Native Americans and French-Canadians threatened to change the face of the university. It just so happens that the kid who tortured me with racial epithets was the son of a professor who disagreed with my father's public position on affirmative action and other progressive programs. Both of my parents took visible stands in the community in favor of civil rights and for more innovative programs in the primary and secondary schools. They were among the white liberals who joined the local chapter of the NAACP. Although they were not "radicals," my family's activities and articulated beliefs signified a set of ideas and practices that challenged certain aspects of the status quo in that location.

In this period of "social change," anxiety about who would suffer some kind of loss and who might benefit often took on gendered as well as racialized aspects. For example, my mother was trying to get a Ph.D. in a male-dominated field and her fundamentalist baptist department chair ridi-

Plate 60: *Triple Silver Yentl (My Elvis)*, 1993
Silkscreen ink and acrylic canvas, 72″ × 94″
Deborah Kass
Photo: Liz Deschenes
Collection of William S. Ehrich and Ruth Lloyds
Courtesy of the artist

culed her constantly in front of the other students, telling her that her children were probably lying dead in the street because she wasn't home to take care of them or that she was just taking space away from a man who needed to support his family. I remember the depth of her outrage over his comments just as I recall how powerless she felt to redress an intolerable situation. In her point of view at that time, her only option was to endure this abuse. I remember my mother's incredible determination and her anger as well as I remember the biochemistry formulas she Scotch-taped to every available surface in the kitchen to help her study for tests while she cooked. "*Get the piece of paper,*" she would urge me later on, drumming in the message that an academic degree would somehow make me less vulnerable to such outrages. Yet, when I got my "piece of paper," I discovered an anti-semite among my most senior colleagues at my first academic job. An equal-opportunity bigot, he was sexist and homophobic for good measure. His sneers and slurred asides were meant to unnerve me. But I had been trained by my mother to get angry but endure (I had snatches of the old Yiddish curse from my grandmother). My father had taught me to temper my anger but keep my principles. With such an array of strategies, brandishing my "pieces of paper," I could stand up to my grown-up bully who wanted to reprise the old anti-semitic refrain, adding his own masculinist twist. (But I like to think the curse I put on him is working . . .)

I know now that in my hometown we weren't just "Jews," we were people who symbolized in our very persons a specific set of changes that many people did not welcome (just as my former colleague feared the consequences of my interdisciplinary feminist training and interests in "his" department). If people harbored anxieties about economic and cultural changes in Maine in the sixties and seventies, why did they express these fears as a hatred for the color of my hair and my ethno-religious background? Paul Gilroy has argued that racial power relations shift during a period of national decline, moving from the more hierarchical distinctions between superior and inferior of high imperialism to the more "subtle and elusive" versions that operate in the present moment.[48] In each era or historical moment, as the work of Gilroy, Stuart Hall, Hazel Carby, and other "Birmingham School" scholars has demonstrated, class and race are intertwined, historically constructed categories that can be read across other key elements to track the power relations of nation-states in crisis.[49] In order to understand the racialization and genderization that I experienced in its fully contradictory and multiply valenced complexity, I have to place my memories of "race" and "gender" in the context of its particular moment.

When I was growing up, throughout the sixties and seventies, a set of specific crises occurred. Decolonization struggles resulted in a restructuring of world economies with the formation of what Wallerstein referred to as a "world system" of center and periphery constituting itself along lines no longer officially dominated by European nation-states but by their financial institutions and interests and the geopolitical alliances that supported those institutions and interests. These shifts from imperialism to neo-imperialism and from colonization to decolonization (with all the attendant tensions and struggles) were apparent to me as a young person only as random, unrelated phenomena: the Cuban Missile Crisis, the war in Indochina, rebellions in U.S. cities and abroad, assassinations of progressive leaders, the gasoline shortage, economic "inflation," and emergent social movements, especially the anti-war, women's, and student movements (in which I participated). Yet, increasing globalization of markets structured the region where I grew up in ways I could hardly grasp at the time. I had no idea that Maine, too, was becoming even more peripheral in the national and world economy in a marked restructuring of industries, services, and markets.

For many people, Maine is symbolized by the slogan on its license plates: "Vacationland." As is common in so many underdeveloped areas, tourism has been and continues to be a primary industry. As a seasonal and fickle industry, it can mask for visitors the economic and social relations that make a landscape "unspoiled," "rural," or "picturesque." But for those of us who live or used to live there, the "undeveloped" shores and woods also signal the threat of poverty. Trying to remember the specificity of this bucolic, rural location during my childhood requires revising my family scripts to demystify the narrative of "race." I have to head to the library and learn how and why the place where I grew up became so unevenly developed. I knew that the period of the sixties and seventies marked a precipitous economic decline from which the region has never recovered. I didn't know exactly how the deindustrialization of the U.S. economy and the move to "off-shore" production affected the Maine textile and shoe industries, for example. Nor did I know just how the paper mills had dominated state economic policy, development, and planning. I loved the rocky coast and the little farms at the edges of enormous forests as authentic signs of a "natural" space just as I loved my romanticized image of the Indians. I knew that my white neighbors down the road lived in what amounted to a shack while my big house featured three bathrooms and picture window views. But I didn't have much of a sense as to how those neighbors might have found themselves moving from working farmers to welfare state dependents. And my fledgling feminism helped me define goals that ensured my own future career (further consolidating my whiteness through class position) but did not yet help me understand why the poor family down the road was headed by a female.

Although Maine's economy is more diversified now than earlier in the century, it is still "colonial" in that Maine produces food and raw materials for use elsewhere and is "dependent" on out-of-state manufacturers for most consumer goods. In addition, most of the capital invested in Maine is generated outside the state.[50] In the seventies, much of that capital came from the seven enormous pulp and paper companies that owned 7.5 million acres, or 37 percent of Maine's land, representing a larger proportion of industry ownership of forest land than in any other state in the country.[51] Throughout the decade, as agriculture and the "traditional" industries of shoe and textile manufacturing declined, a substantial number of families lived on or below the poverty line and Aid to Dependent Children rolls increased. Conditions in the state worsened as the increase in the number of people living in poverty shifted to include the non-elderly population. Thus, throughout the period of economic boom and bust that shaped U.S. national political and cultural agendas, Maine appears to have been consigned to a position of marginality that insured increasing poverty for the young as well as the old and guaranteed uneven, seasonal, and temporary forms of employment. Competition for scarce resources characterized the years of my youth in the state.

In focusing for a moment on economic matters, I do not intend to imply that "class" supercedes "race." As David Roediger argues, "to set race within social formations is absolutely necessary but to reduce race to class is damaging"—damaging, because such a reduction simplifies social relations that are more multi-layered and uneven than such a ranking would indicate.[52] And, as Néstor García Canclini argues, the hegemony of a class cannot "sustain itself solely through economic power."[53] But in shifting the discussion from race/ethnicity to economic conditions, I hope to point to a broader frame for situating the experience of kinds of racism, one that challenges the national parameters of discourses about race and ethnicity. Similarly, gender has to be considered in the scenario I have sketched of underdevelopment and deliberate strategies of economic marginalization. How does gender inflect the policies and local effects of such underdevelopment? When resources become scarce, how are they distributed, contested, and utilized? With the rise of tourism as a primary economic force in the state, what divisions of labor can be seen to be tied to the conventional categories of race, gender, and economic class? Are there emergent categories that inflect specific, contemporary conditions?

Maine can serve as a site for the deconstruction of some categories such as ethnicity because the myths of United States prosperity and homogeneity through diversity are easily disturbed there. Always to one side and peripheral to the nation, it is a state that, nevertheless, tries to stress its centrality to the national project (in relation to party politics, the slogan reads, "As Maine goes, so goes the nation"). If Maine "goes" the way of uneven development, if it is another place of great unemployment and declining opportunities that offers itself as a "vacationland" for "others," then the nation has reason to be concerned. I would not want to read this site as a place where the myths of American uniqueness and promise could be recuperated. For me, reviewing my experiences in one location has made white ethnicity much more complicated, more relational, and, admittedly, far less satisfying. For I have been pressed by this work to give up on some old ideas that I depended upon and I am still unsure about where I am going in this quasi-autobiographical inquiry into the invention of ethnicities. Once I began to research Maine as a site, it threatened to overtake the entire essay project, presenting me with a vast field of old memories and new information. I can still learn a great deal more for, "as Maine goes," so, I hope, goes the feminist cultural critic of transnational subjects.

Rearticulating the National Boundaries of Race and Ethnicity

I began this essay with a rather carnivalesque quotation from Alicia Dujovne Ortiz's wonderful investigation of nation, ethnicity, and gender, *Buenos Aires*. I found this slender, little text with a pale blue cover in a feminist book store in Paris back in the mid-eighties and discovered that its discussion of a Jewish girlhood in Argentina had much to say to me. When I wrote a chapter of my dissertation on this memoir, written in French by a Spanish-speaking political exile, I was interested in its compelling examination of immigration and displacement in the age of imperialism in general and I did not focus on its specifically Jewish qualities. But some of the eastern European Jews from the Pale who emigrated to Argentina might be cousins on my father's side—long-lost and never to be regained in literal fact—and Dujovne Ortiz's sense of humor resonates with my own in ethnically charged ways. So there is plenty in this charming text for me to re-read and re-learn in inventing new kinships and affinities. For example, how can we take this trope of the "wandering Jew" and turn it not into a cornerstone of Eurocentric liberal humanism but into a sign of complex histories of immigration and diaspora? Dujovne Ortiz's image of the crowd, procession, parade, masquerade, works for me because I, too, do not want to anchor a Jewish identity in a territory or in "roots." The motley crew of masqueraders who parade through Dujovne Ortiz's text can't be romanticized as simply nomadic and perpetually wandering. They dwell at once together and in movement, alert to the losses and injuries of history as well as to the ironic pleasures of displacement. "To be a crowd" could be one way of rearticulating Euro-American Jewish whiteness in the current moment. Beyond the "pale" might be another metaphorical route into deconstructing the homogenizing Ashkenazi dominance in U.S. Jewish cultural and political life. Each phrase signals a reworking of identity politics from the singular to the multiple and from the static boundary to the transgressive and transformative inventions of cultural practice.

In seeking to deconstruct "Jewish whiteness" in this essay, then, I want to call into question the erasure of Arab, Latino, African, Asian, and South Asian Jews from the dominant narrative of Jewish identity in U.S. contexts. This eurocentric hegemony itself contains class and national divisions that have divided those descended from peasants and bourgeoisie, rural and metropolitan locations, and western and eastern as well as northern and southern Europe. Asking questions about the process whereby a racially-marked group in Europe eventually gains access to whiteness in another country inevitably raises related concerns about the historical stakes in racialization in the modern nation-state in general but also queries who gets left out of that configuration. As the nation-state becomes increasingly destabilized in the current era, the consolidation and naturalization of identities go hand in hand, as it were. In the face of such recurrent racisms, resurgent patriarchal practices, and widening gaps between rich and poor, the representation of identities must be tied, not to cultural mystification, but to material histories.

It is less and less clear to me how any analysis of "whiteness" can remain within the parameters of a single nation-state, especially within the institutional constructs of "American" or "Ethnic" Studies as they are practiced currently in the United States. As Inderpal Grewal argues, concerns with race solely at the "local/national but not global level" recuperate Euro-American standpoint epistemology.[54] Unless we destabilize such essentialist and ahistorical concepts and categories, our analysis remains nationalist and blind to complex cultural and economic considerations,

Caren Kaplan

working against the formation of links and coalitions between diverse groups and people beyond the borders of the nation. This kind of research project requires a transnational feminist cultural studies methodology: collaborative and multidisciplinary.[55] As Gayatri Spivak suggests, the point is to "negotiate between the national, the global, and the historical as well as the contemporary diasporic"; that is, to move between discussions of domestic/national ethnicities and instances of colonization outside the nation.[56] In that way, "diaspora" cannot be romanticized as the primary practice of postmodern hybridity *or* claimed as the exclusive state of being for any one people.[57]

Similarly, rearticulating "Jewish whiteness" leads to more "relational" studies of ethnicities as linked through histories of transnational cultural and economic circulations. Thus, as Ella Shohat argues in "Staging the Quincentenary," the Middle East and the Americas are always assumed to be entirely separate but they share a relationship to the year 1492 when Spain expelled three hundred thousand Sephardic Jews and launched the conquest of what would be called the "New World."[58] Shohat's references to the critical reluctance to "chart the colonial racial dimensions" of "Euro-Israeli" discourse about the Middle East contextualize the "celebrations of Columbus' 'discovery'" and raise numerous other questions about links between the histories of the Americas and the "Old World."[59] Linking the anti-Muslim projects of the Crusades to anti-semitic pogroms in Europe as well as to the devastation of native populations in the "New World," Shohat argues that Europeans constructed a "conceptual and disciplinary apparatus" that worked first against those who could be marked as other within the nation and then against those brought into contact through imperial ventures.[60] This methodology, "remapping national and ethnic-racial identities," produces exciting new juxtapositions and enables fresh analyses as well as new affinities.

At this moment in the United States, alliances between new religious fundamentalisms and nationalist interests have provoked anti-gay rights legislation and harassment across the nation (including Maine); anti-immigration fervor of a magnitude not seen for several decades; racist backlash and attacks on affirmative action; activist violence in the name of pro-life groups; and the rise in popularity of right-wing "militia" movements. We must not simply struggle to make clear the links between these outrageous acts against public safety and health within the nation. We must also remember how crucial it is for our understanding of present conditions to make the conceptual and analytical move to transnational linkages. Rather than simply call for the "abolition" of whiteness, I would argue for a rearticulation of this category; to destabilize its long-term power as a unified assumption by making its micro-histories into a cacophonous disharmony, to align those in its margins with the struggles of peoples of color not through identificatory desire but through affinities of knowledge and situated experience, and to make whiteness more "crowded" and less "pale." However, Jews of European origin who benefit from "whiteness" in the United States cannot simply deconstruct a national identity. Unless we come to understand how our "whiteness" constructs and supports Arab-Israeli conflicts, for example, or suppresses Sephardic cultural histories, then we only recuperate the centrality of Euro-American colonial discourses. Similarly, feminists who wish to articulate Jewish cultural identities and practices must be alert to histories of imperialism in the eurocentrism of so much U.S. Jewish discourse and in Western feminist rhetoric and representational practice. Then the "Jewish question," the question of particularity and the nature of the nation-state, becomes transformed into the question of postmodern articulation: how do we represent and act through our perceptions of similarity and difference?

Notes

This essay became possible when I began to exchange and explore ideas with Ella Shohat. My thanks to her for friendship and guidance are boundless. Inderpal Grewal's brilliant work on immigration, ethnic studies, race, and gender aided me almost as much as her patient reading of drafts and concrete suggestions. I was also very much helped by generous readings and gifts of information or conversations at key moments with Ken Wissoker, Irit Rogoff, Minoo Moallem, Annette Jaimes-Guerrero, and Nancy Ordover. Karen Sacks, Evelyn Nakano Glenn, and George Yudice were kind enough to share work in progress. Jillian Sandell provided engaged research assistance. My deep thanks to Eric Smoodin for more thoughtful readings and for being my best native informant on jokes from the borscht belt.

1. Alicia Dujovne Ortiz, *Buenos Aires* (Paris: Champ Vallon, 1984). English translation by Caren Kaplan and Aurora Wolfgang, in Philomena Mariani, ed., *Critical Fictions: The Politics of Imaginative Writing* (Seattle, WA: Bay Press, 1991), 126.

2. *The Oxford Universal Dictionary,* 3d. ed. (Oxford: Clarendon Press, 1955,), s.v. "pale."

3. According to the *Encyclopedia Judaica,* a lack of freedom of movement was shared by most inhabitants of czarist Russia when the Pale was first established in

the late eighteenth century. The official limits on where Jews could live and what occupations they could follow were designed to encourage colonization of newly annexed areas and to prevent competition with Russians. The singularly anti-semitic nature of the restrictions intensified in the nineteenth century as peasants were pitted against Jews by corrupt administrations. By the late nineteenth century, the Pale covered an area of approximately four hundred thousand square miles stretching from the Baltic to the Black Sea. The census of 1897 reported approximately five million Jews in the region, constituting 94 percent of the total Jewish population of Russia and approximately 11.6 percent of the general population of the area. Despite their heavy concentration in this border zone, Jews were a minority in every province in the Pale of settlement. Occupation restrictions led to concentrations of Jews in commerce and crafts. Unable to own land by law, the development of a Jewish proletariat with few prospects encouraged migration. The rise in violent pogroms against Jewish communities and anti-Jewish decrees also instigated immigration to such locations as North and South America as well as South Africa. The large numbers of eastern European Jews who migrated from the Pale to North America during the late nineteenth and early twentieth centuries have come to assume a dominant place in the "imagined community" of Jewish life in the United States. Yet their experiences and cultural influences are not the same as German Jews who immigrated earlier in the nineteenth century or Arab Jews, for example. Although the metaphor of "the Pale" is only relevant to one segment of the Jewish population in the United States, it is an important construct in my own formation as a Jewish subject. I am choosing to highlight it as a powerful metaphor in this project of cultural rearticulation. See "Pale of Settlement," *Encyclopedia Judaica*, vol. 13 (Jerusalem: Keter Publishing, 1972), 24–28.

4. Vron Ware, *Beyond the Pale: White Women, Racism, and History* (London: Verso, 1992), xii.

5. Michael Lerner, "Jews Are Not White," *The Village Voice*, May 18, 1993, 33–34.

6. James Baldwin, "On Being 'White' . . . And Other Lies," *Essence* 14, no. 2 (April 1984): 90.

7. Ibid.

8. Richard Dyer, "White," *Screen* 29, no. 4 (Autumn 1988): 45.

9. Ruth Frankenberg, *White Women, Race Matters: The Social Construction of Whiteness* (Minneapolis: University of Minnesota Press, 1993), 14.

10. In addition to Omi and Winant's ground-breaking work on racial formation in the United States, I am also appreciative of the following studies which explore the social construction of race in the history of the United States: Frankenberg, *White Women, Race Matters;* Tomás Almaguer, *Racial Fault Lines: The Historical*

Origins of White Supremacy in California (Berkeley: University of California Press, 1994); Karen Isaksen Leonard, *Making Ethnic Choices: California's Punjabi Mexican Americans* (Philadelphia: Temple University Press, 1992); and Naomi Zack, *Race and Mixed Race* (Philadelphia: Temple University Press, 1993). While these texts differ methodologically and politically, they indicate a growing interest in a cultural studies of ethnicity that moves beyond the conventions of sociology and anthropology. An engaging critique of Leonard's text can be found in Purnima Mankekar's "Reflections on Diasporic Identities: A Prolegomenon to an Analysis of Political Bifocality," *Diaspora* 3, no. 3 (Winter 1994): 349–371.

11. I appreciate Richard Dyer's critique of the two most prevalent "pitfalls" in the current trend in confessional identity memoirs—"guilt and me too-ism": ". . . While writing as a white person about whiteness, I do not mean either to display the expiation of my guilt about being white, nor to hint that it is also awful to be white (because it is an inadequate, limiting definition of being human, because feeling guilty is such a burden). Studies of dominance by the dominant should not deny the place of the writer in relation to what s/he is writing about it, but nor should they be the green light for self-recrimination or trying to get in on the act" (Dyer, "White," 44–45). An outstanding statement on the critically useless properties of guilt can be found in Audre Lorde's essay, "The Uses of Anger: Women Responding to Racism," in *Sister Outsider: Essays and Speeches* (Trumansburg, NY: The Crossing Press, 1984), 124–133. See also Adrienne Rich, "Disloyal to Civilization: Feminism, Racism, Gynephobia," in *On Lies, Secrets, and Silence: Selected Prose, 1966–1978* (New York: Norton, 1979), 275–310; and "Split at the Root: An Essay on Jewish Identity," in *Blood, Bread, and Poetry: Selected Prose, 1979–1985* (New York: Norton, 1986), 100–123; Michelle Cliff, *Claiming an Identity They Taught Me to Despise* (Watertown, MA: Persephone Press, 1980); Ann Russo, "'We Cannot Live Without Our Lives': White Women, Antiracism, and Feminism," in Chandra Talpade Mohanty et al., eds., *Third World Women and the Politics of Feminism* (Bloomington: Indiana University Press, 1991), 297–313; Marilyn Frye, "On Being White: Toward a Feminist Understanding of Race and Race Supremacy," in *The Politics of Reality* (Trumansburg, NY: The Crossing Press, 1983), 110–127; Elly Bulkin, Minnie Bruce Pratt, and Barbara Smith, *Yours in Struggle: Three Feminist Perspectives on Anti-Semitism and Racism* (Brooklyn: Long Haul Press, 1984); bell hooks, "Representations of Whiteness in the Black Imagination," in *Black Looks: Race and Representation* (Boston: South End Press, 1992), 165–78; and C. Margot Hennessy, "Earning It: Black and White Women Coming Together at the Side of the River" (paper delivered at the American Women Writers of Color conference, Ocean City, MD, May 26, 1992).

12. Evelyn Nakano Glenn, "White Women/Women of Color: The Social Construction of Racialized Gender, 1900–1940," unpublished manuscript, 1993, p. 2.

13. Representation of Jews in U.S. popular culture, especially television, is a field that needs more work. Most research homogenizes and essentializes the category

"Jew" in the tradition of ethnic studies or elides class, national, and cultural differences between and among Jews. Extremely useful discussions of ethnicity in early television include Lynne Spigel, *Make Room for Television: Television and the Family Ideal in Postwar America* (Chicago: University of Chicago Press, 1992); and George Lipsitz, "The Meaning of Memory: Family, Class, and Ethnicity in Early Network Television Programs," in Lynne Spigel and Denise Mann, eds., *Private Screenings: Television and the Female Consumer* (Minneapolis: University of Minnesota Press, 1992), 71–110. In film studies, Ella Shohat's work has made the categories of analysis more complex. See her *Israeli Cinema: East/West and the Politics of Representation* (Austin: University of Texas Press, 1989); and essays such as "Ethnicities-in-Relation: Toward a Multicultural Reading of American Cinema," in Lester Friedman, ed., *Unspeakable Images: Ethnicity and the American Cinema* (Urbana: University of Illinois Press, 1991), 215–249; and "Reflections of an Arab Jew," *Emergences* 3/4 (Fall 1992): 39–45. For a problematization of ethnicity, race, and colonial discourse in film and media studies, see Ella Shohat and Robert Stam, *Unthinking Eurocentrism: Multiculturalism and the Media* (New York: Routledge, 1994).

14. U.S. Congress House of Representatives, "Biological Aspects of Immigration," Hearings Before the Committee on Immigration and Naturalization, April 16–17, 1920. Cited in Nancy Ordover, dissertation prospectus (Ethnic Studies, University of California at Berkeley, Spring 1995), 5. For more on the biological, medical, and sexual discourses of anti-semitism, see Sander Gilman, *The Jew's Body* (New York: Routledge, 1991); *Jewish Self Hatred: Anti-Semitism and the Hidden Language of the Jews* (Baltimore: Johns Hopkins University Press, 1986); and *Difference and Pathology: Stereotypes of Sexuality, Race, and Madness* (Ithaca, NY: Cornell University Press, 1985).

15. See Marcia Graham Synnott, "Anti-Semitism and American Universities. Did Quotas Follow the Jews?" in David A. Gerber, ed., *Anti-Semitism in American History* (Urbana: University of Illinois Press, 1986), 233–271.

16. Ibid., 258 259.

17. See Robert Singerman, "The Jew as Racial Alien," in Gerber, *Anti-Semitism*, 103 128.

18. Ironically, many Jewish women who had lived in the Pale had played prominent roles in commerce before emigrating. Generally, upon arrival, eastern European Jewish women in the United States worked in factories or "helped" their families. Having had less access to formal education or craft work, their opportunities were limited accordingly. See Donna Gabaccia, *From the Other Side: Women, Gender, and Immigrant Life in the U.S., 1820–1990* (Bloomington: Indiana University Press, 1994).

19. For an important history of this experience of assimilation and upward mobility see Alan M. Kraut, *The Huddled Masses: The Immigrant in American Society, 1880–*

1921 (Arlington Heights, IL: Harlan Davidson, 1982). Kraut notes that eastern European laws that prevented Jews from owning land had led to a turn to non-agrarian skills that could be transferred from one site or location to another. Thus, Jews arriving at the turn of the century "tended to be skilled artisans or experienced merchants." Jewish women immigrants during this period either did piecework at home or found work in factories and mills, becoming a strong presence in labor organizing (see pp. 74–86).

20. John Bodnar, *The Transplanted: A History of Immigrants in Urban America* (Bloomington: Indiana University Press, 1985), 56.

21. Stephen Steinberg, *The Ethnic Myth: Race, Ethnicity, and Class in America* (New York: Atheneum, 1981), 83.

22. See Bodnar, *The Transplanted,* 20, 31–32.

23. Steinberg, 229.

24. Andrew R. Heinz, *Adapting to Abundance: Jewish Immigrants, Mass Consumption, and the Search for American Identity* (New York: Columbia University Press, 1990), 4.

25. Karen Sacks, "How Did Jews Become White Folks?" in Steven Gregory and Roger Sanjek, eds., *Race* (New Brunswick, NJ: Rutgers University Press, 1994), 79.

26. George Lipsitz, "The Possessive Investment in Whiteness: Racialized Social Democracy and the 'White' Problem in American Studies," *American Quarterly* 47, no. 3 (September 1995): 376.

27. See Lawrence Wright, "One Drop of Blood," *The New Yorker,* July 25, 1994, 46–55. See also, A. Leon Higginbotham, *In the Matter of Color: Race and the American Legal Process—The Colonial Period* (New York: Oxford University Press, 1978); Carl Degler, *Neither Black nor White: Slavery and Race Relations in Brazil and the United States* (New York: MacMillan, 1971); and Virginia R. Dominguez, *White by Definition: Social Classification in Creole Louisiana* (New Brunswick, NJ: Rutgers University Press, 1986).

28. Cheryl L. Harris, "Whiteness as Property," *Harvard Law Review,* 106 (1993): 1713; see also Patricia Williams, "On Being the Object of Property," in *The Alchemy of Race and Rights* (Cambridge, MA: Harvard University Press, 1991), 216–236.

29. Sacks, "How Did Jews Become White Folks?" 98.

30. David A. Gerber, "Introduction," *Anti-Semitism in American History,* 17.

31. See Shohat, *Israeli Cinema.*

32. In a co-authored study on U.S. Immigration, Leonard Dinnerstein, Roger Nichols, and David Reimers argue that for many U.S. Jews who had been aligned

with liberal causes in the past, the late sixties and early seventies represented a period in which many feared the loss of "hard-won gains." "Because many Jews had qualified for professional and executive positions, they interpreted affirmative action as a euphemism for the quota system and, particularly in the contracting economy of the 1970s, as discrimination against them." Here it is possible to see how far the consolidation of whiteness extended and how deeply rooted the property rights of whiteness attached themselves to U.S. Jews of European origin such that those rights could be perceived to be threatened by the claims of people of color. Leonard Dinnerstein, Roger L. Nichols, and David M. Reimers, *Natives and Strangers: Blacks, Indians, and Immigrants in America* (Oxford: Oxford University Press, 1990), 330.

33. Sacks, "How Did Jews Become White Folks?" 86.

34. Harris, "Whiteness as Property," 1714.

35. Another emotion that I identify as I work on this project is shame. Am I complaining too much? Am I exaggerating my perceptions of anti-semitism? In speaking about anti-semitism towards Jews of European origin in the United States am I unintentionally suggesting that it is worse or more important than racism directed against Jews and other people of color? Am I posing myself too much as a victim? Why is it hard to talk about experiences of anti-semitism, experiences that still rock me to the core of my being, that cause me so much pain? David Gerber argues that anti-semitism in the United States has lacked consistent governmental and constitutional sanction (in fact, Jews of European origin have often experienced benefits and aid in this country that people of color have been denied) and, therefore, it has been more difficult to "take seriously or even to detect than its European counterpart." Because exceptions and inconsistencies in the practice and recognition of prejudice and discrimination against Jews in the United States is so widespread, Jews have "received mixed and highly ambiguous signals." I would go so far as to suggest that for some Jews of European origin in the United States, these mixed and ambiguous signals constitute a kind of double bind in which one is both discriminated against and highly privileged. It *is* confusing. See David A. Gerber, "Introduction," *Anti-Semitism in American History*, 19.

36. George Yudice, "Neither Impugning nor Disavowing Whiteness Do a Viable Politics Make: The Limits of Identity Politics," unpublished manuscript, 1993.

37. Lerner, "Jews Are Not White," 33–34. In Lerner's piece, published in a *Village Voice* special issue on "whiteness," Jews are always "white" in the sense that Lerner cannot conceive of Jews who are not part of a specific diaspora. Claiming that anti-semitism and the Nazi extermination of European Jews belie any privileges of whiteness, Lerner argues that "Jews must respond with an equally determined insistence that we are not white, and that those who claim we are and exclude our

history and literature from the newly emerging multicultural canon are our oppressors" (34). On the other side of the disavowal coin, the editors of *Race Traitor,* a journal whose slogan reads, "Treason to whiteness is loyalty to humanity," write that their aim is to serve as an "intellectual center for those seeking to abolish the white race." The journal includes lots of testimonial, autobiographical texts as well as essays, bibliography, reviews, and correspondence. *Race Traitor* is available at newsstands as well as by writing to P.O. Box 603, Cambridge, MA 02140–0005.

38. See Diana Jeater, "Roast Beef and Reggae Music: The Passing of Whiteness," *New Formations* 18 (Winter 1992): 107–121. There is a fine edge between recuperating whiteness and rearticulating it in the progressive sense. Jeater's essay raises many valuable points and questions but I find Yudice's argument to be more complicated and useful.

39. Yudice, "The Limits of Identity Politics," 15.

40. In Allan Bérubé's moving essay, "Intellectual Desire," he records a few of these epithets: "Frenchy, Frog, Creole, Acadien, Métis, Franco, Coonass, Lard-Eater, Dumb Frenchman" (141). Bérubé links the experience of "ethnic shaming" to homophobia: "Growing up Franco, but ashamed to speak our French, gave me the practice I needed in not saying this word that was so often on the tip of my tongue" (145). See Allan Bérubé, "Intellectual Desire," *GLQ* 3, no. 1 (1996): 139–157.

41. Through a treaty agreement in 1777, the U.S. government promised to protect the Maine Indians in exchange for their alliance against the British in the American Revolution. Nevertheless, the government forced the ceding of all Penobscot Indian lands through treaties in 1796 and 1818 and a land sale in 1833. See Duane Champagne, *Native America: Portrait of the Peoples* (Detroit: Visible Ink, 1994), 67–70. For a detailed discussion of the history and culture of the larger Indian nation that included the Penobscots, see Vincent O. Erickson, "Maliseet-Passamaquoddy," in Bruce G. Trigger, ed., *Handbook of North American Indians,* vol. 15 (Washington, D.C.: Smithsonian Institution, 1978), 123–136.

42. For a fascinating look at some little-known histories of Jews in Maine see Judith S. Goldstein, *Crossing Lines: Histories of Jews and Gentiles in Three Communities* (New York: William Morrow, 1992).

43. According to several studies, the Klan reached its apex in membership in 1924. In that year, three to six million men throughout the United States were members of the national movement. Participants in the state of Maine have been estimated at 15,000. The Ku Klux Klan in Maine directed its efforts against French-Canadian and Irish Catholics who had settled in the mill towns and were voting Democrats (upsetting the state's Republican majority); in particular, proposed legislation to divert some state funds to pay for parochial schools excited Klan organiz-

ing and recruiting in the region. See David M. Chalmers, *Hooded Americanism: The History of the Ku Klux Klan* (New York: Franklin Watts, 1965), 274–278; Robert Alan Goldberg, *Hooded Empire: The Ku Klux Klan in Colorado* (Urbana: University of Illinois Press, 1981), 4–5, 178–179; and Charles C. Alexander, *The Ku Klux Klan in the Southwest* (Louisville: University of Kentucky Press, 1965), 176–177.

44. My feelings do not necessarily coincide with my parent's recollections. We all had friends (most of them recent transplants to Maine like ourselves) and there were lots of well-meaning Christians who invited us into their homes and churches for holidays and who treated us with respect and tolerance. I had a best friend who literally drop-kicked my worst anti-semitic tormentor in school and he really did keep a lower profile after her courageous and protective action. I loved her for it—what a pal! But I longed to live in a totally secular site where the blonde Christians did not seem to "rule."

45. A report authored by the Commissioner of the Department of Health and Welfare in 1952 argues that the "principle reason for the current Indian problem" is the "failure of the state of Maine laws relating to the Penobscot and Passama-quoddy Tribes *[sic]* to clearly define the obligations of the State of Maine to these tribes." It is apparent in this report that legal ambiguities about responsibilities and obligations severely hampered Native American standards of living and all economic and cultural development, blocking all kinds of initiatives and change. See David H. Stevens, "Report to Legislative Research Committee regarding Indian Affairs," (Maine Dept. of Health and Welfare, August 4, 1952), 1.

46. See Ward Churchill, "The Earth is Our Mother: Struggles for American Indian Land and Liberation in Contemporary United States," in M. Annette Jaimes, ed., *The State of Native America: Genocide, Colonization, and Resistance* (Boston: South End Press, 1992), 168–69; and John R. Wunder, *"Retained by the People": A History of American Indians and the Bill of Rights* (New York: Oxford University Press, 1994), 167–69.

47. Ella Shohat and Robert Stam have written about the use of Indians as meta-phors for ethnic subjectivity, pointing to the existence of a set of narrative and vis-ual conventions articulated by U.S. Jewish artists and performers. See *Unthinking Eurocentrism*, 240–241.

48. Paul Gilroy, *"There Ain't No Black in the Union Jack": The Cultural Politics of Race and Nation* (Chicago: University of Chicago Press, 1991), 40.

49. For an overview of the "Birmingham School" see Centre for Contempo-rary Cultural Studies, *The Empire Strikes Back: Race and Racism in 70s Britain* (London: Hutchinson, 1982). For a feminist approach, see Floya Anthias and Nira Yuval-Davis, *Racialized Boundaries: Race, Nation, Gender, Color and Class and the Anti-Racist Struggle* (London: Routledge, 1992).

50. University/State Government Partnership Program, *Maine: Fifty Years of Change, 1940–1990* (Orono: University of Maine Press, 1983), 3–5.

51. For a blistering attack on the colonizing properties of the paper industry in Maine, see William C. Osborn, *The Paper Plantation: Ralph Nader's Study Group Report on the Pulp and Paper Industry in Maine* (New York: Viking, 1974), 1.

52. David Roediger, *The Wages of Whiteness: Race and the Making of the American Working Class* (London: Verso, 1991), 8.

53. Néstor García Canclini, *Transforming Modernity: Popular Culture in Mexico* (Austin: University of Texas Press, 1993), 14–15.

54. Inderpal Grewal, "The Postcolonial, Ethnic Studies, and the Diaspora: The Contexts of Ethnic Immigrant/Migrant Cultural Studies in the U.S." *Socialist Review* 24, no. 4 (1994): 46.

55. On the possible practices of such a method, see Caren Kaplan and Inderpal Grewal, "Transnational Feminist Cultural Studies: Beyond the Marxism/Poststructuralism/Feminism Divides," *Positions* 2, no. 2 (Fall 1994): 430–445; and Gayatri Chakravorty Spivak, "Scattered Speculations on the Question of Culture Studies," in *Outside in the Teaching Machine* (New York: Routledge, 1993), 255–284.

56. Spivak, "The Question of Cultural Studies," 278.

57. I have discussed this process of romanticization and mystification in *Questions of Travel: Postmodern Discourses of Displacement* (Durham, NC: Duke University Press, 1996).

58. Ella Shohat, "Staging the Quincentenary: The Middle East and Americas," *Third Text* 21 (Winter 1992–93): 95.

59. Ibid.

60. Ibid., 96.

Chandra Talpade Mohanty

Crafting Feminist Genealogies: On the Geography and Politics of Home, Nation, and Community

Why craft genealogies in conversations about "multicultural feminism?" At a time when globalization (and monoculturalism) is the primary economic and cultural practice to capture and hold hostage the material resources and economic and political choices of vast numbers of the world's population, what are the concrete challenges for feminists of varied genealogies working together? Within the context of the history of feminist struggle in the U.S.A., the 1980s were a period of euphoria and hope for feminists of color, gay and lesbian, and anti-racist, white feminists. Excavating subjugated knowledges and histories in order to craft decolonized, oppositional racial and sexual identities and political strategies that posed direct challenges to the gender, class, race, and sexual regimes of the capitalist U.S. nation-state anchored the practice of anti-racist, multicultural feminisms.

In 1998, however, I believe the challenges are somewhat different. Globalization—or, the unfettered mobility of capital and the accompanying erosion and reconstitution of local and national economic and political resources, and of democratic processes; the post–cold war U.S. imperialist state; and the trajectories of identity-based social movements in the 1980s and 1990s—constitutes the ground for transnational feminist engagement as we approach the twenty-first century. Multicultural feminism that is radical, anti-racist, and non-heterosexist thus needs to take on a hegemonic capitalist regime and conceive of itself as also crossing national and regional borders. Questions of "home," "belonging," "nation," and "community" thus become profoundly complicated.

One concrete task feminist educators, artists, scholars, and activists face is that of historicizing and denaturalizing the ideas, beliefs, and values of global capital such that underlying exploitative social relations and structures are made visible. This means being attentive not only to the grand narrative or "myth" of capitalism as "democracy," but also to the mythologies feminists of various races, nations, classes, and sexualities have inherited about each other. I believe one of the greatest challenges we (feminists) face is this task of recognizing and undoing the ways in which we colonize and objectify our different histories and cultures, thus colluding with hegemonic processes of domination and rule. Dialogue across differences is thus fraught with tension, competitiveness, and pain. Just as radical or critical multiculturalism cannot be the mere sum or coexistence of different cultures in a profoundly unequal, colonized world, multicultural feminism cannot assume the existence of a dialogue among feminists from different communities without specifying a just and ethical basis for such a dialogue.

Undoing ingrained racial and sexual mythologies within feminist communities requires, in Jacqui Alexander's words, that we "become fluent in each other's histories." It also requires seeking "unlikely coalitions" (Angela Davis) and, I would add, clarifying the ethics and meaning of dialogue. What are the conditions, the knowledges, and the attitudes that make a non-colonized dialogue possible? How can we craft a dialogue anchored in equality, respect, and dignity for all peoples? In other words, I want to suggest that one of the most crucial challenges for a critical multicultural feminism is working out how to engage in ethical and caring dialogues (and revolutionary struggles) across the divisions, conflicts, and individualist identity formations that interweave feminist communities in the late twentieth-century U.S.A. And defining genealogies is one crucial element in creating such a dialogue.

Just as the very meaning and basis for dialogue across difference and power needs to be analyzed and carefully crafted, the way we define genealogies also poses a challenge. Genealogies that not only specify and illuminate historical and cultural differences, but also envision and enact common political and intellectual projects *across* these differences constitute a crucial element of the work of building critical multicultural feminism.

To this end I offer a personal, anecdotal meditation on the politics of gender and race in the construction of South Asian identity in North America. My location in the U.S.A. is symptomatic of large numbers of migrants, nomads, immigrants, workers across the globe for whom notions of home, identity, geography, and history are infinitely complicated in the late twentieth century. Questions of nation(ality), and of "belonging" (witness the situation of South Asians in Africa) are constitutive of the Indian diaspora.

Emotional and Political Geographies of Belonging

On a TWA flight on my way back to the U.S. from a conference in the Netherlands, the white professional man sitting next to me asks: a) which school do I go to? and b) when do I plan to go home?—all in the same breath. I put on my most professorial demeanor (somewhat hard in crumpled blue jeans and cotton T-shirt—this uniform only works for white male professors, who, of course, could command authority even in swimwear!) and inform him that I teach at a small liberal arts college in up-state New York, and that I have lived in the U.S. for fifteen years. At this point, my work is in the U.S., not in India. (This is no longer entirely true—my work is also with feminists and grass-roots activists in India, but he doesn't need to know this.) Being "mistaken" for a graduate student seems endemic to my existence in this country: few Third World women are granted professional (i.e., adult) and/or permanent (one is always a student!) status in the U.S., even if we exhibit clear characteristics of adulthood, like grey hair and facial lines. The man ventures a further question: what do I teach? On hearing "women's studies," he becomes quiet and we spend the next eight hours in polite silence. He has decided that I do not fit into any of his categories, but what can you expect from a *Feminist* (an *Asian* one!) anyway? I feel vindicated and a little superior—even though I know he doesn't really feel "put in his place." Why should he? He claims a number of advantages in this situation: white skin, maleness, and citizenship privileges. Judging by his enthusiasm about expensive "ethnic food" in Amsterdam, and his J. Crew clothes, I figured class difference (economic or cultural) wasn't exactly a concern in our interaction. We both appeared to have similar social access as "professionals."

I have been asked the "home" question (when are you going home?) periodically for fifteen years now. Leaving aside the subtly racist implications of the question (go home, you don't belong), I am still not satisfied with my response. What is home? The place I was born? Where I grew up? Where my parents live? Where I live and work as an adult? Where I locate my community, my people? Who are "my people"? Is home a geographical space, a historical space, an emotional, sensory space? Home is always so crucial to immigrants and migrants—I even write about it in scholarly texts, perhaps to avoid addressing it as an issue that is also very personal. What interests me is the meaning of home for immigrants and migrants. I am convinced that this question—how one understands and defines home—is a profoundly political one.

Plate 61: *In 1930 Sue Shee Wong Came* and *You Gotta Be Brave*
from *Baby Jack Rice Story*, 1993
Black and white reproduction from color slide
Mixed media: rice sack, silkscreen, sequins, thread, 20 × 32″ and 26 × 34″
Flo Oy Wong
Courtesy of the artist

Since settled notions of territory, community, geography, and history don't work for us, what does it really mean to be "South Asian" in the U.S.? Obviously, I was not South Asian in India, I was Indian. What else could one be but "Indian" at a time when a successful national independence struggle had given birth to a socialist democratic nation-state? This was the beginning of the decolonization of the Third World. Regional geography (South Asia) appeared less relevant as a mark of identification than citizenship in a postcolonial independent nation on the cusp of economic and political autonomy. However, in North America, identification as South Asian (in addition to Indian, in my case) takes on its own logic. "South Asian" refers to folks of Indian, Pakistani, Sri Lankan, Bangladeshi, Kashmiri, and Burmese (now Myanmar) origin. Identifying as South Asian rather than Indian adds numbers and hence power within the U.S. state. Besides, regional differences among those from different South Asian countries are often less relevant than the commonalities based on our experiences and histories of immigration, treatment, and location in the U.S.

Let me reflect a bit on the way I identify myself, and the way the U.S. state and its institutions categorize me. Perhaps thinking through the various labels will lead me to the question of home and identity. In 1977, I arrived in the U.S. on a F1 visa (a student visa). At that time, my definition of myself—a graduate student in education at the University of Illinois— and the "official" definition of me (a student allowed into the country on a F1 visa) obviously coincided. Then I was called a "foreign student" and expected to go "home" (to India, even though my parents were in Nigeria at the time) after getting my Ph.D. Let's face it, this is the assumed trajectory for a number of Indians, especially the post-independence (my) generation, who come to the U.S. for graduate study.

However, this was not to be my trajectory. I quickly discovered that being a foreign student, and a woman at that, meant being either dismissed as irrelevant (the quiet Asian woman stereotype), treated in racist ways (my teachers asked if I understood English and if they should speak slower and louder so that I could keep up—this in spite of my inheritance of the Queen's English and British colonialism!), or celebrated and exoticized ("You are so smart! Your accent is even better than that of Americans"—a little Anglophilia at work here, even though all my Indian colleagues insist we speak English the Indian way!).

The most significant transition I made at that time was the one from "foreign student" to "student of color." Once I was able to "read" my experiences in terms of race, and to read race and racism as they are written into the social and political fabric of the U.S., practices of racism and sexism became the analytic and political lenses through which I was able to anchor myself here. Of course, none of this happened in isolation; friends, colleagues, comrades, classes, books, films, arguments, and dialogues were constitutive of my political education as a women of color in the U.S.

In the late 1970s and early 1980s feminism was gaining momentum on American campuses, it was in the air, in the classrooms, on the streets. However, what attracted me wasn't feminism as the mainstream media and white women's studies departments defined it. Instead, it was a very specific kind of feminism, the feminism of U.S. women of color and Third World women, that spoke to me. In thinking through the links among gender, race, and class in their U.S. manifestations, I was for the first time able to think through my own gendered, classed, postcolonial history. In the early 1980s, reading Audre Lorde, Nawal el Sadaawi, Cherríe Moraga, bell hooks, Gloria Joseph, Paula Gunn Allen, Barbara Smith, Merle Woo, and Mitsuye Yamada, among others, generated a sort of recognition that was intangible but very inspiring. A number of actions, decisions, and organizing efforts at that time led me to a sense of home and community in relation to women of color in the U.S. Home, not as a comfortable, stable, inherited, and familiar space, but instead as an imaginative, politically charged space in which the familiarity and sense of affection and commitment lay in shared collective analysis of social injustice, as well as a vision of radical transformation. Political solidarity and a sense of family could be melded together imaginatively to create a strategic space I could call "home." Politically, intellectually, and emotionally I owe an enormous debt to feminists of color—especially to the sisters who have sustained me over the years. Even though our attempt to start the Women of Color Institute for Radical Research and Action fell through, the spirit of this vision, and the friendships it generated, still continue to nurture me. A number of us, including Barbara Smith, Papusa Molina, Jacqui Alexander, Gloria Joseph, Mitsuye Yamada, Kesho Scott, among others, met in 1984 to discuss the possibility of such an Institute. The Institute never really happened, but I still hope we will pull it off one day.

For me, engagement as a feminist of color in the U.S. made possible an intellectual and political genealogy of being Indian that was radically challenging as well as profoundly activist. Notions of home and community began to be located within a deeply political space where racialization and gender and class relations and histories became the prism through which I understood, however partially, what it could mean to be South Asian in North America. Interestingly, this recognition also forced me to re-examine the meanings attached to home and community in India.

What I chose to claim, and continue to claim, is a history of anti-colonialist, feminist struggle in India. The stories I recall, the ones that I re-tell and claim as my own, determine the choices and decisions I make in the present and the future. I did not want to accept a history of Hindu chauvinist (bourgeois) upward mobility (even though this characterizes a section of my extended family). We all choose partial, interested stories/histories—perhaps not as deliberately as I am making it sound here, but, consciously or unconsciously, these choices about our past(s) often deter-mine the logic of our present.

Having always kept my distance from conservative, upwardly mobile Indian immigrants to whom the South Asian world was divided into green card holders and non-green card holders, the only South Asian links I allowed and cultivated were with Indians with whom I shared a political vision. This considerably limited my community. Racist and sexist experi-ences in graduate school and after made it imperative that I understand the U.S. in terms of its history of racism, imperialism, and patriarchal relations, specifically in relation to Third World immigrants. After all, we were then into the Reagan–Bush years, when the neo-conservative backlash made it impossible to ignore the rise of racist, anti-feminist, and homophobic atti-tudes, practices, and institutions. Any purely culturalist or nostalgic/senti-mental definition of being "Indian" or "South Asian" was inadequate. Such a definition fueled the "model minority" myth. And this subse-quently constituted us as "outsiders/foreigners" or as interest groups that sought or had obtained the American dream.

In the mid-1980s, the labels changed: I went from being a "foreign student" to being a "resident alien." I have always thought that this designa-tion was a stroke of inspiration on the part of the U.S. state, since it accu-rately names the experience and status of immigrants, especially immigrants of color. The flip side of "resident alien" is "illegal alien," another inspired designation. One can be either a resident or illegal immigrant, but one is al-ways an alien. There is no confusion here, no melting pot ideology or nar-ratives of assimilation: one's status as an "alien" is primary. Being legal requires identity papers. (It is useful to recall that the "passport"—and by extension the concept of nation-states and the sanctity of their borders—came into being after World War I.)

One must be stamped as legitimate (that is, not-gay-or-lesbian and not-communist!) by the Immigration and Naturalization Service (INS). The INS is one of the central disciplinary arms of the U.S. government. It polices the borders and controls all border crossings, especially those into the U.S. In fact, the INS is also one of the primary forces that institutionalizes race differences in the public arena, thus regulating notions of home, legitimacy, and economic access to the "American dream" for many of us. For instance, carrying a green card documenting resident alien status in the U.S. is clearly very different from carrying an American passport, which is proof of U.S. citizenship. The former allows one to enter the U.S. with few hassles; the latter often allows one to breeze through the borders and ports of entry of other countries, especially countries that happen to be trading partners (much of western Europe and Japan, among others), or in an unequal relationship with the U.S. (much of the non-communist Third World). At a time when a capitalist free market economy is seen (falsely) as synonymous with the values attached to democracy, an American passport can open many doors. However, just carrying an American passport is no insurance against racism and unequal and unjust treatment within the U.S. It would be important to compare the racialization of second-generation South Asian Americans. For example, one significant difference between these two generations would be between experiencing racism as a phenomenon specific to the U.S., versus growing up in the ever-present shadow of racism in the case of South Asians born in the U.S. This suggests that the psychic effects of racism would be different for these two constituencies. In addition, questions of home, identity, and history take on very different meanings for South Asians born in North America. But to be fair, this comparison requires a whole other reflection that is beyond the scope of this essay.

Home/Nation/Community: The Politics of being NRI (Non-Resident Indian)

Rather obstinately, I have refused to give up my Indian passport and have chosen to remain a resident alien in the U.S. for the last decade or so. Which leads me to reflect on the complicated meanings attached to holding Indian citizenship while making a life for myself in the U.S.A. In India, what does it mean to have a green card, to be an expatriate? What does it mean to visit Bombay every two to four years, and still call it home? Why does speaking in Marathi (my mother tongue) become a measure and confirmation of home? What are the politics of being a part of the majority and the "absent elite" in India, while being a minority and a racialized "other" in the U.S.? And do feminist politics, or advocating feminism, have the same meanings and urgencies in these different geographical and political contexts?

Some of these questions hit me smack in the face during a recent visit to India, in December 1992, post-Ayodhya (the infamous destruction of the Babri Masjid in Ayodhya by Hindu fundamentalists on December 6, 1992). In earlier, rather infrequent visits (once every four or five years was all I could afford), my green card designated me as an object of envy, privilege, and status within my extended family. Of course, the same green card has always been viewed with suspicion by leftist and feminist friends who (quite understandably) demand evidence of my ongoing commitment to a socialist and democratic India. During this visit, however, with emotions running high within my family, my green card marked me as an outsider who couldn't possibly understand the "Muslim problem" in India. I was made aware of being an "outsider" in two profoundly troubling shouting matches with my uncles, who voiced the most incredibly hostile sentiments against Muslims. Arguing that India was created as a secular state and that democracy had everything to do with equality for all groups (majority and minority) got me nowhere. The very fundamentals of democratic citizenship in India were/are being undermined and redefined as "Hindu."

Bombay was one of the cities hardest hit with waves of communal violence following the events of Ayodhya. The mobilization of Hindu fundamentalists, even paramilitary organizations, over the last century and especially since the mid-1940s, had brought Bombay to a juncture at which the most violently racist discourse about Muslims seemed to be woven into the fabric of acceptable daily life. Racism was normalized in the popular imagination such that it became almost impossible to raise questions in public about the ethics or injustice of racial/ethnic/religious discrimination. I could not assume a distanced posture towards religion anymore. Too many injustices were being committed in my name.

Although born a Hindu, I have always considered myself a non-practicing one—religion had always felt rather repressive when I was growing up. I enjoyed the rituals but resisted the authoritarian hierarchies of organized Hinduism. However, the Hinduism touted by fundamentalist organizations like the RSS (Rashtriya Swayamsevak Sangh, a paramilitary Hindu fundamentalist organization founded in the 1930s) and the Shiv Sena (a Maharashtrian chauvinist, fundamentalist, fascist political organization that has amassed a significant voice in Bombay politics and government) was one that even I, in my ignorance, recognized as reactionary and distorted. But this discourse was real—hate-filled rhetoric against Muslims appeared to be the mark of a "loyal Hindu." It was unbelievably heart-wrenching to see my hometown become a war zone with whole streets set on fire, and a daily death count to rival any major territorial border war. The smells and textures of Bombay, of home, which had always comforted and nurtured me, were violently disrupted. The scent of fish drying on the lines at the fishing village in Danda was submerged in the smell of burning straw and grass as whole *bastis* (*chawls*) were burned to the ground. The very topography, language, and relationships that constituted "home" were exploding. What does community mean in this context? December 1992 both clarified as well as complicated for me the meanings attached to being an Indian citizen, a Hindu, an educated woman, a feminist, and a perma-nent resident in the U.S. in ways that I have yet to resolve. After all, it is often moments of crisis that make us pay careful attention to questions of identity. Sharp polarizations force one to make choices (not in order to take sides, but in order to accept responsibility) and to clarify one's own ana-lytic, political, and emotional topographies.

I learned that combatting the rise of Hindu fundamentalism was a necessary ethical imperative for all socialists, feminists and Hindus of con-science. Secularism, if it meant absence of religion, was no longer a viable position. From a feminist perspective, it became clear that the battle for women's minds and hearts was very much center stage in the Hindu funda-mentalist rhetoric on the social position of women. (The journals *The Eco-nomic and Political Weekly of India* and *Manushi* are good sources for this work.)

Religious fundamentalist constructions of women embody the nexus of morality, sexuality, and *Nation*—a nexus of great importance for femi-nists. Similar to Christian, Islamic, and Jewish fundamentalist discourses, the construction of femininity and masculinity, especially in relation to the idea of the Nation, are central to Hindu fundamentalist rhetoric and mobili-zations. Women are not only mobilized in the "service" of the Nation, but they also become the ground on which discourses of morality and national-ism are written. For instance, the RSS mobilizes primarily middle-class women in the name of a family-oriented, Hindu Nation, much like the Christian Right does in the U.S. But discourses of morality and nation are also embodied in the normative policing of women's sexuality (witness the surveillance and control of women's dress in the name of morality by the contemporary Iranian state). Thus, one of the central challenges In-dian feminists face at this time is how to rethink the relationship of national-

Plate 62: *Look at Me/Look at You*, 1995
Black and white reproduction of installation
Yoshiko Shimada
Photo courtesy of The Power Plant, Contemporary Art Gallery at Harbourfront Centre,
Toronto
Photo: Cheryl O'Brien
Courtesy of the artist and Ota Fine Arts, Tokyo

Chandra Talpade Mohanty

ism and feminism in the context of religious identities. In addition to the fundamentalist mobilization that is tearing the country apart, the recent incursions of the International Monetary Fund and the World Bank, with their structural adjustment programs that are supposed to "discipline" the Indian economy, are redefining the meaning of postcoloniality and of democracy in India. Categories like gender, race, caste/class are profoundly and visibly unstable at such times of crisis. These categories must thus be analyzed in relation to contemporary reconstructions of womanhood and manhood in a *global* arena increasingly dominated by religious fundamentalist movements, the IMF, the World Bank, and the relentless economic and ideological colonization of much of the world by multinationals based in the U.S., Japan, and Europe. In all these global economic and cultural/ideological processes, women occupy a crucial position.

In India, unlike most countries, the sex ratio has declined since the early 1900s. According to the 1991 census, the ratio is now 929 women to 1,000 men, one of the lowest (if not *the* lowest) sex ratios in the world. Women produce seventy to eighty percent of all the food in India, and have always been the hardest hit by environmental degradation and poverty. The contradictions between civil law and Hindu and Muslim personal laws affect women but rarely men. Horrific stories about the deliberate genocide of female infants as a result of sex determination procedures like amniocentesis, and recent incidents of *sati* (self-immolation by women on the funeral pyres of their husbands) have even hit the mainstream American media. Gender and religious (racial) discrimination are thus urgent, life-threatening issues for women in India. In 1998, politically conscious Indian citizenship necessitates taking such fundamentally feminist issues seriously. In fact, these are the very same issues South Asian feminists in the U.S. need to address. My responsibility to combat and organize against the regressive and violent repercussions of Hindu fundamentalist mobilizations in India extends to my life in North America. After all, much of the money that sustains the fundamentalist movement is raised and funneled through organizations in the U.S.

On Race, Color, and Politics: Being South Asian in North America

It is almost exactly three years since I wrote the bulk of this essay,[1] and as I re-read it, I am struck by the presence of the journeys and border-crossings that weave into and anchor my thinking about genealogies. The very crossing of regional, national, cultural, and geographical borders seems to *enable* me to reflect on questions of identity, community, and politics. In the past years I journeyed to and lived among peoples in San Diego, California; Albuquerque, New Mexico; London, England; and Cuttack, India. My appearance as a brown woman with short, dark, greying hair remained the same, but in each of these living spaces I learned something slightly different about being South Asian in North America; about being a brown women in the midst of other brown women with different histories and genealogies.

I want to conclude with a brief reflection on my journeys to California and New Mexico since they complicate further the question of being South Asian in North America. A rather obvious fact, which had not been experientially visible to me earlier, is that the color line differs depending on one's geographical location in the U.S. Having lived on the East Coast these many years, my designation as "brown," "Asian," "South Asian," "Third World," and "immigrant," has everything to do with definitions of "blackness" (understood specifically as African-American). However, San Diego, with its histories of immigration and racial struggle, its shared border with Mexico, its predominantly brown (Chicano and Asian-American) color line, and its virulent anti-immigrant culture unsettled my East Coast definitions of race and racialization. I could pass as Latina until I spoke my "Indian" English, and then being South Asian became a question of (in)visibility and foreignness. Being South Asian here was synonymous with being alien, non-American.

Similarly, in New Mexico, where the normative meanings of race and color find expression in the relations between Native American, Chicano, and Anglo communities, being South Asian was a matter of being simultaneously visible and invisible as a brown woman. Here, too, my browness and facial structure marked me visibly as sometimes Latina, sometimes Native American (evidenced by being hailed numerous times in the street as both). Even Asian, as in being from a part of the world called "Asia," had less meaning in New Mexico, especially since Asian was synonymous with "East Asian," and "South" always fell out. Thus, while I could share some experiences with Latinas and Native American women, for instance, the experience of being an "alien"—an outsider within, a woman outside the purview of legitimate U.S. citizenship—my South Asian genealogy also set me apart. Shifting the color line by crossing the geography and history of the American West and Southwest thus foregrounded questions about being South Asian in a space where, first, my browness was not read against blackness, and second, Asian was already definitively cast as

East Asian. In this context, what is the relation of South Asian to Asian-American (read: East Asian American)? And why does it continue to feel more appropriate, experientially and strategically, to call myself a woman of color or Third World woman? Geographies have never coincided with the politics of race. And claiming racial identities based on history, social location, and experience is always a matter of collective analysis and politics. Thus, while geographical spaces provide historical and cultural anchors (Marathi, Bombay, and India are fundamental to my sense of myself), it is the deeper values and strategic approach to questions of economic and social justice and collective anti-capitalist struggle that constitute my feminism. Perhaps this is why journeys across the borders of regions and nations always provoke reflections on home, identity, and politics for me: there is no clear or obvious *fit* between geography, race, and politics for someone like me. I am always called on to define and redefine these relationships—"race," "Asian-ness," and "browness" are not *embedded* in me, but histories of colonialism, racism, sexism, and nationalism, as well as of priviledge (class and status), are involved in my relation to white people and people of color in the U.S.A.

Let me now circle back to the place I began: defining genealogies as a crucial aspect of crafting critical multicultural feminist practice, and the meanings I have come to give to home, community, and identity. By exploring the relationship between being a South Asian immigrant in America and an expatriate Indian citizen (NRI) in India, I have tried, however partially and anecdotally, to clarify the complexities of home and community for this particular feminist of color/South Asian in North America. The genealogy I have created for myself here is partial and deliberate. It is a genealogy that I find emotionally and politically enabling—it is part of the genealogy that underlies my self-identification as an educator involved in a pedagogy of liberation. Of course, my history and experiences are far messier and not at all as linear as this narrative makes them sound. But then the very process of constructing a narrative for oneself—of telling a story—imposes a certain linearity and coherence that is never entirely there. But that is the lesson, perhaps, especially for us immigrants and migrants: that is, that home, community and identity all fall somewhere between the histories and experiences we inherit and the political choices we make through alliances, solidarities, and friendships.

One very concrete influence on my creating this particular space for myself has been my recent involvement in two grassroots organizations, one in India and the other in the U.S. The former, an organization called

Awareness, is based in Orissa and works to empower the rural poor. The group's focus is political education (similar to Paolo Friere's notion of "conscientization"), and its members have recently begun very consciously to organize rural women. Grassroots Leadership of North Carolina is the U.S. organization I work with. It is a multiracial group of organizers (largely African-American and white) working to build a poor and working people's movement in the American South. While the geographical, historical and political contexts are different in the case of these two organizations, my involvement in them is very similar, as is my sense that there are clear connections to be made between the work of the two organizations. In addition, I think that the issues, analyses, and strategies for organizing for social justice are also quite similar. This particular commitment to work with grassroots organizers in the two places I call home is not accidental. It is very much the result of the genealogy I have traced here. After all, it has taken me over a decade to make these commitments to grassroots work in both spaces. In part, I have defined what it means to be South Asian by educating myself about, and reflecting on, the histories and experiences of African-American, Latina, West Indian, African, European-American, and other constituencies in North America. Such definitions and understandings do provide a genealogy, but a genealogy that is always relational and fluid as well as urgent and necessary.

Note

1. An earlier version of this essay, entitled "Defining Genealogies: Feminist Reflections on Being South Asian in North America," was published in Women of South Asian Descent Collective, eds., *Our Feet Walk the Sky: Writings by Women of the South Asian Diaspora* (San Francisco: Aunt Lute Books, 1993). This essay is dedicated to the memory of Lanubai and Gauribai Vijaykar, maternal grandaunts, who were single, educated, financially independent, and tall (over six feet) at a time when it was against the grain to be any one of these things; and to Audre Lorde, teacher, sister, friend, whose words and presence continue to challenge, inspire, and nurture me.

Inderpal Grewal

On the New Global Feminism and the Family of Nations: Dilemmas of Transnational Feminist Practice

A few years ago in California I attended a conference on human rights in India, organized by a local Sikh group.[1] At that conference, which focused on violations against Sikhs in Punjab and Muslims in Kashmir, I was asked to speak about women and human rights in the Sikh community. Also on the panel was a Euro-American male doctor from a U.S.-based human rights organization who had been to Kashmir and was invited to speak on what he had witnessed and recorded there. I spoke about forms of violence within the community, and the problems of Sikh nationalism when both the police and the insurgency groups were comprised of Sikh men. The doctor presented facts and pictures of women raped by the state authorities, and talked about the ways in which [women's] human rights were being violated by the Indian state.

Most of what I said was not warmly received by the predominantly male Sikh audience since I did not make the "us" and "them" argument about those raped and their rapists, an argument this audience seemed to desire. The doctor, on the other hand, was warmly received. He provided the audience with tangible "information" about Kashmiri women who had been raped by Indian army personnel. He shared statistics, testimonies, and photographs. He presented the Indian army as the rapists and torturers while Kashmiri men and women were portrayed as victims; by implication, the work of his human rights group was to bring these "objective" facts to light.

The language and visual evidence of "human rights violations" was of importance to the doctor's presentation. His slides—mainly of women who he presented as having been raped—enabled a voyeuristic male spectatorship. Such a spectatorship brought together the audience to construct masculinity as the condition of being unrapable and of being protectors of those photographed and enumerated rapable (female) bodies. The visual evidence of human rights violations, so pervasive in discourses used by organizations such as Amnesty International, relies on modernizing First World narratives of the Third World, representing poor women and children as victims in distress and in struggles against overwhelming odds. Such narratives universalize the Third World as a region of aberrant violence, and this notion of aberration occurs in relation to a First World that is seldom included as violating its women. The First World, imperialist, militaristic, violent, and exploitative, is rarely present in this visual evidence of human rights violations. Its absence constructs the authoritative and objective viewer and rescuer, always outside of history.

The masculinities formed by employing this gaze are linked because they depend on a heterosexual discourse of women as nation, as land, as property.[2] To one such as myself, who saw herself more as an activist working in the area of violence against women (which includes economic violence as well) rather than an activist opposed to a singular form of violence such as rape, and as a feminist and a Sikh woman who studies nationalism, this panel was a difficult experience. I was *participating* in the constructions of masculinity as "international protectors" (the doctor), and masculinity as "nationalist protectors" (the audience) within which Sikh women had merely metaphoric existence, i.e., it was in the name of the Sikh women's protection that masculinities and nationalist struggles seemed to be formed. It seemed to me that many elements of the discourse of human rights needed to be questioned. I began to be interested, not only in the objects of rescue created by human rights discourse, but also in the subject formation of those who used and deployed this discourse.

I learned a lot that day. First of all, I learned about the ways in which human rights discourse is applied so differentially by all those who participate in it. I saw that it is an important discourse in contemporary conditions to construct very different subject positions in a linked way—the doctor, as a scientific researcher, fact finder, and "objective" viewer, could make links with the audience, a primarily male, middle-class, Sikh audience of a particular dominant caste, constructing nationalist masculinity. Second, the discourse of rape is acceptable to nationalist discourse only when the perpetrator is an outsider. If human rights violations include the rape of women, the perpetrator of the crime has to be an outsider (the state, a stranger, the opposing side in a struggle); demarcation between public and private is essential. Third, it is important for heterosexual patriarchy to ignore the rape of men as a common but unspoken occurrence in war and as a common method of torture. Torture could include the rapes of men but these are never *seen* as rapes, nor the perpetrators believed to be inflicting same-sex sexual violence, since nationalist discourse within modernity and postmodernity constructs itself as heterosexual. Fourth, within every community that is able to voice its concerns about the violation of rights, there are those groups and individuals who are unable or unwilling to participate in open protest or who are unwittingly incorporated into it (for example, the many women of the Sikh community in that region of California who, for multiple reasons, did not participate in that discussion at the conference). And finally, I learned that one cannot view the practices of "grass-roots" groups, such as this community-based group that had set up the conference, in a celebratory way that ignores the complexity of their positioning as well as the problematic power relations inscribed in their efforts. The discourse of human rights and pain and torture is so dramatically powerful that it can silence many discourses of exploitation and oppression. What are the silences of human rights discourse, I wondered?

It is not unusual for men of the Sikh community in India and elsewhere, who are already seen as violent and aberrantly hypermasculine by a dominant Hindu state nationalism, to set up such a conference.[3] Many nationalisms share the discourse of the protection of women. Stereotypes of Sikh men, who often have beards and wear turbans, abound in India and elsewhere as racism in the West and a dominant Hindu nationalism in India construct their others. I am reminded of a scholar (who might call himself a secular and "modern" "Indian" and believe his religion to be irrelevant to his identity), who one day among all his chauvinism about the greatness of the Indian cricket team, began to tell me about "the first time he had seen a Sikh man." Such ethnocentrism, in addition to the violence used by the Indian state and its repressive measures in Punjab and elsewhere has no doubt contributed to the conference that I participated in. My brothers, cousins, friends, and relatives are by now used to the numbers of names yelled out at them in streets in Calcutta, London, California, and New York; the scars of these experiences are many. These experiences come alive and are recast within Sikh nationalist struggles in India and are also resonant in the United States, since such movements in India create political communities in the diaspora within the context of a problematic and liberal multiculturalism and a racist white America.[4]

While a prime minister of India, Indira Gandhi, began the discourse of Sikh men as terrorists, in the United States, as well as within South

Asian communities, writers such as Bharati Mukherjee,[5] Bhapsi Sidhwa,[6] Chitra Devakaruni,[7] and filmmakers such as Srinivas Krishna[8] and Pratibha Parmar,[9] have continued to use various forms of representational violence against Sikhs. Like so many political issues, the violence of representational practices occurs in complex, intertwined, and related ways. Human rights discourse makes its claims through visual and written representative practices whose power relations must be studied. Therefore, when other human rights movements have come to my attention, I have tried to think about them in terms of what I learned at the conference that day in California.

In this essay, I want to examine the practices used to depict the objects of violations as well as the subject-constitution of those doing the depicting and representing. Who is speaking for whom? What relations of power enable them to speak for others? What forms of violence do these representations perform? If it is not individuals but non-governmental and non-profit groups that are speaking, then we must engage critically with the nature of the "local" and "grass-roots" claims that are being made by these groups. What "community" do they represent? In the United States at present, where the "local" is being fought over by both the Left and the Right, these questions seem to be even more urgent. In attempting to insert critical and progressive feminist politics in thinking and acting within and outside human rights discourse, my focus is the advocacy in the United States of women's rights as human rights and the application of human rights claims for refugee asylum in the United States. I look at the sites within which these discourses are spoken in order to see who uses human rights and for what. Since utterances only make meanings within contexts, I examine the cultural contexts within which human rights can be hailed, instead of examining the legal and political mechanisms of human rights, which have been analyzed by experts in many publications.[10] My concern here is the ways certain goals regarding human rights do not become dominant or lose their direction (e.g., socioeconomic rights of women from "developing countries"), and how those that can be conjoined to problematic discourses (e.g., rights around political asylum linked to domestic violence and rape) do become powerful. I look at the practices of the U.N., the U.S. state (the Immigration and Naturalization Service and gender-based asylum in particular), and non-profit organizations in the United States working on domestic violence issues, to examine how these are limited in their struggle to remove the exploitation and poverty of women worldwide because of connections to the American state and nation. I examine the ways the nation and the state (the U.S. in particular) infiltrate the "grass roots," so that it may be dangerous to romanticize NGOs (Non-Governmental Organizations),[11] such as those that met at the Beijing conference NGO forum, and likewise to romanticize "local" or "grass-roots" groups in their incredible diversity by assuming them to be outside the power/knowledge formations of dominant state frameworks. At the end of the essay, I suggest that NGOs in the United States and elsewhere, because of their increasing global role, would benefit from problematizing state and neo-colonial knowledge formations in their work.

Women and the Universalizing Discourse of Human Rights

As scholars such as Rajni Kothari have argued,[12] the question of human rights remains eurocentric in many of its assumptions and goals, even though it may be one of the few tools available to struggle for the rights of the disenfranchised. As Kothari puts it, human rights are grounded in the assumption of an "individualistic ethic and take as a philosophical given that social formations are homogeneous and hence amenable to universal formulations of individual and community, liberty and democracy."[13] As a formation conceived by liberal democratic states, the claim to human rights has been a means to assert the rights of the individual as a private, autonomous being.[14] Rights discourse thus cannot be adopted for the liberation of many of those outside such notions of a polity, or for those who would argue against such universalizing. Consequently, it is important to ask whether women in many parts of the world can be seen as autonomous individuals outside the structure of the family or whether the problem of their oppression can be addressed by attacking the very families that support many women.[15]

In response to the individualistic assumptions of most dominant forms of human rights, the notion of "group rights" has emerged as a means to preserve "tradition" (for example, in the struggles of the Native Indian groups in North America). However, as Rhoda Howard argues, such a struggle may create incompatibilities and conflicts on issues such as who belongs or does not belong to the group, and redefinitions and representations of traditions that define the group.[16]

It is not clear whether the struggle for women's human rights is to be seen as a group right, since women cannot be seen as one group with a common tradition, and the term woman carries within itself the notion of an autonomous individual.[17] Yet within the modern period, women have

Plate 63: *Women's Rights are Human Rights*
Photo taken at the NGO Forum on Women, Huairou, September 1995
The NGO Forum was held parallel to the Fourth World Conference on Women, Beijing, 1995
Photo: Anne S. Walker (IWTC)
Courtesy of International Women's Tribune Center, Inc.

become constructed and politicized as a group of individuals who articulate their oppression collectively in certain instances, so that their rights are being seen as collective rights rather than group rights. The emergence of collective rights has galvanized the movement for women's rights as human rights to become a new paradigm for organizing women globally. The 1995 Beijing conference highlighted this framework as a unifying one for the NGO conference, suggesting a new impetus in unifying and networking across national and international divides.

The idea of collective rights remains problematic because it assumes that "women" live their lives as "women" solely, rather than as parts of other communities; or, that women see themselves as autonomous individuals.[18] It is not possible to assume that the subjectivity of those persons termed "women" are constructed solely by gender. The multiple subject positions of persons termed "women" argue for differences that include gender as one aspect of their exploitation. Thus, while we may see women's human rights as the struggle of a collectivity, the collective consists more precisely of autonomous individuals believed to be engaged in a common struggle, since it is not tradition or biology that brings them together but it is gender, a highly contingent and diverse formation.

Consequently, the women's human rights struggle attempts to universalize and construct the category of "women," at the same time as it addresses women's situations in important though limited ways. In forming an "international" struggle, in which all women from all nations can speak to or understand each other or work together for a "common" goal, the widely disseminated notion of essential gender finds new impetus, though not always in alignment with all women of the world, since gendering is done by multiple agents in a society and in widely divergent ways. The struggle to keep various kinds of difference alive in the womens' human rights arena is a difficult one, made even more difficult by the asymmetries of power within states, nations, and groups that both construct and fracture contemporary global conditions.[19] It is these asymmetries that become highlighted within various arenas of human rights discourse.

The U.N., the U.S., and NGOs

Human rights discourse took on new impetus with the U.N. World Conference on Human Rights in June 1993. Human rights instruments have become, for the most part, one of the few recourses for many who feel exploited and are able to articulate their feeling in the terms of rights, absent the possibilities of world divided into two camps (Soviet and U.S.) in which alliance with one camp or other was necessary for survival. Human rights struggles seem to be even more urgent now under global economic conditions, when internationalism as a promise of equality, peace and justice among states has receded in the face of a world of transnational corporations, fragmenting yet repressive nation-states, and emerging cosmopolitan groups.[20]

At the same time, given the increasing importance of NGOs, the role of the U.N. has been changing in recent years, with an increasing reliance on the remaining superpower, the United States.[21] Yet in the United States itself, attitudes toward the U.N. remain mixed, given the fragmentation of U.S. nationalism by minority rights, immigration issues, and the importance of race, gender, class, and sexuality in all aspects of political and economic life.[22] The state and the nation are not unified, as many take for granted, especially scholars writing about the "international" arena, who construct it as a unified superpower.[23] The belief in internationalism in the United States and its fragmented communities is tied into race issues and the persistence of nationalist discourse that attempts to keep a hegemonic white America as the "greatest nation in the world." In the United States at the present time, internationalism has decreasing support among many groups from both the Left and the Right. White supremacist groups see the U.N. as an arm of a dangerous "new world order" that is infiltrating the white nation figured as America, revealing within racially dominant groups the split between a cosmopolitan class that benefits directly from global capitalism and a racially dominant group from diverse classes that can retain its power only within a white state.[24]

While organizations such as Amnesty International have waged decades-long battles for political rights, turning to the state and to the U.N. for redress, recent assertions of rights have expanded to socio-economic rights in a global framework, questioning the belief in nation-states as being able to provide for all their citizens, and promoting the rights of all those who are refugees, displaced or stateless. This movement has caused some consternation among conservative supporters of the U.N., especially those alarmed by Clinton's goal of dropping the distinction between "fundamental" rights and the socio-economic ones. The *Wall Street Journal,* for instance, foresees the result to be the United States' becoming "a virtual piggy bank for underdeveloped nations" that could "render the U.N. incapable of sorting out the most basic human-rights problem." While the *Journal* seems to think that socio-economic rights are less "basic" than political ones, and that the U.S. history of opposing any claims for economic rights needs to be continued, it points out for particular condemnation the Clinton Administration's support for collective rights, such as women's rights, and for creating a U.N. High Commissioner on Human Rights. Lumping "economic rights" together with "rights to cultural difference" (as though these are not often diametrically opposed), and representing a veritable "Pandora's box," the *Journal* warns that collective rights discourse is quite powerful and dangerous, especially concerning such topics as women and rape.[25]

Such a conservative take on rights may well lead us to laud the women's rights as human rights approach and to hail human rights internationalism as the answer to global inequalities. However, some caution is needed in pushing this agenda, since it is not clear that this new internationalism is any less dependent on the superpowers than earlier versions, or that the U.N. may be able to exercise greater power than previously or neglect the wishes of the major global powers. Moreover, the history of the U.N. and its participation in pushing development and debt reduction programs through the World Bank and the International Monetary Fund, is hardly encouraging.[26] The U.N. has been in existence for almost half a century, during which initial gains in the lives of women in the 1960s and 1970s have been reversed by increasing poverty, environmental destruction, and the exploitative practices of many transnational corporations.[27] Neo-imperial policies and actions by First World powers have often utilized the U.N. for their interests, even though sections of the U.N. have operated to rescue refugees or protest the actions of certain states. In general, recent U.N. work does not recommend it as the savior of the poor and the women of the world. Rajni Kothari argues, for instance, that the post-cold war period "has given rise to a large and widespread upsurge of nationalist, ethnic, and religious turbulence . . . , which in turn is being used for establishing a new model of hegemony in which the U.N. itself is being made an instrument."[28]

In addition, the U.N. organizations devoted to women and children's welfare, such as UNIFEM, INSTRAW, or UNICEF, seem to have fewer resources and power than the Security Council, the General Assembly, or the IMF, revealing that gender and women's issues are relegated to second place even in the U.N. While the Convention on the Elimination of all Forms of Discrimination Against Women (CEDAW) dictates accountability methods, such as the need for states to report to CEDAW, women's rights organizations report that states are not living up to the stipulations of the Convention. "International pressure" is the means that many argue can be useful for urging states to comply with these treaties. Yet such pressure is often dependent on geopolitics of states and works effectively only when states wish to protect or maximize their own interests, such that it is often the powerful groups within the state system that can bring a problem to international attention.[29]

It is also important to critique the internationalism that the U.N. stands for as the imaginary "family of nations" or of a "global community of nations." The international does not transcend nationality but is a "global social organization that tries to generate a plurality of nations. . . ."[30] Liisa Malkki has pointed out that the global imaginary of the international is shared transnationally but "may have profoundly different significance and uses in specific local sociopolitical contexts."[31] Among white militia groups in the United States it can mean a dangerous and threatening racial commingling of the people of the world, whereas for certain women's human rights organizations it implies a universal category of similarly gendered persons. Thus Malkki points out that for Hutu refugees in Tanzania in 1985, the U.N. occupied a "supralocal moral location" as a buffer between refugees and the Tanzanian state, a location that changed if they were unable to qualify as refugees.[32]

The imaginary of the "international" represented by the U.N. is not unified because the U.N. itself is not a monolithic entity. While the U.N. remains closely tied to the system of nation-states and the power of the Security Council for its highly politicized policies that have benefited the First World rather than the Third, U.N. agencies forge diverse paths and goals. Some U.N. agencies, such as those concerned with women, children, and refugees, seem to be critically aware of power differentials and the problem of economic policies that benefit the North at the expense of the South, while other more powerful agencies have not shown such awareness in their policies. For instance, it is only very recently that the World Bank has recognized the problems of structural adjustment programs being implemented the world over.

Human Rights in the United States, the "American" Nation, and Gender-based Asylum

The international, even in its plethora of meanings, cannot be seen as supra-national[33] since it is reliant on the system of nation-states for its existence and conceptualization. While some resistance to north-south inequalities can come from the states that constitute the "Third World," the struggle for rights must question its own reliance on and recourse to the present system of modern states that has proved to be quite repressive in its participation in the world economy. In the era of multinational capital, it is problematic to assume that Third World nation-states can or will resist the spread of exploitative EPZs, since the states have either maintained these with the use of violence in recent years or have been unable to resist their spread. Furthermore, to presume a "Third World" uniformly opposed to exploitation of the world's poor may also be problematic since global capital is creating new subalterns and new cosmopolitans across national boundaries and north-south divides.

These new "international" alliances enable the deployment of imperial discourses by powerful states. For instance, the sterilization of Chinese women, female infanticide, and abortion of female fetuses were condemned and reviled by Hillary Clinton at the Beijing U.N. Women's conference, not simply to bring to light and to voice the oppression of women. Abuses of Chinese women's rights could be cited only because they fit into long-established Western discourses about Chinese women's backwardness and oppression, and because these abuses revealed the inadequacies of communist rule. It was obvious that such were the underlying agendas in the United States even during the Beijing conference, as indicated by U.S. media coverage. It is part of the U.S. government's political strategy to position America as the site for the authoritative condemnation of such practices. Within U.S. policy, the collaboration between trade and rights is now viewed as effective policy, even though it is presented as a conflictual one. Such a strategy consolidates the United States as the "land of freedom" whose representatives can stand in judgment of the practice of other nation-states. Even though in recent years organizations such as Human Rights Watch have condemned the abuse of women's rights in prisons in the United States, such criticism has neither created much change in the treatment of women in custody nor has it affected U.S. policy of campaigning for human rights in the name of moral superiority.[34] It is unfortunate but unavoidable that the "moral superiority" of U.S. geopolitical discourse has become part of the new global feminism emerging in the United States (and worldwide, though in the interest of diverse agendas). The dominant discourse in regard to international issues constructs U.S. feminists as saviors and rescuers of "oppressed women" elsewhere within a global economy run by powerful states. This new discourse of a global sisterhood misrecognizes the ways many women are treated in the First World itself, without addressing these situations. Furthermore, it creates hegemonic notions of freedom and liberation, refuses to acknowledge the power of dominant groups in the United States, feminist and non-feminist, and wishes to "rescue" "Other" women rather than address the imperial policies and practices of the United States that create conditions of exploitation elsewhere.

The coincidence of this "global" feminist discourse and U.S. governmental goals regarding "international" women's issues emerges more clearly in the discussions of what is being called gender-based asylum, in which new gender-based claims can be made by refugees for asylum in the United States.[35] These claims are long overdue, for women's particular circumstances have been ignored by male-defined asylum laws, which understand the political as a male realm distinct from the domestic (female) domain. It is only recently that arguments by women's groups over women's rights as human rights have pressured the INS to reconsider its refugee asylum guidelines to include women's exploitation and oppression. The INS is bowing to the interpretation of human rights by the "international organizations" (primarily women's NGOs that advise the U.N.), even if these instruments have not been ratified by the U.S. Under the Clinton Administration, the INS has become more open to these claims even as it has become harsher about deportations and persecuting undocumented persons.

Yet even the creation of more gender-sensitive laws can be recuperated by the state. Asylum not only speaks the language of human rights, it also is adjudicated on a case-by-case basis rather than through national quotas or family or kin groups. One change in these laws is that asylum can now be claimed on the basis of belonging to "social groups" that can be proved to be the target of gender-persecution by states or private individuals undeterred by states. One can see that refugee laws present certain possibilities that immigration forecloses—for instance, it can enable gays and lesbians to enter under certain strict guidelines at the same time that immigration constructs and enforces a heterosexual notion of family. On the other hand, a greater emphasis on refugee status and the expansion of refugee guidelines runs the risk of cutting down on immigrants who enter under family categories.

In Canada, feminist and immigrant activists have worked to change male-centered refugee laws to include gender-based asylum claims within which, for instance, female genital surgeries, domestic violence, or rape are included as grounds for asylum. Immigration activists in the United States are also arguing for some version of gender-based asylum, pointing out the arbitrariness and the sexism of the existing categories in refugee law such that only those who have a "well-founded fear of persecution" because of race, religion, nationality, membership in a particular social group, or because of political opinion are eligible for refugee status. Following the Canadian model, they are arguing that women who flee from state-sponsored violence directed at family members or at themselves could qualify for asylum.[36] Domestic violence would also be grounds for asylum, if it were established that the state the claimant lived in would not protect her or that internal flight were impossible. Women who fear persecution because they violate "customary laws and practices in their countries of origin" would also be eligible.[37]

In the practice of ensuring gender-based asylum, as the Canadian case has shown, state power and cultural inequalities that utilize colonial discourses can be recuperated through the work of immigration activists. In Canada, as Sherene Razack reports, the adjudication of claims of gender persecution in the cases of Third World women end up furthering the interests of the First World. In her examination of refugee claims, Razack discovered that these were most likely to be successful when women were "able to present themselves as victims of dysfunctional, unusually patriarchal cultures and states." It is only through "orientalist and imperialist frames" that gender-based persecution established itself.[38] Here the dilemma of feminist practices emerges such that problematic orientalist discourses become the only means to press refugee claims for women from Africa, Latin America, or Asia.

It is apparent that in the United States, the Canadian model will be adopted to a certain extent. The INS is already bringing this model to the attention of its Asylum Officers, instructing them in special gender and cultural considerations in deciding asylum claims. One memorandum on such considerations brings to the notice of Asylum Officers such documents as the U.N. declaration that emphasized the need to incorporate the rights of women as human rights, the 1979 Convention on the Elimination of All Forms of Discrimination Against Women, and the Canadian Guidelines on Gender-Based persecution.[39] In addition, the memorandum suggests that considerations should include "the laws and customs of some countries [that] contain gender-discriminatory provisions." Such statements suggest that the United States remains free of such provisions, since the memo suggests that "some societies require that women live under the protection of male family members"; it is clear that the memo assumes that certain foreign cultures are very oppressive to women, unlike the United States.[40]

Plate 64: *Deductive Object*, 1994
Used clothes and bed covers
Installed at an abandoned Korean traditional house in Kyung Ju
Soo-Ja Kim
Photo: Ju Myung-Duk
Courtesy of the artist

Following U.S. cultural feminist agendas, domestic violence and rape remain dominant categories for establishing refugee claims, closely followed by "infanticide, genital mutilation, forced marriage, slavery, domestic violence and forced abortion." The practices of Islamic fundamentalist regimes against women are also mentioned as grounds, although Christian and other fundamentalisms are not so marked.

The establishment of the United States as a unified nation free of violent practices against women, except for domestic violence and rape, is part of the geopolitical establishment of First World power structures constructed by American nationalism. This notion of America is endemic in popular feminism and derives from U.S. cultural feminism. For instance, in a newspaper column on the Beijing women's conference, Stephanie Salter states that the U.S. is a "relatively enlightened democracy that does not sell women into slavery, mutilate their genitals or deny them the right to vote or to divorce an abusive spouse."[41] Attitudes such as Salter's are present in state policies as well as in popular culture. There have been proposals that the U.S. government compile a list of nations earmarked by their degradation of women for use by the INS in adjudicating asylum claims. As with earlier policies on refugees, U.S. foreign policy and the American establishment of power in the sphere of human rights will no doubt play a large role in the formation of such a list.

Such recuperations of America as a place of freedom for women are in some measure the grounds for the U.S. role as the world's enforcer of human rights, a position that enables power within political and economic spheres. In recent years, women in the United States have begun to struggle against the problems of domestic violence and rape within their borders, but socio-economic concerns of low-income women remain low in priority, as are transnational concerns about the global economy. Within a dominant cultural feminism in the United States, women from the Third World are represented as victims that mark their cultures as anti-women. As Karen Engle argues in her discussion of various approaches to rights concerning female genital surgeries, "Just as Human rights advocates might keep women at the periphery, if not exclude them altogether, women's rights advocates keep the Exotic Other Female at the margins." Engle argues that women's rights advocates categorize variously as this "Exotic Other" the female subjects who support actions that the advocates are working against and who are seen as inaccessible or the victims of false consciousness.[42] The contested terrain of issues such as female genital surgeries become crucial for American women's own construction as subjects.[43]

Refugees and immigrants in the United States, especially the non-Europeans who bring "traditional" and "barbaric" customs with them, are represented as a collective impending crisis within the "civilized" host country that lets in the "barbaric" hordes. Such a practice participates in a xenophobic, racialized American nationalism in which the whiteness, justness, humaneness of a homogeneous "host" nation is established through the presence of its barbaric immigrant or refugee others. A "civilized" and horrified "we" is created through such myths and provides a comfortable standpoint for U.S. feminists that includes feminist multiculturalists arguing for human rights in China or against female genital surgeries among African populations.[44] Within the white homogenizing collectivity of "American" nationalism that requires multiculturalism as economic and social project, practices such as female genital surgeries, conceptualized as violations of women's human rights, find an uneven and varying cathexis.[45] Liberal American multiculturalism creates a new form of global feminism in the context of the U.S. nation-state and a new global economy in which binaries of civilized and barbaric, free-unfree, and West-non-West remain to create new "rescuers" who see themselves as helping their more unfortunate "sisters." At present, such binaries are recast and deployed not only by a "First World" against the "Third World" but also by two somewhat different groups: first, those in the so-called Third World who are part of new cosmopolitan classes emerging in the post-cold war, global economy; and, second, those who see these narratives as part of realpolitik in places such as the United States in order to achieve seemingly laudable goals.

For the latter group, which includes feminist activists and non-profit organizations in the United States that work with immigrant and refugee women, the dilemma is that the discourse in which the needs of these women can be effectively expressed may end up recuperating imperialist narratives of "Third-World" women as victims of patriarchal oppression. Such a discourse is necessary to U.S. imperial agendas as well as to nationalist narratives in many other countries. Since women's bodies have always been used in nationalist agendas, it is important to counter such uses by suggesting the historical contingency of gender formations—to claim that women are not victims but are persons whose agency is differentially constructed within formations that come not only from state and nation, but also from geopolitics, economics, religion, sexuality, etc. The analysis of women's subject positions within institutional formations reveals the specific contexts that allow exploitation and help formulate ways to deal with these contexts.[46]

Yet the problem of immigration activism in the United States (as well as in Europe) remains that the state seems to be the only means to address certain problems, such as who enters and who doesn't, and that anti-nationalist solutions (for instance, the acknowledgment that the U.S. is responsible for poverty and state terrorism in many parts of Latin America and must let in those people who have been exploited in the process, or that it routinely violates the rights of many citizens and non-citizens alike within its borders) do not work as grounds for refugee asylum because they are seen as anti-American. Anti-colonial analyses are unworkable, especially since narratives of immigration to the U.S., including those by feminists, are framed in the dominant paradigm of the movement from non-freedom to freedom.[47] Also unworkable is the discussion of the prevalence of domestic violence in the United States, because then the INS may decide that refugee status should not be given to women if they are subject to violence in the United States as well.[48]

If human rights activism and immigration activism rely on remedies that promote notions of a white, freedom-giving America, then U.S. state power yoked to new imperial and global formations will advance. In such situations, deconstruction of the categories deployed by the state, such as legal, illegal, citizen, alien, nation, seems to be crucial, since by this means we can counter the naturalizing of historically formed contexts. Such examination of categories can be a powerful tool to understand the functioning of gender, race, sexuality, and class in relation to the state. For instance, we can then see how easily a woman who comes into the U.S. with expectations of legal immigration can easily become "illegal" if her husband who sponsors her entry refuses to sign her application papers. Similarly, we can understand that problematic divisions between "political" persecution and "economic" necessity used by the INS and the courts can make one either a "refugee" or an "illegal alien."

Global Feminism, NGOs, and Human Rights Discourse

In the context of the United States, the state and its related nationalist discourses are powerful enough to recuperate many progressive efforts of individual women, dominant and non-dominant groups of women, and also U.S.-based NGOs. Since NGOs and grassroots organizations are separated in U.N. women's conferences from governmental bodies, the NGO forum was at Huairou rather than Beijing. Such a separation makes it possible to ignore the interpellation by the state and its institutions in creating those subjects who participate in NGOs. However, such subjects, in their turn, cannot be seen as pawns of the state since, in many instances, they both protest the state's policies and point out its inadequacies, yet cannot be assumed to have escaped interpellation by the state.[49] The influence of states in creating certain kinds of NGOs and groups is an important one, visible most particularly in the United States and Western Europe within what has been termed "global feminism," that is, the hegemony of First World women's groups to affect women's lives and women's groups worldwide by their interests and their policies.[50] Discourses of American nationalism have widely influenced even those feminist discourses that may see themselves as opposed to particular state policies. As examples of such attitudes, publications from Europe and North America that focus on the issue of women's rights as human rights often rely on agendas that Third World feminist critics such as Chandra Mohanty have critiqued as narrow and eurocentric.[51]

However, many groups, aware of histories of imperialism that promote a notion of "global sisterhood" between colonizing and colonized female subjects, avoid the ethnocentrism of such practices by using discourses of diversity and pluralism. For instance, the Center for Women's Global Leadership, based at Rutgers University in New Jersey, has taken a leading role in pushing this agenda in the United States, and employs very generalized language for organizing in the area of violence against women.[52] One of its reports states that the conception of women's rights as human rights

> provides a framework of reference within which each women's group can place its own existing agenda. It also allows groups to link existing agendas of various women's groups together, to rally people around a common cause, and to project themselves as a unified and unifying force, thereby expanding the vision of each group.
>
> This framework helps connect feminist organizing to activism on other issues such as oppressed groups. . . . It appeals to universal principles and elevates women's rights to a level considered more legitimate by government officials and government policy makers."[53]

Yet even though this group incorporates anti-colonial, anti-racist concerns, its discourse of human rights internationalism claims universalism by ignoring history, contingency, and context and addressing difference solely within a notion of non-conflictual pluralism or of oppressions that can easily fit into a common framework, rather than disrupt it. Crucially, therefore, it becomes problematic for practice, since the ways in which these international instruments are deployed, implemented, and imposed is ignored. The understanding of these deployments is an urgent matter since it is in these contexts that women's agency can be understood; for instance, global feminism constructs U.S. feminist subjects in particular ways and enables them to become agents in the practice of "rescuing" victims of human rights violations. Nuanced understandings of various economic, state, political, and cultural formations that are historically contingent are more useful to activist work than generalized invocations of human rights discourses.[54] As an example, opposition to structural adjustment programs run by the I.M.F. and the World Bank has been gained by analyses of particular ways in which debt reduction has resulted in the erosion of earlier gains in women's health and education in many parts of the world.

Human Rights discourse often seems to take the place of such historically contextualized analyses of women's lives. While groups such as the Center for Women's Global Leadership are struggling to expand the definition of violence against women to include social, cultural, and economic issues, it is also clear that differences between women are such that socioeconomic rights are often given more lip service than serious consideration through sustained campaigns. Furthermore, the ignoring of the context of their own feminist practice within Western feminism, along with a U.S. media that understands only cultural and liberal feminisms, leads to an erasure of other campaigns and gives prominence only to cases of domestic violence and rape.[55] I do not suggest that these crimes are unimportant, but their dominance in the United States media overshadows issues such as socioeconomic, environmental, and health problems that concern poor women in all parts of the world, and which do not receive sustained attention from dominant groups of women everywhere determined to create "common" goals.[56]

It is clear from recent events such as the Beijing conference that in terms of a generalized discourse of women's issues, it is only in areas of activism such as domestic violence and rape that there appears to be unhesitating agreement among women from across the world. Many feminists in the United States, from both minority and mainstream groups, have pressed this agenda, which emerges from U.S. dominant cultural feminists' focus on what they perceive to be issues of the body rather than on socioeconomic issues. Domestic violence is proclaimed to be universal and has been the means for the battered women's movement in the United States to gain strength—by claiming that domestic violence crosses all borders and the boundaries of race, class, and sexuality. This claim, superficially correct though it seems, cannot answer the problem of providing support services to differently constituted women for whom domestic violence is manifested and acknowledged only within particular subject positions. For instance, undocumented women may not acknowledge or report domestic violence for fear of deportation, and to address their needs means confronting questions of immigration status, and economic as well as psychological needs. It is at the level of analysis, policy, and services that non-profit organizations working on domestic violence issues in the United States are quite conflicted, suggesting that coalitions and collaborations are complex even within the United States, let alone in the global arena.

A seemingly global unanimity regarding the prevalence of domestic violence may only be apparent when specificities are not discussed. In the interests of such unanimity, the language of women's rights among U.S. women's groups is startlingly full of laudable goals while absent of the specificities of how these goals will be achieved, rather like the language of inter-governmental agreements. If differences are mentioned they are contained within a non-conflictual model of diversity and pluralism. The many debates and differences among women across the world that argue for different ways to address domestic violence are here ignored. For instance, the role played by the police to prevent domestic violence or come to the aid of battered women can only depend on the specificities of particular states and the particular behavior and position of the police in these states. Attitudes toward battered women are also quite diverse; whereas in some cultures and situations women feel shame for being battered, in others they may not and such feelings affect the nature of services that need to be provided.

Yet the construction of a unified battered women's movement persists both in the United States and globally, bolstered by hegemonic U.S. women's groups situating difference within diversity and liberal multiculturalism. National campaigns may be as universalizing as global ones; in the U.S. context, race, class, and sexuality have led to profound conflicts within the battered women's movement. Differences in the ways women may acknowledge domestic violence, or find remedies for a situation, have not been widely addressed.[57] For instance, resources have been allocated to battered women of color and immigrant women only after a vigorous campaign by women of color and immigrant activists. It is also clear that too few shelters in the United States attend to needs of immigrant women from Asia, Africa, or Latin America. Most of them are run by white, middle-class women who see themselves as raced and classed in very different and problematic ways that reveal the influence of state and nation on their subjectivities. Shelters may offer counseling when the most important priority in a woman's life may be getting training for or finding a job, or finding day care and housing.[58] Many of the short-term programs offered by a shelter may not provide such training, though there are notable exceptions.[59] As a result of deficiencies in established shelters, many women from different communities are setting up their own shelters, though conflicts and concerns arise at every step. For instance, in the shelters and domestic violence programs run by South Asian women in the United States, policy problems arising from class conflicts or generational differences continually crop up.

The mainstream success of the battered women's movement, as indicated by governmental attention to this topic under the Clinton Administration, has led to other problems. The recent Violence Against Women Act, for instance, has allocated most resources to the state law enforcement agencies rather than to women's groups or to women's economic empowerment and education.[60] This is a problem in a culture in which incarceration rather than education seems to be the goal of the state with regard to people of color. Furthermore, domestic violence activism in the courts within the United States sublimates various kinds of cultural stereotypes; the "battered women's syndrome," for instance, deploys rigidified notions of a battered woman that jeopardizes legal remedies for all those who depart from this normative description.[61] Those penalized by this dominant white stereotype may include women from other cultures and races who are gendered very differently.

In cases of global activism or even activism in multicultural contexts such as the United States and Canada, the question of who represents and interprets is an important one and cannot be ignored. As Sherene Razack argues in her examination of the Canadian state's efforts to combat domestic violence, such efforts must begin with an examination of white supremacy and acknowledge that every cross-cultural communication is imbued with power relations.[62] In the United States, the state's increased interest to intervene on behalf of battered women comes at a time of increased conservatism and discrimination against poor women and people of color, and sharpening global inequalities between rich and poor. Consequently, it is important to remember that human rights instruments only occur within politics, not outside them, so that it is essential to understand political and ideological contexts. Consequently, discussions of women's rights as human rights have to include critical and specific illustrations of these contexts that lead to the dilemmas of feminist practice. Since concepts of women and gender are so widely relied upon in the making and remaking of "community," "nation," "tradition," and "culture," they can also be appropriated in different ways.

NGOs and the Grass Roots: A New Global Role

It is clear from the failure of states to improve the conditions of the poor and the women and children of the world, that NGOs utilizing human rights discourses are playing an increasingly important role in the world. They are being positioned as crucial in safeguarding the interests of numbers of people worldwide who are displaced or are refugees or stateless. The numbers of immigrants and refugees in the world today—about twenty million refugees alone, most of them women and children—will certainly increase in the meantime, and the women's NGOs that engage in human rights and other discourses will continue to work as well. Groups putatively outside the states, known as the "TZMO" or "tiz-moes" (transnational social movement organizations), which are coalitions or formal federations of national or regional non-governmental organizations (Medicins sans Frontieres, for example), are also on the increase.[63] Yet to suppose these to be free of national power structures or geopolitical agendas is problematic.

The increased burden and responsibility of such NGOs has led to problems associated with greater professionalization. Professionalizing has benefits, in the form of increased communication among those working in similar agencies and among different communities, and the emergence of common languages for getting resources and connections globally. Yet pressure to professionalize activist work in new and numerous ways, from the search for resources and grants to networking capabilities, creates conditions for work without critical thought as well as an increasing distance from the specificities of communities. Connections to a "community" being served are often believed obvious or transparent, and critical reflection on this connection may be dismissed as an "academic" venture. It is also difficult to assume that one knows the needs of a community or that one represents a community. At best this representation can only be an approximation; at worst it may become a deafness to those marginalized in the community. Debates on the consolidation of academic discourses and elite scholarship in international arenas have focused on similar problems of conducting scholarly work.[64] Grass-roots groups may indeed encapsulate a romantic notion of community, having little to do with the pressures of work and constant search for resources experienced by women's NGOs.

The continued valorization of "activism" in a binary of "activism" and "theory" that is constantly being set up in various arenas of feminist work in the United States, is no doubt a response to elite groups' discursive control over subaltern women. However, it may also lead to a refusal to question positivist knowledge systems, and a rejection of critique and self-examination of the structures of power in which all subjectivities are embedded. Furthermore, such questionings may threaten the certainties of evaluations of the extent to which women are exploited or oppressed in various parts of the world.

In the area of women's human rights, an important feminist practice would involve work by feminist scholars, lawyers, social scientists, activists, historians, and social workers. Although it may be contentious, this work will necessitate coalitions across many institutionalized "borders." Networking could be most useful if global inequalities and questions of power and self-critique are figured in as practices of critical reflection and rethinking. In such reflection, women's rights as human rights may be a small part of the struggle, and the examining of gendering practices in various societies as both enabling and disciplining may emerge as crucial. What needs to be examined is how gendering is a disciplinary practice in all societies, without relying on notions of First World "freedoms" and "Third World" repressions.

Within such conditions, it seems important not to romanticize the practices of grassroots groups. Such groups—for example, the one that set up the California conference on human rights that I mentioned at the beginning of my essay—have complex positionings as well as problematic power relations inscribed in their efforts. Yet these have to be carefully scrutinized in order to examine the practices and work of both grassroots and non-governmental organizations, not with the view that they may not be authentically grass-roots, but with the belief that complex subjectivities, positions, and power relations are endemic to all groups, whether in the north or south, First World or Third.

Notes

This project is the result of concerns that have emerged from many conversations with colleagues and friends. In particular, I am deeply indebted to Deana Jang, Leti Volpp, and Jayne Lee, who articulated important issues resulting from their work with immigrant Asian women and who gave me inspiration as well as information; and to Caren Kaplan, for her careful and detailed readings and discussions, important suggestions, and encouragement; Ella Shohat, for nurturing this project through all my distractions and hesitations and for being a meticulous editor and an engaged intellectual; Minoo Moallem, for her useful and encouraging and incisive conversations; Sherene Razack for sharing her important work; and Narika for giving me insights into the concerns of this essay.

1. Sikhs belong to a religious group from the North of India, residing mostly in Punjab but also in far-flung communities in the U.K., Canada, the U.S., Hong Kong, East Africa, Malaysia, Singapore, Philippines, New Zealand, and Australia. Twelve million Sikhs live in India and about four million elsewhere. Since the 1980s they have been involved in a separatist movement that has been repressed by the removal of civil liberties and massive Indian governmental counter-insurgency movements in the state of Punjab.

2. Mary Layoun, "The Female Body and 'Transnational' Reproduction Or, Rape by Any Other Name?" in Inderpal Grewal and Caren Kaplan, eds., *Scattered Hegemonies: Postmodernity and Transnational Feminist Practices* (Minneapolis: University of Minnesota Press, 1994), 63–75.

3. A noteworthy point here is that the organizers were second-generation professionalized Sikh men, for whom discourses of human rights violations are an important part of their socialization into U.S. global human rights discourses, and for whom being Sikh enables an non-white, patriarchal, modern, subjectivity in relation to white patriarchal cultures in the U.S.

4. See Ella Shohat and Robert Stam, *Unthinking Eurocentrism* (New York: Routledge, 1994); and Inderpal Grewal, "The Postcolonial, Ethnic Studies, and the Diaspora: The Contexts of Ethnic Immigrant/Migrant Cultural Studies in the U.S.," *Socialist Review* 24, no. 4 (1994): 45–74.

5. Bharati Mukherjee, *Jasmine* (New York: Fawcett Crest, 1989).

6. Bhapsi Sidhwa, *Cracking India,* Minneapolis: Milkweed Edition, 1992.

7. Chitra Devakaruni, "Yuba City School," in Women of South Asian Descent Collective, eds., *Our Feet Walk the Sky* (San Francisco: Aunt Lute Foundation Books, 1993), 120–121.

8. Srinivas Krishna, *Masala,* 1990.

9. Parmar's film *Sari Red* (1988) takes as its topic the murder of an Indian (Punjabi Sikh) woman in England. However, it erases the woman by using the sari as a symbol of this woman, even though Punjabi Sikh women do not wear saris for the most part and wear the *salw-kameez* instead. Parmar seems unable to conceptualize violence against Indian women through the heterogeneity of their cultural formations but instead has to subsume their differences under a dominant sign (the sari).

10. Two recent anthologies among many are: Abdullahi Ahmed An-Na'Im, ed., *Human Rights in Cross-Cultural Perspectives* (Philadelphia: University of Pennsylvania Press, 1992); and Rebecca J. Cook, ed., *Human Rights of Women: National and International Perspectives* (Philadelphia: University of Pennsylvania Press, 1994).

11. The term NGO is officially used by the U.N. to refer to the functions rather than the membership of organizations (since governmental members and branches may be members of NGOs, for instance, in sports organizations such as the International Table Tennis Federation). NGOs operate under rules of private law instead of public law, and the U.N. grants them consultation rights.

12. See, for example, the essays in Smitu Kothari and Harsh Sethi, eds., *Rethinking Human Rights* (Delhi: Likayan, 1991).

13. Rajni Kothari, "Human Rights—a Movement in Search of a Theory," in *Rethinking Human Rights,* 19–29.

14. Rhoda E. Howard, "Dignity, Community, and Human Rights," in *Human Rights in Cross-Cultural Perspectives,* 81–102.

15. Smitu Kothari and Harsh Sethi, "Categories and Interventions," in *Rethinking Human Rights,* 1–17.

16. Howard, "Dignity, Community, and Human Rights," 81–102.

17. Norma Alarcon, "The Theoretical Subject(s) of *This Bridge Called Our Back* and Anglo-American Feminism," in Gloria Anzaldúa, ed., *Making Face, Making Soul/Haciendo Caras* (San Francisco: Aunt Lute Books, 1990), 356–369.

18. Ibid.

19. Hilary Charlesworth, "What are 'Women's International Human Rights,'?" in *Human Rights of Women,* 58–84.

20. Rajni Kothari, "Globalization and 'New World Order': What Future for the United Nations?" *Economic and Political Weekly,* October 7, 1995, 2513–2517.

21. Ibid., 2513–2517.

22. For an extended discussion within the field of International Relations as it pertains to matters of U.S. nationalism, race, immigration, and the transnational, see Michael J. Shapiro and Hayward R. Alker, eds., *Challenging Boundaries* (Minneapolis: University of Minnesota Press, 1996).

23. See Rajni Kothari, "Globalization and 'New World Order,'" 2513–2517.

24. Among some white militia organizations, it is believed that army helicopters and all-terrain vehicles painted black or white signal a U.N. invasion force, and the U.N. is seen as a representation of Third World nations as well as a multinational, often supposedly Jewish-dominated, global economy. It is revealing of the complicity between some elements of the state and such racist national imaginary that the

New York Times reports that the military attaché of the U.S. mission to the U.N. had to write to the leader of the Michigan Militia to assure him that the U.N. was not taking over a Michigan camp for training its troops (June 25, 1995). Such courtesy as writing to reassure the Militia reveals the importance of a racist white constituency to politicians in Congress. Both Democrats and Republicans in congress hesitate to support the U.N., although President Clinton seems somewhat more of an advocate. While the conservatives in the U.S. Congress—in the midst of their onslaught on so-called wasteful bureaucracies that they assert should be replaced by private sector organizations which are supposedly efficient—target the U.N. as a bureaucratic institution that wastes and misuses money, the Democrats have not been able to give the U.N. the share the U.S. owes to its maintenance. Recent attempts to remit to the U.N. the more than one billion dollars owed by the U.S. have evolved into a grass-roots matter, with every U.S. citizen being asked to send a check for approximately five dollars on his or her own initiative.

25. *Wall Street Journal,* May 19, 1993.

26. Gita Sen and Karen Grown, *Development Crises and Alternative Visions: Third World Women's Perspectives* (New York: Monthly Review Press, 1987).

27. Rajni Kothari, "Globalization and 'New World Order,'" 2513–2517.

28. Ibid.

29. Andrew Byrnes, "Toward a More Effective Enforcement of Women's Human Rights through the Use of International Human Rights Law and Procedures," in *Human Rights of Women,* 189–227.

30. Jonathan Ree, "Internationality," *Radical Philosophy,* 60 (1992): 3–11.

31. Liisa Malkki, "Citizens of Humanity: Internationalism and the Imagined Community of Nations," *Diaspora* 3, no. 1 (1994): 41–68.

32. Ibid.

33. For a more detailed discussion of this term see David Morley and Kevin Robins, *Spaces of Identity: Global Media, Electronic Landscapes and Cultural Boundaries* (London: Routledge, 1995).

34. Human Rights Watch Women's Rights Project, *The Human Rights Watch Global Report on Women's Human Rights* (Human Rights Watch, 1995).

35. Extensive discussions of this and following points can be found in Nancy Kelly, "Gender-Related Persecution: Assessing the Asylum Claims of Women," *Cornell International Law Journal* 26 (1993); and "Guidelines for Women's Asylum Claims," *Interpreter Releases* 71, no. 24 (June 27, 1994).

36. Pamela Goldberg, "Refugee and Migrant Women around the Globe," in Leni Marin and Blandina Lansang-De Mesa, eds., *Women on the Move: Proceeding of the*

Workshop on Human Rights Abuses against Immigrant and Refugee Women (San Francisco: Family Violence Prevention Fund, 1993), 1–4.

37. Nurjehan Mawani, "Women Refugee Claimants Fearing Gender-related Persecution: The Canadian Experience," in *Women on the Move,* 1–4.

38. Sherene Razack, "Domestic Violence as Gender Persecution: Policing the Borders of Nation, Race, and Gender," *Canadian Journal of Women and the Law* 8 (1995): 45–88.

39. U.S. Immigration and Naturalization Service, Washington, D.C., "Considerations for Asylum Officers Adjudicating Asylum Claims from Women" by Phillis Coven (May 26, 1995).

40. Leti Volpp, "(Mis)Identifying Culture: Asian Women and the "Cultural Defense," *Harvard Women's Law Journal* 17 (1994): 57–101.

41. *San Francisco Examiner,* September 7, 1995.

42. Karen Engle, "Female Subjects of Public International Law: Human Rights and the Exotic Other Female," in Dan Danielsen and Karen Engle, eds., *After Identity* (New York: Routledge, 1995), 210–228.

43. Isabelle Gunning, "Arrogant Perception, World-Traveling and Multicultural Feminism: The Case of Female Genital Surgeries," *Columbia Human Rights Law Review* 23 (1992): 189–248. See also Razack, "Domestic Violence as Gender Persecution."

44. An example is the film *Warrior Marks* (1993), collaboratively produced and directed by Alice Walker and Pratibha Parmar. In the film, we hear and see Amanata Diop, who was able to get refugee status to live in France, mainly through the efforts of French feminist lawyer, Linda Weil-Curiel. Yet questions remain about Weil-Curiel's racial politics. In an interview in *Vanity Fair,* which does not figure in the film, Weil-Curiel claims that African and Muslim immigrants in France know female genital surgery is illegal through a grapevine that Weil-Curiel and other activists in her group call "Radio Tom-Tom." For Weil-Curiel, the validity and "human" universality of French law is established through its enforcement in prohibiting this procedure. She says, therefore, that "the best way to stop racism is to treat the crimes of these people as firmly as we treat the crimes of French people, to say that we welcome you to France, but you must respect French law." A racialized binary configuration of "hosts" and "guests," in which the hybridity of the nation is denied and its racial homogeneity proclaimed as white, is established here, one that is ubiquitous in much scholarship and popular discourse on immigrants and migrants. *Warrior Marks* shares this crisis of "unspeakable" practices entering the "free" country, stating at one point that we, the audience, need to know that such practices can happen "here," too. Thus, toward the end of the film, Tracy

Chapman consolidates such the binary between the free American and the unfree African woman when standing in the slave fort on Goree Island by saying, "I stand here a free person as much as it's possible in the world and it's possible that things will change and that women will have control over their bodies and have whole bodies and a new beginning." In this scene only a body sexualized in the same way as Chapman's can be imagined as free, so that not only is the U.S. hegemonic feminist project validated but the scene also embodies a statement often cited in INS documents: U.S. citizenship enables freedom, which is a privilege.

45. This theme is continued in the forthcoming essay by Caren Kaplan and Inderpal Grewal, *"Warrior Marks:* Neo-Colonial discourse and Global Feminism's 'Lesbian' Body."

46. For instance, U.S. immigration laws make it possible for immigrant or undocumented women to be exploited in particular ways, and immigration activists have pushed for ways to address this situation by policies such as waivers for domestic violence and self-petitioning for immigrant status. The work of many groups, such as Family Violence Prevention Fund and the Coalition for Immigrant and Refugee Rights and Services, both in San Francisco, has made these changes possible. In addition, see the testimonials and statements in Marin and Lansang-De Mesa, *Women on the Move.*

47. For more on these narratives see Grewal, "The Postcolonial, Ethnic Studies, and the Diaspora."

48. My thanks to Deanna Jang for her identification and critique of this issue.

49. In Beijing, the use of English, the protests about substandard accommodations by many groups from the U.S., the continued focus on Chinese women as victims of their government and on Chinese censorship, as well as the emphasis on human rights as governing agenda are some indications of the clout of U.S. (and European) women's groups in the NGO forum. Yet women's groups from other parts of the world are also using these frameworks, partly because they come from nonsubaltern groups in their nations and partly because nothing else seems to work to get their particular and diverse goals. Thus "global" feminism is being used by a wide variety of women globally, albeit in vastly different ways.

50. See our introduction, "Transnational Feminist Practices and Questions of Postmodernity," in Inderpal Grewal and Caren Kaplan, eds., *Scattered Hegemonies: Post-Modernity and Transnational Feminist Practices* (Minneapolis: University of Minnesota Press, 1994), 1–33; see also Chandra Talpade Mohanty, "Feminist Encounters: Locating the Politics of Experience," *Copyright* 1 (Fall 1987): 30–44.

51. Chandra Talpade Mohanty, "Under Western Eyes: Feminist Scholarship and Colonial Discourses," in Chandra Mohanty, et al., eds., *Third World Women and the*

Politics of Feminism (Bloomington and Indianapolis: Indiana University Press, 1991), 51–80. For instance, one publication from Zed Press, titled *Women and Human Rights,* erases inequalities emerging from racism and colonialism for a focus on ahistorical and decontextualized notions of population or poverty, and enact many of the problems Mohanty critiques in her essays (Katarina Tomasevski, *Women and Human Rights* [London: Zed Press, 1993]). This text, while acknowledging that poverty and health issues are also central to rights as much as "political liberty," implies that gender is the sole and primary category of analysis. Ignoring race, for instance, or imperialism, or global asymmetries, it adopts a simplistic notion of politics and culture and ignores their interconnections to argue for a "top down" enforcement of these rights. In this work, all the discussions, illustrations, and issues focus on women in the Third World, suggesting that, much as Amnesty International does, the issue of human rights is one that concerns women in parts of the world other than North America or Western Europe.

52. See the publications of this group for more information: Center for Women's Global Leadership, Douglass College, Rutgers University, New Jersey, *International Campaign for Women's Human Rights 1992–1993 Report, Women, Violence and Human Rights* (1992), *From Vienna to Beijing: The Cairo Hearing on Reproductive Health and Human Rights* (1995).

53. Center for Women's Global Leadership, *International Campaign for Women's Human Rights 1992–1993 Report,* 11.

54. For some excellent examples of economic organizing in particular contexts, see Sheila Rowbotham and Swasti Mitter, eds., *Dignity and Daily Bread* (London: Routledge, 1994).

55. Groups such as W.E.A.P. (The Women's Economic Agenda Project) based in Oakland, California, and addressing the needs of poor women in the U.S., are much less visible in the news than groups working on domestic violence, rape, or abortion rights, such as National Abortion Action Rights League, B.A.W.A.R. (Bay Area Women against Rape), etc. The worldwide focus on S.A.P. (Structural Adjustment Programs) was initiated by women from developing countries at the NGO forum at Huairou.

56. Even though such a search for "common" ground is a problem everywhere, women's groups in India, even if they are formed by middle-class women, tend to focus on economic issues much more than do dominant women's groups in the U.S.

57. Kimberle Crenshaw, "Mapping the Margins: Intersectionality, Identity Politics and Violence against Women of Color," in *After Identity,* 332–354.

58. Johanna Finney, "Domestic Violence and Shelter Services," Unpublished paper. 1995.

59. For instance, the Asian Women's Shelter in San Francisco has made noteworthy progress in providing specialized services for certain groups of women.

60. My thanks to Jayne Lee for making this important point, among many others.

61. Jayne Lee, "Constructing Battered Women Who Kill: The Interaction of Feminism, Psychiatry and the Law" (paper delivered in the workshop, "Questions of Women, Culture and Difference," Seattle, University of Washington, May 16–17, 1995).

62. Sherene Razack, "What Is to Be Gained by Looking White People in the Eye? Culture, Race, and Gender in Cases of Sexual Violence," *Signs* 19, no. 1 (Summer 1994): 894–921.

63. George Lopez, et al., "The Global Tide," *Bulletin of the Atomic Scientists* 51, no. 4 (July–August 1995): 33–39.

64. The debates of the effects of disciplinary formations on academic production are numerous. For excellent analysis of them see Gayatri Spivak, *In Other Worlds* (New York: Methuen, 1987); and *Outside in the Teaching Machine* (New York: Routledge, 1993).

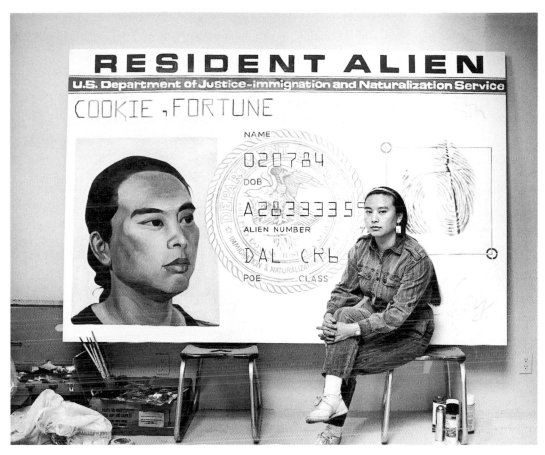

Plate 65· *Resident Alien*, 1988
Oil on canvas, 60 × 90"
© Hung Liu
Photo. Ben Blackwell
Courtesy Steinbaum Krauss Gallery, New York

Selected Bibliography

Abu-Lughod, Lila. *Writing Women's Worlds: Bedouin Stories.* Berkeley and Los Angeles: University of California Press, 1993.

Afkhami, Mahnaz. *Women in Exile.* Charlottesville and London: University Press of Virginia, 1994.

Ahmed, Leila. *Women and Gender in Islam: Historical Roots of a Modern Debate.* New Haven, CT: Yale University Press, 1992.

Alarcon, Norma, ed. *The Sexuality of Latinas.* Berkeley, CA: Third Woman Press, 1993.

Albrecht, Lisa, and Rose M. Brewer, eds. *Bridges of Power: Women's Multicultural Alliances.* Philadelphia: New Society Publishers, 1990.

Alexander, M Jacqui, and Chandra Talpade Mohanty, eds. *Feminist Genealogies, Colonial Legacies, Democratic Futures.* New York: Routledge, 1996,

Alexander, Meena. *The Shock of Arrival: Reflections on Postcolonial Experience.* Boston. South End Press, 1996.

Al-Hibri, Azizah, ed. *Women and Islam.* New York: Pergamon Press, 1992.

Allen, Paula Gunn. *The Sacred Hoop: Recovering the Feminine in American Indian Traditions.* Boston: Beacon Press, 1986.

———, ed. *Spider Woman's Granddaughters: Traditional Tales and Contemporary Writing by Native American Women.* Boston: Beacon Press, 1986.

Alloula, Malek. *The Colonial Harem.* Minneapolis: University of Minnesota Press, 1986.

Al-Qazzaz, Ayad. *Women in the Middle East and North Africa: An Annotated Bibliography.* Austin: Center for Middle Eastern Studies, University of Texas, Austin, 1977.

Altorki, Soraya, and Camillia Fawzi El-Solh. *Arab Women in the Field: Studying Your Own Society.* Syracuse, NY: Syracuse University Press, 1988.

Anzaldùa, Gloria. *Borderlands/La Frontera: The New Mestiza.* San Francisco: Spinsters/Aunt Lute, 1987.

————, ed. *Making Face, Making Soul/Haciendo Caras: Creative and Critical Perspectives by Women of Color.* San Francisco: Aunt Lute Books, 1990.

Arenal, Electa, and Stacey Schlau, eds. *Untold Sisters: Hispanic Nuns in Their Own Works.* Albuquerque: University of New Mexico Press, 1989.

Asian Women United of California, eds. *Making Waves: An Anthology of Writings By and About Asian American Women.* Boston: Beacon Press, 1989.

Bad Object-Choices, eds. *How Do I Look: Queer Film and Video.* Seattle: Bay Press, 1991.

Badran, M., and M. Cooke. *Opening the Gates: A Century of Arab Feminist Writing.* Indianapolis: Indiana University Press, 1990.

Barrett, Michele. *Women's Oppression Today: The Marxist/Feminist Encounter.* New York and London: Verso, 1980.

Barry, Kathleen. *The Prostitution of Sexuality: The Global Exploitation of Women.* New York and London: New York University Press, 1995.

Bartkowski, Frances. *Travelers, Immigrants, Inmates: Essays in Estrangement.* Minneapolis: University of Minnesota Press, 1995.

Beck, Lois, and Nikki Keddie, eds. *Women in the Muslim World.* Cambridge, MA, and London: Harvard University Press, 1978.

Beemyn, Brett, and Mickey Eliason, eds. *Queer Studies: A Lesbian, Gay, Bisexual and Transgender Anthology.* New York and London: New York University Press, 1996.

Belsey, Catherine, and Jane Moore, eds. *The Feminist Reader: Essays in Gender and the Politics of Literary Criticism.* New York: Basil Blackwell, 1989.

Behar, Ruth, and Deborah A. Gordon, eds. *Women Writing Culture.* Berkeley: University of California Press, 1995.

Betaille, Gretchen, and Kathleen Mullen Sands. *American Indian Women: Telling Their Lives.* Lincoln: University of Nebraska Press, 1984.

Blea, Irene I. *La Chicana and the Intersection of Race, Class, and Gender.* Westport, CT, and London: Praeger, 1992.

Blunt, Alison. *Travel, Gender and Imperialism: Mary Kingsley and West Africa.* New York and London: The Guilford Press, 1994.

————, and Gillian Rose, eds. *Writing Women and Space: Colonial and Post-Colonial Geographies.* New York and London: The Guilford Press, 1994.

Bobo, Jacqueline. *Black Women as Cultural Readers.* New York: Columbia University Press, 1995.

Broe, Mary Lynn, and Angela Ingram, eds. *Women's Writing in Exile.* Chapel Hill and London: The University of North Carolina Press, 1989.

Brown, Elaine. *A Taste of Power: A Black Woman's Story.* New York: Anchor Books/ Doubleday, 1992.

Bulkin, Elly, Minnie Bruce Pratt, and Barbara Smith, eds. *Yours in Struggle: Three Feminist Perspectives on Anti-Semitism and Racism.* Ithaca, NY: Firebrand Books, 1984.

Butler-Evans, Elliott. *Race, Gender and Desire: Narrative Strategies in the Fiction of Tony Cade Bambara, Toni Morrison and Alice Walker.* Philadelphia: Temple University Press, 1970.

Callaway, Helen. *Gender, Culture and Empire: European Women in Nigeria.* Urbana and Chicago: University of Illinois Press, 1987.

Carby, Hazel. *Reconstructing Womanhood: The Emergence of the Afro-American Woman Novelist.* Oxford: Oxford University Press, 1987.

Castillo, Ana. *Massacre of the Dreamers: Essays on Xicanisma.* Albuquerque: University of New Mexico Press, 1994.

Cha, Theresa Hak Kyung. *Dictée.* New York: Tanam Press, 1982.

Chaudhury, Nupur, and Margaret Strobel, eds. *Western Women and Imperialism: Complicity and Resistance.* Bloomington and Indianapolis: Indiana University Press, 1992.

Chow, Rey. *Writing Diaspora. Tactics of Intervention in Contemporary Cultural Studies.* Bloomington: Indiana University Press, 1993.

Christian, Barbara. *Black Feminist Criticism: Perspectives of Black Women Writers.* New York: Pergamon Press, 1985.

Collins, Patricia Hill. *Black Feminist Thought: Knowledge, Consciousness, and the Politics of Empowerment.* New York: Routledge, 1990.

Cohen, Cathy, Kathleen B. Jones, and Joan C. Tronto, eds. *Women Transforming Politics: An Alternative Reader.* New York: New York University Press, 1997.

Cohen, Colleen Ballerino, Richard Wilk, and Beverly Stoeltje. *Beauty Queens on the Global Stage: Gender, Contests, and Power.* New York and London: Routledge, 1996.

Cooke, Miriam, and Roshni Rustomji-Kerns, eds. *Blood Into Ink: South Asian and Middle Eastern Women Write War*. Boulder, CO, San Francisco, and Oxford: Westview Press, 1994.

Cooper, Carolyn. *Noises in the Blood: Orality, Gender and the "Vulgar" Body of Jamaican Popular Culture*. Durham, NC: Duke University Press, 1993.

Crenshaw, Kimberle, Neil Gotanda, and Gary Peller, eds. *Critical Race Theory: The Key Writings That Formed the Movement*. New York: The New Press, 1996.

Cudjoe, Selwyn R., ed. *Caribbean Women Writers: Essays from the First International Conference*. Wellesley, MA: Calaloux Publications, 1990.

Davies, Miranda. *Third World-Second Sex*. London: Zed Books, 1983.

Davis, Angela. *Angela Davis: An Autobiography*. New York: International Publishers, 1988.

———. *Women, Culture, and Politics*. New York: Vintage Books, 1990.

———. *Women, Race and Class*. New York: Vintage Books/Random House, 1981.

Dearborn, Mary V. *Pocahontas's Daughters: Gender and Ethnicity in American Culture*. New York: Oxford University Press, 1986.

Deepwell, Katy, ed. *New Feminist Art Criticism: Critical Strategies*. Manchester, England: St. Martin's Press, 1995.

di Leonardo, Micaela, ed. *Gender at the Crossroads of Knowledge: Feminist Anthropology in the Postmodern Era*. Berkeley, Los Angeles, and Oxford: University of California Press, 1991.

Dion, Mark, Renée Green, and Larry Johnson. *True Stories*. London: ICA Editions, 1994.

Djebar, Assia. *A Sister to Scheherazade*. London and New York: Quartet Books, 1987.

———. *Fantasia: An Algerian Cavalcade*. London: Quartet Books, 1985.

———. *Women of Algiers in their Apartment*. Charlottesville: University Press of Virginia, 1992.

Donaldson, Laura E. *Decolonizing Feminisms: Race, Gender and Empire Building*. Chapel Hill: University of North Carolina Press, 1992.

DuBois, Ellen Carol, and Vicki L. Ruiz, eds. *Unequal Sisters: A Multicultural Reader in U.S. Women's History*. New York: Routledge, 1990.

DuCille, Ann. *The Coupling Convention: Sex, Text and Tradition in Black Women's Fiction*. New York: Oxford University Press, 1993.

———. *Skin Trade*. Cambridge, MA: Harvard University Press, 1993.

Dunham, Katherine. *Island Possessed*. Chicago and London: The University of Chicago Press, 1969.

Ehrenrich, Barbara, and Annette Fuentes. *Women in Global Factory*. Boston: South End Press, 1983.

Eisenstein, Zillah R. *Hatreds: Racialized and Sexualized Conflicts in the 21st Century*. New York: Routledge, 1996.

El Saadawi, Nawal. *The Hidden Face of Eve: Women in the Arab World*. London: Zed Books, 1980.

Enloe, Cynthia. *Bananas, Beaches and Bases: Making Feminist Sense of International Politics*. Berkeley: University of California Press, 1989.

Etienne, Mona, ed. *Women and Colonization: Anthropological Perspectives*. New York: Bergin & Garvey Publishers, Inc. 1980.

Essed, Philomena and Rita Gircour. *Diversity: Gender, Color, and Culture*. Amherst: University of Massachusetts Press, 1996.

Ferguson, Russell, Martha Gever, Trinh T. Minh-ha, Cornel West, eds. *Out There: Marginalization and Contemporary Cultures*. New York: The New Museum of Contemporary Art; Cambridge, MA: The MIT Press, 1991.

Fisher, Dexter. *The Third Woman: Minority Women Writers of the United States*. Boston: Houghton-Mifflin, 1980.

Franco, Jean. *Plotting Women: Gender and Representation in Mexico*. New York: Columbia University Press, 1989.

Frankenberg, Ruth. *White Women, Race Matters*. Minneapolis: University of Minnesota Press, 1993.

Fusco, Coco. *English is Broken Here: Notes on Cultural Fusion in the Americas*. New York: The New Press, 1995.

Gadant, Monique. *Women of the Mediterranean*. London and New Jersey: Zed Books, 1984.

Garber, Linda, ed. *Tilting the Tower: Lesbians/Teaching/Queer Subjects*. New York: Routledge, 1994.

Giddings, Paula. *When and Where I Enter: The Impact of Black Women on Race and Sex in America*. New York: Bantam Books, 1984.

Gilman, Sander L. *Difference and Pathology: Stereotypes of Sexuality, Race, and Madness*. Ithaca, NY: Cornell University Press, 1985.

Ginsburg, Faye, and Rayna Rapp, eds. *Conceiving the New World Order: The Global Politics of Reproduction*. Berkeley, Los Angeles, and London: University of California Press, 1995.

Golden, Thelma. *Black Male: Representation of Masculinity in Contemporary American Art*. New York: Whitney Museum of American Art, 1994.

Gossett, Hattie. *Sister No Blues*. Ithaca, NY: Firebrand Books, 1988.

Graham-Brown, Sarah. *Images of Women: The Portrayal of Women in Photography of the Middle East, 1860–1950*. New York: Columbia University Press, 1988.

Green, Mary Jean, Karen Gould, Micheline Rice-Maximin, Keith L. Walker, Jack A. Yearger, eds. *Post-Colonial Subjects: Francophone Women Writers*. Minneapolis and London: University of Minnesota Press, 1996.

Green, Rayna. *Native American Women: A Contextual Bibliography*. Bloomington: Indiana University Press, 1983.

———, ed. *That's What She Said: Contemporary Poetry and Fiction by Native American Women*. Bloomington: Indiana University Press, 1984.

———. *Indians of North America: Women in American Indian Society*. New York and Philadelphia: Chelsea House Publishers, 1992.

Grewal, Inderpal, and Caren Kaplan, eds. *Scattered Hegemonies: Postmodernity and Transnational Feminist Practices*. Minneapolis: University of Minnesota Press, 1994.

Grewal, Inderpal. *Home and the Harem*. Durham, NC: Duke University Press, 1996.

Gunew, Sneja, and Anna Yeatman. *Feminism and the Politics of Difference*. St. Leonards, N.S.W.: Allen and Unwin, 1993.

Haraway, Donna J. *Primate Visions: Gender, Race, and Nature in the World of Modern Science*. New York: Routledge, 1989.

———. *Simians, Cyborgs, and Women: The Re-invention of Nature*. New York: Routledge, 1991.

Harlow, Barbara. *Barred: Women, Writing, and Political Detention*. Hanover, NH, and London: University Press of New England, 1993.

Hernton, Calvin C. *The Sexual Mountain and Black Women Writers: Adventures in Sex, Literature, and Real Life*. New York: Anchor Books/Doubleday, 1987.

Hongo, Garrett, ed. *Under Western Eyes: Personal Essays From Asian-Americans*. New York: Anchor Books, 1995.

hooks, bell. *Ain't I a Woman: Black Women and Feminism*. Boston: South End Press, 1984.

———. *Art on My Mind: Visual Politics*. New York: The New Press, 1995.

———. *Black Looks: Race and Representation*. Boston: South End Press, 1992.

———. *Feminist Theory: From Margin to Center*. Boston: South End Press, 1984.

————. *Talking Back: Thinking Feminist, Thinking Black*. Boston: South End Press, 1989.

————. *Yearning: Race, Gender and Cultural Politics*. Boston: South End Press, 1990.

Hossain, Rokeya Sakhwat. *Sultana's Dream and Selections From the Secluded Ones*. New York: Feminist Press at the City University of New York, 1988.

Hull, Gloria T., Patricia Bell Scott, and Barbara Smith, eds. *All the Women Are White, All the Blacks Are Men, But Some of Us Are Brave*. New York: Feminist Press at the City University of New York, 1982.

Hurston, Zora Neale. *Dust Tracks on a Road: An Autobiography*. Second Edition. Urbana and Chicago: University of Illinois Press, 1984.

Jayawardena, Kumari. *Feminism and Nationalism in the Third World*. London and New Jersey: Zed Books, 1986.

Jaimes, Annette M., ed. *The State of Native America: Genocide, Colonization and Resistance*. Boston: South End Press, 1992.

James, Joy. *Transcending the Talented Tenth: Black Leaders and American Intellectuals*. New York: Routledge, 1996.

————, and Ruth Farmer, eds. *Spirit, Space, and Survival: African American Women in (White) Academe*. New York: Routledge, 1993.

James, Stanlie M., and Abena P.A. Busia, eds. *Theorizing Black Feminisms: The Visionary Pragmatism of Black Women*. New York and London: Routledge, 1993.

Jones, Lisa. *Bulletproof Diva: Tales of Race, Sex and Hair*. New York: Doubleday, 1994.

Jordan, June. *Affirmative Acts: Political Essays*. New York: Doubleday, 1998.

————. *Moving Towards Home: Political Essays*. New York: Virago Press, 1994.

Juhasz, Alexandra. *AIDS TV: Identity, Community, and Alternative Video*. Durham, NC, and London: Duke University Press, 1995.

Kadi, Joanna, ed. *Food for our Grandmothers: Writings by Arab-American and Arab-Canadian Feminists*. Boston: South End Press, 1994.

Kandiyoti, Deniz, ed. *Women, Islam and the State*. Philadelphia: Temple University Press, 1991.

Kaplan, Caren. *Questions of Travel: Postmodern Discourses of Displacement*. Durham, NC: Duke University Press, 1996.

Kaye-Kantrowitz, Melanie. *The Issue Is Power: Essays on Women, Jews, Violence and Resistance*. San Francisco: Aunt Lute Books, 1992.

Kim, Elaine H. *Asian American Literature: An Introduction to the Writings and Their Social Context*. Philadelphia: Temple University Press, 1984.

Kim, Elaine H., and Lilia V. Villanueva, eds. *Making More Waves: New Asian American Writing by Asian Women.* Boston: Beacon Press, 1997.

Kim, Elaine H., and Norma Alarcon, eds. *Writing Self Writing Nation: Essays on Theresa Hak Kyung Cha's Dictée.* Berkeley: Third Woman Press, 1992.

Kim, Elaine H., Laurie Fendrich, Jo Goodman, Minne Hone, Young C. Lee, eds. *Across the Pacific: Contemporary Korean and Korean American Art.* Exhibition Catalogue. New York: Queens Museum of Art, 1993.

King, Katie. *Theory in Its Feminist Travels: Conversations in U.S. Women's Movements.* Indianapolis: Indiana University Press, 1994.

Lamphere, Louise, Helena Ragoné, and Patricia Zavella, eds. *Situated Lives: Gender and Culture in Everyday Life.* New York and London: Routledge, 1997.

Larsen, Nella. *Quicksand and Passing.* New Brunswick, NJ: Rutgers University Press, 1986.

Lazreg, Marnia. *The Eloquence of Silence: Algerian Women in Question.* New York and London: Routledge, 1994.

Levine, S., and T. Ybarra Frausto, eds. *Museums and Their Communities.* Washington, D.C.: Smithsonian Institution Press.

Lippard, Lucy R. *Mixed Blessings: New Art in a Multicultural America.* New York: Pantheon, 1990.

———. *The Pink Glass Swan: Selected Feminist Essays on Art.* New York: The New Press, 1995.

Loomba, Ania. *Gender, Race, Renaissance Drama.* Manchester, England, and New York: Manchester University Press/St. Martin's Press, 1989.

Lorde, Audre. *The Black Unicorn.* New York and London: W. W. Norton, 1978.

———. *A Burst of Light.* Ithaca, NY: Firebrand Books, 1988.

———. *The Cancer Journals.* San Francisco: Spinsters/Aunt Lute, 1980.

———. *I Am Your Sister: Black Women Organizing Across Sexualities.* New York: Kitchen Table/Women of Color Press, 1985.

———. *The Marvelous Arithmetics of Distance: Poems, 1987–1992.* New York and London: W. W. Norton, 1993.

———. *Need: A Chorale for Black Woman Voices.* New York: Kitchen Table/Women of Color Press, 1990.

———. *Sister Outsider.* Freedom, CA: The Crossing Press, 1984.

———. *Undersong: Chosen Poems Old and New.* New York and London: W. W. Norton, 1992.

————. *Uses of the Erotic: The Erotic As Power.* Freedom, CA: The Crossing Press, 1981.

————. *Zami, A New Spelling of My Name: A Biomythography.* Freedom, CA: The Crossing Press, 1982.

Lowe, Lisa. *Critical Terrains: French and British Orientalisms.* Ithaca, NY, and London: Cornell University Press, 1991.

————. *Immigrant Acts: On Asian American Cultural Politics.* Durham, NC: Duke University Press, 1996.

Lubiano, Wahneema. *Missing With the Machine: Modernism, Postmodernism, and Black American Fiction.* New York: Verso, 1996.

————. *The House That Race Built: Black Americans, U.S. Terrain.* New York: Pantheon Books, 1997.

MacDonald, Sharon, Pat Holden and Shirley Ardener, eds. *Images of Women in Peace and War: Cross-Cultural and Historical Perspectives.* Madison: The University of Wisconsin Press, 1987.

Mahone, Sydne, ed. *Moon Marked and Touched by Sun: Plays by African-American Women.* New York: Theatre Communications Group, 1994.

Malti-Douglas, Fedwa. *Woman's Body, Woman's Word: Gender and Discourse in Arabo-Islamic Writing.* Princeton, NJ: Princeton University Press, 1991.

Marchetti, Gina. *Romance and the "Yellow Peril": Race, Sex, and Discursive Strategies in Hollywood Fiction.* Los Angeles and Berkeley: University of California Press, 1994.

Martinez-Alier, Verena. *Marriage, Class and Colour in Nineteenth-Century Cuba: A Study of Racial Attitudes and Sexual Values in a Slave Society.* Ann Arbor: The University of Michigan Press, 1989.

McClintock, Anne. *Imperial Leather: Race, Gender and Sexuality in the Colonial Context.* New York and London: Routledge, 1995.

————, Aamir Mufti, and Ella Shohat, eds. *Dangerous Liasons: Gender, Nation, and Post-Colonial Perspectives.* Minneapolis: University of Minnesota Press, 1997.

McDowell, Deborah E., ed. *Quicksand and Passing: Nella Larson.* New Brunswick, NJ: Rutgers University Press, 1986.

Mendus, Susan, and Jane Rendall. *Sexuality and Subordination.* New York and London: Routledge, 1989.

Mernissi, Fatima. *Beyond the Veil: Male-Female Dynamics in Modern Muslim Society.* Bloomington and Indianapolis: Indiana University Press, 1987.

————. *Dreams of Trespass: Tales of a Harem Girlhood.* New York: Addison Wesley Publishing Company, 1994.

———. *The Forgotten Queens of Islam.* Minneapolis, Minnesota: University of Minnesota Press, 1993.

———. *Women and Islam: A Historical and Theological Inquiry.* London: Blackwell Publishers, 1991.

Milani, Farzaneh. *Veils and Words: The Emerging Voices of Iranian Women Writers.* Syracuse, NY: Syracuse University Press, 1992.

Minh-ha, Trinh T. *Framer, Framed.* New York: Routledge, 1992.

———. *When the Moon Waxes Red: Representation, Gender and Cultural Politics.* New York and London: Routledge, 1991.

———. *Woman, Native, Other.* Bloomington and Indianapolis: Indiana University Press, 1989.

Mohanty, Chandra Talpade, Ann Russo, and Lourdes Torres, eds. *Third World Women and the Politics of Feminism.* Bloomington and Indianapolis: Indiana University Press, 1991.

Moraga, Cherríe. *Loving in the War Years: Lo Que Nunca Paso Por Sus Labios.* Boston: South End Press, 1983.

———, and Gloria Anzaldúa, eds. *This Bridge Called My Back: Writings by Radical Women of Color.* Latham, NY: Kitchen Table/Women of Color Press, 1981.

Morrison, Toni. *The Bluest Eye.* New York and London: Plume/Penguin, 1970.

———, ed. *Race-ing Justice, En-gendering Power: Essays on Anita Hill, Clarence Thomas, and the Construction of Social Reality.* New York: Pantheon Books, 1992.

———, and Claudia Brodsky Lacour, eds. *Birth of a Nation'hood: Gaze, Script, and the Spectacle in the O. J. Simpson Case.* New York: Pantheon Books, 1997.

Ong, Aihwa. *Spirits of Resistance and Capitalist Discipline: Factory Women in Malaysia.* Albany: State University of New York Press, 1987.

Morton, Patricia. *Disfigured Images: The Historical Assault on Afro-American Women.* Westport, CT, and London: Praeger, 1991.

Nah, June, and Maria Patricia Fernandez-Kelly. *Women, Men and the International Division of Labor.* Albany: State University of New York Press, 1983.

Parker, Andrew, Mary Russo, Doris Sommer, and Patricia Yeager, eds. *Nationalisms and Sexualities.* New York and London: Routledge, 1992.

Parmar, Pratibha, and Alice Walker. *Warrior Marks: Female Genital Mutilation and the Sexual Mutilation of Women.* New York: Harcourt Brace, 1993.

Peteet, Julie M. *Gender in Crisis: Women and the Palestinian Resistance Movement.* New York: Columbia University Press, 1991.

Ramazanoglu, Caroline. *Feminism and the Contradictions of Oppression*. London and New York: Routledge, 1989.

Ramos, Juanita, ed. *Compañeras: Latina Lesbians*. New York: Latina Lesbian History Project, 1987.

Out El Kouloub. Ramza (Contemporary Issues in the Middle East) Nayra Atiya, trans. Syracuse, NY: Syracuse University Press, 1994.

Rose, Phyllis. *Jazz Cleopatra: Josephine Baker in Her Time*. New York: Vintage Books/Random House, 1989.

Rose, Tricia. *Black Noise: Rap Music and Black Culture in Contemporary America*. Middletown, CT: Wesleyan University Press, 1994.

Sangari, Kumkum, and Sudesh Vaid. *Recasting Women: Essays in Colonial History*. New Delhi: Kali for Women's Press, 1989.

Sarris, Greg. *Keeping Slug Women Alive: A Holistic Approach to American Indian Texts*. Berkeley, Los Angeles, and Oxford: University of California Press, 1993.

Savigliano, Marta E. *Tango and the Political Economy of Passion*. Boulder, CO, San Francisco, and Oxford: Westview Press, 1995.

Shaarawi, Huda. *Harem Years: The Memoirs of an Egyptian Feminist*. New York: The Feminist Press at the City University of New York, 1986.

Shakur, Assata. *Assata: An Autobiography*. Westport, CT: Lawrence Hill & Company, Publishers, Inc., 1987.

Sharpe, Jenny. *Allegories of Empire: The Figure of Woman in the Colonial Text*. Minneapolis: University of Minnesota Press, 1993.

Shepard, Verene, Bridget Brereton, and Barbara Bailey, eds. *Engendering History: Caribbean Women in Historical Perspective*. New York: St. Martin's Press, 1995.

Shohat, Ella, and Robert Stam. *Unthinking Eurocentrism: Multiculturalism and the Media*. London and New York: Routledge, 1994.

Silko, Leslie Marmon. *Ceremony*. New York: Penguin, 1977.

———. *Yellow Woman and a Beauty of Spirit: Essays on Native American Life Today*. New York: Touchstone/Simon and Schuster, 1997.

Sinclair, M. Thea, ed. *Gender, Work, and Tourism*. London and New York: Routledge, 1997.

Sister Souljah. *No Disrespect*. New York: Vintage Books/Random House, 1994.

Siverblatt, Irene. *Moon, Sun, and Witches: Gender Ideologies and Class in Inca Peru*. Princeton, NJ: Princeton University Press, 1987.

Smith, Anna Deavere. *Fires in the Mirror.* New York: Anchor Books/Doubleday, 1993.

Smith, Barbara, ed. *Home Girls: A Black Feminist Anthology.* Lantham, NY: Kitchen Table/Women of Color Press, 1983.

Sommer, Doris. *Foundational Fictions: The National Romances of Latin America.* Berkeley and Los Angeles: University of California Press, 1991.

Spivak, Gayatri Chakravorty. *In Other Worlds: Essays in Cultural Politics.* New York and London: Methuen, 1987.

————. *Outside in the Teaching Machine.* New York and London: Routledge, 1993.

————. *The Post-Colonial Critic: Interviews, Strategies, Dialogues.* New York and London: Routledge, 1990.

Stoler, Ann Laura. *Race and the Education of Desire: Foucault's History of Sexuality and the Colonial Order of Things.* Durham, NC: Duke University Press, 1995.

Spillers, Hortense J. *Comparative American Identities: Race, Sex and Nationality in Modern Text.* New York: Routledge, 1991.

Stasiulis, Daiva, and Nira Yuval-Davis, eds. *Unsettling Settler Societies: Articulations of Gender, Race and Class.* London: Sage Publications, 1995.

Tarabishi, Georges. *Woman Against Her Sex: A Critique of Nawal El-Saadawi.* New York: Saqi Books, 1988.

Tate, Claudia, ed. *Black Women Writers at Work.* New York: Continuum, 1985.

Terry, Jennifer, and Jacqueline Urla, eds. *Deviant Bodies: Critical Perspectives on Difference in Science and Popular Culture.* Bloomington and Indianapolis: Indiana University Press, 1995.

Trask, Haunani-Kay. *From a Native Daughter: Colonialism and Sovereignty in Hawaii.* Monroe, ME: Common Courage Press, 1993.

Treichler, Paula A., Cheris Kramarae, and Beth Stafford. *For Alma Mater: Theory and Practice in Feminist Scholarship.* Urbana and Chicago: University of Illinois Press, 1985.

Trujillo, Carla, ed. *Chicana Lesbians: The Girls Our Mothers Warned Us About.* Berkeley: Third Woman Press, 1991.

Utas, Bo, ed. *Women in Islamic Societies: Social Attitudes and Historical Perspectives.* New York: Olive Branch Press, 1983.

Visweswaran, Kamala. *Fictions of Feminist Ethnography.* Minneapolis and London: University of Minnesota Press, 1994.

Wallace, Michele. *Black Macho and the Myth of the Superwoman.* London and New York. Verso, 1990.

―――. *Invisibility Blues: From Pop to Theory.* London and New York: Verso, 1990.

Ware, Vron. *Beyond the Pale: White Women, Racism and History.* New York and London: Verso, 1992.

Warland, Betsey, ed. *Inversions: Writing by Dykes, Queers & Lesbians.* Vancouver: Press Gang Publishers, 1991.

Wiegman, Robyn. *American Anatomies: Theorizing Race and Gender.* Durham, NC: Duke University Press, 1995.

Williams, Patricia J. *The Alchemy of Race and Rights: Diary of a Law Professor.* Cambridge, MA: Harvard University Press, 1991.

―――. *The Rooster's Egg: On the Persistence of Prejudice.* Cambridge, MA, and London: Harvard University Press, 1995.

Williams, Walter W. *The Spirit of the Flesh: Sexual Diversity in American Indian Culture.* Boston: Beacon Press, 1992.

Willis, Susan. *Specifying: Black Women Writing the American Experience.* Madison: University of Wisconsin Press, 1987.

Wing, Adrien Katherine, ed. *Critical Race Feminism: A Reader.* New York and London: New York University Press, 1997.

With Silk Wings: Asian American Women at Work. Illustrated by Elaine H. Kim. San Francisco: San Francisco Study Center, 1983.

Women of South Asian Descent Collective, eds. *Our Feet Walk the Sky: Women of the South Asian Diaspora.* San Francisco: Aunt Lute Books, 1993.

Wong, Diane Yen-Mei. *Dear Diane: Letters from Our Daughters.* San Francisco: San Francisco Study Center, 1983.

―――. *Dear Diane: Questions and Answers for Asian American Women.* San Francisco: San Francisco Study Center, 1983.

Yaeger, Patricia, ed. *The Geography of Identity.* Ann Arbor: University of Michigan Press, 1996.

Yuval-Davis N., and F. Anthias, eds. *Woman-Nation-State.* New York: St. Martin's Press, 1989.

Zinn, Maxine Baca, and Bonnie Thornton Dill, eds. *Women of Color in U.S. Society.* Philadelphia: Temple University Press, 1994.

Contributors

Laura Aguilar is a widely exhibited photographer. She has organized and curated art-related events, participated in lectures and panel discussions, and her photography has appeared in several feminist publications. Over the past several years, her photographs have come to focus on portraiture as social commentary. By focusing on the lives of lesbian women, gay men, and people of color, she seeks to create visual images that compassionately reflect the diversity of human experience and express self-acceptance in spite of societal repression. She has received numerous grants, including the James D. Phelan Art Award (1995) and the California Arts Council Fellowship (1994–95).

Meena Alexander is a widely published poet and prosewriter whose works have been translated into several languages including Malayalam, Hindi, Arabic, German, and Italian. She was born in India and lives in New York City, where she is Professor of English and Women's Studies at the Graduate Center, City University of New York. She is the author most recently of *Manhattan Music* (Mercury House, 1997).

M. Jacqui Alexander is an scholar-activist, teacher, writer whose work has focused on the ways in which law has been used by the neocolonial state, particularly in the Caribbean, in the interest of heterosexual nation building. She now holds the Fuller Maathai Chair in Gender and Women's Studies at Connecticut College. She is a long-time member of the Caribbean Association for Feminist Research and Action (CAFRA) and has been active in the struggle for lesbian and gay self-determination in the United States. She is a co-editor with Chandra Talpade Mohanty of *Feminist Genealogies, Colonial Legacies, Democratic Futures* (Routledge, 1996). She is recipient of a 1997 Guggenheim Fellowship and is now at work on a project that deals with memory and spirit within Kongo systems in the Caribbean. She is currently Director of the Gender and Women's Studies Program at Connecticut College.

Petra Allende is one of the most respected leaders of the Latino community. She was born in 1920 in San Juan, Puerto Rico, and in 1949 moved to New York City where she began working in factories and later in city government. She has been a major activist in the Puerto Rican community since the 1960s. Since 1982, she has dedicated her time to protecting the rights of women and improving the quality of services for non-privileged elderly in the city. She is a volunteer at the Gaylord White Senior Center in East Harlem and at the East Harlem Interagency Council. She is also the Legislative Coordinator of the Hispanic Senior Action Council. She is involved in outreach and advocacy and currently in voter education and registration. She has won numerous awards for her community work.

Rocío Aranda-Alvarado is a Ph.D. student in the Art History Department at the Graduate Center of the City University of New York. She is also a dissertation fellow of the National Museum of American Art. She has researched and written on U.S. Latino Art and on modernism in the Americas. She is now working on her dissertation, which offers a comparative study of avant-garde movements in Havana and Harlem.

Marina Alvarez is an AIDS educator and community organizer. Her activism on behalf of the health care needs of women and families with AIDS and HIV infection derives from her considerable personal experience. She co-directed *(In)Visible Women,* a video documentary on Latina Women with AIDS, and was content director of *Positive: Living With AIDS,* a PBS series on the experiences of diverse communities with AIDS. She sits on the Board of various AIDS organizations. In 1993, she received the AIDS Institute's Distinguished Service Award, and in 1998 she was awarded the Voz de Compromiso Award from the Latino Commission on AIDS.

Yolanda Andrade is a Mexican photographer. Her work has emphasized women who freely exercise their sexuality. The image included here, *La Tetona Mendoza,* was taken on Earth Day, 1990, and forms part of her series on popular culture and street theater. The title alludes to the comic strip character created by the Mexican cartoon artists, Jis and Trino. (The blanket on the right side has the face of Borola Burron, of the popular Mexican comic strip, The Burron Family.) She has published a book entitled *Los Velos Transparentes, Las Transparencias Veladas* and has been awarded numerous fellowships, including those from the National Endowment for Culture and the Arts in Mexico City (1993) and the John Simon Guggenheim Memorial Foundation (1994).

Nina Barnett, born and raised in Manhattan, grew up on the streets and in the museums of the city. Her first career was as an art-production editor and designer of photography books. She became a professional photographer in the 1980s. She has worked on many generational, educational, and family related stories. The image included in this volume was taken at the Casa Linda Community Center in New Haven, Connecticut.

Maria Beatty is a filmmaker whose films reflect the dark side of her sexuality as well as her personal views on sex, eroticism, and fantasy. Her films and videos have been shown at The Whitney Museum, The Museum of Modern Art, and various galleries and international film festivals. Some of her titles include *Le Petit Marquis, The Black Glove, The Elegant Spanking, Imaging Her Erotics,* and *Sphinxes Without Secrets.*

Catherine Benamou is a film scholar, producer and critic who specializes in Latin American, inter-American, and indigenous film, television, and video. In the early eighties, she was co-founder of the Punto de Vista: Latina, a distribution project devoted to the work of Latin American women filmmakers at Women Make Movies, Inc. Her articles on Latin American women's cinema have appeared in *Frontiers, Symposium,* and *Trasimagen.* She is currently Assistant Professor of Latin American and Latino/a Film studies at the University of Michigan.

Maria Magdalena Campos-Pons is a Cuban-born Boston-based artist. She studied at the Higher Institute of Art in Havana as well as in Boston at Mass College of Art. She has exhibited extensively in Cuba and abroad. She has received a number of fellowships, including The Louis Comfort Tiffany Foundation Grant (1997) and a Foreign Visiting Artists Media Grant, Canada Council (1992–96). She is currently living and working in Boston, where she is a Professor at the School of the Museum of Fine Arts.

Ginetta E. B. Candelario is a Ph.D. candidate in Sociology at the City University of New York Graduate School, writing her dissertation on Dominican race ideologies. Her creative and scholarly work on the Latina experience in the U.S. has appeared in *Bilingual Review/Revista Bilingue, Dominicana USA,* and *Phoebe: Journal of Feminist Scholarship, Theory and Aesthetics.* She co-directed and co-produced *De Welfare no vive nadie,* a video documentary on Dominican women receiving public assistance in New York City. Currently, she is a Rockefeller Fellow at the Dominican Studies Institute of City College and a Mendenhall Fellow at Smith College.

Teresa Carrillo is completing a manuscript titled *Gendered Unions: The Rise and Demise of the Mexican Garment Workers Movement* (forthcoming from University of Texas Press), which follows the "19th of September" Garment Workers Union from its dramatic emergence after the 1985 Mexico City earthquake through its transformation to a more enduring women's organization and social movement in the early 1990s. Her Chicana roots are in Tucson, Arizona, and she now teaches government courses as an Associate Professor of La Raza Studies at the College of Ethnic Studies, San Francisco State University.

Shu Lea Cheang is a filmmaker and installation artist based in New York City. Her video installations *Color Schemes* (1990) and *Those Fluttering Objects of Desire* (1993) were both exhibited at The Whitney Museum of American Art. Her first feature film, *Fresh Kill,* billed as "eco-cybernoia," premiered at the Berlin International Film Festival in 1994. *Bowling Alley* (1995), a cybernetic installation that sends actual bowling balls to strike virtual landscape, was commissioned by the Walker Art

Center and funded by AT&T's New Vision/New Vision. She has recently received funding from the Rockefeller Foundation for a one year WWW installation project at The Whitney Museum and Banff Centre for the Arts in Canada. Currently, she is working in Okinawa on a public project titled *Elephant Cage Butterfly Locker,* a Tokyo Metropolitan government sponsored art project.

Renée Cox, born in Jamaica, West Indies, received her B.A. from Syracuse University, her M.F.A. in photography from the School of Visual Arts, New York, and participated in the Whitney Independent Study Program (1992). In addition to her commitment to photography and other visual arts, and to addressing in her work issues such as racism and sexism, she has also curated, taught, lectured, and acted. She has been awarded numerous prestigious grants, fellowships, and residencies, including the New York Foundation for the Arts' Artist Fellowship Award and Lightwork, and Artists in Residency Program (1996). Her work has been widely exhibited in the United States and featured in various publications, such as *The New York Times, The Village Voice, Art in America,* and *Camera International* (Austria).

Allan deSouza is an artist and writer living in Los Angeles. He was an active participant in the Black Arts movement in Britain during the 1980s and has exhibited extensively in Britain as well as in the U.S., Canada, Cuba, the Philippines, and Germany. His fiction and critical writings have been published in various journals and anthologies.

Abbe Don holds a Master's degree from the Interactive Telecommunications Program at New York University. From 1988 to 1991, she pioneered the use of characters in the interface as a member of the Guides Team for Apple Computer's Advanced Technology Group. She was also producer of *Voices of the 30s,* an educational CD-ROM about the 1930s. She spent a year doing research in the Agents Group at the MIT Media Lab before leaving to become Senior Interface Designer for Network Service at Kaleida Labs. She is best known for her innovative interactive family album, *We Make Memories,* which has been exhibited in the United States and Europe. Her most recent foray into interactive family storytelling, *Bubbe's Back Porch,* can be viewed and added to on the World Wide Web at http://www.bubbe.com.

Mallika Dutt has been an organizer and activist in the U.S. women's movement for more than a decade. She was the Associate Director of the Center for Women's Global Leadership and is the author of several publications, including a manual for women's human rights. Mallika serves on the boards of Asian American Pacific Islanders in Philanthropy (AAPIP) and Sister Fund. A founding member of Sakhi for South Asian Women, Mallika is now the Program Officer for the Rights and Social Justice Program at the Ford Foundation in New Delhi, India.

Nicole Eisenman's art has been seen across the United States and Europe. She is known for her loosely improvised installations and her gigantic murals that effortlessly roam across walls, combining dozens of heavily-modeled figures in frenzied scenes. Her work is confrontational and humorous; no subject is too sensitive to be spared. She was the recipient of the John Simon Guggenheim Grant (1996) and has had solo shows in the last year at the Jack Tilton Gallery, New York; the Centraal Museum, Utrecht; and with Cokkie Snoei in the Netherlands. Her work has also been featured in the group exhibitions *Picassoid* at the Whitney Museum of American Art and *Screen* at the Friedrich Petzel Gallery.

Coco Fusco is a writer and interdisciplinary artist based in New York. She is the author of *English is Broken Here: Notes on Cultural Fusion in the Americas* (New York: The New Press, 1995). Her videos include *Pochonovela* (1995) and (with Paula Heredia) *The Couple in the Cage* (1993). She has performed, published, exhibited, curated, and lectured throughout the U.S., Europe, and Latin America.

Renée Green is an artist and writer. Her work and writings circulate internationally. Her publications include *World Tour* (Museum of Contemporary Art, Los Angeles, 1993); *Camino Road* (Centro de Arte Reina Sofia, Madrid, 1994); *After the Ten Thousand Things* (Stroom, The Hague/Idea Books, Amsterdam, 1994); and *Certain Miscellanies,* (DAAD, Berlin, and Stichting de Appel, Amsterdam, in 1996). She is based in New York.

Inderpal Grewal is Professor and Chair of Women's Studies at San Francisco State University. She is author of *Home and Harem: Nation, Gender, Empire and the Cultures of Travel* (Duke University Press, 1996) and co-editor (with Caren Kaplan) of *Scattered Hegemonies: Postmodernity and Transnational Feminist Practices* (University of Minnesota Press, 1994). She also works with Narika, a referral service for South Asian Women in the San Francisco Bay Area.

M. A. Jaimes * Guerrero is a scholar, professor, activist, and contemporary critic of eurocentric colonialism in the United States, from a Native American and Southwestern *mestiza* perspective. She is a professor of the Humanities and Women's Studies at San Francisco State University. She is the editor of the internationally awarded *The State of Native America* (Boston: South End Press, 1992), and has written numerous contributions in multicultural anthologies focusing on issues of race, ethnicity, class, and gender. Her most recent research project is at the Australian National University, Humanities Research Centre (Canberra, ACT). She is currently developing a comparison of "indigenous knowledge systems" between Native Pueblo cultures in the Southwest U.S. and the Aborigines of Australia.

Guerrilla Girls are an anonymous, collaborative group of women artists and art professionals. They remain anonymous to protect their identities and to focus on issues rather than personalities. Dubbing themselves "The Conscience of the Art World," they began making posters in 1985 that bluntly stated the facts of discrimination. They appear wearing Gorilla masks and use humor to convey information, provoke discussion and to show that feminists can be funny. They have been the subject of countless feature articles, television programs, and a documentary film, *Guerrillas in Our Midst.* They have received numerous awards, have had exhibitions at numerous museums and schools all over the world, and have released a book, *Confessions of the Guerrilla Girls* (Harper Collins, 1995).

Isabelle R. Gunning is a professor of law at the Southwestern University School of Law in Los Angeles, California. Her teaching areas include international human rights, evidence, immigration, alternative dispute resolution, and skills training. Her research interests encompass female genital surgeries and broader concerns to multicultural feminism along with questions of diversity and multiculturalism in the context of mediation. Her current community activities are also largely involved with mediation and dispute resolution in specific cross-cultural disputes within communities of color.

Marina Gutierrez is a mixed media artist from New York City. She has exhibited internationally and created public art and design projects. Her work constructs personal and historical narratives, interweaving the multiple influences of popular, traditional, and conceptual arts. As part of her art practice, Gutierrez directs a free art program for New York City public high school students.

Donna Han, after leaving art school in 1992, made low income art by herself and with friends. While living in New York from 1994 to 1995, she continued to make art while noodling in a rock band and writing a bad first novel. She said "ciao" to her overpriced Manhattan studio and headed back to California. Somehow she received a couple of grants and awards and so, indulged in unemployment. But it didn't last long. Another round-trip cross-country bus ride later, she licked her pen nib and took to stringing works and pictures together again in San Francisco, California. Life as meditation, feline worship, and scatological curiosity are predominant themes in her recent work. She has had exhibitions in California, New York, and the Netherlands.

Jamelie Hassan's diverse mixed-media works have addressed questions of colonialism, patriarchy, militarism, censorship, sexuality, and cultural identity. She is based in London, Ontario, Canada, and travel in the Americas, Europe, the Middle East, and other parts of Asia have strongly influenced her work. Her work has been exhibited since the early 1970s and is included in numerous public collections, including the National Gallery of Canada, Ottawa; the Art Gallery of Ontario, Toronto; and The New Museum of Contemporary Art, New York.

Mervat F. Hatem is originally from Egypt, but has lived, studied, and worked in the U.S. since 1974. She is presently working on a manuscript that critically examines the relationship between the modernization discourse and forms of (gendered and ethnic) governmentalities developed in Egypt since 1952. She is Associate Professor of Political Science at Howard University, Washington, D.C..

Mona Hatoum is a Palestinian video, performance, and installation artist, born in Lebanon. She has exhibited extensively throughout the world, including in solo shows at Centre Georges Pompidou (Paris); and her recent traveling survey organized by the Museum of Contemporary Art (Chicago, 1997–98). Her work has been included in numerous prestigious group exhibitions, including *Sense and Sensibility: Women Artists and Minimalism in the Nineties* at the Museum of Modern Art (New York); *Cocido y Crudo* at the Centro de Arte Reina Sofia (Madrid); *Identity and Alterity* at the 1995 Venice Biennale; and *Rites of Passage* at the Tate Gallery (London). Her work has been written about in a wide range of periodicals and in a monograph on the artist's work published by Phaidan Press (1997). Themes in her work include the exploration of complex identities generated from exile.

Janet Henry is a working artist and former art administrator. Her work has been shown in New York at Pulse Art, The Drawing Center, Art in General, Just Above Midtown, The New Museum, and the Studio Museum in Harlem. She attended the School of Visual Arts and the Fashion Institute of Technology, and received a Rockefeller Foundation Fellowship in Museum Education at the Metropolitan Museum of Art. She has worked at a variety of cultural institutions: the New York State Council on the Arts Visual Artists Program, Children's Art Carnival, Jamaica Art Center, the Studio Museum in Harlem, the Brooklyn Children's Museum, among others.

Maria Hinojosa, an award-winning correspondent, was with National Public Radio in New York City until 1997 when she became an urban affairs correspondent for CNN. She has been frequently heard on *All Things Considered, Morning Edition,* and as the host of NPR's *Latino USA,* a nationally broadcast program covering news and culture in the Latino community. A frequent guest on local and national TV news analysis programs, Hinojosa, has focused on urban affairs, youth issues, multiculturalism, labor, politics, and Latino people. She received a Robert F. Kennedy Award for her story *Manhood Behind Bars,* a New York Society of Professional Journalists Deadline Award for her piece *Kids and Guns,* and a Unity Award and a Top Story of the Year honor from the National Association of Hispanic Journalists for her piece *Crews,* which ran on *All Things Considered.* In January 1995, Harcourt Brace published her book *Crews—Gang Members Talk with Maria Hinojosa,* which was based on the award-winning story. Her latest book, *Raising Raul: A Motherhood Memoirs of Raising a Latino Child in a Multicultural Society,* is forthcoming from Viking-Penguin Books in 1999.

Patricia Hoffbauer is a Brazilian-born choreographer, director, writer, and educator living in New York City. Her work has been shown extensively in New York and throughout Latin America and Canada. The *Architecture of Seeing,* a collaboration with writer/performer George Emilio Sanchez, was presented in New York at Dance Theater and will be touring to different cities in 1998. The last installment of her series *"Who Killed Carmen?"—Carmenland, the Saga Continues,* was part of the Whitney Museum of American Art at Philip Morris Performance Series, *Second Sight*. She is focused on the development of a hybrid theatrical language that uses choreography, text, and music to deconstruct media representations of current events and to examine cultural references.

bell hooks is currently Distinguished Professor of English at City College in New York. She is the author of several books, including *Talking Back* (Boston: South End Press, 1989), *Black Looks* (South End Press, 1992), *Outlaw Culture* (Routledge, 1994), *Art On My Mind* (New York: New Press, 1995), and *Killing Rage* (New York: Henry Holt and Company, 1995). Her most recent writing includes *Reel to Reel: Race, Sex and Class at the Movies* (Routledge, 1996) and the memoir, *Bone Black: Memories of Girlhood* (Henry Holt and Company, 1996).

Lisa Jones writes for print, theater, and film. She is the author of *Bulletproof Diva: Tales of Race, Sex, and Hair* (Doubleday, 1995). Her writing is collected in numerous anthologies, including *Contemporary Plays by Women of Color* (Routledge, 1996). *Stained,* her music-theater collaboration with Alva Rogers, won a 1995 Bessie Award. She is a staff writer at the *Village Voice*.

May Joseph is a playwright and director teaching in the Department of Performance Studies, New York University. She edited *New Hybrid Identities* (a special double issue of *Women and Performance:* A Journal of Feminist Theory, Vol. 1, No. 2–Vol. 8, No. 1, Issue 14–15). Her essays have appeared in *Women and Performance, Oxford Literary Review, Late Imperial Culture,* and *Journal of Dramatic Theory and Criticism.* Her book *Nomadic Identities* and a co-edited anthology titled *Performing Hybridity* are forthcoming from the University of Minnesota Press. Joseph is on the editorial committees of *Cultural Studies* and *The Journal of Sports and Social Issues.*

Caren Kaplan is the author of *Questions of Travel: Postmodern Discourses of Displacement,* a monograph on contemporary theory and the politics of location (Duke University Press, 1996), and the co-editor with Inderpal Grewal of *Scattered Hegemonies: Postmodernity and Transnational Feminist Practices,* a collection of essays (University of Minnesota Press, 1994). She is an Associate Professor of Women's Studies at the University of California, Berkeley.

Deborah Kass is an artist who lives and works in New York City. Her work has been exhibited nationally and internationally and is included in the collections of New York's Museum of Modern Art, Whitney Museum, Guggenheim Museum, and the Jewish Museum, as well as the Museum of Fine Arts, Boston, and the Cincinnati Museum, among others. She has lectured and taught throughout the United States, including at the Whitney Museum, the Jewish Museum, Museum of Fine Arts, Boston, the Cincinnati Museum, Kansas City Arts Institute, the Rhode Island School of Design Museum of Art, California Institute of the Arts, the Art Institute of Chicago, and Skowhegan School of Sculpture and Painting. She has received grants from the National Endowment for the Arts, the New York State Council on the Arts, and Art Matters, Inc.

Soo-Ja Kim was born in Taegu, Korea, and is currently based in Seoul. She works mainly with Korean fabrics and used clothing, exhibiting in Asia, Europe, and New York. Her solo shows include *Sewing Into Walking,* Gallery Seomi (Seoul, 1994) and *A Laundry Field—Looking Into Sewing,* Oakville Galleries (Toronto, 1997). Her group exhibitions include *Ten Contemporary Korean Women Artists* at the National Museum for Women in the Arts (Washington, D.C., 1991); The Fifth Istanbul Biennial (Istanbul, Turkey, 1997); *Tradition/Tensions* at the Queens Museum of Art (New York, 1998); and Cities on the Move at the Musee d'Art Contemporain de Bordeau (France, 1998) which was recently released as a book. She has received numerous grants and awards, including two Korean Culture and Arts Foundation Grants (1992–93, 1996–97).

Indu Krishnan's first independently-produced video, *Knowing Her Place,* has been screened at a number of international festivals and was broadcast on public television. She co-produced *First World Order,* a television program that critically evaluates the role of the U.S. media in the Gulf War. She participated in Shu Lea Cheang's *That Obscure Object of Desire,* a video installation on interracial sexuality, featured at the Whitney Biennial and the Museum of Modern Art, New York. She is currently completing a documentary on a community of courtesans in south India, which looks at the colonialist and nationalist restructurings of religion and sexuality. She received a Bachelor's degree in psychology from the University of Delhi and a Master's degree in media studies from the New School for Social Research. She currently lives and works in New York City.

Maria del Carmen de Lara is a Mexican independent filmmaker. She began making independent films about women's issues in 1980. The themes of her documentaries have included prostitution, women and work, Indian women leaders, women peasants and health, the earthquake and Seamstress Movement, AIDS, reproductive rights, and abortion. She has received awards in various national and international festivals.

Walter Lima Jr. is a Brazilian documentary, short, and feature filmmaker. He began his career as a member of Brazil's Cinema Novo movement. The image included here is from his film, *Chico Rey,* a fiction feature about slavery and resistance in eighteenth century Brazil

Hung Liu was born in Changchun, China. She received her M.F.A. from the University of California, San Diego, and is currently an Associate Professor of Art at Mills College in Oakland, California. Selected solo exhibitions include a traveling ten year survey of her work, hosted by the Wooster College Museum of Art (1997); the University of Nevada, Donna Beam Fine Art Gallery, Las Vegas, Nevada; and the Steinbaum Krauss Gallery, New York. She has participated in a number of group exhibitions, including *American Kaleidoscope: Themes and Perspectives in Recent Art,* at the National Museum of American Art, Smithsonian Institution

(Washington, D.C., 1996); and *Gender Beyond Memory* at the Tokyo Metropolitan Museum of Photography (1996). Her work can be found in museums and corporate and private collections throughout the United States.

Maria Milagros Lopez is Professor of Social Psychology in the Psychology Department of the Rio Pietras Campus of the University of Puerto Rico. She is also a visiting researcher at the Social Sciences Research Center at the same university. In 1977 she was the founding director of the Center de Ayuda a Victimas de Violacion (rape crisis center) at the Comisión para los Asuntos de la Mujer (Women's Affairs Commission). Her work confronts issues of gender, faith, and politics, and is never predictable. She has written on such topics as women and welfare, agency among Puerto Rican women, and Puerto Rican women in literature. She presently teaches courses on the psychology of women and feminist theory. Her interests center around the collapse of the wage structure in Puerto Rico.

Wahneema Lubiano teaches in the programs in Literature and African-American Studies at Duke University. She has edited a collection of essays on race titled, *The House That Race Built: Black Americans, U.S. Terrain* (New York: Pantheon Books, 1997) and is author of *Like Being Mugged by a Metaphor: "Deep Cover" and Other Fictions of Black American Life* (forthcoming from Duke University Press), and *Missing With the Machine: Modernism, Postmodernism, and Black American Fiction* (forthcoming from Verso Press).

Amalia Mesa-Bains was born in Santa Clara, California. She received her Ph.D. from the Wright Institute in Berkeley, California. Among numerous awards, she received the distinguished MacArthur Fellowship from the John D. and Catherine T. MacArthur Foundation, Chicago, and the Distinguished Service to the Field Award from the Association of Hispanic Artists, New York (1992). In addition to many group exhibitions, her selected solo exhibitions include those at the Steinbaum Krauss Gallery, New York (1995); Williams College Museum of Art in Williamstown, Massachusetts (1994); and Artspace in Phoenix, AZ (1990).

Yong Soon Min, born in South Korea and currently based in Los Angeles, is an artist and Assistant Professor in the Department of Studio Art at the University of California, Irvine. She works in a wide range of media and was a recipient of an NEA Artists Grant in New Genre (1989–90). One of her current projects is a Percent for Art commission for a public library in Queens, New York.

Chandra Talpade Mohanty is Associate Professor of Women's Studies at Hamilton College, Clinton, New York, and Core Faculty at the Graduate School of the Union Institute, Cincinnati, Ohio. She is co-editor with Ann Russo and Lourdes Torres of *Third World Women and the Politics of Feminism* (Indiana University Press, 1991) and with M. Jacqui Alexander, of *Feminist Genealogies, Colonial Legacies, Democratic Futures* (Routledge 1997).

Lillian Mulero is a 1995 New York Foundation on the Arts Fellow in sculpture. She graduated from SUNY at Albany in 1983, and since then has exhibited widely across the U.S. She has shown at Feature Gallery in New York City and Chicago, the New Langton Arts Center in San Francisco, the Walker Art Center in Minneapolis, as well as many universities and museums in New York state. Her 1995 solo exhibition at the Jersey City Museum was a multimedia installation titled, *Body and Soul of Lolita Lebron* (a Puerto Rican Revolutionary).

Annie Nash is an artist and writer living in Corrales, New Mexico. She is a non-federally recognized Quinault-Cowlitz Indian and unenrolled Celtic-American. She has had her work exhibited at the Musenhof Poppendorf, Germany; the Southwest Museum, Los Angeles; the Center of Contemporary Art, St. Louis, Missouri; Art in General, New York; and the Center for Photography at Woodstock, New York. Her paintings are published in *Native American Painters of the Twentieth Century* (McFarland and Co., Inc., 1995), *In My Own Voice: Multicultural Poets on Identity* (CD-ROM, Jefferson, NC: Sunburst Communications, 1996), and *Proteus: A Journal of Ideas* (Shippenburg, PA: Shippenburg University Press, Fall 1993). She has received awards from the National Endowment for the Arts, the Rockefeller Foundation, the Fulbright Foundation, the Southwest Museum, and the Council for Basic Education.

Shirin Neshat was born in Qazvin, Iran. She received her M.F.A. from the University of California, Berkeley. Her work has been featured at the Venice Biennale (1995), Istanbul Biennial (1995/1997), Sydney Biennale (1996), Africas 97 in South Africa, Whitney Museum (1998) and Tate Gallery in London (1998), among other venues. Her work has been widely published, including in the World Art (Spring, 1998 issue #16), *Flash Art* (December 1994), and the *New York Times* (February 1994). Her photographic and video work investigate meanings, complexities, and paradoxes that exist behind the lives of contemporary Islamic women and Islamic identities at large. She has been the recipient of grants from the New York Foundation for the Arts (1996), Tiffany Foundation (1996), Art Matters, Inc. (1995), and Mid-Atlantic Art Foundation (1995).

Lorraine O'Grady is a conceptual artist whose work most often argues against the dualism of Western culture by using the diptych as form, and colonialism, hybridity, and diaspora as content. Trained in economics and literature, she began making visual art in 1980 with her performances *Mlle Bourgeoise Noire* and *Nefertiti/Devonia Evangeline*. In 1991 she turned to photo-based installations. In 1995–96 she held the Fellowship in Visual Art of the Bunting Institute at Harvard.

Catherine Opie is a Los Angeles photographer whose work represents ideas related to identity, gender, and sexuality. She shows her work internationally and exhibits her work at Regen Projects in Los Angeles. Her work was included in the 1995

Biennial at the Whitney Museum of American Art, New York, and was recently shown at the Museum of Contemporary Art, Los Angeles.

Tatiana Parcero was born in Mexico City in 1967. She completed an M.A. in Photography at the International Center of Photography at New York University. She has received several photography and video awards in Mexico and her work has been exhibited in Mexico, Cuba, Great Britain, Italy, and Spain.

Marta María Pérez Bravo is a Cuban photographer. Most of her work refers to a Cuban syncretic mythological context that addresses superstitious beliefs and taboos. Her photography is not used to capture a moment in time but rather to document a constructed situation. She has produced autobiographical series that investigate issues of motherhood, womanhood, and the self, often in relation to popular Santería rituals in which her body is used as a personal altar.

Hanh Thi Pham is a naturalized U.S. citizen born in Vietnam. She is a nonconformist of anarchist persuasion. She has identified herself as a transsexual, female-to-female queer Vietnamese, and as an Asian-American vampire. She uses photography and her life experiences to develop strategies that may ignite necessary revolts. Hanh was a Rockefeller Foundation Fellow at the Asian American Studies Center at the University of California, Los Angeles (1992–93). She received her M.F.A. in photography in 1986, from California State University, Fullerton. Hanh says she is in exile, homeless, but horny and fierce.

Adrian Piper is a conceptual artist who works in a variety of media on racial stereotyping and xenophobia, and a Professor of Philosophy at Wellesley College, specializing in meta-ethics and Kant. Her *Out of Order, Out of Sight, Volume I: Selected Writings in Meta-Art 1968–1992* and *Volume II: Selected Writings in Art Criticisms 1967–1992* have just been published by The MIT Press.

Liliana Porter, born in Buenos Aires, Argentina, 1941, has lived in New York since 1964. She is a printmaker, painter, photographer, filmmaker, as well as a Professor of Art at Queens College, CUNY. Her work has been exhibited in New York, Argentina, Colombia, Uruguay, Panama, Switzerland, among other places worldwide. Her work is included in the collections of the Metropolitan Museum, New York; Clouste Gulbenkian Foundation, Lisbon, Portugal; Museu de Arte Moderna, Rio de Janeiro; Museo de Bellas Artes, Buenos Aires, among others.

Ernesto Pujol received a B.A. from the University of Puerto Rico in 1979. He has done graduate work in art therapy at Pratt Institute, New York; in media studies at Hunter College, New York; and in art history at Complutense University, Madrid. He received a Joan Mitchell Fellowship (1997), a National Endowment for the Arts Regional Fellowship in Painting (1994), two Pollock-Krasner Foundation Grants (1993/1997), two CINTAS Foundation Awards (1991/1997). In 1991, he

Subject Index

Note: Pages where figures appear are in boldface.

Plate 66: *House on Wheels*, 1991
Cast and painted aluminum, 12 × 8.5 × .5"
Zarina
Photo: D. James Dee
Courtesy of the artist

participated in the Artist in the Marketplace Program, Bronx Museum of the Arts, and the Studio Scholarship Program, Bronx Council on the Arts. His work has had more exposure in Havana than that of any other Cuban-American artist. In 1995–96, Pujol accomplished four exhibitions on the issue of national reconciliation: *The Children of Peter Pan* (Casa de las Americas, 1995); *Trophies of the Cold War* (Espacio Aglutinador, 1995); *Saturn's Table* (Centro de Desarrollo de las Artes Visuales, 1996); and The Void (Sixth Havana Biennial, 1997). He is based in New York.

Tricia Rose is the author of *Black Noise: Rap Music and Black Culture in Contemporary America* (Wesleyan University Press, 1994), which won an American Book Award from the Before Columbus Foundation in 1995. An Assistant Professor of History and Africana Studies at New York University, Rose is currently working in a new project on black women, intimacy, and sexuality.

Celia Rumsey is an artist who lives in Santa Fe, New Mexico. Her work has been exhibited throughout the United States in private and corporate collections, and in museums including the Smithsonian. Her installation, *Chronic,* expresses through sculptural forms the pain, endurance, and fear of someone living with a chronic illness. Like other contemporary artists who deal with issues relating to the body, Ms. Rumsey's work alludes to broader medical issues affecting many lives around the world. Ms. Rumsey is a magna cum laude graduate of Bryn Mawr College and a Fulbright Scholar.

Juan Sanchez is a painter/photographer whose RICAN/STRUCTION mixed media paintings explore his Puerto Rican heritage and the issue of colonialism and Puerto Rican independence. Sanchez's art has been exhibited in numerous exhibitions throughout the U.S., Latin America, and Europe. His works are included in many collections, such as the Metropolitan Museum of Art, the Museum of Modern Art, and El Museo del Barrio, New York City. In 1988, Juan Sanchez became the recipient of the John Simon Guggenheim Foundation Fellowship in painting. He is currently a Professor of Art at Hunter College, CUNY.

Joyce Scott is a visual and performing artist living and working in Baltimore, Maryland. She teaches, lectures, and performs internationally. Much of her work addresses social and political issues. Her visual art leaves meaning to the imagination of the viewer while her performance art takes an in-your-face approach to audiences.

Yoshiko Shimada was born in Tokyo in 1959 and graduated from Scripps College in 1982. In 1994 she was a guest artist at the Kunstlerhaus Bethanien in Berlin and received a Berlin Senatsverwaltung für Kulturelle Angelegenheiten Kunstlennenprogramme grant in 1995. Solo exhibitions of her work include those at the Kunsthaus Tacheles, Berlin (1995); Ota Fine Arts, Tokyo (1995, 96, 98); and Hiraya Gallery, Manila (1997). Her work has also been included in many group exhibitions, such as *The Age of Anxiety at the Power Plant* (Toronto, 1995), *Gender Beyond Memory* at Tokyo Metropolitan Museum of Art (1996), *Flexible Coexistence* at Art Tower Mito (1997), and *Lord of the Rim* at Hsin-Cuang Center for Arts (Taiwan, 1997). She is currently an artist-in-residence at P.S.1 New York.

Ella Habiba Shohat is Professor of Cultural Studies and Women's Studies at the City University of New York. A writer, curator, and activist, she has published and lectured extensively on the intersection of post/colonialism, gender, and sexuality. She is the author of *Israeli Cinema: East/West and the Politics of Representation* (1989) and the co-author (with Robert Stam) of the award winning *Unthinking Eurocentrism: Multiculturalism and the Media* (1994). On the editorial board of the journals *Social Text, Critique,* and *Merip,* she has co-edited *Dangerous Liaisons: Gender, Nation and Postcolonial Reflections* (1997). Her work has been translated into French, Spanish, Portuguese, Arabic, Hebrew, and German.

Lorna Simpson's art has earned her significant recognition. In 1990, at age 30, she was the first African-American woman to exhibit at the Venice Biennale. She was also the first African-American woman to have a Projects show at the Museum of Modern Art, New York. In 1992, the Museum of Contemporary Art in Chicago organized a nationally traveling retrospective of her work. That same year a book about her work was published by The Friends of Photography. Her work is featured in the October 10, 1994, *Time* magazine cover story, "Black Renaissance," and in the February 1995 issue of the *New Art Examiner.* Her work is included in the collections of several major art museums and in private collections.

Teri Slotkin is a New York City-based freelance photographer specializing in studio and environmental portraiture, as well as community, corporate, and art world documentation. She is currently engaged in an ongoing project titled, *Mixed Doubles*—studio portraits of pairs, people connected by birth, marriage, or social, business, and other ties. Her work has been widely exhibited and published.

Jaune Quick-to-See Smith, painter/printmaker, was born on the Indian Mission Reservation, Montana. She is an enrolled member of the confederate Salish and Kootenai Nation in Western Montana. Smith is an activist and spokesperson for Contemporary Native American Art. She received her M.A. in Art in 1980 from the University of New Mexico, Albuquerque. She has founded two Native co-ops; organized and curated numerous touring exhibitions of Native art; lectured at over 100 Universities internationally; juried for numerous organizations; printed at workshops nationwide; and served on many boards. Smith has received numerous awards, including the 1997 Award for Outstanding Achievement in the Visual Arts from the Women's Caucus for Art, and an Honorary Doctorate from the Minneapolis College of Art and Design. Her work can be seen in many private and public collections internationally.

Ellen Spiro is an independent filmmaker whose work has won numerous awards. Her works have been screened internationally on television and in museums. Her documentaries include *DiAna's Hair Ego, Greetings From Out Here,* and *Roam Sweet Home.* She currently lives in New York.

Annie Sprinkle has been passionately researching and exploring sex for the past twenty-five years. She has documented her findings through film, writing, performance, teaching, publishing, and photography. She has appeared in 150 X-rated feature films, has written and directed several films, has written and published over three hundred articles about sex, and has taught and lectured at many museums, universities, and holistic healing centers.

Maud Sulter was born in Glasgow, Scotland, and is currently living and working in England. She is Principal Lecturer in Fine Art and Head of Fine Printmaking at the Manchester Metropolitan University. She writes and lectures extensively on Art History, specializing in Photographic Theory and Women's Art Practice from 1840–1990. Her work has been written about in various publications by diverse authors. She has received numerous awards and commissions; has appeared on television and radio; and has exhibited in England, Ireland, Canada, and the United States.

Diane Tani, photographer and activist, is a former member of the Board of Directors at San Francisco Camerawork and the recipient of a 1991 Eureka Fellowship from the Fleishhacker Foundation. She received a B.A. from San Francisco State University in Art/Photography with a minor in Asian-American Studies. Since completing her M.A. at the University of New Mexico, she has exhibited at the Museum of Modern Art, New York, SF Camerawork, California Museum of Photography, and the Smithsonian Institution. Currently, she is a Digital Imaging Specialist for the Lawrence Berkeley National Laboratory.

Jocelyn Taylor is a video artist living in New York. Her videos, *Bodily Functions, Frankie and Jocie,* and *Father Knows Best* have shown at The New Museum, the Whitney Museum of American Art, and the Museum of Modern Art in New York City. Internationally, her videos have been screened at the Institute for Contemporary Art in London, CURARE in Mexico City, and at film festivals in São Paulo, Tokyo, Toronto, Paris, and Berlin. Her video installations, *Alien at Rest* and *Something Private* have been shown at Deitch Projects and Franklin Furnace in New York. She has written for *Art Papers, Felix Magazine,* the *SF Cameraworks Journal,* and has also contributed essays to the anthologies *Afrekete* (Doubleday, 1995) and *Policing Public Sex* (South End Press, 1996). She has received numerous awards and fellowships.

Tiana (Thi Thanh Nga) was born in Saigon and lived there until 1966 when she moved with her family to America and became a U.S. citizen. She studied acting and directing and worked with Asian-American filmmakers such as Wayne Wang and Emiko Omari. As an actress, she has appeared in a variety of feature films and TV series. She began work on *From Hollywood to Hanoi* as a "search for roots and identity" in 1988 when she first returned to Vietnam. She subsequently made more than twelve trips to her homeland, filming over seventy hours of footage with a Vietnamese crew, which she and her cameramen trained, and spent a year and a half editing the film in New York.

Pamela Tom is a fifth-generation Chinese American filmmaker and writer whose work includes documentary and narrative film and video. She received her B.A. in Third World Development from Brown University and an M.F.A. in film production from the University of California, Los Angeles. Much of her work explores the lives of women and Asians in America. *Two Lies* was her graduate thesis film. She lives in Los Angeles with her husband and daughter, Isabela.

Carmelita Tropicana, a Cuban-American, has collaborated with Ela Troyano and Uzi Parnes in creating multi-media spectacles. She has received a fellowship from the Cintas Foundation, and will have a collection of plays, monologues and stories published by Beacon Press in 1999. The script for *Milk of Amnesia* was reprinted in *The Drama Review.* The film *Carmelita Tropicana: Your Kunst is Your Waffen,* co-written with Ela Troyano, won the prize for best short film at the Berlin Film Festival in 1994.

Ela Troyano is a New York-based, Cuban-born, Latina filmmaker whose films and performances have been shown throughout the U.S. and at international festivals. Troyano recently completed her first feature film project, *Latin Boys Go To Hell,* and two half-hour films funded by the Independent Television Service (ITVS) for public television: *Once Upon a Time in the Bronx* and *Carmelita Tropicana: Your Kunst is Your Waffen.* She is a recipient of a Rockefeller Foundation Fellowship and has previously received support from the New York State Council on the Arts, Jerome Foundation, the National Endowment for the Arts, and the Film Fund.

Josette Urso is a painter/mixed-media artist residing in New York City. In her work, animal/human creatures act out the dramas of life: love/death, celebration/mourning, feast/famine. Urso has exhibited and has held artist residencies in numerous locations in the United States, Europe, and Latin America. In 1994, she received a Mid-Atlantic Arts Foundation/NEA Regional Fellowship. In 1996, she received funding from the Pollock-Krasner Foundation, Inc.

Dr. Anne S. Walker, feminist activist, educationalist, photographer, artist, and writer, has been the Executive Director of the International Women's Tribune Center (IWTC) since its inception in 1976. She has spearheaded IWTC's efforts to support the initiatives of women worldwide with a program of technical assistance and training, collaborative projects, skill-sharing, and the collecting, producing, and disseminating of information on a wide range of concerns regarding women and development. She has also participated in each of the four UN Women's Conferences and NGO Forums, and IWTC has produced slide-tapes using a selection of photographs taken by her at each of these world gatherings.

Kara Walker, installation artist, draftsperson, and printmaker, was born in Stockton, California. She received her B.A. from the Atlanta College of Art and her M.F.A. from Rhode Island School of Design. She has participated in numerous solo and group exhibitions. Her most recent solo exhibitions include those at Wooster Gardens in New York (1998) and the San Francisco Museum of Modern Art (1997). Her most recent group exhibitions include the 1997 Whitney Biennial; *no place (like home)* at the Walker Arts Center, Minneapolis (1997) and Strange Days at The Art Gallery of New South Wales, Sydney (1998). Her work has been written about and featured in the *New York Times,* the *Village Voice, Frieze, The Source, Artnews,* among other publications.

Flo Oy Wong, contemporary installation artist and painter, was born and raised in Oakland, California's Chinatown. She began her art career at the age of forty. Wong is a co-founder of the Northern California-based Asian American Women Artists Association, and is a national board member of the Women's Caucus for Art (WCA), serving on the WCA's Women of Color in Art Committee and the Honors Award Committee. Her work is shown nationally and internationally. One of her installations, *The Baby Rice Jack Story,* was shown at the inaugural exhibition of the National African American Museum Project at the Smithsonian Institution in 1994 and 1995. Wong, with Omaha-based artists Pam J. Berry and Reese Crawford, is a recipient of a 1997 Multicultural Awareness Grant from the Nebraska Arts Council. Wong is also the recipient of a 1997–98 California Arts Council Multi-Residency Grant.

Lynne Yamamoto, born and raised in Honolulu, Hawai'i, is an artist and educator based in New York City. Her work in installation and sculpture originates from narratives about women in her family who worked as laundresses and domestics. She received her M.A. from New York University and participated in the Whitney Independent Study Program. She has exhibited widely nationally and internationally. Her recent solo exhibitions include *Submissions* at The Contemporary Museum in Honolulu (1996); *They all fall down* at articule in Montreal (1997); an exhibition and website (curated by high school students) for P.S.1 Contemporary Art Center (1997); *Grasp* at George Suyama Architect Space and *New Work* at Greg Kucera Gallery in Seattle (1998). Her current projects include an installation for the Whitney Museum of American Art at Philip Morris (1999).

Kathleen C. J. Zane was born on Maui and grew up in Honolulu, Hawai'i. After completing her university studies in New York City, she taught at universities in New York, Mexico, Spain, and Japan. A Rockefeller Foundation Fellowship in gender and visual culture at the University of Rochester, New York supported her earlier research on cosmetic surgery. As a Research Associate at the Five College Women's Studies Research Center, she continues culturally mapping the Asian body and is currently collaborating on an interactive installation project about Hello Kitty.

Zarina was born in Aligarh, India in 1937. She has lived, worked, and exhibited in Europe, Southeast Asia, and the United States. She has taught at Bennington College, Cornell University, and at the University of California, Santa Cruz. Her work is about "moving homes," inspired by her experiences of navigating between cultures and watching others move in search of safety and "home."

Dolores Zorreguieta was born in Argentina in 1965. She grew up in Buenos Aires and in 1987 she graduated from the National School of Fine Arts. In 1992, she came to New York to pursue graduate studies at New York University. She has exhibited her work in several solo and group shows in the U.S. as well as in Argentina. In 1994, she received a grant from Franklin Furnace in New York. Her range of production goes from painting, objects, and installations, to choreography and stage investigations.

Name Index